# Integrated Advertising, Promotion, and Marketing Communications

# Integrated Advertising, Promotion, and Marketing Communications

**KENNETH E. CLOW**
University of Louisiana at Monroe

**DONALD BAACK**
Pittsburg State University

PEARSON
Prentice Hall

Upper Saddle River, New Jersey 07458

**Library of Congress Cataloging-in-Publication Data**

Clow, Kenneth E.
   Integrated advertising, promotion, & marketing communications/Kenneth E.Clow, Donald Baack.—3rd ed.
     p. cm.
   ISBN 0-13-186622-2
   1. Communication in marketing.  2. Advertising.  I. Title: Integrated advertising, promotion,
and marketing communications.  II. Baack, Donald.  III. Title.

HF5415.123.C58 2007
659.1—dc22                                                  2005053427

**Senior Editor:** Katie Stevens
**VP/Publisher:** Jeff Shelstad
**Product Development Manager:** Ashley Santora
**Editorial Assistant:** Christine Letto
**Senior Media Project Manager:** Peter Snell
**Marketing Manager:** Ashaki Charles
**Marketing Assistant:** Joanna Sabella
**Associate Director, Production Editorial:** Judy Leale
**Managing Editor (Production):** Renata Butera
**Production Editor:** Kelly Warsak
**Permissions Supervisor:** Charles Morris
**Manufacturing Buyer:** Diane Peirano
**Design/Composition Manager:** Christy Mahon
**Art Director:** Kevin Kall
**Interior Design:** Kevin Kall
**Cover Design:** Kevin Kall
**Composition Liaison:** Nancy Thompson
**Illustrator (Interior):** Integra Software Services
**Director, Image Resource Center:** Melinda Reo
**Manager, Rights and Permissions:** Zina Arabia
**Manager, Visual Research:** Beth Brenzel
**Manager, Cover Visual Research and Permissions:** Karen Sanatar
**Image Permission Coordinator:** Debbie Hewitson
**Photo Researcher:** Teri Stratford
**Composition:** Integra Software Services
**Full-Service Project Management:** Jennifer Welsch/BookMasters, Inc.
**Printer/Binder:** Quebecor World
**Typeface:** 10.5/12 Times

Credits and acknowledgments borrowed from other sources and reproduced, with permission, in this textbook appear on the appropriate page within text or on page 491.

Pearson Education LTD.
Pearson Education Singapore, Pte. Ltd
Pearson Education, Canada, Ltd
Pearson Education—Japan

Pearson Education Australia PTY, Limited
Pearson Education North Asia Ltd
Pearson Educación de Mexico, S.A. de C.V.
Pearson Education Malaysia, Pte. Ltd

10 9 8 7 6 5 4 3 2 1
ISBN 0-13-186622-2

*To my sons Dallas, Wes, Tim, and Roy, who provided encouragement, and especially to my wife, Susan, whose sacrifice and love made this textbook possible.*
**—Kenneth E. Clow**

*I would like to dedicate my efforts and contributions to the book to my wife Pam; children Jessica, Daniel, and David; and grandchildren Danielle, Rile, and Andrew.*
**—Donald Baack**

# Brief Contents

# Contents

# Preface

We created *Integrated Advertising, Promotion, and Marketing Communications*, in part, to deal with what we believed were three problems with the integrated marketing communications course. First, we thought the textbooks available did not always practice exactly what they preached: They included large sections on advertising and marketing communications, but these two key ingredients were not completely blended together. Without this integration, students would be unable to see why everyone made such a fuss about integrated marketing communications. We wanted to provide a more carefully *integrated* marketing communications text.

Second, we believe that an IMC course requires students to apply concepts as often as possible in order for the ideas to be clearly understood and retained. As a result, we have created end-of-chapter materials designed to help students practice using the concepts. These materials include integrated learning exercises, critical thinking exercises, and short cases.

Third, we found that integrated marketing communications texts sometimes have disjointed supplements packages. Too often, we have heard professors complain that there were unpleasant surprises teaching with these supplements. We wanted to provide a more useful and *integrated* supplements package.

This, then, was the mandate for the third edition of *Integrated Advertising, Promotion, and Marketing Communications*: Provide a true integrated marketing communications text that integrated student learning and integrated the supplements used to teach the course. Hopefully we have accomplished this by providing an integrated text, building a project into every chapter, providing commercial software to bring this project to fruition, and putting together a supplements package ourselves.

## WHAT IS NEW IN THE THIRD EDITION?

Based on extensive review from users of our textbook and professionals in the field, we have made the following improvements to the text:

- **Improved organization.** We have reorganized the chapters in response to feedback from various constituents. In the foundations section of the text (Part 1), we combined the chapters on consumer buying behavior and business-to-business buyer behavior (Chapter 3). Most students have taken a course in buyer behavior and reviews indicated too much space was being devoted to these topics.
- **Enhanced discussion of customer relationship management (CRM).** A section of Chapter 12 describes the concept of CRM and how it is being used by businesses. CRM is designed to be a cost-effective method of interacting with customers to better serve key customers and generate higher profits for the firm. When combined with information regarding database marketing, CRM programs are effective methods of integrating communications with members of various target markets.

▶ **A new approach to integrating ethics into IMC programs.** The first edition of this text contained a stand-alone chapter on regulations and ethics. This edition features ethics issues that are part of each chapter. The Ethical Issues boxes are designed to identify key issues in the chapter that raise ethical concerns. The legal issues associated with advertising regulation are located in Chapter 12, where they are discussed in conjunction with public relations. Having already covered the major forms of marketing communications, students are better able to understand the role of regulations at this point in the course.

▶ **Greater emphasis on brands.** Brand management is presented throughout the text where it is applicable to the IMC issue involved. This discussion builds on materials presented in Chapter 2 regarding corporate image, brand management, brand equity, and brand parity.

▶ **Visual appeal.** This edition contains a substantial number of ads and illustrations. These items make the book visually appealing and provide students with examples of various advertising and promotional tactics. We are especially indebted to Bobbie Snodgrass from the *Joplin Globe*, who gave us access to numerous ads that support Chapter 15 regarding small business IMC programs.

In all, we think these improvements and additions help to make *Integrated Advertising, Promotion, and Marketing Communication* the most integrated and effective IMC teaching and learning package available.

## INTEGRATED LEARNING PACKAGE

To learn the material properly, students must first have a text that engages them. Next, students must go outside of the text and learn by doing. Because of this, we have created the following features with the student in mind:

▶ **Lead-in vignettes.** Each chapter begins with a vignette that is related to the topic being presented. The majority of the vignettes revolve around success stories in companies students will recognize, such as Starbucks and AFLAC. In this edition, new vignettes have been introduced and include features on Ron Jon Surf Shop, M&M's, and Google to keep the stories fresh and recognizable.

▶ **Business-to-business marketing concepts.** Many marketing students are likely to hold jobs that emphasize sales to other businesses. Therefore, business-to-business components have been incorporated in many of the discussions throughout the text. Examples, cases, text illustrations, and Internet exercises have been woven into the materials. In addition, a complete examination of business-to-business buyer behavior is provided in Chapter 3.

▶ **International marketing discussions.** Students are curious about the world around them. Many marketing texts address international issues as an add-on. Although there are some separate discussions of international issues, this book features international concerns where they correlate with the materials being presented. Further international cases are found

**8**

Advertising Media Selection

**Chapter Objectives**

*Master* the process of creating a media strategy.

*Understand* the roles media planners and media buyers play in an advertising program.

*Utilize* reach, frequency, continuity, impressions, and other objectives in the preparation of an advertising program.

*Study* and incorporate the advantages of various media in developing an ad program.

*Recognize* the value of an effective mix of media in an advertising campaign.

**M&M'S: THE SWEET TASK OF MEDIA SELECTION**

Can you remember the first time you ate M&M's? Most probably cannot, because it happened so early in life. The M&M's brand is one of the most famous and popular candies offered by Mars, Incorporated. Today, the brand enjoys an international presence that continues to grow.

M&M's began with a global flavor. According to legend, Forrest Mars Sr. was in Spain visiting soldiers fighting the Spanish Civil War. He noted that they were eating pieces of chocolate that were encased in a hard sugary coating. Using this as inspiration, Mars returned to the United States and refined the recipe for M&M's. The first packages were sold in 1941 in the United States. They were a favorite of many GIs serving in World War II. The original candies were sold in a cardboard tube. The famous brown and white label package didn't emerge until the late 1940s.

The legend of M&M's grew when colors were added to the original brown. In the 1960s, red, green, and yellow were created. Eventually, these and other colors developed into advertising spokescandies, including the egomaniac Red, the lovely female Green, the amazing Crispy Orange, Cool Blue, and, of course, nutty Yellow.

Red disappeared for a time from the M&M's mix after some research suggested concerns about red food dye, even though the problem was not associated with M&M's. In 1987, Red triumphantly returned, much to the joy of candy lovers around the world.

The advertising program for M&M's has been long-lasting, noteworthy, and award-winning. Practically any baby boomer remembers the original M&M's tagline: "Melts in your mouth, not in your hand." Television advertisements have long been the staple of M&M's. Using a natural tie-in with candy consumption at Christmas, an intense burst of M&M's advertising takes place each December. Most of these ads include a guest visit from Santa.

230

in several chapters. These end-of-chapter features lead students to discover a more integrated approach to advertising, promotions, and marketing communications in both domestic and international markets.

▶ **Communication Action boxes.** In each chapter, one key illustration of the subject matter in a real-world setting is presented as a Communication Action box. These features include business-to-business, consumer, and international examples. In addition, interviews of professionals from the worlds of advertising and marketing are presented as Communication Action boxes in some chapters.

▶ **Critical thinking exercises and Discussion Questions.** The end-of-chapter materials also contain several short scenarios and exercises to help students review chapter concepts by applying them in various settings. Internet exercises lead students to Web sites where advertisements can be assessed for quality. Innovative approaches, such as asking students to prepare and evaluate various kinds of advertisements and advertising campaigns, are also suggested.

▶ **Integrated learning exercises.** At the end of each chapter, questions guide students to the Internet to access information that ties into the subject matter covered in the particular chapters. These exercises also provide an opportunity for students to keep abreast of new material.

▶ **Cases.** At the conclusion of each chapter, two cases are available as assignments or to generate discussion. These cases assist student learning by providing plausible scenarios that require thought and review of chapter materials. The short cases are designed to help students conceptually understand chapter components as well as larger, more general marketing issues. Each chapter contains one new case that replaces a case from the second edition. The old case is included in the Instructor's Manual.

# ORGANIZATION OF THE TEXTBOOK

## Part 1: The IMC Foundation

Being heard in a cluttered marketplace is one of the major obstacles most firms face. The past decade has introduced numerous new ways to vend products and many new venues to promote those products. The key to an effective advertising, promotions, and integrated marketing communications program is to develop the one clear voice that will be heard over the din of so many ads and marketing tactics. Meeting this challenge involves bringing together every aspect of the firm's marketing efforts and having them focus as a team on one message.

**Chapter 1, "Integrated Marketing Communications,"** presents a basic model of communication and describes how it applies to marketing goods and services. An overview of the entire IMC approach is presented. It contains four parts: the foundation, advertising tools, promotional tools, and integration tools.

---

### COMMUNICATION ACTION

**Hewlett-Packard: "We Understand"**

An excellent example of an integrated marketing communications program is provided by the software systems engineering division (SSED) of Hewlett-Packard (H-P). This group initiated its IMC process through workshops designed to help H-P's employees better understand the dilemmas faced by its customers. These workshops were directed by representatives from sales, product marketing, engineering, and customer support departments within H-P. Each had a different perspective of the customer and provided valuable input into the various dilemmas faced by end users. The team approach allowed everyone to see the customer from a more holistic perspective.

Based on input from these departments, a creative strategy emerged with a strong focus on customer needs. The theme "we understand" was adopted. H-P's marketing emphasis centered on the idea that members of the company understood the issues, pressures, and constraints that software developers faced. Knowing about unrealistic deadlines, hidden-code errors, and other problems and how to cope with these issues was the key. H-P's leaders believed they could solve transition problems for customers by moving to object-oriented programming and simultaneously developing multiple applications of company software. The theme was integrated into all of H-P's marketing programs. It was launched in an advertising campaign and then reinforced in three direct mailings. The same message was used in trade show handouts and displays. H-P's Web site was redesigned around the same principle.

The "we understand" idea served as an umbrella for all marketing strategies and tactics. The integrated approach allowed H-P to speak with one voice regardless of the communication method customers encountered when they contacted the firm. This more fully integrated program was more than just the theme, however. It began with effective communication within and built outward to the point where H-P's end users (other business) could see and experience a real difference in the products and services that were being provided.

**Source:** P. Griffeth Lindell, "You Need an Integrated Attitude to Develop IMC," *Marketing News* 31, no. 11 (May 26, 1997), p. 6.

---

### CASE 1

**A HEALTHY IMAGE**

Mary Wilson was both nervous and excited as she opened her first staff meeting in the marketing department of St. Margaret's General Hospital. Mary's new role was Director of Marketing and Communications. Her primary task was to increase the visibility of St. Margaret's Hospital in order to raise the image of the institution in the eyes of the many publics served. The long-term goal was to attract the best possible physicians while increasing use of the hospital's facilities and attracting more patients.

The world of health care has dramatically changed in the past decade. Governmental regulations and support, concerns about lawsuits, evolving and expensive technologies, and changes in health insurance provisions affect hospitals of all sizes. In addition, St. Margaret's faced strong competition. The hospital's primary location is in a major metropolitan area in Minnesota. Two other large hospitals also offer comparable services in the same city. Each seeks to sign physicians to exclusive contracts in which they will only provide care with one organization.

The other significant challenge to St. Margaret's is its proximity to the Mayo Clinic. Clearly Mayo holds the highest level of prestige in the state and even in the region. Most physicians are inclined to think of Mayo first when making referrals for patients with difficult medical conditions. Mayo would be viewed by most publics as the "best" care possible.

The key issues in the image of any health organization are developing trust and a feeling of confidence in the quality of care that will be received. Beyond technological advantages, other, more subtle elements of an image could have an influence. Mary noted that to most patients the nurse plays a primary role in determining how the hospital is viewed. An uncaring and inattentive nurse is likely to drive away both the patient who encountered the nurse and all of the patient's family and friends. Negative word-of-mouth, Mary said, must be held to an absolute minimum.

Mary believed St. Margaret's needed to overcome two problems. First, the name "Margaret" is not commonly used anymore. Some publics may view it as an "old-fashioned" name. Second, there was nothing distinctive about the hospital's image. The overlap in services provided (heart care, cancer treatment) made it difficult to differentiate St. Margaret's from other providers.

If there was any advantage, Mary believed it was that St. Margaret's was affiliated with the Catholic Church. It was the only nonprofit hospital of the three major competitors. This attracted both Catholic patients and some Catholic physicians. Also, the hospital was able to utilize the services of a wide variety of volunteers.

As the marketing meeting opened, the agenda was to discuss all of the ways St. Margaret's could build its client base. The task would not be easy, but everyone in the room believed the hospital offered high-quality services in a caring atmosphere.

1. What are the image issues in this case?
2. What are the brand-name issues? Should the brand name be changed? If so, to what?
3. What types of advertisements should Mary develop for St. Margaret's General Hospital?
4. What other types of activities could St. Margaret's pursue to build a strong and positive corporate image?

**Chapter 2, "Corporate Image and Brand Management,"** describes these two key marketing ingredients. The role of the brand name, package, label, company logos, and other branding issues are described.

**Chapter 3, "Buyer Behaviors,"** reviews the steps of the consumer buyer behavior process as well as the business-to-business buying process. Individual decision-making models are identified. Tactics to influence buyers are also described. In the business-to-business area, buyer–seller relationships are discussed. The roles played by members of the buying center are noted. Methods that can be used to reach individual members are suggested.

**Chapter 4, "Promotions Opportunity Analysis,"** discusses the nature of a promotions opportunity analysis program. Market segmentation in consumer and business-to-business settings is also presented.

## Part 2: IMC Advertising Tools

**Chapter 5, "Advertising Management,"** describes the overall process of managing an ad campaign. Selection criteria used in choosing an agency are provided.

**Chapter 6, "Advertising Design: Theoretical Frameworks and Types of Appeals,"** analyzes the various kinds of appeals that can be used in creating ads. Sex, fear, rational approaches, and other methods are noted. Advantages and appropriate usage of each type of appeal are discussed.

**Chapter 7, "Advertising Design: Message Strategies and Executional Frameworks,"** explains the individual executional frameworks that are available, such as the slice-of-life, demonstration, and testimonial forms. Also, sources and spokespersons are analyzed.

**Chapter 8, "Advertising Media Selection,"** completes the advertising section by reviewing the various media that are available, including both more conventional methods such as television and radio as well as more recent venues such as the Internet and guerilla marketing programs.

## Part 3: IMC Promotional Tools

A fully integrated marketing communications program requires the inclusion of other company activities. Many customers are persuaded to make purchases through the use of marketing tactics other than advertising. This is also true in the business-to-business sector.

**Chapter 9, "Trade Promotions,"** details the various kinds of promotional tactics that are useful to marketing teams. Advantages and costs of each are defined.

**Chapter 10, "Consumer Promotions,"** notes the connections between consumer promotions, advertisements, and effective IMC programs. Benefits and costs of consumer promotions tactics are identified.

**Chapter 11, "Personal Selling, Database Marketing, and Customer Relationship Management,"** examines all of these buyer-focused activities that must be integrated with other communications that consumers experience.

**Chapter 12, "Public Relations, Sponsorship Programs, and Regulations,"** notes the importance of quality public relations efforts and the role of government and industry regulations within the integrated marketing communications plan. Individual sponsorship programs are noted in light of their contributions and costs.

## Part 4: IMC Integration Tools

The strings that tie together a complete IMC program include other important marketing activities as well as the assessment of the levels of success of a company's efforts. This final section provides information about the Internet, special concerns for small businesses, and assessment programs.

**Chapter 13, "Internet Marketing,"** gives special attention to Internet marketing and e-commerce programs. This form of marketing must be carefully integrated with other company activities.

**Chapter 14, "IMC for Small Businesses and Entrepreneurial Ventures,"** is devoted to the special IMC challenges these companies encounter. Limited budgets and limited customer awareness must be overcome to successfully build and sustain a new firm.

**Chapter 15, "Evaluating an Integrated Marketing Program,"** is the assessment chapter. Managers who are faced with accountability issues require quality methods for analyzing the effectiveness of their IMC programs. This chapter describes the tools that are available.

## THE INSTRUCTOR'S INTEGRATED TEACHING PACKAGE

The best way to teach IMC is with an integrated teaching package. We have prepared all of the supplements to make sure everything works together. The textbook includes the following instructional supplements:

▶ **The IMC Plan Pro Handbook.** This supplemental package consists of a booklet and disk, and is available from Prentice Hall. The IMC Plan Pro disk provides an exercise that requires a student or businessperson to prepare an entire marketing communications program. The booklet provides step-by-step instructions on how to use the disk and gives brief explanations of the IMC concepts that are part of the program.

▶ **Media Rich PowerPoint Presentation (on CD only).** This PowerPoint presentation features print advertisements, slides that build concepts over several steps, discussion questions, Web links, and video snippets. The PowerPoint not only include ads from the text but also additional ads. The slides, Web site links, video clips,

The IMC PlanPro Handbook

Kenneth E. Clow | Donald Baack

Featuring *IMC PlanPro* Software

and questions form a coherent presentation for the class. The print advertisements are accompanied by questions or captions relating them to the concepts within the chapter. Integrated learning experiences take the class to Web sites referenced in the text. These files are available on the Instructor's Resource CD-ROM, and a download version may be found on the Companion Website.

▶ **PowerPoint BASIC.** This simple presentation includes only basic outlines and key points from each chapter. No animation or forms of rich media are integrated, which makes the total file size manageable and easier to share online or via e-mail. BASIC was also designed for instructors who prefer to customize PowerPoint and want to be spared from having to strip out animation, embedded files, or other media rich features.

▶ **PowerPoint for Classroom Response Systems (CRS).** These Q&A–style slides are designed for classrooms using "clickers," or classroom response systems. Instructors who are interested in making CRS a part of their course should contact their Prentice Hall representative for details and a demonstration. CRS is a fun and easy way to make your classroom more interactive.

▶ **Web Site.** The Companion Website (www.prenhall.com/clow) contains chapter objectives, faculty resources, and links to company sites referenced in the text. Study guide questions for each chapter are available, and students can receive e-mail results, complete with grade reports, directly from professors. The Companion Website also includes details and information to direct students through the process of building an IMC campaign, and serves as an alternative for those who desire not to use the IMC Plan Pro disk, which is now located in a separate IMC supplement. Faculty may access the PowerPoint slides, *Instructor's Manual*, and other resources.

▶ *Instructor's Manual.* This resource provides support and suggestions for instructors. A complete outline is provided for each chapter, including key words and their definitions, important themes, references to text figures, and the material's implications for marketing professionals. Review questions, discussion questions, and application questions are all answered thoroughly by the authors, and the chapter-opening vignettes are also explained. A case from each chapter that was removed from the second edition appears in the *Instructor's Manual.*

▶ **Test Item File.** The test file has been expanded to include approxmiately 3,500 true-false, multiple-choice, and short-answer questions. It includes page references and difficulty level so that instructors can provide greater feedback to students. The test item file itself is available in print and electronic formats. The new TestGen-EQ test generation software is a computerized package that allows instructors to custom design, save, and generate classroom tests. The test program permits instructors to edit, add, and delete questions from the test bank; analyze test results; and organize a database of tests and student results. The new software allows for greater flexibility and ease of use. It provides many options for organizing and displaying tests, along with a search and sort feature.

▶ **Instructor's Resource CD-ROM.** The Instructor's Resource CD-ROM contains additional presentation materials for instructors to bring into class, including figures from the book and a version of the electronic test bank. This is in addition to inclusion of the electronic files for the *Instructor's Manual* and Media Rich PowerPoint Presentation.

▶ **IMC Video Library.** A video library is available for use in the classroom. Using today's popular news magazine format, students are taken on location and behind closed doors. Each news story profiles a well-known or up-and-coming company leading the way in its industry. Teaching materials to accompany the video library are available on the Companion Website and in the *Instructor's Manual*. Videos included are:

Angela Talley, DDB Worldwide

Inken Hollman-Peters, Nivea/Biersdorf, Inc.

Starbucks

Marriott

Motorola

Accenture

Reebok

American Express

Hasbro

Sony Metreon

Eaton Corporation

NFL

eGO Bikes

Honest Tea

Burke, Inc.

Strawberry Frog: Inside an Advertising Agency

Strawberry Frog: Behind the Scenes of an Advertising Campaign

Dunkin' Donuts

AFLAC

## ACKNOWLEDGMENTS

We would like to thank the following individuals who assisted in the development of both the second and third editions through their careful and thoughtful reviews:

Robert W. Armstrong, University of North Alabama

Jerome Christa, Coastal Carolina University

Stefanie Garcia, University of Central Florida

Robert J. Gulovsen, Washington University—Saint Louis

Sreedhar Kavil, St. John's University

Franklin Krohn, SUNY—Buffalo

Tom Laughon, Florida State University

William C. Lesch, University of North Dakota

James M. Maskulka, Lehigh University

Darrel D. Muehling, Washington State University

Esther S. Page-Wood, Western Michigan University

Venkatesh Shankar, University of Maryland

Albert J. Taylor, Austin Peay State University

Jerald Weaver, SUNY—Brockport

We are grateful to these reviewers of the first edition:

Craig Andrews, Marquette University

Ronald Bauerly, Western Illinois University

Mary Ellen Campbell, University of Montana

Les Carlson, Clemson University

Newell Chiesl, Indiana State University

John Cragin, Oklahoma Baptist College

J. Charlene Davis, Trinity University

Steven Edwards, Michigan State University

P. Everett Fergenson, Iona College

James Finch, University of Wisconsin—La Crosse

Thomas Jensen, University of Arkansas

Russell W. Jones, University of Central Oklahoma

Dave Kurtz, University of Arkansas

Monle Lee, Indiana University—South Bend

Ron Lennon, Barry University

Charles L. Martin, Wichita State University

Robert D. Montgomery, University of Evansville

S. Scott Nadler, University of Alabama

Ben Oumlil, University of Dayton

Melodie R. Phillips, Middle Tennessee State University

Don Roy, Middle Tennessee State University

Elise Sautter, New Mexico State University

Janice E. Taylor, Miami University

Robert L. Underwood, Bradley University

Robert Welch, California State University—Long Beach

Although there were many individuals who helped us with advertising programs, we want to thank a few who were especially helpful. These include the Bozell Advertising Agency for giving us access to the "Got Milk" advertisements. Special thanks goes to Kerri Martin of BWM motorcycles and Gretchen Hoag of Publics Technology for taking time to share with us their thoughts concerning their work and the IMC process. We appreciate the owners and employees of advertising agencies Newcomer, Morris, and Young, and Sartor Associates for providing us with a large number of advertisements. We also appreciate the staff at the *Joplin Globe* for providing many local advertisements.

On a personal note, we would like to thank Leah Johnson, who signed us for the first edition of the book. Katie Stevens and her team have rendered insightful opinions and given us a great deal of quality advice as this edition has moved forward. We would also like to thank the entire Prentice Hall production group.

Kenneth Clow would like to thank the University of Louisiana at Monroe for providing a supportive environment to work on this text. He is thankful to his sons Dallas, Wes, Tim, and Roy, who always provided encouragement and support.

Donald Baack would like to thank Mimi Morrison for her continued assistance in all his work at Pittsburg State University. Christine Fogliasso has been a great help in her role as department chairperson. She helped make the workload manageable during the preparation of the manuscript. Rachel Peterson, graduate assistant, and Dan Baack, his son, also contributed to this work.

We would like to especially thank our wives, Susan Clow and Pam Baack, for being patient and supportive during those times when we were swamped by the work involved in completing this edition. They have been enthusiastic and understanding throughout this entire journey.

# Integrated Advertising, Promotion, and Marketing Communications

# 1 Integrated Marketing Communications

## Chapter Objectives

*Recognize* the critical role communication plays in marketing programs.

*Review* the nature of the communication process.

*Apply* a communications model to marketing issues.

*Discover* the nature of a totally integrated advertising and marketing communications approach.

*Expand* the concept of integrated marketing communications to the global level.

## RON JON SURF SHOP

### IMC and Brand-Building Go to the Beach

If there is one common trend in beachside communities, it would be that there are plenty of surfing and swimwear shops located nearby. Most people couldn't tell you the name of any one store, unless they have visited a Ron Jon Surf Shop. Ron Jon is a prime example of how to develop and build strong brand awareness and loyalty in an industry in which mostly small, single-owner stores are located along the shorelines of beaches and lake-towns across the United States.

In the 1960s, surfboard technology was changing. Homemade wooden boards were being replaced with mass-produced fiberglass models. A surfer-dude name Ron DiMenna was frustrated that he could not buy one of these new and improved rides. As a result, he founded the first Ron Jon Surf Shop in New Jersey. In the early days, DiMenna would buy three boards and sell two with a markup that gave him the third board for "free." As time passed, the company grew and additional locations were opened on both the East and West Coast.

The center of the Ron Jon empire is located in Cocoa Beach, Florida. At the Ron Jon Surf Shop near the beach, surfer and beach-lover figures that look like sand sculptures greet customers as they approach. Huge billboards showing images of happy and relaxed swimmers and beautiful beach-people line the top of the building. The store itself covers more than 52,000 square feet. It is filled with an amazing variety of items. Swimsuits, sunglasses, toys, surfboards, towels, shirts, and even beach-themed home decorations are available. There is also a refreshment stand with picnic tables located outside the store for patrons to enjoy. This Ron Jon unit is open 24 hours per day, 365 days per year—just like the beach.

One of the most memorable Ron Jon images is its logo. The company's beach-themed, fun-loving image has led loyal customers to attach Ron Jon decals carrying the

logo practically everywhere, including one near the top of the Eiffel Tower and another aboard the U.S. space station. Many of the products sold in the store also display the logo.

The Ron Jon marketing team effectively utilizes advertising by creating cooperative programs with other companies. In 2003, the Cocoa Beach store celebrated its 40th anniversary. The Chrysler Corporation united with the firm to create a limited edition Ron Jon PT Cruiser. The autos were customized to display Ron Jon decal art on the outside. Inside, numerous items were added, including a Ron Jon sports bag, blankets, license plates, bumper stickers, key chains, and a t-shirt that guaranteed the car owner special bragging rights: Only 1,000 cars were made. One was given away as the grand prize of a local surfing event.

The 40th anniversary celebration also featured a contest in which Ron Jon memorabilia were solicited. Entrants sent in old photos, news articles, postcards, and personal stories. Each item gave the person a chance at a gift certificate for Ron Jon merchandise.

Ron Jon sponsors events that tie in with the company's primary business. This includes a natural alliance with professional surfing contests and other beachwear manufacturers, such as Billabong. In the early 2000s, one contest, called the "Rip Curl Trip Giveaway," was held in Southern California. The event featured free prizes for those who attended, including a drawing for a trip for two to view another professional surfing contest at Sunset Beach in Hawaii. The Rip Curl event included a radio remote for the general public, an autograph-signing session with professional surfers, and a chance to be one of 200 special guests at a VIP party featuring world championship surfer C. J. Hobgood and his Rusty Team Riders.

Awareness of Ron Jon presence has grown through innovative marketing programs. At one point, Ron Jon Surf Shop were featured in a MasterCard commercial. Now,

Ron Jon is expanding to reach international customers. The company has received in-store visits from people all around the world. Part of the reason, according to vice president for corporate development Bill Bieberbach, is that international customers prefer name-brand items. Ron Jon is a powerful brand that reaches beach lovers in other countries.

In this decade, Ron Jon has expanded into land-based sports. In the mid-2000s, the company sponsored an "End of Summer Skateboard Contest" in Florida. Skateboarders competed for cash prizes and merchandise. Pepsi was a co-sponsor of the event. Later, the two companies also held autograph sessions with Globe Pro Skateboarding. These events were aimed at new, young customers who enjoy skateboarding as much as surfing.[1]

The future of Ron Jon Surf Shops remains bright. The overall theme of fun, relaxation, and enjoyment makes the Ron Jon brand a major force in what is often a no-name marketplace.

The global marketplace consists of a complex set of competitors battling for customers in a rapidly changing environment. New companies are formed on a daily basis. Small businesses, Internet-based operations, and global conglomerates that have expanded through takeovers and mergers are all part of a worldwide marketing environment.

A wide variety of media beckon the leaders of these companies to spend advertising and marketing dollars. Marketing methods range from approaches as simple as stand-alone billboard advertisements to complex multilingual global Web sites. The number of ways to reach potential customers continually increases.

In the face of these sophisticated and cluttered market conditions, firms try to be heard. Marketing experts know that a company's communications must speak with a clear voice. Customers need to understand the essence of a business and the benefits that will come from using that firm's goods and services. With so many advertising and promotional venues available, and so many companies bombarding potential customers with messages, the task is challenging.

Two trends have emerged in this turbulent new marketing context. First, *accountability* is the primary focus. Advertising agencies are expected to produce tangible results. The company leaders who hire advertising agencies recognize that they cannot spend unlimited dollars on marketing programs. The funds must be spent wisely. A coupon program, contest, rebate program, or advertising campaign must yield measurable gains in sales, brand awareness, or customer loyalty to be considered successful.

The push for accountability is being driven by chief executive officers (CEOs), chief financial officers (CFOs), and boards of directors. Both large and small companies need visible, measurable results from marketing expenditures. According to Martyn Straw, chief strategy officer of the advertising agency BBDO Worldwide, corporate executives and business owners are tired of "funneling cash into TV commercials and glossy ads" that keep increasing in cost and seem to do less and less. As a result, companies like DaimlerChrysler are less likely to rely on 30-second television spots. Instead, communication venues (such as the Internet) and events where names, profiles, and addresses of prospective car buyers can be collected and tracked are utilized. Straw believes that "marketing has gone from being a cost or expense to an investment." Promotional dollars must add value as they generate new sales and higher profits.[2]

The second new trend in advertising is tied to the first. There have been major changes in the *tasks performed* by all of the key players in advertising programs. The first person who faces a new type of job is the account executive. The *account executive* is the person in an advertising agency who directs and oversees advertising and promotional programs for client companies. The strong demand for accountability has put the advertising or marketing account manager on the hot seat. He or she must respond to the scrutiny placed on each marketing campaign. This increased responsibility has changed the account executive's day-to-day activities. In the past, an account executive mainly served as a liaison between the people who prepared commercials and client companies. Now, the account manager is involved in developing overall strategic communication plans while, at the same time, trying to make sure each individual promotional activity achieves tangible results.

Another person facing greater accountability is the brand or product manager. The *brand manager* is the individual who manages a specific brand or line of products for the client company. When sales of a brand slow down, the brand manager looks for ways to boost them. The brand manager must work diligently with the advertising agency, the trade promotion specialist, the consumer promotion specialist, and any other individual or agency involved in conveying that brand image to customers. The brand manager must be a master at organizing the activities of many individuals while integrating each marketing campaign. Every promotional effort is coordinated so that each message about the brand speaks with the same voice.

A third set of individuals facing new responsibilities are creatives. *Creatives* are the people who develop the actual advertising and promotional campaigns. Although most creatives are employed by advertising agencies, some work for individual companies. Others are freelancers. In this new era where attracting attention to a company, good, or service is so difficult, creatives are being asked to perform additional functions. They are now often required to contribute ideas about the strategic marketing direction of the firm while developing individual advertisements. Creatives are also held accountable, along with account executives, for the effectiveness of an advertising campaign.

As a result, a new partnership among account executives, brand managers, and creatives has emerged. Most advertising and marketing agencies are expected to do more than create ads. They are assigned the task of helping a client company develop a totally integrated communications program. This trend toward a more integrated approach to advertising and communication will continue.

This textbook is devoted to explaining marketing communications from the strategic perspective of the decision makers both inside and outside the firm. Various topics are viewed from the vantage points of the key individuals involved, including account managers, brand managers, creatives, media buyers, and the Web master.

This chapter explains the nature of an integrated advertising and marketing communications program. First, communication processes are described. Understanding how communication works helps build the foundation for the rest of an integrated marketing program. Next, a totally integrated marketing communications program is described. Finally, the integrated marketing communications process is applied to global or international operations, generating the term *GIMC,* or globally integrated marketing communications.

## COMMUNICATION AND IMC PROGRAMS

**Communication** can be defined as transmitting, receiving, and processing information. When a person, group, or organization attempts to transfer an idea or message, communication occurs when the receiver (another person or group) is able to comprehend the

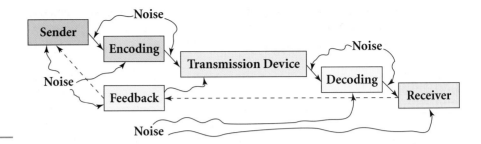

information. The model of communication shown in Figure 1.1 suggests that communication takes place when the message that was sent reaches its destination in a form that is understood by the intended audience.[3]

The communication process is part of any advertising or marketing program. For example, think about a person who plans to buy a new pair of athletic shoes. Using the communications model displayed in Figure 1.1, the **senders** are companies that manufacture and sell shoes. New Balance, ASICS, Reebok, and Skechers all try to gain the customer's attention. Most of these firms hire advertising agencies to construct messages. In other situations, the firm may have its own in-house marketing group.

Various advertisements for shoes.
*Source:* Courtesy of New Balance Athletic Shoes Inc. Photograph by Paul Wakefield; ASICS Tiger Corporation; Reebok International; Skechers USA Inc.

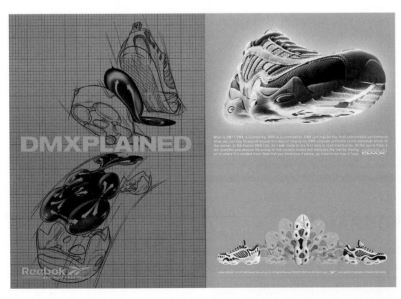

**Encoding** the message is the second step in the communications process. A creative takes the idea and transforms it into attention-getting advertisements designed for various media (television, radio, magazines, and others). The athletic shoe advertisements that are shown in this section are examples of encoding.

Messages travel to audiences through various **transmission devices**. The third stage of the marketing communication process occurs when a channel or medium delivers the message. The channel may be a television carrying an advertisement, a billboard, a Sunday paper with a coupon placed in it, or a letter to the purchasing agent of a large retail store. The shoe ads displayed in this section were transmitted through various magazines.

**Decoding** occurs when the message reaches one or more of the receiver's senses. Consumers both hear and see television ads. Others consumers handle (touch) and read (see) a coupon offer. It is even possible to "smell" a message. A well-placed perfume sample may entice a buyer to purchase both the magazine containing the sample and the perfume being advertised. People who are interested in purchasing athletic shoes pay closer attention to advertisements and other information about shoes. Study the athletic shoe advertisements shown in this section. Then, answer the following questions:

1. Which advertisement most dramatically attracted your attention? Why?
2. Which advertisement is the least appealing? Why?
3. How important is the brand name in each ad? Why?
4. What is the major message of each individual advertisement?
5. What makes each advertisement effective or ineffective?
6. Discuss your thoughts about each advertisement with other students.

When students discuss the advertisements, they sometimes discover that the same advertisement has been interpreted differently by other members of the group. In other words, the message is not being decoded in the same way. Quality marketing communication occurs when customers (the **receivers**) decode or understand the message as it was intended by the sender. In the case of the shoe ads, effective marketing communications depends upon receivers getting the right message and responding in the desired fashion (such as shopping, buying, or telling their friends about the shoes).

Examine the Web sites of the four athletic shoe companies featured in the advertisements.

▶ Reebok (www.rbk.com)
▶ ASICS (www.asics.com)
▶ New Balance (www.newbalance.com)
▶ Skechers (www.skechers.com)

The sites provide additional insights about the messages these companies are trying to send. Compare the materials on the Web sites to the shoe advertisements shown here. You should be able to see how the two messages were designed to go together. If they do not, the IMC program is not completely developed or fully integrated.

One obstacle that prevents marketing messages from being efficient and effective is called **noise**. Noise is anything that distorts or disrupts a message. It can occur at any stage in the communication process, as displayed in Figure 1.1. Examples of noise are provided in Figure 1.2.

The most common form of noise affecting marketing communications is **clutter**. Modern consumers are exposed to hundreds of marketing messages each day. Most are tuned out. Clutter includes:

▶ Eight minutes of commercials per half hour of television and radio programs
▶ A Sunday newspaper jammed with advertising supplements
▶ An endless barrage of billboards on a major street
▶ The inside of a bus or subway car papered with ads
▶ Web sites and servers loaded with commercials

> ▶ **The viewer is talking on the phone.**
> ▶ **The viewer is getting something to eat during the ad.**
> ▶ **The viewer of the ad dislikes or is offended by the nature of the ad.**
> ▶ **The ad is placed on a TV show that is seldom watched by the producer's target audience.**
> ▶ **The advertisement is placed next to an ad by a competitor.**
> ▶ **The creative designed an ad that the target audience did not get.**
> ▶ **The person in the ad overpowers the message.**
> ▶ **The producer of the ad changed the background of the ad from what the creative wanted.**

**FIGURE 1.2**
**Communication Noise in Television Advertising**

The final component of the communication process is **feedback**. It takes the forms of purchases, inquiries, complaints, questions, visits to the store, and hits on a Web site. Each indicates that the message has reached the receiver and that the receiver is now responding.

Account managers, creatives, brand managers, and others involved in the marketing process should pay attention to every part of the communications model. They should make sure that the proper audiences receive the messages. The message also must cut through all of the noise and clutter. In the case of athletic shoes, increases in market share, sales, and brand loyalty are common outcomes the marketing team tries to achieve.

Remember, however, that communicating with consumers and other businesses requires more than simply creating attractive advertisements. In the next section, the nature of a fully developed integrated marketing communications program is described. An effective IMC process integrates numerous marketing activities into a single package. This makes it possible for companies to reach target markets and other audiences more effectively.

## INTEGRATED MARKETING COMMUNICATIONS

An integrated marketing communications program can be built on the foundation provided by the communications model. Some marketing scholars argue that the integrated marketing communications (IMC) approach is a recent phenomenon. Others suggest the name is new, but the concept has been around for a long time. They note that the value of effectively coordinating all marketing functions and promotional activities has been mentioned in marketing literature for many years.[4]

Although IMC programs have been described in several ways, the consensus is to define them as follows: **Integrated marketing communications (IMC)** is the coordination and integration of all marketing communication tools, avenues, and sources within a company into a seamless program that maximizes the impact on consumers and other end users at a minimal cost. This integration affects all of a firm's business-to-business, marketing channel, customer-focused, and internally directed communications.

Before further examining the IMC concept, first consider the traditional framework of marketing from which it originated. The **marketing mix** is the starting point. As shown in Figure 1.3, promotion is one of the four components of the mix. For years the traditional view was that promotional activities included advertising, sales promotions, and personal selling activities. Sales promotions actually includes both sales and trade promotions, with sales promotions aimed at end users or consumers of goods and services, and trade promotions directed toward distributors and retailers. This traditional

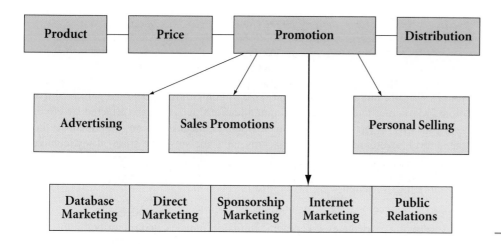

**FIGURE 1.3**
**The Components of Promotion**

view has changed some, due to the accountability issue that was discussed earlier in this chapter. The need to integrate all promotional efforts has expanded beyond the three traditional elements of advertising, sales promotions, and personal selling. Now, promotion also includes activities such as database marketing, direct marketing, sponsorship marketing, Internet marketing, and public relations.

A complete IMC plan incorporates every element of the marketing mix: products, prices, distribution methods, and promotions. This textbook primarily deals with the promotions component. Keep in mind, however, that to present a unified message the other three elements of the marketing mix must be blended into the program.

## AN INTEGRATED MARKETING COMMUNICATIONS PLAN

Integrated marketing is based on a master marketing plan. This plan should coordinate efforts in all components of the marketing mix. The purpose of the marketing plan is to achieve harmony in relaying messages to customers and other publics. The same plan integrates all promotional efforts. The idea is to keep the company's total communication program in synch.

Figure 1.4 lists the steps required to complete a marketing plan. The first step is a *situational analysis,* which is the process of examining factors from the organization's internal and external environments. The analysis identifies marketing problems and opportunities present in the external environment as well as internal company strengths and weaknesses.

When the situation is fully understood, the second step is to define primary *marketing objectives.* These objectives normally include targets such as higher sales, an increase in market share, a new competitive position, or desired customer actions, such as visiting the store and making a purchase.

Based on the marketing objectives, a *marketing budget* is prepared and *marketing strategies* are finalized. Marketing strategies apply to all the ingredients of the marketing mix plus any positioning, differentiation, or branding strategies the marketing team wishes to add.

▶ Situation analysis
▶ Marketing objectives
▶ Marketing budget
▶ Marketing strategies
▶ Marketing tactics
▶ Evaluation of performance

**FIGURE 1.4**
**The Marketing Plan**

## ETHICAL ISSUES

### Ethics, Morals, and IMC

*Morals* are beliefs or principles that individuals hold concerning what is right and what is wrong. *Ethics* are moral principles that serve as guidelines for both individuals and organizations. Marketing and marketing communications activities are affected by ethical and moral concerns. In each chapter of this textbook, ethical issues are described. At the most general level, several major ethical concerns and criticisms have arisen. They include:

1. Marketing causes people to buy more than they can afford.
2. Marketing overemphasizes materialism.
3. Marketing increases the costs of goods and services.
4. Advertising perpetuates stereotyping of males, females, and minority groups.
5. Marketers too often create advertisements that are offensive.
6. Advertisements often make bad habits (such as smoking) seem attractive.
7. Marketers use unfair tactics (such as bait and switch programs).
8. Too many advertisements are deceptive or misleading.
9. Advertising to children is unethical.
10. Salespeople use too many deceptive practices.

While reading about the nature of integrated marketing communications, consider these and other ethical issues. The time to start thinking about the ethical and moral basis of a career in marketing is now.

From these strategies, *marketing tactics* guide the day-by-day activities necessary to support marketing strategies. The final step in the marketing plan is stating how to *evaluate performance.*

These six steps of the marketing plan are similar to those used in creating management strategies. Both are designed to integrate all company activities into one consistent effort. Also, both provide guidance to company leaders and marketing experts as they try to ensure that the firm's total communications package is fully integrated. Once the marketing plan has been established, the firm can prepare its integrated marketing communications program.

## IMC COMPONENTS

Figure 1.5 presents on overview of the IMC approach that will be used in this textbook and presented in subsequent chapters. A brief description of each aspect follows. As shown, the foundation of an IMC program consists of a careful review of the company's image, the buyers to be served, and the markets in which the buyers are located.

Advertising programs are then built on this foundation, as are the other elements of the promotional mix. Finally, the integration tools located at the peak of the pyramid help the company's marketing team make certain that the elements of the plan are consistent and effective.

### The Foundation

The first section of this text builds the foundation for the rest of an IMC program. Chapter 2 describes the corporate image and brand management elements. Strengthening the firm's image and brands answers the key questions, "Who are we and what message are we trying to send?" From there it is possible to identify target markets.

Chapter 3 describes buyer behaviors. The steps of the consumer purchasing process can be used to explain how individuals make choices. Marketers identify which motives lead to purchase decisions and which factors affect those decisions. Then, the IMC program

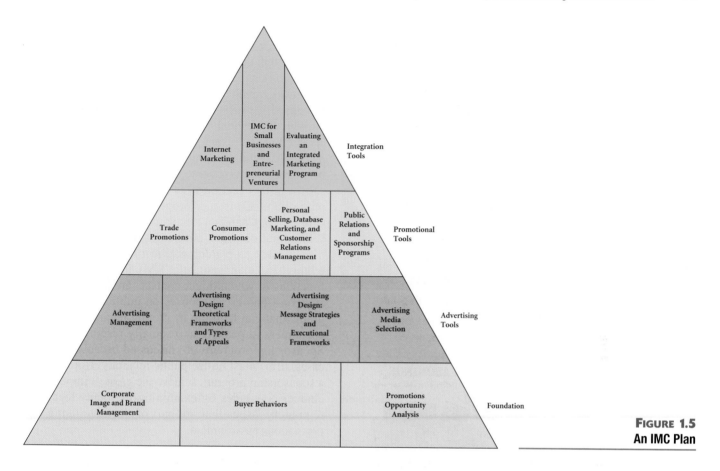

**FIGURE 1.5**
**An IMC Plan**

can be designed in a manner that best influences consumer choices. Business-to-business buyer behavior is also examined. Knowing how to reach purchasing managers and other decision makers within target businesses is another critical element in the development of a totally integrated communications plan. Discovering viable business-to-business marketing opportunities plays a vital role in implementing the IMC plan.

Chapter 4 describes the promotions opportunity analysis element of the IMC program. This task includes identifying all target markets. Consumer market segments are often distinguished by demographics, income, social class, and various psychographic variables. Business markets can also be segmented by understanding the demographics of the company's buying team, noting who the end users will be, and by determining the benefits other businesses expect to receive from the products and services they buy.

## Advertising Tools

The second section of this text is devoted to advertising issues. Advertising management, as described in Chapter 5, addresses the major functions of advertising and directs the general path the company will take. Advertising design and media selection (Chapters 6 through 8) involve matching the message, media, and audience, so that the right people see and/or hear the ads. Many appeals can be used, including those oriented toward fear, humor, sex, music, and logic. These should be conveyed by attractive, credible, likable, and authoritative sources. Effective advertising is based on a foundation of understanding consumer and business buyer behaviors. Advertising reinforces or projects the specific brand and firm image stated in the marketing plan.

## Promotional Tools

The next level of the IMC pyramid adds trade promotions, consumer promotions, personal selling, database marketing, public relations, and sponsorships into the program. When marketing managers carefully design all of the steps taken up to this point, the firm

Celestial Seasonings 'Greens just keep getting better' Green Tea.
*Source:* Courtesy of Celestial Seasonings.

The Internet is an important communication tool for companies such as WeddingChannel.com.
*Source:* Courtesy of WeddingChannel.com.

is in a better position to integrate these activities. Messages presented in the advertising campaign can be reinforced in the trade and consumer promotions. Trade promotions, as described in Chapter 9, include contests, incentives, vendor support programs, and other fees and discounts that help the manufacturer push the product through the channel. Consumer promotions are directly oriented to end users and include coupons, contests, premiums, refunds, rebates, free samples, and price-off offers. The advertisement for Celestial Seasonings shown in this section illustrates the use of consumer promotions. Consumer promotions are the subject of Chapter 10. Chapter 11 explains the nature of personal selling and database marketing in terms of database management, data mining, direct marketing, customer relationship management (CRM) activities, and other functions in which direct contacts are made with consumers. Chapter 12 focuses on public relations programs that can help the marketing team connect with consumers in positive and socially responsible ways. Sponsorship programs are discussed because, in many cases, firms must utilize public relations efforts to help a sponsorship program achieve the greatest impact. The chapter concludes by examining the many legal and regulatory issues that are part of the advertising and promotions environment.

## Integration Tools

The "top" level of the IMC program includes the integration tools needed to make sure all customers are effectively being served. Internet marketing, the topic of Chapter 13, has become a critical activity in nearly every firm. Consumers look for companies to have an Internet presence. For businesses, it is even more critical as increasingly business-to-business transactions, sales, and service are being conducted online. Chapter 14 is devoted to small businesses and entrepreneurial ventures. All of the IMC tasks are included in managing a small business; however, the emphasis changes due to special challenges such as limited funds for promotions.

Chapter 15, the final chapter of this textbook, explains how to evaluate an integrated marketing program. It is crucial to make decisions about how a communication program will be evaluated *prior to* any promotional campaign. Then, evaluation materials can be designed accordingly. A promotions evaluation process holds everything together. It drives the entire IMC process as much as does preparing the core business plan. Fully integrated marketing requires a careful linkage between planning and evaluation processes; one cannot occur without the other.

## Refining the IMC Program

Integrated marketing communications (IMC) involves more than simply writing a plan. It is also not a program limited to the company's marketing department. IMC is a company-wide activity. To be successful,

# COMMUNICATION ACTION

## Hewlett-Packard: "We Understand"

An excellent example of an integrated marketing communications program is provided by the software systems engineering division (SSED) of Hewlett-Packard (H-P). This group initiated its IMC process through workshops designed to help H-P's employees better understand the dilemmas faced by its customers. These workshops were directed by representatives from sales, product marketing, engineering, and customer support departments within H-P. Each had a different perspective of the customer and provided valuable input into the various dilemmas faced by end users. The team approach allowed everyone to see the customer from a more holistic perspective.

Based on input from these departments, a creative strategy emerged with a strong focus on customer needs. The theme "we understand" was adopted. H-P's marketing emphasis centered on the idea that members of the company understood the issues, pressures, and constraints that software developers faced. Knowing about unrealistic deadlines, hidden-code errors, and other problems and how to cope with these issues was the key. H-P's leaders believed they could solve transition problems for customers by moving to object-oriented programming and simultaneously developing multiple applications of company software. The theme was integrated into all of H-P's marketing programs. It was launched in an advertising campaign and then reinforced in three direct mailings. The same message was used in trade show handouts and displays. H-P's Web site was redesigned around the same principle.

The "we understand" idea served as an umbrella for all marketing strategies and tactics. The integrated approach allowed H-P to speak with one voice regardless of the communication method customers encountered when they contacted the firm. This more fully integrated program was more than just the theme, however. It began with effective communication within and built outward to the point where H-P's end users (other business) could see and experience a real difference in the products and services that were being provided.

**Source:** P. Griffeth Lindell, "You Need an Integrated Attitude to Develop IMC," *Marketing News* 31, no. 11 (May 26, 1997), p. 6.

every part of the organization's operation must be included. A study conducted by the American Productivity & Quality Center of Houston of the best integrated marketing firms indicates that four stages are involved in designing an effective integrated marketing communications system.[5]

The first stage is to identify, coordinate, and manage all forms of marketing communication. The objective is to bring all of the company's communication elements together under one umbrella. This includes advertising, promotions, direct marketing, Internet and e-commerce programs, public relations, sponsorships, and other marketing activities. During this stage of IMC development, the marketing team must be sure that all promotional materials deliver a unified message and speak with one voice. The theme should also be present in the logos, colors, letterhead, and every other message the company sends. The goal is to make sure there is consistency in and synergy among all communication venues.

In the second stage, communications are examined from the perspective of the customer. The marketing team should analyze every contact method that might influence customers as they form opinions and make decisions about the company. This means studying employees who work at the company, the firm's Web site, and the product itself. Even those who answer the phone deserve scrutiny. The idea is to be certain external communications match internal communications. The IMC umbrella covers every internal and external group that might affect perceptions of the company and its products. Employees, distributors, retailers, dealers, product package designers, and others need to be observed.

Advertising is a crucial component of a firm's IMC program.
*Source:* Courtesy of Newcomer, Morris & Young, Inc.

Information technology comes to the forefront in the third stage. Company leaders should find ways to apply information technology to IMC programs. This provides the basis for identifying and evaluating the impact of communication programs with respect to key customer segments. The third step is a critical part of an IMC program because now customer input is being gathered and used to make marketing and communication decisions. This means the best IMC companies involve customers in planning processes. Consumer goods companies seek inputs from consumers. Business-to-business firms invite target members from other businesses. As a result, the potentially adversarial relationship between business buyers and sellers is replaced by a cooperative, "let's work together" mentality.

The fourth and final stage of IMC development occurs when the organization uses customer data information and insights to drive corporate strategic planning. Return-on-customer investment is calculated for the various marketing initiatives. The information guides marketing decisions and the communication approaches aimed at individual customer segments. Firms reaching this stage, such as Dow Chemical, FedEx, and Hewlett-Packard, take databases and use them to calculate and establish a customer value for each buyer. All customers are not equally valuable. In contrast to a typical marketing program designed to win customers by sending the same marketing message to everyone, Dow Chemical, FedEx, and Hewlett-Packard allocate sales and marketing communication resources to those customers with the greatest potential for return, based on calculations of customer values. This process helps company leaders understand each customer's worth and treat each one individually, resulting in the highest possible return on investment for marketing expenditures.

After the internal marketing activities have been completed, the marketing team should address other parts of the company. A study by the American Productivity & Quality Center notes that successful IMC programs require cross-functional communication. In other words, communication lines must be open between marketing and other departments. Every employee in the company must become part of the emphasis on quality communications and customer orientation.[6]

One final ingredient is found in successful IMC companies. The marketing team clearly understands as many of the company's customers' needs as possible. This makes them customers of the whole company, not just the SBU, operating division, or outlet in which they are doing business. Seeing a patron as a customer of the total company encourages the cross-selling of goods and services. Using this method, ServiceMaster, which provides janitorial services to various companies, was able to increase revenues. The marketing team

Rapid delivery systems and other innovations have caused shifts in market channel power.

> ▶ Development of information technology
> ▶ Changes in channel power
> ▶ Increase in competition (global competitors)
> ▶ Maturing markets
> ▶ Brand parity
> ▶ Integration of information by consumers
> ▶ Decline in effectiveness of mass-media advertising

**FIGURE 1.6**
**Factors Affecting the Value of IMC Programs**

encouraged cross-selling of pest control and lawn services to customers already using the firm's janitorial services. This approach also assists selling in other countries when the firm is a multinational operation. Thus, a customer who buys from Hewlett-Packard in the United States is an excellent prospect in other countries where both H-P and that customer operate. When members of the company think in these terms, marketing dollars are spent wisely.

## THE VALUE OF IMC PLANS

Why are IMC programs so crucial to marketing success? Figure 1.6 lists several trends that are linked to the increasing importance of integrated advertising and marketing communications programs. A major force compelling firms to seek greater integration of advertising and marketing communications is *information technology*. Computers, the World Wide Web, and telecommunications have moved the world into an information age where businesses and most consumers have access to an abundance of marketing information. The challenge for marketers in the future will not just be gathering information; the challenge will also involve sifting through an avalanche of statistics, ideas, and messages and putting them into a format that company leaders can use. When this is accomplished, business leaders can make intelligent, informed decisions about how to market products.

### Information Technology

Technology allows instant communications among business executives, employees, and others around the world. It has also created new opportunities for marketing communications. For example, predicting the purchasing behaviors of consumers in the past was based on the results of test markets, attitudinal research, and intention-to-buy surveys. Although these are excellent means of obtaining information about consumers, they often are slow, costly, and are potentially unreliable.

Today, predicting purchase behavior is more precise due to the development of the UPC (universal product code) bar-coding system. The technology was originally used to manage inventories. Scanning every sale meant retailers were better able to develop efficient inventory control systems. They did not have to rely on human counting of merchandise.

At the same time, UPC codes combined with other technology programs allow huge amounts of data and information about customers to be gathered. Advanced statistical software helps company leaders analyze these data files. Connections between financial (credit card, banking) and business firms make it possible to collect purchasing data. Using this information, demographic and psychographic information about consumers can be correlated with the items they buy, when they make purchases, and where they make purchases. Consequently, marketers can quickly determine who is buying a company's products and identify the best communication channels to reach those customers.

### Changes in Channel Power

Technological developments also served as catalysts for changes in channel power. Two typical market channels are:

Producer → Wholesaler → Retailer → Consumer

and

Producer → Business Agent → Business Merchant → Business User

With the advancement of the World Wide Web and information technology, the power has shifted to the consumer.[7] Currently, consumers can obtain information about goods and services from their homes or businesses and purchase almost anything over the Internet. For example, the Visa advertisement in this section encourages consumers to book hotel rooms, air travel, and car rentals online. Internet-driven sales have grown at a tremendous rate. In fact, since 1999 Internet retail sales have expanded at annual rate of 44.4 percent. By 2003, total global retail sales were $232.4 billion. The most concentrated spending is in the areas of computers, electronics, tickets, and travel.[8] Figure 1.7 highlights the major segments of global Internet retail sales and what percentage each category represents of the total global Internet retail sales.

To illustrate how technology has changed channel power, think about an individual in the market for a new stereo. First, she goes to the Internet and searches for information. She then identifies several possible brands and narrows them down to three. Next, she travels to a local mall and investigates the three brands. Asking questions of the salesclerks helps her gather additional product information. Going home, she then logs onto the Web sites of the three manufacturers to learn about warranties and company policies. Having gathered sufficient information to make a decision, she can utilize Internet sources or a catalog to finalize the purchase either via the

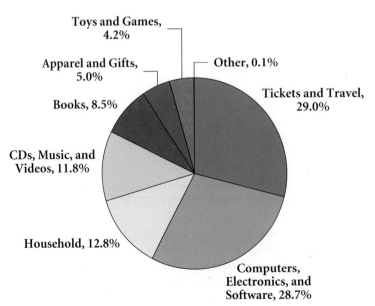

**FIGURE 1.7**
**Global Internet Retail Sales by Product Type**

*Source:* "Global Internet Retail: Industry Profile," *Datamonitor* (May 2004), p. 10.

Web or by telephone. Within 3 days, the new stereo arrives complete with a money-back guarantee if she is not satisfied. The result is that the buyer is in charge of the entire process, not the retailer or the wholesaler.

The same principles apply to business-to-business purchasing activities. Buyers who shop on behalf of organizations and other company members seeking business-to-business services are able to tap into the same resources (Web sites, databases). This means that the same kind of shift in channel power is taking place in the business-to-business sector.

## Increases in Competition

Information technology has dramatically changed the marketplace in other ways. Consumers can purchase goods and services from anywhere in the world. Competition no longer comes from the company just down the street—it can come from a firm 10,000 miles away that can supply a product faster and cheaper. People want quality, but they also want a low price. The company that delivers on both quality and price gets the business, regardless of location. Advancements in delivery systems make it possible for purchases to arrive almost anywhere in a matter of days.

In this type of market, the only way one firm can gain sales is to take customers away from another firm. Integrating advertising and other marketing communications becomes extremely important in such an environment. Advertising alone is not enough to maintain sales. This situation is further complicated for manufacturers when retailers hold stronger channel power and control the flow of merchandise to consumers. In that situation, manufacturers have to invest in trade promotions (dealer incentives, slotting allowances, discounts) to keep their products in various retail outlets. Encouraging retailers to promote a manufacturer's brand or prominently display it for consumer viewing requires even greater promotional dollars. Manufacturers also must invest heavily in consumer promotions to keep end users loyal to their companies and encourage them to purchase their brands because they know that the more they promote their own products, the more attractive those products become to retailers.

The U.S. athletic shoe market provides an excellent example of how growth for any given company comes at the expense of competing brands. Figure 1.8 displays market shares for the top four athletic shoe brands over an 18-year period. Although Nike remains the leading brand, its share and lead over competing brands have been reduced from 48 percent of the total market in 1997 to 36 percent market share in 2003. On the

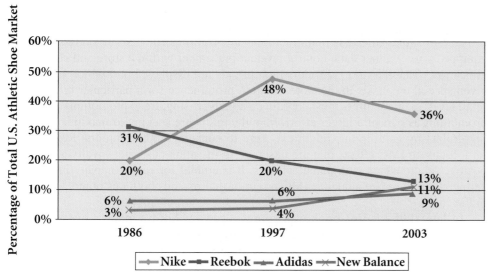

**FIGURE 1.8**
**Market Share of Top Four Brands in 2003 in the U.S. Athletic Shoe Market**

*Source:* Greg Lindsay, "The Rebirth of Cool," *Business 2.0* 5, no. 8 (September 2004), pp. 108–113.

## COMMUNICATION ACTION

### Reebok: The Cool Campaign

Realizing the difficulty of competing head-to-head with Nike, Reebok has chosen a new marketing approach. Through a re-branding strategy and image repositioning, Reebok hopes to become the shoe of choice for hip-hoppers, hipsters, and other fashion-forward urbanites. It is a risky strategy. Still, in 2003, of the top four athletic shoe brands, only Reebok had increases in sales.

Reebok's first move into the new arena of fashion was signing hip-hop artists Jay-Z and 50 Cent to endorsement deals. Reebok then signed Japanese clothing designer Nigo to develop a new line, which was branded "Ice Creams." Although bold, this new approach has captured a segment of consumers who liked the new fresh look, the new endorsers, and the fashion-forward statements. The new line was targeted primarily to males. It accounted for 15 percent of Reebok's 2003 sales.

In Asia–Pacific, the company used another program. Reebok teamed with MTV to bring basketball programming to Asia. Reebok signed a 10-year pact with the National Basketball Association to not only provide programming, but also to design, manufacture, market, and sell official NBA sportswear in the Asia–Pacific region. According to Siddarth Varma, vice president of marketing for Asia–Pacific Reebok International, "Reebok has been gaining inroads into the world of basketball and hip-hop music with the sponsorship of various prominent NBA players and hip-hop artists."

A third objective was to reach tech-savvy fans. Reebok signed a multiyear sponsorship with entertainment software company Electronic Arts, Inc. Advertisements featuring Reebok shoes and gear in video games were developed. Brain Povinelli, vice president of integrated marketing at Reebok, stated that combining Reebok's products with video games was "an effective part of our integrated marketing model." This new integrated approach may be just the right approach to rejuvenate the Reebok brand.

**Source:** Greg Lindsay, "The Rebirth of Cool," *Business 2.0* 5, no. 8 (September 2004), pp. 108–113; "Reebok's New Game," *WWD: Women's Wear Daily* 188, no. 132 (December 23, 2004), p. 3; Amy White, "Reebok, MTV Line for Brand Hoopla," *Media Asia* (April 9, 2004), p. 3.

other hand, Reebok's market share declined from 31 percent in 1986 (when the brand was the market leader) to 13 percent in 2003. As a result of this drop, Reebok has chosen not to compete with Nike in the hard-core sports market. Instead, Reebok now focuses on becoming the brand of choice for hip-hoppers, hipsters, and other fashion-forward urbanites. The Communication Action box in this section contains more information about Reebok's strategy and new integrated marketing communication plan.

At the same time that manufacturers are fighting for market share, retailers, equipped with scanner data, control product placement within a store and shelf space allocation.[9] Retailers now decide which brands are displayed and which brands are given special emphasis in the store. To gain prominence for a particular brand at the retail level, manufacturers must coordinate all advertising, trade promotions, and sales promotions as part of a larger effort. Manufacturers are seeking to maximize marketing dollars by gaining maximum exposure to consumers and retailers. Retailers, in turn, focus on IMC efforts that are designed to maintain customer loyalty along with positive relationships with manufacturers. It is crucial for each company in the marketing chain to create a quality IMC program that reaches both customers and others in the chain.

In late 2005 (as this book was going to press), Adidas made a bid to acquire Reebok. In the near future, it appears that Reebok will remain a separate brand alongside Adidas. This purchase enables Adidas/Reebok to increase total market share and more effectively compete with Nike because each brand has different strengths and different target markets.

## Brand Parity

The increase in national and global competition is due to the availability of multiple brands. Many of these products have nearly identical benefits. When consumers believe that most brands offer the same set of attributes, the result is called **brand parity.** From the consumer's perspective, this means shoppers will purchase from a *group* of accepted brands rather than one specific brand. When brand parity is present, quality is often not a major concern because consumers believe that only minor quality differences exist. Consumers often view quality levels of products as being nearly equal. As a result, they often base purchase decisions on other criteria such as price, availability, or a specific promotional deal. The net effect is that brand loyalty has experienced a steady decline.[10] Brand loyalty has also been reduced because of a growing acceptance of private brands.

A survey conducted by Top Brands in 2004 revealed higher levels of interest in brand switching in 13 of 17 major product categories.[11] The lowest levels of brand loyalty were present for greeting cards, groceries, and canned foods. When asked "If you didn't find the brand you wanted, would you be likely to buy another brand," 68 percent of the consumers surveyed said they would be willing to switch to another greeting card brand if their favorite was not available. For groceries and canned foods, 67 percent were willing to switch.

In response, the marketing team should try to create a message that expresses how the company's products are clearly different. They must convince consumers that the company's brand is superior. They must also convince consumers that the product is not the same as the competition's. A quality IMC program is, in part, designed to gain the benefits associated with a strong brand name.

## Integration of Information

Today's consumers have a variety of choices regarding where they obtain information about a brand. If consumers are not satisfied with what they hear, they can seek additional information. They may go to the Internet and read about other brands and companies. As a result, most companies now list Internet addresses on advertisements. In the McCormick's ad shown in this section, notice the address: www.mccormick.com. The Web site contains additional information about McCormick seasonings along with ideas and recipes for consumers. Web users can discuss products and companies with other customers in chat rooms or in Web logs. They may also travel to retail stores and discuss various options with the salesclerk. Others may consult independent sources of information such as *Consumer Reports.*

The marketing team should be concerned with the ways consumers integrate the information they receive. Company leaders should make sure that every contact point projects the same message. **Contact points** are

Many companies such as McCormick now list their Web address on advertisements to encourage customers to visit company Web sites.
*Source:* Courtesy of McCormick & Co., Inc.

**Positive Responses**

▶ Ads have potential to be entertaining (45%)

▶ Sit and watch ads (16%)

**Negative Responses**

▶ Get up and do something else (54%)

▶ Get annoyed (52%)

▶ Switch channels (40%)

▶ Talk to others in the room (34%)

▶ Turn down the sound on the TV (19%)

▶ Read (11%)

▶ Use the computer (5%)

**FIGURE 1.9**
**Viewer Activities**
**During TV Commercials**

*Source:* Jennifer Lach, "Commercial Overload," *American Demographics* 21, no. 9 (September 1999) p. 20.

the places where customers interact with or acquire additional information from a company. These contacts may be direct or indirect, planned or unplanned. An effective IMC program sends a consistent message about the nature of the company, its products, and the benefits that result from making a purchase from the organization.

## Decline in the Effectiveness of Mass-Media Advertising

The influence of mass-media advertising has dramatically declined. VCRs and TIVO systems allow consumers to watch programs without commercials. The rise in popularity of cable TV, DVR recorders, and satellite dishes means consumers have a wider variety of viewing choices. Using the remote while watching television means it is likely that, during most commercials, the viewer is surfing other channels to see what else is on. Many television advertisements are not seen, even by those people watching a particular program. In a recent survey by conducted by *Brandweek* magazine, only 16 percent of viewers said that they watch commercials during a program. Figure 1.9 displays the results of this study.[12] To overcome this problem, it is vital to create new and innovative communications programs.

Many firms employ advertising agencies to assist in marketing efforts. Until 1970, almost all advertising agencies focused only on the advertising aspect of the marketing plan. Now, however, many advertising agencies spend substantial amounts of time assisting clients in the development of IMC programs.[13] In addition to advertisements, these agencies design consumer promotion materials and direct-marketing programs, along with other marketing tactics.

## GLOBALLY INTEGRATED MARKETING COMMUNICATIONS

The same trend that exists among advertising agencies in the United States also occurs in the international arena. Instead of being called "IMC," however, it is known as *GIMC,* or a globally integrated marketing communications program.[14] The goal is still the same— to coordinate marketing efforts. The challenges are greater due to larger national and cultural differences in target markets.

In the past, marketers could employ two different strategies for global companies. The first approach was called **standardization,** in which the idea was to standardize the product and message across countries. The goal of this approach was generating economies of scale in production while creating a global product using the same promotional theme. The language would be different, but the basic marketing message would be the same.

The second approach to global marketing was called **adaptation**. Products and marketing messages were designed for and adapted to individual countries. Thus, the manner in which a product was marketed in France was different than in Italy, India, or Australia.

The GIMC approach is easier to apply when a company relies on the standardization method; however, GIMC can and should be used with either adaptation or standardization.[15] To reduce costs, careful coordination of marketing efforts should occur across countries. Even when a firm uses the adaptation strategy, marketers from various countries can learn from each other. Members of the marketing department should not feel like they have to reinvent the wheel. Synergy can occur between countries. More importantly, learning can occur. As telecommunications continue to expand, contacts between peoples of different countries are much more frequent.

Remember, a commercial targeted for customers in France may also be viewed by citizens of Spain because of satellite technologies. Therefore, a company should try to transmit a consistent theme, even when there are differences in local messages. In terms of marketing, the philosophy many companies use is "market globally, but act locally." When marketers design or encode messages for local markets, they need to have the freedom to tailor or alter the message so that it fits the local culture and the target market. Thus, although Pepsi portrays a global image around a theme of "Generation Next," the final message conveyed to each country often varies. Development of a GIMC is the final extension to an IMC plan. With its completion, companies are able to compete more effectively both at home and abroad.

## SUMMARY

A new era is unfolding in the fields of advertising, promotions, and marketing communications. Marketing departments and advertising agencies, as well as individual account managers, brand managers, and creatives, encounter strong pressures. They are being held accountable for expenditures of marketing communications dollars. Company leaders expect tangible results from promotional campaigns and other marketing programs. As a result, new partnerships form between account executives, creatives, and the companies that hire them. The duties of the account manager have expanded in the direction of a more strategically oriented approach to the advertising and marketing communications. Those preparing to become advertising or promotions professionals must be aware of both accountability issues and the new aspects of these jobs.[16]

Communication is transmitting, receiving, and processing information. It is a two-way street in which a sender must establish a clear connection with a receiver. Effective communication is the glue holding the relationship between two entities together. When communication breaks down, conflicts, misunderstandings, and other problems may develop.

The components of the communication process include the sender, an encoding process, the transmission device, the decoding process, and the receiver. Noise is anything that distorts or disrupts the flow of information from the sender to the receiver.

In the marketing arena, senders are companies seeking to transmit ideas to consumers, employees, other companies, retail outlets, and others. Encoding devices are the means of transmitting information, and include advertisements, public relations efforts, press releases, sales activities, promotions, and a wide variety of additional verbal and nonverbal cues sent to receivers. Transmission devices are the media and spokespersons who carry the message. Decoding occurs when the receivers (such as customers or retailers) encounter the message. Noise takes many forms in marketing, most notably the clutter of an overabundance of messages in every available channel.

Integrated marketing communications (IMC) takes advantage of the effective management of the communications channel. Within the marketing mix of products, prices, distribution systems, and promotions, firms that speak with one clear voice are able to coordinate and integrate all marketing tools. The goal is to have a strong and positive impact on consumers, businesses, and other end users.

IMC plans are vital to achieving success. The reasons for their importance begin with the explosion of information technologies. Channel power has shifted from manufacturers to retailers to consumers. Company leaders must adjust in order to maintain a strong market standing, and IMC programs can assist in this effort. New levels of competition drive marketers to better understand their customers and be certain those end users are hearing a clear and consistent message from the firm. As consumers develop a stronger sense of brand parity, whereby no real differences in product–service quality are perceived, marketers must recreate a situation in which their brand holds a distinct advantage over others. This is difficult, because consumers now can collect and integrate information about products from a wide variety of sources, including technological outlets (Internet Web sites) and interpersonal (sales reps) sources. Quality IMC programs help maintain the strong voice companies need to be certain their messages are heard. An additional challenge is the decline in effectiveness of mass-media advertising. IMC helps company leaders find new ways to contact consumers with a unified message.

When a firm is involved in an international setting, a GIMC, or globally integrated marketing communications system, can be of great value. By developing one strong theme and then adapting that theme to individual countries, the firm conveys a message that integrates international operations into a more coherent package.

Most of this text explains the issues involved in establishing an effective IMC program. The importance of business-to-business marketing efforts is noted, because many firms market their wares as much to other companies as they do to consumers. Successful development of an IMC program should help firms remain profitable and vibrant, even when the complexities of the marketplace make these goals much more difficult to reach.

## REVIEW QUESTIONS

1. Define *communication*. Why does it play such a crucial role in business?

2. What are the parts of an individual communications model?

3. Who are the typical senders in marketing communications? Who are the typical receivers?

4. Name the transmission devices, both human and nonhuman, that carry marketing messages. How can the human element become a problem?

5. Define *clutter*. Name some of the forms of clutter in marketing communications.

6. Define *integrated marketing communications*.

7. What are the four parts of the marketing mix?

8. What steps are required to write a marketing plan?

9. Describe a promotions opportunity analysis.

10. Describe firm and brand image.

11. What are the three main components of advertising?

12. Why has the growth of information technology made IMC programs so important for marketing efforts?

13. What reasons were given to explain the growth of IMC plans and their importance?

14. What is channel power? How has it changed in the past few decades?

15. What is brand parity? How is it related to successful marketing efforts?

16. What is a GIMC? Why is it important for multinational firms?

17. What is the difference between *standardization* and *adaptation* in GIMC programs?

18. How has the job of an advertising account executive changed? How has the job of a creative changed? How has the job of a brand manager changed? How do the three jobs interact in this new environment?

## KEY TERMS

**communication**   Transmitting, receiving, and processing information.

**senders**   The person(s) attempting to deliver a message or idea.

**encoding**   The verbal (words, sounds) and nonverbal (gestures, facial expressions, posture) cues that the sender utilizes in dispatching the message.

**transmission devices**   All of the items that carry the message from the sender to the receiver.

**decoding**   Takes place when the receiver employs any set of his or her senses (hearing, seeing, feeling) in the attempt to capture the message.

**receivers**   The intended audience for a message.

**noise**   Anything that distorts or disrupts a message.

**clutter**   Exists when consumers are exposed to hundreds of marketing messages per day, and most are tuned out.

**feedback**   Information the sender obtains from the receiver regarding the receiver's perception or interpretation of a message.

**integrated marketing communications (IMC)**   The coordination and integration of all marketing communication tools, avenues, and sources within a company into a seamless program that maximizes the impact on consumers and other end users at a minimal cost. This affects all of a firm's business-to-business, marketing channel, customer-focused, and internally oriented communications.

**marketing mix**   Consists of products, prices, places (the distribution system), and promotions.

**brand parity**   Occurs when there is the perception that most products and services are essentially the same.

**contact points**   The places where customers may interact with or acquire additional information about a firm.

**standardization**   When a firm standardizes its products and market offerings across countries with the goal of generating economies of scale in production while using the same promotional theme.

**adaptation**   Occurs when products and marketing messages are designed for and adapted to individual countries.

# CRITICAL THINKING EXERCISES

**Discussion Questions**

1. The marketing director for a furniture manufacturer is assigned the task of developing an integrated marketing communications program to emphasize the furniture's natural look. Discuss the problems the director may encounter in developing this message and in ensuring that consumers understand the message correctly. Refer to the communication process in Figure 1.1 for ideas. What kind of noise may interfere with the communication process?

2. Referring to Exercise 1, assume the director wants to develop an integrated marketing communications program emphasizing a theme focused on the furniture's natural look. This theme applies to all of their markets, that is, both retailers and consumers. Using Figure 1.5 as a guide, briefly discuss each element of the integrated marketing communications plan and how to incorporate it into an overall theme.

3. The marketing director for a manufacturer of automobile tires wants to integrate its marketing program internationally. Should the director use a standardization or adaptation approach? How could the company be certain that its marketing program will effectively be integrated among the different countries where it sells tires?

4. Hewlett-Packard's IMC theme is "we understand." Do you think this conveys a clear message about the company's operations in the software industry?

5. Reebok is moving away from direct competition with other companies in the athletic shoe market. Instead, the goal is to position the shoes as being cutting-edge fashion. Do you think this is a wise move? What kinds of problems or obstacles could this repositioning effort encounter?

# INTEGRATED LEARNING EXERCISES

1. Ron Jon Surf Shop is probably the best known retail store brand for ocean gear in Florida. In Hawaii, the dominant name is Hilo Hattie. Go to the Hilo Hattie Web site at www.hilohattie.com. Compare it to the Ron Jon site at www.ronjons.com. Do the two sites have relatively common themes? Which is the more attractive site? Why?

2. How do marketing experts integrate advertisements with Web sites? Access each of the following company sites. Compare the appearance and content of the Web sites to the four shoe advertisements on page 6 of this chapter. Also, compare the sites to other ads you have seen for each of the four brands.
   a. Reebok (www.reebok.com)
   b. ASICS (www.asics.com)
   c. New Balance (www.newbalance.com)
   d. Skechers (www.skechers.com)

3. Find each of the following companies on the Internet. For each company, discuss how effective its Web site is in communicating an overall message. Also, discuss how well the marketing team integrates the material on the Web site. How well does the Web site integrate the company's advertising with other marketing communications?
   a. Revlon (www.revlon.com)
   b. J.B. Hunt (www.jbhunt.com)
   c. United Airlines (www.united.com)
   d. Steamboat Resorts (www.steamboatresorts.com)

4. Information is one key to developing a successful integrated marketing communications program. Access each of the following Web sites and examine the information and news available on each site. How would this information help in developing an integrated marketing campaign?
   a. *Brandweek* (www.brandweek.com)
   b. *Adweek* (www.adweek.com)
   c. *Mediaweek* (www.mediaweek.com)
   d. *Branding Asia* (www.brandingasia.com)

# STUDENT PROJECT

**IMC Plan Pro**

Are you interested in becoming an award-winning advertiser? Help is available. A supplement package called "IMC Plan Pro" is designed to help students create an entire advertising and communications program. A disk is part of the package. The booklet and disk will guide you through the entire process. The authors of this textbook developed the IMC Plan Pro package,

which means the materials match the topics presented in the upcoming chapters.

The advertisement shown here promoting the annual Student ADDY Awards competition, as sponsored by the American Advertising Federation, was designed by a creative at French Creative Advertising Agency. This advertisement won an ADDY at the Monroe, Louisiana, advertising competition. With some

An advertisement designed by French
Creative Advertising Agency promoting
the ADDY Student Competition.
*Source:* Courtesy of French Creative Group, Ltd.

hard work, creativity, and help, it is possible that next year's winning ad in the student competition will be the one you designed. Ask your instructor about the Student ADDY Awards sponsored by the American Advertising Federation and what you can do to enter. Also, ask the instructor how to obtain the IMC Plan Pro booklet and disk, or log onto the Prentice Hall Web site at www.prenhall.com, or e-mail Kenneth Clow at clow@ulm.edu. The best way to be prepared for a job when you graduate is to develop your creative talent now.

## CASE 1

## THE CABLE COMPANY

Rachel Peterson knew she faced several major challenges as she took the job of marketing director for CableNOW. The company was the sole cable provider for six communities in northeast Louisiana. All of the cities were essentially "licensed monopolies," in the sense that no other cable company could compete within the city limits. In spite of this edge, however, competition was becoming a major problem.

Satellite television was the primary competitor for CableNOW's customers. Both DirecTV and the Dish Network had set up operations in the six communities. The two providers were able to charge lower prices for basic services. They had also started to compete by offering price reductions on installations. This made switching from cable to satellite much easier for local residents.

CableNOW's primary selling point was in the delivery of programming during bad weather. Thunderstorms and snowstorms completely disrupt a satellite signal. Severe weather is common in that part of Louisiana. The same weather events do not affect a cable picture. CableNOW also held a competitive advantage because the company offered local business and real estate listings to subscribers. The firm also was able to provide local radar and weather forecasts during the "Local on the 8s" segments on the Weather Channel. The satellite companies could not provide these special options.

When Rachel took the job, she knew another issue was about to unfold. CableNOW had been able to transmit each city's local channels as part of the basic cable package. Until this year, the satellite companies could not. Dish Network was changing the mix. Dish Network had just signed a contract to provide the local stations to subscribers. DirecTV did not, but did offer a greater number of channels in the company's basic package.

The final piece of this changing landscape was changing technology. It was becoming clear that HDTV (high definition television) was the future. CableNOW had not yet developed the capacity to deliver high definition signals. Both DirecTV and the Dish Network had this capability. It was going to take a substantial investment to make the change at CableNOW. As a result, Rachel knew she had her work cut out as the marketing department struggled to maintain its market share in each city.

1. What image or theme should CableNOW portray to subscribers?

2. Can you think of a way to emphasize the advantages CableNOW has in an advertising campaign?

3. Do you believe CableNOW will survive these changes over the next 10 years? Why or why not?

## CASE 2

## MARKETING MINI-CDS

Craft-tech Technologies was on the verge of a major expansion. The company's management team invested heavily in compact disk technology and created what they believed was a viable product for the mini-CD marketplace. Company leaders were certain that mini-CDs soon would outsell the traditional-size version, giving them inroads into numerous markets, including the:

▶ Music industry
▶ Computer industry
▶ CD player market (both Walkman and larger versions for home use)

(continued)

The company's president, Merv Watson, contacted a full-service advertising agency. Merv asked the agency manager, Susan Ashbacher, to describe the meaning of full service. Susan responded, "We will take care of every aspect of your company's integrated marketing communications program. We'll either prepare the material ourselves, or outsource it and manage the process."

Merv was still confused. "What exactly does that mean?" he asked.

Susan handed him a worksheet (Figure 1.10). She responded, "We will sit down with you and figure out your company's primary message. Do you want to represent yourself as a high-quality leader in technology? Or is your focus more toward this particular product, and how you serve that niche better than anyone else? What we'll ask you to do is define yourself, and then we'll help you develop a marketing program to get that message out."

Merv studied the worksheet. He was amazed to see all of the items listed. Noting his interest, Susan said, "Every single thing on that page should speak with the same voice. Every one of your customers, from businesses to end users, should know your main message. Your customers should buy from you because they have confidence in your brand. We want to make sure you stand out. After all, it's pretty crowded out there in the world of technology."

Merv hired Susan, and the process began. The IMC program was to integrate a marketing plan to other businesses, individual users, and international markets.

1. What image or theme should Craft-tech Technologies portray?

2. Design an IMC approach and state how it will affect all of the items shown in Figure 1.10.

3. Choose another good or service. Consider every IMC aspect of that good or service as you read the following chapters.

**FIGURE 1.10**
**Items to Be Included in an IMC Program**

- Company logo
- Product brand name and company name
- Business cards
- Letterhead
- Carry home bags (paper or plastic)
- Wrapping paper
- Coupons
- Promotional giveaways (Coffee mugs, pens, pencils, calendars)
- Design of booth for trade shows
- Advertisements (billboards, space used on cars and busses, television, radio, magazines, and newspapers)
- Toll-free 800 or 888 number
- Company database
- Cooperative advertising with other businesses
- Personal selling pitches
- Characteristics of target market buyers
- Characteristics of business buyers
- Sales incentives provided to salesforce (contests, prizes, bonuses, and commissions)
- Internal messages
- Company magazines and newspapers
- Statements to shareholders
- Speeches by company leaders
- Public relations releases
- Sponsorship programs
- Web site

## ENDNOTES

1. Ron Jon Surf Shop (www.ronjons.com, accessed February 22, 2005); Donald Baack, "Ron Jon's Surf Shop: Brand Building in a No Name Marketplace," *IMC Communique* (Spring 2005), p. 5.

2. Diane Brady, "Making Marketing Measure Up," *BusinessWeek* (December 13, 2004), pp. 112–113.

3. Donald Baack, "Communication Processes," *Organizational Behavior,* Chapter 13 (1998), pp. 313–37.

4. James G. Hutton, "Integrated Marketing Communications and the Evolution of Marketing Thought," *Journal of Business Research* 37 (November 1996), pp. 155–162.

5. Don Schultz, "Invest in Integration," *Industry Week* 247, no. 10 (May 18, 1998), p. 20; "Integrated Marketing Communications," *Consortium Benchmarking Study,* American Productivity & Quality Center (1999).

6. Ibid.

7. Lauren Keller Johnson, "Harnessing the Power of the Customer," *Harvard Management Update* 9 (March 2004), pp. 3–5; Patricia Seybold, *The Customer Revolution,* London: Random House Business Books.

8. "Global Internet Retail: Industry Profile," *Datamonitor* (May 2004), p.10.

9. Tammy Mastroberte, "Cool Control," *Convenience Store News* 38, no. 8 (July 14, 2003), pp. 49–53.

10. David J. Lipke, "Pledge of Allegiance," *American Demographics* 22, no. 11 (November 2000), pp. 40–42.

11. Debbie Howell, "Today's Consumers More Open to Try New Brands," *DSN Retailing Today* 43, no. 20 (October 25, 2004), pp. 29–32.

12. Sandy Brown, "Study: DVR Users Skip Live Ads, Too," *Brandweek* 45, no. 37 (October 18, 2004), p. 7; Jennifer Lach, "Commercial Overload," *American Demographics* 21, no. 9 (September 1999), p. 20.

13. Don E. Schultz and Philip J. Kitchen, "Integrated Marketing Communications in U.S. Advertising Agencies: An Exploratory Study," *Journal of Advertising Research* (September–October 1997), pp. 7–18.

14. Stephen J. Gould, Dawn B. Lerman, and Andreas F. Grein, "Agency Perceptions and Practices on Global IMC," *Journal of Advertising Research* (January–February 1999), pp. 7–26.

15. Ibid.

16. Laura Petrecca, "Agencies Urged to Show the Worth of Their Work," *Advertising Age* 68, no. 15 (April 14, 1997), pp. 2–3; Joseph A. Tradii, "Get the Most from Your Agency," *Marketing News* 28, no. 22 (October 24, 1994), p. 4; Pete Millard, "Gauging Ad Success: Bean Counters Eclipse Agency Creatives," *Business Journal Serving Greater Milwaukee: Marketing Resource Guide* 14, no. 29 (April 18, 1997), p. 4; Robert L. Gustafson, "Better Leaders Make Better Account Execs," *Indianapolis Business Journal* 16, no. 15 (March 4, 1996), p. 15; John Bissell, "Agency Creatives: A Strategic Resource?" *Brandweek* 39, no. 19 (May 11, 1998), p. 18.

## Chapter Objectives

*Understand* the nature of a corporation's image and why it is important.

*Develop* tactics and plans to build an effective corporate image.

*Cultivate* effective brand names, family brands, brand extensions, flanker brands, co-brands, private brands, brand equity, and brand recognition.

*Discover* the advantages of a quality logo, package, and label.

*Recognize* the importance of effective brand and product positioning, and utilize strategies to help establish a positive position.

# Corporate Image and Brand Management

## GUCCI: ONE STRONG BRAND WORKS WITH OTHERS

How many Gucci items do you own? Before you answer, remember that Gucci stores also sell Yves Saint Laurent, Sergio Rossi, Alexander McQueen, Oscar de la Renta, and other brands. From the humble beginnings of a single-product firm, Gucci has grown and evolved into a dominant player in the fashion industry. The path was not always easy. Gucci started in Italy, took a detour through Bahrain, and has ended up in The Netherlands.

The House of Gucci was founded by Guccio Gucci in Florence, Italy, in 1921. Gucci was the son of a leather craftsman. While visiting Paris and London, he was impressed by the sophistication of the cultures he encountered. He returned to Italy to open his store, which sold small luggage and saddlery. Soon Gucci was a widely popular store, selling exclusive leather goods.

As the Gucci company grew, the line of products continued to expand, as did the locations. Rome and Milan were two of the new sites. Guccio Gucci died in 1953, leaving his company to his brothers and family members. The Gucci heirs opened new stores in London, Paris, New York, and Palm Beach.

When the Gucci family sold all its interests in the 1980s, the firm that purchased it was located in Bahrain. Unfortunately, the company had expanded so quickly that it lost control over quality and distribution.

The newest owners are the Gucci Group NV, located in Amsterdam. The corporation fixed many problems by issuing shares of stock to finance growth. Currently the Gucci line includes watches, leather goods, perfumes, jewelry, and other items. Gucci Group NV now owns 348 directly operated stores around the world.

In the United States, Gucci is marketed as a seductive, high fashion brand. A visit to the company's Web site allows the visitor to view the many products and stores that are all part of Gucci's image. High fashion is a major feature of the Gucci line. All of Gucci's products are advertised to enhance the same position.

Recently, Gucci appointed three new creative directors. One was to direct a Women's Ready-to-Wear Collection, a second leads the Men's Ready-to-Wear Collection, and the third manages the company's fashion accessories.

Gucci provides an excellent example of how the leaders of one company were able to take a single line of products and eventually build a powerful international presence featuring dozens of products and brand names. Maintaining a cutting-edge position and image drives the marketing team at Gucci to innovate and grow with each new fashion trend.[1]

One of the most critical ingredients in the successful development of an integrated marketing communications plan is effective management of an organization's image. A firm's **image** is based on the feelings consumers and businesses have about the overall organization and its individual brands. Advertising, consumer promotions, trade promotions, personal selling, and other marketing activities all affect consumer perceptions of the firm. When the image of an organization or one of its brands is somehow tarnished, sales revenues and profits often plummet. Rebuilding or revitalizing an image is a momentous task.

Brand managers and advertising account executives are responsible for developing and maintaining a quality image. Image has a "bottom line" that can even be assigned a value on accounting statements. Advertising managers and other marketing experts are expected to create messages that (1) sell products in the short term and (2) build a firm's image over time. Advertising creatives must think about both goals as they design advertisements and promotional campaigns.

Company leaders study the firm's image during the promotions opportunity analysis (see Chapter 4) phase of the IMC program. Image is connected to a company's strengths and weaknesses. A strong image can be combined with an opportunity discovered in the external environment to create a major strategic advantage for the firm.

When the marketing team is able to clearly understand the firm's image and has knowledge about the strengths of individual brands, it is easier to make solid connections with consumers and business-to-business customers. A strong IMC foundation is based on combining ideas about a firm's image and brand with assessments of consumer and business buyer behaviors. Then, the marketing team can prepare consistent messages designed to reach all of the individuals who may purchase a company's goods and services.

The first part of this chapter examines the activities involved in managing a corporation's image. The second part addresses ways to develop and promote the various forms of brand names. Brand equity and brand parity are also described. Brand names, company logos, packages, and labels are closely tied to a firm's image.

## CORPORATE IMAGE

Effective marketing communication is based on a clearly defined corporate image. The image summarizes what the company stands for and how well its position has been established. Whether it is the "good hands" of Allstate Insurance or the "good neighbors" at State Farm Insurance, the goal of image management is to create a stable impression in the minds of clients and customers (in the case of insurance companies, helpfulness, safety, and security are most prevalent).

The first thing to remember is that what *consumers* believe about a firm is far more important than how company officials view the image. Corporate names such as IBM, Apple Computers, Toyota, Nike, and Enron all conjure images in the minds of consumers. Although the specific version of the image varies from consumer to consumer or business buyer to business buyer, the overall or most general image of a firm is determined by the combined views of all publics. A firm's image can have a positive or a negative influence on customers as they make purchase decisions.

### Components of a Corporate Image

Consumers see many things as they encounter a company or an organization. One primary component of a corporate image is customer perceptions of the goods or services offered by the organization. In a study conducted by Edelman Asia Pacific, the quality of a company's goods and services ranked as the most important component of corporate image. A close second was the willingness of a firm to stand behind its goods and services when something went wrong. Third on the list was how the firm dealt with customers (pleasant, helpful, professional, etc.).[2]

Every firm's image consists of a unique set of components. The corporate image of an automobile manufacturer such as Mazda, Subaru, or General Motors might be based on: (1) evaluations of vehicles, (2) whether the company is foreign or domestic, (3) customer views of each company's advertisements, and (4) reactions to the local dealership. Further, the corporation's image may include assessments of employees. In fact, the mechanic trying to repair a vehicle at a local Mr. Goodwrench garage could become the dominant factor that shaped an individual customer's image of General Motors.

Recently, both Subaru and Mazda began to emphasize the importance of the dealership as an influence on consumer assessments of an automobile company's corporate image. As a result, both firms launched aggressive remodeling plans for local dealerships. The goal was to provide a more inviting shopping environment. These new look dealerships helped boost the images of both Subaru and Mazda. Sales also increased. Subaru dealers that remodeled using the new retail format sold 54 percent more vehicles in the following year. Mazda dealers that adopted the new retail design sold 30 percent more cars.[3]

A corporate image also contains invisible and intangible elements (see Figure 2.1). A pharmaceutical or cosmetic company policy prohibiting product testing using animals will be integrated into consumer attitudes toward the firm. Personnel policies and practices impact the firm's image. Strikes and labor disputes often have a negative impact on a firm's image. The business philosophies of Bill Gates at Microsoft and Martha Stewart of Martha Stewart Living Omnimedia affect the images consumers have of the two companies. The beliefs and attitudes consumers have about Japan may influence views of companies such as Sony and Toyota.

Any negative publicity has the potential to stain or damage consumer perceptions of a corporation's image. Powerful examples of these events took place at Enron, WorldCom, and Tyco as the new millennium began to unfold. Some writers believe the problems at these companies created an overall distrust of all corporations.

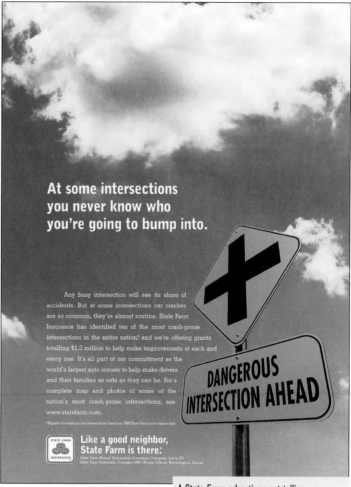

A State Farm advertisement telling consumers about the company's goal of making driving safer.
*Source:* Courtesy of State Farm Insurance Companies. State Farm Mutual Automobile Insurance Company, 1999. Used by permission.

| Tangible Elements | Intangible Elements |
|---|---|
| 1. Goods and services sold | 1. Corporate, personnel, and environmental policies |
| 2. Retail outlets where the product is sold | 2. Ideals and beliefs of corporate personnel |
| 3. Factories where the product is produced | 3. Culture of country and location of company |
| 4. Advertising, promotions, and other forms of communications | 4. Media reports |
| 5. Corporate name and logo | |
| 6. Packages and labels | |
| 7. Employees | |

**FIGURE 2.1**
**Components of a Corporate Image**

## The Role of a Corporate Image—Consumer Perspective

From a consumer's perspective, the corporate image serves several useful functions. These include:

▶ Providing assurance regarding purchase decisions of familiar products in unfamiliar settings

▶ Giving assurance about the purchase when the buyer has little or no previous experience with the good or service

▶ Reducing search time in purchase decisions

▶ Providing psychological reinforcement and social acceptance of purchases

A well-known corporate image provides consumers with positive assurance of what they can expect from the firm. A can of Coke or Pepsi purchased in Anchorage, Alaska, has a comparable taste to one purchased in Liverpool, England, or Kuala Lumpur, Malaysia. McDonald's serves the same or similar value meals in San Francisco as the ones sold in Minneapolis or Paris. Consumers on vacation know that if they make purchase from a Wal-Mart in Texas, a defective item can be returned to a local store in Toronto, Canada.

This assurance has even greater value when consumers purchase goods or services with which they have little experience. For example, consider a family on vacation. Often travelers in another state or country look for signs or logos of companies from their native area. Purchasing from a familiar corporation is perceived to be a "safer" strategy than purchasing from an unknown. Patronizing a hotel or restaurant that the consumer has never heard of will be seen as riskier than would be utilizing a familiar one. Thus a family visiting Brazil may normally not stay at the Holiday Inn, but because they have heard of the name, they feel it is a lower-risk alternative than an unknown hotel.

Another significant role corporate image plays for the consumer is reducing search time. Purchasing a product from a familiar firm saves the consumer considerable time and effort. An individual loyal to Ford is going to spend fewer hours searching for a new car than does someone with no loyalty to any particular automobile manufacturer. The same principle holds in purchasing low-cost items such as groceries. A great deal of search time is saved when a consumer purchases brands and items from the same organization, such as Kellogg or Nabisco.

For many individuals, purchasing from a highly recognized company provides psychological reinforcement and social acceptance. Psychological reinforcement comes from feeling that a wise choice was made and believing that the good or service will perform well. Social acceptance is derived from knowing that many other individuals also purchased from the well-known firm. More importantly, other people, such as family and friends, are likely to accept the choice.

Who are the most reputable firms? *Forbes,* in conjunction with Predictiv and FactSet Research Systems, produced a list of the top 25 corporate brands. Procter & Gamble (P&G) was at the top, with a corporate brand value of $107.4 billion. Second on the list was Microsoft, with a brand

The well-established Yamaha corporate name provides consumers assurance of quality and dependability for the Skeeter boat brand.
*Source:* Courtesy of Newcomer, Morris & Young, Inc.

| Rank | Company | Corporate Brand Value (Billions) | Sales (Billions) | Behind the Brand |
|---|---|---|---|---|
| 1 | Procter & Gamble | $107.4 | $47.0 | Pampers, Crest, Tide, and other products that are used 2 billion times daily |
| 2 | Microsoft | $103.1 | $34.3 | World's largest software producer with Windows; also has MSNBC cable channel and Xbox video game |
| 3 | Merck | $91.3 | $22.5 | Pharmaceutical company; 22% of sales was cholesterol-lowering drug Zocor |
| 4 | Intel | $80.2 | $30.1 | Producer of microprocessors |
| 5 | Eli Lilly | $76.4 | $12.6 | Pharmaceutical company; biggest seller was Zyprexa, a schizophrenia drug |
| 6 | IBM | $71.0 | $89.1 | In one year, IBM was issued 3,415 patents, 1,400 more than any other company |
| 7 | Cisco Systems | $69.6 | $19.8 | Has 81% of the worldwide router market |
| 8 | Medtronic | $61.4 | $8.6 | Developed groundbreaking products, such as the first completely automatic pacemaker |
| 9 | UPS | $58.2 | $33.5 | Has gone high tech with a Web site that averages 115 million hits per day |
| 10 | PepsiCo | $56.1 | $27.0 | Accounts for nearly $1/3$ of total soft drink sales in the United States |

**TABLE 2.1**

**Top 10 Corporate Brands**

*Source:* Forbes.com (www.forbes.com/forbes/2004/0419.html, February 8, 2005).

value of $103.1 billion. Rounding out the top five were Merck, Intel, and Eli Lilly. For a complete listing of the top 10 brands, see Table 2.1.

## The Role of a Corporate Image—Business-to-Business Perspective

A strong corporate image creates a major competitive advantage in the business-to-business marketplace. Many of the same processes that affect individual consumers also affect business buyers. This means that purchasing from a well-known company reduces the feelings of risk that are part of the buying process. A firm with a well-established image makes the choice easier for business customers seeking to reduce search time during the purchasing process. Psychological reinforcement and social acceptance may also be present. Company buyers who make quality purchases receive praise from organizational leaders and others involved in the process. Therefore, once again, a strong company image or brand name can make the difference in a choice between competitors.

Brand image is especially valuable to a company that is expanding internationally. Foreign businesses are likely to feel more comfortable making transactions with a firm from a different country that has a strong corporate image. Risk and uncertainty are reduced when the buyer knows something about the seller. Therefore, a company such as IBM can expand into a new country and more quickly gain the confidence of consumers and businesses.

## The Role of a Corporate Image—Company Perspective

From the viewpoint of the firm itself, a highly reputable image generates many benefits. These include:

▶ Extension of positive consumer feelings to new products
▶ The ability to charge a higher price or fee

The strong General Mills brand name makes the introduction of new products easier

*Source:* Reprinted with the permission of General Mills, Inc.

▶ Consumer loyalty leading to more frequent purchases

▶ Positive word-of-mouth endorsements

▶ The ability to attract quality employees

▶ More favorable ratings by financial observers and analysts

A quality corporate image provides the basis for the development of new goods and services. When consumers are already familiar with the corporate name and image, the introduction of a new product becomes much easier, because long-term customers are willing to give something new a try. Customers normally transfer their trust in and beliefs about the corporation to a new product.

A strong corporate image allows a company to charge more for its goods and services. Most customers believe they "get what they pay for." Higher quality is often associated with a higher price. This, in turn, can lead to better markup margins and greater profits for the firm with a strong corporate image.

Further, firms with well-developed images have customers who are more loyal. A higher level of customer loyalty results in patrons purchasing more products over time. There will be less substitution purchasing taking place when other companies offer discounts, sales, and other enticements to switch brands.

Heightened levels of customer loyalty are often associated with positive word-of-mouth endorsements of the company and its products. These favorable comments about the firm help generate additional sales and attract new customers. Most consumers have more faith in the personal references they receive than in any form of advertising or promotion.

Another advantage of a strong corporate image is that it attracts quality employees. Just as consumers are drawn to strong firms, potential workers will apply for jobs at companies with solid reputations. Consequently, recruiting costs are reduced because there is less employee turnover. Then, fewer advertising dollars are needed to attract new applicants.

An additional value of a strong corporate reputation is a more favorable rating by Wall Street analysts. A strong corporate image can also lead to higher evaluations by financial institutions. This is especially helpful when a company tries to obtain capital for financing. Further, legislators and governmental agencies tend to act in a more supportive manner toward companies with strong and positive reputations. Lawmakers are less inclined to pursue actions that may hurt the business. Regulatory agencies are less likely to believe rumors of wrongdoing.

Building a strong corporate image provides tangible and intangible benefits. Both customers and organizations benefit from a well-known firm with an established reputation. Organizational leaders devote considerable amounts of time and energy to building and maintaining a positive organizational image. Client companies expect advertising account managers and creatives to help design marketing programs that take advantage of the benefits of a strong corporate image.

## PROMOTING THE DESIRED IMAGE

The right image can be a major part of an organization's success. The marketing team should try to understand the nature of the company's current image. The goal is to make sure that

BMW Motorcycle carefully plans all of its communication materials to ensure that a consistent brand image is projected.

*Source:* Courtesy of BMW of North America, LLC.

# COMMUNICATION ACTION

## Wal-Mart's Image Issues

For many years, Wal-Mart enjoyed a positive image in the eyes of most publics. After all, the company offered low prices in a friendly atmosphere. The legendary Sam Walton was the focal point of a company that was viewed favorably by consumers, the government, and others.

In the past few years, however, Wal-Mart's image has been tarnished. The company faced a gender discrimination class action lawsuit along with charges that Wal-Mart employed illegal immigrants in some locations. Also, many local communities experienced complaints that Wal-Mart was so dominant, much in the same way as a monopoly, that small companies were being driven out of business.

To combat these image issues, Wal-Mart is aggressively pursuing a corporate image-building campaign. Television advertisements noting that Wal-Mart really is a good corporate citizen and a great place to work have been widely circulated. In areas where local governments challenge new stores, Wal-Mart's publicity team notes the vast amount of sales tax revenue the company generates, and how the firm offers medical insurance to full- and part-time employees. In the future, with new efforts to unionize employees underway, expect Wal-Mart's marketing and publicity department to work hard to maintain the company's positive image that it took Sam Walton a lifetime to build.

**Sources:** Michelle Dalton Tyree, "Wal-Mart's Woes," *Women's Wear Daily* 188, no. 118 (December 7, 2004), p. 24; Aaron Bernstein, "Declaring War on Wal-Mart," *BusinessWeek,* no. 3919 (February 7, 2005), p. 31.

future communications clearly promote the image. These communications should reach every constituency. This includes customers, suppliers, and employees.

As the advertising team studies a company's image, other consumers, especially noncustomers of the firm, should be approached to ascertain their views. Once those in the firm understand how others see the company, they can make decisions about how to correct any misperceptions and/or build on the image that customers currently hold. In making decisions about the image to be projected, marketers should remember four things:

1. The image being projected must accurately portray the firm and coincide with the goods and services being offered.
2. Reinforcing or rejuvenating a current image that is consistent with the view of consumers is easier to accomplish than changing a well-established image.
3. It is very difficult to change the images people hold about a given company. In some cases, modifying the current image or trying to create an entirely new image is not possible.
4. Any negative or bad press can quickly destroy an image that took years to build. Reestablishing or rebuilding the firm's image takes a great deal of time once its reputation has been damaged.

## Creating the Right Image

In each industry, the right image is one that sends a clear message about the unique nature of an organization and its products. A strong image is one that accurately portrays what the firm sells. For example, notice the BMW advertisement in this section. The goal of the ad is to reinforce the image that BMW is a quality product and the top brand in the motorcycle industry. The idea is that "BMW Motorcycles are the indisputable mark of a real ride," according to BMW brand manager Kerri Martin.[4] Because the image is well established, other promotions can be built around the reputation. This fuels long-term customer loyalty and future sales.

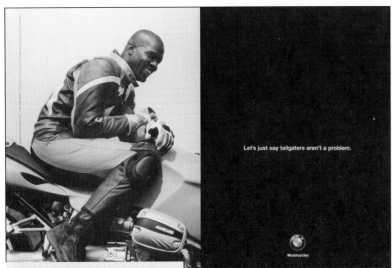

An image-building advertisement for BMW Motorcycles.

*Sources:* Courtesy of BMW of North America, LIC. © 1999 BMW of North America, Inc. All Rights Reserved. The BMW trademark and logo are registered. This advertisement is reproduced with the permission of BMW of North America, Inc. for promotional purposes only.

Creating the right image is often challenging for a small business. Many times no image exists. For example, Portillo's Hot Dogs had been operating in Chicago for 42 years. When owner Dick Portillo decided to open a new outlet, he was shocked to learn that 30 percent of the consumers in the area had never heard of Portillo's. With over 2,300 places in Chicago offering hot dogs, it was going to be difficult to attract the attention of potential buyers.

Portillo met with an advertising agency. Together they decided to create television and radio advertisements that would project an image in which Portillo's restaurants were "warm and fun." The result was, that although actual sales figures were not released, Portillo stated that the integrated image advertising program put his chain of restaurants "on a roll."[5]

## Rejuvenating an Image

Rejuvenating an image helps a firm sell new products and can attract new customers. At the same time, reinforcing previous aspects of an image assists the company in retaining loyal patrons comfortable with the firm's original image. The key to successful image reengineering is to keep consistent with a previous image while at the same time building to incorporate new elements to expand the firm's target audience.

Rejuvenating a firm's image can be difficult. There are some success stories, however. Hewlett-Packard's former CEO Carly Fiorina worked with marketing executive Allison Johnson to help transform H-P's image. The goal was to move from being seen as a staid company run by engineers into an ultimate lifestyle technology company in tune with pop culture. H-P started by launching innovative new products, including the co-branded iPod (with Apple Computers). Then, the new H-P advertising became much edgier than any used in the past. This image overhaul turned a company that was struggling into a profitable organization that is recognized as the one of the best lifestyle technology companies.[6]

Rejuvenating a well-established image takes time and effort. McDonald's faced this problem when the company encountered negative publicity about health-related concerns and its menu. According to Wendy Cook, McDonald's vice president of U.S. menu innovations and marketing, the key to rejuvenating the company's image was to send the message that it is possible to buy healthy food at McDonald's. The main product leading the effort was a series of salads. Before launching the new salad line, McDonald's marketing team talked to women, the primary customers. The team learned that women notice details such as all-natural dressings with low-fat options and the 16 different kinds of lettuce. Using this information, new advertisements were developed using a "girl talk" approach where women discovered a great salad with a variety of options. This integrated marketing approach helped modify McDonald's image for working women who might stop there for lunch.[7]

## Changing an Image

It is very difficult to completely change the image people have about a company. Changing an image becomes necessary, however, when target markets have begun to shrink or disappear, or the firm's image no longer matches industry trends and consumer expectations. At that point, company leaders must carefully consider what they wish to change, why they wish to make a change, and how they intend to accomplish the task.

One company that successfully changed its image is Bluenotes, a Canadian retailer that caters to the 14- to 22-year-old market. The chain's original name was "Thrifty's."

Unfortunately Thrifty's marketing strategy was weak. Company messages did not appeal to young people. Advertisements focused on clothes rather than customers. Eventually, the 111-retail chain outlet was purchased by the U.S.–based company American Eagle Outfitters.

The first step in changing the firm's image was to rename the stores. "Bluenotes" was the name of the store's private brand of jeans. Along with the new name came a new logo. Still, the marketing team recognized that just changing the name and logo would not be enough. Bluenotes' HR department began hiring younger people. These new, hip employees were closer in age to the target market. They could identify with the store's patrons. Next, Bluenotes added "lifestyle areas" where magazines, message boards high-lighting Bluenotes' involvement in local events, sitting areas, and music-listening areas were located. Bluenotes began promoting popular Canadian bands and music festivals. At those events, the marketing team was able to collect customer names and e-mail addresses.

Bluenotes stores began featuring an expanded set of product offerings. This included outside brands as well as the company's six private labels. The product strategy was to have a brand for every kind of youth: preppy, skater, hip-hopper, rocker, or athlete. Apparently, many young consumers have responded. Bluenotes has gained in popularity. A recent survey by a Toronto-based youth marketing firm revealed that Bluenotes was the most frequented place to shop for the 13- to 19-year-old age group.[8]

Changing an image requires more than one well-made ad or press release. It begins with internal company personnel and products and then moves outward to suppliers, other businesses, and especially to consumers.[9]

## Conveying an Image to Business Customers

Corporate advertising sends important signals to other businesses. Corporate image advertising is designed to build the organization's reputation with the general public and with other firms. Robert Worcester, chair of the British marketing research group MORI, reports that the more a company advertises, the more it is admired. The U.S.–based Opinion Research Corporation notes that "knowing a company very well" is a key reason to award new business. Therefore, image advertising is a crucial ingredient in business-to-business marketing. Stephen Greyser, from the Harvard Business School, states that corporate image advertising should be aimed at three constituencies: opinion formers (customers, politicians, investors), employees, and *other businesses.*[10]

## CORPORATE NAME

A corporate name is the overall banner under which all other operations occur. According to David Placek, president and founder of Lexicon, Inc., "The corporate name is really the cornerstone of a company's relationship with its customers. It sets an attitude and tone and is the first step toward a personality."[11] Corporate names can be divided into the following four categories based on their actual, implied, or visionary meaning.[12]

*Overt names* reveal what the company does, such as American Airlines or BMW Motorcycles USA. *Implied names* contain recognizable words or word parts that imply what the company is about, such as FedEx and IBM (International Business Machines). *Conceptual names,* including Lucent Technologies, Google, and Krispy Kreme, try to capture the essence of the idea behind the brand. Lucent conveys the idea of glowing light, Google portrays the idea of a place where an endless number of items can be found, and Krispy Kreme suggests confectionaries filled with tasty crème. The last category, *iconoclastic names,* does

Haik Humble Eye Center uses an overt corporate name.
*Source:* Courtesy of Sartor Associates, Inc.

Focus. Vision. Dedication.

Haik Humble Eye Center
*Total Eye Care for Life*

# COMMUNICATION ACTION

## Silly Names Are a No-No

What's in a name? A great deal, according to Javed Naseem, writing in *Marketing Magazine*. Cute names like Boo.com, Blahblah.com, clickmago, purplefrog, and pinkrhino may lead to creative advertisements, but consumers don't remember them and the names soon tend to die. Naseem suggests that branding is an important marketing exercise, one that should not be confused with graphics, colors, logos, or packages. The marketing department should appoint an expert to conduct the kind of quality research that will lead to a successful brand name. The three golden rules of creating brand names are:

1. Do not copy others.
2. Do not get too creative.
3. Only accept global names.

Naseem concludes that there is no shortage of unique, powerful, one-of-a-kind names that can be trademarked. It just takes hard work and a serious marketing leader to identify the right one for the company.

**Source:** Javed Naseem, "The Death of Silly Names," *Marketing Magazine* 106, no. 36 (September 10, 2001), p. 35.

not reflect the company's goods or services, but instead something that is unique, different, and memorable. Apple Computers, Monstor.com, and Gucci are examples of iconoclastic names. The first two categories (overt and implied) are easier to market. They make it easier for consumers to recall the good or service. The other two categories (conceptual and iconoclastic) require a greater marketing effort to ensure that consumers connect the corporate name with the goods and services that are being sold.

## CORPORATE LOGOS

Another aspect of a corporation's image is its logo. A **corporate logo** is a symbol used to identify a company and its brands, helping to convey the overall corporate image. The logo should be carefully designed to be compatible with the corporation's name. Many organizations have spent millions of dollars selecting and promoting corporate names and logos. Consumers are flooded with numerous advertisements every day. A strong corporate name featuring a well-designed logo can be a powerful aid that helps the consumer remember specific brands and company advertisements. Search time may also be reduced as consumers look for specific corporate products that are easily identified by logos and names. Quality logos and corporate names should meet four tests. They should be: (1) easily recognizable, (2) familiar, (3) elicit a consensual meaning among those in the firm's target market, and (4) evoke positive feelings.[13]

Logos are especially important for in-store shopping. Pictures can be processed in the mind faster than words; thus, corporate logos are more readily recognized by shoppers. Logo recognition can occur at two levels. First, a consumer may remember seeing the logo in the past. It is stored in memory, and when it is seen at the store, that memory is jogged. Second, a logo may remind the consumer of the brand or corporate name. This reminder can elicit positive feelings regarding either the retailer's brand name or manufacturer's brand name.

Successful logos elicit shared meanings across consumers. When a logo elicits a consensual meaning among customers, the process is known as **stimulus codability**. Logos with high

Sartor Associates designed five different logos for Achievers, Inc
*Source:* Courtesy of Sartor Associates, Inc.

- ▶ **Apple**—Created by Rob Janoff of Regis McKenna Advertising in 1977. Some people think the bite represents Adam and Eve, but it was actually placed there so people wouldn't mistake it for a tomato.
- ▶ **Coke**—One of the most preeminent logos in the world. It was created in 1886 by Frank Robinson, who was the bookkeeper for John Pemberton, creator of Coca-Cola. Robinson was selected to design the logo because he had good handwriting.
- ▶ **FedEx**—Created by Landor Associates in 1994. The logo designers kept the orange and purple color but shortened the name to "FedEx" as a verb.
- ▶ **McDonald's**—Before it was adopted by McDonald's, the arches represented military triumph. Now they represent the triumph of the cheeseburger. The arches were adopted in 1962 as the logo. Before the arches, McDonald's used the cartoon mascot Speedee.
- ▶ **Nike**—The swoosh was designed in 1971 by Carolyn Davidson, a graphic-design student. She was paid $35 for the design by Phil Knight, founder of Nike. In 1983, she was rewarded with shares of Nike stock.
- ▶ *Playboy*—Hugh Hefner originally planned on calling the magazine *Stag Party* and used a stag as the logo. Just before the first issue was published, his attorney advised against the name and logo. The bunny logo was created by art director Art Paul in just 30 minutes. It was placed on the second issue of the magazine.
- ▶ **Starbucks**—The stylized mermaid logo was created in 1971. At the original store in Seattle, the mermaid is topless and her hair is different. The logo was based on work done by Hadank, a graphic designer in Germany.

**FIGURE 2.2**
**How Were These Logos Developed?**

*Source:* From "The Logo" By Gavin Edwards from *Rolling Stone*, May 15, 2003 © Rolling Stone LLC 2003. All Rights Reserved. Reprinted by Permission.

stimulus codability evoke consensual meanings within a culture or subculture (such as the Prudential Rock). Logos with a high degree of codability are more easily recognized, such as Apple, McDonald's, and Coke. Company with logos having a low degree of codability must spend more money on advertising. Recognition will come from familiarity rather than stimulus codability. For example, Nike spent a considerable amount of resources making the "swoosh" recognizable to those in various target markets. Early in its life, the swoosh by itself did not conjure any specific image of the firm.

Figure 2.2 provides insights about the creation of some famous logos. Notice that the Apple logo created by Rob Janoff of Regis McKenna Advertising in 1977, had a bite taken from the apple so consumers wouldn't mistake it for a tomato. The Nike swoosh logo was created in 1971 by Carolyn Davidson, a graphic-design student. She was only paid $35 for the design. Later, however, Phil Knight, founder of Nike, decided that she should receive additional compensation.

## BRANDING

Many of the benefits of a strong corporate image also apply to brands. The primary difference between the two is that of scope. **Brands** are names generally assigned to an individual good or service or to a group of complementary products. A corporation's image covers every aspect of the firm's operations. The corporation Procter & Gamble carries many brands, including Tide, Cheer, Bold, and Dreft laundry detergents; Crest and Gleem toothpastes; and Old Spice, Secret, and Sure deodorants.

An effective brand name allows a company to charge more for products, which in turn increases gross margins. Strong brands provide customers with assurances of quality and reduction of search time in the purchasing process.

One primary feature that keeps a brand strong is that it contains something that has **salience** to customers. Salience occurs when customers are aware of the brand and the brand has attributes they desire. Salience comes from several sources. One is that the product or brand has benefits consumers consider important. Another comes from the view that the brand is a good value. A third is that consumers buy the item and use it on a regular basis. Consumers recommend salient brands to their families and friends.[14]

In international markets, branding is more complex. As discussed in Chapter 1, firms can either use an *adaptation* strategy or a *standardization* strategy in promotional programs. These two approaches can be applied to product brand names. With standardization, the same brand name is used in all countries. With adaptation, the brand is different in each country or region. This can mean it will be viewed as a local brand. Mr. Clean uses the adaptation brand approach. It is sold under the names of "Mr. Proper" and "Maestro Limpio," as well as other names in various countries.

Using a standardized global brand reduces costs. Instead of advertising each local brand with a separate communication strategy, one standardized message can be sent. Standardized global brands also allow for the transference of best practices from one country to another. Further, purchasing a standardized global brand can be viewed as a better choice than buying a local brand. The global brand may have a higher perceived quality. The consumer's self-concept of being cosmopolitan, sophisticated, and modern can be enhanced when buying a global brand.[15] As the world continues to shrink through advances in telecommunications, consumers are becoming increasingly similar, displaying similar consumer characteristics and purchase behaviors. This may lead to even greater use of standardized global brands.

Despite all of the advantages of global brands, some efforts to standardize brand names have met with resistance. There have been global brands that were introduced that were not received with enthusiasm. Although consumer behavior may have converged somewhat throughout the world, there are still many local idiosyncrasies. Global brands enjoy the most success in high-profile, high-involvement products. Local brands have performed the best in low-involvement everyday products. Automobiles and computers have done well as global brands. Food, candy, and some soft drinks have done better using a local brand approach.[16] Chapter 1 suggested that a solid GIMC strategy is to "think globally, but act locally." This approach may also be applied to branding. Developing global brands may be the ultimate goal; still the marketing team should consider each local market's unique features and be sensitive to supporting and developing local brands.

## Developing a Strong Brand Name

Developing a strong brand begins with discovering why consumers buy a brand and why they rebuy the brand. Questions to be asked include:

- What are the brand's most compelling benefits?
- What emotions are elicited by the brand either during or after the purchase?
- What one word best describes the brand?
- What is important to consumers in the purchase of the product?

Once the answers to these questions are known, a company's marketing team can cultivate a stronger brand position.

Two important processes help establish stronger brand prestige. First, the brand name must be prominently promoted through repetitious ads. The colossal number of brands and advertisements consumers see makes repetition essential to capturing the buyer's attention. Repetition increases the odds that a message will be stored in memory and recalled.

Second, the brand name should be associated with the product or service's most prominent characteristic.[17] Many consumers associate Crest with "cavity prevention." Coca-Cola seeks to associate its name with a product that is "refreshing." For Volvo, the impression is "safety." For BMW, it is "performance driving."

Brands develop histories. They have personalities. They include strengths, weaknesses, and flaws. Many brands produce family trees. A **family brand** is one in which a company offers a series or group of products under one brand name. The Black & Decker brand is present on numerous power tools. The advantage of a family brand is that consumers usually transfer the image associated with the brand name to any new products added to current lines. When Black & Decker offers a new power tool, the new item automatically assumes the reputation associated with the Black & Decker name. These transfer associations occur as long as the new product is within the same product category. When additional products are not related to the brand's core merchandise, the transfer of loyalty may not occur as easily.

The goal of branding is to set a product apart from its competitors. Market researchers must seek to identify the "one thing" the brand can stand for, that consumers recognize, and that is salient to consumers. When these tasks are successfully completed, more powerful brand recognition occurs. Notice the Hertz advertisement in this section directed to small-business owners. The advertisement promotes the Hertz brand name as well as highlighting special low rates that are available to small businesses.

After brand recognition has been achieved, the next step is to prolong its success. The secret to a long brand life is finding one unique selling point and sticking with it. Crest has been touting its cavity-fighting ability almost since its inception. Tide has been viewed as a powerful laundry detergent for years. Remember that some brands experience decline. If the company waits too long to respond, the result may be eventual brand death. If caught in time, a brand can be revived and given new life. The marketing team must pay careful attention to how each brand is perceived and how it is performing over time.[18]

The Hertz brand name is easily recognized by consumers and small-business owners.
**Source:** Courtesy of the Hertz Corporation.

## BRAND EQUITY

One major problem many established companies encounter is called *brand parity*. Brand parity occurs when there are few tangible distinctions between competing brands in mature markets. Brand parity means only minor product differences exist. In many product categories, even minor variations are hard to find.

One major force that can help fight the problem of brand parity is called brand equity. **Brand equity** is a set of characteristics that are unique to a brand. In essence, brand equity is the perception that a good or service with a given brand name is different and better.

Brand equity creates several benefits. First, brand equity allows the company to charge a higher price. The company may retain a greater market share than would otherwise be expected for an undifferentiated product. Brand equity is a source of channel power as the company deals with retailers. This power, in turn, leads to an improved position in terms of shelf space and displays. Brand equity also influences wholesalers by affecting what they stock and which brands they encourage their customers to purchase. Wholesalers often will stock several brands but place greater emphasis on high-equity brands.

In business-to-business markets, brand equity often allows a company to charge a higher price. Equity also influences selections in the buying decision-making process. Products with strong brand equity are often selected over products with low brand equity or brands that firms know little about. The same scenario is present in international markets. Brand equity opens doors of foreign firms, brokers, and retailers and provides privileges that products with low brand equity cannot obtain.

Brand equity is a strong weapon that might dissuade consumers from looking for a cheaper product or for special deals or incentives to purchase another brand. Brand equity

1. Allows manufacturers to charge more for products
2. Creates higher gross margins
3. Provides power with retailers and wholesalers
4. Captures additional retail shelf space
5. Serves as a weapon against consumers switching due to sales promotions
6. Prevents erosion of market share

**FIGURE 2.3**
**Benefits of Brand Equity**

prevents erosion of a product's market share, even when there is a proliferation of brands coupled with endless promotional maneuvers by competitors. Additional benefits of brand equity are displayed in Figure 2.3.

## Steps to Building Brand Equity

Brand-name recognition and recall can be built through repetitive advertising. Building brand equity, however, requires the company to achieve more than brand recognition. Recognition is only the first phase of the marketing program. Building brand equity includes the following steps:[19]

1. Research and analyze what it would take to make the brand distinctive.
2. Engage in continuous innovation.
3. Move fast.
4. Minimize reliance on any one customer.
5. Integrate new and old media.
6. Focus on domination.

The first step to building brand equity is having a distinctive brand and deciding what unique selling point should be promoted. Part of this analysis involves the need to continually innovate. Many products compete in mature markets. Companies that are not innovating and not moving forward quickly fall behind. For example, it may be tempting for Procter & Gamble not to tinker with Tide, the best-selling laundry detergent on the market. Doing so, however, might mean a steady erosion of its market share to upstart brands with unique new features. Instead, Procter & Gamble's management team widened the Tide family of detergents to include new products such as Tide Coldwater and Tide Kick. Tide Kick is a combination measuring cup and stain penetrator. The result of this continuous innovation was a 2.6 percent gain in sales when the industry sales increased less than 1 percent.[20]

In today's society, customers want innovations and new products. They also want them *fast*. Handbag designer Coach used to introduce new products quarterly. Now they come out monthly. Coach CEO Lew Frankfort states that "For brands to stay relevant, they have to stay on their toes. Complacency has no place in this market." In any given month, new products account for up to 30 percent of U.S. retail store sales.[21]

The fourth element in building brand equity is minimizing reliance on any one customer. For many consumer product manufacturers, Wal-Mart is the vital customer. To achieve long-term success, however, the supplier should balance sales to Wal-Mart with sales to other customers. A recent study revealed that firms whose sales to Wal-Mart constituted more than 10 percent of the company's total sales often experienced negative effects on profitability and shareholder returns.[22]

The same concept applies to business-to-business customers. When one customer dominates a company's sales, the company becomes a slave to the customer. Eventually the customer may try to dictate product features, delivery, and prices. It is extremely difficult to build brand equity when one customer gains too much power over the product.

Another ingredient in building brand equity is to integrate new and old media. Consumers are bombarded with advertising messages from a multitude of sources. Therefore, the marketing team must try to integrate all messages while looking for new, nontraditional methods of communicating. Although television, radio, magazines, and newspapers will always remain key media, newer alternative advertising methods can help strengthen a brand name. Procter & Gamble uses "surround-sound marketing" to reach consumers everywhere they go (surround them). Therefore, more than just television advertising is needed. Surround-sound marketing includes in-store demonstrations of products and messages on Wal-Mart's in-store televisions. P&G also used product placement in the TV show *The Apprentice.* Crest Whitening Expressions Refreshing Vanilla Mint was featured in the program. From consumer research, the P&G marketing team learned that younger girls wanted to know more about Tampax. To reach them, advertising dollars were shifted from television to magazines. Also, a Web site called Beinggirl.com was developed. This new approach resulted in an dramatic increase in sales.

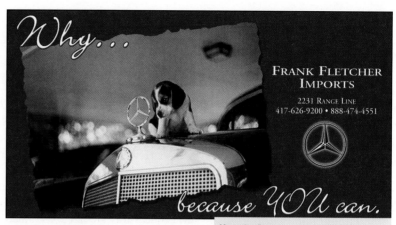

Mercedes Benz is a prominent brand in the luxury vehicle class.
*Source:* Courtesy of *The Joplin Globe,* Joplin, MO.

Brand equity involves domination. *Domination* is a strongly held view that the brand is number one in its product category. Domination can take place in a geographic region or in a smaller product category or market niche. To dominate, the brand must be viewed as number one in some way by consumers. For instance, Crest is viewed as the number-one cavity fighter in the toothpaste category. For automobiles, the number-one car in terms of safety is Volvo. Domination means delivering on the promise. Because Crest promotes itself as the cavity fighter, then it must deliver on that promise. Consumers have to believe that Crest does a better job of preventing cavities than does any other brand of toothpaste.

Developing brand equity in today's competitive global market requires a different approach than was used in the past. Companies must always be on the cutting edge, innovating new products, moving faster than the competition, and effectively reaching consumers. No matter where they are, the brand message must come through. Brand equity grows when the same integrated message that was heard before reaches consumers in a new place, through a different medium.

## Measuring Brand Equity

Trying to find out whether or not brand equity exists is difficult. One method marketing experts use is called brand metrics. **Brand metrics** measure returns on branding investments. Attitudinal measures associated with branding may be used to track awareness, recall, and recognition. To increase their power, these factors can be tied with other variables (for example, brand awareness coupled with intent to buy). Brand awareness may also be connected to use of either the product class (mustard) or the brand (Kraft, Grey Poupon). Remember that, when measuring awareness, recall, and recognition, a brand can be recalled for negative as well as positive reasons.[23]

In Quebec, a group of advertising agencies developed a measure, called "Equi* Marques," to display the importance of brand equity to clients. The measure shows that American products, which are the recipients of greater marketing investments, score higher than Quebec-based brands in many instances. In other words, U.S. firms have an advantage in Quebec due to brand equity. The head of the organization, Paul Paré, noted, "If Quebec brands want to penetrate the U.S. market, they'll find themselves up against players who invest much more in marketing." He called for a "quiet revolution" in the classroom and the boardroom to fend off this disadvantage.[24]

Brand equity has also been studied on a global scale. The primary features of brand equity include the consumers' sensory, utilitarian, symbolic, and economic needs at the national and global level. Global brand equity exists when there is a cohesive image of the brand across nations and across cultures.[25]

Although these methods of measuring brand equity can provide valid information, CEOs and other corporate leaders often want real, hard numbers. One such method is called *revenue premium.* The method compares a branded product to the same product without a

---

### ETHICAL ISSUES

#### Brand Infringement

There have always been ethical issues associated with brand management. For years, the most common problem was *brand infringement*. Brand infringement occurs when a company creates a brand name that closely resembles a popular or successful brand, such as when the Korrs beer company was formed. In that case, the courts deemed the brand an intentional infringement, and the name was abandoned. Another brand-infringing company that was forced by the courts to give up its name was Victor's Secret.

The brand infringement issue becomes more complex when a brand is so well established that it may be considered a generic term, such as a Kleenex tissue or a Xerox copy. Band-Aid encountered the problem in the 1970s, forcing the marketing team to make sure the product was identified as "Band-Aid Brand Strips" rather than simply "band aids," to keep the competition from being able to use the name. The most vulnerable new brand name may be Google, as in, "I Googled myself," or "I Googled it."

The newest form of unethical behavior, at least according to some sources, is called *domain squatting* or *cyber squatting* on the Internet. This is the controversial practice of buying domain names (barnesandnoble.com, kohls.com, labronjames.com, etc.) that are valuable to specific people or businesses in the hopes of making a profit by reselling the name. At the extreme, whitehouse.com was a pornographic Web site. Any new company trying to build a presence in the marketplace may find itself stifled by domain squatters. Names matter, and cyber squatters are willing to take advantage of that to make profits at someone else's expense.

**Source:** Internet Marketing Register (www.marketing-register.com, February 28, 2005).

---

brand name. To calculate a brand's revenue premium, the revenue generated by a particular brand is compared to a private label brand. The difference is the revenue premium, or value, of that brand and would equate to the brand equity that has accrued.[26] There are two problems with the revenue premium approach. First, it is sometimes difficult to pick the right benchmark private label to be used for comparison. Second, many private labels are no longer generic brands with no names. These private labels have some brand status and have built considerable brand equity of their own. Despite these drawbacks, the revenue premium is one of the best methods currently available to actually measure brand equity.

## BRAND EXTENSIONS AND FLANKER BRANDS

One common approach a firm can use to enter a new market is a *brand extension strategy*. Figure 2.4 identifies several types of brand strategies. **Brand extension** is the use of an established brand name on goods or services not related to the core brand. For

---

- ▶ Family brands—A group of related products sold under one name.
- ▶ Brand extension—The use of an established brand name on products or services not related to the core brand.
- ▶ Flanker brand—The development of a new brand sold in the same category as another product.
- ▶ Co-branding—The offering of two or more brands in a single marketing offer.
- ▶ Ingredient branding—The placement of one brand within another brand.
- ▶ Cooperative branding—The joint venture of two or more brands into a new product or service.
- ▶ Complementary branding—The marketing of two brands together for co-consumption.
- ▶ Private brands—Proprietary brands marketed by an organization and sold within the organization's outlets.

**FIGURE 2.4**
**Types of Brands**

example, Nike has been successful in extending its brand name to a line of clothing. Black & Decker has been somewhat successful in extending its brand name to a line of small kitchen appliances. The brand extension program used by Singer in Europe to move from producing only sewing machines to refrigerators, ranges, and televisions was less successful, at least in the initial stages.

An alternative to a brand extension program is a flanker brand. A **flanker brand** is the development of a new brand by a company in a good or service category in which it currently has a brand offering. For example, Procter & Gamble's primary laundry detergents are Cheer and Tide. Over the years, P&G introduced a number of additional brands such as Ivory Snow. In total, P&G offers 11 different brands of detergents in North America; 16 in Latin America; 12 in Asia; and 17 in Europe, the Middle East, and Africa. Table 2.2 lists Procter & Gamble's various brands of laundry detergents, cosmetics, and hair-care products. The company's marketing team introduced these flanker brands to appeal to target markets that Procter & Gamble believed its main brand in each product category was not reaching. Thus, using a set of flanker brands can help a company offer a more complete line of products. This creates barriers to entry for competing firms.

Sometimes a flanker brand is introduced when company leaders think that offering the product under the current brand name may adversely affect the overall marketing program. Hallmark created a flanker brand known as Shoebox Greetings. These cards sell in discount stores as well as Hallmark out-

A brand extension of the Skin-So-Soft bath line to a line of Skin-So-Soft Bug Guard products.
*Source:* Courtesy of Avon.

lets; however, the Hallmark brand sells only in its named retail stores. Shoebox Greeting cards are lower priced and allow Hallmark to attract a larger percentage of the market. Firms often use this type of strategy in high-end markets that want to compete in low-end markets. It is also used in international expansion. For example, Procter & Gamble sells Ariel laundry detergent in Latin America, Asia, Europe, the Middle East, and Africa, but not in North America. Offering different brands for specific markets is a common flanker brand strategy that helps a firm expand to international markets using more than its current brands.

## CO-BRANDING

There are other ways to brand products besides flanker brands. **Co-branding** takes three forms: ingredient branding, cooperative branding, and complementary branding. **Ingredient branding** is the placement of one brand within another brand, such as Intel microprocessors in Compaq computers. **Cooperative branding** is the joint venture of two or more brands into a new good or service. Study the advertisement featuring a cooperating branding venture by American Airlines, Citibank, and MasterCard in this section. **Complementary branding** is the marketing of two brands together to encourage co-consumption or co-purchases, such as Seagram's 7 encouraging 7-Up as a compatible mixer or Oreo milkshakes sold in Dairy Queen stores.[27] Locating Subway sandwich shops in convenience stores, Little Caesar's in Kmart outlets, and McDonald's in Wal-Mart stores is another type of co-branding trend.

Co-branding succeeds when it builds the brand equity of both brands. For example, when Monsanto created NutraSweet, consumer trust was built by placing the NutraSweet

**TABLE 2.2**

Brands Sold by Procter & Gamble

| Product Category | North America | Latin America | Asia | Europe, Middle East, and Africa |
|---|---|---|---|---|
| Laundry and cleaning brands | Bold | Ace | Ariel | Ace |
| | Bounce | Ariel | Bonus | Alo |
| | Cheer | Bold | Bounce | Ariel |
| | Downy | Downy | Cheer | Azurit |
| | Dreft | Duplex | Doll | Bold |
| | Dryel | InExtra | Ezee | Bonux |
| | Era | Limay | Gaofuli | Bounce |
| | Gain | Magia Blanca | Lanxiang | Dash |
| | Ivory Snow | ODD Fases | Panda | Daz |
| | Oxydol | Pop | Perla | Dreft |
| | Tide | Quanto | Tide | Fairy |
| | | Rapido | Trilo | Lenor |
| | | Ridex | | Maintax |
| | | Romtensid | | Myth |
| | | Supermo | | Rei |
| | | Tide | | Tide |
| | | | | Tix |
| Cosmetics | Cover | Cover Girl | Cover Girl | Cover Girl |
| | Max Factor | Max Factor | Max Factor | Max Factor |
| | Oil of Olay | | | Ellen Betrix |
| Hair Care | Head & Shoulders | Drene | Head & Shoulders | Head & Shoulders |
| | Mediker | Head & Shoulders | Mediker | Mediker |
| | Pantene Pro-V | Pantene Pro-V | Pantene Pro-V | Pantene Pro-V |
| | Physique | Pert Plus | Rejoy–Rejoice | Rejoy–Rejoice |
| | Rejoy–Rejoice | | Pert Plus | Pert Plus |
| | Pert Plus | | Vidal Sassoon | Vidal Sassoon |
| | Vidal Sassoon | | | |

logo on venerable brands consumers trusted, such as Diet Coke, Wrigley's Chewing Gum (Wrigley's Extra), and Crystal Light. The strategy worked so well that NutraSweet is now the standard of quality in the sweetener industry.[28]

Conversely, there can be risks in co-branding. If the relationship fails to do well in the marketplace, normally both brands suffer. To reduce the risk of failure, co-branding should be undertaken only with well-known brands. Co-branding of goods and services that are highly compatible generally will be less risky. Ingredient and cooperative branding tend to be less risky than complementary branding because both companies have more at stake and devote greater resources to ensure success.

For small companies and brands that are not as well known, co-branding is an excellent strategy. The difficult part is finding a well-known brand that is willing to take on a lesser-known product as a co-brand. Yet, if such an alliance can be made, the co-brand relationship often builds brand equity for the lesser-known brand, as in the case of NutraSweet. Co-branding also provides access to distribution channels that may be difficult to obtain either because of lack of size or dominance by the major brands.

# PRIVATE BRANDS

**Private brands** (also known as *private labels*) are proprietary brands marketed by an organization and normally distributed exclusively within the organization's outlets. Over the last 50 years, private brands have experienced a roller-coaster ride in terms of popularity and sales. To many individuals, private brands carry the connotation of a lower price and inferior quality. Historically, the primary audience for private labels was price-sensitive individuals. That is no longer true; retailers now are investing marketing dollars to develop their private brands, which now account for approximately 13 percent of all U.S. supermarket sales and 20 percent of Canadian supermarket sales.[29]

Over the past few years, several changes have occurred in the private brand arena, which Figure 2.5 summarizes. The first change is that the quality levels of private label products have improved. In some cases, the quality is perceived to be equal to or better than that of national brands. For example, consumers believe Sears' Kenmore and Craftsman brands and Gap's private label of clothing are high-quality products.

Although private labels still tend to be priced between 15 percent and 30 percent lower than national brands, they also tend to have higher gross margins than national brands. This allows the retailer to earn higher profits on its private brands. It also provides retailers with an opportunity to use some of the markup to advertise and promote the private brands.

An example of cooperative branding.
*Source:* Courtesy of CitiBank.

Not all national brands have done well. When they do poorly, it is the retailer that is forced to offer discounts on the merchandise. National brands that do not sell well reflect negatively on the retailer that carries them. As a result, several retailers have placed greater emphasis on private brands. Saks, Inc., receives 15 percent of total sales dollars from the company's private brands. For Dillard's, it is 18 percent.[30] See Figure 2.6 for additional information on private labels by department stores.

Another emerging trend in retailing is that loyalty toward retail stores has been gaining while loyalty toward individual brands has been declining. Rather than going to outlets that sell specific brands, many shoppers go to specific stores and are willing to buy from the brands offered by that store. The increase in loyalty to retailers has caused several department and specialty stores to expand the number of private brand products that are offered. To do so, however, requires that the retailer develop a private brand that is congruent with customers' image of the retailer.[31] A high-end department store should offer private brands that are considered high quality. A discount store will sell private brands that fit with the lower price, lower quality image of the retailer

Private labeling is experiencing new trends in the areas of advertising and promotions. Many private labels have more favorable images. Consequently, retailers are treating private brands more like national brands. Marketing dollars are spent on improving the actual label and on more

An advertisement by Dell with both Microsoft and Intel brands included in the ad.
*Source:* © 2005 Dell Inc. All Rights Reserved.

**FIGURE 2.5**
**Changes in Private Brands**

1. Improved quality
2. Priced 25 percent below manufacturer's brands
3. Loyalty toward retail outlets increased while loyalty toward specific brands decreased
4. Increase in advertising of private brands
5. Increase in quality of in-store displays of private brands

noticeable in-store displays.[32] At the extreme, the private brand displays may be more attractive than national brand displays.

Some private brand advertising is being designed apart from the store's regular advertising program. The purpose of this approach is to help establish the name as a bona fide brand competing head-to-head with national products. Recently, Sears launched a series of advertisements featuring its Kenmore and Craftsman brands. Sears was only mentioned in the context of being the place to purchase Kenmore and Craftsman products. Kmart heavily promotes its private lines, including Martha Stewart Everyday, Chic, Jaclyn Smith, Kathy Ireland, Expressions, Route 66, and Sesame Street. Wal-Mart has 14 private labels of clothing, including labels such as Basic Image, Bobbie Brooks, Catalina, Jordache, and Kathy Lee.

Private labeling has exploded in the area of active lifestyle–related clothing. The successes of Nike, Reebok, and Adidas apparel lines have enticed sports retailers to create competing private labels. By adding fresh, original private label products, the store competes against other manufacturer brands. Retailers make higher margins from these lower-priced (but still premium) goods.

Some manufacturers have responded aggressively to the inroads made by private labels in the clothing industry. Wrangler and Lee have increased company advertising budgets to restore their brand-name advantage in order to make sure retailers offer the proper mix of private label and brand-name jeans. It is likely that new partnerships between manufacturers and retailers looking to carry private brands will follow.[33]

Some manufacturers seek to reduce the impact of private labels on sales by expanding product offerings. The Sara Lee Corporation—which owns a number of branded apparel companies such as Bali, Playtex, Champion, Ocean, and Hanes—has expanded into the active wear market with the Hanes Sport casual collection. The surge in popularity of active lifestyle clothing created an increase in sales of other related products such as the sports underwear featured in the Hanes ad in this section. Hanes Sport now manufactures products for women, men, and children.

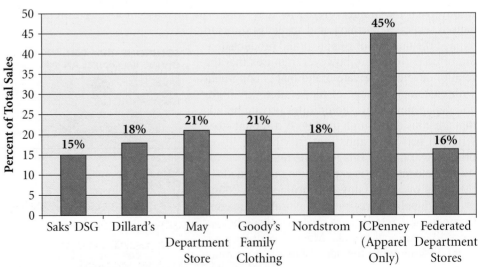

**FIGURE 2.6**
**Private Label Sales As a Percentage of Total Sales**

*Source:* Thomas J. Ryan, "Private Labels: Strong, Strategic & Growing," *Apparel Magazine* 44, no. 10 (June 2003), pp. 32–39.

The success of private brands has influenced both manufacturers and retailers. Each type of company must pay careful attention to where this trend leads in the next decade.

## PACKAGING

In many large retail stores, most employees are either stockers or cashiers. Few know anything about the products that are on the shelves. Therefore, the product's package is the last opportunity to make an impression on a consumer. Marketing surveys have revealed that only 31 percent of purchases are planned prior to reaching a store. This means 69 percent of purchase decisions are made in the store. Other research indicates that when consumers walk within 10 to 15 feet of a product, the brand has three seconds to make contact with the consumer.[34]

A package design must stand out. It must tell consumers what is inside and why the brand should be purchased. Traditionally, the primary purposes of packaging were those shown in Figure 2.7. Now, however, packages and labels are increasingly viewed as a key part of a company's integrated marketing communications program. It makes little sense to spend millions of dollars on advertising only to lose the sale in the store because of a lackluster, dull package design that does not communicate to potential customers.

The Reynolds Company recognized the value of a tie-in with packaging during the early 2000s. The entire wraps category was experiencing declining sales. The marketing team at Reynolds discovered that consumers enjoy using products that make them feel like experts. The firm created a new brand message that Reynolds was a "helper in the kitchen." This new brand message was extended and reinforced in ads showing how to use the product to prepare foods as well as by printing recipes into the design on the package. When tied to the perception that Reynolds was the premium brand in the marketplace, strong sales were continued.[35]

Most retail purchase decisions are made based on familiarity with a brand or product at the retail store. Consequently, a unique package that is attractive or captures the buyer's attention increases the chances the product will be purchased, sometimes as an impulse buy. For many years, winemakers strongly resisted the use of marketing tactics for fear of being perceived as having questionable quality. Products such as Blue Nun, Ripple, and Boone's Farm were major marketing successes but did not enjoy reputations for high quality. Recently, however, some wineries have begun to accept the value of a quality package. Many Australian wineries captured market share based on the knowledge that men (who are more likely to make the wine purchase) look at a wine's country of origin, followed by grape variety, and finally

Hanes Sport is one of many companies that have introduced new products into the active lifestyle wear market.

*Source:* Courtesy of Sara Lee Corporation.

▶ **Protect the product inside.**

▶ **Provide for ease of shipping, moving, and handling.**

▶ **Provide for easy placement on store shelves.**

▶ **Prevent or reduce the possibility of theft.**

▶ **Prevent tampering (drugs and foods).**

**FIGURE 2.7**
Traditional Elements of a Package

FIGURE 2.8
New Trends in Packaging

▶ Meets consumer needs for speed, convenience, and portability
▶ Must be contemporary and striking
▶ Must be designed for ease of use

aesthetics. Australian wine is perceived as new, different, and of sufficient quality, especially in the Shiraz lines. As a result, attractive bottles featuring names such as Vale, Valley Hill, and Cloudy Bay with images of mountain peaks and vineyards receding in the distance have been designed. Bottle color is crucial, because buyers prefer dark, warm, and intense colors (red and blue). These changes and the successes of the Australians have caused French and German winemakers to change their packages and labels to compete.[36]

## New Trends in Packaging

Some of the new trends in packaging are based on changes in the ways in which consumers use products (see Figure 2.8). In the foods market, foods that are fast, convenient, and portable are selling quickly. The package must accommodate these needs. The same is true for soft drinks.

The marketing team at Alcoa Rigid Packaging watched consumers as they bought groceries and stocked refrigerators. The team noticed that the standard 3- × 4-can (12-pack) box was too large for the refrigerator. This meant that consumers took out only a few cans at a time to cool. It seemed logical that if more cans were cold, consumers might drink more. This observation led to the design of a box that was easier and more convenient to use, the 6- × 2-can box, which is longer and slimmer. This newly designed 12-pack fits into the refrigerator door or on a shelf. It is also self-dispensing. As a can is taken out, a new one automatically slides down to the front of the box. This innovation improved sales for both Alcoa and several soft-drink manufacturers, who loved the new package.[37]

Consumers tend to buy packages that are eye-catching and contemporary. When Nestle created a new line of products called Nescafé Original, one primary consideration was the package. The goal was to create a package that would protect the contents but would also stand out. The result was a container with a unique geometrical set of shapes designed to appeal to younger consumers. The approach was very successful.[38]

The trends in packaging in international markets are much the same as in the United States. Ease of use is a key feature. When shipping products overseas, however, one key issue is that the buyer must feel reassured the package will not break or become contaminated.[39]

## LABELS

Labels on packages serve several functions. First, they must meet legal requirements. This includes identifying the product contained in the package and any other specific information about content, such as nutritional information on foods. The Food and Drug Administration (FDA) regulates food labels in the United States. Also, many times warranties and guarantees are printed on the label.

The label represents another marketing opportunity. Many times a label is the only distinguishing feature of a product, such as a 12-ounce bottle of beer or a 1-gallon container of milk. An attractive label is an attention-getting device that may draw the consumer to the product. This feature is vitally important in the United States as well as in other nations. For example, many Asian purchases are, in part, driven by the appeal of the label.[40] The company's logo and the brand name must appear prominently. Labels often contain special offers and other tie-ins, such as a box of cereal with a toy contained inside. The consumer is notified of the offer on the label.

Labels often carry terms designed to build consumer interest and confidence in making the purchase. Word such as "gourmet," "natural," "premium," "adult formula," and "industrial strength" make the product seem like a better buy. At the same time, consumers are used to such puffery. A private brand's label is often very plain. This type of label matches the buyer's perception that the price is being held down by lesser use of marketing tools. In general, a company's image, brand, logo, and theme should carry through to the design of the package and label. Doing so allows the marketing team one more chance to make the sale when the consumer is in the store making a final purchasing decision.

## POSITIONING

A final element in corporate and brand image management is product positioning. **Positioning** is the process of creating a perception in the consumer's mind regarding the nature of a company and its products relative to competitors. Positioning is created by variables such as the quality of products, prices charged, methods of distribution, image, and other factors. A product's position is based on two elements: (1) the product's standing relative to the competition and (2) how the product is perceived by consumers.

Consumers ultimately determine the position a product holds. Marketing programs are designed to position effectively. To do so, marketing communications must either reinforce what consumers already believe about a product and its brand name or shift consumer views toward a more desirable position. The first strategy is certainly easier to accomplish. The goal of positioning is to find that niche in a consumer's mind that a product can occupy.

To prevent cannibalism, Campbell's must position each version of its V8 juice for individual target markets.
*Source:* Courtesy of Campbell Soup Company.

Positioning is vital for companies such as Procter & Gamble, VF Corporation, Sara Lee Corporation, and Campbell Soup because it helps prevent cannibalism among various brands within a product category. Campbell's produces five different types of V8 juice. The one pictured in this section is being marketed to individuals who are concerned about calories and fat content. Campbell's offers a low-sodium version of V8 for individuals on a low-sodium diet, a spicy hot version for consumers who want something with more taste or who need a mixer, and a calcium-enriched version for those who desire more calcium, potassium, or vitamins A and C.

Effective positioning can be achieved in seven different ways (see Figure 2.9). Although companies may try two or three approaches, such efforts generally only manage to confuse customers. The best method is to use one of these approaches consistently.

▶ **Attributes**

▶ **Competitors**

▶ **Use or application**

▶ **Price–quality relationship**

▶ **Product user**

▶ **Product class**

▶ **Cultural symbol**

**FIGURE 2.9**
**Product Positioning Strategies**

An advertisement by Echo positioning the automobile on the basis of high gas mileage.
**Source:** Courtesy of Toyota Motor Sales and Charles Hopkins Photography, Inc.

A business-to-business advertisement positioned based on the product's attributes.
**Source:** Courtesy of Sony Electronics, Inc.

An *attribute* is a product trait or characteristic that sets it apart from other products. In the Toyota advertisement shown above the Echo is positioned based on the attribute of gas mileage, because the car gets 41 miles per gallon. The Sony ad is aimed at business customers. The advertisement promotes the attribute of quality, because the projector provides stronger light. Both ads attempt to convey the message that the attribute featured by the brand outperforms the competition.

Another common tactic is using *competitors* to establish position. This is done by contrasting the company's product against others. For years Avis ran advertisements comparing the company to Hertz. Avis admitted they were not number one, but turned that position into an advantage, because Avis was willing to "try harder" for business.

*Use* or *application* positioning involves creating a memorable set of uses for a product. Arm & Hammer has long utilized this approach in the attempt to convince consumers to use its baking soda as a deodorizer in the refrigerator. Arm & Hammer has also been featured as a co-brand in toothpaste, creating yet another use for the product.

Businesses on the extremes of the price range often use the *price–quality relationship*. At the top end, businesses emphasize high quality while at the bottom end, low prices are emphasized. Hallmark cards cost more but are for those who "only want to send the very best." Other firms seek to be a "low-price leader," with no corresponding statement about quality.

A *product user* positioning strategy distinguishes a brand or product by clearly specifying who might use it. Apple Computers originally positioned itself as the computer for educational institutions. Although this strategy helped the company to grow rapidly, Apple had a difficult time convincing businesses to use its computers. Apple's marketing team had done such a good job creating the company's original position strategy that changing people's minds was difficult.

Sometimes firms seek to position themselves in a particular *product class.* Orange juice was long considered part of the breakfast drink product class. Years ago, those in the industry decided to create advertisements designed to move orange juice into a new product class, with slogans such as "it's not just for breakfast anymore." This repositioning has been fairly successful. Many consumers drink orange juice at other times during the day. This result was due, in part, to the perception that orange juice is a healthy drink. Orange juice cannot compete with Pepsi or Coke. Instead, it must be viewed as an alternative to a sugary soft drink.

Identifying a product with a *cultural symbol* is difficult but, if done successfully, can become a strong competitive advantage for a firm. Chevrolet used this type of positioning strategy. For years, Chevrolet was advertised as being as American as baseball and apple pie during the summer. Playboy has evolved into an entertainment empire by becoming a cultural symbol, albeit a controversial one. In its advertisement shown in this section, Stetson cologne is tied to the American cowboy and the spirit of the West. The ad copy reads that "The attraction is legendary." The purpose of placing this ad in *Glamour* magazine was to entice women to purchase the product for the men in their lives.

An advertisement by Stetson using the cultural symbolism of the cowboy as the positioning strategy.
*Source:* Courtesy of J.B. Stetson Company.

## Other Elements of Positioning

A brand's position is never completely fixed. It can be changed. Gillette is a brand that has been traditionally firmly entrenched with men. Recently, the company launched a massive campaign to position itself in the women's market. New products, including the Sensor Excel razor and Satin Care Shave Gel, were offered by mail to consumer homes, and free samples were placed in homeroom bags for 14- and 15-year-old girls at school. Gillette's advertisements encouraged women to view the products as a key part of being physically and psychologically ready for anything. The ad copy asked "Are you ready?" and answered "Yes, I am!" This positioning matches with the position of Gillette's products for men, which are marketed using the "Best a man can get" slogan.[41]

Understanding how consumers view a product is important to successful positioning. Market researchers discovered that although the Lexus was known for quality and luxury, the brand position was still ill-defined in consumers' minds. Lexus launched a $50 million brand blitz designed to hammer home the high-end "pursuit of perfection" position. According to Mike Wells, vice president of marketing, "These ads, in a sense, celebrate and restate our commitment to the pursuit of perfection by demonstrating how Lexus has taken that pursuit to the next level with new innovations and technologies."[42]

Brand positioning must also be applied to business-to-business marketing efforts. InterContinental Hotels Group, which owns InterContinental, Crowne Plaza, Holiday Inn, Holiday Inn Express, Staybridge Suites, and Candlewood Suites, understands the

This advertisement for NetSuite is a direct
challenge to the position held by QuickBooks.

*Source:* Courtesy of NetSuite Inc.

needs of business travelers and offers unique
services that add value to the businessperson's
stay. High-speed Internet access is available at all
of the properties, and at the Crowne Plaza wireless
connections are available at any location on the
property. Understanding that time and convenience are important to business travelers,
InterContinental Hotels offers an online wireless
reservation system that allows business guests to
review, cancel, or modify reservations online. To
ensure that business guests have a good night's
sleep, Crowne Plaza offers a guaranteed wake-up
call, quiet zone floors, sleep amenities, sleep CDs,
and relaxation tips.[43] These all emphasize the
attribute and product user–based positions associated with offering all of the conveniences and services a businessperson would want.

Effective positioning is vitally important in
the international arena. Plans must be made to
build an effective position when a firm expands
into new countries. Often the positioning strategy
used in one country will not work in another.
Marketing experts carefully analyze the competition as well as the consumers or businesses
that are potential customers. After this analysis,
the marketing team is better able to choose a positioning strategy. Although the positioning strategy
may need to be modified for each country, the
company's overall theme and the brand image
should be consistent.

Brand positioning is a critical part of image
and brand-name management. Consumers have
an extensive set of purchasing options. This
means consumers can try products with spe-
cific advantages or attributes. Effective positioning, by whatever tactic chosen,
increases sales and strengthens the long-term positions of both individual products and
the total organization.

## SUMMARY

An effective integrated marketing communications plan must
emphasize a strong and positive company or corporate image
as part of the program. An image consists of consumer and
business-to-business feelings toward the overall organization
as well as evaluations of each individual brand the firm carries.
An image has both tangible and intangible components.
Tangible ingredients include products, advertisements, names,
logos, and services provided. Intangible elements consist of
policies and practices that change or enhance the company's
image in the consumer's mind. A well-developed and well-
established image benefits both customers and the company in
many ways.

Creating an effective image is a difficult task. It is important to
know how all publics view the firm before seeking to build or

enhance an image. Rejuvenating the image involves reminding
customers of their previous conceptions of the company while at
the same time expanding into a closely related area of concern.
Once an image is strongly pressed into the minds of customers, it
becomes difficult, if not impossible, to change.

A corporate name is the overall banner under which all other
operations occur. The corporate logo accompanying the name is
the symbol used to identify a company and its brands, helping to
convey the overall corporate image. The firm's name and image
are important not only to general customers but also to any firms
that may make purchases from or conduct business with a manufacturer or service provider.

Brands are names given to goods or services, or groups of
complementary products. Effective brands give the firm an

advantage, especially in mature markets containing fewer actual products or where service differences exist. Strong brands convey the most compelling benefits of the product, elicit proper consumer emotions, and help create loyalty. There are many versions of brands, including family brands, flanker brands, and co-brands. In each, brand equity is built by domination, or the recognition that the brand has one key advantage or characteristic.

Recently, private brands or private labels have become an important component in the success rates of both producers and retailers. Consumers now view private brands as having quality equal to or close to that of more famous manufacturer brand names. At the same time, customers expect price advantages in private label products. Consequently, effective management of brands and products includes creating a mix of offerings that both end users and retailers recognize as a beneficial range of choices.

Positioning is the relative psychological location of the good or service as compared to its competitors' in the views of customers. Marketing managers must select a positioning strategy that highlights the best features of the company's products. Positioning is never fixed, because markets evolve over time. Positioning can be established with both the general public and business-to-business customers.

## REVIEW QUESTIONS

1. What is meant by "corporate image"? What are the tangible aspects of a corporate image?

2. How does a corporation's image help customers? How does it help the specific company?

3. How will company leaders know when they have created the "right" image for their firm?

4. What is a corporate logo? What are the characteristics of an effective corporate logo?

5. What is meant by the term *stimulus codability?*

6. What is the difference between a brand name and a corporation's overall image?

7. What are the characteristics of a strong and effective brand name?

8. What is the difference between brand equity and brand parity?

9. Why is brand equity important? How is it measured?

10. Describe the use of brand extension and flanker brand strategies.

11. Name and describe three types of co-brands.

12. How has private branding, or private labeling, changed in the past decade?

13. What role does a product's package play in the marketing program?

14. How can a label support an IMC program or advertising campaign?

15. What is product–brand positioning? Give examples of various types of positioning strategies.

## KEY TERMS

**image**  Overall consumer perceptions or end-user feelings toward a company along with its goods and services.

**corporate logo**  The symbol used to identify a company and its brands, helping to convey the overall corporate image.

**stimulus codability**  Items that easily evoke consensually held meanings within a culture or subculture.

**brands**  Names generally assigned to a good or service or a group of complementary products.

**salience**  When consumers are aware of the brand, have it in their consideration sets (things they consider when making purchases), regard the product and brand as a good value, buy it or use it on a regular basis, and recommend it to others.

**family brand**  When a company offers a series or group of products under one brand name.

**brand equity**  A set of brand assets that add to the value assigned to a product.

**brand metrics**  Measures of returns on brand investments.

**brand extension**  The use of an established brand name on goods or services not related to the core brand.

**flanker brand**  The development of a new brand by a company in a good or service category in which it currently has a brand offering.

**co-branding**  Offering two or more brands in a single marketing effort.

**ingredient branding**  A form of co-branding in which the name of one brand is placed within another brand.

**cooperative branding**  A form of co-branding in which two firms create a joint venture of two or more brands into a new good or service.

**complementary branding**  A form of co-branding in which the marketing of two brands together encourages co-consumption or co-purchases.

**private brands**  (also known as *private labels*) Proprietary brands marketed by an organization and normally distributed exclusively within the organization's outlets.

**positioning**  The process of creating a perception in the consumer's mind about the nature of a company and its products relative to the competition. It is created by the quality of products, prices charged, methods of distribution, image, and other factors.

## CRITICAL THINKING EXERCISES

### Discussion Questions

1. Dalton Office Supply Company has been in operation for over 50 years and has been the predominant office supply company in its region during that time. Approximately 85 percent of Dalton's business is based on providing materials to other businesses. Only 15 percent comes from walk-in customers. Recently, low-cost providers such as Office Depot have cut into Dalton's market share. Surveys of consumers indicate that Dalton has an image of being outdated and pricey. Consumers did report that Dalton's customer service was above average. What image should Dalton project to regain its market share? Outline a plan to rejuvenate the company's image.

2. Henry and Becky Thompson plan to open a new floral and gift shop in Orlando, Florida. They want to project an image of being trendy, upscale, and fashionable. They are trying to decide on a name and logo. What should be the name of their company? What kind of logo should they develop?

3. Go to a local retail store. Choose five packages that are effective. Describe the reasons they are effective. Choose five labels that are effective at capturing attention. What are the attention-getting aspects of the label?

4. Suppose Terminix Pest Control wants to expand through co-branding. To gather more information about Terminix, access its Web site at www.terminix.net. What kind of co-branding would you suggest? Which companies should Terminix contact?

## INTEGRATED LEARNING EXERCISES

1. Web sites are an important element of a company's image. Access the Web sites of the following companies to get a feel for the image each company tries to project. Is the image projected on the Web site consistent with the image portrayed in the company's advertisements?

   a. Bluenotes (www.bluenotesjeans.com)

   b. Portillo's Restaurants (www.portillos.com)

   c. BMW Motorcycles (www.bmwmotorcycles.com)

   d. McDonald's (www.mcdonalds.com)

   e. Hewlett-Packard (www.hp.com)

2. A major consulting firm that has been a leader in extending marketing knowledge and in the area of brand development is the Boston Consulting Group. Other companies that have actively been involved in brand development are Lexicon Branding and Corporate Branding. Access each of these Web sites. What kinds of services does each provide?

   a. Boston Consulting Group (www.bcg.com)

   b. Lexicon Branding, Inc. (www.lexicon-branding.com)

   c. Corporate Branding (www.corebrand.com)

3. Brand extension and flanker branding are common strategies for large corporations. Access the following Web sites. Identify the various brand extension strategies and flanker brands used by each company.

   a. Marriott Hotels (www.marriott.com)

   b. Procter & Gamble (www.pg.com)

   c. Sara Lee Corporation (www.saralee.com)

   d. VF Corporation (www.vfc.com)

4. Private labels are an important source of revenue for many retail stores and manufacturers. The Private Label Manufacturers' Association promotes manufacturers that produce private labels. From the Web site at www.plma.com, identify the press updates, store brands, and upcoming events that illustrate the importance of private labels for both retailers and manufactures.

5. Look up one of the following companies on the Internet. Discuss the image conveyed by the Web site. What positioning strategy does it use? What changes or improvements could it make?

   a. Scubaworld (www.scubaworld.com)

   b. Union Pacific Railroad (www.uprr.com)

   c. Bicycle Museum of America (www.bicyclemuseum.com)

   d. Metropolitan Transportation Commission (www.mtc.ca.gov)

   e. Canyon Beachwear (www.canyonbeachwear.com)

## STUDENT PROJECT

### IMC Plan Pro

Advertising and promotion begin with the big picture. The IMC Plan Pro disk and booklet available from Prentice Hall have a section devoted to making sure a company has a strong sense of image, brand, and position. This strong foundation helps you get started creating an advertising and communications program that is best for your company.

## CASE 1

## A HEALTHY IMAGE

Mary Wilson was both nervous and excited as she opened her first staff meeting in the marketing department of St. Margaret's General Hospital. Mary's new role was Director of Marketing and Communications. Her primary task was to increase the visibility of St. Margaret's Hospital in order to raise the image of the institution in the eyes of the many publics served. The long-term goal was to attract the best possible physicians while increasing use of the hospital's facilities and attracting more patients.

The world of health care has dramatically changed in the past decade. Governmental regulations and support, concerns about lawsuits, evolving and expensive technologies, and changes in health insurance provisions affect hospitals of all sizes. In addition, St. Margaret's faced strong competition. The hospital's primary location is in a major metropolitan area in Minnesota. Two other large hospitals also offer comparable services in the same city. Each seeks to sign physicians to exclusive contracts in which they will only provide care with one organization.

The other significant challenge to St. Margaret's is its proximity to the Mayo Clinic. Clearly Mayo holds the highest level of prestige in the state and even in the region. Most physicians are inclined to think of Mayo first when making referrals for patients with difficult medical problems. Mayo would be viewed by most publics as the "best" care possible.

The key issues in the image of any health organization are developing trust and a feeling of confidence in the quality of care that will be received. Beyond technological advantages, other, more subtle elements of an image could have an influence. Mary noted that to most patients the nurse plays a primary role in determining how the hospital is viewed. An uncaring and inattentive nurse is likely to drive away both the patient who encountered the nurse and all of the patient's family and friends. Negative word-of-mouth, Mary said, must be held to an absolute minimum.

Mary believed St. Margaret's needed to overcome two problems. First, the name "Margaret" is not commonly used anymore. Some publics may view it as an "old-fashioned" name. Second, there was nothing distinctive about the hospital's image. The overlap in services provided (heart care, cancer treatment) made it difficult to differentiate St. Margaret's from other providers.

If there was any advantage, Mary believed it was that St. Margaret's was affiliated with the Catholic Church. It was the only nonprofit hospital of the three major competitors. This attracted both Catholic patients and some Catholic physicians. Also, the hospital was able to utilize the services of a wide variety of volunteers.

As the marketing meeting opened, the agenda was to discuss all of the ways St. Margaret's could build its client base. The task would not be easy, but everyone in the room believed the hospital offered high-quality services in a caring atmosphere.

1. What are the image issues in this case?

2. What are the brand-name issues? Should the brand name be changed? If so, to what?

3. What types of advertisements should Mary develop for St. Margaret's General Hospital?

4. What other types of activities could St. Margaret's pursue to build a strong and positive corporate image?

## DAVE'S SCUBA SHOP

"For sale," read the sign in front of Dave's Scuba Shop. Dave Dishman, who loved his business, sadly had to admit that he could not continue operating with the kinds of losses he had been experiencing. He was left to ponder what had gone wrong.

From what he could tell, Dave's problems came in three areas: turnover, inconsistency, and bad public relations. He had tried to deal with all of the issues, but with no success.

The company had begun with a promising opening weekend. Dave had set up shop on the south side of Arlington, Texas, with a small store containing basic scuba equipment items for sale and the offer to make repairs and provide routine maintenance for scuba gear. Early traffic through the store had been encouraging, partly due to radio remote features of a local disk jockey, who was an avid diver.

In the first year, Dave sponsored a dive and also provided funds for a diving-for-charity event. He was trying to build a name for his store as the center of activity when it came to diving in the region. He posted billboards promoting his outlet as where the "best scuba gear and repair" could be found.

The first bad break came when Dave's key repairman, John, had to quit. John was a first-class repairman who took the time to do a job right. He never compromised on the quality of a repair, even if the store lost money on the deal. John's wife, who was their major source of income, had gotten a promotion, which meant they had to move. John's talent was easily transferred to another city. Consequently, he agreed to move on.

Dave tried three new maintenance and repair workers in the next 6 months. Two were male, one was female, and all three were unacceptable. There was either sloppy work to contend with, or the work took too long. Dave had to soothe the feelings of many unhappy customers during that time period.

Because Dave couldn't find a good repairperson, he decided to do all of the repair work personally. He hired a sales rep to run the front of the store. Mimi was an attractive snorkeling enthusiast. Her only drawback was a great interest in talking about diving rather than selling gear. She was not highly productive in terms of other chores, such as checking out the drawer or restocking shelves. Dave ended up spending longer hours at night fixing things in the "front room." He was also inclined to make mistakes when he was tired, meaning even some of his repairs were suspect.

Word around town was that customers would get an overpriced diving suit with marginal service at Dave's Scuba Shop. Business slowed, and Dave was forced to fire Mimi, leaving him to run the entire operation by himself. Mimi quickly began spreading rumors that Dave was a "jerk," not a good thing to happen in a tightly knit diving community.

Dave decided to try big discounts. He cut prices on all of his products and took out several ads showing how his products were comparably priced with those in major discount stores. To offset his margin losses on scuba equipment, Dave raised the price for his repairs. He soon was spending too much time on the sales floor and not enough in the repair room.

Finally, Dave found a competent maintenance person. He could again focus on selling. He lowered the rates for his repair business, but word around town was that his was the highest price in the area.

Dave tried getting more involved in the diving community to offset the negative image Mimi was creating. He had some limited success, enticing a few former customers to come back.

By then Dave pretty well knew that there was insufficient demand to continue operations in the same way. He was at a loss about how to proceed. Before he could even offer a new program, his rent was 3 months overdue and several suppliers had "cut him off" until he paid some back bills. He knew the store's credit rating was ruined. Even the utility companies were unhappy.

At that point, Dave had no choice. He had lost his investment and knew his store was about to become one of those nameless and faceless statistics of failed entrepreneurial ventures.

1. What image did Dave try to establish in his store?
2. What image did Dave's Scuba Shop end up projecting?
3. What could Dave have done to maintain and improve the image of his store and his company?
4. Could Dave's Scuba Shop have been salvaged? How?

# ENDNOTES

1. Gucci (www.gucci.com, accessed February 28, 2005).

2. Arun Sudhaman, "Brand Quality Still Key to Corporate Reputation: Edelman," *Media Asia* (November 19, 2004), p. 8.

3. Kari Greenberg, "Mazda, Subaru Racing to Upgrade Dealerships," *Brandweek* 45, no. 39 (November 1, 2004), p. 10.

4. Interview with Kerri L. Martin, brand manager for BMW Motorcycles USA (October 12, 2002).

5. Gregg Cebrzynski, "Low Brand Awareness Prompts Portillo's Image Ads," *Nation's Restaurant News* 38, no. 26 (June 28, 2004), p. 18.

6. Beth Snyder Bulik, "Hewlett-Packard," *Advertising Age* 75, no. 50 (December 13, 2004), p. S-10.

7. Kate MacArthur, "Salad Days at McDonald's," *Advertising Age* 75, no. 50 (December 13, 2004), p. S-2.

8. Michelle Halpern, "Hip Huggers," *Marketing Magazine* 109, no. 27 (August 23–30, 2004), p. 6.

9. Jennifer McFarland, "Branding from the Inside Out, and from the Outside In," *Harvard Management Update* 7, no. 2 (February 2002), pp. 3–4.

10. "Puffed Up," *The Economist* (March 21, 1998), p. 82.

11. Paul McNamara, "The Name Game," *Network World* (April 20, 1998), pp. 77–78.

12. Max Du Bois, "Making Your Company One in a Million," *Brand Strategy,* no. 153 (November 2001), pp. 10–11.

13. Pamela W. Henderson and Joseph A. Cote, "Guidelines for Selecting or Modifying Logos," *Journal of Marketing* (April 1998), pp. 14–30.

14. Andrew Ehrenberg, Neil Barnard, and John Scriven, "Differentiation or Salience," *Journal of Advertising Research* (November–December 1997), pp. 7–14.

15. Johnny K. Johansson and Ilkka A. Ronkainen, "Consider Implications of Local Brands in a Global Arena," *Marketing News* 38 (May 15, 2004), pp. 46–48.

16. Ibid.

17. Chuck Pettis, "Making Ignorance an Opportunity," *MC Technology Marketing Intelligence* (February 1998), pp. 52–53; David Marting, "Branding: Finding That 'One Thing,'" *Brandweek* (February 16, 1998), p. 18.

18. Debra Semans, "The Brand You Save," *Marketing Management* 13, no. 3 (May–June 2004), pp. 29–32.

19. Nanette Byrnes, Robert Berner, Wendy Zellner, and William C. Symonds, "Branding: Five New Lessons," *BusinessWeek* (February 14, 2005), pp. 26–28; Marsha Lindsay, "Five Ways to Build Brand Equity," *Electrical World* (March 1998), p. 15.

20. Nanette Byrnes, Robert Berner, Wendy Zellner, and William C. Symonds, "Branding: Five New Lessons," *BusinessWeek* (February 14, 2005), pp. 26–28.

21. Ibid.

22. Ibid.

23. Don E. Schultz, "Mastering Brand Metrics," *Marketing Management* 11, no. 3 (May–June 2002), pp. 8–9; Daniel Baack and Mark N. Hatala, "Predictors of Brand Rating and Brand Recall: An Empirical Investigation," *Regional Business Review* 17 (1998), pp. 17–34.

24. Danny Kucharsky, "AAPQ Study Highlights Brand Value," *Marketing Magazine* 107, no. 13 (April 1, 2002), p. 3.

25. Ming H. Hsieh, "Identifying Brand Image Dimensionality and Measuring the Degree of Brand Globalization: A Cross-National Study," *Journal of International Marketing* 10, no. 2 (2002), pp. 46–68.

26. Kusum L. Ailawaldi, Scott A. Neslin, and Donald R. Lehman, "Revenue Premium As an Outcome Measure of Brand Equity," *Journal of Marketing* 67, no. 4 (October 2003), pp. 1–18.

27. Stephanie Thompson, "Brand Buddies," *Brandweek* (February 23, 1998), pp. 22–30.

28. Ibid.

29. Dongdae Lee, "Image Congruence and Attitude Toward Private Brands," *Advances in Consumer Research* 31 (2004), pp. 435–441.

30. Thomas J. Ryan, "Private Labels: Strong, Strategic & Growing, *Apparel Magazine* 44, no. 10 (June 2003), pp. 32–39.

31. Dongdae Lee, "Image Congruence and Attitude Toward Private Brands," *Advances in Consumer Research* 31 (2004), pp. 435–441.

32. Thomas J. Ryan, "Private Labels: Strong, Strategic & Growing, *Apparel Magazine* 44, no. 10 (June 2003), pp. 32–39.

33. Mark Henricks, "Private Labeling: Who Said the Stores Would Get Tired of Manufacturing . . . " *Apparel Industry Magazine* (March 1998), pp. 20–28.

34. Kris Perry, "Do You Help Your Customers Sell or Market?" *Paperboard Packaging* 89, no. 11 (November 2004), p. 8.

35. Ibid.

36. Victoria Moore and Frances Stonor Saunders, "Message on a Bottle," *New Statesman* 130, no. 4538 (May 21, 2001), pp. 49–53.

37. Andrea Zoe Aster, "Good Drinks Come in Smart Packaging," *Marketing Magazine* 109, no. 32 (October 4–11, 2004), pp. 13–15.

38. "A Sleek Look for Nescafe," *Food Manufacture* 76, no. 11 (November 2001), p. 21.

39. Michael Kahn, "Super Convenience," *Frozen Food Age* 49, no. 6 (January 2001), p. 16.

40. Ibid.

41. Pat Sloan, "Gillette Bets $80 Mil on Women," *Advertising Age* (May 4, 1998), p. 63.

42. Jean Halliday, "Lexus Readies Launch of $50M Brand Effort," *Advertising Age* 74, no. 49 (December 8, 2003), p. 6.

43. "Intercontinental Hotels Group," *Business Travel News* 21, no. 6 (April 19, 2004), p. 67.

# 3

# Buyer Behaviors

## Chapter Objectives

*Understand* **the consumer buying decision-making process.**

*Learn* **how attitudes and values influence buyer behaviors.**

*Discover* **how traditional factors and new trends affect consumer purchasing decisions.**

*Create* **effective marketing messages targeted to business buyers.**

*Integrate* **business and consumer markets into an effective dual channel marketing program.**

## HOW STARBUCKS CREATED A NEW COFFEE CULTURE

How was it possible to convince ordinary Americans, who routinely open 3-pound "value" cans of coffee, shovel the grounds into a paper filter, push a button, and then go about their business, to suddenly change their coffee-drinking ways? Why would they suddenly be willing to spend $2 or more per day on what used to be a convenience good? What would cause people to change personal buying habits to include $1,400 per year purchases of *lattes* and scones? The answers to these questions explain how Starbucks became more than a coffee shop. Starbucks has created a new coffee culture.

Starbucks began as a coffee-importing firm. Howard Schultz, an employee in the organization, toured Italy in the early 1980s. He watched with interest as crowds of city dwellers began each morning with a stop at a coffee bar. Schultz tried to convince the owners of Starbucks to do something similar in the United States. He was strongly rejected. Schulz quit the firm and set out on his own. The move quickly turned into a lucrative decision. Schultz raised money from a variety of investors and opened a café in Seattle using the name *Il Giornale*. Success came rapidly. Schultz eventually wound up buying the original importing business and renaming his cafés "Starbucks."

Within 15 years, Starbucks Coffee Company expanded to over 1,200 retail outlets. The firm achieved this remarkable growth because of several key marketing activities. The product itself, locations, employees, sourcing, and effective marketing communications all worked together to help the firm prosper in a saturated marketplace. The nonchalance of major competitors was also a factor.

Until Starbucks entered the market, coffee was a rather banal commodity to most consumers. Purchase price was traditionally the primary decision variable. Starbucks needed to convince prospective buyers of the differences in its offerings. After studying the basics of coffee (flavor, acidity, and body), the company's leadership sought the best beans in the world. Then, other aspects of the product changed, including steaming milk

and brewing coffee in a plunger pot. *Espresso* is an acquired taste for most consumers. To build the market, Starbucks offered straight *espresso* along with diluted, creamy drinks. For example, *caffe latte* is *espresso* mixed with steamed milk and covered with a topping of milk foam. Other featured products are *cappuccino* and *caffe mocha*. When any one of these Starbucks products is sold, the basic ingredient, coffee, is never more than an hour old.

Location is another key ingredient in Starbucks' success. Cafés are located on commuter routes and in other places where people can gather to socialize. Each café features numerous enticements, including jazz music in the background and merchandise to examine, such as stainless steel thermoses, commuter mugs, filters, natural hairbrushes for cleaning coffee grinders, and home *espresso* machines.

Starbucks attracts employees who enjoy coffee. They are retained through a variety of motivational programs, including buy-in options. Workers are called *baristas*, Italian for "bar person." Starbucks continually encourages these *baristas* to provide high-quality, pleasant service to patrons. Extensive training helps ensure that they become experts in all aspects of coffee vending. The company also insists on a diverse workforce reflecting the makeup of the local community.

Starbucks holds a major advantage of sourcing. The firm is vertically integrated and relies on quality suppliers from around the world. Each region grows beans with distinct flavors for coffee connoisseurs, and Starbucks brings all of the flavors to a single location for purchase.

The most impressive aspect of Starbucks may be its marketing communications program. The firm had to convince price-conscious buyers to shift away from old purchasing decision rules in order to part with a great deal more money each day. Starbucks also needed to convince some consumers to develop a habit that, to many, seemed like a bad one because of the caffeine involved.

To achieve these goals, Starbucks noted two primary target markets. The first was the younger, grunge-dominated Generation X types inhabiting the Seattle area. Many people of this generation found coffee shops to be an alternative to the bar scene and made purchases accordingly. Coffee-shop regulars tend to hang out for longer periods of time, reading, talking, and listening to the background music. Next, the baby boom generation became a target as people in their 40s and 50s began consuming less alcohol and looking for other products with a degree of "snob appeal." Coffee became an excellent choice. The most loyal boomer customers can discuss coffees such as Jamaican Blue Mountain with as much sophistication as they used to describe wines such as Châteauneuf du Pape. Starbucks customers appear to agree that this more expensive but higher-quality coffee makes regular joe seem almost distasteful.

Coffee giants Maxwell House (owned by General Foods) and Folgers (owned by Procter & Gamble) simply ignored the potential of gourmet coffee. The idea of vending coffee in a café seemed so far-fetched to these firms that they did not view Starbucks as a threat, even as Seattle became known as "Latteland." Failing to see the growing market for whole bean coffee as a retail product led to lost market share. In 1990, gourmet coffee companies had a 13.5 percent share of the market. By 1991, the share was up to 17.1 percent. The trend has continued through the new millennium. Today, Starbucks easily has as much name recognition and more brand loyalty compared to its major competitors.

Starbucks has continued to expand through business-to-business marketing efforts based on the strength of the company's name. New customers include United Airlines, the Holland America cruise line, Chicago's Wrigley Field, and an alliance with Barnes & Noble bookstores. What started as essentially a small blip on the competitive radar is now a major force in the coffee industry. Consumers continue to happily part with extra dollars to support coffee habits that represent something far more complex than simply buying a beverage in the morning. As a result, the coffee landscape will never be the same.[1]

**overview**

A primary goal of an integrated marketing communications program is to develop effective methods of persuading people to purchase goods and services. The best way to reach the goal is to clearly understand how a buyer makes the decision to purchase from a particular vendor. This chapter reviews two types of buyer behaviors: (1) consumer buyer behaviors and (2) business-to-business buyer behaviors. When the steps followed in making purchasing decisions are more fully understood, it becomes possible to develop better marketing communications programs.

The first half of this chapter is devoted to consumer purchasing processes. The focus is on two stages in that process. The first is the information search stage where the customer goes through previous memories and experiences looking for acceptable ways to meet a need by buying a product. The second stage is the evaluation of alternatives process, where the individual compares various purchasing possibilities. An effective IMC program targets potential buyers as they are involved in these processes. To help the marketing team, a review of the traditional factors that affect consumers is presented along with a discussion of some of the newer trends that are present in the consumer buying environment.

The second part of this chapter examines business-to-business buyer behaviors. A review of the five major roles played in business buying is presented first. These roles make up what is called the buying center. Next, the types of purchases companies make are noted along with the steps involved in the purchasing process. Finally, dual channel marketing is described. Dual channel marketing involves selling the same product to both consumers and business buyers. Effective IMC programs identify every potential customer. This helps a company increase sales and maintain a strong presence in the marketplace.

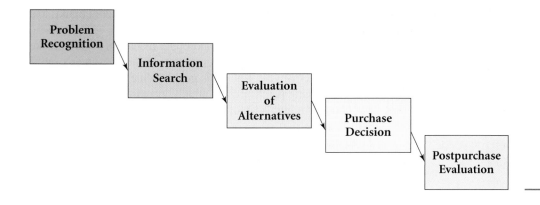

**FIGURE 3.1**
Consumer Decision-Making
Process

# CONSUMER PURCHASING PROCESS

A key activity in marketing communications is finding ways to influence consumer purchasing decisions. Many marketers are being held directly accountable for results of individual campaigns. Consequently, it is important to carefully develop messages that will entice customers to buy products.

Figure 3.1 models the consumer buying decision-making process. As shown, the steps include recognizing a need, searching for information, evaluating alternatives, making a purchase decision, and evaluating that decision. Each step of the decision-making process is important; however, two of the components are most directly related to developing quality integrated marketing communications:

▶ Information search
▶ Evaluation of alternatives

In this section, these two steps are examined in detail. Understanding how customers seek out product information and then evaluate that information is the key to creating effective advertisements.

# INFORMATION SEARCH

As the buying decision-making process begins, the first step occurs when the consumer notices a need or want. Then, the consumer conducts a search for information. Typically, a consumer starts with an *internal search*. In other words, the person mentally recalls products that might satisfy or meet the need. Often, the individual remembers how the need was met in the past. If a particular brand was chosen and the experience with that brand was positive, the consumer is likely to make the same purchase decision. When this happens, there is no further search for information. On the other hand, if the previous experience did not work out, the consumer conducts a more complete internal search. This includes memories of past experiences as well as the examination of other brands.

Once the problem recognition stage has been triggered by an ad such as this one by Bell, consumers will begin their search for information.

## Internal Search

When conducting the internal search, a consumer first thinks about the brands he or she is willing to consider during the information search and evaluation processes. This group does not normally contain every possible brand the consumer has experienced. The consumer often removes brands that have been tried that did not provide a positive experience. The consumer will also eliminate brands he or she knows little about. This means that during the information

THE #1
ANTI-WRINKLE CREAM
BECAUSE IT WORKS.

#1
WITH BEAUTY
EDITORS.
Winner of Allure Editors'
"Best of Beauty" Award.

Neutrogena
HEALTHY
SKIN®

ANTI-WRINKLE
CREAM

SPF 15

#1
WITH
DERMATOLOGISTS.
The first Retinol
anti-wrinkle cream
with SPF 15.

#1
SELLER.
Clinically proven to both
treat and help prevent
fine lines and wrinkles.

A Retinol
Facial Treatment with
Multi-Vitamins

Neutrogena®

A Neutrogena ad designed to convince
consumers that the product should be the first
choice when selecting an antiwrinkle cream.
**Source**: Courtesy of Neutrogena Corporation.

search process, the consumer is reducing the number of brands to a group that is mentally manageable.

A key objective creatives and brand managers set is to make sure the company's brand becomes part of the consumer's set of potential alternatives. When this goal is achieved, the chances of the brand being purchased are greatly increased. Also, if a brand has obtained a high level of brand equity, it is likely that the brand will become part of a consumer's set of potential alternatives. High-quality, reasonably priced goods and services, when accompanied by attractive and powerful advertising messages, will become finalists in the purchasing decision. The Neutrogena advertisement shown in this section uses "#1" four times to persuade consumers that Neutrogena is the number-one antiwrinkle cream. The idea is to cause consumers who want an antiwrinkle cream to think about Neutrogena, hopefully as the first and best choice.

## External Search

Following an internal search, consumers will make a mental decision about an *external search.* If the customer has sufficient internal information, he or she moves to the next step of the decision-making process: evaluating the alternatives. When the consumer feels uncertain about the right brand to purchase, an external search takes place.

External information comes from a variety of sources including friends, relatives, experts, books, magazines, newspapers, advertisements, exposures to public relations activities, in-store displays, salespeople, and the Internet. The amount of time a consumer spends on an external search depends on three factors: (1) ability, (2) motivation, (3) costs and benefits (see also Figure 3.2).[2]

The first factor that determines the extent of a search for information is the *ability to search.* Ability is related to a person's educational level combined with the specific knowledge he or she has about a product and the brands in that product's category. Educated individuals are more likely to spend time searching for information. They are also more inclined to visit stores prior to making a decision. Consumers having extensive knowledge about individual brands and product categories are better able to conduct a more involved external search. For example, someone who knows a great deal about digital cameras has a more sophisticated ability to examine information than does someone who knows little about digital technology. In addition, people with more comprehensive knowledge of a product area often collect additional data even when they are not in the market for the product.[3]

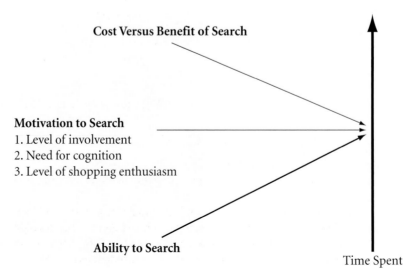

Cost Versus Benefit of Search

Motivation to Search
1. Level of involvement
2. Need for cognition
3. Level of shopping enthusiasm

Ability to Search

Time Spent

**FIGURE 3.2**
**Factors Impacting the Amount
of Time Consumers Spend
Conducting an External Search**

In terms of the amount of time an individual devotes to the external search process, a different phenomenon occurs. Although extensive product category knowledge provides individuals with a greater ability to search for external information, these consumers will normally spend less time during the external search process. With knowledge already stored internally, there is no need to conduct an extensive external search for additional information. Consumers at the other end of the spectrum will also spend less time during the external search process, but for the opposite reason. They lack knowledge about the product category and do not know what type of information to ask for or what type of information is even needed. They lack the ability to search for information. Individuals in the middle, who have some knowledge of a product category but feel they need additional information to make an intelligent decision, will spend the most time searching for an external information.

The degree to which an external search takes place also depends on the customer's *level of motivation*. The greater the motivation, the greater the extent of an external search. Motivation is determined by the consumer's:

- Level of involvement
- Need for cognition
- Level of shopping enthusiasm

Individuals are motivated to search for information when their involvement levels are high. **Involvement** is the extent to which a stimulus or task is relevant to a consumer's existing needs, wants, or values. The more important a product is to a consumer, the more likely he or she will engage in an external search. The amount of involvement is based on factors such as the *cost* and its *importance*. The more a product costs, the more time an individual will spend searching for information.

The same is true about importance. Choosing clothes may not be regarded as a highly important decision to some young males. This means clothing purchases will typically have low involvement. Still, picking a tux for the high school prom may spur greater involvement and a higher level of information search due to the social ramifications of dressing poorly at such an important event. Higher involvement is present due to the addition of the new element, a major occasion in the person's life.

The **need for cognition** is a personality characteristic an individual displays when he or she engages in and enjoys mental activities. These mental exercises have a positive impact on the information search process. People with high needs for cognition gather more information and search more thoroughly than do individuals with a lower need for cognition.

The search also depends on a person's **enthusiasm for shopping**. Customers who like to shop will undertake a more in-depth search for goods and services. Involvement, need for cognition, and enthusiasm for shopping determine the individual's motivation to search for information.[4]

The final factors that influence an information search are the *perceived costs* and the *perceived benefits* of the search. Higher perceived benefits increase the tendency to search. One benefit that a consumer often looks for while examining external information is the ability to reduce purchase risk. This means that by obtaining additional information, a customer can lower the chances of making a mistake in the purchase selection. The cost of the search consists of several items:

- The actual cost of the good or service
- The subjective costs associated with the search, including time spent and anxiety experienced while making a decision
- The opportunity cost of foregoing other activities to search for information (e.g., going shopping instead of playing golf or watching a movie)

The greater the perceived subjective cost of the external information search, the less likely the consumer will conduct a search.[5]

The four factors that make up an external search (ability, motivation, costs, and benefits) are normally all considered simultaneously. When the perceived cost of a search is low and the perceived benefit high, a consumer has a higher motivation to search for information. A consumer with a minimal amount of product knowledge and a low level

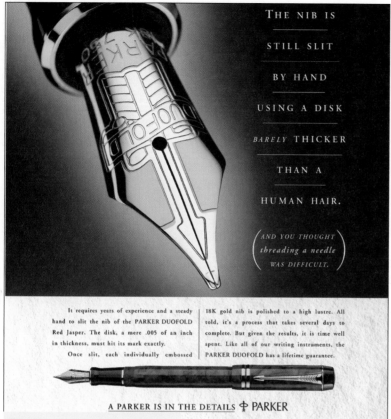

THE NIB IS

STILL SLIT

BY HAND

USING A DISK

*BARELY* THICKER

THAN A

HUMAN HAIR.

*(AND YOU THOUGHT threading a needle WAS DIFFICULT.)*

It requires years of experience and a steady hand to slit the nib of the PARKER DUOFOLD Red Jasper. The disk, a mere .005 of an inch in thickness, must hit its mark exactly. Once slit, each individually embossed

18K gold nib is polished to a high lustre. All told, it's a process that takes several days to complete. But given the results, it is time well spent. Like all of our writing instruments, the PARKER DUOFOLD has a lifetime guarantee.

A PARKER IS IN THE DETAILS ✦ PARKER

This Parker advertisement uses a cognitive appeal.
*Source:* Courtesy of Parker Pens.

of education is less likely to undertake an external search, because the consumer lacks the ability to find the right information.

From an integrated marketing communication perspective, the search process is an important time to reach the consumer with information about a particular brand. In the opening vignette featuring Starbucks, consumer behaviors changed after perceptions of involvement in coffee-buying decisions were changed. Also, consumer calculations of the benefits and costs of more expensive coffees were affected.

The consumer's goal in making the effort to perform an external search is to acquire information leading to a better, more informed decision. The goal of marketers is to provide information that allows consumers to make the right choice. When a consumer has not yet made up his or her mind, it is an ideal time for marketers to influence the decision-making process. The key is to provide the right information at the right time. Marketing experts need to consider three additional concepts that are important in the information search process: (1) attitudes, (2) values, and (3) cognitive mapping.

## Consumer Attitudes

Consumer attitudes can be influenced by effective marketing communications. An **attitude** is a mental position taken toward a topic, person, or event that influences the holder's feelings, perceptions, learning processes, and subsequent behaviors.[6] From a marketing communications perspective, attitudes can drive purchase decisions. If a consumer has a positive attitude toward a brand, the propensity to actually purchase the brand is higher. If a consumer likes an advertisement, the probability of purchasing the product being featured increases.

Attitude consists of three components: (1) affective, (2) cognitive, and (3) conative.[7] The *affective* component contains the feelings or emotions a person has about the object, topic, or idea. The *cognitive* component refers to a person's mental images, understanding, and interpretations of the person, object, or issue. The *conative* component is an individual's intentions, actions, or behavior. A common sequence of events that takes place as an attitude forms is:

Cognitive → Affective → Conative

Most of the time, a person first develops an understanding about an idea or object. In the case of marketing, these ideas center on the nature of the good or service. Thoughts about the product emerge from watching or reading advertisements. Other thoughts may result from exposures to information from other sources, such as the Internet or a friend's referral. Eventually, these ideas become beliefs the consumer has about a particular product. For instance, a consumer seeing the Parker advertisement shown in this section may develop the impression that a Parker is a precisely designed and manufactured quality writing instrument.

The affective part of the attitude is the general feeling or emotion a person attaches to the idea. In the case of goods and services, the product, its name, and other features all can generate emotions. For example, consider your emotional reactions to these goods and services:

▶ Cough medicine
▶ Diaper wipes
▶ Motorcycles

▶ Baseball and apple pie

▶ *Sports Illustrated*'s annual swimsuit issue

▶ Condoms

What emotions and thoughts did you associate with diaper wipes? The goal of the Pampers diaper wipe advertisement shown on this page is to influence your emotions. Does the picture in the ad change your feelings about Pampers or diaper wipes? As you consider the items listed here, some of your emotions or attitudes about them are relatively benign. Others are more strongly held. It is likely that cough medicine does not evoke much of an emotional response, but the swimsuit issue or condoms may generate a much stronger response.

Decision and action tendencies are the conative parts of attitudes. Therefore, if a person feels strongly enough about the swimsuit issue, he or she may cancel a subscription to *Sports Illustrated* or buy extra copies for friends. Many times attitudes are not held that strongly. Some may feel favorably about a topic, such as green marketing, but not be moved to change their purchasing behaviors.

Attitudes can develop in other ways. An alternative process may be:

Affective → Conative → Cognitive

In marketing, advertisements and other communications often appeal first to the emotions or feelings of consumers. The goal is to get a consumer to "like" a product and then make the purchase (the conative component). The cognitive understanding of the product follows. For example, a young woman may be exposed to a feminine hygiene product advertisement featuring soft, gentle images of nature; the ad actually may not show the physical product. Still, the ad conjures favorable emotions. The person eventually purchases the product and finally learns more about it by using it and reading directions, instructions, and other information on the package or label.

Some attitudes result from a third combination of the components, as follows:

Conative → Cognitive → Affective

Purchases that require little thought, have a low price, or those that do not require a great deal of emotional involvement might follow this path. For instance, while shopping for groceries, a customer may notice a new brand of cookies on sale. The person may have never seen the brand or flavor before but, because it is on sale, decides to give it a try. As the consumer eats the cookies, he or she develops a greater understanding of the product's taste, texture, and other qualities. Finally, the consumer reads the package to learn more about contents, including how many calories were devoured in one short gulp. Then the buyer finally establishes feeling toward the cookies that will affect future cookie purchases.

No matter which path is taken to develop attitudes, each component is present to some extent. Some attitudes are relatively trivial (e.g., "I like table tennis, even though I hardly ever get to play"). Others are staunchly held, such as "*I hate cigarette smoking!*" Both are associated with feelings toward things, including products in the marketplace that may eventually result in behaviors (purchases).

What emotions does this ad for Pampers Wipes elicit?

*Source:* Courtesy of D'Arcy Masius Benton & Bowles Inc. © Procter & Gamble Productions, Inc. 1999. Photograph by Penny Gentjeu.

## Consumer Values

Attitudes are shaped, in part, by an individual's personal values. **Values** are strongly held beliefs about various topics or concepts. Values contribute to attitudes and lead to the judgments that guide personal behaviors. Values tend to be enduring and normally form during childhood, although they can change as a person ages and experiences life.

**FIGURE 3.3**
**Personal Values**

Figure 3.3 lists some of the more commonly recognized personal values. Individuals hold these values to differing degrees. Factors that affect a person's values include the individual's personality, temperament, environment, and culture. These values will be discussed in greater detail in Chapter 6 in the context of advertising design. By appealing to basic values, marketers hope to convince prospective customers that the company's products can help them achieve a desirable outcome. At the same time, creatives know marketing communications are considerably more effective in changing a person's attitude about a product than they are in changing a consumer's value structure.

In terms of consumer decision-making processes, both attitudes and values help marketing experts. If a good or service can be tied to a relatively universal *value,* such as patriotism, then the firm can take advantage of the linkage to present a positive image of the product. A recent advertisement for Lucky Brand jeans used the slogan "Always America's favorite" and the fact that "every pair [is] American made" in the attempt to tie into the patriotism value.

*Attitudes* may also be used in marketing communications. Most people consider being "put on hold" to be a nuisance. A marketing creative may be able to tap that attitude and use it to present a good or service in a more favorable light. Making the time pass pleasantly while on hold turns a negative attitude into a more positive experience.

## Cognitive Mapping

The manner in which individuals store information further affects decisions because it impacts what is recalled. Knowing how people store, retrieve, and evaluate information can help a company's marketing team develop advertisements and other marketing communications. The first step is to understand how various thought processes and memories work.

**Cognitive maps** are simulations of the knowledge structures and memories embedded in an individual's brain.[8] These structures contain a person's assumptions, beliefs, interpretations of facts, feelings, and attitudes about the larger world. People use these thought processes to interpret new information and to determine an appropriate response to fresh information or a novel situation. Figure 3.4 is a hypothetical cognitive map for an individual thinking about a Ruby Tuesday restaurant.

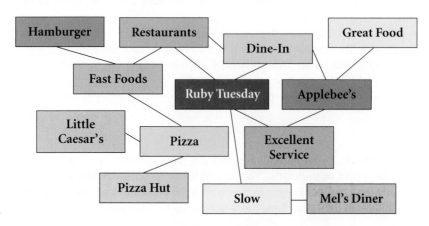

**FIGURE 3.4**
**Cognitive Map for Ruby Tuesday**

Based on the cognitive structures illustrated in Figure 3.4, when this customer thinks about Ruby Tuesday, she connects images of it to other restaurants offering fast food and others that provide dine-in services. In this case, the individual recognizes Ruby Tuesday as a dine-in establishment. The consumer also believes that Ruby Tuesday offers excellent service, but that the service is slow. Next, when the person thinks of slow service, her thoughts turn to Mel's Diner. When she thinks of excellent service, she recalls Applebee's.

Cognitive structures contain many linkages and can exist on several levels. For instance, one level of cognition is the map with the linkages in Figure 3.4. At another level, the cognitive map is more spatial and conjures images of the actual physical location of Ruby Tuesday along with the surrounding businesses. A third cognitive level related to Ruby Tuesday is the person's recall of the interior of the restaurant along with other linkages that occur at that level. The consumer can even have thoughts about Ruby Tuesday that focus on employees, including a relationship she had with a server who is a friend. Therefore, cognitive processing occurs on many levels using highly complex mechanisms.

Consumers use cognitive mapping to assess and evaluate information.

As a marketing message reaches a consumer, there are several ways the person may consider the information. If the new information is consistent with current information, then the new information primarily tends to strengthen an existing linkage. For example, when a consumer views a Ruby Tuesday ad promoting great service, the result may be that the ad will strengthen an existing belief, because the consumer already concluded that Ruby Tuesday offers great service.

A different response can occur in other situations, including times when a message has no current linkages. For example, if a consumer sees an advertisement featuring Ruby Tuesday's seafood selection, and the consumer did not know that Ruby Tuesday offers seafood, a different reaction occurs. In order for this information to remain in the consumer's mind and to become linked to Ruby Tuesday, the customer must create a new linkage between previous Ruby Tuesday images with other images of seafood.

Hearing something once is usually not enough to cause it to be retained in a person's long-term memory. This is due to differences between short-term recall and long-term memories. The cognitive mapping process explains the knowledge structures embedded in a person's long-term memory. Ordinarily, information is retained in short-term memory for only a few seconds. As stimuli reach an individual's senses, short-term memory processes them. Short-term memory can retain only five to nine bits of information. These new messages are either soon forgotten or eventually have to be added to long-term memory. When a message is repeated, an individual is more likely to remember it, because the message will be processed into long-term memory and fitted into previously developed cognitive maps.

As a result, when a company attempts to introduce consumers to a new brand, the advertisements and other marketing messages should repeat the name of the brand several times during the presentation. This repetition improves the chances of its recall at a later time. To illustrate how this works, consider what happens when a person gives a phone number to a friend. To help remember it, the individual repeats the number several times to place it into longer-term recall.

Another way a consumer can process information is to link the message to a new concept. For example, if a consumer sees an advertisement from Ruby Tuesday emphasizing that it has great food but has never thought about the restaurant in terms of quality food, that linkage is not currently present. If the advertisement persuades the consumer, she may construct a linkage between Ruby Tuesday and good food without even traveling to the restaurant. If she does not believe the message, she will ignore or forget the information, and no new linkage evolves. A third possibility is that the consumer recalls the advertisement at a later time and decides to try Ruby Tuesday. If the food is great, then the link is established at

The affect referral model also explains purchases of higher priced items as well as purchases of products that are "socially visible." It is the emotional bond that has been established between the consumer and the brand that leads to a purchase under those circumstances.

The affect referral model explains three things. First, using this approach to product evaluation saves mental energy. A quick choice is easier than going through the mental process of evaluating every possible alternative. Some purchases basically don't deserve much effort. The affect referral model is useful in explaining those situations.

Second, a multiattribute model type of approach may have been previously used when making a purchase. This means the person has already spent a great deal of time considering various product attributes, deciding which are most critical, and reaching a decision about the brand with the greatest number of advantages. Therefore, going through the process again would be "reinventing the wheel." For example, a teenager buying jeans may have already spent considerable time evaluating styles, prices, colors, durability levels, and "fit" of various brands. After making the purchase, this teenager continues to purchase that same brand as long as the experience remains positive. The affect referral model explains this buying behavior, because a repurchase is simple and convenient.

Third, consumers often develop emotional bonds with brands. In terms of the purchase decision, an emotional bond with a product can be the strongest and most salient factor in the decision.[10] It is more important than any attribute or benefit the product can offer. The most successful brands are those that establish emotional bonds with consumers. The bond generates brand loyalty, enhances brand equity, and reduces brand parity. This means consumers do not have to evaluate alternatives because of their bond with the brand. Harley-Davidson has developed such a bond with many of the company's customers. So has Nike. For these customers, these feelings toward Harley-Davidson and Nike are so strong that they do not even think about other alternatives. Again, the affect referral model explains this type of buying behavior.

## TRENDS IN THE CONSUMER BUYING ENVIRONMENT

Studying the steps consumers take while making purchasing decisions is a useful activity when creating marketing communications. At the same time, the environment in which purchases are made rapidly changes and constantly evolves. Several trends in the consumer buying environment may affect purchasing patterns. Some of these are listed in Figure 3.5.[11]

### Age Complexity

Information has changed the ways children grow up. Children are bombarded with advertisements, video games, television shows, movies, and a myriad of other sensory perceptions at an early age. Most know more about sex by the age of 12 than their parents did at age 20. Fashions such as cropped tops, miniskirts, and low-rider jeans were worn by many teenagers and even preteens over the past 5 years. The result is that many believe children are "growing up" at a much earlier age.

At the other end of the spectrum, many adults are refusing to "grow old." They still wear the fashions that resemble those worn by college students. Some still drive fast cars, sports cars, or convertibles. Many middle-aged adults apparently do not want to age anymore. They try to remain young by acting like young people and buying products normally

**FIGURE 3.5**
**Trends Affecting Consumer Buying Behavior**

- Age complexity
- Gender complexity
- Individualism
- Active, busy lifestyles
- Cocooning
- Pleasure pursuits
- Health emphasis

# COMMUNICATION ACTION

## The Belly Button Fad

Some say it started with Shania Twain; others claim it was Britney Spears. Others still blame/credit advertising. While there may be arguments about where it started, no one doubts the presence of the belly button fad. Eager to be noticed among myriads of advertisements, companies including Levi Strauss, mLife, and JCPenney jumped at the chance to take advantage of this new trend.

One of the first ads to capture the new fad was a television spot entitled "Belly Button." The ad showed people's stomachs, paying careful attention to their navels. The first image was of an older woman's belly and, with each succeeding scene, the person got younger. The last scene was a woman who had just given birth. As the doctor prepared to cut the umbilical cord, the voiceover explained that people were meant to live wireless lives and that AT&T with mLife could make that a reality.

Soon after, Levi Strauss used an ad that focused on the midriffs of young women dressed in Levi's Superlow jeans. According to Levi's director of marketing, Anna Brockway, "The belly button spot is a lighthearted ad that showcases Superlow jeans as a confident, sexy, fun way to make a statement."

Not all of the advertisements were successful. One produced for JCPenney featured a curly-haired preteen admiring her outfit—low-rider jeans and a crop top—in front of a mirror. Her mother came in and explained that the daughter could not go to school like that. Rushing over to her daughter, she yanked the girl's jeans down another inch or so. "There, that's better," she exclaimed. A strongly negative reaction by parents followed. JCPenney quickly pulled the ad, afraid it would damage sales instead of boosting them. In Louisiana, State Representative Danny Martiny even introduced a bill to get rid of low-riding jeans and exposed underwear.

It is clear that advertising did not create the "belly button" fad. Still, some companies have been able to take advantage of the phenomenon. At the same time, as the JCPenney case indicates, advertisers must be careful not to push the fashion envelope too far, especially with teen and preteen targets.

**Sources:** Margarita Bauza, "Skimpy School Wear Frustrates Parents," *The Detroit News* (www.detnews.com/2004/schools/0405/28-a01–164586.htm, accessed May 26, 1004); Michelle Krupa, "Bill Would Ban Low-Riding Pants," *New Orleans Times-Picayune* (April 22, 2004), p. F3; Justin M. Norton, "TBWA\C\D Debuts Singing Belly Buttons for Levi's," *Adweek Eastern Edition* 42, no. 25 (June 18, 2001), pp. 25–26; Christine Champagne, "Launching Mobility," *Shoot* 43, no. 8 (February 22, 2002), pp. 26–27.

purchased by youth. This trend challenges marketers to create messages that reflect these behaviors but not offend the traditional middle-aged component of society.

## Gender Complexity

A second new trend in the consumer buying environment can be labeled gender complexity. This means that the traditional roles, lifestyles, and interests of both men and women are becoming blurred. Women increasingly enter occupations that were the domain of men. Men now work in occupations that were once considered only for women. Many women attend college, delay marriage, and wait to start families. Some do not marry or have children, choosing instead to focus on moving up the corporate ladder.

Men, meanwhile, are more likely to play an active role in parenting and help more with household work. Today's men spend more on personal care products and plastic surgery. Traditionally, a company like General Foods would advertise food and grocery shopping to women and an automaker like General Motors would target car ads to men. That type of approach is no longer as useful. Advertisements for food manufacturers may be targeted to the large percentage of men who do the grocery shopping. Ads for automobiles may be targeted at the large number of women who either purchase cars or have a major influence on vehicle purchases.

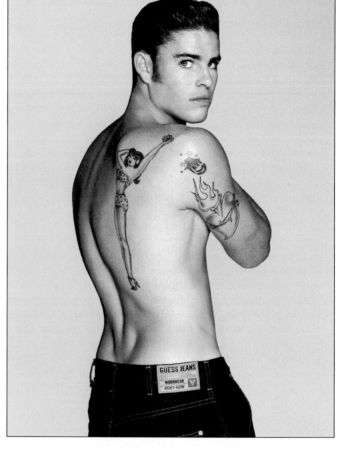

Understanding the issues created by age and gender complexity, Guess created these two advertisements.

**Source:** Courtesy of Guess.

## Individualism

Individualism has become more pronounced, especially in the purchase of goods and services. Customers want companies to develop products just for them. To meet this trend, Nike now allows consumers to design their own shoes using the company's Web site. Levi Strauss allows for personalized jeans, made to fit the exact measurements given to them by the consumer, again over the Internet. Recognizing this trend, food manufacturers have increased the varieties, sizes, and flavors of foods.

## Active, Busy Lifestyles

Active lifestyles have had a dramatic impact on consumer behaviors. In one survey, 47 percent of the respondents stated that they would prefer additional free time over more money. In another poll, 53 percent of the respondents said they would be willing to give up one day's wages per week in exchange for a day off to spend with family and friends. Many consumers now focus less on material possessions and more on experiences such as vacations, entertainment, and events with friends and family.[12]

Time pressures account for increases in sales of convenience items, such as microwave ovens, drive-through dry-cleaning establishments, and one-stop shopping outlets, most notably Wal-Mart's Supercenters. People on the go utilize cell phones and answering machines to make sure they don't miss messages during their busy days. The demand for convenience continues to increase.

## Cocooning

One of the side effects of a busy and hectic lifestyle is cocooning. The stress of long hours at work with additional hours spent fighting commuter traffic has led many individuals to retreat and cocoon in their homes. A major part of cocooning is making the home environment as soothing as possible. Evidence of cocooning includes major expenditures on elaborate homes, expensive sound systems, satellite systems with big-screen televisions, swimming pools, saunas, hot tubs, gourmet kitchens with large dining rooms, decks and porches, and moving to the country or to a gated community.

At the same time, shopping, going out on the town, and even visiting with neighbors is out.[13] Many advertisements emphasize cocooning aspects of shops and services. Recently, Internet ads focused on the utility of shopping from home during the Christmas season to offer the consumer a method to avoid the hustle and bustle of the holidays.

Divorce and remarriage have altered many family units. Remarried divorcees represent about 10 percent of the population. Divorcees tend to develop a new outlook on life. They often desire to cocoon, which changes their purchasing patterns. This group, called *second chancers,* is usually between the ages of 40 and 59 and has a higher household income. Second chancers are more content with life than are average adults. They tend to be happy with their new families but also have a different life focus. Second chancers spend less time trying to please others and more time seeking fuller, more enriching lives for themselves and their children or spouse. Although the home and cocooning is a major emphasis, entertainment and vacation services also appeal to this group.[14]

## Pleasure Pursuits

Some people handle the stress caused by a hectic, busy lifestyle through occasional indulgences or pleasure binges such as expensive dinners out and smaller luxury purchases. Pleasure pursuits also include "getaway" weekends in resorts and on short cruises. These self-rewarding activities make the consumer feel that all the work and effort is "worth it." The implications for marketing experts are to note the indulgence aspects of products. Clairol's Herbal Essence shampoo and conditioner commercials played to the emotions of pleasure and self-indulgence, with the "yes, Yes, YES!" approach.

Many people respond to stress through exciting adventures. From theme parks to virtual reality playrooms, consumers enjoy the mental relaxation of experiencing things that seem almost unreal. Many gambling establishments cater to these more exotic types of vacations. IMAX theaters generate a much more exciting experience than do normal movie theaters. As the technology of fantasy continues to develop, more firms enter the marketplace to profit from consumer desires to "get away from it all."

## Health Emphasis

The U.S. population continues to age. Two outcomes of this trend are a blossoming interest in health and maintaining one's youthful appearance. Many consumers are trying to

develop a balanced lifestyle. This includes a regular emphasis on nutrition, exercise, and staying active without feeling too guilty about an occasional overindulgence.

Developing better eating habits has had an impact on many families. Some companies were caught off guard by this change. Kraft, whose best-selling products included macaroni and cheese, Oscar Mayer hot dogs, Philadelphia cream cheese, and Kool-aid, faced a new landscape. The rising level of concern about obesity caused the company to shift its approach. Kraft began to produce healthy, diet-oriented foods. Also, Kraft reduced the fat content in over 200 products. The marketing message was changed to promote Kraft foods as part of a proper diet.[15]

In sum, these new trends in the consumer buying environment create several challenges for marketing

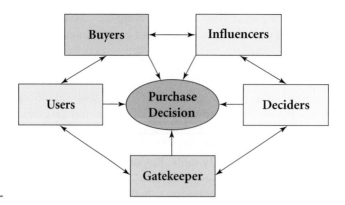

**FIGURE 3.6**
**The Buying Center**

experts. The first is to monitor for changes so that the company is not surprised by them. The second is to create goods and services that are compatible with changing values. The third is to design marketing messages that reflect and build on the values people in various target markets express. The idea is to incorporate new trends into the marketing program while at the same time being careful not to alienate current customers who may not like the trends.

## BUSINESS-TO-BUSINESS BUYER BEHAVIOR

The main thing to remember about business-to-business (B-to-B) purchases is that *people* still make the decisions. At the same time, when selling to a business organization the marketing team must be aware that several individuals normally become involved in the purchasing process. Further, corporate policies will provide restrictions and decision rules that affect purchasing activities. Factors such as budgets, costs, and profit considerations will also influence the final choice.

The buying decision-making process for businesses is more complex because of the number of people involved. A **buying center** is the group of individuals who make a purchase decision on behalf of a business. The buying center consists of five different individuals playing various roles in the process, as shown in Figure 3.6. The five roles involved in the buying center are:

> *Users:* Members of the organization who actually use the good or service

> *Buyers:* Individuals given the formal responsibility of making the purchase

> *Influencers:* People who shape purchasing decisions by providing the information or criteria utilized in evaluating alternatives, such as engineers

> *Deciders:* Individuals who authorize the purchase decisions

> *Gatekeepers:* Individuals who control the flow of information to members of the buying center

Many times, these five roles overlap. A gatekeeper may also be the user. Often the gatekeeper is the entire purchasing department. This group often determines what information will reach members of the buying center. The department usually controls the amount of access a salesperson has to members of the buying center.

Several individuals can occupy the same role in a buying center, especially when a large or critical purchase is being made. It is not unusual for a variety of members of the organization to serve as influencers, because these roles usually are not fixed and formal. Roles change as the purchase decision changes.

The buying behavior process is unique in each organization. It varies within an organization from

A B-to B advertisement directed to buyers in the apparel industry.
**Source:** Courtesy of Kimberly-Clark.

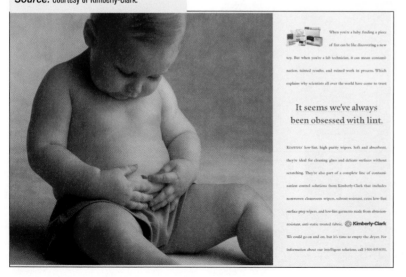

one purchasing decision to the next. Salespeople calling on a business must be able to locate members of the buying center and understand their roles in the process. These roles often change from one purchase situation to another, making the marketing task more difficult than one might expect.[16]

Social interactions impact the way business purchase decisions are made.

## FACTORS AFFECTING MEMBERS OF BUSINESS BUYING CENTERS

The behaviors of each member in the buying center are influenced by a series of organizational and individual factors.[17] These influences change the manner in which decisions are made and often affect the eventual outcome or alternative chosen. A discussion of these factors follows.

### Organizational Influences

Several organizational factors affect the ways in which individuals make purchasing decisions for a company. These organizational factors include the company's goals and its operating environment (recession, growth period, lawsuits pending, etc.). Decisions are further constrained by the organization's finances, capital assets, market position, the quality of its human resources, and the country in which the firm operates.

Studies of organizational decision making indicate that employees tend to adopt *heuristics,* which are decision rules designed to reduce the number of viable options to a smaller, manageable set. Company goals, rules, budgets, and other organizational factors create heuristics. One decision rule often employed is called *satisficing,* which means that when an acceptable alternative has been identified, it is taken and the search is completed. Rather than spending a great deal of time looking for an optimal solution, decision makers tend to favor expedience.[18]

### Individual Factors

At least seven factors affect each member of the business buying center: (1) personality features, (2) roles and perceived roles, (3) motivational levels, (4) levels of power, (5) attitudes toward risk, (6) levels of cognitive involvement, and (7) personal objectives. (See Figure 3.7.)[19] Each impacts how the individual interacts with other members of the center.

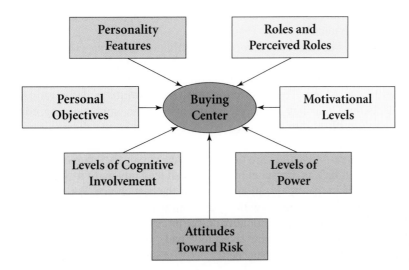

**FIGURE 3.7**
**Individual Factors Affecting the Behaviors of Buying Center Members**

The first individual factor is *personality*. This means, for example, that a decisive person will make a purchase decision in a manner different from someone who vacillates. Confidence, extroversion, shyness, and other personality features affect both the person performing the decision-making role and others in the process. An aggressive "know it all" type affects the other members of a decision-making team, and such a personality feature does not always benefit the organization. An extrovert tends to become more involved in the buying process than a more introverted individual. The extrovert spends more time talking, and the introvert spends more time listening to sellers. The introvert might be too timid with salespeople and consequently may not ask important questions.

The *roles* people play are influenced by an individual's age, heredity, ethnicity, gender, cultural memberships, and patterns of social interaction. Roles are socially constructed, which means people define how they intend to play roles as part of the negotiation process with others nearby. It is not just the role itself that affects decisions. A person's perception of how the role fits into the buying center process and the overall organization is important. When a buying center member perceives the role as merely giving approval to decisions made by the boss (the decider), then the individual will not be an active member of the group. When members feel their inputs are important and wanted, they become more active. A person can believe his role is to provide information. Another might perceive his role as being the person who synthesizes information provided by vendors and then relates it to the buying center to save the other members time. Roles and perceptions of roles are major factors determining how members of the buying center go about their business.

*Motivation* depends on how well the individual's goals match the organization's goals. If a factory foreman has a personal goal of becoming the vice president of operations, that foreman is more likely to become involved in all purchasing decisions that affect his performance and that of his department. If a purchasing agent has been charged by the CEO to cut expenses, she may take a more active role to ensure cost-cutting selections are made. Many individuals also are motivated by needs for recognition. The goal of making successful purchasing decisions is to ensure that others recognize their efforts. They may believe recognition is linked to getting promotions and pay raises.

A person's *level of power* in the buying process depends on his or her role in the buying center, official position in the organization, and the impact of the purchase decision on a specific job. When a particular purchase decision directly affects an employee, that person tries to gain more power in the buying process. For instance, a factory foreman has greater power within the buying center in the purchase of raw materials, whereas the maintenance foreman has more power in the purchase of maintenance supplies. In these situations, each strives to influence the decision that affects his or her area.

*Risk* is another factor that affects members of the buying center. Many vendors are chosen because buyers believe the choice has the lowest risk. Also, risk avoidance means that firms tend to stay with current vendors rather than switching. In marketing to businesses, reducing risk is a major concern, especially when signing large contracts or when the purchase might affect company profits. People tend to think taking risks (especially when a failure follows) can affect performance appraisals, promotions, and other aspects of an individual's job.

*Levels of cognitive involvement* influence not only consumer buyer behaviors but also business buyers. Individuals with higher levels of cognitive capacity want more information prior to making decisions. They also ask more questions when interacting with a sales rep. These individuals spend more time deliberating prior to making a decision. Clear key message arguments are the important ingredients in persuading people with higher cognitive levels (as noted in the discussion of consumer buyer behaviors).

*Personal objectives* are tied to motives, personality, perceptions of risk, and the other individual factors. Personal objectives can lead buyers to make purchases that help them politically in the organization, but aren't the best choice. For example, if someone knows his or her boss is friends with a particular vendor, the buyer can choose that vendor even when others offer higher quality, lower prices, or both. Personal objectives can be tied to getting promotions, making rivals look bad, "brown-nosing" a boss, or the genuine desire to help the organization succeed.

Account executives are expected to understand the client's business as well as the target markets that can be tapped. Expanding marketing programs from business customers to include consumer markets, or vice versa, is one way to respond to the increasing insistence on immediate results.

## Importance of E-Commerce

The second major trend in the business-to-business buying environment is the expansion of e-commerce and increased Web-based marketing. One business executive recently noted that the electronic commerce revolution is probably doing more to integrate business-to-business marketing communications than any other marketing force. Engaging in Web-based commerce is no longer an option. Firms must either get involved, or it is likely that they will not stay in business.

In addition to print advertisements, Volvo uses a Web site to market products.
*Source:* Courtesy of Volvo Cars of North America.

Part of the e-commerce revolution is the creation of more effective Web sites. Web sites must be more than merely a catalog placed online. Sites must be truly interactive, allowing business customers to gain information, product specifications, prices, and other key information. The Internet's technology saves time and money for both customers and vendors.

## Global Branding

Building a powerful brand is important for a successful IMC program. This is especially true in business-to-business marketing, where a global brand presence is a crucial. The existence of multiple vendors, increasing perceptions of brand parity, and growing use of the Internet have made it impossible for a company to succeed using only price differentiation. A strong brand presence is practically a necessity in the new global environment.

Most markets contain numerous competitors. Each forces the other to improve the quality of the good or service being offered. Over time, fewer perceived differences exist. Perceptions of brand parity in the marketplace are the result. In those circumstances, the brand plays a vital role. A strong brand inspires recall when a purchase is about to be made. If perceptions of brand equity can be built, the company has a major advantage. For example, Acme Brick is still able to charge 10 percent more than competitors due to business customer perceptions that the company's products are superior. Builders do not want to risk using an inferior brick, even though few differences exist.[24]

The Internet allows business buyers to search for more potential providers. Without a strong brand, it is nearly impossible to stand out in the marketplace. As Robert Duboff writes, "It is no longer sufficient to be a great company; *you must be a great brand.*"[25]

James Hardie Siding Products is a small company that has built a strong brand presence. In an industry dominated by price and delivery, James Hardie used a different approach. Market research about the industry indicates that consumers are quite emotional about their homes. They look for products that provide safety, security, warmth, and stability. Consequently, James Hardie developed advertisements for *Southern Living, Coastal Living,* and *Sunset* magazines, emphasizing strong, weather-resistant materials in the company's siding. The salesforce emphasized these product features rather than price and delivery. Over time, James Hardie was able to gain co-branding inroads by displaying company products on model homes and builder design centers. The net result was growth in the strength of the brand, which in turn resulted in a 30 percent increase in annual sales.[26]

## Database Mining

Database mining (see Chapter 11) has been integrated into many business-to-business marketing programs. Computers are being used to access databases containing information about customers and prospects. Database mining programs identify buyer behavior patterns that can be then be matched with business communication programs. Additional analyses segment business customers into target groups. A distinct appeal can be created for each group. The new business-to-business data mining programs allow companies to customize messages to individual customers based on the customer's needs and past purchase behaviors.

## Alternative Methods of Communication

There are several alternative methods that can be utilized to communicate with customers. Paying salespeople to call on customers is expensive and time-consuming. Consequently, personal sales calls have been reduced and other methods of making contact have been increased. Direct mail, telephone calls, faxes, interactive Internet sites, and e-mail are some of the new, alternative methods of sending out communications. Effective IMC programs include these methods in order to maximize company exposure to potential clients while making it easier for customers to contact the firm. Alternative methods of communication also help marketers to bypass gatekeepers in the business buying center. Making direct contact with users, deciders, and influencers increases the chances of making a sale.

One key element of an advertising program is choosing media that match the target audience. Generally, the audience can be divided into three categories: (1) chief executive officers, (2) members of the top management team, and (3) the middle-level managers. Many CEOs are involved in buying decisions due to the need to integrate purchases. To reach CEOs, the *Wall Street Journal* is a common venue. Ninety-two percent of CEOs report that they read the publication. CEOs are less likely to read other publications, such as *Forbes, BusinessWeek,* and *Fortune.* Instead, CEOs tend to use Internet sites to obtain hard information about products.

On the other hand, middle managers, where other members of the buying center are likely to be found, watch sports (70%), view documentaries (65%), and listen to news radio (68%), and public radio (48%). Reaching these members of the buying center with attention-getting information requires different media than those used to reach CEOs.

The New York–based Siemens Corporation used a unique approach to raise brand awareness among middle-level managers. Instead of spending funds on trade shows and industry magazines, the company placed ads in lifestyle magazines such as the *New Yorker* and sponsored various events, such as the U.S. Open golf tournament and the NCAA basketball tournament. The idea was that the best way to strengthen the brand in the business-to-business arena was to stay away from the clutter that dominates typical business venues.[27]

## Focus on Internal Marketing Communications

The final emerging B-to-B buying environment trend is the growing importance of internal integrated marketing communications. *Internal marketing communications* efforts include creating, packaging, and delivering the organization's IMC marketing message (including its business-to-business components) to all employees of the organization. Employees must understand and believe in the firm's image and its marketing position. Employees need to comprehend what each company brand stands for and the benefits it offers customers. Most importantly, each employee must believe in the company and its mission. Spending more time marketing internally produces more knowledgeable and dedicated employees who will, in turn, seek the goal of providing excellent service to customers.[28]

## DUAL CHANNEL MARKETING

When firms sell virtually the same goods or services to both consumers and businesses, it is known as **dual channel marketing**.[29] The approach is used in several situations. Perhaps the most common scenario occurs when a product is first sold in business markets and then is adapted to consumer markets. New products often have high start-up costs including R&D expenditures, market research, and so forth. Businesses tend to be less price-sensitive than are retail consumers. Thus it is logical to sell to them first.

As sales grow, economies of scale can be created. Larger purchases of raw materials combined with more standardized methods of production make it possible to enter consumer markets. The benefits of economies of scale entice manufacturers to sell products previously supplied to the business sector in the retail markets. Products such as digital cameras, calculators, computers, fax machines, and cellular phones first were marketed to businesses and then later to consumers. To make the move to the retail arena possible, prices must come down and products need to be user-friendly. For example, consumers can now have their photos put on a CD rather than obtain prints. The imaging technology developed by Kodak and Intel was first sold to various businesses and now is being offered to retail customers. By forming an alliance with Intel, Kodak brought the cost down and developed the economies of scale needed for consumer markets.

Another type of dual channel marketing results from *spin-off sales.* Individuals who buy a particular product at work often have positive experiences and, as a result, purchase the product for personal use. This situation often occurs with computers and computer software. Favorable feelings about more expensive items can also result in spin-off sales. A salesperson who drives a Buick LeSabre to work may like it so well that one is purchased for personal use. Holiday Inn's marketing team discovered that many of its private stays come from business-related spin-offs. Approximately 30 percent of Holiday Inn's business customers also stay with the chain on private vacations.[30]

In dual channel marketing, a primary decision to make is how to represent the product in each channel. The firm can either emphasize similarities between the two markets or focus on differences. Consumers and businesses looking for the same benefits and product features probably will see marketing messages quite similar in both channels. When consumers and business buyers value different product attributes or desire different benefits, the marketing strategy develops more customized messages for the separate markets.

When there are substantial differences between the two channels, the typical tactics are to:

- Use different communication messages
- Create different brands
- Use multiple channels or different channels

In many instances the product attributes are the same, but the value or benefit of each attribute is different. Messages should focus on the benefits each segment can derive from the product. Cellular phones marketed to businesses can stress the area coverage and service options. For consumers, cell phone messages can center on the fashionable design of the product, its ease of use, or a lower price.

## Simple. Indispensable. Effective.

3M Promotional Products provide a simple way to get noticed. Whether at home, in the office, or on the road, your message stays within reach. Indispensable. Effective. We've recently added Post-it® Angle Note Pads to our exceptional line of Post-it® Products.

If you've never worked with 3M before, come on board and experience the service, turnaround and 3M quality so many have come to rely on.

For information on Post-it® Custom Printed Products including product samples, please call **1-800-328-2407** or visit **www.3M.com/ideas**

Post-it notes are a product that is sold to both retail customers and in the business-to-business market.
*Source:* Courtesy of 3M.

Approximately 30 percent of Holiday Inn's business customers also stay with the chain on private vacations.

To avoid confusing individuals who may see both messages from the same producer, companies often utilize dual branding. For instance, when Black & Decker decided to launch a professional line of power tools, it used the DeWalt brand name. This avoided confusion with the Black & Decker name and prevented any negative image transfer from home tools to professional tools.

In most cases, business customers and consumers want the same basic benefits from products. In these situations, a single strategy for both markets is best. Tactics include:

- Integrating communications messages
- Selling the same brand in both markets
- Scanning both markets for dual marketing opportunities

Although Midwest Express's primary market is business travelers, the airline promotes the same benefits to leisure travelers.
*Source:* © Midwest Airlines, Inc.

In addition to creating economies of scale, integrating consumer markets has an additional advantage: the potential to create synergies. Synergies arise from increased brand identity and equity. An image developed in the consumer market can then be used to enter a business market, or vice versa. Using one brand makes it easier to develop brand awareness and brand loyalty. A business customer who uses a company-owned American Express Card is likely to have a separate card from the same company for personal use.

Scanning both types of customers for new opportunities is an important part of dual channel marketing. For example, the firm Intuit, which sells Quicken software, discovered that individuals who use Quicken at home also are willing to use a similar version for their small businesses. Capitalizing on this need or demand, Quicken added features such as payroll and inventory control to a business software package. At the same time, Quicken maintained its easy-to-use format. By finding business needs for a consumer product, Quicken adapted a current product and captured 70 percent of the small-business accounting software market.[31]

Dual channel marketing can create a major competitive advantage as products are sold in both markets. A complete IMC planning process includes the evaluation of potential business market segments as well as consumer market segments. Firms that integrate messages across these markets take a major step toward reaching every potential user of the company's goods or services.

## SUMMARY

Buyer behaviors are part of the purchasing process in both consumer markets and business-to-business transactions. An effective IMC program accounts for the ways in which goods and services are purchased in both markets. The goal is to tailor marketing messages to target audiences in the appropriate media.

The consumer buying decision-making process consists of five steps. Marketing experts and especially creatives must be aware of each step and prepare effective communications that will lead most directly to the decision to buy. Two of the most important steps, for the purposes of creating effective marketing communications, are the information search stage and the evaluation of alternatives stage.

After a consumer recognizes a want or need, the individual searches for information, internally and externally. Marketing messages must be directed to placing the product or service in the consumer's evoked set of viable purchasing prospects. The more involved the customer feels in the search, the more likely the product will have a longer-lasting impact once purchased. Those with greater needs for cognition are attracted to the process of thinking through a decision. Those with a greater degree of enthusiasm for shopping spend more time analyzing the available alternatives. Customers consider the benefits and costs of searches and make more or less rational decisions about how extensively they will seek out information.

Evoked sets, attitudes and values, and cognitive maps explain how an individual evaluates various purchasing choices. Evoked sets reveal which products "make the cut" and receive consideration. Attitudes and values predispose consumers toward some products and companies and away from others. Cognitive maps help the customer link what the company says about itself with other experiences. Marketing experts must identify consumer attitudes and values that affect purchase decisions and make sure they do not offend prospects with their messages. Stronger ties can be built with customers when the good or service is favorably attached to strongly held attitudes and values.

The new millennium presents a changing buying decision-making environment to marketers. New cultural values and attitudes, time pressures, and busy lifestyles influence what people buy, how they buy, and the manner in which they can be enticed to buy. Many families try to isolate themselves from everyday pressures by cocooning. They also try to escape through indulgences and pleasure binges, by finding excitement or fantasy, and by clanning to meet social needs. An aging baby boom population is more focused on lasting values and on health issues. Marketing experts can address these needs and lead customers to purchases based on them.

By understanding business buyer behaviors, the marketing team can construct a more complete and integrated marketing communications program. Business purchases are driven by members of the buying center. These members include users, buyers, influencers, deciders, and gatekeepers. Each role is important, even when a single person plays more than one role. Members of the buying center are human beings. This means they are influenced by both organizational and individual factors that affect various marketing decisions.

Business-to-business sales take three forms. A straight rebuy occurs when the firm has previously chosen a vendor and intends to place a reorder. A modified rebuy occurs when the purchasing group is willing to consider and evaluate new alternatives. This decision is usually based on dissatisfaction with a current vendor. A new task purchase is one in which the company buys a good or service for the first time, and the product involved is one with which organizational members have no experience.

The business-to-business buying process is similar to consumer purchase decisions. A more formal purchasing process includes formal specifications, bids from potential vendors, and a contract finalizing the purchasing agreement. Marketing to businesses is affected by several new trends, including an emphasis on accountability, the importance of e-commerce and a strong brand presence, new efforts in database mining, the use of alternative methods of communication with business buyers, and a greater focus on internal marketing communications.

Dual channel marketing means that the firm sells virtually the same goods or services to both consumers and businesses. Dual channel marketing creates both economies of scale and synergies for the vendor company. It also enhances the chances that a product will be sold to every available customer. The challenge to the marketing team is to create strong and consistent marketing messages to every potential buyer, accounting for how buyer behaviors are present in purchasing processes.

## REVIEW QUESTIONS

1. What are the five steps of the consumer buying decision-making process? Which two steps are the most important with regard to developing quality integrated marketing communications?

2. What is the difference between an internal search and an external search in a purchasing decision?

3. Define *attitude*. What are the three main components of attitudes, and how are they related to purchasing decisions?

4. How do values differ from attitudes? Name some personal values related to purchasing decisions.

5. Develop and explain a cognitive map of your own mind about your most recent major purchase (car, stereo, computer, etc.).

6. What is an evoked set? Why are evoked sets, inept sets, and inert sets so important to the marketing department?

7. What are the key features of the multiattribute approach to evaluating purchasing alternatives?

8. What is meant by affect referral? When is a person likely to rely on such a cognitive approach to evaluating purchasing alternatives?

9. What traditional factors and new trends in the consumer buying environment affect consumer purchasing decisions?

10. Name and describe the five roles played in a buying center.

11. What organizational and individual factors affect members of the business buying center?

12. Describe the three main forms of business-to-business sales.

13. Name the steps in the business-to-business buying process.

14. What new trends are affecting the business-to-business buying environment?

15. Describe dual channel marketing and explain why it is important to a company's well-being.

## KEY TERMS

**involvement**   The extent to which a stimulus or task is relevant to a consumer's existing needs, wants, or values.

**need for cognition**   A personality characteristic an individual displays when he or she engages in and enjoys mental activities.

**enthusiasm for shopping**   Customers who like to shop will undertake a more in-depth search for details about goods and services.

**attitude**   A mental position taken toward a topic, person, or event that influences the holder's feelings, perceptions, learning processes, and subsequent behaviors.

**values**   Strongly held beliefs about various topics or concepts.

**cognitive maps**   Simulations of the knowledge structures embedded in an individual's brain.

**evoked set**    Consists of the set of brands a consumer considers during the information search and evaluation processes.

**inept set**    Part of a memory set that consists of the brands that are held in a person's memory but are *not considered,* because they elicit negative feelings.

**inert set**    Part of a memory set of brands that holds the brands that the consumer has awareness of but has neither negative nor positive feelings about.

**affect referral**    A purchasing decision model in which the consumer chooses the brand for which he or she has the strongest liking or feelings.

**buying center**    The group of individuals who make a purchase decision on behalf of a business.

**straight rebuy**    Occurs when the firm has previously chosen a vendor and intends to place a reorder.

**modified rebuy**    The company buying team considers and evaluates new purchasing alternatives.

**new task**    The company buys a good or service for the first time, and the product involved is one with which organizational members have no experience.

**derived demand**    Demand based on, linked to, or generated by the production and sale of some other good or service.

**dual channel marketing**    Selling virtually the same goods or services to both consumers and businesses.

**compensatory heuristics**    A purchasing decision model that assumes that no one single brand will score high on every desirable attribute and further that individual attributes vary in terms of their importance to the consumer.

**conjunctive heuristics**    A purchasing decision model that establishes a minimum or threshold rating that brands must meet in order to be considered.

**phased heuristics**    A purchasing decision model that is a combination of the compensatory and conjunctive heuristics models.

# CRITICAL THINKING EXERCISES

## Discussion Questions

1. In a study of compulsive buying behaviors among college students, a primary influence was the family. Often one or both parents were compulsive shoppers. Families that displayed other forms of dysfunctional behaviors such as alcoholism, bulimia, extreme nervousness, or depression produced children who were more inclined to exhibit compulsive shopping behaviors. Why do dysfunctional behaviors among parents produce compulsive shopping behavior among children? Another component of compulsive buying behaviors is self-esteem. Again, self-esteem is partly inherited but also develops in the home environment.[32] How would self-esteem be related to compulsive shopping behaviors? What other influences other than family might contribute to compulsive shopping behaviors? If an individual has a tendency to be a compulsive shopper, what can (or should) be done?

2. Study the list of personal values presented in Figure 3.3. Identify the five most important to you. Rank them from first to last. Beside each value, identify at least two products or services you have purchased to satisfy those values. Then, gather into small groups of three to five students. Using the information from your list of values, discuss differences among members of the group. Identify a way to send a marketing message that will appeal to the top value from each person's list.

3. Cultural values and norms constantly change. In groups of three to five students, discuss the cultural values and norms that have changed in the last 10 years. Are these values and norms different from those held by most parents? If so, why? What caused these changes to occur?

4. A member of the buying center for a large shoe manufacturer tries to purchase soles for shoes from an outside vendor (or vendors). Study the individual and organizational factors that affect buying center members. Discuss the effect of each factor on the roles of members in the shoe company's buying center. How does the factory foreman's role differ from the purchasing agent's role? How do these roles differ from the company president's role?

5. A purchasing agent for a clothing manufacturer is in the process of selecting a vendor (or vendors) to supply the materials to produce about 30 percent of its clothes. The clothing manufacturer employs about 300 people. As the audit nears completion, what factors are most important to the purchasing agent?

# INTEGRATED LEARNING EXERCISES

1. Consumers and businesses conduct external searches when they lack sufficient internal knowledge to make a wise decision. Assume you have $50,000 to $70,000 to spend on a sailboat. Locate four Web sites that sell sailboats. Select a sailboat in your price range. Why did you select that particular brand? What features are attractive to you? Would you want any additional information before making a final purchase decision?

2. Almost everyone has an opinion about tattoos. Some attitudes are positive while others are negative. Few are neutral. Go to www.tattoos.com and examine the material that is on the Web site. Did this information modify your attitude toward tattoos? What factors on the Web site influenced your attitude?

3. United Raw Material Solutions, Inc., is a business-to-business marketplace that brings together buyers and seller of textiles, petrochemicals, plastics, and electronics. Access the Web site at www.urms.com. Which members of the buying center would be most interested in this site? What services and benefits do you see for buyers? For suppliers?

4. Examine the following Web sites. What kind of information is provided? Which component of attitude is the site designed to affect: cognitive, affective, or conative?

   a. Kenneth Cole (www.kennethcole.com)

   b. Starbucks (www.starbucks.com)

   c. Cadillac (www.cadillac.com)

   d. IKEA (www.ikea.com)

   e. Baby Gap (www.babygap.com)

5. A member of the buying center has been asked to gather information about possible shipping companies for international shipments. Go to the following Internet addresses. What companies have the most appealing Web sites? Beyond Internet materials, what additional information do they need to supply to the buying center in order to win the contract?

   a. ABC India Limited (www.abcindia.com)

   b. BDP International (www.bdpint.com)

   c. Falcon Transportation & Forwarding Corp. (www.falcontrans.com)

   d. Global Freight Systems (www.globalfreightsystems.com)

# STUDENT PROJECT

## IMC Plan Pro

Any advertising project requires a solid understanding of what leads individual consumers and other businesses to make buying decisions. The IMC Plan Pro disk and booklet available through Prentice Hall are designed to help you assess these buyer behaviors before moving forward with other elements of your advertising and communications program.

# CASE 1

## BUYING A TELEVISION? IT'S NOT THAT SIMPLE

Kelli is evaluating four console television brands. The multiattribute approach to processing information helps explain Kelli's final purchasing decision. In making this purchase, she bases her evaluation on five criteria: (1) quality of sound, (2) quality of picture, (3) style of cabinet, (4) other features, and (5) the price or value of the television. The importance ratings in Table 3.2 indicate that Kelli is most interested in the quality of the sound, because she gave it a 5 rating. Quality of picture and style of cabinet are next, with ratings of 4. Other television features and price are the least important to Kelli.

The next column of numbers shows her evaluation of each attribute for each brand. In terms of quality of sound, Brand A was the best (Kelli gave it a score of 5). Brands B and D were next. The score of 4 each received indicates approximately equal sound quality. Brand C had the lowest sound quality and thus she gave it a score of 3.

After evaluating all the brands across all the criteria, Kelli will make a decision. Kelli can calculate these scores in several ways. One method is to multiply each attribute's importance rating times the corresponding evaluation for each brand. Summing these results in the scores is shown in the row labeled Compensatory Score. Using this method, she would choose Brand D because of its overall score. This method of evaluating alternatives is called **compensatory heuristics**.

The compensatory heuristics method assumes that no one single brand scores high on every attribute and that individual attributes vary in importance. When considering several brands, consumers make trade-offs. Notice that, in Table 3.2, Kelli rates Brand A as having the best quality of sound, her most important product attribute. At the same time, Brand A has the worst quality picture and she ranked it lowest in terms of television features. Although Brand A had the best sound, it was not the best brand for Kelli because of the poor ratings on other attributes.

When Kelli considers Brand D, she concludes it has good sound, although the sound is not as good as in Brand A. Brand D does have the best-quality picture. In terms of price and television features, it is not the best but is still good. The worst rating Kelli gives Brand D is for the cabinet style. But even there, Brand C's cabinet style rating is lower. To get the best overall television, Kelli has to make trade-offs and choose the best one of the attributes evaluated. Consumers are not likely to draw a table like Table 3.2, but they go through a similar process mentally.

A second computational form Kelli can use to make her evaluation is called **conjunctive heuristics**. In this method, Kelli establishes a minimum or threshold rating. She considers only brands that meet the threshold, even when one product ranks high in individual criteria. Going back to Table 3.2, assume Kelli has mentally established a minimum threshold of 4.

## TABLE 3.2

Example of a Multiattribute Approach Evaluation of Console Televisions by Kelli

| Attribute[b] | Importance[a] | Brand A | Brand B | Brand C | Brand D |
|---|---|---|---|---|---|
| Quality of sound | 5 | 5 | 4 | 3 | 4 |
| Quality of picture | 4 | 3 | 4 | 4 | 5 |
| Style of cabinet | 4 | 4 | 5 | 2 | 3 |
| Television features | 3 | 3 | 3 | 5 | 4 |
| Price of television (good value) | 3 | 4 | 2 | 5 | 4 |
| Compensatory Score[c] | | 74 | 71 | 69 | 76 |

[a] Ranked from 1 to 5 with 5 being highly important and 1 being unimportant.
[b] Each attribute is rated on a score from 1 to 5 with 5 being high performance and 1 being poor performance.
[c] Scores are cumulative sums of the importance rating times the brand evaluation.

She discards a brand if it scores 3 or lower on any criterion important to her. Using this method, she would eliminate all five brands because of low scores on individual attributes.

Consequently, consumers can use an *iterative approach.* Quality of sound is most important to Kelli and so she starts there. She rated Brand C a 3, and because this is below the minimum, Kelli eliminates Brand C. Next, Kelli looks closely at Brands A, B, and D. All have good or excellent sound. Therefore, Kelli goes to her next most important criterion—quality of the picture. She ranks both quality of picture and style of cabinet with a 4 in terms of importance. Before Kelli can eliminate any more brands, she has to decide which of those two criteria is more important. Assuming that quality of picture is next, she would eliminate Brand A due to its rating below the threshold. Now Kelli has narrowed her choice to two models, Brand B and Brand D. The next attribute she considers is style of cabinet. Because Brand D is below the threshold, she eliminates it. Thus, she chooses Brand B because it is the only one left.

Another calculation can be made using a **phased heuristic** approach. This method is a combination of the others. Going back to Table 3.2, assume that Kelli eliminates any brand with a score lower than a 3 on any criterion. Notice Brand B's rating of 2 on price and Brand C's rating of 2 on style of cabinet. Kelli immediately discards them (Brand B because it is too expensive and Brand C because she does not like its cabinet). This leaves Brands A and D. To make the decision between these two brands, she can use the compensatory heuristic approach. Consumers often use a phased approach similar to this when they have many brands to evaluate. This method easily reduces the evoked set to a smaller and more manageable subset.

Buying a television isn't easy. The same mental gymnastics are part of many purchases. Marketing experts spend a great deal of time trying to make sure that the characteristics consumers value appear in their products, services, and marketing messages.

1. Go through Table 3.2 and make sure you can explain how Kelli makes her purchase decision, whether product A, B, C, or D is chosen, using the various heuristic models.

2. Construct a similar table for one of the following products:
   a. An automobile
   b. A night out for dinner
   c. A drinking establishment
   d. A new clothing outfit
   e. A spring break vacation

3. For each product listed in Question 2, identify a recent purchase. Explain the process you used to make the purchase decision. Which heuristic model did you use?

## CASE 2

**TAKING THE NEXT STEP IN THE DEATH INDUSTRY**

Nancy Hines was always reluctant to tell people about the business she was starting, even though she was convinced it would be a valuable service people would appreciate. It also might be quite lucrative. Still, many of her friends viewed her work as maudlin, or worse.

For the past 7 years, Nancy had worked as a reporter for a local newspaper. Among her duties was preparation of the daily obituary column. She made phone calls to the local mortuaries, and they would provide the basic

(continued)

information for each newly deceased person. Then, Nancy would rewrite or edit the materials to fit the space requirement for the paper.

During the past year, however, the paper had made substantial cuts. The standard of 8 to 12 column inches to use for an obit was reduced to 1 to 1 1/2 column inches, which would normally contain about 80 words. The paper charged a fee for the family to have a complete obituary printed. In spite of initial objections from the community, the new system was soon in place, and Nancy was relieved of her duties for that area of the paper.

A close friend of Nancy's, Margo Youker, had recently completed a series of courses in the area of e-commerce. Margo saw a great opportunity for the two of them to pursue. They established a new company, Remembrances.com, a Web site dedicated to the mortuary industry.

The "death industry," as it is known, has peaks and valleys, which are based on how many people die in any given month or year. Fees are collected for gravesites, cremations, embalming, caskets, memorial services, and limousine services for family members and the deceased (the hearse). Margo and Nancy believed they could add to the revenues of these companies by offering an additional service: a Web site for the family of the deceased.

The Web site would contain a full-length obituary, photos, directions to the church and gravesite, and requests for memorial contribution allocations. It would also allow long-distance friends to send online notes and comments. The mortuary would provide a homepage directing people to the site for each individual person. It also would set up links to the newspaper (for a fee) in which the newspaper would print the Web address as part of the short obituary. The text would appear as follows:

> Fred Johnson, age 83, died on Monday, June 6, 2005 from natural causes. He was a lifelong resident of Oxnard, California. He retired from Montgomery Ward in 1981. Further information may be obtained at Remembrances.com.

Nancy and Margo would sell their Web site service to individual mortuaries. They would charge a fee for each person, and the cost would be passed along to the family as part of the burial price. Nancy would manage the Web site, including writing full-length obits for each person. Margo would help with additional information and make sales calls. Their intention was to build a base of operations in Southern California and to expand outward from there.

1. Describe how various morticians could use the buying decision-making process as they considered a sales pitch from Remembrances.com.

2. Is this a dual channel program? Should Nancy and Margo promote this service directly to potential patrons? If so, how?

3. Will this business succeed? Why or why not?

## ENDNOTES

1. Len Lewis, "Coffee Culture," *Progressive Grocer* 76, no. 11 (November 1997), pp. 20–22; "Starbucks Roasts the Competition," *Journal of Business Strategy* 16, no. 6 (November–December 1995); Kate Rounds, "Starbucks Coffee," *Incentive* 167, no. 7 (July 1993), pp. 22–23; Ingrid Abramovitch, "Miracles of Marketing," *Success* 40, no. 3 (April 1993), pp. 22–27; Jennifer Rose, "Starbucks: Inside the Coffee Cult," *Fortune* 134, no. 11 (December 9, 1996), pp. 190–200.

2. Jeffrey B. Schmidt and Richard A. Spreng, "A Proposed Model of External Consumer Information Search," *Journal of Academy of Marketing Science* 24, no. 3 (Summer 1996), pp. 246–56.

3. Merrie Brucks, "The Effect of Product Class Knowledge on Information Search Behavior," *Journal of Consumer Research* 12 (June 1985), pp. 1–15; Schmidt and Spreng, "A Proposed Model of External Consumer Information Search."

4. Laura M. Buchholz and Robert E. Smith, "The Role of Consumer Involvement in Determining Cognitive Responses to Broadcast Advertising," *Journal of Advertising* 20, no. 1 (1991), pp. 4–17; Schmidt and Spreng, "A Proposed Model of External Consumer Information Search"; Jeffrey J. Inman, Leigh McAllister, and Wayne D. Hoyer, "Promotion Signal: Proxy for a Price Cut," *Journal of Consumer Research* 17 (June 1990), pp. 74–81; Barry

J. Babin, William R. Darden, and Mitch Griffin, "Work and/or Fun: Measuring Hedonic and Utilitarian Shopping Value," *Journal of Consumer Research* 20 (March 1994), pp. 644–56.

5. Schmidt and Spreng, "A Proposed Model of External Consumer Information Search."

6. M. Fishbein and Icek Ajzen, *Belief, Attitude, Intention, and Behavior: An Introduction to Theory and Research* (Reading, MA: Addison-Wesley, 1975).

7. Richard P. Bagozzi, Alice M. Tybout, C. Samuel Craig, and Brian Sternathal, "The Construct Validity of the Tripartite Classification of Attitudes," *Journal of Marketing* 16, no. 1 (February 1979), pp. 88–95.

8. Discussion of cognitive mapping based on Anne R. Kearny and Stephan Kaplan, "Toward a Methodology for the Measurement of Knowledge Structures of Ordinary People: The Conceptual Content Cognitive Map (3CM)," *Environment and Behavior* 29, no. 5 (September 1997), pp. 579–617; Stephan Kaplan and R. Kaplan, *Cognition and Environment, Functioning in an Uncertain World* (Ann Arbor, MI: Ulrich's, 1982, 1989).

9. Discussion of heuristics and multiattribute model based on William L. Wilkie and Edgar A. Pessemier, "Issues in Marketing's Use of Multiattribute Models," *Journal of Marketing Research* 10 (November 1983), pp. 428–41; Peter L. Wright, "Consumer Choice Strategies: Simplifying vs. Optimizing," *Journal of Marketing Research* 11 (February 1975), pp. 60–67; James B. Bettman, *An Information Processing Theory of Consumer Choice* (Reading, MA: Addison-Wesley, 1979).

10. Mark Sneider, "Create Emotional Ties with Brand for Sales," *Marketing News* 38 (May 15, 2004), pp. 44–45.

11. This section is based on "Are Latest 'Megatrends' a Road Map for New Products?" *Candy Industry* 170, no. 1 (January 2005), pp. 14–15; "The Changing Face of 2005," *International Food Ingredients* (February–March 2005), p. 20; "Global Consumer Trends," *Datamonitor* (**www.market-research-report.com/datamonitor/DMCM0683.htm**, July 21, 2004).

12. Mark Dolliver, "Alas, Free Time Comes at a Price," *Adweek* 45, no. 34 (September 13, 2004), p. 42; Mark Dolliver, "More Money or More Time?" *Adweek* 42, no. 11 (March 12, 2001), p. 44.

13. Hester Cooper and Ann Holway, "Consumer Behaviour: The Seven Key Trends," *New Zealand Marketing Magazine* 18, no. 2 (March 1999), pp. 27–30.

14. Discussion of second chancers based on Richard Halverson, "The Customer Connection: Second-Chancers," *Discount Store News* 37, no. 20 (October 26, 1998), pp. 91–95.

15. Dave Carpenter, "Diets Force Kraft to Change Marketing Approach," *Marketing News* 38 (September 15, 2004), p. 37.

16. Discussion based on Frederick E. Webster, Jr., and Yoram Wind, "A General Model for Understanding Organizational Buyer Behavior," *Marketing Management* 4, no. 4 (Winter–Spring 1996), pp. 52–57. Patricia M. Doney and Gary M. Armstrong, "Effects of Accountability on Symbolic Information Search and

Information Analysis by Organizational Buyers," *Journal of the Academy of Marketing Science* 24, no. 1 (Winter 1996), pp. 57–66; Rob Smith, "For Best Results, Treat Business Decision Makers As Individuals," *Advertising Age's Business Marketing* 84, no. 3 (1998), p. 39.

17. Patricia M. Doney and Gary M. Armstrong, "Effects of Accountability on Symbolic Information Search and Information Analysis by Organizational Buyers," *Journal of the Academy of Marketing Science* 24, no. 1 (Winter 1996), pp. 57–66.

18. Herbert Simon, *The New Science of Management Decisions,* rev. ed. (Upper Saddle River, NJ: Prentice Hall, 1977).

19. Webster and Wind, "A General Model for Understanding Organizational Buyer Behavior"; Doney and Armstrong, "Effects of Accountability on Symbolic Information Search and Information Analysis by Organizational Buyers"; James A. Eckert and Thomas J. Goldsby, "Using the Elaboration Likelihood Model to Guide Customer Service-Based Segmentation," *International Journal of Physical Distribution & Logistics Management* 27, no. 9–10 (1997), pp. 600–615.

20. Patrick J. Robinson, Charles W. Faris, and Yoram Wind, "Industrial Buying and Creative Marketing," *Marketing Science Institute Series* (Boston: Allyn & Bacon, 1967).

21. Adapted from Webster and Wind, "A General Model for Understanding Organizational Buyer Behavior."

22. Eugene F. Brigham and James L. Pappas, *Managerial Economics,* 2d ed. (Hinsdale, IL: Dryden Press, 1976).

23. Charles A. Weber, John R. Current, and Desai Anand, "Vendor: A Structured Approach to Vendor Selection and Negotiation," *Journal of Business Logistics* 21, no. 1 (2000), pp. 134–69.

24. Bob Lamons, "Another Story About an Unlikely Brand," *Marketing News* 30, no. 11 (May 27, 2002), p. 8.

25. Robert Duboff, "True Brand Strategies Do Much More Than Name," *Marketing News* 35, no. 11 (May 21, 2001), p. 16.

26. Ibid.

27. Dana James, "Something in Common," *Marketing News* 36, no. 11 (May 27, 2002), pp. 11–12.

28. Discussion of trends based on Laurie Freeman, "Technology Influences Top Trends for 1999," *Advertising Age's Business Marketing* 84, no. 1 (January 1999), pp. 1–2; John Obrecht, "Speculations for the Millennium," *Advertising Age's Business Marketing* 84, no. 6 (June 1999), p. 13; Laurie Freeman, "Agencies See 37 Percent Growth Amid B-to-B Revolution," *Advertising Age's Business Marketing* 84, no. 7 (July 1999), pp. 1–2.

29. Discussion of dual channel marketing is based on Wim G. Biemans, "Marketing in the Twilight Zone," *Business Horizons* 41, no. 6 (November–December 1998), pp. 69–76.

30. Ibid.

31. Biemans, "Marketing in the Twilight Zone."

32. Schmidt and Spreng, "A Proposed Model of External Consumer Information Search."

# Promotions Opportunity Analysis

## Chapter Objectives

*Prepare* **a complete promotions opportunity analysis.**

*Compare* **the relationship between a company's promotional efforts and the efforts of the competition.**

*Identify* **the characteristics of various consumer market segments.**

*Reach* **key business-to-business market segments.**

*Expand* **IMC and promotions to the global level.**

## THE HALLMARK DIFFERENCE

### Sending "The Very Best" to New Target Markets

Hallmark has a long-standing tradition of excellence in the greeting card industry. For many years, the company's overall theme has been "For people who only want to send the very best." The "very best" extends to the quality of cards, the types of employees who are hired, and a variety of promotional tactics. Hallmark stores, which are found in both freestanding locations and malls, are clean, well lit, and upscale. They provide a variety of products besides greeting cards. Each store offers keepsakes, wedding items, and other specialty goods that blend together to reinforce the theme of quality.

The greeting card business has changed dramatically in the past 40 years. To keep pace, Hallmark has adjusted its approach to the marketplace. The result has been that Hallmark remains an excellent example of an effective integrated marketing communications program.

One consumer market segment buys humorous cards with lighter, less sentimental messages. In response, Hallmark created the Shoebox Greetings line in 1986. Shoebox cards are funny and distinctive. Hallmark hired highly creative and productive writers to prepare punch lines for them on a daily basis.

Another market segment buys cards at specialty stores such as Factory Card Outlet and Card$mart. To meet this competitive threat, Hallmark entered the "alternative" card market, which features cards offering offbeat humor and inspirational messages. These cards are often impulse buys. To be noticed, the cards are displayed in prominent locations. The Hallmark Expressions brand features many alternative card lines. When a particular card works well, the verse and other artistic components are reproduced

in more conventional cards. The Expressions brand reaches the marketplace quickly and offers cards featuring recent events.

Hallmark also sells cards to drugstores and discount retailers. To strengthen its position in these retail outlets, Hallmark competes with both products and prices. The marketing team points to the ambience in-store cards give to retail outlets, heightening the store's colors and image. Walgreen's regards Hallmark cards as a major draw to complement its drugstore, cosmetics, and photo-finishing departments.

Hallmark offers point-of-purchase-generated information to various retail outlets. The company provides demographic and sales data to companies that agree to carry Hallmark's products. This led to the discovery that there are local preferences for certain types of cards. Through data mining, it is possible to find out which cards sell best in each type of outlet. Both the retailer and Hallmark understand the customer base more clearly as a result. Shoppers are more satisfied with the products, and retailers are able to customize promotional activities and reduce unnecessary inventories.

Hallmark entered the international arena with its first foreign location in Japan. Now Hallmark products are sold in at least 40 other nations, including China, Germany, Brazil, Australia, Greece, and smaller countries. Besides greeting cards, the company sells calendars, gifts, giftwrap, ribbons, stationery, and party goods.

Hallmark has recently developed a "Touch Screen Greeting" card. It allows the customer to create an individualized card at an automated outlet. Consumers use this new technology to express their creative impulses on a high-markup card. Men and younger consumers in their teens and early 20s are the most likely to use the touch screen. The product allows Hallmark to compete with the "Create-A-Card" program of American Greetings.

One goal of an IMC program is to identify opportunities and threats in the environment. By doing so, Hallmark has been able to maintain a competitive advantage in the marketplace. Company strengths and weaknesses are studied as part of the planning process. Hallmark consistently takes advantage of the firm's primary strength: a high-quality image that appeals to both customers and retailers. As a result, Hallmark has been able to build on a strong past and work toward a more lucrative future, even as competitive pressures intensify.[1]

**overview**

Individual customers and businesses receive a myriad of promotional materials every day. From pens marked with logos to letterhead embossed with a company's mission statement, to calendars containing both advertisements and tear-off discount coupons, consumers and businesses encounter marketing materials in an increasing variety of ways. These marketing contacts do not occur by accident. At some point, a marketing official decided to distribute pens or calendars, or the printing department was asked to design letterhead. Beyond the world of advertising and personal selling, successful marketing efforts occur because *someone identified an opportunity to make a quality contact with a customer.* IMC is a program designed to help find the places to make those contacts and to present the customer with a well-defined message spoken in a clear voice by a firm.

This chapter describes the nature of a promotions opportunity analysis. The purpose is to identify customers and competitors in the marketplace and to discover new promotional opportunities. When these new opportunities are found, the firm's overall IMC message can be structured to fit various target markets. An effective promotional analysis specifies the audiences and markets the company intends to serve. Locating key market segments helps the company's leaders more accurately define whom they are trying to reach with an IMC program.

In this section, target markets and promotional opportunities are described. Each of these activities is a key component in preparing IMC program.

## PROMOTIONS OPPORTUNITY ANALYSIS

One primary task in creating an effective marketing plan is examining promotional opportunities. A **promotions opportunity analysis** is the process marketers use to identify target audiences for a company's goods and services and the communication strategies needed to reach these audiences. People are different and have unique uses for various products. The same is true for businesses. These special features are especially pronounced in global markets; therefore, communication to each group requires distinct and somewhat customized approaches. An effective promotional analysis identifies the approach or appeal that is best suited to each set of customers.

A promotions opportunity analysis must accomplish two objectives: (1) determine which promotional opportunities exist for the company and (2) identify the characteristics of each target audience so that precise advertising and marketing communications messages can reach them. The more a marketer knows about an audience, the greater the chance a message will be heard, understood, and result in the desired outcome (a purchase, increased brand loyalty, etc.).

There are five steps in developing a promotions opportunity analysis, Figure 4.1 displays these steps. The upcoming sections describe each part of this planning process in greater detail.

> **Promotions Opportunity Analysis**
> ▶ **Conduct a communication market analysis**
> ▶ **Establish communication objectives**
> ▶ **Create communications budget**
> ▶ **Prepare promotional strategies**
> ▶ **Match tactics with strategies**

**FIGURE 4.1**
**Promotions Opportunity Analysis Steps**

## COMMUNICATION MARKET ANALYSIS

The first step of a promotions opportunity analysis is a communication market analysis. A **communication market analysis** is the process of discovering the organization's strengths and weaknesses in the area of marketing communication and combining that information with an analysis of the opportunities and threats present in the firm's external environment. This process is quite similar to a managerial approach called *SWOT analysis* (strengths, weaknesses, opportunities, threats). The primary difference is that instead of looking at the environment from a company-wide or strategic business unit's (SBU) point of view, the analysis is from a communication perspective. A communication market analysis examines five areas:

▶ Competitors
▶ Opportunities
▶ Target markets
▶ Customers
▶ Product positioning

These five ingredients are studied together rather than sequentially. Each contributes key information about the marketplace.

### Competitors

When examining competitors, the objective is to discover who the competition is and what they are doing in the areas of advertising and communication. The marketing tactics that competitors use must be identified to understand how they are attacking the marketplace. Consumers integrate information from a variety of sources. It is helpful to know what potential customers see, hear, and read about the competition.

Every domestic and foreign competitor should be identified. After a listing of all the competing firms, the competitive analysis should include *secondary data* about those companies. The first items to look at are statements competitors make about themselves. These statements can be found in:

▶ Advertisements
▶ Promotional materials
▶ Annual reports
▶ A prospectus for a publicly held corporation
▶ Web sites

The idea is to obtain as much information as possible about the competition, including what they say to their customers.

Intense competition in the cellular phone industry makes a communication market analysis important for T-Mobile.
*Source:* Courtesy of Scott Foreman, Publicis West Advertising.

The next task is to study what *other people* say about the competition. Marketers should read trade journals. The library may yield additional news articles and press releases about competitor activities. The marketing team should try to find out how companies close to the competition view them. This provides a sense of how any given company is viewed in comparison with its competition.

Another part of an analysis of the competition is *primary research.* In the retail business, it is helpful to visit competing stores to see how merchandise is displayed and to observe as the store's personnel deal with customers. The marketing team should also visit the vendors and suppliers who have dealt with the competition or who have read the competition's statements. For businesses other than retail, marketers can talk to salespeople in the field to obtain additional information about the competition. They also may talk to channel members such as wholesalers, distributors, and agents.

## Opportunities

A second component of a communication market analysis is the search for opportunities. This includes carefully watching for new marketing communication opportunities by examining all of the available data and information about the market. Some of the questions the marketing team asks include:

1. Are there customers that the competition is ignoring or not serving?
2. Which markets are heavily saturated and have intense competition?
3. Are the benefits of our goods and services being clearly articulated to the various customer market segments?
4. Are there opportunities to build relationships with customers using a slightly different marketing approach?
5. Are there opportunities that are not being pursued, or is our brand positioned with a cluster of other companies in such a manner that it cannot stand out?

The purpose of asking these questions is to explore new communication opportunities. These opportunities are present when there is an unfilled market niche, when the competition is doing a poor job of meeting the needs of some customers, when the company has a distinct competence to offer, or when a market niche is not being targeted with effective marketing communications.

One firm that has recently identified a new and unique communication opportunity is Digital Lifestyles Group, Inc., of Austin, Texas. The opportunity was marketing computers to teens. Most computer companies treat teens like all other market segments. Digital Lifestyles started by offering the hip-e computer, which is almost all white, but the screen and keyboard are framed in fuzzy pink fur, or leopard skin, or a graffiti-themed pattern. Besides this unique design, the hip-e includes a prepaid debit account that teens or parents can use to fund cell phone time, online

These ads were developed by BMW Motorcycles after an opportunity analysis revealed that females were not being targeted as important influences on purchase decisions of motorcycles.
*Source:* Courtesy of BMW Motorcycles.

shopping, or music downloads. The hip-e relies heavily on viral marketing, which is advertisements and recommendations spread through e-mail.[2]

## Target Markets

A third communication market analysis activity is examining various target markets. This analysis requires the marketing department to recognize the needs of various consumer and business groups. Company marketers must discover the benefits customers are seeking and determine the various ways in which the customers can be reached.

The questions asked during this part of the analysis are similar to those posed while looking for opportunities. The difference is that the focus now shifts to defining target markets more precisely. Beyond target market groups, the marketing team should try to decipher the needs and wants of individual groups. The goal is to divide the overall market into smaller market segments. Then the company can develop marketing programs and advertising campaigns for each of these smaller groups. The advertisement for A.G. Edwards shown on this page is based on the idea that grandparents are a target market that can be reached in more than one way. In the ad, the focus is on investments that grandparents can make to provide funds to help a grandchild attend college rather than investing solely for personal benefit. By understanding the makeup, personalities, and interests of grandparents, the marketing team created an advertisement that appeals to these seniors in a unique new way.

## Customers

Another ingredient in examining a target market is conducting an in-depth analysis of customers. There are three types of customers to study:

1. Current company customers
2. The competition's customers
3. Potential new customers

The point is to understand how people in each group think, why they buy, when they buy, where they buy, and how they evaluate a product after a purchase. Creating effective advertisements and marketing communications requires knowing everything that goes on in the minds of customers. The easiest group to study is a firm's current customers; however, the other two groups are equally, if not, more important. Members of these groups may think differently or make decisions differently from a firm's current customers. They may also evaluate products and advertisements differently. The objective of this part of the analysis is to find out what type of message works for each customer group.

It is helpful to ascertain how customers perceive individual advertisements as well as what they think about the larger company. Service Metrics (see the advertisement on the next page) examines a firm's Web site from the customer's perspective and, more importantly, compares the Web site to the competitions'. This type of analysis identifies all of a firm's

**GRANDPARENTS...**

**HOW CAN YOUR GRANDCHILD POSSIBLY SAVE THE $320,000[1] NEEDED FOR COLLEGE?**

**WITH YOUR HELP.**

Provide for your family while benefiting yourself with a 529 college savings plan. 529 plans help you give your grandchildren the gift of a quality education while you reduce potential estate taxes.*

**THE PLAN LETS YOU:**
- Make first-year contributions of up to $55,000 ($110,000 for a couple) per beneficiary without incurring federal gift taxes[2]
- Reduce your total taxable estate by the amount of your gifts[3]
- Keep control over how and when the money is spent
- Control taxes – Pay no taxes on earnings or withdrawals when used for college expenses[4]

**CALL ME TODAY** to learn more about this personalized college savings investment strategy.

[1]Projected four-year private college expenses for the academic years 2020-2024 based on College Board estimates for 2003-2004. Future years assume a 6.5% annual increase. [2]Gift will apply for five years. No other gifts may be made to the same beneficiary during this five-year period. [3]Gifts are subject to recapture if the donor dies within five years. [4]Nonqualified withdrawals will be subject to a 10% IRS penalty and income taxes.

As with any investment, your 529 plan's value will fluctuate. When you redeem your shares, you may receive more or less than the value of your original investment, and there is no guarantee that your account will grow enough to cover higher education expenses. Before you invest in a 529 plan, be sure to read the plan's offering document carefully for more information about fees, charges and expenses.

FC Name
Title
E-mail
Address, City, State
**Phone**

2005 A.G. Edwards & Sons, Inc. • Member SIPC

This advertisement by A.G. Edwards was developed after identifying a viable target market (grandparents) and the needs of that market.
*Source:* Courtesy of A.G. Edwards.

Part of a customer analysis includes an analysis of a firm's Web site from the customer's perspective.
*Source:* Courtesy of Service Metrics.

communication avenues. It also tells the company how its Web site compares to the competitions'.

## Product Positioning

Part of a communications analysis is examining the position a firm has relative to its competition. As defined in Chapter 2, product positioning is the perception created in the consumer's mind regarding the nature of a company and its products relative to the competition. The seven possible positioning strategies are listed in Figure 4.2.

The quality of products, prices charged, methods of distribution, image, communication tactics, and other factors create positioning and are, in turn, affected by the brand's position. In examining the brand's positioning, the marketing firm should determine how the brand's position is viewed by consumers, businesses, and customers. It is important to make sure the position being promoted is consistent with current views by the various constituencies and is also consistent with various elements of the IMC program. A problem exists when customers view the brand's position differently from the manner in which the company sees itself.

An effective communication market analysis lays the foundation for the development of communication objectives, the next step of a promotions opportunities analysis. A poor analysis results in something similar to shooting at a target with a blindfold on. It is nearly impossible to find the target, and the chances of hitting the bull's-eye are very slim.

## ESTABLISHING MARKETING COMMUNICATIONS OBJECTIVES

The second step of a promotions opportunity analysis is to identify objectives. Communication objectives help account executives and advertising creatives design effective messages. Figure 4.3 lists some of the more common objectives found in profit-seeking organizations.

A communications plan is often oriented toward a single objective. It is possible, however, for a program to accomplish more than one goal at a time. Logical combinations of communication objectives are possible. For example, advertising is an excellent means of developing brand awareness and enhancing a brand's image. Further, increasing sales can be accomplished through price changes, contests, or coupons. The key is to match the objective to the medium and the message.

▶ Attributes
▶ Competitors
▶ Use or application
▶ Price–quality relationship
▶ Product user
▶ Product class
▶ Cultural symbol

**FIGURE 4.2**
**Product Positioning Strategies**

> ▶ Develop brand awareness
> ▶ Increase category demand
> ▶ Change customer beliefs or attitudes
> ▶ Enhance purchase actions
> ▶ Encourage repeat purchases
> ▶ Build customer traffic
> ▶ Enhance firm image
> ▶ Increase market share
> ▶ Increase sales
> ▶ Reinforce purchase decisions

**FIGURE 4.3**
**Communication Objectives**

The process of defining and establishing communication objectives is a crucial element of a promotional opportunities analysis. Without clearly specified objectives, the company can quickly drift off course or lose its focus on the overall IMC program. Objectives serve as reminders of what the firm is attempting to do with its communications to various customers.

Communication objectives are derived from marketing objectives, which tend to be general because they relate to the entire marketing plan. They also must be measurable. Marketing objectives address:

▶ Sales volume

▶ Market share

▶ Profits

▶ Return on investment

Many marketing professionals believe **benchmark measures** are helpful. A benchmark is a starting point that is studied in relation to the degree of change following a promotional campaign. For example, through market research a dry cleaning company may discover that during its first year only 20 percent of the community's population is aware of the company and that the company has an 8 percent share of the city's total market. Following a campaign featuring advertisements, coupons, and discounts for certain days of the week (Tuesday specials) and to senior citizens, the company could hope to achieve 30 percent awareness and a 10 percent share. This would indicate a level of success compared to the previously established benchmarks.

## ESTABLISHING A COMMUNICATIONS BUDGET

The third step of a promotions opportunity analysis is preparing a communications budget. Budgets are based on communication objectives as well as marketing objectives. Communications budgets differ between consumer markets and business-to-business markets. A much larger percentage of the budget for B-to-B is allocated for telephone marketing than in the consumer market. Television and newspapers are primary venues for consumer markets. See Figure 4.4 for examples of the differences between the two areas.

Managers often make unrealistic assumptions about a communications budget. This occurs, for example, when a manager assumes there is a direct relationship between expenditures on advertising communications and subsequent sales revenues, which is highly unlikely. A more realistic relationship is shown in Figure 4.5. Several factors influence the relationship between expenditures on promotions and sales, including:

▶ The goal of the promotion

▶ Threshold effects

▶ Carryover effects

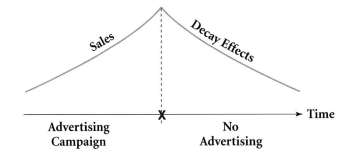

**FIGURE 4.6**
**A Decay Effects Model**

decay is dramatic. In others, the carryover effects are strong enough that some time can lapse before the brand drops out of the consciousness of the consumer. The promotional budget must be structured to avoid the problems of decay effects, which are illustrated graphically in Figure 4.6.

Finally, random events affect promotions. The September 11, 2001, attacks affected a variety of industries and individual companies. Promotional expenditures were, in some cases, cut back as the nation recovered. It would be impossible to demonstrate the relationship between promotions and sales in such circumstances. Some new products were successfully launched almost immediately after September 11; in other cases, the advertisements did not result in additional sales.

Therefore, as the marketing team constructs the budget, the assumptions that drive the process should be considered. The newness of the product, the economy, and other complicating factors must be considered during the process of tying budgeting expenditures to marketing and communication objectives.

## TYPES OF BUDGETS

There are many ways to prepare a communications budget. Figure 4.7 provides a list of the various methods that are used.[5]

### The Percentage of Sales Method

One common approach to setting the communications budget is the **percentage of sales method**. Companies using this form prepare communications budgets for coming years based on either: (1) sales from the previous year or (2) anticipated sales for the next year. A major reason for using this type of budget is its simplicity. A percentage of sales budget is relatively easy to prepare.

The approach also has problems. First, this type of budget tends to change in the opposite direction of what may be needed. That is, when sales go up, so does the communications budget. When sales decline, the communications budget also declines. In most cases, the communications budget should be the opposite. It should be increased during periods of declining sales to help reverse the trend. Further, during growth periods the communications budget may not need to be increased. The second major disadvantage of this method is that it does not allocate money for special needs or to combat competitive

**FIGURE 4.7**

**Methods of Determining a Marketing Communications Budget**

▶ Percentage of sales
▶ Meet the competition
▶ "What we can afford"
▶ Objective and task
▶ Payout planning
▶ Quantitative models

pressures. Therefore, many marketing experts believe the disadvantages of the percentage of sales method tend to outweigh its advantages.

## The Meet-the-Competition Method

Some firms use the **meet-the-competition** method of budgeting. The primary goal of this form of budgeting is to prevent the loss of market share. It is often used in highly competitive markets where rivalries between competitors are intense.

The potential drawback to meet-the-competition budgeting is that marketing dollars may not be spent efficiently. Matching the competition's spending does not guarantee success, which means market share can still be lost. The concept to remember is that it is not *how much* is spent, but rather *how well* the money is allocated and how effectively the marketing campaign works at retaining customers and market share.

## The "What We Can Afford" Method

A third type of budgeting is the **"what we can afford" method**. This technique sets the marketing budget after all of the company's other budgets have been determined. Money is allocated based on what the company leaders feel they can afford.

This method suggests management does not recognize the benefits of marketing. Instead, company leaders may view marketing expenditures as non-revenue-generating activities. Newer and smaller companies with limited finances often use the "what we can afford" approach.

## The Objective and Task Method

Another form is the **objective and task method**. To prepare this type of communications budget, management first lists all of the objectives it intends to pursue during the year; then, they calculate the cost of accomplishing each objective. The communications budget is the cumulative sum of the estimated costs for all objectives.

For a small business like Ozark Decorative Paving, budgeting adequate dollars to advertising is essential to build brand awareness.
*Source:* Used with permission of the *Joplin Globe*, Joplin, Missouri.

Many marketing experts believe the objective and task method is the best method of budgeting because it relates dollar costs to achieving specific objectives. Unfortunately, it is difficult for a large company, such as Procter & Gamble, to use. With hundreds of products on the market, producing a budget based on objectives for each brand and product category is very time-consuming. Despite the challenge, some form of the objective and task method of setting marketing budgets is used by about 50 percent of the firms, approximately equal to the percentage of companies that use the percentage of sales technique.[6]

## Payout Planning

**Payout planning** establishes a ratio of advertising to sales or market share. This method normally allocates greater amounts in early years to yield payouts in later years.[7] By allocating larger amounts at the beginning of a new product introduction, brand awareness and brand equity are built. Then, as the brand is accepted and sales build, a lower percentage of advertising dollars is needed to maintain a target growth. This budgeting approach is based on the threshold effects concept and the idea of diminishing returns. A company that has reached the maximum threshold point should not continue pouring money into advertising that only results in diminishing returns. Instead, a company can maintain awareness and brand equity level by more effective expenditures of marketing dollars. Future promotions and advertisement will target specific market segments and consumer groups rather than the company simply increasing the volume of marketing dollars spent.

## Quantitative Models

In some instances, computer simulations may be developed to model the relationship between advertising or promotional expenditures with sales and profits. These models are far from perfect. They do have the advantage of accounting for the type of industry and product as the model is created. Normally quantitative models are limited to larger organizations with strong computer and statistical departments.

# BUDGETING EXPENDITURES

A budget is finalized when the company has specified how funds will be spent on each of the major communications tools. Media advertising normally accounts for 25 percent of a communications budget. Trade promotions receive about 50 percent, and consumer promotions on average about 25 percent. These percentages, however, vary considerably from industry to industry.[8] Consumer product manufacturers spend more on trade promotions directed toward retailers. Service companies tend to spend more on media advertising. Budgets also vary by product types. For example, for dolls and stuffed toys, the average expenditure on media advertising as a percentage of sales is 11.2 percent, whereas for men's clothing, expenditures on media advertising represent only 3.3 percent of sales.[9]

The United States leads the world in annual advertising expenditures at $137.2 billion. This figure is over three times more than the next closest nation. Japan spends $32.4 billion, followed by the United Kingdom ($20 billion), Germany ($18.3 billion), and France ($11.1 billion). Figure 4.8 provides data about the average expenditure per capita for 10 selected nations as well as total overall expenditures. The United States averages $468 per person in annual advertising expenditures as compared to Japan's $254 per person, the United Kingdom's $332, and Germany's $221.

Marketing allocations for business-to-business firms are not the same as those of consumer-oriented firms. Approximately 20 percent of all business-to-business ads emphasize or promote the corporate image; 80 percent focus on specific goods or services.[10] The major goals of many business-to-business advertisements are to create awareness of new products or brands and to heighten awareness of the company. Many advertising creatives believe it is difficult to design effective business-to-business advertisements because they don't have the creative freedom possible with consumer advertisements. Also, because most business ads are print ads in trade journals, the flexibility of television and radio advertisements is not available.

Many firms aim marketing programs at both consumers and businesses. Revlon produces television and print ads directed to consumers while trade promotion dollars are directed toward retailers. On average, a company spends about 30 percent of its total communications budget on marketing to other businesses. In service industries, the percentage is much higher (70%). In some technology-based industries, business-to-business allocations account for as little as 13 percent of the total marketing budget.[11]

When the budgeting process is complete, company leaders should believe they have wisely allocated funds to increase the effectiveness of the marketing communications program. Although specific dollar amounts and percentages vary, the overall goal remains the same—to achieve the marketing objectives as established in the plan.

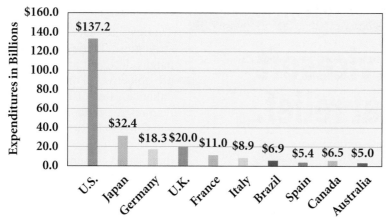

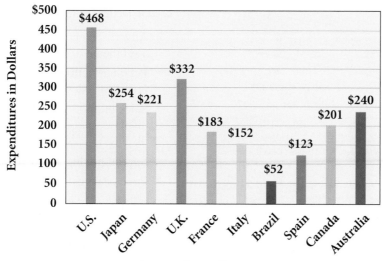

**FIGURE 4.8**
**Global Advertising Expenditures**

*Source:* Adapted from "Global Adspend Trends: Adspend in G7 Countries," *International Journal of Marketing* 23 (2004), pp. 534–536.

# PREPARING PROMOTIONAL STRATEGIES

The fourth step of a promotions opportunity analysis program is to prepare a general communication strategy for the company and its products. **Strategies** are sweeping guidelines concerning the essence of the company's marketing efforts. Strategies provide the long-term direction for all marketing activities.

An excellent example of a general communications strategy is found in the marketing efforts of Mountain Dew. The primary market for Mountain Dew is teenagers and young adults. As a result, communications efforts are directed to that market using slogans such as "Do the Dew" to "Been There Done That" and so forth. Action-oriented commercials featuring higher-risk activities are designed to attract younger people (and the young at heart), who are more willing to take "risks" in the products they sample and adopt. The overall theme of the Mountain Dew communications program guides all other activities.

It is critical that the company's communication strategies mesh with its overall message and be carefully linked to the opportunities identified by a communication market analysis. Communications strategies should be directly related to a firm's marketing objectives. Strategies must be achievable using the allocations available in the marketing and communications budgets. Once strategies have been implemented, they are not changed unless major new events occur. Only changes in the marketplace, new competitive forces, or new promotional opportunities should cause companies to alter strategies.

108   Part 1   The IMC Foundation

## SUFFERING FROM CUSTOMER E-MAIL OVERLOAD?

# Only Servicesoft offers real relief.

### Comparison of e-mail features

| | Servicesoft | Kana | eGain |
|---|---|---|---|
| Interactive e-mail | ✓ | — | — |
| Sophisticated knowledge engine | ✓ | — | — |
| Intelligent routing rules | ✓ | ✓ | ✓ |
| Auto response | ✓ | ✓ | ✓ |
| Auto suggestion | ✓ | ✓ | ✓ |
| Auto acknowledgement | ✓ | ✓ | ✓ |

Service*soft*®
www.servicesoft.com

**Don't just manage your customer e-mail problem. Solve it with Servicesoft interactive e-mail.**

It's amazing. But the so-called "leading" e-mail systems don't address the real reason e-mail volumes grow out of control. The culprit? Ambiguous e-mails that can't be handled with an auto response. These e-mails require agents to start a back-and-forth e-mail dialogue. Delaying responses. And resulting in what Aberdeen Group calls "e-mail ping-pong" that actually *increases* your e-mail volume.

The solution? Servicesoft interactive e-mail, with its sophisticated knowledge engine and intelligent routing rules. The power to answer customer e-mails through your Web site. Accurately. Without delays. And without expensive agents having to handle every message.

**Get a real solution to your e-mail problem. Register today for a free Web seminar at www.servicesoft.com/e-mail. Or call 1-800-737-8738, ext. 1.**

Servicesoft is a registered trademark of Servicesoft, Inc. All other registered trademarks or trademarks are the property of their respective owners. © 2000 Servicesoft, Inc., Natick, Massachusetts, USA.

In this business-to-business advertisement, Servicesoft reinforces its corporate image while promoting its interactive e-mail system.
*Source:* Courtesy of Servicesoft Inc.

## Matching Tactics with Strategies

**Tactics** are activities performed to support strategies. Tactics include promotional campaigns designed around themes based on strategic objectives. For example, Kellogg's seeks to enhance sales of cereals by designing unusual features for certain holidays, such as Halloween and Christmas Rice Krispies.

Tactics do not replace strategies, nor should they distract consumers from the consistent message or theme the company is trying to create. At the same time, they add excitement or interest to what the company is ordinarily doing. Holiday promotions, anniversary sales, and a variety of other events can be the basis for a promotional effort. Methods used in tactical campaigns include:

▸ Advertisements based on the major theme or a subtheme
▸ Personal selling enticements (bonuses and prizes for sales reps)
▸ Sales promotions (posters, point-of-purchase displays, end-of-aisle displays, freestanding displays)
▸ Special product packaging and labeling
▸ Price changes

Besides the methods of communicating with consumers and sales reps who offer the products, companies are able to add other enticements. Items that may be included in tactical efforts include:

▸ Coupons
▸ Gift certificates
▸ Bonus packs (a second product attached to a first)
▸ Special containers (e.g., holiday decanters or soft-drink glasses)
▸ Contests and prizes
▸ Rebates
▸ Volume discounts (larger-size packages, "buy three, get one free" promotions, etc.)

The Gold Bond advertisement shown on the next page uses a manufacturer's coupon to encourage people to purchase the product. The creative use of a snowy, winter scene highlights the product benefits of Gold Bond. The more creative the campaign the better the chance the company can overcome clutter and become recognized in the marketplace.

When a promotions opportunity analysis is complete, company leaders and the marketing department should have a grasp of the organization's marketing situation, along with specific information about internal strengths and weaknesses in the promotions area. They should also be aware of communication opportunities present in the environment along with any threats to the company's marketing program. They must study and understand the organization's competition to the greatest degree possible. Target markets must be defined and budgets set. Then, the marketing leaders of the company can establish strategies and tactics to guide efforts to reach specific marketing objectives and performance targets.

The next sections describe in greater detail two key ingredients of the promotional opportunities analysis process. The first is the study of consumer and business-to-business market segmentation. The second is to extend promotional opportunities analysis to global or international markets.

## MARKET SEGMENTATION

IMC experts use market segmentation to distinguish between specific purchasing groups. **Market segmentation** is the process of identifying specific purchasing groups based on their needs, attitudes, and interests. A **market segment** is a set of businesses or group of individual consumers with distinct characteristics. Market segmentation efforts are of great value in completing a promotions opportunity analysis. These advantages include:

A creative message strategy is combined with the marketing tactic of a coupon to stimulate sales of Gold Bond Medicated Body Lotion.
*Source:* Courtesy of Chattem, Inc.

1. Helping marketers identify company strengths and weaknesses as well as opportunities in the marketplace
2. Working toward the goal of matching what the firm does best with the most lucrative sets of customers
3. Clarifying marketing objectives associated with individual target markets
4. Focusing budgeting expenditures or consumer groups and business segments more precisely
5. Linking company strategies and tactics to select groups of customers

Segmentation should be designed to build brand loyalty and improve the odds of success of a marketing plan. For a market segment to be considered a viable target for a specific marketing communications campaign, it should pass the following tests:

▸ The individuals or businesses within the market segment should be similar in nature, having the same needs, attitudes, interests, and opinions. This means persons or businesses *within* the segment are *homogenous*.

▸ The market segment differs from the population as a whole. Segments are distinct from other segments and the general population.

---

### ETHICAL ISSUES

#### Is Segmentation the Same as Stereotyping?

In an era in which the term "political correctness" has been tossed about by political parties and other social critics, questions remain regarding what it means to be culturally aware. This issue has emerged in the area of marketing. Consider some of the primary categories in which segments are identified: age, race, gender, social status, and income. Of these, many are cultural characteristics.

Should there be a "black," "Hispanic," or "Caucasian" market? Should there be "male" and "female" markets? What about "teenagers," "Generation Y," and "baby boomers"? Are these markets distinct enough to require special advertisements and marketing promotions? Or should the general message be universal enough to reach people from all backgrounds?

Advertisements often depict teenagers in one-dimensional ways rather than reflecting the complexities of young adulthood. Rebellious, carefree, and sexually starved are common depictions. For baby boomers, the image presented is of a white, well-educated, well-off person with a spacious home and expensive cars and toys instead of the complex makeup of multiple nationalities of all income levels. From a marketing perspective, it is much easier to group people into smaller subgroups with common interests. Is it unethical, bad business, or simply a practical matter to pigeonhole consumer types in these ways?

FIGURE 4.9
**Methods of Segmenting Consumer Markets**

▶ **Demographics**
▶ **Psychographics**
▶ **Generations**
▶ **Geographic**
▶ **Geodemographics**
▶ **Benefits**
▶ **Usage**

▶ The market segment must be large enough to be financially viable to target with a separate marketing campaign.

▶ The market segment must be reachable through some type of media or marketing communications method.

Marketers engaged in research spend considerable resources and amounts of time working to identify quality market segments. These groups are specified in two general areas: (1) consumer markets and (2) business-to-business markets. The following section describes each of these segments in greater detail.

## MARKET SEGMENTATION BY CONSUMER GROUPS

In many instances, end users are the primary target market for a firm's offerings. Effective IMC programs identify sets of consumers who are potential buyers and who have things in common, such as attitudes, interests, or needs. These consumer market segmentation approaches are listed in Figure 4.9.

An advertisement by Bijan targeted to females.
*Source:* Courtesy of Bijan Fragrances, Inc.

### Segments Based on Demographics

As shown, the first method of segmentation uses demographics. **Demographics** are population characteristics. Typical demographic segmentation variables include gender, age, education, income, race, and ethnicity. Consumer market segmentation approaches to demographic groups are based on the idea that people with distinguishable characteristics have different needs. Companies create goods and services to meet the needs of individual demographic segments.

### Gender

One demographic category is gender. Males and females purchase different products, buy similar products with different features (e.g., deodorants), buy the same products for dissimilar reasons (stereos, televisions), and buy the same products after being influenced by different kinds of appeals through different media.

Women constitute a major market, especially as the number of working women establishing successful careers continues to rise. Nearly 70 percent of the women in the workforce express concerns about balancing work and family. This worry has led to a change in how many companies market their products to women. Goods and services that offer convenience, flexibility, and independence are in demand. Marketing appeals using these hooks have been successful. At the same time, many working women do feel a certain need to reward themselves. Consequently, they also are willing to indulge in purchases of CDs and other perks or seek out services including health spas and beauty salons to obtain these rewards.[12] In the Bijan ad shown on the previous page the company sends a message to women in three different ways.

Marketing to women is more than creating and selling female-oriented products. A recent study revealed that women have an enormous impact on the spending habits of men. Males who are sports fans attend 57 percent more sporting events if their wives are also sports fans, as compared to men who are avid sports fans but their wives are not. The number of times a man attends a professional sporting event is directly related to his spouse's attitude toward sports. Therefore, to boost attendance, many professional sports teams realize they should market the team, event, or sport to women. This approach can have a double impact. First, more women will attend sporting events, and second, men who are zealous sports fans will attend more games.[13]

A BMW Motorcycle ad targeted toward men as the primary purchasers and women as the decision-making influencers.
*Source:* Courtesy of BMW of North America, LLC. © 1999 BMW of North America, Inc. All Rights Reserved. The BMW trademark and logo are registered. This advertisement is reproduced with the permission of BMW of North America, Inc. for promotional purposes only.

BMW Motorcycles recognized that women exert a considerable amount of influence on purchasing decisions for luxury touring motorcycles. A subject in one of the company's research programs explained that "If mama ain't happy, nobody's happy." Couples most often use luxury touring motorcycles for long-distance touring. This became an important factor in the development of a new motorcycle and in creating its market position. BMW's K 1200 LT has heated seats and backrests, with separate controls for both the passenger and the rider. A man tends to look at a motorcycle in terms of style, horsepower, torque, and handling. A woman has other concerns—most notably, comfort. In this case, BMW Motorcycles took what was learned from market research and made sure the motorcycle reached two target audiences: men as the primary purchasers and women as the decision-making influencers. Each was an important part of the promotional campaign.[14]

Some messages are directly targeted at men because the products are masculine (after-shave) or because more men will use the product (e.g., athlete's foot remedies). Appeals aimed only at men speak in a different tone than do more general ads and messages. Notice the advertisement for milk on the next page that is directed toward men and how it differs from the one aimed at women.

### Age

Age is a second demographic characteristic. Marketing campaigns target children, young adults, middle-age adults, and senior citizens. Some campaigns combine age-related factors with other demographics such as gender. Creating logical combinations with other segments is a common segmentation approach. For example, older women may be primary targets for specific types of vitamins and other age-related products. Young working women with children are more likely to notice ads for conveniences (ready-made foods and snacks, quick lube oil change facilities, etc.). Other groups may buy vitamins, snack foods, and change their car's oil. Still, individual segments can be targeted with messages that reach a particular set of needs.

*Children* have a major impact on the purchasing decisions of their parents. Appeals to children can tie several items together, including advertisements, merchandise based on the ads, and selections from other media. Children attracted to Harry Potter can buy toys, watch the movies, buy the books, and witness advertisements using the Harry Potter theme, such as when Burger King, KFC, and Taco Bell all combined to sponsor a campaign.

Besides children, another age-based demographic group that appeals to many firms is *seniors,* defined as individuals over age 55. In the past, all seniors were treated as one market and tended to be stereotyped in ads. Often they were pictured as elderly grand-parents or as feeble but avid gardeners. Several firms discovered that many seniors lead active lives and many are not gardeners. Nearly 60 percent are volunteers, and many have begun dating following the loss of a spouse. More than 25 percent in the 65 to 72 age

Great for growing chicks.

Want strong bones?
Your bones grow until about
age 35 and the calcium in
milk helps. After that,
it helps keep them strong.
Chicks rule.

got milk?

An advertisement for milk based on
nutritional benefits directed to women.
*Source:* Courtesy of Bozell Worldwide, Inc.

Your bones may be in jeopardy.

One in five
osteoporosis victims
is male. Luckily, fat free
milk has the calcium bones
need to help beat it.
Beating your Harvard Ph.D.
opponents? Well, that's
another story.

got milk?

An advertisement for milk based on
nutritional benefits directed to men.
*Source:* Courtesy of Bozell Worldwide, Inc.

group still work and 14 million seniors care for grandchildren.[15] In marketing to seniors, it is important to recognize that they are not one unified group. Ads must be targeted to more specific groups within the senior citizen category.

### Income

Income is an important demographic segmentation variable for many goods and services. Spending is normally directed at three large categories of goods: (1) necessities, (2) sundries, and (3) luxuries. Lower levels of income mean consumers purchase mostly necessities, such as food, clothing, cleaning supplies, and so forth. With increased income, households can buy more items categorized as sundries, such as those things that are "nice to own," but not absolutely necessary. Sundries include televisions, computers, CD players, and other similar goods. Vacation spending also is a sundry expenditure. Luxuries are things most people cannot afford or can afford only once in a lifetime, unless the family is a high-income household. Luxuries include yachts, expensive automobiles, extravagant resort vacations and other high-cost goods and services. Marketers work closely with creatives to tailor messages to various income groups and to select media that match those groups.

### Ethnic Groups

By the year 2010, most Americans will be nonwhite. Currently, many advertisements and marketing communications are still written from a white, Anglo-Saxon perspective. This represents both an opportunity and a threat: an opportunity for companies able to adapt their messages to other cultures and heritages. It is a threat to those that do not.

Ethnic marketing is more than spending money with ethnically owned radio stations or hiring ethnically owned advertising agencies. It is more than translating an advertisement from English into Spanish. It is more than including African-Americans or Asian-Americans in advertisements. Successful ethnic marketing requires understanding various ethnic groups and writing marketing communications that speak to specific cultures and values.

The three major ethnic groups in the United States are African-Americans, Hispanics, and Asian-Americans. African-American economic power exceeds $800 billion annually, Hispanic-sector purchases are in excess of $900 billion, and Asian-American spending is more than $400 billion.[16] In addition, a large number of immigrants are arriving from India and Pakistan. Another large group is coming from the Middle East and Eastern European countries. Each ethnic group contains multiple subgroups. Within the Asian community are individuals of Korean, Japanese, Filipino, Vietnamese, and Chinese descent. The Hispanic community is made up of individuals from Latin America, Mexico, Cuba, and Puerto Rico.

Although different in many ways, several common threads exist among these ethnic groups. They all tend to be more brand loyal than their white counterparts. They value quality and are willing to pay a higher price for quality and brand identity. They value relationships with companies and are loyal to those that make the effort to establish a connection with them.

To market effectively to ethnic groups, it is important to develop new creative approaches that respect America's ethnic differences while also highlighting its similarities. Achieving this requires advertising and marketing agencies that understand the subtleties of multiculturalism. Becoming involved in sponsorships of minority and ethnic events goes a long way toward establishing ties with specific ethnic groups. Indications are strong that ethnic consumers reward companies that invest in them. In addition to sponsorships, becoming involved in ethnic community groups and civic and trade associations should prove beneficial.[17]

A Skechers advertisement featuring a multiethnic approach.
*Source:* Courtesy of Skechers USA Inc.

Ethnic marketing is similar in some ways to global marketing. It is important to present one overall message that is then tailored to fit the needs and values of various groups. Successfully achieving this integration of the overall message with characteristics of individual cultures should result in valuable gains in loyalty to a company and its brands, and diversify the markets the company can effectively serve.

## Psychographics

Demographics are typically easy to identify. They do not, however, fully explain why people buy particular products or specific brands, or the type of appeal that can be used to reach them. To assist in the marketing effort while building on demographic information, psychographic profiles have been developed. **Psychographics** emerge from patterns of responses that reveal a person's attitudes, interests, and opinions (AIO). AIO measures can be combined with demographic information to provide marketers with a more complete understanding of the market to be targeted.[18] The Communication Action box titled "Psychographics and Technology" provides an example of marketing psychographic segmentation.

SRI Consulting Business Intelligence provides a popular classification of lifestyles using psychographic segmentation. The VALS2 typology categorizes respondents into eight different groups based on resources and on the extent to which they are action-oriented.[19] The VALS2 typology includes the following segments:

▶ *Innovators*—Successful, sophisticated, and receptive to new technologies. Their purchases reflect cultivated tastes for upscale products.

▶ *Thinkers*—Educated, conservative, practical consumers who value knowledge and responsibility. They look for durability, functionality, and value.

▶ *Achievers*—Goal-oriented, conservative consumers committed to career and family. They favor established prestige products that demonstrate success to peers.

▶ *Experiencers*—Young, enthusiastic, and impulsive consumers who seek variety and excitement, and spend substantially on fashion, entertainment, and socializing.

▶ *Believers*—Conservative, conventional consumers who focus on tradition, family, religion, and community. They prefer established brands and favor American-made products.

▶ *Strivers*—Trendy, fun-loving consumers who are concerned about others' opinions and approval. They demonstrate to peers their ability to buy.

▶ *Makers*—Self-sufficient consumers who have the skill and energy to carry out projects, respect authority, and are unimpressed by material possessions.

▶ *Survivors*—Concerned with safety and security, focus on meeting needs rather than fulfilling desires. They are brand loyal, and purchase discounted products.

Having this type of information about consumers allows marketers to design communications that will be more effective. For instance, reaching strivers requires ads that convey fun and trendy products. Ads for believers should focus more on tradition and American values.

## COMMUNICATION ACTION

### Psychographics and Technology

Odyssey is a multimedia technology company. The company's marketing team conducted psychographic research while developing a marketing program. The research revealed that instead of one market, there were six unique market segments, each with a distinct attitude about technology. In other words, consumers may have identical demographic characteristics but differ greatly in how they view multimedia technology. Understanding the six different segments allowed Odyssey's marketing group to create advertising and promotional themes geared to each segment. The six segments that Odyssey identified were:

1. *New Enthusiasts.* These households enjoy being on the cutting edge of technology and are eager to purchase the most recent version of any new technology. Members of this group tend to have high incomes and higher levels of education.

2. *Hopefuls.* These households also like to be on the cutting edge of technology but lack the financial means to make extensive purchases. They are concerned that a new technology may be too difficult to use.

3. *Faithful.* These households are not eager to try new technologies but are not averse to trying something new.

4. *Oldliners.* These households are not interested in new technologies. Finances also concern this group.

5. *Independents.* These individuals have higher incomes and higher educational levels but do not value new forms of technology. They are unwilling to try new things.

6. *Surfers.* These households are ambivalent about new technologies and tend to be cynical about business and privacy issues. They have above-average incomes and are able to afford new technologies, but don't trust them.

Each segment clearly requires a distinct advertising appeal. In this case, similar people have differing psychological attitudes and needs for a product, even though the product itself is the same for each group.

**Source:** Marilyn A. Gillen, "Tracking Multimedia's Fragmented Audience," *Billboard* 106, no. 10 (March 5, 1994), p. 60.

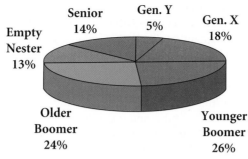

**FIGURE 4.10**
**Spending Power of U.S. Generation Segments**

Source: *American Demographics* 24, No. 7 (July–August 2002) pp. S3–S10.

## Segments Based on Generations

Beyond using gender, age, income, ethnic heritage, education, or other demographic variables for segmentation, many marketers target generational cohorts. This approach does not require the use of psychographic information to enrich the demographics. It does possess some of the richness of the psychographics. The concept behind marketing to generational cohorts is that common experiences and events create bonds between people who are about the same age.

Segmentation based on generations notes that as people experience significant external events during their late adolescence or early adulthood, these events impact their social values, attitudes, and preferences. Based on similar experiences, these cohorts of individuals develop common preferences for music, foods, and other products. They also tend to respond to the same types of marketing appeals. Based on this idea, six cohorts or generations have been identified. Figure 4.10 identifies these cohorts along with their sizes relative to U.S. population.

*Generation Y* (individuals 18–24 years old) contributes only 5 percent of the total spending power. It is the smallest of the six generational cohorts, but it is growing both in size and wealth. Clothes, automobiles, and college are the big-ticket items for this group. Nearly 90 percent of Generation Y lives in a rental or with parents. Buying a home and home furnishings is a low priority. Generation Y spends substantial amounts on television sets and stereo systems and products that enhance personal appearance and fun.[20]

*Generation X* (individuals 25–34 years old) contributes 18 percent of the total spending power of consumers in the United States. Members focus on family and children. Food, housing, transportation, and personal services are the important categories for this generation segment. Time pressures are intense for this generation as they strive to balance work and family; therefore, they outsource many of the daily tasks such as house cleaning, lawn mowing, babysitting, and other domestic chores.[21]

*Younger boomers* (individuals 35–44 years old) have an estimated spending power of $1.1 trillion. The home and family is the focus of younger

An advertisement directed to Generation Y's desire to enhance their personal appearance.
*Source:* Courtesy of Gillette.

boomers' spending. The majority (60%) own homes. Consequently, a considerable amount of income is allocated to mortgage expenditures, home furnishings, and home renovations. The remaining disposable income is spent on family purchases such as pets, toys, playground equipment, or a large recreational item such as a boat or 4-wheel-drive vehicle.[22]

*Older boomers* (individuals 45–54 years old) account for 24 percent of the total spending, an estimated $1 trillion. The priorities of this group include upgrading homes, ensuring education and independence for their children, buying luxury items such as boats or hot tubs, and taking more exotic vacations. With fewer responsibilities at home, older boomers spend considerably more on recreation than any of the other generation groups. Insurance and investments are also high-ticket items as boomers begin to think about their later years and retirement.[23]

*Empty nesters* (individuals 55–64 years old) contribute 13 percent of the total spending and spend heavily on home mortgages, new furniture, new automobiles, and personal indulgence items. Over 80 percent own homes. Many have paid the mortgage in full. Investments and insurance are high-ticket items, and their attention is now focused on things such as the fancy, nice automobile they could not afford earlier because of children.[24]

*Seniors* (individuals over age 65) account for 14 percent of all spending in the United States. Because of fixed incomes and tighter budgets, household income and spending decline sharply. Drugs, health insurance, and health care constitute the top three categories of spending for this group, followed closely by medical supplies and medical expenses.[25]

## Segmentation by Geographic Area

Another form of segmentation is by geographic area or region. This method is especially useful for retailers that want to limit marketing communications programs to specific areas. It also helps a company conduct a direct-mail campaign in a target area. The primary disadvantage of this approach is that everyone in a geographic area receives the marketing communication or is exposed to the advertisement, regardless of interest in the product or service. Geographic segmentation does not allow a firm to focus in on a more specific target market containing only those most likely to make purchases.

Geographic segmentation should be reserved for more basic products (restaurants, foods) or items of specific interest to a region. For example, *Sports Illustrated* now offers "Championship Editions" in limited geographic regions when college and professional football or basketball teams win championships.

## Geodemographic Segmentation

A hybrid form of geographic segmentation allows companies to enrich geographic approaches to segmentation. This new form of segmentation, called *geodemographics,* combines census data with psychographic information. This method is more powerful in finding potential customers because it combines census demographic information, geographic information, and psychographic information into one package.

Geodemographic segmentation is especially beneficial for national firms conducting direct-mail campaigns or using a sampling promotion. Normally, it is too expensive and unwise to mail a sample to every household. Through geodemographics, a firm can send samples to the households that match the profile of a target market. For instance, colleges and universities use geodemographics to locate ZIP codes of communities that match student profiles.

One firm, PRIZM (Potential Rating Index by Zip Marketing) specializes in geodemographics. PRIZM has identified 62 different market segments in the United States. The company has categorized every U.S. ZIP code. The concept behind PRIZM is that ZIP codes represent neighborhoods containing people with relatively uniform characteristics. Consumers tend to be attracted to neighborhoods consisting of people similar to them. Recognizing that more than one market segment may live within a ZIP code, PRIZM identifies the top market segments within each ZIP code.

A PRIZM-coded map of downtown Jackson, Mississippi, identifies two primary clusters. The more predominant is the "Southside City" residents. This cluster is mainly young and elderly African-Americans employed in low-paying blue-collar jobs. They tend to have lower levels of formal education, rent apartments, and read sports and fashion magazines. The second cluster within downtown Jackson is labeled as the "Towns and Gowns" neighborhoods. Towns and Gowns inhabitants also rent apartments, but members tend to be college graduates with better-paying white-collar jobs. This group likes to ski, reads beauty and fitness magazines, and frequently use ATM cards.[26]

Geodemographic marketing has been expanded to the Internet. Adfinity is a program designed by Intelligent Interactions. It allows an advertiser to direct specific ads to Web users based on user-defined demographics. Often, when users visit Web sites, they provide their names and addresses along with other demographic information. While the user is surfing a site, Adfinity's software can access the user's file in order to place a targeted ad on the page. To extend its power and effectiveness, Adfinity formed a strategic alliance with PRIZM. When a user accesses a Web site, the user is matched with data from the 62 PRIZM clusters. Based on the lifestyle and interests of that cluster, messages are sent that match the user. A person from the cluster "Executive Suites" will see advertisements about jazz or business books, because people in the Executive Suites cluster prefer those items.

## Benefit Segmentation

Benefit segmentation focuses on the advantages consumers receive from a product rather than the characteristics of consumers themselves. Demographic and psychographic information can be combined with benefit information to better identify segments. Then, the company can seek to further understand each segment's consumers.

Benefit segmentation has been used in the fitness market. Regular exercisers belong in one of three benefit segments. The first group, called "winners," do whatever it takes to stay physically fit. This segment tends to be younger, upwardly mobile, and career oriented. The second group, "dieters," exercise to maintain weight control and physical appearance. This group tends to be females over the age of 35. They are primarily interested in reliable wellness programs offered by hospitals and weight control nutritionists. The third group, "self-improvers," exercise to feel better and to control medical costs.[27] Understanding that individuals exercise for different reasons provides excellent material for a fitness center to design a marketing program.

Benefit segmentation can be very helpful in understanding what customers seek from a product. By tying these benefits to demographic and psychographic data, companies can use the information to design targeted messages for each market segment.

## Usage Segmentation

The final type of consumer segmentation is based on customer usage or purchases. The goal of usage segmentation is to provide the highest level of service to a firm's best customers while promoting the company to casual or light users. Usage segmentation is also designed to maximize sales to all user groups.

Many company marketing teams identify heavy users by utilizing internal databases. With bar-code scanners, point-of-sale systems, and data from credit, debit, and transaction cards, in-house marketers can accumulate a wealth of information about customers. Many have learned that between 10 percent and 30 percent of company customers generate 70 percent to 90 percent of total sales. Instead of using firms such as PRIZM to create customer clusters, firms develop customer clusters from these databases. Customers are placed in clusters based on common attitudes, lifestyles, and past purchase behaviors. This technique offers a business the following advantages:[28]

1. A meaningful classification scheme to cluster customers based on a firm's actual customers
2. The ability to reduce large volumes of customer data down to a few concise, usable clusters

3. The ability to assign a cluster code number to each customer in the database. Each number is based on the customer's actual purchases and other characteristics (address, amount spent, credit versus cash, etc.).

4. The capacity to measure the growth and migration of customers over time and from one cluster to another, which allows for the evaluation of marketing programs

5. The capability of using a database to develop multiple clusters based on different benefits or usages

Not all businesses have such extensive databases. For these types of businesses, several companies sell and provide consumer databases. These consumer databases can be linked to a customer's records through a name, address, or social security number. These commercial databases contain typical information such as the household's income, the ages of household members, the length and type of residence, information about car ownership, and telephone numbers.

In summary, there are many ways to identify consumer market segments. Each segment presents opportunities and problems. The best segmentation approaches are based on the company's circumstances. In choosing market segments to approach, a marketer should look for groups that best match the company's goods and services as well as the overall marketing message. Then the message can be structured to meet the needs of the various market segments.

## BUSINESS-TO-BUSINESS SEGMENTATION

Some approaches that help identify consumer market segments can also be used to discover business-to-business market segments. There are also alternate methods. Figure 4.11 lists the various types of business-to-business market segments. Keep in mind that, as with consumer markets, the primary goals of segmentation are to provide better customer service and to group homogeneous customers into clusters to enhance the marketing effort.

### Segmentation by Industry

One method used to examine potential customers is by industry. Many marketers use the NAICS (North American Industry Classification System) coding system. NAICS allows the marketing team to examine specific industries such as construction (23) or wholesale trade (42). They also can study segments within specific categories. For example, NAICS codes health care and social assistance services as 62. A company that manufactures health-related products can divide the market into four segments based on the subsections. These four market segments are:

621    Ambulatory Health Care Services

622    Hospitals

623    Nursing and Residential Care Facilities

624    Social Assistance

If these segments are too broad, a company can break each segment down into smaller subcomponents. For example, Ambulatory Health Care Services includes physicians, dentists, chiropractors, and optometrists.

**FIGURE 4.11**
**Methods of Segmenting
Business-to-Business Markets**

▶ **Industry (NAICS/CIS codes)**
▶ **Size of business**
▶ **Geographic location**
▶ **Product usage**
▶ **Customer value**

The NAICS divides the economy into 20 broad sectors using a 6-digit code rather than the SIC 4-digit code. The 6-digit code allows greater stratification of industries and provides greater flexibility in creating classifications. The federal government records corporate information and data using the NAICS, making it a logical system to choose for identifying market segments.

## Segmentation by Size

Another set of market segments can be identified based on the size of company. The rationale for this view is that large firms have needs that are different from smaller companies. Each should be contacted in a different manner. This means that the marketing effort is often focused on the company's purchasing department when the firm is large. For smaller firms, the owner or general manager often makes the purchase decisions and is therefore the target of marketing messages.

B&J Food Service Equipment can use the NAICS code to locate firms in the food service industry.
*Source:* Courtesy of *The Joplin Globe,* Joplin, MD.

## Segmentation by Geographic Location

As with consumer segmentation, identifying market segments by geographic location can be a successful tactic. This approach especially benefits businesses with customers that are concentrated in geographic pockets such as the Silicon Valley area of California. It works for other firms as well. When the Applied Microbiology firm developed a new antimicrobial agent, the goal was to market the product to dairy farmers. The traditional agricultural marketing and distribution channel required to launch such a new product nationally was estimated at $3 million. Such a traditional marketing plan involved national advertising in agriculture magazines plus recruiting sales agents and brokers to introduce the product. Instead, Applied Microbiology used geodemographics, which combined geographic areas with demographic and psychographic data. Applied Microbiology used geodemographics to find areas with dairy herds consisting of 1,000 or more cows per ranch. These farmers were contacted for two reasons. First, large dairy farmers who adopted the product would buy greater quantities of it. Second, the company's leaders believed that the larger farmers were opinion leaders who would influence smaller farmers, thereby causing them to adopt the product as well.

Several separate direct-response pieces offering discounts for and samples of Applied Microbiology's new product were sent to larger farms. After sales started rising, farmers were asked for testimonials. The testimonials were extremely powerful, and they were then incorporated into new direct-marketing pieces. One brochure contained three testimonials and validation of the product by Cornell University. After a dairy farmer adopted the product, direct-marketing pieces were sent to farmers in the surrounding area. Not only did this method bring excellent results, but the marketing costs were also one-third of the traditional approach. Using geodemographics cost only $1 million rather than the proposed $3 million.[29]

## Segmentation by Product Usage

Business markets can be segmented based on the manner in which the good or service is used. Many services (financial, transportation, shipping, etc.) have a variety of uses for distinct customers. For example, in the hotel industry, a major source of revenue is booking business events and conferences. A hotel or resort may identify business market segments based on various types of events. Single-day seminars require only a meeting room and refreshments. A full conference may involve renting rooms for lodging, preparing banquets, furnishing meeting rooms, and planning sightseeing excursions. By segmenting the market based on the use of the hotel's facilities and staff, a manager can prepare marketing materials

An advertisement targeted to the large business conference segment.
*Source:* Courtesy of Edgewater Beach Resort.

that address the needs of each specific type of conference. The advertisement for Edgewater Beach Resort, shown in this section, is an example of this type of approach.

## Segmentation by Customer Value

The final method of business segmentation is based on customer value. This approach is much easier for business-to-business firms to utilize than it is for consumer businesses, due to the availability of in-depth data about each business customer. A more precise value can be assigned to each individual business through sales records and other sources of data and information. Customer value segmentation is illustrated in Case 1, "Commercial Consolidated," at the end of this chapter.

In summary, when choosing the communication objective, it is important to decide what the desired response should be. Sometimes a company wants customers to quickly purchase a good or service. In others, marketing managers try to persuade customers that the company's product is better than the competitions'. For other companies, the goal is to convince a retail store to allocate more shelf space for certain products. The desired response should be based on the communication market analysis discussed in the previous section.

## IMPLICATIONS FOR GIMC PROGRAMS

As was first presented in Chapter 1, globally integrated marketing communications (GIMC) programs are vital for international firms. The world consists of many different languages and cultures. Brand names, marketing ideas, and advertising campaigns designed for one country do not always translate correctly to another. Consequently, understanding the international market is essential. Figure 4.12 highlights the ingredients of successful globally integrated marketing communications plans.

Recognizing the many cultural nuances throughout the world is one key. This does not mean that different marketing campaigns must always be developed for each country and each cultural group within a country. Still, marketers must understand the region and its culture in order to tailor messages to individual areas.

A borderless marketing plan suggests that the firm should use the same basic marketing approach for all of its various markets. At the same time, it allows each subsidiary the freedom to determine how to implement that marketing plan. This presents the opportunity to maintain a theme while targeting the message carefully.

Another key to a successful GIMC is developing local partnerships. Local partners can be marketing research firms or advertising firms that are familiar with the local language

**FIGURE 4.12**
**Successful Globally Integrated Marketing Communications Tactics**

▶ Understand the international market

▶ A borderless marketing plan

▶ Thinking globally but acting locally

▶ Local partnerships

▶ Communication segmentation strategies

▶ Market communications analysis

▶ Solid communication objectives

and culture. These partnerships sometimes are formed by hiring someone from a particular country with a full understanding of the market. Such a person is sometimes referred to as a **cultural assimilator**. It is also vital that the chosen individual has a clear understanding of the English language or the language of the parent firm and the parent firm's business.

As with domestic markets, segmentation is critical. The goal is to design a communications package that effectively reaches every market segment. Target markets in other countries should be identified. In most instances there will be both consumer and business-to-business segments.

A well-designed market communications analysis process is another key factor in the success of a GIMC program. Marketing managers must identify strengths and weaknesses of local competitors and places in which opportunities exist. They must also develop an understanding of how the firm is perceived in the international marketplace.

Finally, solid communication objectives based on an effective market communication analysis greatly improve the chances that a GIMC program will be successful. Linguistics is a major hurdle to overcome. Translating an English advertisement into another language requires expertise, because exact word translations often do not exist. For example, the slogan of Ruth's Steak House, "We sell sizzle as well as steaks," could not be translated into Spanish, because there is no equivalent word for sizzle. Therefore, the translator found a Spanish idiom conveying a similar meaning in order to solve the problem.

The promotions opportunity analysis process is difficult in international settings; however, it is crucial in creating an effective GIMC. Language, culture, norms, beliefs, and laws all must be taken into consideration in the development of the GIMC program. Literal translation of a commercial's tagline may not be acceptable within a given culture. Laws concerning advertising and promotions vary by country. Further, cultures view ideas and objects differently. These differences must be considered when designing an integrated program.

Without a solid market communication analysis, international communication programs are more likely to fail. One good thing about international markets is that many of the communications objectives will be the same as those for domestic operations. In all countries, marketers must make consumers aware of the company's products. Advertisements must break through local clutter and capture the attention of the target audience. Effective communication means a product's features and advantages are clearly understood. Ads can also present the product using the emotions and imagery that speak effectively to the target audience. The ultimate goal is to persuade members of the target audience to purchase the company's products.

## SUMMARY

A promotions opportunity analysis is the process by which marketers identify target audiences for the goods and services produced by the company. It consists of five steps: conduct a communication market analysis, establish communications objectives, create a communications budget, prepare promotional strategies, and match tactics with strategies. Along the way, marketing managers should review competitors, opportunities, target markets, customers, and the company's positioning.

Market segmentation is identifying sets of business or consumer groups with distinct characteristics. Segments must be clearly different, large enough to support a marketing campaign, and reachable through some type of media. Consumer groups that can be segmented include those identified by demographics, including gender, age, income, and ethnic heritage. Markets can also be identified using psychographic, generational, and geographic delineations. Geodemographic segmentation combines demographic, psychographic, and geographic information together. Other ways to categorize consumers are by the benefits they receive from goods or services and by the ways they use products.

Business-to-business segmentation can be accomplished by targeting business customers by industry, business type, the size of the company, geographic location, usage, and customer value calculations. Marketing managers should carefully specify the company's consumer and business market segments. All other promotions opportunity analysis processes are tied to the identification of key customers.

Globally integrated marketing communications efforts must also be linked to promotions opportunities analysis programs. National differences, cultural concerns, language issues, and other challenges must be viewed in light of the target markets an individual company intends to serve.

A promotions opportunity analysis program is the first step in developing a complete IMC package. Based on an overall marketing plan, company leaders gather information and generate decisions regarding target markets and marketing opportunities.

They proceed to develop a further understanding of the company's image and dig deeper into the process of revealing key consumer and business buyer behaviors. They should address the company's message to tie in with the overall IMC theme. A promotions opportunity analysis is the foundation stage for the rest of the IMC program. A solid promotions opportunity analysis program greatly increases the chances that marketing messages will reach the right audiences. This leads to increased sales, customer loyalty, and a stronger long-term standing in the marketplace.

# REVIEW QUESTIONS

1. What is a promotions opportunities analysis? Why is it a critical part of a company's marketing effort?

2. What are the five parts of a promotions opportunities analysis planning process?

3. What common marketing communications objectives do firms establish?

4. Name and describe the types of communications budgets. Which is best? Why?

5. What is a strategy? Give an example of a promotional strategy.

6. What are tactics? How are they related to strategies?

7. Define *demographics*. How are they used to segment consumer markets?

8. How can firms take advantage of target markets by gender?

9. What generational cohorts have marketing experts identified?

10. What problems are associated with markets segmented according to geographic areas?

11. What are geodemographics? Why have they been so successful in defining marketing segments?

12. Describe usage segmentation and benefit segmentation.

13. What are the common business-to-business market segments?

14. Describe the NAICS approach to business market segmentation.

15. Describe a usage segmentation approach in a business-to-business setting.

16. Describe a segmentation approach based on company size.

17. How does the idea of a promotions opportunities analysis fit with a GIMC program?

# KEY TERMS

**promotions opportunity analysis** The process marketers use to identify target audiences for a company's goods and services and the communication strategies needed to reach these audiences.

**communication market analysis** The process of discovering the organization's strengths and weaknesses in the area of marketing communication, and combining that information with an analysis of opportunities and threats that are present in the firm's external environment.

**benchmark measures** Starting points that are studied in relation to the degree of change following a promotional campaign.

**threshold effects** For new products, initial advertisements yield little behavioral response; however, over time, a consumer who is exposed enough times to a company's marketing message will recall the company and eventually become willing to make a purchase.

**sales-response function curve** An S-shaped curve that indicates when threshold effects are present and when diminishing returns are present.

**concave downward function** A model of the diminishing returns of advertisements on sales.

**marginal analysis** A model that shows when additional expenditures on advertising and promotions have an adverse affect on profits.

**carryover effects** When products are only purchased when needed, promotions for those products must be designed to generate a situation in which the consumer has been exposed to the company's message for so long that when the time comes to buy, the consumer remembers the key company.

**wear-out effects** Declines in advertising effectiveness that occur when an ad or marketing communication becomes "old" or "boring."

**decay effects** Declines in advertising effectiveness that occur when advertising stops and consumers begin to forget about the company.

**percentage of sales method** A form of communications budgeting in which budgeting is based on the sales from the previous year or anticipated sales for the coming year.

**meet-the-competition** A method of communications budgeting in which the primary rationale is to prevent the loss of market share, which occurs in highly competitive markets where rivalries between competitors are intense.

**"what we can afford" method** A method of communications budgeting in which the marketing budget is set after all of the company's other budgets have been determined and communications monies are allocated based on what the firm feels it can afford to spend.

**objective and task method** A form of communications budgeting in which management first lists all of the objectives it wants to accomplish during the year and then allocates budget to meet those objectives.

**payout planning** A budgeting method that establishes a ratio of advertising to sales or market share.

**strategies** Sweeping guidelines concerning the essence of the company's marketing efforts.

**tactics** The activities companies do to support overall promotional strategies.

**market segmentation** The identification of specific purchasing groups based on their needs, attitudes, and interests.

**market segment** A set of businesses or group of individual consumers with distinct characteristics.

**demographics** The study of population characteristics.

**psychographics** The study of patterns of responses that reveal a person's attitudes, interests, and opinions (AIO).

**cultural assimilator** A person who is familiar with the local language and culture of a given country who can help marketing efforts in that particular country.

# CRITICAL THINKING EXERCISES

## Discussion Questions

1. Use a search engine to locate five companies on the Internet that sell swimwear. Perform a competitive analysis of these five companies to find the types of products sold, the types of promotional appeals that are used, and the types of special offers used to entice buyers. What type of advertising strategy would you use to sell swimwear over the Internet?

2. A promotions opportunity analysis of movie theaters reveals the primary moviegoer to be between 18 and 24 years of age. In 1986, 44 percent of the individuals in this age bracket went to movies frequently. Today, less than 34 percent are frequent moviegoers.[30] Conduct a customer analysis by interviewing five individuals between the ages of 18 and 24. Based on their responses, what suggestions would you make to movie theaters to reverse this declining trend?

3. Make a list of five consumer goods or services segmented on the basis of gender but sold to both genders. Are there any differences in the product or service attributes? Are there differences in how they are marketed? What are those differences? Do you think using a different marketing approach has worked?

4. For each of the following goods or services, identify the various benefits that consumers may derive from the good or service. Can you think of an advertisement or other marketing communication that has used the benefit as the central part of its appeal?
   a. Seafood restaurant
   b. Auto insurance
   c. Optometrist or eye-care clinic
   d. Soft drink
   e. Aspirin or other pain reliever

# INTEGRATED LEARNING EXERCISES

1. Adage.com provides the latest ad agency news and account news. Go to the Web site at www.adage.com. Scan through the news articles about advertising, accounts, and ad agencies. Pick two that interest you and write a short summary report about the contents of each article.

2. For consumer markets, a leading geodemographic firm is Claritas. Go to the Web site at www.claritas.com and explore the various methods of segmentation. What information does Claritas provide? How would it help a company develop an integrated marketing communication plan?

3. Values and lifestyles (VALS) psychographic segmentation can be a valuable tool for marketers as they prepare their marketing materials. Access VALS2 through the Business Intelligence Center at www.sric-bi.com/VALS/presurvey.shtml. Once at the VALS site, examine the characteristics of each of the groups. Then take the test to determine which group you belong to. How can VALS2 help marketers develop advertising messages?

4. A current trend for many companies is the development of marketing messages for specific demographic, ethnic, or lifestyle groups. This allows for a more targeted message than is possible for the mass audience. Go to the following Web sites. What types of marketing messages are on each site? How could the information on these Web sites be used to developed integrated marketing communication plans?
   a. Women (www.iVillage.com)
   b. Hispanics (www.hispaniconline.com)
   c. African-Americans (www.targetmarketnews.com)
   d. Gays and lesbians (www.planetout.com)

5. Choose one of the following Internet companies. Examine the company's Web site to determine what segmentation strategy the firm uses. Describe the intended target market for the Web site. Using Figure 4.3 as a guide, what communication objective(s) do you think the company is trying to accomplish?
   a. Sports Spectrum Greeting Cards (www.sportsgreetingcards.com)
   b. Ty Beanie Babies (www.ty.com)
   c. Advanced Hardware Architectures (www.aha.com)
   d. Dr. James J. Romano (www.jromano.com)

# STUDENT PROJECT

## IMC Plan Pro

The third cornerstone in the IMC foundation is a promotions opportunity analysis. You need these guidelines in order to make sure the money you spend on advertising and promotions is carefully budgeted to match the situation, objectives, strategies, and tactics that drive the company's marketing efforts. The IMC Plan Pro booklet and disk available through Prentice Hall have an entire section developed to helping you formulate an effective promotions opportunity analysis. This includes making sure you have identified all of the viable target markets.

## COMMERCIAL CONSOLIDATED

# CASE 1

John Mulvaney had been a marketing account manager for many years. He left a private firm to take a position at a local bank, Commercial Consolidated. Bank officials concluded that because the marketplace for financial services had become so competitive, they needed an on-staff marketing executive to continually fine-tune the bank's advertising program. The company's headquarters were in John's hometown, only 12 blocks from his house. John saw the opportunity to make a "lifestyle" move while staying active in his chosen profession.

Once he was settled in, the first issue John pursued was a promotional analysis, focusing on various customers. His research indicated that in most banks, 10 percent to 20 percent of the small-business accounts yielded 80 percent to 90 percent of the bank's profitability. Upon being informed of this statistic, bank officials set the goal of moving some of the small businesses within the 80 percent that was not currently profitable to become more like the 10 percent to 20 percent.

John told the bank's leaders that he wanted to pursue a customer valuation segmentation approach, assigning each business a value related to the bank's level of profitability. To illustrate how this segmentation method works, John described the ways banks could market to small businesses. He noted that the first step in customer value segmentation is to identify the drivers that impact each business customer's profitability potential. For a bank providing financial services to small businesses, the primary value drivers are:

1. Deposit balances wherein interest and other revenues exceed requirements for servicing the account
2. Consistent fee income from sundry banking and financial services
3. Efficient lending practices emphasizing underwriting, approval, and processing of profitable loans
4. Targeted customer development focusing on building relationships that would lead to profitable transactions between the bank and the small business
5. Sales and service delivery programs that match the bank's profitability goals

John told Commercial Consolidated's management team that not all customers have the potential to be highly profitable accounts. He noted that by segmenting its small customers into customer value clusters, the bank could design different marketing programs for each segment to maximize effectiveness while minimizing marketing costs. He suggested putting a greater marketing effort into an account with high profitability potential than into one with low potential for profitability.

The marketing team decided to segment various small-business customers along several dimensions. Codes placed in each customer's data file allowed for easy clustering. The team used seven characteristics to code the bank's small-business customers. Account managers were given the following instructions for each account and its particular characteristics:

1. *Value segment.* Code the account based on how profitable it has been over the last 12 months. Codes range from highly profitable to unprofitable.
2. *Long-term value segment.* Code the account based on profitability potential for the next 5 years.
3. *Industry growth potential segment.* Code the growth potential of the industry in which the firm operates, from high-growth industry to negative anticipated growth.

(continued)

4. *Industry position segment.* Relative to the industry, code the size of the firm from large to small within the same industry.

5. *Transaction frequency segment.* Code the business customers from high to low based on frequency of transactions with the bank over the past 6 months.

6. *Product propensity segment.* Code the business customers based on their propensity to purchase a 401(k) plan with the bank. This code would be based on the firm's size and growth characteristics, from high potential for a 401(k) to low potential.

7. *Creditworthiness segment.* The code indicates the businesses' relative credit risk.

This coding system allowed the bank greater flexibility in designing its marketing program. The codes identified customers with the highest profit potential based on these factors.

Commercial Consolidated's overall theme had always been focused on its "hometown" bank image. Advertisements and other promotions restated the message that dollars invested locally were more valuable to the community than those shipped to the home office of a competitor in another city or state.

Using this technique, a bank could assign customers to clusters based on loan usage. Another set of clusters could be developed for investment services. A bank could develop many different clusters with customers assigned to clusters based on their purchase behavior of that particular type of service.

From there the bank generated an aggressive marketing program including advertising, direct-mail pieces, and some personal visits to companies with high profit potential. Customers with a medium level of transaction frequency could be targeted to increase their transactions with the bank if their potential was high. The bank aimed the direct marketing program at its top 20 customers; advertising was designed to reach the next 100 customers (in terms of profit potential); and the remainder of the firm's advertising funds were spent on brand awareness commercials.

Next, individual consumers were segmented and targeted. The bank was most interested in increasing use of their highly profitable consumer credit card. To do so, it needed to understand the usage of the credit card. The bank's customer cluster analysis identified the following seven clusters:

1. **The uncommitted.** The newest users of the credit card, these individuals tended to use the card infrequently and make relatively small purchases. This cluster primarily consisted of retired persons and individuals with low incomes.

2. **Convenience users.** These customers used their cards frequently and normally paid off their balances at the end of each monthly billing cycle. This cluster tended to have below average assets and slightly less than average household income.

3. **Starting out.** This cluster was predominantly young adults with lower than average incomes and low assets. They tended to have high purchases and carry moderate to high balances on their cards.

4. **Channel shoppers.** Consisting of older cardholders, these individuals had the highest income levels and were primarily females or married couples. This cluster had a low level of delinquency, low service charges, and moderate card activity.

5. **Credit addicts.** This group had the longest tenure of cardholders in the bank. They had the highest credit limits, the greatest spending, and the highest payments due each month. This cluster was of average age with above average income.

6. ***Cash driven.*** As the cash-hungry cluster, these individuals tended to pay off account balances slowly, had moderate credit limits, and used the card frequently to garner cash advances. This cluster generally included younger males and other singles with low assets.

7. ***Borderline.*** The youngest of the clusters with the lowest card activity, these customers had a high delinquency rate and had low incomes.

Using the cluster information, the bank sought to expand revenues by targeting current customers. They developed specialty marketing communication pieces for each cluster. Based on the demographic and psychographic information from each cluster, marketing pieces were designed to elicit responses. This clustering information helped the bank prevent customer defections to the competition by meeting the needs of each individual segment. To maximize the success of the program, the firm's marketing team made sure that the correct services were matched with customer needs. This information was used to focus media and advertising strategies creating specific messages for specific customers.

Within a few months, bank profits had risen significantly. John received a healthy raise and concluded he had made a wise choice in moving to this particular organization.

1. Explain how the steps of a promotions opportunity analysis are present in this case.

2. Explain why John and Commercial Consolidated were so successful.

3. Based on information in this case, design a business-to-business print advertisement offering local businesses "loans" or "investment services." Where should the ad be placed? Why?

4. Choose one of the credit-card customer clusters listed in the case. Design a print advertisement to reach this group. Where should the print ad be placed? What other marketing tools could be used with the print advertisement?

**Sources:** Sandy Berry and Kathryn Britney, "Market Segmentation," *Bank Management* 72, no. 1 (January–February 1996), pp. 36–40; "Study Reveals Wide Use of Value-Added Cards," *America's Community Banker* 6, no. 9 (September 1997), p. 43.

# CASE 2

## RED HOT MARKETING

Mary Wilson could not believe her company was suddenly facing a competitive threat. For years, her small retail shop, called Red and Purple Adventures, was the only store in town catering to members of the city's numerous chapters of the Red Hat Society. Now, a rival firm had opened up a competing outlet across town. Mary knew she had to work harder and smarter to keep an edge in what had always been a prosperous business.

The Red Hat Society was formed in 1998. In 1997, Sue Ellen Cooper, a resident of Fullerton, California, on vacation in Tucson, Arizona, bought a red fedora at a thrift shop. She was acquainted with a poem, called "Warning," written by Jenny Joseph. The poem is about an older woman wearing a purple dress and a bright red hat. The poem advises older women to free themselves to be silly and have fun. Bright, daring clothes are the order of the day. Sue Ellen Cooper was so enamored with the concept that she began giving red hats and copies of the poem to friends as birthday presents. Soon after, the Red Hat Society was born when the group got together for tea.

Sue Ellen Cooper's credo for the Red Hat Society states: "We believe silliness is the comedy relief of life, and since we are all in it together, we

(continued)

Come in for your
"3 Ingredient"
Cookbook!

Smell of
Spring
Potpourri
arriving
soon!

Red Hat Society
Gifts

The Lily Pad Gift Shop

1921 South Garrison, Carthage, MO (Inside All Occasions Floral and Bakery) • (417) 358-1866

An example of an advertisement directed to the members of the Red Hat Society.
*Source:* Courtesy of *The Joplin Globe,* Joplin, Missouri.

might as well join red-gloved hands and go for the gusto together. Underneath the frivolity, we share a bond of affection, forged by common life experiences and a genuine enthusiasm for wherever life takes us next."

Besides red hats, members of the Red Hat Society wear purple outfits. Those who join the Red Hat Society before the age of 50 adorn themselves with pink hats and lavender clothes. Most activities for members of the Red Hat Society are scheduled by individual chapters, with a heavy emphasis on fun-loving events.

Mary Wilson had been selling both licensed and unlicensed red and pink hats and gloves along with purple and lavender outfits to the under- and over-50 women's crowd for several years. Her quirky store included not only clothes and hats, but also jewelry and perfume. Mary always had fresh pastries available for visiting clients. She served tea to anyone who wished to stay for a while and visit. Light "oldies" music from the 1930s, 40s and 50s played in the background. Mary always believed the key to her success was a warm, friendly atmosphere that was highly compatible with the goals of the Red Hat Society.

The new competitor in town took a different approach. The company's advertisements featured low prices and specials. Mary also believed the other store had a better location in a small but busy shopping mall where parking was easier to find. She worried new Red Hat Society members would be enticed by convenience and price. Although it made Mary uncomfortable, she knew for the first time that her business had to be more than just warm and friendly. She needed a competitive marketing strategy to fight off this new threat.

1. Conduct a promotions opportunity analysis for Red and Purple Adventures.

2. Identify the market segments that Red and Purple Adventures must continue to maintain.

3. Describe the ways to reach Mary's key market segments effectively.

4. Should Mary expand her business to the Internet and sell her merchandise nationwide via e-commerce?

**Source:** Red Hat Society (www.redhatsociety.com, April 7, 2005).

# ENDNOTES

1. Christy Edison, "Thinking Out of the (Shoe) Box," *Across the Board* 36, no. 3 (March 1999), pp. 9–10; Mike Troy, "New Cards Alter Discount Convention," *Discount Store News* 37, no. 16 (August 24, 1998), p. 35; Seth Mendelson, "Card Sharks," *Discount Merchandiser* 38, no. 8 (August 1998), pp. 73–77; Mike Troy, "An Ideal Dose of Consistency," *Discount Store News* 37, no. 23 (December 14, 1998), pp. 57, 74; Joe Dysart, "Getting the Most from Your Greeting Card Department," *Drug Topics* 137, no. 14 (July 19, 1993), pp. 48–50.

2. Brian Bergstein and May Wong, "PC Firm Designs Computer Just for Teens," *Marketing News* 38 (September 15, 2004), p. 29.

3. Margaret Henderson Blair, "An Empirical Investigation of Advertising Wearin and Wearout," *Journal of Advertising Research* 40, no. 6 (November–December 2000), pp. 95–100.

4. Ibid.

5. Lionell A. Mitchell, "An Examination of Methods of Setting Advertising Budgets: Practice and Literature," *European Journal of Marketing* 27, no. 5 (1993), pp. 5–22.

6. James E. Lynch and Graham J. Hooley, "Increased Sophistication in Advertising Budget Setting," *Journal of Advertising Research* 30, no. 1 (February–March 1990), pp. 67–76.

7. James O. Peckham, "Can We Relate Advertising Dollars to Market Share Objectives?" *How Much to Spend for Advertising,* M. A. McNiver (ed). (New York: Association of National Advertisers, 1969), p. 30.

8. "Upward Bound," *Promo Magazine* (www.promomagazine.com, accessed April 2004).

9. "2004 Advertising to Sales Ratios for 200 Largest Ad Spending Industries," *Adage* (www.adage.com, accessed February 26, 2005).

10. Laurie Freeman, "B-to-B Marketing Communication Budgets Grow 14.5 Percent As Overall Spending Reaches $73 Billion," *Advertising Age's Business Marketing* 84, no. 5 (May 1999), pp. S3–S4.

11. Matthew Martinez, "Reed Study Sees Where Ad Dollars Go," *Advertising Age's Business Marketing* 82, no. 9 (October 1997), p. 46.

12. Cyndee Miller, "Study Dispels '80s Stereotypes of Women," *Marketing News* 29 (May 22, 1995), p. 3.

13. Andy Bernstein, "Study: Women Vital to Pro Sports," *Denver Business Journal* 50, no. 14 (December 4, 1998), p. 62.

14. Interview with Kerri Martin, brand manager of BMW Motorcycles, July 18, 2000.

15. Rick Adler, "Stereotypes Won't Work with Seniors Anymore," *Advertising Age* 67, no. 46 (November 11, 1996), p. 32.

16. Deborah L. Vence, "Top Niche: Growth in Asian-American Spending Fuels Targeted Marketing," *Marketing News* 38 (June 1, 2004), pp. 11–13.

17. Alf Nucifora, "Ethnic Markets Are Lands of Opportunity," *Business Journal Serving Phoenix & the Valley of the Sun* 18, no. 52 (October 16, 1998), p. 31; Steve Climons and David O'Connor, "Marketers Lose Out by Ignoring Ethnic Segments," *Advertising Age* 70, no. 10 (May 10, 1999), p. 40.

18. Rebecca Piirto Heath, "Psychographics," *Marketing Tools* (November–December 1995), pp. 74–81.

19. SRI Consulting Business Intelligence (www.sric-bi.com, accessed February 26, 2005); Dana-Nicoleta Lascu and Kenneth E. Clow, *Marketing Frontiers: Concepts and Tools* (Cincinnati, OH: Atomic Dog Publishing, 2004), p. 175.

20. "The Gen Y Budget," *American Demographics* 24, no. 7 (July–August 2002), p. S4.

21. "The Gen X Budget," *American Demographics* 24, no. 7 (July–August 2002), p. S5.

22. "The Younger Boomer Budget," *American Demographics* 24, no. 7 (July–August 2002), p. S6.

23. "The Older Boomer Budget," *American Demographics* 24, no. 7 (July–August 2002), p. S7.

24. "The Empty Nester Budget," *American Demographics* 24, no. 7 (July–August 2002), p. S8.

25. "The Senior Budget," *American Demographics* 24, no. 7 (July–August 2002), p. S10.

26. Susan Mitchell, "Birds of a Feather," *American Demographics* 17, no. 2 (February 1995), pp. 40–45.

27. Ronald L. Zallocco, "Benefit Segmentation of the Fitness Market," *Journal of Health Care Marketing* 12, no. 4 (December 1992), p. 80.

28. Susan Pechman, "Custom Clusters: Finding Your True Customer Segments," *Bank Marketing* 26, no. 7 (July 1994), pp. 33–35.

29. Gene Koprowski, "Bovine Inspiration," *Marketing Tools* (October 1996), pp. 10–11.

30. Shannon Dortch, "Going to the Movies," *American Demographics* 18, no. 12 (December 1996), pp. 4–8.

# Advertising Management

## Chapter Objectives

*Understand* the steps of an effective advertising management process.

*Study* the roles that the company's overall mission, products, and services play in advertising programs.

*Recognize* when to use an in-house advertising approach and when to employ an external advertising agency.

*Review* the steps of effective advertising campaign management programs.

*Analyze* the functions performed by the advertising account manager and the advertising creative in preparing an advertising campaign.

## MARKETING POWER

### Women Plus 40

Over half of all women buying new cars are over the age of 40. The same is true for computers. Of all women who use facial moisturizers, 60 percent are also 40 plus. These statistics fly in the face of traditional marketing wisdom suggesting that the 18- to 34-year-old female demographic is the only one that matters. Young women are strong spenders, but their buying clout is smaller than those over age 40. As Annette Simon of GSD&M Advertising in Austin, Texas, notes, "I make most of the buying decisions, as do my friends and my mom—let's talk to women like they have a brain." Simon, who is over 40, has created ads for Southwest Airlines, Wal-Mart, and Charles Schwab.

Art director Stuart Pittman from the Kaplan Thaler Group, Ltd., in New York, which is the agency that created the Herbal Essences "yes, Yes, YES!" commercials and the AFLAC duck, states, "I like to think of 40-plus as the cocktail hour of your life. Now you're up for a good time." He believes women over 40 are "energized, terrific, and self-assured. Their humor is developed and their attitudes are out there." Jeff Weekly, from D'Arcy Los Angeles, who creates ads for both NBC and Paramount, calls this group "vibrant yet powerful."

The buying potential of women over 40 extends across all ethnic groups. For example, Louis Miguel Messianu, from the Del Rivero Messianu DDB agency in Coral Gables, Florida, suggests, "Hispanic women over 40 can be viewed as 'chief operating officers' of the household." He believes this group is confident, in control, and discerning.

*MORE* magazine, which targets women over 40, recently featured a unique approach to understanding the over-40 market. Author Mary Lou Quinlan, a former ad agency CEO, noted the bias that has been a part of traditional marketing thinking. She states, "I've sat in too many casting sessions where I'd hear, 'We need one older woman to round out these models. How about so-and-so? She must be 32.' "

Quinlan and *MORE* magazine arranged for five advertising agencies to create campaigns for the 40-plus group. The point of the ad had to be to change corporate decision makers' minds about them. The advertising copy that resulted:

- ▶ "These Babies Have Boom." (The Kaplan Thaler Group, Ltd., New York)
- ▶ "Spring Chickens Have Smaller Nest Eggs." (GSD&M Advertising, Austin)
- ▶ "If you want my money, stop showing me pictures of my daughter in underwear." (Dimassimo Brand Advertising, New York)
- ▶ "At 42, I still kick butt. I just do it in a more expensive shoe." (D'Arcy, Los Angeles)
- ▶ "In my house I always have the last word . . . Yes, mi vida (yes honey)." (Del Rivero Messianu, DDB, Coral Gables)

As the baby boom generation continues to age, the 40- and even 50-plus crowd grows larger. Affluence, self-indulgence, and comfort characterize typical boomer buying habits. In the future, more advertisers, who aren't getting any younger themselves, may shift toward this group in growing numbers.[1]

Renew, Refresh, Restore, Rejuvenate, Revitalize...*Remember*

# Microdermabrasion
## Call today **623-7171**

**$35** PER TREATMENT

A simple easy way
to have a youthful, healthy,
complexion. No chemicals,
or discomfort, just a quick
treatment to look fantastic
and feel terrific.

## Call us now at **623-7171**

Two advertisements directed at 40-plus
women using middle-aged models.
*Source:* Used with permission of *The Joplin
Globe,* Joplin, Missouri.

*Source:* Courtesy of Cox Target Media.

## overview

The average person encounters more than 600 advertisements per day. As every marketing manager knows, these messages are delivered through an expanding variety of media. Television and radio have long been the staples of advertising programs. They compete with newspaper and magazine ads, billboards, signs, direct-mail campaigns, and other traditional channels. Recently, the number of ways to contact customers has grown. Ads on the Internet, clothing lines with messages printed on them, telemarketing programs, and even messages heard while someone is on hold on the telephone create numerous new ways to attract potential customers.

Today's marketers face a tremendous challenge. A company simply cannot afford to prepare ads for every possible medium. Choices must be made. The messages must be designed to give the company an advantage in a highly cluttered world, a world in which people are becoming increasingly proficient at simply tuning ads out.

To be effective, an ad first must be noticed. Next, it must be remembered. Then, the message of the advertisement should incite some kind of action, such as a purchase, a shift in brand loyalty, or at least find a place in the buyer's long-term memory.

Part 2 of this textbook describes the role advertising plays in an integrated marketing communications program. Figure 5.1 is a reminder of the overall IMC approach. The four chapters in this section detail the relationship between a company's advertising program and its overall IMC plan.

Two major topics are covered in this chapter. The first is to describe three theoretical approaches to advertising design. They are:

▶ Hierarchy of effects model

▶ Means–end theory

▶ Visual and verbal imaging

The second topic is to review, in detail, the major appeals advertisers use. Many of these approaches may seem familiar. The goal of the advertising agency is to select the appeal that has the best chance of achieving a desired outcome. From there, the actual message content is developed. Before beginning the process of creating the ad, it is important to remember the steps taken up to this point. These activities can be summarized by reviewing the items in a creative brief.

# THE CREATIVE BRIEF

Figure 6.1 summarizes the elements of the creative brief that was introduced in Chapter 5. The brief provides the background for the creative. Designing an effective advertising message begins with understanding the *objective* of the ad and the *target audience.* Then, the advertising group agrees on the *message theme*, which is the outline of the key ideas the commercial will convey. The account executive or client must provide the *support* and documentation for the advertising theme or claim. Finally, the creative must be aware of any *constraints* to be included. With these key components in mind, the creative can move forward and prepare the ad. The following section describes three theoretical approaches that may assist the creative in the design process.

# ADVERTISING THEORY

In developing an advertisement for an advertising campaign, several theoretical frameworks are useful. The first theory is the hierarchy of effects model. The second is a means-end chain. Both the hierarchy of effects model and a means–end chain can be used to develop leverage points. A **leverage point** moves the consumer from understanding a product's benefits to linking those benefits with personal values. Finally, the third theoretical perspective involves the visual and verbal images present in an advertisement.

## Hierarchy of Effects

The **hierarchy of effects model** clarifies the objectives of an advertising campaign and for each individual advertisement. The model aids the marketing team in identifying the best message strategy (see Chapter 7). The model suggests that there are six steps a consumer or a business buyer moves through when making a purchase. The steps are:

1. Awareness

2. Knowledge

3. Liking

▶ The objective
▶ The target audience
▶ The message theme
▶ The support
▶ The constraints

**FIGURE 6.1**
**Creative Brief**

4. Preference

5. Conviction

6. The actual purchase

These steps are sequential. A consumer will spend a period of time at each step before moving to the next. Thus, before a person can develop a liking for a product, he or she must first have sufficient knowledge of the product. Once the individual has the knowledge and develops liking for the product, the advertiser can try to influence the consumer to favor a particular brand or company.

The hierarchy of effects approach can help a creative understand how a consumer reaches purchase decisions; however, some of the theory's assumptions have been questioned. For one, it is possible that these six steps are not always the route taken by consumers. For instance, a person makes a purchase (such as an impulse buy) and then later develops knowledge, liking, preference, and conviction. Also, shoppers may purchase products when little or no preference is involved, because coupons, discounts, or other purchase incentives cause them to choose one brand instead of another. At other times, someone may not even remember the name of the brand purchased. This is often the case with commodity products such as sugar and flour or even clothing purchases such as socks and shirts.

Still, the major benefit of the hierarchy of effects model is that it is one method used to identify the typical steps consumers and businesses take when making purchases. To encourage brand loyalty, all six steps must be included. A consumer or business is unlikely to be loyal to a particular brand without sufficient knowledge of the brand. Purchasers must like the brand and build a strong preference for it. Next, they must cultivate strong convictions that the particular brand is superior to the other brands on the market. None of this occurs without first becoming aware of the product.

An advertisement for Curves featuring a 50 percent service fee discount for a workout program designed to help consumers lose weight.
*Source:* Courtesy of Curves.

# What if you could change your life in 30 minutes?

At Curves, we give the support you need to achieve 30-minute fitness and commonsense weight loss.

The power to
amaze yourself.®

*Over 9,000 locations worldwide.*

Join Now
**50% Off***
Service Fee

©2005 Curves International

curves.com

*Offer based on first visit enrollment, minimum 12 mo. c.d. program. Not valid with any other offer. Valid only at participating locations.

Thus, the components of the hierarchy of effects approach highlight the various responses that advertising or other marketing communications must stimulate. This is true in both consumer and business markets.

The hierarchy of effects model has many similarities with theories about attitudes and attitudinal change. Chapter 3 defined the concepts of cognitive, affective, and conative elements of attitudes. The *affective* component contains the feelings or emotions a person has about the object, topic, or idea. The *cognitive* component is the person's mental images, understanding, and interpretations of the person, object, or issue. The *conative* component is the individual's intentions, actions, or behavior. The most common sequence that takes place when an attitude forms is:

Cognitive → Affective → Conative

It is important to remember that any combination of these components is possible. Again, this suggests that the structured six-step process of the hierarchy of effects model may be more rigid than is actually the case. Keep in mind that sometimes an advertisement breaks out of the mold. In other words, an ad can be very different and highly successful because of how it captures an individual's attention. As a general guideline, however, cognitive-oriented ads work best for advertising objectives addressing brand awareness and brand

| | | |
|---|---|---|
| ▶ Comfortable life | ▶ Inner peace | ▶ Self-fulfillment |
| ▶ Equality | ▶ Mature love | ▶ Self-respect |
| ▶ Excitement | ▶ Personal accomplishment | ▶ Sense of belonging |
| ▶ Freedom | ▶ Pleasure | ▶ Social acceptance |
| ▶ Fun, exciting life | ▶ Salvation | ▶ Wisdom |
| ▶ Happiness | ▶ Security | |

**FIGURE 6.2**
**Personal Values**

knowledge. Affective-oriented ads are superior in developing liking, preference, and conviction for a product. Conative-oriented ads are best for facilitating actual product purchases or other types of buyer actions.

## Means–End Theory

A second theoretical approach a creative can use to design an advertisement is a **means–end chain.** This approach suggests that an advertisement should contain a message or *means* that leads the consumer to a desired end state. These *end* states include the personal values presented in Chapter 3 and listed again in Figure 6.2. The purpose of the means–end chain is to start a process in which viewing the ad leads the consumer to believe that using the product will help him or her reach one of these personal values.

Means–end theory is the basis of a model called the **Means–End Conceptualization of Components for Advertising Strategy (MECCAS).**[2] The MECCAS model suggests using five elements in creating ads:

▶ The product's attributes
▶ Consumer benefits
▶ Leverage points
▶ Personal values
▶ The executional framework

The MECCAS approach moves consumers through the five elements. The attributes of the product are linked to the specific benefits consumers can derive. These benefits, in turn, lead to the attainment of a personal value.

To illustrate the MECCAS method, consider Figure 6.3 and the milk advertisement shown. The product attribute calcium is linked to the benefits of being strong and healthy. The personal value the consumer obtains from healthy bones is feeling wise for using the product. The leverage point in the advertisement is the link between the benefit of health and the personal value of feeling wise. The white mustache and the text in the advertisement are designed to help the viewer remember that drinking milk is healthy. In this case, the specific issue is preventing osteoporosis in women.

The MECCAS approach can also be applied to business-to-business advertisements. As discussed in

A Got Milk? advertisement illustrating the use of a means–end chain.
*Source:* Courtesy of Bozell Worldwide, Inc.

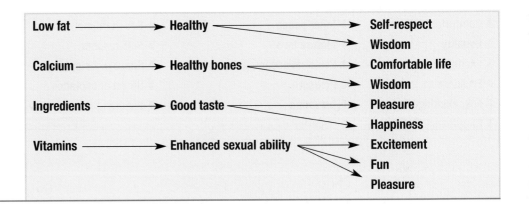

**FIGURE 6.3**
**Means–End Chain for Milk**

Chapter 3, members of the buying center can be influenced by personal values, organizational values, and corporate goals. Consider the advertisement for Greenfield Online on the next page and the means–end chain in Figure 6.4. Each attribute is presented in terms of the benefits business customers can obtain. Although not explicitly stated, the personal values of members of the buying center choosing Greenfield Online might include job security for making good decisions, self-fulfillment, wisdom, and social acceptance by other members of the buying group.

## Leverage Points

Both the hierarchy of effects model and the means–end chain approach are associated with leverage points. Remember that a leverage point is designed to move the consumer from understanding a product's benefits to linking those benefits with personal values. To construct a quality leverage point, the creative builds the pathway that connects a product benefit with the potential buyer's value system.

In terms of the hierarchy of effects model, the initial level of awareness begins the process of exposing consumers to product benefits. As the viewer moves through the six stages, he or she eventually develops the conviction to buy the product. At that point, the benefit has indeed been linked with a personal value. In the milk advertisement used to illustrate the means–end chain, the leverage point is the phrase "There's one person I won't be," which is tied with the copy message "a woman with osteoporosis." The copy goes on to explain that because of calcium (a product attribute), women can have healthy bones (product benefit). Making a conscious decision to use milk to prevent osteoporosis demonstrates the personal values of wisdom and seeking a healthy lifestyle.

In the Greenfield Online business-to-business advertisement, the leverage point is the picture of an old-fashioned woman using an old telephone sandwiched between the headline "Are you still buying marketing research done the old-fashioned way?" and the first sentence of the copy explaining that companies can "Do it better on the Internet." The picture creates an excellent mental image of marketing research done the old-fashioned way and the opportunities Greenfield Online can provide.

The means–end chain and MECCAS approaches begin with the product's attributes and the benefits to the consumer. The leverage point is the message in the ad that links these attributes and benefits with consumer values. In the ad itself, the executional framework is the plot or scenario used to convey the message designed to complete the linkage.

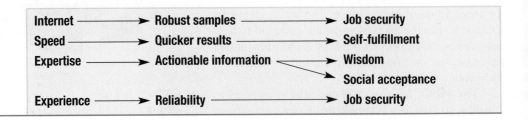

**FIGURE 6.4**
**B-to-B Means–End Chain**
**for Greenfield Online**

A Greenfield Online business advertisement illustrating the use of a means–end chain in a business ad.
*Source:* Courtesy of Greenfield Online Inc.

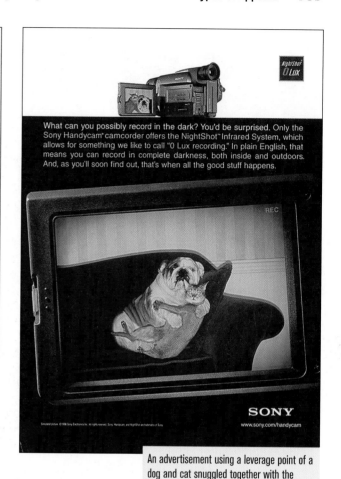

An advertisement using a leverage point of a dog and cat snuggled together with the opening sentence "What can you possibly record in the dark?"
*Source:* Courtesy of Sony Electronics Inc.

Chapter 7 presents executional frameworks in detail, in which dramatizations and other methods of telling the ad story help build successful leverage points.

An effective leverage point can also be associated with an attitudinal change, especially when the sequence is cognitive → affective → conative. As the attitude is formed, the individual first understands, then is moved emotionally, and then takes action. A leverage point can help the viewer of an ad move through these three stages, thereby tying cognitive knowledge of the product to more emotional and personal values.

Creatives spend considerable amounts of time designing ads with powerful leverage points. Executional frameworks and various types of appeals, as described in the upcoming pages, are the tools creatives use to help consumers make the transition from being aware of a product's benefits to incorporating them with personal value systems.

## Verbal and Visual Images

A third theoretical approach to advertising design contains the decision the creative makes about the degree of emphasis given to the visual part of the ad versus the verbal element. Most major forms of advertising have both visual and verbal elements, with the obvious exception of radio. A visually-biased ad places the greatest emphasis on the picture or visual element of the ad.

Visual images often lead to more favorable attitudes toward both the advertisement and the brand. Visuals also tend to be more easily remembered than verbal copy. Visual elements are stored in the brain as both pictures and words. This dual-coding

This ASICS ad blends visual imagery with the verbal copy.

*Source:* Courtesy of ASICS Tiger Corporation.

process makes it easier for people to recall the message. Further, visual images are usually stored in both the left and right sides of the brain; verbal messages tend be stored in the left side of the brain only.

Visual images can range from concrete and realistic to highly abstract. A concrete visual is one in which the subject is easily recognizable as a person, place, or thing. In an abstract picture or image, the subject is more difficult to recognize. Concrete pictures have a higher level of recall than do abstract images because of the dual-coding process whereby the image is stored in the brain as both a visual and a verbal representation. For example, viewers process an ad with a picture of spaghetti used in promoting a restaurant as both a picture and a verbal representation. Ads with concrete images lead to more favorable attitudes than ads with no pictures or abstract pictures. Research offers many reasons for creatives to include visual images in advertisements.[3]

Radio does not have a visual component. As a result, radio advertisers often try to create visual images for the audience. Pepsi produced an ad in which listeners hear a can being opened, the soft drink being poured, and the sizzle of the carbonation—an excellent example of creating a visual image. If consumers can see the image in their minds, the effect is greater than actual visual portrayal. An actual visual event requires less brain activity than using one's imagination to develop the image. The secret is getting the person to think beyond the ad and picture the scene being simulated.

Visual imagery is especially important in international marketing. Global advertising agencies try to create what is called **visual esperanto**, a universal language that makes global advertising possible for any good or service. Visual esperanto advertising recognizes that visual images are more powerful than verbal descriptions. Visual images are more likely to transcend cultural differences.[4] To illustrate the power of a visual image compared to a verbal account, think of the word *exotic*. To some, exotic means a white beach in Hawaii with young people in sexy swimsuits. To others, it may be a small cabin in the snow-capped mountains of Switzerland. To others still, exotic may be a close-up of a tribal village in Africa. The verbal word can vary in meaning. At the same time, a picture of a couple holding hands in front of Niagara Falls has practically the same meaning across all cultures. A young child smiling after eating a piece of candy also conveys an almost universal message.

Finding the appropriate image is the most important task in creating visual esperanto. The creative looks for an image that conveys the intended meaning or message. The goal is to create a brand identity through visuals rather than words. Then the creative uses words to support the visual image. For example, the creative may decide that a boy and his father at a sports event illustrate the priceless treasure of a shared family moment. In Mexico, the setting could be a soccer match instead of a baseball game in the United States. The specific copy (the words) can then be adapted to the country involved. The difficult part of obtaining visual esperanto is choosing an image that transcends cultures. Once a universal image is found, creatives in each of the countries represented can take the visual image and modify it to appeal to the local target audience.

In the past, creatives designing business-to-business advertisements relied heavily on the verbal element rather than on visuals. The basis of this approach was the idea that business decisions are made in a rational, cognitive manner. In recent years, more business ads have incorporated strong visual elements to heighten the emotional aspects of making a purchase.

In summary, all of the theoretical models presented in this section provide useful ideas for the advertising creative. Each one suggests that some kind of sequence must be followed as the ad is prepared. The endpoint of the ad should be a situation in which the viewer is enticed to remember the product, to think favorably about it, and to look for that product when making a purchase decision. Various kinds of advertising messages, or appeals, can be utilized to reach such key advertising objectives.

# TYPES OF ADVERTISING APPEALS

Throughout the years, advertisers have employed a wide variety of advertising approaches. Seven major types of **advertising appeals** have been the most successful. Advertisers usually select from one of these types of appeals as they develop the advertisement:

- Fear
- Humor
- Sex
- Music
- Rationality
- Emotions
- Scarcity

The particular appeal to use should be based on a review of the creative brief, the objective of the advertisement, and the means–end chain to be conveyed. The actual choice depends on a number of factors, including the product being sold, the personal preferences of the advertising creative and the account executive, as well as the wishes of the client. In determining the best appeal to use, it is often a question of which type of appeal is most inappropriate. Advertising experts know that certain appeals are less effective at various times. For example, research indicates that sex appeals tend not to be as effective for goods and services that are not related to sex.

This section provides descriptions of the types of advertising appeals that are available. Each has been successfully used in some ads and has failed in others. The key responsibility of the marketer is to make sure, to whatever degree is possible, that the appeal is the right choice for the brand and the target audience.

## Fear

Advertisers use fear to sell a variety of products. Life insurance companies focus on the consequences of not having life insurance if a person dies. Shampoo and mouthwash ads invoke fears of dandruff and bad breath. These problems can make a person a social outcast. Fear is used more often than most casual observers realize.

Simply stated, advertisers use fear appeals because they work. Fear increases both the viewer's interest in an advertisement and the persuasiveness of the ad. Many individuals remember advertisements with fear appeals better than they do warm, upbeat messages.[5] Consumers who pay more attention to an advertisement are more likely to process the information it presents. This information processing makes it possible to accomplish the ad's main objective.

A theoretical explanation regarding the way fear works is the *behavioral response model* (see Figure 6.5).[6] As shown, various incidents can lead to negative or positive consequences, which then affect future behaviors. For an example, see the Communication Action box called "Smoking and Fear: Which Wins Out?"

In developing fear advertisements, the idea is to include as many aspects of the behavioral response model as possible. A business-to-business advertiser offering Internet services tries to focus on the **severity** of downtime if a company's Internet server goes down. Another ad describes the firm's **vulnerability** by showing the high

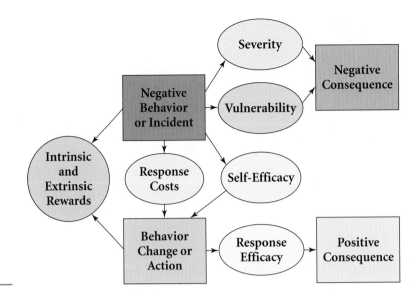

**FIGURE 6.5**
**Behavioral Response Model**

probability that a company's server is going to crash. The Service Metrics advertisement on this page features a picture of a blindfolded man ready to step into a manhole to illustrate the danger of e-business pitfalls. The goal of the advertisement is to make business leaders realize their companies are more vulnerable than they think. Service Metrics can help them identify these potential problems before they turn into disasters.

When using fear, one issue is the strength of the appeal. Most advertisers believe a moderate level of fear is the most effective. A low level of fear may not be noticed, and the fear level may not be convincing in terms of severity or vulnerability. On the other hand, an advertisement with too high of a fear level can backfire, because the message is so strong that it causes feelings of anxiety. This leads the viewer to avoid watching the ad, by changing the channel or muting the sound.[7] The goal of a fear ad is to be powerful enough to get a viewer's attention and to influence his or her thinking, but not so scary that the person avoids seeing the advertisement.

Fear ads match well with certain types of goods and services, especially products that eliminate problems or threats to a consumer's sense of personal security. Account executives, creatives, and company leaders must decide if fear is a good choice or if some other type of appeal offers greater promise.

## Humor

Clutter is a significant problem in every advertising medium. Capturing a viewer's attention is difficult. Even after an advertiser has garnered the audiences' attention, keeping that attention is even more challenging. Humor has proven to be one of the best techniques for cutting through clutter. Humor can be effective at both getting

A business-to-business advertisement using a fear appeal to promote.
*Source:* Courtesy of Service Metrics.

What you **can't see** about your e-business **performance** can hurt.

HOW'S your site?

Let Service Metrics™ remove the blindfold. We measure Web site performance from your customer's perspective, revealing potential problems before they become e-business pitfalls. With Service Metrics, you can see exactly where you stand. We don't just help you compete, we give you an unfair advantage.

**SERVICE METRICS**
an Exodus Communications Company

*The Best Measure of Performance™*
www.servicemetrics.com

# COMMUNICATION ACTION

## Smoking and Fear: Which Wins Out?

The American Cancer Society has attempted to develop more effective antismoking advertisements for many years. The behavioral response model (Figure 6.5) can be a useful guide in developing such ads. The negative behavior addressed is smoking. The goal becomes to portray negative consequences associated with smoking, such as heart problems, lung cancer, or throat cancer. The severity is the degree of possible physical or psychological harm. The severity is quite high. Lung cancer often results in death. The vulnerability is the probability that the consequence will occur. Unfortunately, the American Cancer Society knows that many people continue smoking because they do not see themselves as being highly vulnerable.

One side of the behavioral response model includes the intrinsic and extrinsic rewards associated with various activities. Extrinsic rewards are those given by other people. Young people often begin smoking because of the social rewards they obtain, such as social acceptance by peers. Intrinsic rewards are internally generated (the ones you give yourself). Teenagers gain an intrinsic psychological reward from smoking when it makes them feel like they are adults.

The fight to curb tobacco usage among teenagers is extremely difficult because of these intrinsic and extrinsic rewards. Recent antismoking ads attempted to tackle the problem by changing the nature of extrinsic rewards. These ads show teenagers who smoke as being undesirable to those of the opposite sex. The idea is that a teenager who believes his or her peers will not accept the smoking behavior is more inclined to quit or never start.

In general, smokers engage in the negative behavior because of the intrinsic and extrinsic rewards they receive and because they either minimize the severity of the consequences or do not see themselves as being vulnerable. To change their behavior requires three things. First is the response cost. In other words, what would it cost to quit smoking? Teenagers can be influenced through fear of losing social acceptance. Adults may worry that if they quit smoking, they will gain weight or become nervous and irritable. These fears must be overcome for a campaign to succeed.

Another element of the behavioral response model is self-efficacy, or a person's ability to change a behavior. Many smokers do not believe they can quit, even when they want to. In a similar fashion, some people who want to lose weight often do not even try because they feel they do not have enough willpower to stick with a diet. To convince a person to quit smoking is to build up enough self-efficacy to make it seem possible. Many recent antismoking ads use phrases such as "The power to quit!" to build self-efficacy in the target audience.

Another behavioral response model ingredient is response efficacy. This is the belief that the change in behavior will result in the positive consequence that is being espoused. If a person does not believe that quitting smoking results in better health or a happier life, then there is little incentive to change behaviors.

For both teenagers and adults, antismoking ads must tackle the combined problems of peer pressure, low self-efficacy, and the physical addiction to the product. Therefore, one clear goal should be to use models such as the behavioral response approach to convince young people never to start.

attention and keeping it. Consumers, as a whole, enjoy advertisements that make them laugh. Something that is funny has intrusive value and grabs attention.

Humor is used in about 24 percent of prime time television advertisements and 35 percent of radio ads. Humorous ads often win awards and tend to be favorites among judges at the International Advertising Film Festival at Cannes as well as for other types of advertising awards. At a recent Clio Awards ceremony for radio ads, 62 percent of the winners used some type of humor.[8] In *USA Today*'s consumer survey of the most likeable advertising campaigns for the year, three of the top four used humor.[9]

**Brand manager eliminates pilot costs, becomes hero**

Testing new package designs online with rotating 3-D images not only saved the client expensive tooling costs but also saved time. Now manufacturers can design today and test tomorrow. Eliminating pilot costs and shortening "time to market" are just some of the many ways that Greenfield Online quantitative research beats the old-fashioned kind.

Put our expert consultants and advanced technology to work for you.

www.greenfield.com

888.291.9997

*Greenfield Online*
Leading the Research Revolution®

• Quantitative Studies
• Qualitative Studies
• Media Research
• Self-Directed Research
• Syndicated Studies
• Website Evaluations

A Greenfield Online ad using a humor appeal.
*Source:* Greenfield Online. Used with permission.

A humorous ad by Boeri directed to skiers and snowboarders about the need to wear helmets.
*Source:* Courtesy of Craig Orsini.

Remember to ski and snowboard responsibly. www.boeriusa.com

**boeri**
it's your head

The success of humor as an advertising appeal is based on three things. Humor causes consumers to: (1) watch, (2) laugh, and, most importantly, (3) remember. In recall tests, consumers most often remember humorous ads. To be successful, the humor should be connected directly to the product's benefits. It should tie together the product features, the advantage to customers, and the personal values of the means–end chain.

Humorous ads pique viewer interest. This makes it is easier to gain more careful consumer consideration to the message in the ad. A funny ad capture's the viewer's attention, which leads to improved comprehension and recall of the advertising message and tagline. Advertising research indicates that humor elevates people's moods. Happy consumers associate a good mood with the advertiser's products. Humor helps fix the company in the consumer's cognitive structure with links to positive feelings.[10]

Although humor captures the viewer's attention, cuts through ad clutter, and enhances recall, unfortunately, humorous ads can also go wrong. Advertisers must be careful to avoid letting the humor overpower the advertisement. When humor fails, it is usually because the joke in the ad is remembered but the product or brand is not. In other words, the ad is so funny that the audience forgets or does not catch the sponsor's name. Although funny ads often win awards, they can fail in terms of accomplishing advertising objectives. To avoid this problem, the humor used in the ad should focus on a component of the means–end chain. The humor should relate either to a product's attributes, a customer benefit, or the personal value obtained from the product. The most effective ads are those in which the humor incorporates all three elements.

Sarcasm and jokes made at someone's expense are often popular with younger audiences, but are not well received by baby boom and older generations, especially among the more affluent. For example, an advertisement by Miller Lite featuring an elderly couple passionately necking on a sofa was designed to be funny to the young, male beer-drinking audience. Unfortunately, the ad offended some older consumers. With age and maturity comes empathy. Put-downs and cruel jokes are not seen as funny by older people. Understanding these different nuances helps advertisers keep from making mistakes in the use of humor.[11]

There is some evidence that suggests that humor is universal; however, other research indicates that particular executions of humor may not be. Humor is often based in one's culture. It is sometimes difficult to transfer what is funny in one culture to another culture. Not all audiences will see a humorous ad in the same way. It is important for advertisers to pretest an advertisement before it is launched in another country to ensure it will be liked and, more importantly, that it will be seen as funny and not offensive.[12]

| Good or Service | Hints |
|---|---|
| ▶ Beer | ▶ Miller Lite, Keystone, Budweiser, Heineken |
| ▶ Restaurants | ▶ Wendy's, Shoney's, Long John Silver's |
| ▶ NBA | ▶ It's Fantastic! |
| ▶ Telephone | ▶ U.S. Cellular |
| ▶ Motels | ▶ Holiday Inn, Red Roof Inn |
| Can you remember a funny advertisement for each product or service? | |

**FIGURE 6.6**
**Humorous Ads Quiz**

Humor is being used more frequently in various countries. A humorous ad developed for McDonald's in Singapore had the highest recall rate (90 percent) of all other ads shown in the month it was released. In Germany, Ford deviated from traditional ads that concentrated on promoting product quality and value to a humorous ad approach. The humorous ad shows a pigeon sitting on tree branch with a Ford Ka parked nearby. The bird swoops down to bomb the car, but at the last minute the car hood springs up and knocks the bird out. The advertisement was first shown on Ford's U.K. Web site. Word about the ad quickly spread until more than 1 million people had visited the Web site to see the ad. German dealers requested the ad so they could show it on television. The feedback and popularity of the ad in the United Kingdom caused Ford's marketing bosses to agree to run the ad in Germany. The ad resonated with young, affluent buyers, which Ford had been trying to reach. The new ad was seen as witty, gutsy, and edgy, which worked well with Ford's theme of projecting the Ka as a stylish car.[13]

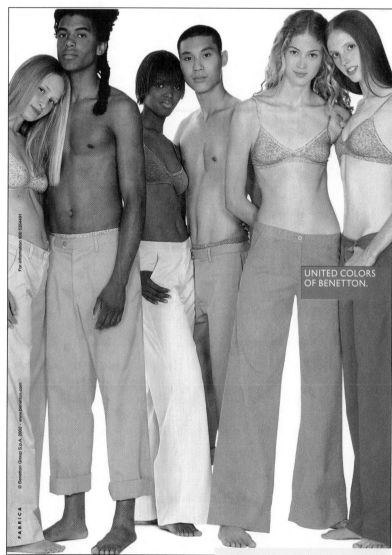

Humorous ads are difficult to design. One cynic once noted that there are only 12 funny people in the United States. Humor that doesn't work often creates a negative image for the company. Consequently, account executives must be certain that the creatives they hire are truly among those who can write and execute funny and effective ads (see Figure 6.6).

## Sex

Sexual appeals are often used as a means to break through clutter. Advertisements in the United States and other countries throughout the world contain more visual sexual themes than they have in the past. Nudity and other sexual approaches are common. Sex, however, no longer sells the way it used to. It no longer has shock value. Today's teens are growing up in societies immersed in sex. Seeing another sexually oriented ad gets very little attention. Using raw sex to sell a product has nearly reached a saturation point. Currently, many advertisers are shifting to more subtle sexual cues, suggestions, and innuendos. For instance, several recent television ads for jewelry depict a woman wearing a nightgown in the bedroom, looking very passionate and aroused. Then, a ring and the price of the ring are shown with the company's name. Viewers are left to their own imagination as to what occurred.[14]

An advertisement by Benetton using partial nudity.
*Source:* © 2002 Benetton Group SpA, Ph. James Mollison.

Bo Derek is wearing Bijan Eau de Parfum and nothing else!!

A Bijan perfume advertisement featuring a sexual theme.
**Source:** Courtesy of Bijan Fragrances, Inc.

Sexuality has been employed in advertising in five ways, including:

▶ Subliminal techniques

▶ Nudity or partial nudity

▶ Overt sexuality

▶ Sexual suggestiveness

▶ Sensuality

*Subliminal approaches* place sexual cues or icons in advertisements in the attempt to affect a viewer's subconscious mind. In an odd paradox, truly subliminal cues are not strong enough to be noticed or create any effects. Consumers pay little attention to ads already. A subliminal message that registers only in the subconscious mind is not going to be effective. If it did, there would not be the need for such strong sexual content in advertising.

*Nudity or partial nudity* is still used to sell products that have sexual connotations, such as clothing, perfume, and cologne. Some ads are designed to solicit a sexual response. Others are not. For example, starting in 1987, underwear companies could use live models in television ads. The first commercials were modest and informational, emphasizing the design or materials used in the undergarment. The first Playtex bra commercials using live models drew strong criticism from organizations such as the American Family Association. Now, advertisements for underwear go much further. Ads do much more than show models wearing undergarments. In a recent issue of *Interview* magazine, the underwear model Raina is reclining on a couch, her back arched and pinkie finger tucked below her panty line. Victoria's Secret has launched a number of ads featuring girls in underwear in provocative poses, both on television and on billboards.[15]

Using *overt sexuality* in ads for products that are sexually oriented is normally accepted, but it often becomes controversial when used for other types of products. When Procter & Gamble launched a television advertising campaign for

Dentyne, eyebrows were raised. The ad shows two teens in a living room. The girl pops a piece of Dentyne Fire bubble gum into her mouth and then rips off her blouse and jumps on her boyfriend. At first the parents stare in shock. Then, the mom tries a piece of Dentyne Fire and promptly jumps on the dad. The controversy centered on whether the ad promoted teenage sexuality by suggesting that parents should openly display sexual feelings and desires.[16]

Today, many ads use a *sexually suggestive* approach. The Bijan ad shown on the previous page features Bo Derek. The ad states, "Bo Derek is wearing Bijan Eau de Parfum and nothing else," which is a sexually suggestive message. In a similar manner, the Clairol Herbal Essence Shampoo ads borrowed the "yes, Yes, YES!" scene from the movie *When Harry Met Sally* to make the product seem more sensuous by suggesting sexual activity.

A recent trend in sexual suggestiveness is to use gay and lesbian themes. Swedish retailer IKEA was the first in the United States to use a gay theme. A television commercial showing two gay men shopping for a dining room table together first appeared in 1994. Now, a number of companies use homosexuality in advertising. New York City–based Daily Soup restaurant ran an advertisement that featured a woman meeting a blind date at a park. She sits next to an attractive man who she thinks may be her date, but instead he is met by a biker guy who gives him a kiss. Levi Strauss, in an effort to reach younger con-

Forever on the lips, never on the hips.

Exceptionally great taste – with 75% less carbs, calories and sugar. Introducing Old Orchard LoCarb juice cocktails – nine delicious blends sweetened with Splenda® no-calorie sweetener – the perfect juice for a low-carb, low-sugar lifestyle.
www.oldorchardjuice.com  OLD ORCHARD  We make apple interesting.™

An advertisement by Old Orchard using a sensuality sex appeal.
*Source:* Courtesy of Old Orchard Brands, LLC.

sumers, introduced a campaign featuring interviews with real teenagers. In one ad, a young man admits to being gay while explaining that his neighbors didn't like him. Many other ads hint at gay themes.[17]

Sexual appeals can also be based on *sensuality*. Many women respond more favorably to a sensual suggestion than an overtly sexual approach. An alluring glance across a crowded room can be sensual and draw attention to a product. Many view sensuality as a more sophisticated approach because it relies on the imagination. Images of romance and love can be more enticing than raw sexuality.

## Are Sex Appeals Effective?

There have been numerous studies of sexual appeals and nudity. Almost all of them conclude that sex and nudity do increase attention, regardless of the gender of the individual in the advertisement or the gender of the audience. Normally, the attention is greater for opposite-sex situations than same-sex situations. That is, a male viewing a female in a sexually provocative advertisement pays more attention than a male viewing another male in a sexually provocative ad. The same is true for females. To encourage both males and females to pay attention to its ads, Guess often uses both a male and female in a sexually provocative manner in a single advertisement.

Although sexually oriented ads attract attention, brand recall for ads using a sex appeal is lower than ads using some other type of appeal. Thus, it appears that although people watch the advertisement, the sexual theme distracts them from paying attention to the brand name.[18]

Sexually oriented advertisements are often rated as being more interesting. Those ads deemed to be highly controversial in terms of their sexual content were rated as more interesting by both males and females. The paradox, however, is that although the controversial

A Guess advertisement featuring both a male and a female model using a sexual appeal.
*Source:* Courtesy of Guess?, Inc.

ads are more interesting, they fail to increase the transmission of information. Respondents could not remember any more about the message of the ad than could individuals who viewed the same ad but without a controversial sexual theme.[19]

Advertisements using overt sexual stimuli or containing nudity produce higher levels of physiological arousal responses. These arousal responses have been linked to the formation of both affective and cognitive responses. If the viewer is male and the sexual stimulus is female, such as a naked female in an ad for cologne, then the viewer tends to develop a strong feeling toward the ad based on the arousal response his body experiences. Female viewers of male nudity in an ad often experience the same type of response, although the arousal response tends not to be as strong.

The cognitive impression made on viewers of a sexually oriented ad depends on whether the viewer feels the advertisement is pleasant or offensive. If a viewer likes the ad, then a positive impression of the brand will result. If, on the other hand, the viewer thinks the ad is in poor taste, then negative feelings and beliefs about the brand may result. In an effort to gain attention, DaimlerChrysler has recently launched several bolder ads that have progressed from sexual suggestiveness to an R-rated spot. The first sexually oriented ad by DaimlerChrysler in this series was of a young girl learning that her sister had been conceived in the back seat of a Chrysler Concorde. The next ad had a dialogue in a minivan that suggested wife swapping. Later an R-rated spot was created for Dodge Durango featuring two men standing at urinals making comments such as "Man, that's big" and "My girlfriend loves it." Because of the R-rating of the ad, it was shown only on late night television and in theaters on R-rated movies. Dodge's marketing officials expected 11 million moviegoers to see the ad. If it works, the ad should increase sales. If it does not, the ad may create strong negative feelings toward the company.[20]

A common sexual appeal in advertising is to use decorative models. **Decorative models** are individuals in an advertisement whose primary purpose is to adorn the product as a sexual or attractive stimulus. The model serves no functional purpose in the ad except to attract attention. Automobiles, tools, and beer commercials in the past often used female models dressed in bikinis to stand by their products. Figure 6.7 covers the basic conclusions of studies looking at the impact of decorative models.[21]

In determining the level of sex appeal to use in an advertisement, it is important to consider society's view and level of acceptance.[22] Just as economies go through cycles, attitudes toward sex in advertising experience acceptance swings. The use and acceptance of sexual themes in advertising had swung to a high level of tolerance in the early part of the 2000s, until the Super Bowl of 2004. The public reaction to Janet Jackson's breast-baring halftime show sent ripples all the way to Madison Avenue. Shortly afterward, Victoria's Secret dropped its TV lingerie fashion show. Abercrombie & Fitch killed the company's quarterly catalog, which had been strongly criticized for featuring models in sexually suggestive poses. Anheuser-Busch dropped some more risqué ads.[23] The pendulum was still swinging in the opposite direction a year later when ads for Super Bowl 2005 were unveiled. Fewer ads used sexual appeals. Those that featured sex were much tamer. The only controversial ad was by GoDaddy.com. Only one of the two ads for GoDaddy.com was shown; the other was rejected by the network because of its highly sexual content. The network feared upsetting the Super Bowl audience.

Many researchers, both in academia and in industry, believe society is becoming more conservative and that youth are returning to more traditional values. Recent research suggests that many teens are offended by the widespread use of sexually provocative advertising and are often embarrassed by sexual innuendos in advertising. Many teens are tired of being bombarded by sexual themes from television, movies, and advertising. As one study concluded, "Sexually explicit advertising has lost its potency. Young people of today are more interested in traditional family values and wholesome ad messages than the flash of a nipple to sell shampoo or the promise of limitless sex if your engine is big enough."[24]

On the other hand, in an experimental study by Reactorz Research of clothing ads, teens had a stronger, more favorable opinion of brands featuring sexually oriented messages. A 17-year-old male, upon seeing a non–sexually oriented clothing ad, complained that the ad was ". . . too boring. If I saw it somewhere, it wouldn't stick in my mind. A good ad is either funny, sexy, or provocative. This is neither. The models aren't even sexy—what is this, a Wal-Mart ad?"[25]

It is clear that the use of sex in advertising will continue. Advertisers must carefully determine the level and the type of sexuality to use. They must know society is on the pendulum of acceptance and, more importantly, where their target audience is. What will work at one particular point in time may not work at another.

An advertisement in a woman's magazine using a partially nude male model to sell Stetson cologne.
*Source:* Courtesy of J. B. Stetson Company.

## Sex Appeals in International Advertising

What is deemed appropriate in terms of sexual appeal varies across countries. Something that is acceptable in one country may not be in another. In Chile, a campaign

> ▶ The presence of female (or male) decorative models improves ad recognition, but not brand recognition.
>
> ▶ The presence of a decorative model influences emotional and objective evaluations of the product among both male and female audiences.
>
> ▶ Attractive models produce a higher level of attention to ads than do less attractive models.
>
> ▶ The presence of an attractive model produces higher purchase intentions when the product is sexually relevant than if it is not sexually relevant.

**FIGURE 6.7**
**Factors to Consider Before Using Decorative Models**

In selling swim and active wear products on the Internet, Jantzen is utilizing a sexual appeal.

*Source:* © 2001 Jantzen, Inc., A VF Company.

featuring nude celebrities touting the benefits of drinking milk was recently launched. The ads' producers stated, "Chile is a country of stuffed shirts, so this campaign is going to shake them up, and at a relatively low cost, thanks to nudity." The Chilean dairy federation believed the idea of rebellion rather than nudity is an easy sell to Chilean youth. As more Chilean kids travel and see a world filled with teens wearing green and blue hair and body piercings, public nudity will become associated with freedom. Despite opposition by conservatives, the new "naked" milk campaign aroused the attention of Chilean young people and milk sales grew.[26]

Religions, cultures, and value systems determine the levels of nudity, sexual references, and gender-specific issues that are permitted in a country. Moslem nations tend to reject any kind of nudity and any reference to sexuality and other gender-related issues. They also do not permit any type of advertising for personal goods, such as female hygiene products, contraceptives, and undergarments. Any hint of sexuality or display of the female body is strictly forbidden.

Moslem countries are not the only ones with restrictive advertising for sex appeals. Many Christian countries such as Ireland, Spain, South Africa, Mexico, and the Philippines have similar standards. In Malaysia, if a man and woman are shown in the same room alone together for more than 3 seconds, it implies they had intercourse.

In other countries, standards on sexually-oriented advertising are quite liberal but sometimes confusing. In France, sex is everywhere. Advertisers can feature seminude or completely nude models in advertisements if they can be justified. There must be a relationship between the product and the nude model. It does not take much of a justification in France, where sex is viewed as healthy, innocent, and natural. One difference in France, however, is that sex and humor are not mixed. The French do not see sex as silly or funny.[27]

In many Middle Eastern countries, sex and gender issues are taboo subjects. Sexual appeals are not used in advertising and even sexually related products are difficult to advertise. In Egypt, Procter & Gamble hosted a call-in TV show directed toward young girls. The show's panel contained health experts, and topics ranged from marriage to menopause. The call-in show was followed up with a TV talk show (called *Frankly Speaking*) about feminine hygiene. The goal of the show was to tackle some of the more sensitive issues facing young Egyptian girls. Although the show discussed what happens during puberty, it was P&G's policy not to discuss sexuality. P&G sponsored the show and the primary product advertised, P&G's feminine sanitary pads, Always.[28]

## Disadvantages of Sex Appeals

Everyone has heard that "sex sells." Although this may be true, it is a less powerful force today. Seeing another naked person in an advertisement is much less likely to cause a viewer to pay more attention.

One major criticism of sexually based advertising is that it perpetuates dissatisfaction with one's body. Females in print advertisements and models in television advertising are often thin. The key to success seems to be the thinner the better. As advertising models have gotten thinner, body dissatisfaction and eating disorders among women have risen. Research indicates that women feel unhappy about their own bodies and believe they are too fat after viewing advertisements showing thin models. What is interesting is that these same ads have an impact on men, but the reverse. Men feel they are not muscular enough and are too thin or too fat. It does not make any difference if the male is viewing a male model or a female model in advertisements.[29]

In response, some firms have begun using "regular person" models in ads. Wal-Mart and Kmart have employees pose in clothing to be sold and with other products. This approach has met with many positive results, which means other companies may need to rethink their positions on body image advertising.

Bijan employed an extreme approach in one series of advertisements. Instead of either a superthin model or a regular person, Bijan's advertisement featured a nude overweight female. Several magazine editors refused to carry the advertisement at first but then changed their minds. Of the more than 1,000 e-mails received by Cynthia Miller, the creative who designed the ads for Bijan, only a few were negative. The vast majority were very supportive of the move to think outside of the typical female model stereotype.

The problem with the stereotyping of females in ads takes a different twist in other countries. For example, in Saudi Arabia and Malaysia, women must be shown in family settings. They cannot be depicted as being carefree or desirable to the opposite sex. In Canada, France, and Sweden, sexism should be avoided in any advertising directed toward children. Advertisers refrain from associating toys with a particular gender, such as dolls for girls or soldier figures for boys.[30]

In general, the use of sex to make products more appealing is a legitimate tactic for many companies, products, and advertising firms. The goal should be to use sex in a manner that is interesting, germane to the product, and within the ethical standards of the region. From there, taste and other more personalized standards serve as guides. The U.S. milk industry advertisement shown above has been very effective. Although the model is dressed in a swimsuit, it is germane to the product. It is a very effective way to persuade women that milk not only is good for healthy bones but also enhances one's appearance. By telling women that bones continue to develop until the age of 35, the ad reinforces the reasons to consume milk.

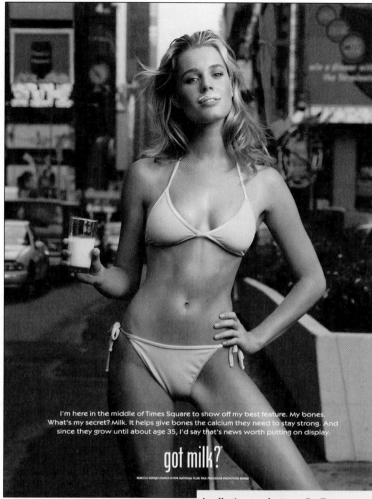

I'm here in the middle of Times Square to show off my best feature. My bones. What's my secret? Milk. It helps give bones the calcium they need to stay strong. And since they grow until about age 35, I'd say that's news worth putting on display.

**got milk?**

REBECCA ROMIJN-STAMOS ©1998 NATIONAL FLUID MILK PROCESSOR PROMOTION BOARD

An effective use of sex to sell milk.
*Source:* Courtesy of Bozell Worldwide, Inc.

## Musical Appeals

Music is an extremely important advertising ingredient. Music helps capture the listener's attention. It is easily linked to emotions, memories, and other experiences. Music can be intrusive, which means it will gain the attention of someone who previously was not listening to or watching a program. Music can be the stimulus that ties a particular musical arrangement, jingle, or song to a certain product or company. As soon as the tune begins, consumers know what product is being advertised because they have been conditioned to tie the product to the music. For example, the song "Like a Rock" is often quickly linked to Chevrolet's trucks for many people, and the Intel "tune" is readily noticed by computer buffs.

Music gains attention and increases the retention of information as it becomes strongly intertwined with the product. For example, think of the McDonald's jingle, "For a good time, and a great place, try McDonald's." Most remember the song along with images of the Golden Arches or Ronald McDonald. Even when consumers do not recall the ad message argument, music can lead to a better recall of the visual and emotional aspects of an ad. Music can also increase the persuasiveness of an argument. Subjects asked to compare ads with music to identical ads without music almost always rated those with music higher in terms of persuasiveness.[31]

**See if you can think of the tune that matches each of the following taglines:**

▶ Like a good neighbor, State Farm is there.

▶ Feel like a woman (Revlon).

▶ Come see the softer side of Sears.

▶ The ABC News theme (also used in commercials for the news).

▶ I am stuck on BAND-AIDs, 'cause BAND-AID's stuck on me.

**Now, ask your parents to sing the tune and identify the products from these jingles.**

▶ You can trust your car to the man who wears the Star, the big bright **** Star!

▶ Hold the pickle, hold the lettuce, special orders don't upset us, all we ask is that you let us serve it your way.

▶ Take it off. Take it all off.

▶ My bologna has a first name, it's O S C A R. . . .

▶ **** tastes good, like a cigarette should.

▶ Plop, plop, fizz, fizz. Oh what a relief it is.

▶ It's not how long you make it, it's how you make it long.

▶ Double your pleasure, double your fun, with ****.

▶ M'm! M'm! Good! M'm! M'm! Good! That's what **** are! M'm! M'm! Good!

▶ From the land of the sky blue waters, **** the beer refreshing.

▶ I'd like to teach the world to sing, in perfect harmony.

**FIGURE 6.8**
**Tunes and Taglines**

Musical memories are often stored in long-term recall areas of the brain. Most people can remember tunes even from their childhood days. For examples, consider the musical approaches displayed in Figure 6.8.

Several decisions are made when selecting music for ads. They include answering questions such as these:

▶ What role will music play in the ad?

▶ Will a familiar song be used, or will something original be created?

▶ What emotional pitch should the music reach?

▶ How does the music fit with the message of the ad?

Music plays a number of roles in advertisements. Sometimes the music is incidental. In others, it is the primary theme of the ad. Occasionally, the use of music misdirects the audience so a surprise ending can be used. For instance, a Volkswagen television commercial showed people on the streets of New Orleans doing things in time to the music (sweeping, bouncing a basketball, unloading a truck) with the end line "That was interesting," and the VW logo followed. The creative must select the correct type of music, from whimsical, to dramatic, to romantic. Just as using the wrong plot or wrong actors in an advertisement can mean disaster, so can selecting the wrong music. Conversely, a quality match between the music and the ad theme can lead to a strongly favorable reaction by the viewer or listener.

Another important decision involves the selection of a familiar tune versus creating original music for the ad. The most common method is to write a jingle or music specifically for the advertisement. Background or mood-inducing music is usually instrumental, and advertisers often pay musicians to write music that matches the scenes in the ad. Also, some companies use the same instrumental tune for each commercial, such as United Airlines, which for years featured "Rhapsody in Blue" in television and radio ads.

Using a well-known song in an ad has certain advantages. The primary benefit is that consumers already have developed an affinity for the song. Brand awareness, brand equity, and brand loyalty are easier to develop when consumers are familiar with the music. This happens when consumers transfer an emotional affinity for the song to the product. One variation on this approach is to purchase an existing song and adapt the ad to the music.[32] Using popular songs is often costly. The average price for rights to an established song is $250,000. The Internet company Excite paid $7 million for the rights to Jimi Hendrix's song "Are You Experienced," and Microsoft paid about $12 million for "Start Me Up."[33]

Not all writers and musicians are willing to sell their songs for advertising. Ben McDonald rejected a $150,000 offer from Bausch & Lomb and $450,000 from Clairol for the Top 40 hit "The Future's So Bright I Gotta Wear Shades." Bruce Springsteen rejected offers in the millions for his hit song "Born in the USA." The estate of Johnny Cash refused to allow the classic "Ring of Fire" to be used in a campaign for hemorrhoid products. These and other songwriters feel strongly about preventing their music from becoming part of an ad. To them, it is selling out.[34]

The relationship between the advertising and music industries in the United Kingdom is different from that in the United States. Artists in the United Kingdom believe that if their songs are played in an advertisement, the attention leads radio programmers to play the song on the air as a single. For many artists, this can be a path to stardom. Ladysmith Black Mambazo reached the U.K. Top 30 with "The Star and the Wiseman" after the song played in a TV ad for Heinz beans. Now companies such as Virgin Records have special departments dedicated to placing songs with advertising agencies.[35]

Music is an important ingredient in ads produced for television, radio, and even for the Internet. When a company becomes associated with a popular theme or tune, recall is enhanced and often the firm is seen as delivering higher quality. Creatives must either prepare music themselves or contract for it in some form. Currently, very few organizations use long-standing musical taglines. Instead, each ad or campaign has its own music. This makes the job of the creative more difficult. He or she must try to "hit a home run" every time a new ad is produced. Other advertising forms, most notably print and billboard, do not use music. Consequently, other appeals become a better match.

## Rational Appeals

A rational appeal follows the hierarchy of effects stages of awareness, knowledge, liking, preference, conviction, and purchase. Creatives design ads for one of the six steps. An ad oriented to the knowledge stage will transmit basic product information. In the preference stage, the ad shifts to presenting logical reasons why one particular brand is superior, such as the superior gas mileage of an automobile or a better safety record. A rational ad leads to a stronger conviction about a product's benefits, so that the purchase is eventually made.

Rational appeals rely on consumers actively processing the information presented in the advertisement. The consumer must pay attention to the commercial, comprehend the message, and compare the message to knowledge embedded in a cognitive map. Messages consistent with the current concepts in the cognitive map strengthen key linkages. New messages help the person form cognitive beliefs about the brand and establish a new linkage from his or her current map to the new product. For example, a business customer who sees a Kinko's advertisement about videoconferencing services already may have the company in his cognitive structure. The business customer may have used Kinko's in the past but was not aware that the company offers videoconferencing. When Kinko's is already established in this person's cognitive map, it is only a matter of creating a new linkage to entice the customer to try its videoconferencing services.

Print media offer the best outlets for rational appeals. Print ads allow readers greater opportunities to process copy information. They can pause and take time to read the verbal content. Television and radio commercials are so short that it is difficult for viewers to process message arguments. Also, if television viewers miss the ad, they must wait until the ad is broadcast again to view it.

We started here.
We stayed here.

Clyde R. White, CEO
Neville High School
Class of 1966.

# We're still here.

Over the years, banks have come and gone – big banks, small banks, local banks, and national banks.

However, the north Louisiana bank that started here in 1997 has stayed here, locally owned and locally managed. No other bank can come close to having the level of OIB's community roots among its leadership.

What does that mean to you?

Simply, the folks at OIB understand local customers and community expectations. We cater to your account needs and make local loan decisions quickly. That means better service for you.

It's easy to make the switch using our OIB *QuickChange! Kit*. Call, come by or log-on today.

**OIB**
OUACHITA INDEPENDENT BANK

**Local people.**
**Local trust.**

OIB QuickChange

Member FDIC | Bastrop (318) 283-5500 | Monroe/West Monroe (318) 338-3000 | Shreveport/Bossier City (318) 459-3000 | www.oibank.com

An advertisement for Ouachita Independent Bank that uses an emotional appeal.
*Source:* Courtesy of Newcomer, Morris & Young.

has the horse thinking, "I will prove them wrong. I will run again. I will mend my spirits."[39]

The underlying principle for changing to more emotional business-to-business ads is that emotions can be part of every type of purchase decision. Members of the buying center consider product information in making decisions but, at the same time, they are likely to be affected by emotions. Although a member of the buying center may try to minimize the emotional side of a purchase, the person is still likely to be affected. The affective component of attitudes is just as important as the cognitive component. In the past, business-to-business advertisers tended to ignore the affective element.

Television is one of the best media for emotional appeals. Television offers advertisers intrusion value and can utilize both sound and sight. Models in the ads can be "real people." Facial expressions can convey emotions and attitudes. Consumers learn about a particular product and develop attitudes based on these vicarious experiences. Television ads also are more vivid, more lifelike, and they can create dynamic situations that pull the viewer into the ad. Music may be incorporated to make the ad more dramatic. Peripheral cues are important components of emotional appeals. These peripheral cues (such as music and background visuals) also capture the viewer's attention.

Emotions are tied with humor, fear, music, and other appeals to make a compelling case for a product. The same ad can influence a consumer both emotionally and rationally. The goal of the creative is to select the most appropriate emotional appeal for the product and company.

## Scarcity Appeals

Scarcity appeals urge consumers to buy a particular product because of a limitation. It can be a limited number of the products available or, more often, that the product is available for only a limited time. When there is a limited supply of a product, the value of that product increases. In 1996, General Mills introduced USA Olympic Crunch cereal and Betty Crocker Team USA desserts for a limited time. Then, at the turn of the century, General Mills introduced a Cheerios line called *Millenios* as a limited time product. Tiny "2s" were added to the familiar O-shaped cereal Cheerios.[40] McDonald's, Wendy's, and Burger King offer sandwiches (McRib, Hot N' Spicy Chicken, Dollar Whoppers) for limited time periods throughout the year. The scarcity concept is also used for musical compilations, encouraging consumers to buy the product because of its limited availability. By making sure it is not available in retail stores, marketers increase its scarcity value.

A scarcity appeal is often tied to other promotional tools. For example, a manufacturer may advertise a limited price discount offer to retailers who stock up early for Christmas or some other holiday season. Contests and sweepstakes also run for limited

## COMMUNICATION ACTION

### The Super Bowl and Advertising Appeals

The Super Bowl is the most watched event on television. Nielsen ratings suggest that more than 40 percent of U.S. households tune in to the game. With so many viewers, it is no wonder that some companies make the Super Bowl a premier venue for new ads. Many viewers watch just to see the ads. The result is that the Super Bowl commands advertising rates in excess of $2.4 million for a 30-second ad.

The major stage offered by the Super Bowl creates pressures on advertising agencies. The ads must be seen as being innovative and still be effective at reaching marketing objectives. In a 7-year study of Super Bowl ads, the most frequently used appeal was humor, followed by emotions.

An examination of the "best" ads versus the "worst" ads provides additional insights into which ads were effective. In terms of humor, 76 percent of the best ads used some type of humor, compared to only 26.3 percent of the worst ads. In terms of emotions, 67.3 percent of the best ads used some type of emotional appeal, compared to only 33 percent of the worst. A rational appeal was used in only 5.1 percent of the ads rated as "best" compared to 94.9 percent in ads that were rated the "worst."

These findings indicate that during the Super Bowl, the "best" ads featured humor and/or emotional appeals. Ads with rational appeals did not work. The reason may be that emotional advertisements do well within a positive-mood-inducing environment. The Super Bowl is a festive occasion. It tends to generate positive moods, strong feelings, and emotional reactions. Consequently, humor and emotional appeals are a better fit. Rational appeals are not effective because viewers are not in the mood or willing to take time to process information provided.

**Source:** Scott W. Kelley and L. W. Turley, "The Effect of Content on Perceived Affect of Super Bowl Commercials," *Journal of Sports Management* 18 (2004), pp. 398–420.

times. The primary benefit of scarcity appeals is that they encourage consumers to take action. Creatives normally receive information about scarcity issues in the creative brief or from the account executive who has consulted with the company.

## THE STRUCTURE OF AN ADVERTISEMENT

The majority of ads prepared for publication or broadcast tend to contain five elements. These ingredients create the structure of an advertisement. They are:

- The promise of a benefit, or the headline
- The spelling out of the promise, a subheadline
- Amplification
- Proof of the claim
- Action to take

In print advertising, the *headline* is crucial. A typical reader is going to look at the artwork, figure, or illustration first. Next, the reader scans the headline. To keep the potential customer interested means finding some method (rational, emotional, humor, etc.) that moves the reader to the rest of the copy. Typical features of a headline are that the words are short, simple, and limited (less than 12), inviting or interest-provoking, and

---

**STAND-ALONE HEADLINES**

Now you can shave your legs half as often. *(the promise of a benefit by Jergens)*

Just when you thought laundry couldn't get any more fun. *(benefit promised by Tide)*

It's so delicious you'll wish bagels didn't have holes. *(enticement, Brummel & Brown spread)*

Can Opener *(provocative, Maxwell House—the opener is one finger)*

Why macaroni was invented. *(presents an existing benefit, Kraft Macaroni and Cheese Dinner Delux)*

**HEADLINES WITH SUBHEADINGS**

| | |
|---|---|
| 1. Headline: | Whipped up. Fluffy. Now with better-tasting chocolate. *(presents a new benefit, 3 Musketeers)* |
| Subheadline: | It could be better if Mr. Right fed it to you. *(targets women in Redbook, a magazine oriented to women)* |
| 2. Headline: | Chemo was stealing the energy I needed for my grandson. *(emotional, Procrit)* |
| Subheadline: | Until I talked to my doctor about getting it back. |
| 3. Headline: | Free face-lifts. *(creates intrigue, FTD florists)* |
| Subheadline: | With every bouquet from your FTD florist. |

**FIGURE 6.10**
**Advertising Headlines and Subheadlines**

action-oriented and portray enough information to let the buyer know about the product while appealing most directly to the target audience.

A headline should not be mistaken for a tagline. The **tagline** is the key phrase within the advertising copy, a television ad, or radio ad. Examples of headlines are shown in Figure 6.10.

The *subheadline*, or spelling out of the promise, accompanies the headline. In some instances, the headline is powerful enough by itself, so this step is skipped. A subheadline is similar to a second headline in a newspaper story. It delivers additional information and leads the reader to the copy. Examples of subheadlines are also shown in Figure 6.10.

The *amplification* is the text or body copy of the advertisement. The wording should be concise. The *unique selling proposition* or the *major selling idea* is portrayed in the copy. The company can be factual, imaginative, or emotional in its approach. Factual copy often is part of comparison advertising, where one product or company is directly contrasted with another. Amplification copy is especially important in business-to-business advertisements, in which more complex features of a product must be explained or summarized.

*Proof of the claim* can be generated from many sources. These include seals of approval (e.g., Good Housekeeping), guarantees (money back if not fully satisfied), trial offers and samples, warranties, demonstrations, and testimonials. A company with strong brand equity is in a better position to make a claim because of the brand's power.

Finally, the consumer must be made aware of the *action to take.* "Buy now," "stop by for a free sample," and "tell your friends" are statements declaring the action the consumer should take. Less direct actions might be "give us a try" or "stop by for a test drive." The action should mirror the stage in the hierarchy of effects model: awareness, knowledge, liking, preference, conviction, or purchase.

These five parts of the structure of an advertisement must also be contained in the use of message strategies and executional frameworks, which are presented in the following chapter. The account executive, creative, and company presenting the ad know that every advertisement cannot contain every component. Instead, these factors and features should appear as an advertising campaign progresses over time.[41]

## SUMMARY

Developing effective advertisements is the culmination of a series of integrated marketing communications efforts. They include knowing the objective of the ad, the target audience, the message theme used, the type of support needed, and any constraints that apply. Then, a creative must work within the context of key advertising theories in selecting the correct media and designing the leverage point and message appeal that work effectively within each medium.

Three important theoretical approaches drive the development of many advertisements. The hierarchy of effects model suggests consumers move through a series of stages as they are persuaded to make a purchase. The steps are: (1) awareness, (2) knowledge, (3) liking, (4) preference, (5) conviction, and (6) the actual purchase. Although the process probably is not a lock-step model that every buyer follows, the hierarchy of effects approach does provide important information about which mental issues to account for in various advertising campaigns. The hierarchy of effects model can be combined with the three main elements present in attitudes: (1) cognitive, (2) affective, and (3) conative components. Ads are designed to influence affective feelings, cognitive knowledge, or conative intentions to act or behave based on an attitude. A means–end chain displays the linkages between a means to achieve a desired state and the end or personal value at issue. Advertisers can select personal values that mesh with the key characteristics of the target market and then construct ads designed to provide them the means to achieve these ends by purchasing the good or service. These ideas help the creative develop a leverage point to move the buyer from understanding the product's benefits to incorporating those benefits with his or her personal values.

Visual and verbal issues should also be considered in the formation of an ad. Concrete visual images are easily recognized and recalled. Abstract images may be linked with values or emotions the product creates or the feeling the buyer should experience that may be associated with the product or company. Visual elements are key components in almost every form of advertising. Verbal elements must reach the more rational, central route of the audience's mental processing procedures.

Beyond these components, advertising creatives must form messages using one (or more) of the seven major appeals: (1) fear, (2) humor, (3) sex, (4) music, (5) rationality, (6) emotions, or (7) scarcity. Just as there are logical combinations of media, there are logical combinations of these appeals for various messages. Often, music is the backdrop for messages invoking fear, humor, sex, and emotions. Humor can be linked with sex, music, rationality (by showing how being illogical is silly or funny), and scarcity. Rationality combines with fear in many commercials. The goal of the creative is to design a message argument that takes advantage of the various characteristics of these appeals, breaks through clutter, and convinces the audience to buy the item involved. Mismatches of message tactics are to be avoided, such as combining sex with humor in France, as mentioned in this chapter.

Business-to-business ads often appear in print and many times include rational approaches in the copy because the purchase decision variables are more complex. At the same time, many advertisers have recently discovered that emotional ads can be effective, which expands business-to-business advertising into other venues, such as television, radio, and the Internet.

The process of designing ads for international markets is quite similar to that for domestic ads. The major difference is careful consideration of local attitudes and customers, with due care given to the language, slang, and symbols of the area. For example, Sega recently discovered that its product's name is slang for "masturbation" in Italian, after a major advertising campaign had started. These types of mistakes should be carefully avoided.

Every marketer knows that some ad campaigns, no matter how carefully conceived, still fail. The goal is to try to reach a point where the failure of one specific ad or campaign does not have long-lasting effects on the company. To do so, a thoughtfully designed IMC program can build a firm's image in such a manner that brand and product loyalty, along with customer recognition, can reduce the ill effects of one "lead balloon" advertising campaign. In the end, advertising is only one component of an IMC program. Although it is clearly a major and important ingredient, it should be considered in the context of a long-term plan to strengthen the company, its products, and its overall image in the customer's mind.

## REVIEW QUESTIONS

1. What are the five main elements of a creative brief? How do they affect the choice of advertising appeals?

2. What are the six stages of the hierarchy of effects model? Do they always occur in that order? Why or why not?

3. How are the three components of attitudes related to the hierarchy of effects model?

4. In a means–end chain, what are the means? The ends? How do they affect advertising design?

5. What is a leverage point? How are leverage points related to the hierarchy of effects model, attitudinal changes, and means–end chains?

6. Why are visual elements in advertisement important? What is the relationship between visual and verbal elements? Can there be one without the other?

7. What are the advantages and disadvantages of fear appeals in advertising?

8. When does humor work in an ad? What pitfalls should companies avoid in using humorous appeals?

9. What types of sexual appeals can advertisers use?

10. When are sexual appeals most likely to succeed? To fail?

11. What should international advertisers consider when thinking about using sexual appeals?

12. Name the different ways music can play a role in an advertisement. Explain how each role should match individual appeals, media, and the other elements in the design of the ad.

13. What are the advantages and disadvantages of rational appeals? Which media do they best match?

14. How can emotions accentuate advertisements? Why are they being used more often in business-to-business advertisements?

15. What is scarcity? How do scarcity ads lead to buyer action?

16. Name four combinations of appeals that are logical combinations for advertisers.

17. What five components make up the structure of an advertisement? Explain each one.

# KEY TERMS

**white space**    The absence of copy in a printed text.

**leverage point**    The feature of the ad that leads the viewer to relate the product's benefits with personal values.

**hierarchy of effects model**    A marketing approach suggesting that a consumer moves through a series of six steps when becoming convinced to make a purchase, including: (1) awareness, (2) knowledge, (3) liking, (4) preference, (5) conviction, and (6) the actual purchase.

**means–end chain**    An advertisement approach in which the message contains a means (a reasoning or mental process) to lead the consumer to a desired end state, such as a key personal value.

**Means–End Conceptualization of Components for Advertising Strategy (MECCAS)**    An advertising approach that suggests using five elements in creating ads, including: (1) the product's attributes, (2) consumer benefits, (3) leverage points, (4) personal values, and (5) the executional framework.

**visual esperanto**    A universal language that makes global advertising possible for any good or service by recognizing that visual images are more powerful than verbal descriptions.

**advertising appeals**    Approaches to reaching consumers with ads. The seven major appeals are: (1) fear, (2) humor, (3) sex, (4) music, (5) rationality, (6) emotions, and (7) scarcity.

**severity**    Part of the fear behavioral response model that leads the individual to consider how strong certain negative consequences of an action will be.

**vulnerability**    Part of the fear behavioral response model that leads the individual to consider the odds of being affected by the negative consequences of an action.

**decorative models**    Models in an advertisement whose primary purpose is to adorn the product as a sexual or attractive stimulus without serving a functional purpose.

**tagline**    The final key phrase in an ad, used to make the key point and reinforce the company's image to the consumer.

# CRITICAL THINKING EXERCISES

## Discussion Questions

1. Develop a means–end chain similar to the one in Figure 6.3 for each of the following branded products:

   **a.** Clorox bleach

   **b.** Zippo lighters

   **c.** Kool-Aid

   **d.** Sony stereos

   Share your results with the class. How were your means–end chains similar or dissimilar to others in class?

2. Evaluate the balance of visual and verbal elements of 5 advertisements shown in this chapter. Which is predominant? Which images are considered appropriate for international advertising because they have the characteristic of visual esperanto? Do they use white space effectively?

3. Try to recall five outstanding television commercials. Identify the appeal used in each one. Why were these five ads effective? Compare your list with those of other classmates. What was their reaction to your list? How did you feel about theirs?

4. Develop a print advertisement for vitamins using a fear appeal. Be sure to consider the means–end chain prior to starting on the advertisement. After completing the means–end chain and

advertisement, to what other media could the advertisement be adapted? How?

5. Borrow a camcorder and develop a 30- or 45-second television spot for one of the following products, using the suggested appeal. Be sure to develop a means–end chain prior to creating the advertisement.

   **a.**  Denim skirt, sex appeal

   **b.**  Tennis racket, humor appeal

   **c.**  Ice cream, emotional appeal

   **d.**  Stockbroker, fear appeal

   **e.**  Dress shoes, musical appeal

6. Using a VCR, record five television commercials. Identify which appeal each advertisement uses. Discuss the quality of the advertisement and its best and worst aspects. For each ad, present another possible appeal and how it could be used. What personal values and customer benefits does each advertisement present?

7. Record five television commercials or find five print advertisements that use sex appeal. Identify which of the five ways sexuality was used. Evaluate each ad in terms of the appropriateness and effectiveness of the sex appeal.

# INTEGRATED LEARNING EXERCISES

1. Greenfield Online is one of the leading online research firms. Access the Web site at www.greenfieldcentral.com. What types of products does the company offer? How would this information help a creative in developing an advertisement? How would this information assist an advertising agency in understanding the target audience for an advertisement?

2. Examine Figure 6.3, and then access the following Web sites for the milk industry. What differences do you see in the Web sites? What do you believe is the intended audience for each Web site?

    a. www.got-milk.com

    b. www.gotmilk.com

    c. www.whymilk.com

3. Look up each of the following Internet Web sites. Identify which type of appeal each site uses. Evaluate the quality of that appeal. What other appeals can be used to make the site more appealing? Discuss the balance of visual and verbal elements on the Web site and ad.

    a. Service Metrics (www.servicemetrics.com)

    b. Trashy Lingerie (www.trashy.com)

    c. Skechers (www.skechers.com)

    d. Bijan Fragrances (www.bijan.com)

    e. Guess (www.guess.com)

    f. Aetna Inc. (www.aetna.com)

    g. Liz Claiborne (www.lizclaiborne.com)

4. Access an online database search engine through your library. Pick one of the appeals listed in the chapter. Find at least three different articles that discuss the appeal. Write a report of your findings.

# STUDENT PROJECT

## IMC Plan Pro

How is your advertising campaign going to make a difference? Which theory will you use to drive customers to the Web site or store and make a purchase? Using the Prentice Hall IMC Plan Pro disk and booklet as a guide, you can think your way through to choose the best theory and the right type of appeal to reach your target customers. Each year the American Advertising Federation (AAF) holds competition for students. You can win an ADDY award. As this advertisement says: "Prove Your Professors Wrong." This year may be your year to enter and win the competition.

Heath Poole of French Creative Advertising Agency designed this ad to encourage students to enter the student ADDY competition.
*Source:* Courtesy of French Creative Group, Ltd.

Jon Johnson came from an unusual background. As an undergraduate at Missouri State University, Jon studied accounting for a year before changing his major to marketing. His musical talents plus a whimsical creative streak made him an ideal candidate to work in an advertising agency.

The most recent client Jon was asked to serve was the CPA firm Burns, Connors, and Morris, or BCM, located in St. Louis, Missouri. The firm was quite large but was not affiliated with any of the large national accounting companies. Jon's task was to find a way to compete effectively with the services offered by the major national companies in the local market.

At his first meeting with BCM officials and Jon's account manager, they reviewed what is known as the AIDA methodology. AIDA stands for Attention-Interest-Desire-Action. Clearly, the ad must garner the prospective client's attention and incite interest. Desire and action are much more difficult to achieve, because a business customer must be moved to consider changing accounting firms or giving some activities to the BCM firm. Jon commented that the AIDA approach seemed quite similar to a hierarchy of effects model.

BCM officials pointed out that their business was more likely to grow by capturing new clients rather than getting long-standing large firms to change. They wanted Jon and his company to stress BCM's areas of expertise (tax accounting and advice) along with the idea that the company has a quality staff, affordable fees, excellent seminars, and the ability to handle international clients. BCM was also proud of its collaborative efforts with prominent local business leaders, politicians in St. Louis, and local law firms and insurance companies.

BCM faced the unique challenge of finding outlets to reach a target market that was smaller and growing firms in need of CPA services. The traditional approach had always been to seek out print media to present ads. Thus, BCM would reach physicians through ads in medical journals (which could be regionally, but not locally, targeted). New businesses might be enticed through ads published in local magazines and specialty journals, insurance companies could be contacted through trade journals, and small businesses through small business magazines and journals. Such an approach was costly, because of the difficulty in reaching all prospective customers in an across-the-board fashion.

In spite of these obstacles, BCM asked Jon and his firm to prepare a series of print ads for a winter campaign. This was a logical time. The key tax season begins in January and ends in April. Jon decided his print ad campaign must have an effective banner or headline. He knew 80 percent of readers read only that part of an ad. Most CPA firms create ads emphasizing the cost savings or quality of using their services. The copy of these ads focused on the advantages each company held in the marketplace. Successful campaigns generally had attractive logos as well as a type of layout that made the company distinct.

Jon prepared the campaign BCM wanted, using the banner "Small Enough to Know You, Large Enough to Serve Your Financial Needs." The print ad campaign was geared to four primary markets: (1) physicians, (2) small businesses, (3) attorneys, and (4) local restaurants. Each could be reached by magazine–trade journal advertising. The medical campaign centered on special programs and seminars for doctors and featured a photo of a physician meeting with an accountant. The small business ad showed the BCM president working in a storefront setting at a ribbon-cutting ceremony; the same ad was used for restaurants. The attorney ad photo was shot in a law library.

Jon then offered an alternative. He suggested that rather than using such a traditional approach, the company might be able to attract attention and desire with a more sexy and less rational approach. He showed BCM officials a storyboard (six stop-frame pictures in sequence used to represent a television ad) for local television and cable outlets. The ad showed BCM's office and people working diligently in it, followed by several local business clients during a regular day of work. The copy featured the same advantages as the print ads. The final board displayed the same business-man from one of the local companies sitting on a beach with a phone–fax–laptop setup. He was working but also sunning himself. Behind the businessman was a woman wearing a skimpy bikini lounging with a drink. The tagline was "We take care of business, so you can take care of yours."

Jon suggested that billboards and print ads could feature the same photo as the final storyboard frame and use the same, more provocative tagline. The same photo and ad could be sent by direct-mail flyer, by fax, and as the main page of BCM's Web site. Jon reported to BCM and to his company that he would be comfortable preparing either approach.

1. Did Jon meet the AIDA model with his television campaign?
2. Did Jon meet the AIDA model with his print campaign?
3. Which campaign would you run for BCM? Why?
4. What other appeal besides sex or rationality might fit BCM?

**Source:** Some of the case information came from the following article: Jay P. Granat, "How to Create an Effective Advertisement," *CPA Journal* 61, no. 1 (January 1991), pp. 68–80.

# CASE 2

## THE AUTO ADVANTAGE

**B**arry Farber has pretty much "seen it all" in his 30 years of selling used cars. His business, The Auto Advantage, had experienced a series of high and low points related to buyer whims and the nature of the industry. Barry is quick to point out that his strongest ally has always been a local advertising company in Sacramento that has helped him negotiate the troubled waters.

From the beginning, Barry has seen opportunities rise up and drift away. When he opened his modest lot in 1973, the first gas crisis was just emerging. People were dumping gas-hog cars and diligently looking for high-mileage cars and those fueled by diesel. In fact, Barry distinctly remembers offering a practically brand-new Ford LTD II, one of the most popular models of the time, at $3,000 below its "blue book" value and not being able to find a buyer for weeks due to consumer fears about oil shortages and rising gas prices.

At that time, Barry's new advertising agency manager, Wendy Mozden, pointed out an old technique that had worked wonders for years. She called it "turning a disadvantage into an advantage." She learned the tactic by watching old Volkswagen commercials. The original "bug" was promoted as being ugly, but economical. Many restaurants during that era bought ads pointing out that the reason they were so "slow" was due to their higher-quality food, making it "worth the wait."

Consequently, The Auto Advantage placed ads in newspapers and on the radio focusing on the "value" an individual could obtain by trading down or across. Sales reps were instructed to convey to individual buyers that a person would have to buy an awfully large amount of gas at 55 cents per gallon before a large car would actually be costly, especially when mpg (miles per gallon) differences between midsize and smaller cars were so small. The Auto Advantage managed to buy cars that other companies did not want to carry at drastically reduced prices and sell them to the customers they could educate concerning the shift from disadvantage to advantage. Within a few years, those high-priced (and hard to maintain) diesel cars disappeared, and people once again fell in love with larger gas hogs. By then Barry's company was well established in the marketplace.

Barry weathered the invasion of foreign cars into the United States by once again seeing an advantage in the disadvantage. Using patriotic themes, his company subtly pointed out that people buying foreign-made cars hurt the local economy, especially because one of the major

(continued)

manufacturers in the Sacramento area made replacement parts for GM cars. Sales presentations always included the question "Are you in a union?" Those who responded "yes" were easy targets for the company's "Buy American" theme during the early 1980s.

From there, Barry spent a great deal of energy making sure he understood the needs of his aging client base. Those who started families in the 1980s needed minivans in the 1990s. Those who were older and facing retirement often wanted low-maintenance cars. By carefully constructing his original message, that a person would gain an advantage by shopping at his lot, the business continued to succeed.

The next major challenge for The Auto Advantage may become the same one in which the company began. Oil prices started to rise, and the U.S. government created tighter pollution standards for almost every make and model of car. Some consumers again looked for more efficient autos, even hybrid gas–electric models as the new century began. Barry knew he would need to continue to adapt as the marketplace evolved. He continued to look for turnaround situations to find the edge to keep his clients happy with what they bought from The Auto Advantage.

1. Describe an advertisement that you have seen in which the firm attempted to turn a disadvantage into an advantage.

2. If gas prices doubled in a 1-year time period, how should The Auto Advantage respond? Design an ad using the various strategies described in this chapter that promote fuel economy.

3. Should The Auto Advantage continue to advertise to baby boomer and older clients? How would they attract Generation X or Generation Y customers to the lot? In other words, how would the advertisements be different? Design an advertisement for the Generation X or Generation Y customers.

4. Pick one of the following appeals. Design a print advertisement for The Auto Advantage using that appeal.

   a. Fear

   b. Humor

   c. Sex

   d. Emotional

# ENDNOTES

1. Arundhati Parmar, "Marketers Ask: Hues on First?" *Marketing News* 28, no. 3 (February 15, 2004), p. 8; G. Douglas Olsen, "Observations: The Sounds of Silence: Functions and Use of Silence in Television Advertising," *Journal of Advertising Research* 34, no. 5 (September–October 1994), pp. 89–95.

2. Jerry Olson and Thomas J. Reynolds, "Understanding Consumers' Cognitive Structures: Implications for Advertising Strategy," *Advertising Consumer Psychology*, L. Percy and A. Woodside, eds. (Lexington, MA: Lexington Books, 1983), pp. 77–90; Thomas J. Reynolds and Alyce Craddock, "The Application of the MECCAS Model to Development and Assessment of Advertising Strategy," *Journal of Advertising Research* 28, no. 2 (1988), pp. 43–54.

3. Laurie A. Babin and Alvin C. Burns, "Effects of Print Ad Pictures and Copy Containing Instructions to Imagine on Mental Imagery That Mediates Attitudes," *Journal of Advertising* 26, no. 3 (Fall 1997), pp. 33–44.

4. Marc Bourgery and George Guimaraes, "Global Ads: Say It with Pictures," *Journal of European Business* 4, no. 5 (May–June 1993), pp. 22–26.

5. Olson and Reynolds, "Understanding Consumers' Cognitive Structures"; Reynolds and Craddock, "The Application of the MECCAS Model to Development and Assessment of Advertising Strategy."

6. Based on Rosemary M. Murtaugh, "Designing Effective Health Promotion Messages Using Components of Protection Motivation Theory," *Proceedings of the Atlantic Marketing Association* (1999), pp. 553–557; R. W. Rogers and S. Prentice-Dunn, "Protection Motivation Theory," *Handbook of Health Behavior Research I: Personal and Social Determinants,* D. Gochman, ed. (New York: Plenum Press, 1997), pp. 130–132.

7. Michael S. Latour and Robin L. Snipes, "Don't Be Afraid to Use Fear Appeals: An Experimental Study," *Journal of Advertising Research* 36, no. 2 (March–April 1996), pp. 59–68.

8. Karen Flaherty, Marc G. Weinberger, and Charles S. Gulas, "The Impact of Perceived Humor, Product Type, and Humor Style in Radio Advertising," *Journal of Current Issues and Research in Advertising* 26, no. 1 (Spring 2004), pp. 25–37.

9. Theresa Howard, "Most Likable Ads of '03 Had a Bit of Laughter," *USA Today* (December 29, 2003), p. 06B.

10. Hillary Chura and Mercedes M. Cardona, "Online Broker Datek Stakes 'Serious Turf' with $80 Mil," *Advertising Age* 70, no. 10 (October 18, 1999), pp. 1–2.

11. David B. Wolfe, "Boomer Humor," *American Demographics* 20, no. 7 (July 1998), pp. 22–23.

12. Karen Flaherty, Marc G. Weinberger, and Charles S. Gulas, "The Impact of Perceived Humor, Product Type, and Humor Style in Radio Advertising," *Journal of Current Issues and Research in Advertising* 26, no. 1 (Spring 2004), pp. 25–37.

13. Jimmy Yap, "McDonald's Finds Humor a Hit with Singapore Viewers," *Media Asia* (February 7, 2004), p. 22; Bill Britt, "Ford Tries Witty, Edgy Advertising to Promote the Kia," *Automotive News Europe* 9, no. 2 (January 26, 2004), p. 4.

14. "Sex Doesn't Sell," *The Economist* 373, no. 8399 (October 30, 2004), pp. 62–63.

15. Pat Sloan and Carol Krol, "Underwear Ads Caught in Bind over Sex Appeal," *Advertising Age* 67, no. 28 (July 8, 1996), p. 27.

16. Bob Garfield, "Dentyne Spot Makes It Seem That Naysayers Have a Point," *Advertising Age* 76, no. 5 (January 31, 2005), p. 41.

17. Laurel Wentz, "Global Village," *Advertising Age* 68, no. 10 (March 10, 1997), p. 3; Michael Wilke, "A Kiss Before Buying," *Advocate* (April 27, 1999), pp. 34–35.

18. Jessica Severn, George E. Belch, and Michael A. Belch, "The Effects of Sexual and Non-Sexual Advertising Appeals and Information Level on Cognitive Processing and Communication Effectiveness," *Journal of Advertising* 19, no. 1 (1990), pp. 14–22.

19. Tom Reichart, "Sex in Advertising Research: A Review of Content, Effects, and Functions of Sexual Information in Consumer Advertising," *Annual Review of Sex Research* 13 (2002), pp. 242–274; D. C. Bello, R. E. Pitts, and M. J. Etzel, "The Communication Effects of Controversial Sexual Content in Television Programs and Commercials," *Journal of Advertising* 3, no. 12 (1983), pp. 32–42.

20. "Note to Chrysler: Gutter Humor Has No Place in Ads," *Automotive News* 78, no. 6064 (October 27, 2003), p. 12.

21. Based on G. Smith and R. Engel, "Influence of a Female Model on Perceived Characteristics of an Automobile," *Proceedings of the 76th Annual Convention of the American Psychological Association* 15, no. 3 (1968), pp. 46–54; Leonard Reid and Lawrence C. Soley, "Decorative Models and the Readership of Magazine Ads," *Journal of Advertising Research* 23, (April–May 1983), pp. 27–32; R. Chestnut, C. LaChance, and A. Lubitz, "The Decorative Female Model: Sexual Stimuli and the Recognition of Advertisements," *Journal of Advertising* 6 (Fall 1977), pp. 11–14.

22. Tom Reichart, "Sex in Advertising Research: A Review of Content, Effects, and Functions of Sexual Information in Consumer Advertising," *Annual Review of Sex Research* 13 (2002), pp. 242–274; Andrew A. Mitchell, "The Effect of Verbal and Visual Components of Advertisements on Brand Attitude and Attitude Toward the Advertisement," *Journal of Consumer Research* 13 (June 1986), pp. 12–24.

23. Bruce Horovitz, "Risque May Be Too Risky for Ads," *USA Today* (April 16, 2004), p. 1B.

24. Bruce Horovitz, "Risque May Be Too Risky for Ads," *USA Today* (April 16, 2004), p. 1B; Claire Beale, "What Now for Ad Industry As Sex No Longer Sells?" *Campaign (UK)*, no. 36 (September 3, 2004), p. 23.

25. Kelly Lynne Ashton, "Wise to the Game," *Marketing Magazine* 108, no. 28 (August 11, 2003), pp. 22–23; "Teens Deconstruct Two Clothing Ads," *Marketing Magazine* 108, no. 28 (August 11, 2003), p. 22.

26. Daniel A. Joelson, "Rebel Sell," *Latin Trade* 12, no. 8 (August 2004), p. 16.

27. Gerard Stamp and Mark Stockdale, "Sex in Advertising," *Advertising Age's Creativity* 7, no. 6 (July–August 1999), pp. 35–36; Bob Garfield, "Pushing the Envelope: The Performing Penis," *Advertising Age International*, (July 12, 1999), p. 4. Jean J. Boddewyn, "Sex and Decency Issues in Advertising: General and International Dimensions," *Business Horizons* 34, no. 5 (September–October 1991), pp. 13–20.

28. Elizabeth Bryant, "P&G Pushes the Envelope in Egypt with TV Show on Feminine Hygiene," *Advertising Age International* (December 14, 1998), p. 2.

29. Howard Levine, Donna Sweeney, and Stephen H. Wagner, "Depicting Women as Sex Objects in Television Advertising," *Personality and Social Psychology Bulletin* 25, no. 8 (August 1999), pp. 1049–1058.

30. Boddewyn, "Sex and Decency Issues in Advertising: General and International Dimensions."

31. G. Douglas Olsen, "Observations: The Sounds of Silence: Functions and Use of Silence in Television Advertising," *Journal of Advertising Research* 34, no. 5 (September–October 1994), pp. 89–95.

32. Felicity Shea, "Reaching Youth with Music," *B&T Weekly* 54, no. 2491 (October 1, 2004), pp. 16–17.

33. Michael Miller, "Even out of Context, the Beat Goes On (and On)," *Pittsburgh Business Times* 18, no. 18 (November 27, 1998), p. 12.

34. Simon Morrissey, "Jingles in the Jungle," *Campaign (UK)*, no. 38 (September 17, 2004), p. 37; John Marks, "Shake, Rattle, and Please Buy My Product," *U.S. News & World Report* 124, no. 20 (May 25, 1998), p. 51.

35. Paul Sexton, "This Is How They Do It in the U.K.," *Adweek Eastern Edition* 39, no. 43 (October 26, 1998), pp. SPS14–SPS15.

36. Joy Dietrich, "Western Union Retraces Roots: The Emotions of Money Transfers," *Advertising Age International* (October 1999), pp. 24–25.

37. Scott Rockwood, "For Better Ad Success, Try Getting Emotional," *Marketing News* 30, no. 22 (October 21, 1996), p. 4.

38. Mae Anderson, "A Priceless Promotion," *Adweek* 45, no. 44 (November 22, 2004), pp. 24–25.

39. Joanne Lynch and Leslie de Chernatony, "The Power of Emotion: Brand Communication in Business-to-Business Markets," *Journal of Brand Management* 11, no. 5 (May 2004), pp. 403–420; Karalynn Ott, "B-to-B Marketers Display Their Creative Side," *Advertising Age's Business Marketing* 84, no. 1 (January 1999), pp. 3–4.

40. Stephanie Thompson, "Big Deal," *Mediaweek* 7, no. 44 (November 24, 1997), p. 36; Judann Pollack, "Big G Has Special Cheerios for Big '00,'" *Advertising Age* (June 14, 1999), pp. 1–2.

41. J. Thomas Russell and W. Ronald Lane, *Kleppner's Advertising Procedure,* 15th ed. (Upper Saddle River, NJ: Prentice Hall), pp. 423–437.

# Advertising Design: Message Strategies and Executional Frameworks

## Chapter Objectives

*Develop* **awareness of three types of message strategies (cognitive, affective, and conative) and match them with the media chosen for an advertising campaign.**

*Study* **the roles message strategies play in designing effective leverage points and executional frameworks.**

*Apply* **every executional framework described in this chapter in the right situation.**

*Learn* **the value of an effective source or spokesperson, plus the criteria to use in selecting the individual.**

*Utilize* **the principles of effective advertising to be certain the message has the best chance of reaching and affecting the audience.**

## THE AFLAC DUCK MAKES A BIG SPLASH

Just a few years ago, AFLAC advertised the company's insurance in a manner similar to practically every other insurer. Images of happy families looking lovingly at each other and having warm, fuzzy interactions with an insurance agent were common. After all, supplemental health insurance is supposed to provide peace of mind; matching the message to the theme with soothing music seemed the most logical choice.

In 1999, the marketing team working with AFLAC took a bold step. They noticed that AFLAC ads were competing for viewers' attention in a barrage of television advertisements, some of which were stacked 10 to 15 deep during a commercial break. Many of these competing images were funny and smart.

Enter the duck.

Linda Kaplan Thaler, CEO of the Kaplan Thaler Group Ltd., a New York–based agency, has a track record of developing innovative and attention-grabbing advertising approaches. Kaplan Thaler said that the biggest challenge was trying to find some way to build the AFLAC brand, which is an acronym, not a word. Finally, when a creative employee said the name sounds like the squawking of a duck, the team was off and running.

In addition to buying time on national television, the media buyer suggested buying spots on CNN Airport news and on in-flight television shown on American Airlines, Delta, United, and Continental. The target market for the company's product is employees who work in businesses with fewer than 500 employees. A number of these individuals are underinsured or not insured with health coverage. AFLAC's supplemental policies cover loss of income, deductibles, and non-medical expenses that are sometimes not covered by standard health, life, and disability policies. Many of these employees and leaders of those companies spend time in airports and on airplanes.

The white Pekin duck, which appears in key spots of commercials, shouts out the company's name in response to a problem. For example, an early spot features a passenger

in an airport tripping over a piece of luggage. The flight attendants standing nearby discuss a friend who was hurt on the job and did not have supplemental insurance. At the end of the spot, the duck is flying alongside the plane, still trying to get the attention of the people involved. In another, the duck rides a roller coaster trying to get the message to a couple taking a thrill ride.

"He's the underduck," Linda Kaplan Thaler reports. "We can rant and rave against policies and institutions, but as one person, we never feel as if we're heard. That's the role of the duck. He'll even go on a roller coaster to tell the world about supplemental insurance."

To make sure every ingredient of the plan was in place, the company featured the duck in its annual report, including footprints and feathers on every page. The theme presented to the company was, "If it ain't broke . . . fix it anyway!" The duck image was shown throughout the organization before the campaign even began.

The advertisements have been a major success. Sales have risen by 27 percent since the ads began running. The company's name shows up on late-night talk shows as well as a list of ads (prepared by the *Wall Street Journal*) that have made an impact on popular culture. Lewis Lazre, a writer for the *Chicago Sun-Times,* notes, "The duck does stick in the mind, and you can remember it and the name of the company."

Currently, AFLAC sells a stuffed toy duck and other duck-related merchandise on its Web site. This process, known as *merchandising the advertising,* features another twist: The profits from the sales of the merchandise support the AFLAC Cancer and Blood Disorder Center at Children's Healthcare of Atlanta hospital.

The advertising team continues to look for new ways to feature the duck, including ads with Olympic-like skaters during the 2002 Olympics and another starring Yogi Berra during the baseball season. AFLAC's media budget was more than $40 million in 2002.

With creativity, careful media selection, and a strong "spokesperson," AFLAC has built a stronger brand in a market where differentiation is difficult to achieve. "He has very long legs," reports one AFLAC employee. It would be hard to argue with that.[1]

The essence of an integrated marketing communications program is designing messages that effectively reaches the target audience. Many of these messages are, in a very real sense, quite personal. They are designed to change or shape attitudes. They must be remembered. They should lead to some kind of short- or long-term action.

Marketing messages travel in two ways. First, a personal message can be delivered through a personal medium. A sales rep closing the deal, shaking the hand of the buyer, giving a reassuring tap on the shoulder, and smiling while talking is delivering a message in an intimate, warm, human fashion. Clearly, personal media (sales reps, repair department personnel, customer services representatives, etc.) must be included in the overall IMC program and approach.

The second way marketing messages travel is through the various forms of advertising media. Many of these media are completely *impersonal*. Television sets are indifferent as to what appears on the screen. Radios deliver any sound that can be transmitted. Computer screens are nothing more than special-purpose television screens. The challenge to the marketing account executive, the company, and especially the creative is to design a personal message, even while it is being delivered through an impersonal medium.

Account executives are acutely aware of the importance of effectively reaching a target audience. It is not simply a matter of reach, frequency, and continuity. The message must engage the targeted buyer and influence the individual to the point that he or she will recall and purchase the product.

Beyond the goal of making a message personal, many marketers are interested in tangible, measurable results that can be reported to clients and to prospective new customers. Therefore, the relationship between the executive and the creative reaches a critical point at the stage in which an advertisement is developed.

This chapter focuses on several major topics. First, three types of message strategies are described. Each may be used to help convince the consumer to make a purchase, either through reason, emotion, or an action-inducing advertisement. Second, the major types of executional frameworks are noted. These forms of advertising presentations help the creative prepare original, convincing, and memorable ads. Third, the four types of sources or spokespersons that appear in various advertisements are described, and the criteria used to select them are reviewed. Fourth and finally, the principles of effective advertising campaigns are presented. When advertisements are combined with other elements of the promotions mix in an integrated fashion, the net result is a stronger company image and a clear IMC theme.

## MESSAGE STRATEGIES

As noted in Chapter 5, the **message theme**, or the outline of the key ideas in the ad, is a central part of the creative brief. The message theme can be created using a number of message strategies. A **message strategy** is the primary tactic or approach used to deliver the message theme. There are three broad categories of message strategies:[2]

1. Cognitive strategies
2. Affective strategies
3. Conative strategies

| Cognitive Strategies | Affective Strategies |
|---|---|
| ▶ Generic | ▶ Resonance |
| ▶ Preemptive | ▶ Emotional |
| ▶ Unique selling proposition | Conative Strategies |
| ▶ Hyberbole | ▶ Action-inducing |
| ▶ Comparative | ▶ Promotional support |

**FIGURE 7.1**
**Message Strategies**

The categories represent the components of attitudes as described earlier. All three of the message strategies are described in this section. Figure 7.1 lists the three message strategies along with various forms or approaches from each category.

## Cognitive Strategies

A **cognitive message strategy** is the presentation of rational arguments or pieces of information to consumers. These ideas require cognitive processing. When a cognitive message strategy is used, the advertisement's key message is about the product's attributes or the benefits. Customers can obtain these benefits by using the product.

The goal of the cognitive message strategy approach is to design an ad that will have an impact on a person's beliefs and/or knowledge structure. This can be accomplished by suggesting any one of a wide variety of potential product benefits. Foods may be described as healthful, pleasant tasting, or low calorie. A tool can be shown as durable, convenient, or handy to use. A drill press machine used in a manufacturing operation may be portrayed as being more reliable or faster than comparable machines on the market. Cognitive message strategies make these benefits clear to potential customers. There are five major forms of cognitive strategies:

1. Generic messages
2. Preemptive messages
3. Unique selling proposition
4. Hyperbole
5. Comparative advertisements

**Generic messages** are direct promotions of product attributes or benefits without any claim of superiority. This type of strategy works best for a firm that is clearly the brand leader and is the dominant company in the industry. The goal of the generic message is to make the brand synonymous with the product category. Thus, Campbell's Soups can declare "Soup is good food" without making any claim to superiority. This is because the company so strongly dominates the industry. When most consumers think of soup, they think of Campbell's. Out of the top 10 ready-to-serve soups, three are Campbell's products, accounting for 43.1 percent of the total market share.[3] Nintendo uses a similar strategy because the company dominates the handheld game category with more than 98 percent of the market share.[4]

Generic message strategies are seldom found in business-to-business advertisements, because few firms dominate an industry to the extent of Campbell's or Nintendo. One major exception is Intel, which controls 13.7 percent of the global microconductor market, which is double its closest competitor, Samsung (6.7% market share). The generic message "Intel inside" has been used for years to convey to both businesses and end users that the processor inside is made by Intel. The Intel name is synonymous with quality. One of Intel's major customers is IBM. For several years IBM's marketing team wanted to discontinue displaying the Intel logo, because they thought it distracted from the IBM's brand. IBM, however, was compelled to continue to display the Intel inside logo to assure buyers that IBM computers contain Intel microprocessors. Forcing IBM to display the Intel inside logo on IBM's products illustrates the power a generic message has when the firm dominates the market.[5]

An advertisement using a preemptive message strategy.
*Source:* Courtesy of DaimlerChrysler Corporation.

An advertisement for Bonne Bell featuring a unique selling proposition.
*Source:* Courtesy of Bonne Bell.

Generic message strategies can also be used to create brand awareness. The goal of the advertiser may be to develop a cognitive linkage between a specific brand name and a product category, such as Skechers and sporty footwear. The ad may contain very little information about the product's attributes. The intent of the ad is simply to put the brand name in a person's cognitive memory and cognitive map.

**Preemptive messages** claim superiority based on a product's specific attribute or benefit. The idea is to prevent the competition from making the same or a similar statement. For example, Crest toothpaste is so well-known as "the cavity fighter" that the brand preempts other companies from making similar-sounding claims, even though all toothpastes fight cavities. The key to effectively using a preemptive strategy is to be the first company to state the advantage. This keeps competitors from saying the same thing. Those that do are viewed as "me-too" brands or copycats.

A **unique selling proposition (USP)** is an explicit, testable claim of uniqueness or superiority that can be supported or substantiated in some manner. Brand parity makes a unique selling proposition more difficult to establish. Reebok claims it is the only shoe that uses DMX technology, which provides for a better fit. Reebok can use this unique selling proposition because the company holds patents on DMX technology. In the Bonne Bell advertisement shown on this page, the company proposes a unique selling proposition aimed at teenagers. The message that Bonne Bell Lipshade is "your 1 and only, 1 handed, sleek sweep flipstick" stresses a unique product feature.

The **hyperbole** approach makes an untestable claim based upon some attribute or benefit. When NBC claims that its Thursday night lineup is "America's favorite night of television," the claim is a hyperbole. These claims do not have to be substantiated, which makes this cognitive strategy quite popular.

The final cognitive message strategy is a **comparative advertisement**. When an advertiser directly or indirectly compares a good or service to the competition, it is the comparative method. The advertisement may or may not mention the competitor by name. Sometimes, an advertiser simply presents a "make-believe" competitor, giving it a name like product *X*. This approach, however, is not as effective as comparative advertising that states the actual competitor's name. To provide protection from lawsuits, company leaders must be sure any claim concerning the competition can be clearly substantiated.

AT&T and MCI compare rates. VISA brags that many merchants using the card will not accept American Express. Burger King explains the advantages of flame broiling as opposed to frying, which McDonald's and Wendy's use. In the business-to-business sector, shipping companies compare delivery times and accuracy rates.

The major advantage of comparative ads is that they often capture the consumer's attention. When comparisons are made, both brand awareness and message awareness increase. Consumers tend to remember more of what the ad says about a brand than when the same information is presented in a non-comparative ad format.

The negative side of using comparative ads is in the areas of believability and consumer attitudes. Many consumers think comparative ads are less believable. They view the information about the sponsor brand as exaggerated and conclude that the information about the comparison brand probably is misstated to make the sponsor brand appear superior.

Another danger of comparative ads is the negative attitudes consumers may develop toward the ad. If viewers acquire negative attitudes toward the advertisement, these negative attitudes can transfer to the sponsor's product. This is especially true when the sponsor runs a *negative comparative ad.* This form of advertisement portrays the competition's product in a negative light. Research has shown that negative comparative ads typically result in lower believability of the ad claims and create less favorable attitudes toward the brand.[6]

In psychology, the concept of *spontaneous trait transference* suggests that when someone calls another person dishonest, other people tend to remember the speaker as also being less than honest. When a comparative ad criticizes the competition's brand based upon some particular attribute, viewers of the ad may attribute that deficiency to the sponsor brand as well. This is most likely to occur when the consumer uses the comparative brand, not the sponsored brand.[7] Companies must be careful in choosing an appropriate comparison firm and must be even more careful about using a negative comparative ad format.

Comparison ads are less common in other countries. This is due to both social and cultural differences as well as legal restrictions. It is critical to be aware of these issues. For example, many governments in Europe classify comparative advertising as illegal. In Japan, it is not illegal, but it runs against the society's cultural preferences. In Brazil, the advertising industry is so powerful that any attempt to create a comparative advertisement has been challenged and stopped. Often, international consumers not only dislike the advertisements but often transfer that dislike to the company sponsoring the ad.[8]

The comparative message strategy can be beneficial if used with caution. The comparison brand must be picked carefully to ensure consumers see it is a viable competing brand. Actual product attributes and customer benefits must be used, without stretching the information or providing misleading information. If there are actual differences to compare, then comparative advertising works well. If the comparisons are all hype and opinion, with no substantial differences, comparative advertising does not work as well. If the comparison is misleading, the Federal Trade Commission (FTC) may step in and investigate. The largest number of complaints that the FTC hears are about potentially misleading comparison advertisements.

In general, comparing a low-market share brand to the market leader works well, because viewers concentrate more carefully on the content and message of the ad. On the other hand, comparing a high-market share brand with another high-market share brand is often not effective. In these cases, a better strategy may be to simply make the comparison without naming the competitor.

Several years ago, comparative advertising worked well for Avis. When Avis was tenth in market share in the rental car industry, a series of ads was developed for Avis, comparing its service to the market leader, Hertz, mentioning the Hertz name specifically. Consumers began to believe that Avis provided the same level of quality as Hertz. After gaining market share and becoming one of the top three brands, Avis changed its approach and now usually does not mention Hertz in advertisements. Still, when comparisons are made, consumers still know which competitor is involved.[9]

All five of these cognitive message strategies are based on some type of rational logic. The message is designed to make sure consumers pay attention to the ad and take the time to cognitively process the information. In terms of attitudes, the sequence of cognitive → affective → conative is the plan of attack when developing a rational approach. The intention of a cognitive message strategy is first to present consumers with rational information about a good, service, or company, and then to help them develop positive feelings about the same product or company.

A Cheerios advertisement utilizing a resonance affective message strategy.
*Source:* Courtesy of General Mills.

## Affective Strategies

**Affective message strategies** invoke feelings or emotions and match those feelings with the good, service, or company. Such ads are prepared to enhance the likeability of the product, recall of the appeal, or comprehension of the advertisement. Affective strategies elicit emotions that, in turn, lead the consumer to act, preferably to buy the product, and subsequently affect the consumer's reasoning process.

An emotion such as love can be used to convince consumers that a product such as Cheerios is a superior breakfast cereal for loved ones. The consumer group is then led to believe Cheerios is a rational choice because the company's advertisements mention the cereal's positive effects on cholesterol levels. This approach is demonstrated by the advertisement for Cheerios in this section. Three generations of a family in the picture combined with the words "Your heart has better things to do than deal with heart disease." Family memories and emotions combine with the product feature of being a heart-smart cereal. Affective strategies fall into two categories: (1) resonance and (2) emotional.

**Resonance advertising** attempts to connect a product with a consumer's experiences to develop stronger ties between the product and the consumer. The use of music from the 1960s takes baby boomers back to that time and the experiences they had growing up. Any strongly held memory or emotional attachment is a candidate for resonance advertising.

**Emotional advertising** attempts to elicit powerful emotions that eventually lead to product recall and choice. Many emotions can be connected to products, including trust, reliability, friendship, happiness, security, glamour, luxury, serenity, pleasure, romance, and passion.

As noted in Chapter 6, emotional appeals can be used in both consumer-oriented and business-to-business ads. Members of the buying center in a business are also human beings. They do not always make decisions based solely on rational thought processes. Emotions and feelings also affect decisions. If the product's benefits can be presented within an emotional framework, the advertisement is normally more effective, even in business-to-business ads.[10]

Affective strategies are a common approach to developing a strong brand name. When an advertisement gets you to like a brand and have positive feelings for a brand, then the hope is that you will also purchase that brand. Cognitive beliefs about the brand then follow. This approach relies on the attitude development sequence of affective → conative → cognitive. For some products, affective ads are an effective approach because there are no real tangible differences among the brands. Coke and Pepsi primarily use affective message strategies. The ads are made to evoke liking, positive emotions, and favorable feelings toward the products and the companies who sell them. Few ads focus on physical attributes of the soft drink. Skechers Sport Footwear is using a similar strategy in the advertisement on this page. The ad depicts social acceptance and the idea that Skechers shoes will make you a part of the in-crowd. The ad is supposed to create positive feelings for the Skechers Sport brand.

An advertisement for Skechers Sport Footwear using a brand image message strategy.
*Source:* Courtesy of Skechers USA Inc.

## COMMUNICATION ACTION

### Corporate Advertising and Image-Building

Corporate advertising promotes the corporate name and image rather than the individual brand. Corporate advertising often contains an affective message strategy. As companies continue to face public pressure to be more socially responsible, corporate advertising is an increasingly important tactic. Recently Microsoft launched a global corporate advertising campaign created by the McCann-Erickson advertising agency. The ads appeared in China, Japan, Australia, Korea, India, and the United States. Each message highlights the company's efforts to build programs and partnerships with communities around the world. The tagline used is "Your Potential. Our Passion." Each advertisement features video showing people involved in various activities. The video is then overlaid with drawings. In one ad children are participating in various school events. White lines are drawn around each student to illustrate what that student could become (doctor, lawyer, chemist) through education and technology.[11] The goal is to tie emotions about success and taking care of children with using Microsoft products, all the while believing Microsoft is concerned about young people.

GlaxoSmithKline launched a corporate advertising campaign highlighting the company's investments in pharmaceutical research. The idea was to make sure consumers realize that people depend on pharmaceutical companies to develop medicines that improve the quality of life and fight disease. The message of the ads is that although developing medicines is an expensive process, the results are immeasurable. The tagline in the advertisements was "Today's medicines finance tomorrow's miracles."[12]

These "Big Sale" signs are a conative strategy designed to encourage customers to make a purchase.

## Conative Strategies

Conative message strategies are designed to lead more directly to some type of consumer response. They can be used to support other promotional efforts, such as coupon redemption programs, Internet "hits" and orders, and in-store offers such as buy-one-get-one-free. The goal of a conative advertisement is to elicit behavior. A conative strategy is present in any television advertisement for music CDs that seeks to persuade viewers to call a toll-free number to purchase the music. These ads typically encourage quick action by stating that the CD cannot be purchased at stores and is available for only a limited time.

**Action-inducing conative advertisements** create situations in which cognitive knowledge of the product or affective liking of the product may come later (after the actual purchase) or during product usage. For instance, a point-of-purchase display is designed (sometimes through advertising tie-ins) to cause people to make *impulse buys*. The goal is to make the sale, with cognitive knowledge and affective feelings forming as the product is used. In terms of an attitude sequence, conative message strategies typically utilize the conative → cognitive → affective approach.

**Promotional support conative advertisements** are used to support other promotional efforts. Besides coupons and phone-in promotions, a company may advertise a sweepstakes that a consumer enters by filling out the form on the advertisement or by going to a particular retail store.

Cognitive, affective, and conative strategies can be matched with the hierarchy of effects approach described in the previous chapter. The hierarchy of effects model suggests that consumers pass through a series of stages, from awareness to knowledge, liking, preference, conviction, and finally to the purchase. As shown in Figure 7.2, each message strategy can highlight a different stage of the hierarchy of effects model.

Choosing the right message strategy is a key ingredient in creating a successful advertising program. To be effective, the message strategy must be carefully matched with the leverage point and executional framework that have been selected as well as with the media that will be utilized. The creative and the account executive must remain in constant contact

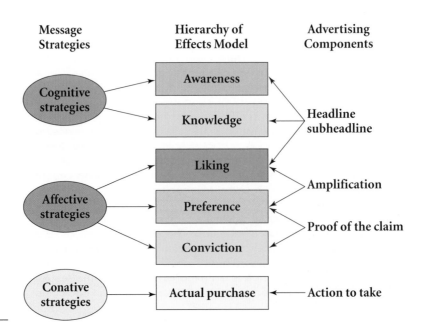

**FIGURE 7.2**
**The Hierarchy of Effects Model, Message Strategies, and Advertising Components**

▶ **Animation**
▶ **Slice-of-life**
▶ **Dramatization**
▶ **Testimonial**
▶ **Authoritative**
▶ **Demonstration**
▶ **Fantasy**
▶ **Informative**

**FIGURE 7.3**
**Executional Frameworks**

throughout the process to be certain all of these advertising ingredients are consistent. In the following section, the next element, the executional framework, is described.

## EXECUTIONAL FRAMEWORKS

An **executional framework** is the manner in which an ad appeal is presented. The executional framework is chosen after an advertising appeal has been selected. In Chapter 6, the types of appeals that are most commonly used were described, including fear, humor, sex, music, rationality, emotions, and scarcity. Each appeal can be matched with the appropriate executional framework. Figure 7.3 displays the various frameworks that are described in this section.

### Animation

Animation is a popular type of executional framework. In recent years, the use of animation in advertising has dramatically increased. This is due in part to the growing sophistication of computer graphics programs. The animation technologies available to advertising creatives are far superior to the cartoon-type that was previously used.

One new animation technique is called *rotoscoping*. Rotoscoping is the process of digitally painting or sketching figures into live sequences.[13] This makes it possible to present both live actors and animated characters in the same frame. The creative can also merge or modify various live scenes within the same frame.

Rotoscoping was used in Budweiser's "Born a Donkey" commercial, which was voted the viewer's favorite in the 2004 Super Bowl. The ad features a donkey that wants to be a Clydesdale and lead the Clydesdales pulling the Budweiser beer wagon. Almost all of the scenes involving the donkey and the Clydesdale horses were filmed separately. They were then merged. Rotoscoping helped enhance various actions, such as when all of the Clydesdales turn their heads simultaneously to listen to the donkey speak. In reality, it would be almost impossible to get that many horses to turn their heads in concert with each other.[14]

An advertisement using an animation character.
*Source:* Used with permission of *The Joplin Globe*, Joplin, Missouri.

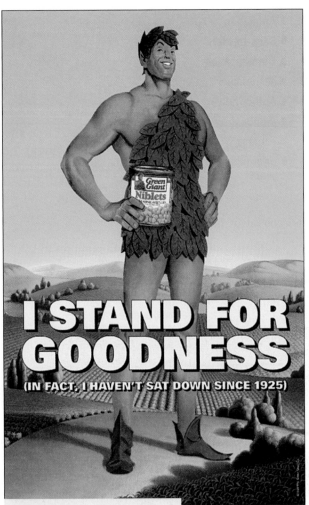

A Green Giant advertisement using animation.

**Source:** Reprinted with the permission of General Mills, Inc.

Animation characters can be human, animal, or product personifications. Animation was originally a last-resort technique for advertisers who did not have money to prepare a live commercial. Most agencies did not hold it in high regard. Currently animation is one of the most popular advertising techniques. Successful films such as *The Incredibles* and *Finding Nemo* generated a great deal of interest in animation advertising.

Besides cartoons, another method of animation, made popular by the California Raisins commercials, is *clay animation*. Although expensive to create, clay animation has been successful. One well-known product personification is the Pillsbury Doughboy. Computer graphics technology now allows production companies to superimpose these personifications in live scenes.

Animation is used mostly in television spots. It can be utilized in movie trailers and Internet ads. Single shots of animated characters, such as Tony the Tiger, are also placed into print ads. For years animation was rarely used in business-to-business advertising. Many advertising agencies had negative views of it. Agency leaders tended to believe animation appealed to children but not to businesspeople. These views have changed. Business ads shown on television can now take advantage of high-quality graphics technologies to illustrate a product's uses with animated figures and graphics.

## Slice-of-Life

In slice-of-life commercials, advertisers attempt to provide solutions to the everyday problems consumers or businesses face. This format was made famous by Procter & Gamble during the early days of television advertising in the 1950s. The advertisements normally show the common experiences and especially the problems people encounter. Then, the good or service is made available to solve the problem. The most common slice-of-life format has four components:

1. Encounter
2. Problem
3. Interaction
4. Solution

In some of the ads, the actors portray the dilemma or problem and solve the problems themselves. In others, a voice-over explains the benefits or solution to the problem that the good, service, or company provides.

A typical slice-of-life commercial could start with a child playing soccer and her parents cheering (the encounter). Her dirty uniform is then shown with comments by the child that it will never come clean for the championship game, or a voice-over can be used to state the same message (the problem). Another parent or the announcer then introduces the benefits of the new laundry detergent (the interaction). The commercial ends with the proud parents taking their daughter to a championship game in a clean uniform (the solution). Note that this commercial could be shot in various ways. The actors can talk to each other in the scenario, making the audience the third party who essentially is "eavesdropping" on the conversation. Or, the commercial can be shot using a voice-over to highlight the problem and solution portions of the commercial, with the announcer speaking directly to the audience.

In print advertisements, slice-of-life frameworks are difficult, but not impossible to prepare. In the business-to-business advertisement for Messagemedia shown on the next page, the encounter is the potential female customer. The problem is that the "average single female breaks up with 4.3 men, avoids 237 phone calls, and ignores approximately 79 red lights per year." The interaction occurs through the copy "What are the chances she'll read your e-mail message?" The solution to this problem is Messagemedia's "E-messaging campaign."

The slice-of-life executional framework has become popular in Japan in recent years. The slice-of-life style is suited to Japan's soft-sell approach to marketing. A more hard-sell attitude is often found in the United States. Japanese advertising tends to be more indirect, and the slice-of-life approach allows advertisers to present a product in a typical everyday situation. Benefits can be presented in a positive light without making brazen or harsh claims and without directly disparaging the competition.[15]

Business-to-business advertisements also heavily use the slice-of-life method. The executional framework is popular because it allows the advertiser to highlight the ways a product can meet business needs. For example, a typical business-to-business ad begins with a routine business experience, such as a sales manager making a presentation to the board of directors. Then, the projector being used by the salesperson does not have a clear picture. The ad offers the solution: a projector from Sony. The presentation is made with great clarity, and the board of directors accepts the customer's bid for the account. As with all slice-of-life commercials, disaster is avoided and, by using the advertised brand, a happy ending results.

Slice-of-life executional frameworks are possible in most media, including magazines or billboards, because a single picture can depict a normal, everyday situation or problem. The challenge is creating one image that can tell the entire story, with the product being the solution.

A business-to-business advertisement for Messagemedia.com containing a slice-of-life executional framework.
*Source:* Courtesy of MessageMedia.

## Dramatization

A dramatization is similar to the slice-of-life executional framework. It uses the same format in which a problem is first presented and then a solution is offered. The difference lies in the intensity and story format. Dramatization uses a higher level of excitement and suspense to tell the story. A dramatization story normally builds to a crisis point.

An example of a dramatization is a recent Maytag commercial, which did not use the "lonely repairman" theme the company had featured for decades. The ad was designed to launch a new product—the Gemini range. Thirty- and sixty-second spots featured children carrying pizzas, yelling and rushing toward a throng of adults carrying casserole dishes. The groups run toward each other on a battlefield. The two groups are ready to break into battle when the Maytag representative intervenes with the dual-oven range that accommodates the needs of both groups.[16] The commercial contains all of the critical components of a drama execution. It tells a story in a dramatic way, leading up to a suspenseful climax. Suddenly, the Maytag product provides a solution to the crisis.

An effective and dramatic advertisement is difficult to create, because the drama must be completed in either 30 or 60 seconds. Building a story to a climatic moment is challenging, given such a short time period. The first "What's in Your Wallet" advertisements for Capital One credit cards did manage to create the level of excitement needed. Not all dramatic execution styles can, however, accomplish the high level of suspense required to make them successful. It is often easier to simply produce the ad using the slice-of-life framework.

## Testimonials

The testimonial type of executional framework has been successful for many years, especially in the business-to-business and service sectors. When a customer is presented in an advertisement telling about a positive experience with a product, it is a testimonial. In the business-to-business sector, testimonials from current customers add credibility to the claims being made. In many business buying situations, prospective vendors are asked for references. Testimonials provide references in advance. Further, most buyers believe what others say about a company more than they believe what a company says about itself. Thus, testimonials by someone else offer greater credibility than self-proclamations.

Testimonials also are an effective method for promoting services. Services are intangible; they cannot be seen or touched. Consumers cannot examine services before making decisions. A testimony from a current customer is an effective method of describing the benefits or attributes of the service. This matches the method most consumers use in selecting a service. When choosing a dentist, an attorney, or an automobile repair shop, consumers often ask friends, relatives, or coworkers. A testimonial ad for a service simulates this type of word-of-mouth recommendation.

One major reason companies choose testimonials is that they enhance company credibility. Endorsers and famous individuals do not always have high levels of credibility, because consumers know they are being paid for their endorsements. In testimonials, everyday people, often actual customers, are the main characters. At other times, they are paid actors who look like everyday consumers.

## Authoritative

When using the authoritative executional framework, the advertiser is seeking to convince viewers that a given product is superior to other brands. One form is **expert authority**. These ads employ a physician, dentist, engineer, or chemist to state the particular brand's advantages compared to other brands. Firms also can feature less recognized experts such as automobile mechanics, professional house painters, nurses, or even aerobics instructors. Advertising presents each of these as an expert or authority in a particular field. These experts normally talk about the brand attributes that make the product superior.

Many authoritative advertisements include some type of scientific or survey evidence. Independent organizations such as the American Medical Association undertake a variety of product studies. Quoting the results gives an ad greater credibility. Survey results are less credible. Stating that four out of five dentists recommend a particular toothbrush or toothpaste is less effective, because consumers do not have details about how the survey was conducted or even how many dentists were surveyed (5 or 50). On the other hand, when the American Medical Association states that an aspirin a day reduces the risk of a second heart attack, it is highly credible. A company such as Bayer can take advantage of the finding by including the information in the company's ads. The same is true when a magazine such as *Consumer Reports* ranks a particular brand as the best.

Any scientific, independent, unpaid source makes an advertising claim more powerful. For example, Wachovia Bank recently created advertisements featuring the Bank's rating as the number one community development lender in the United States. The rating was given by the Federal Financial Institutions Examining Council.[17] The ad was more credible because the rating was made by a federal agency, which was an independent source.

Authoritative advertisements have been widely incorporated into business-to-business sector ads,

An advertisement by St. Francis Medical Center promoting its orthopedics unit.
*Source:* Courtesy of Newcomer, Morris & Young, Inc.

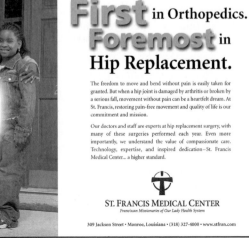

**First** in Orthopedics.
**Foremost** in **Hip Replacement.**

The freedom to move and bend without pain is easily taken for granted. But when a hip joint is damaged by arthritis or broken by a serious fall, movement without pain can be a heartfelt dream. At St. Francis, restoring pain-free movement and quality of life is our commitment and mission.

Our doctors and staff are experts at hip replacement surgery, with many of these surgeries performed each year. Even more importantly, we understand the value of compassionate care. Technology, expertise, and inspired dedication–St. Francis Medical Center... a higher standard.

**ST. FRANCIS MEDICAL CENTER**
*Franciscan Missionaries of Our Lady Health System*

309 Jackson Street • Monroe, Louisiana • (318) 327-4000 • www.stfran.com

especially when scientific findings are available to support a company's product claims. Independent test results are likely to have a more profound influence on members of the buying center, especially if they are actively looking for rational information to help them make decisions.

The authoritative approach assumes consumers and business decision makers rely on cognitive processes when making purchase decisions. This means that they will pay attention to an ad and carefully think about the information conveyed in the advertisement. The authoritative approach works most effectively in print ads, because the buyers are willing to take the time to read the claim or findings provided in the advertisement.

Authoritative ads work especially well in specialty magazines. For example, in a hunting magazine, having an expert hunter discuss the superiority of a particular gun is effective, because readers have an interest in hunting. Brides observe the endorsements of wedding experts in special bridal magazines. Readers notice these specialized advertisements, and the claims made have greater credibility. The same is true in business-to-business magazines. Trade journals in the business world are similar to specialty magazines in the consumer world.

## Demonstration

A demonstration execution shows how a product works. A demonstration is an effective way to communicate the attributes of a product to viewers. Other product benefits can be described as the product is exhibited. For example, one recent advertisement featured a new form of dust cloth that could be attached to a handle or used separately. The demonstration highlighted the product's multiple uses by cleaning a television screen, a wooden floor, a saxophone, and light fixtures on the ceiling. Thus, consumers were being shown how to use the product while at the same time hearing about its advantages.

Business-to-business ads often present demonstrations. They allow a business to illustrate how a product can meet the specific needs of another business. For example, GoldTouch, Inc., can demonstrate the InstaGold Flash System, which deposits a bright and uniform gold surface finish on products such as jewelry, through a nonelectrical current process of immersion plating. Such demonstrations can be offered via television ads or Flash media ads on the Internet.

Demonstration ads are especially well suited to television and Internet Flash ads. To a limited extent, the print media can feature demonstrations, especially when a series of photos outline the sequence of product usage.

## Fantasy

Some products lend themselves to a fantasy-type of executional framework. Fantasy executions are designed to lift the audience beyond the real world to a make-believe experience. Some fantasies are meant to be realistic. Others are completely irrational. Often, the more irrational and illogical ads are, the more clearly consumers recall them. Fantasies can deal with anything from a dream vacation spot or cruise ships to a juicy hamburger or an enticing DiGiorno pizza. The Jantzen ad to the right encourages consumers to fantasize about what the world would be like if they ruled. People are even encouraged to share their fantasies by contacting Jantzen at www.jantzen.com.

The most common fantasy themes, however, still involve sex, love, and romance. According to some marketing experts, raw sex and nudity in advertisements are losing their impact. Instead, advertisers can feature a softer, more subtle

A Jantzen ad utilizing a fantasy executional framework.
**Source:** Courtesy of Jantzen Inc.

This advertisement for bottled water uses a fantasy appeal.
**Source:** Courtesy of Coca-Cola.

presentation of sex. Fantasy fits nicely with preferences for a tamer sexuality, which primarily are found in older members of the population. For some senior citizens, raw sex and nudity simply are offensive. Fantasy is an excellent way to approach older individuals by taking them into a world of romantic make-believe rather than hard-driving sexuality.[18]

One product category that frequently uses fantasy executions is the perfume and cologne industry. In the past, the most common theme was that splashing on a certain cologne causes women to flock to a man. For women, the reverse was suggested. Although used extensively, these ads were not particularly effective because people didn't believe them. Currently, perfume advertisers tend to portray the product as enhancing the love life of a couple or even making a man or woman feel more sensuous, rather than turning a man into a "babe magnet" or a woman into a "diva."

Television fantasy ads for cruise lines show couples enjoying romantic, sensuous vacations together, swimming, jet skiing, and necking. The goal is to make the cruise into more than just a vacation—it should become a romantic fantasy trip. Fantasy ads also can show people experiencing the thrill of winning a major sports event or sharing a common product (beer, pizza) with a beautiful model. Effective fantasies can inspire both recall and action.

The business-to-business advertising field has not used fantasy a great deal primarily because of fear that members of a buying center would not take it seriously. At the same time, creatives are sometimes able to feature a fantasy in a business-to-business ad by showing a product helping the buyer achieve some type of unrealistic result or outcome. For example, being promoted from janitor to president because of the correct choice of a cleaning product would be a fantasy aimed at people using or purchasing janitorial supplies.

An advertisement for Security Finance using an informative appeal.
**Source:** Used with permission of *The Joplin Globe,* Joplin, Missouri.

## Informative

A common advertising executional framework is an informative advertisement. Informative ads present information to the audience in a straightforward manner. Agencies prepare informative messages extensively for radio advertisements, where only verbal communication is possible. Informative ads are less common in television and print because consumers tend to ignore them. With so many ads bombarding the consumer, it takes more than just the presentation of information to capture someone's attention.

Consumers highly involved in a particular product category pay more attention to an informational ad. Such is often the case when business buyers are in the process of gathering information for either a new buy or modified rebuy. On the other hand, if the business is not in the market for a particular product, buying center members do not pay much attention to informative ads. Thus, informative ads tend to work well only in high-involvement situations. Many advertisers believe that business buyers need detailed information to make intelligent buying decisions. As a result, the informative framework continues to be a popular approach for business-to-business advertisers.

One of the keys to informative advertising is the placement of the ad. An informative advertisement about a restaurant placed on a radio station just before noon is listened to more carefully than if it runs at 3:00 P.M. An informative ad about a diet product in an issue of *Glamour* that has a special article on weight control or exercising will be noticed more than if it is placed in the fashion section of the magazine. An informative business ad featuring a new piece of industrial equipment works well next to an article about the capital costs of equipment. Consequently, informative ads have limited uses but can be effective when placed properly.

Beyond these types of executional frameworks, the creative decides about all of the other ingredients, including music, copy, color, motion, light, and the size of a print ad. Remember that almost any of these executional frameworks can be used within the format of one of the various appeals. A slice-of-life can depict fear, as can a dramatization. Informative ads can be humorous, but so can animations. Testimonials or demonstrations are rational or emotional, and so forth. As the advertisement comes together, one element remains: the choice of a source or spokesperson.

## SOURCES AND SPOKESPERSONS

One final major issue remains for the creative, the company, and the account executive. Selecting the right **source and spokesperson** to use in an advertisement is a critical decision. Four types of sources are available to advertisers:

1. Celebrities
2. CEOs
3. Experts
4. Typical persons

Approximately 20 percent of all advertisements use some type of *celebrity spokesperson*. Payments to celebrities account for around 10 percent of all advertising dollars spent.[19] A celebrity endorser is used because his or her stamp of approval on a product can enhance the product's brand equity. Celebrities also help create emotional bonds with the products. The idea is to transfer the bond that exists between the celebrity and the audience to the product being endorsed. This bond transfer often is more profound for younger consumers. Older consumers are not as likely to be influenced by celebrity endorsements. Still, many advertisers believe they are effective. Figure 7.4 lists some major brands and their endorsers.

Agencies also utilize celebrities to help establish a "personality" for a brand. The trick is to the tie the brand's characteristics to those of the spokesperson, such as Elizabeth Taylor's love of the finer things in life being attached to her line of scents and

▶ Ace Hardware: John Madden

▶ Adidas: Steffi Graf

▶ American Express: Robert DeNiro

▶ Amway: Shaquille O'Neal

▶ Campbell Soup: Donovan McNabb

▶ Converse: Larry Bird, Larry Johnson

▶ Danskin: Nadia Comaneci

▶ Fila: Naomi Campbell, Grant Hill, Kathy Ireland, Vendela

▶ Ford Trucks: Toby Keith

▶ Hanes: Fran Drescher, Marisa Tomei

▶ Hanes Underwear: Michael Jordan

▶ MasterCard: Tom Watson

▶ Nintendo: Ken Griffey Jr.

▶ Outback Steakhouse: Rachel Hunter

▶ Revlon: Cindy Crawford

▶ Subaru: Paul Hogan

▶ Sprite: LeBron James

▶ Taco Bell: Spike Lee, Shaquille O'Neal

**FIGURE 7.4**
**Celebrity Endorsers**

# COMMUNICATION ACTION

## The Changing World of the Creative

The advertising landscape is changing. New pressures have affected the role of the creative. For some, the most dramatic shift is in the center of power of the entire industry. For many decades Madison Avenue agencies were viewed as being on the cutting edge of innovation in advertising. Currently, if you believe renowned creatives Bob Kuperman and Roy Grace, the shift has most of the "action" to the west.

Kuperman says, "The Madison Avenue label may play to middle America. But any client or marketing head knows he doesn't have to go to New York to get what he wants in terms of creativity." Grace is more blunt. He states that too many creative decisions fall within a safety zone of familiar styles, concepts, and sales techniques, especially in the Big Apple.

One of the reasons for the change is the shift to market research–driven advertising development. Focus groups and other forms of testing have made it so that, according to Grace, "There's too much testing and too much research. Advertising is too much of a science and not as much of an art." This frustration appears to be growing throughout the industry. Winston Fletcher notes that every major creative decision is subjected to research. When things get modified, creatives can scream themselves hoarse, but they don't necessarily convince the focus group.

To regain control, some creatives have moved into the role of director, splitting their time between commercial development and commercial production. In this new role, creatives limit themselves to one company per industry. For example, one creative noted that he had just prepared a $50 million campaign for Jack in the Box and therefore would not film for clients such as McDonald's or Burger King. The Chicago-based Fusion Idea Lab, which creates a number of Bud Light spots, will not film ads for other breweries.

Assuming the new role of director also puts the creative more directly in the line of fire, in terms of reporting tangible results. Unfortunately, "Creatives are probably the worst judges of their own work," states Don Williams, creative director at the PI Design agency. The new accountability may force some creatives away from directing and back into simple development.

Creative Stuart Burnett concludes that the best route to take is to find a marketing communications firm rather than a simple ad agency. He states that "marketing communications agencies are best at responding to the [new] challenges. Their media-neutral, integrated approach is winning more and more fans and is getting them sexier work, bigger budgets, and meatier problems to solve."

No matter who employs the creative, the goal is to keep things original. According to Jeff Goodby, a major creative in San Francisco, "Advertising very quickly turns into formulas, and the real enemy of the creative organization is the formulaic feeling." Consequently, the firm Goodby, Silverstein & Partners is working to make sure the agency's creatives take risks and work to sell themselves to clients.

If you are looking for a dynamic, interesting, and evolving career, the job of creative offers many challenges and opportunities. As the next generation of creatives moves forward, the nature of the advertising game will continue to shift with the times, making things exciting for everyone involved.

**Sources:** Alice Z. Cuneo, "Goody Grows Up," *Advertising Age*, Crain Communications (2000), at www.webinfo@adage.com; Winston Fletcher, "Drop in Creative Tension May Kill Off Imagination," *Marketing*, Haymarket Publishing, Ltd. (August 27, 1998); Stuart Burnett, "Comment," *Marketing*, Haymarket Publishing, Ltd. (December 16, 1999); Kathy Desalvo, "Two-timers," *SHOOT*, BPI Communications (March 26, 1999); Justin Elias, "Now and Then," *SHOOT*, BPI Communications (September 10, 1999); Robert Mcluhand, "Creatives Can Sharpen Focus," *Marketing*, Haymarket Publishing Ltd. (April 20, 2000).

perfumes as well as other products. In developing a brand personality, the brand must already be established. The celebrity merely helps to define the brand more clearly. Using celebrities for new products does not always work as well as for already established brands.

There are three variations of celebrity endorsements: (1) unpaid spokespersons, (2) celebrity voice-overs, and (3) what may be called *dead-person endorsements.* Unpaid spokespersons are those celebrities who support a charity or cause by appearing in an ad. These types of endorsements are highly credible and can entice significant contributions to a cause. Politicians, actors, and musicians all appear in these ads. VH1's "Save the Music" ads are a recent campaign of this type.

Many celebrities also provide voice-overs for television and radio ads without being shown or identified. Listeners often respond to the ads and try to figure out who is reading the copy. This adds interest to the ad but may also serve as a distraction, when the individual does not hear the message while trying to identify the speaker.

A dead-person endorsement occurs when a sponsor uses an image, or past video or film, featuring an actor or personality who has died. Dead-person endorsements are somewhat controversial but are becoming more common. Bob Marley, Marilyn Monroe, John Wayne, John Lennon, Elvis Presley, and many others have appeared in ads and even become spokespersons for products after dying. Colonel Sanders has become a spokesperson in animation for KFC. Figure 7.5 identifies the top-earning dead celebrities and the amount each of their estates earned in endorsements in just one year.

Instead of celebrities, advertisers can use a CEO as the spokesperson or source. Dave Thomas of Wendy's was possibly the most famous CEO in commercials in the 1990s. For many years, Lee Iacocca was the spokesperson for Chrysler, and Michael Eisner served as the main voice for Disney. A highly visible and personable CEO can become a major

An ad by The Record Exchange promoting a Britney Spears record.
*Source:* Courtesy of Elberson Partners.

| 1. Elvis Presley | $40 million |
|---|---|
| 2. Charles Schulz | $35 million |
| 3. J. R. Richard | $23 million |
| 4. John Lennon | $21 million |
| 5. Theodore Seuss Geisel | $18 million |
| 6. Marilyn Monroe | $ 8 million |
| 7. George Harrison | $ 7 million |
| 8. Bob Marley | $ 7 million |
| 9. Irving Berlin | $ 7 million |
| 10. Richard Rodgers | $6.5 million |

**FIGURE 7.5**
**Top 10 Earnings of Dead Celebrities**

*Source:* Lisa DiCarlo, "Death's Upside," *Forbes* 174, no. 10 (November 15, 2004), p. 58.

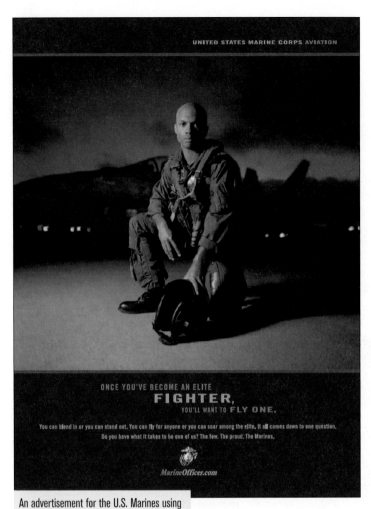

An advertisement for the U.S. Marines using a typical person spokesperson.
*Source:* Courtesy of the U.S. Marine Corps.

asset for the firm and its products. Many local companies succeed, in part, because their owners are out front in small market television commercials. They then begin to take on the status of local celebrities.

*Expert sources* include physicians, lawyers, accountants, and financial planners. These experts tend not to be famous celebrities or CEOs. Experts provide backing for testimonials, serve as authoritative figures, demonstrate products, and enhance the credibility of informative advertisements.

The final category of spokesperson is *typical-person sources.* Typical persons are one of two types. The first category consists of paid actors or models that portray or resemble everyday people. The second is actual, typical, everyday people used in advertisements. Wal-Mart, as already mentioned, features its own store employees in freestanding insert advertisements. Agencies also create many "man-on-the-street" types of advertisements. For example, PERT shampoo recently prepared ads showing an individual asking people if they would like their hair washed. Dr. Scholl's interviews people about foot problems that might be resolved with cushioned shoe inserts.

Real people sources are becoming more common. One reason for this is the overuse of celebrities. Many experts believe that consumers have become saturated with celebrity endorsers and that the positive impact today is not as strong as it was in the past. One study conducted in Great Britain indicated that 55 percent of the consumers surveyed reported that a famous face was not enough to hold their attention. Celebrities held a greater appeal for the 15- to 24-year-old age bracket. Sixty-two percent of that group stated that a famous person in an ad would get their attention.[20]

## Source Characteristics

In evaluating sources, most account executives and companies consider several characteristics. The effectiveness of an advertisement that utilizes a spokesperson depends on the degree to which the person has one or more of the characteristics. As illustrated in Figure 7.6, the source selection characteristic of a spokesperson's *credibility* is derived from the composite of attractiveness, likablity, trustworthiness, and expertise. Credibility affects a receiver's acceptance of the spokesperson and message. A credible source is believable. Most sources do not score highly on all four attributes, yet they need to score highly on multiple characteristics to be viewed as credible. One reason for using celebrities is that they are more likely to possess at least an element of all characteristics.

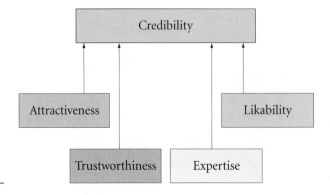

**FIGURE 7.6**
**Characteristics of Effective Spokespersons**

A CEO, expert, or typical person probably lacks one or more of them.

*Attractiveness* has two forms: (1) physical characteristics and (2) personality characteristics. Physical attractiveness is usually an important asset for an endorser. Bijan used Michael Jordan's and Bo Derek's physical attractiveness to promote its line of menswear, perfume, and jewelry. Advertisements with physically attractive spokespersons fare better than advertisements with less attractive people. This is true for both male and female audiences. At the same time, the attractiveness of the spokesperson's personality is also important to many consumers. This personality component helps viewers form emotional bonds with the spokesperson. If the spokesperson is seen as having a sour personality, even if physically beautiful, consumers are less likely to develop an emotional bond with the individual and the product.

Closely related to attractiveness is the concept of **similarity**. Consumers are more inclined to be influenced by a message delivered by a person who is somehow similar. For example, a "stay at home" mom is more likely to be influenced by an advertisement that starts out with a woman saying, "Since I made the decision to stop working and care for my family full-time. . . . " Both similarity and attractiveness can create **identification**, in which the receiver is able, in some manner, to identify with the source. At times this may involve the fantasy of identifying with a rich person buying a BMW. At others, identification is based on believing the source has similar beliefs, attitudes, preferences, or behaviors, or is in the same or a similar situation as the customer.

A Bijan perfume advertisement featuring celebrity Bo Derek.
*Source:* Courtesy of Bijan Fragrances, Inc.

Closely related to the personality component of attractiveness is *likeability*. Consumers respond more positively to spokespersons they like. This liking arises from various sources, including situations in which viewers like either the actor or the character played by the actor in a movie. An athlete gains likeability if he or she plays on the consumer's favorite team. Other individuals are likable because they support the favorite charities of consumers. If consumers do not like a particular spokesperson, they are likely to transfer that dislike to the product the celebrity endorses. This is not an automatic transfer, because consumers recognize that endorsers are paid spokespersons. Still, there is almost always a negative impact on attitudes toward the brand.

A celebrity may be likable or attractive, but he or she may not be viewed as *trustworthy*. Trustworthiness is the degree of confidence or the level of acceptance consumers place in the spokesperson's message. A trustworthy spokesperson helps consumers believe the message. In the early 2000s, two of the most trusted celebrities were Michael Jordan and Bill Cosby. Likeability and trustworthiness are highly related. People who are liked tend to be trusted and people who are disliked tend not to be trusted.

The fourth characteristic advertisers look for when examining sources is *expertise*. Spokespersons with higher levels of expertise are more believable than sources with low expertise. Richard Petty and Jeff Gordon are seen as experts when automobile products and lubricants are advertised. Often when expertise is desired in an ad, the ad agency opts for the CEO or a trained or educated expert in the field. American Express features Maria Barraza, a small-business owner and designer, to promote its Small Business Services.

A potential negative side to using a CEO as the spokesperson may be present. Although he or she has a high degree of expertise, the individual may lack some of the other key characteristics (attractiveness, likeability, or trustworthiness). Expertise can be valuable in persuasive advertisements designed to change opinions or attitudes.

| Celebs People Most Likely to Buy From | Celebs People Least Likely to Buy From |
|---|---|
| 1. Jon Stewart | 1. Donald Trump |
| 2. Oprah Winfrey | 2. Dick Cheney |
| 3. Bill Clinton | 3. Terrell Owens |
| 4. P. Diddy | 4. Teresa Heinz Kerry |
| 5. Martha Stewart | 5. Ashlee Simpson |
| 6. Ashton Kutcher | 6. David Ortiz |
| 7. Arnold Schwarzenegger | 7. Ryan Seacrest |
| 8. Christina Aguilera | 8. Rosie O'Donnell |
| 9. Rudy Giuliani | 9. Tom Cruise |
| 10. Madonna | 10. Sarah Jessica Parker |

**FIGURE 7.7**
Celebrities People Would Most Likely and Least Likely Purchase a Product From

*Source:* "Celebs People Would Most (Least) Likely Buy a Product From," *Advertising Age* 75, no. 51 (December 20, 2004), p. 2.

Spokespersons with high levels of expertise are more capable of persuading an audience than someone with zero or low expertise.[21]

## Matching Source Types and Characteristics

The account executive, ad agency, and corporate sponsor, individually or jointly, may choose the type of spokesperson. They can choose a celebrity, CEO, expert, or typical person, and the specific individual must have the key characteristics. This section matches source types with various characteristics.

*Celebrities* normally score well in terms of trustworthiness, believability, persuasiveness, and likeability. These virtues increase if the match between the product and celebrity is a logical and proper fit. For example, Phil Mickelson endorsing golf merchandise is a good fit. An athlete endorsing any type of athletic product fits well. Companies can be creative but also use common sense in making quality matches. For instance, the match of boxer George Foreman to his Lean Mean Grilling Machine is a great success. Figure 7.7 lists the top 10 celebrities people would most likely buy a product from and the 10 celebrities people would least likely buy a product from. Both lists were compiled from a random survey conducted by *Advertising Age* magazine.

Several dangers exist in using celebrities. The first is negative publicity about the celebrity caused by inappropriate conduct. For example, prior to the 2004–05 basketball season, numerous NBA basketball stars served as spokespersons and endorsers. The Kobe Bryant trial and the brawl between several members of the Indiana Pacers and spectators in the stands at the start of the season quickly changed the landscape. Shortly afterwards, a survey of marketing executives revealed that 31 percent of those contacted said they would consider reducing associations with the NBA and specific players. Twenty-one percent of those surveyed said the incident caused them to rethink using any professional athlete.[22]

The potential for negative publicity has led some advertisers to use deceased celebrities, because what was

Michael Jordan is one of only a few celebrities who was able to endorse a number of products and maintain a high level of credibility.
*Source:* Courtesy of Bijan Fragrances, Inc.

essentially *negative likeability* became attached to the company and its products. Many companies concluded that there was no need to risk bringing embarrassment or injury to themselves or the brand. It is also a reason that more ads use cartoon characters. Practically everyone likes cartoons.

The second danger of using celebrities is that their endorsement of too many products tarnishes their credibility.[23] Only a few exceptional celebrities, such as Michael Jordan and Bill Cosby, have been able to successfully endorse a variety of products.

Another problem associated with celebrity endorsements is credibility. Consumers know celebrities are paid, which detracts from their believability. If the celebrity endorses a number of products, consumer evaluations of that person's credibility decline further. Some advertising research indicates that when a celebrity endorses multiple products, it tends to reduce his or her credibility and likeability as well as consumers' attitudes toward the ad.[24]

As a result, careful consideration must be given to the choice of a celebrity. The individual cannot simply be famous. The person should possess as many of the characteristics as possible, match the good or service being advertised, not be "spread too thin" or overexposed, and promote a positive image that can be transferred to the good, service, or company.

A *CEO* or other prominent corporate official may or may not possess the characteristics of attractiveness and likeability. CEOs should, however, appear to be trustworthy, have expertise, and maintain a degree of credibility. A CEO is not a professional actor or model. Coming across well in a commercial may be difficult.

Companies must be aware of the trustworthiness issue. For example, many times the owner of a local auto dealership represents it as the spokesperson. The primary problem is that many consumers view used-car salespeople as those who cannot be trusted. Other local business owners may be highly trustworthy, such as restaurant owners, physicians, eye care professionals, and so forth.

Advertising creatives and account executives should be careful about asking a CEO or business owner to serve as a source. They first must be convinced that the individual has enough key characteristics to promote the product and gain the consumer's interest and trust.

*Experts,* first and foremost, should be credible. The ad agency should seek out an expert who is also attractive, likable, and trustworthy. Experts are helpful in promoting health-care products and complicated products that require explanations. In other situations, consumers will place a degree of trust in the company when purchasing the product or service recommended by an expert. An expert who is unattractive and dislikable cannot convince consumers that he or she can be trusted, and credibility drops as a result. Business-to-business ads often feature experts. The agency should be certain that an expert spokesperson has valid credentials and will be able to clearly explain a product's benefits. Then the source's trustworthiness and credibility rise.

*Typical-person* ads are sometimes difficult to prepare, especially when they use real persons. First, typical-person sources do not have the name recognition of celebrities. Consequently, advertisers often use multiple sources within one advertisement to build credibility. Increasing the number of sources in the ad makes the ad more effective. Hearing three people talk about a good dentist is more believable than hearing it from only one person. By using multiple sources, viewers are motivated to pay attention to the ad and to process its arguments.[25]

Real person ads are a kind of two-edged sword. On the one hand, trustworthiness and credibility rise when the source is bald, overweight, or has some other physical

This Jockey advertisement features an older typical-person model.
***Source:*** Courtesy of Jockey International.

"Jockey For Her is the best fitting underwear I've ever worn. It's so comfortable. And now my favorite granddaughters wear Jockey For Girls®. Just Jockey."

Catherine Councell Moll
Grandmother/Banker
Sheboygan, Wisconsin

So Comfortable
JOCKEY
For Her

For Pantyhose That Fit . . . Wear Jockey For Her Pantyhose with Lycra®

imperfections. This can be especially valuable when the bald person promotes a hair replacement program or the overweight source talks about a diet program. On the other hand, attractiveness and likeability may be lower.

Using customers in ads can be difficult, because they will flub lines and look less natural on the screen. These difficulties with actual customers and employees lead many ad agencies to turn to professional models and actors to portray ordinary people. Professional actors make filming and photographing much easier. Also, the agency is in the position to choose a likable but plain person. The desired effects (trustworthiness and credibility) are often easier to create using professional actors and models.

In general, the ad agency should seek to be certain that the source or spokesperson has the major characteristics the ad needs. When the appeal is humor, likeability is very important. In a rational or informational ad, expertise and credibility are crucial, especially in business-to-business ads. In each case, the goal is to try to include as many of the characteristics as possible when retaining a spokesperson.

## CREATING AN ADVERTISEMENT

Figure 7.8 illustrates the process a creative uses in preparing an advertisement. The work begins with the creative brief, which outlines the message theme of the advertisement as well as other pertinent information. Using the creative brief blueprint, the creative develops a means–end chain, starting with an attribute of the product that generates a specific customer benefit and eventually produces a desirable end state. This means–end chain is the foundation on which all other decisions will be made.

Following the development of the means–end chain, the creative selects a message strategy, the appeal, and the executional framework. He or she also chooses a source or spokesperson at this point, because the choice usually affects other creative decisions. Development of the leverage point is usually undertaken after the creative begins work on the advertisement. The leverage point moves the consumer from the product attribute or customer benefit to the desired end state. The type of leverage point used depends on the message strategy, appeal, and executional framework.

Although certain combinations tend to work well together, the creative has an almost infinite number of options when preparing an advertisement or campaign. For example, if the creative wants to use a cognitive message strategy, the most logical appeal is rationality. The creative, however, could use fear, humor, sex, music, or even scarcity. The one appeal that would not work as well is emotions. The emotional part of the advertisement tends to overpower the cognitive message the creative is trying to send to the viewer. If the creative decides to use a humor approach with a cognitive strategy, other logical and illogical combinations emerge. In terms of the executional framework, dramatization and authoritative

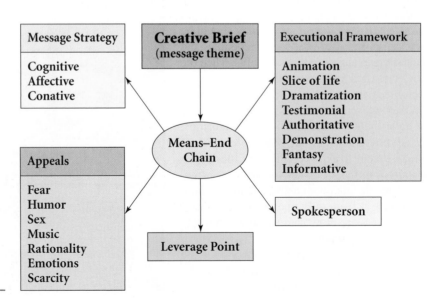

**FIGURE 7.8**
**Creating an Advertisement**

▶ **Visual consistency**

▶ **Campaign duration**

▶ **Repeated taglines**

▶ **Consistent positioning—avoid ambiguity**

▶ **Simplicity**

▶ **Identifiable selling point**

▶ **Create an effective flow**

**FIGURE 7.9**
**Principles of Effective Advertising**

tend not to work as well with humor. Any of the other executional frameworks are suitable. This flexibility allows a variety of advertisements to emerge from a single means–end chain. The combination to use depends on the creatives' expertise and experience as well as the creatives' opinion about the best way to accomplish the client's advertising objectives.

## ADVERTISING EFFECTIVENESS

Producing effective ads requires the joint efforts of the account executive, creative, media planner, and media buyer. Working independently can produce some award-winning ads, but often they will not be effective ads that meet a client's objectives. One major problem ad agencies face is producing a commercial that will stand out among the thousands of existing ads. If an advertisement can break through the clutter, half the battle is won. All that remains is finding a way to lead consumers or businesses to react to the ad in the desired manner.

An effective advertisement accomplishes the objectives desired by the client. The task of making sure the ad accomplishes the IMC objectives is a major challenge. Seven basic principles of advertising effectiveness, as shown in Figure 7.9, should be followed. Each of these principles is described in greater detail next.

The first principle is to maintain **visual consistency**. Repeatedly seeing a specific image or visual display helps embed it in long-term memory. Visual consistency is important because consumers, whether individual consumers or members of a business buying center, spend very little time viewing or listening to an advertisement. In most cases, it is just a casual glance at a print advertisement or a cursory glimpse at a television ad. Visual consistency causes the viewer to move the advertising message from short-term memory to long-term memory. Consistently used logos and other long-standing images help fix the brand or company in the consumer's mind. For example, people remember Frosted Flakes because of the visually consistent use of Tony the Tiger. They know Green Giant products by their cartoon spokesperson. Logos such as the Nike swoosh and the Prudential Rock emblems are well established in the minds of many consumers.

The second principle of effective advertising is concerned with *campaign duration.* Consumers often do not pay attention to advertisements. This makes the length or duration of a campaign important. Using the same advertisement for an appropriate period of time helps embed the message in the consumer's long-term memory. Account executives give careful thought to how long to run an advertisement. The ad should be changed before it becomes stale and viewers become bored with it; however, changing ads too frequently impedes the retention process. Reach and frequency affect the duration of a campaign. Higher frequency usually leads to a shorter duration. Low reach may be associated with a longer duration. In any case, typical campaigns last 1 to 2 months, but there are exceptions. Marlboro and Camel still use the same visual imagery and have never changed their basic advertisements, but these are rare examples.

Haik Humble Eye Center maintains visual consistency by using the same headlines in a number of different ads.
*Source:* Courtesy of Sartor Associates, Inc.

> ▶ It's everywhere you want to be.
> ▶ Are you feeling it?
> ▶ Just do it.
> ▶ You're in good hands.
> ▶ The brushing that works between brushings.
> ▶ Driving excitement.
> ▶ A different kind of company. A different kind of car.
> ▶ When you care enough to send the very best.
> ▶ The ultimate driving machine.
> ▶ It takes a licking and keeps on ticking.

**FIGURE 7.10**
**Which Taglines Can You Identify?**

Answers: VISA, Reebok, Nike, Allstate, Colgate, Pontiac, Saturn, Hallmark, BMW, Timex.

The third method used to build effective advertising campaigns is *repeated taglines*. Visual consistency combined with consistent taglines can be a powerful approach. The advertisement may change, but either the visual imagery or the tagline remains the same. The U.S. Army has promoted the tagline "Be all that you can be" for many years, and the Marines are known as "The few. The proud. The Marines." Taglines help consumers tie the advertisement into current knowledge structure nodes that already exist in their minds. Figure 7.10 contains some of the more common taglines. See how many you can identify.

A fourth advertising principle is *consistent positioning*. Maintaining consistent positioning throughout a product's life makes it easier for consumers to place the product in a cognitive map. When the firm emphasizes quality in every ad, it becomes easier to tie the product into the consumer's cognitive map than if the firm stresses quality in some ads, price in others, and convenience in a third campaign. This inconsistency in positioning makes the brand and company appear more confused and harder to remember. Consistent positioning avoids ambiguity, and the message stays clear and understandable.

*Simplicity* is the fifth principle of effective advertising. Simple advertisements are easier to comprehend than are complex ads. A print ad with a simple tagline and limited copy is much easier to read than an overloaded or complex one. Consequently, advertisers must resist the temptation to relate all of a product's attributes in a single advertisement. This practice is more prevalent in business-to-business print advertisements, but it should be avoided there as well. Further, consumer ads on radio or television spots often are so verbally overloaded that the announcer is forced to talk faster. This is usually ineffective, because the listener has too much information to grasp in such a short time period.

The principle of simplicity should be carefully applied to Internet advertising. The primary reason for simplicity with the Internet is load time. Individuals surfing the Internet will not wait more than a few seconds for something to load; if it doesn't load quickly, they move on to another site.

The next principle of effective advertising is the concept of an *identifiable selling point*. The emphasis should be placed on all three of the words: (1) identifiable, (2) selling, and (3) point. The advertisement should have a selling point (price, quality, convenience, luxury, etc.) that is easily identifiable to the viewer of the ad. It is important to remember that an advertisement should sell a product's *benefits* as much as the product itself. Also, the concept is a selling point, not selling *points*. The best advertisements are those that emphasize one major point and do not confuse the viewer by trying to present too many ideas. An advertisement's primary goal is to fix the product into the cognitive map of the viewer through establishing new linkages or strengthening current linkages. An identifiable selling point helps reach that goal.

The final principle is to *create an effective flow*. In a print ad, the reader's eye should move easily to all of the key points in the ad. In a television ad, the points to be made should flow in a manner that leads the consumer to the appropriate action or conclusion. Ads without flow confuse the consumer or are simply tuned out.

## Beating Ad Clutter

Overcoming clutter is a major challenge when creating an effective advertising campaign. The presence of a competitor's ad within the same medium or time slot makes the ad clutter problem worse. A recent survey of television advertising revealed that during prime-time programming, 42 percent of the ads shown had one or more of their competitors also advertising during the same hour. Research suggests that an advertisement's effectiveness is significantly reduced when a competitor's advertisement runs during the same time slot.[26]

One method advertisers use to overcome this brand interference is repetition. Repeating an ad can increase brand and ad recall. In advertising studies, repetition is effective in increasing recall if no competitor ads are present. When competitor ads are present, repetition does not help the competitive ad interference problem and does not stimulate greater recall.

Mere repetition of an ad does not always work. Therefore, advertisers have begun to emphasize the principles present in **variability theory**.[27] The theory suggests that variable encoding occurs when a consumer sees the same advertisement in different environments. These varied environments increase an ad's recall and effectiveness by encoding it into the brain through various methods. Creatives can generate the effect by varying the situational context of a particular ad. For example, the MasterCard campaign noted previously uses various settings to convey the same basic message, "There are some things money can't buy. For everything else, there's MasterCard." Varying the context of the ad increases recall, which is an effective method for overcoming competitive ad interference.[28]

These two advertisements for Absolut Vodka beat ad clutter through repetition and through the use of variability theory in using more than one message.

*Source:* Under permission by V&S Vin & Spirit AB. Absolut country of Sweden Vodka & Logo, Absolut, Absolut Bottle Design and Absolut Calligraphy are trademarks owned by V&S Vin Spirit AB © 2002 V&S Vin & Spirit AB.

Another method designed to decrease the impact of competing ads is to use a second medium. Using two media to convey a message generally is more effective than repeating an advertisement within the same medium. An ad placed in more than one medium also reduces competing ad interference. In other words, an ad that appears on television and in magazines works better than one that appears only on television. Consumers seeing an advertisement in a different medium are more likely to recall the ad than if it is always seen in only one medium.

Clutter remains a difficult problem in advertising. Creatives who are able to capture the attention of the audience and transmit messages successfully are in great demand. Companies constantly experiment with various approaches to reach audiences. When a program works, the advertising firm and its client have a great deal to celebrate.

## SUMMARY

Advertising is the process of transmitting a personal message through one or more impersonal media. The message should reflect the image that occurs throughout an IMC program. Three types of message strategies are present in advertisements. Cognitive strategies emphasize rational and logical arguments to compel consumers to make purchases. Affective strategies are oriented toward buyer emotions and feelings. Conative strategies are linked to more direct responses, behaviors, and actions. These strategies should be integrated with various types of appeals through the media selected for the campaign.

Executional frameworks tell the story in the ad. Animation has become more sophisticated and provides many new creative approaches in the design of ads. The slice-of-life approach and dramatizations are problem-solving types of ads, leading the consumer to something better by using the product. Testimonials are rendered by individuals who have realized the benefits of a product. An authoritative expert can build consumer confidence in a product or company. Demonstrations show how products can be used. A fantasy takes people away from the real world to a make-believe place. This makes the product more exotic and desirable. Informative ads render basic information about the product. Each execution can be used effectively to persuade consumers and business-to-business buyers to consider a company's offerings.

Celebrities, CEOs, experts, and typical persons can be chosen to be "out front" in the advertisement. Each has advantages and disadvantages. The marketing team selects sources or spokespersons based on the individual's attractiveness, likeability, trustworthiness, expertise, or credibility. The more of these characteristics that are present, the better off the advertiser will be.

Effective ad campaigns are based on the seven principles of visual consistency, sufficient campaign duration, repeated taglines, consistent positioning, simplicity, presentation of an identifiable selling point, and creation of an effective flow. Creatives and account executives must incorporate these principles into the advertising campaign to enhance the odds of success. Also, clutter must be overcome by repeating ads and showing them in various media, or in some other way.

Designing ads is often considered the most glamorous part of the advertising industry, and it is in many ways. Remember, however, that the other side of the glamour coin is hard work and the constant pressure to perform. Many people think being a creative is a burnout-type of job. At the same time, those who have proven track records of success are well rewarded for their efforts. Utilizing the principles presented in this chapter can be key to success in the highly competitive and exciting business of advertising design.

## REVIEW QUESTIONS

1. Name the three types of message strategies creatives can use. How are message strategies related to the message theme?

2. What types of products or services best match cognitive message strategies? Name the five types of cognitive approaches.

3. When will an affective message strategy be most effective? What two types of affective messages can creatives design? Give an example of each.

4. What is the primary goal of a conative message strategy?

5. How is an executional framework different from an ad appeal? How are they related?

6. List as many uses of animation-based advertisements as possible. What forms of animation are possible with the available technology?

7. How are slice-of-life and dramatization executional frameworks similar? How are they different?

8. How are authoritative and informational executional frameworks similar? How are they different?

9. What types of testimonials can advertisers use? Give an example of each.

10. Which media are best for demonstration-type ads?

11. What kinds of products or services are best suited to fantasy-based executional frameworks? What products or services are poor candidates for fantasies?

12. Name the four main types of sources or spokespersons. What are the advantages and disadvantages of each?

13. Name the five key criteria used when selecting a spokesperson. Which four build to the fifth?

14. Name the tactics available to overcome clutter. How does variability theory assist in this process?

## KEY TERMS

**message theme**  The outline of the key idea(s) that the advertising program is supposed to convey.

**message strategy**  The primary tactic used to deliver the message theme.

**cognitive message strategy**  The presentation of rational arguments or pieces of information to consumers.

**generic messages**  Direct promotions of product attributes or benefits without any claim of superiority.

**preemptive messages**  Claims of superiority based on a specific attribute or benefit of a product that preempts the competition from making the same claim.

**unique selling proposition**  An explicit, testable claim of uniqueness or superiority that can be supported or substantiated in some manner.

**hyperbole**  Making an untestable claim based upon some attribute or benefit.

**comparative advertisement**  The direct or indirect comparison of a good or service to the competition.

**affective message strategies**  Ads designed to invoke feelings and emotions and match them with the good, service, or company.

**resonance advertising**  Attempting to connect a product with a consumer's experiences to develop stronger ties between the product and the consumer.

**emotional advertising**  Attempting to elicit powerful emotions that eventually lead to brand recall and choice.

**action-inducing conative advertisements**  Advertisements that create situations in which cognitive knowledge of the product or affective liking of the product follow the actual purchase or arise during usage of the product.

**promotional support conative advertisements**  Ads designed to support other promotional efforts.

**executional framework**  The manner in which an ad appeal is presented.

**expert authority**  When an advertiser seeks to convince viewers that a given product is superior to other brands in some authoritative manner.

**sources and spokespersons**  Persons in the advertisement who make the actual presentation.

**similarity (source)**  Consumers are more inclined to be influenced by a message delivered by a person who is somehow similar.

**identification (source)**  Occurs when the receiver is able, in some manner, to identify with the source, either through a fantasy or by similar beliefs, attitudes, preferences, behaviors, or by being in the same or a similar situation.

**visual consistency**  Occurs when consumers see a specific image or visual display repeatedly.

**variability theory**  A theory stating that when a consumer sees the same advertisement in different environments, the ad will be more effective.

## CRITICAL THINKING EXERCISES

### Discussion Questions

1. Mark five advertisements in a magazine. Identify the message strategy, appeal, and executional framework each uses. Did the creative select the right combination for the advertisement? What other message strategies or executional frameworks could have been used?

2. Record five television advertisements on videotape. Identify the message strategy, appeal, and executional framework each uses. Did the creative select the right combination for the advertisement? What other message strategies or executional frameworks could have been used?

3. Studies involving comparative advertisements as compared to non-comparative ads produced the following findings.[29] Discuss why you think each statement is true. Try to think of comparative ads you have seen that substantiate these claims.

   a. Message awareness was higher for comparative ads than for non-comparative ads if the brands were already established brands.

   b. Brand recall was higher for comparative ads than for non-comparative ads.

   c. Comparative ads were viewed as less believable than non-comparative ads.

   d. Attitudes toward comparative ads were more negative than toward non-comparative ads.

4. Suppose Charles Schwab wants to develop an advertisement with the message theme that Charles Schwab understands the

needs of individual consumers and can design an investment strategy to meet each person's particular needs. Which type of message strategy should Schwab choose? Why? Based on the message strategy chosen, which executional framework should the company use? Why? What type of source or spokesperson should Schwab use? Why? Would the type of media being used for the advertisement affect the message strategy choice? Explain your answer.

5. A resort in Florida wants to develop an advertisement highlighting scuba diving classes. Pick one of the following combinations of message strategy, appeal, and executional framework. Then design an advertisement using those components.

   **a.** Hyperbole cognitive message strategy, humor appeal, and demonstration execution

   **b.** Emotional message strategy, emotional appeal, and slice-of-life execution

   **c.** Conative message strategy, scarcity appeal, and informative execution

   **d.** Emotional or resonance message strategy, sex appeal, and fantasy execution

   **e.** Comparative message strategy, fear appeal, and a testimonial execution

6. Name three influential commercial spokespersons. For each one, discuss the five characteristics used to evaluate spokespersons. Next, make a list of three individuals who are poor spokespersons. Discuss each of the five evaluation characteristics for each of these individuals. What differences exist between an effective and a poor spokesperson?

7. Find a copy of a business journal such as *BusinessWeek* or *Fortune,* or a trade journal. Also locate a copy of a consumer journal such as *Glamour, Time, Sports Illustrated,* or a specialty magazine. Look through an entire issue. What differences between the advertisements in the business journal and consumer journals are readily noticeable? For each of the concepts that follow, discuss specific differences you noted between the two types of magazines. Explain why the differences exist.

   **a.** Message strategies

   **b.** Executional frameworks

   **c.** Sources and spokespersons

# INTEGRATED LEARNING EXERCISES

1. Animation is often used on a Web site to add to its appeal. Two sources of free animation that can be used for your personal Web site or for a commercial Web site are at www.camelotdesign.com and www.animationlibrary.com. Access each site. What types of animation are available? How could animation be used to enhance a commercial Web site?

2. Current as well as past Super Bowl ads are available at www.superbowl-ads.com. Access the site and compare Super Bowl ads for the last several years. What types of message strategies were used? What types of executions were used? Who and what types of endorsers were used? Compare and contrast these three elements of ads.

3. Most advertising agencies provide examples of advertisements on company Web pages. The goal is to display the agency's creative abilities to potential clients. Using a search engine, locate three different advertising agencies. Locate samples of their work. Compare the ads produced by your three agencies in terms of message appeals, executions, and spokespersons. What similarities do you see? What differences do you see? Which agency, in your opinion, is the most creative? Why?

4. Access the following Web sites. For each one, identify the primary message strategy used. What type of executional framework is present? Does the site use any sources or spokespersons? What type of appeal is used? For each Web site, suggest how the site could be improved by changing either the message strategy, the executional framework, or both. Be specific. Explain how the change would improve the site.

   **a.** Georgia–Pacific (www.gp.com)

   **b.** Playland International (www.playland-inc.com)

   **c.** MGM Grand (www.mgmgrand.com)

   **d.** The Exotic Body (www.exoticbody.com)

   **e.** CoverGirl (www.covergirl.com)

   **f.** American Supercamp (www.americansupercamp.com)

   **g.** Windmill Hill Tennis & Golf Academy (www.windmillhill.co.uk)

5. Identify a commercial that uses each of the following executional frameworks. Evaluate the advertisement in terms of how well it is executed. Also, did the appeal and message strategy fit well with the executional framework? Was the ad memorable? What made it memorable?

   **a.** Animation

   **b.** Slice-of-life

   **c.** Dramatization

   **d.** Testimonial

   **e.** Authoritative

   **f.** Demonstration

   **g.** Fantasy

   **h.** Informative

## STUDENT PROJECT

### IMC Plan Pro

Emotion, reason, or action. One of these driving forces will be the main ingredient in the theme of an advertising campaign. Once you select the main strategy, you can develop an advertising program that will resonate with the right customers, whether they are individual buyers or other companies. The IMC Plan Pro booklet and disk available from Prentice Hall are designed to help you make logical, consistent choices for your advertising program.

# CASE 1

## CHARITABLE COMPETITION

John Mulvaney was placed in charge of his company's newest account, the United Way Charities of Savannah, Georgia. This branch of the United Way had never retained the services of an advertising agency but had gotten caught in the crush of competitive problems in the past decade. Consequently, the organization decided it was necessary to prepare more professional advertisements in order to succeed in the new millennium.

At the first meeting with the organization's leaders, John discovered a world of competition he had never envisioned. First of all, the number of charities competing for contributions had grown exponentially in the past decade. Relief for terrorism and disaster victims, women's shelters, homeless shelters, performing arts facilities, veterans groups, colleges and universities, minority organizations, Girl Scouts, Boy Scouts, and dozens of other charities were in the marketplace for charitable dollars. Illnesses alone included heart disease, lung disease, AIDS, MD (Jerry Lewis telethon), blindness, and many others. Organizations representing these causes contact small and large donors alike.

Second, bad publicity had tainted the entire industry. Church scams combined with spending abuses by leaders of other charities had created a negative impact. Many people believe charities simply fund themselves, with very few of the dollars actually reaching people in need. As a result, contributions had declined.

Third, a booming economy had created an odd effect. On the one hand, the number of extremely rich people had grown, especially those associated with Silicon Valley. Many of these individuals were actually trying to be effective altruists. Unfortunately, far too many of these givers wanted to see their names on buildings rather than simply making contributions to operating budgets. Also, prosperity (lower unemployment, fewer people in poverty) had created a kind of complacency in which many regular givers had begun to assume there was simply less need for charity.

The United Way had received major support from the NFL for more than 2 decades. Visibility was high, and the organization had a solid base of donations. The goal was to build on this base and combat the problems that had grown. John contacted his best creative, Tom Prasch, to see what could be done.

Tom argued that the primary problem with United Way ads was that they were boring. They typically showed a football player visiting a sick child or shaking hands with some community leader. Viewers could tune them out easily. Tom said the United Way needed something that would recapture the attention of John Q. Public. Tom told John and the United Way that he believed strongly in the use of seven attention-getting factors:

1. Intensity
2. Size
3. Contrast
4. Repetition
5. Motion
6. Novelty
7. Familiarity

Intensity means that bright, loud, strong stimuli capture the attention of the audience. A large-size billboard or full-page newspaper ad is more likely to be noticed than something normal or small. Contrast is the difference between dark and light or loud and soft. Repetition means something repeated has attention-getting value. Motion captures attention, even in print ads where the illusion of movement can be created. Novelty occurs when someone encounters a novel stimulus in a familiar setting (a new piece of furniture in a living room will be immediately noticed). Familiarity means finding something familiar in an unfamiliar setting such as seeing the Golden Arches in a foreign country.

Tom suggested that the United Way had only one solid attention-getting factor: its logo. It was highly recognizable from being repeated for so many years. None of the other factors was featured in the ads.

John gave the United Way a major discount in billing for services. He also constructed a very conservative budget. The group agreed that any endorser must volunteer his or her time in order to serve. Then, they turned Tom loose to create a new local campaign.

1. Design a campaign for the United Way of Savannah. Use Tom's attention-getting factors to create the ads.

2. Which media should the United Way use? Why?

3. What kind of message strategy would be best? Why?

4. What kind of executional framework should be used? Why?

5. What kind of source or spokesperson is best for this campaign? Defend your choice.

# CASE 2

## HANK'S FURNITURE MART

Hank Freeman was excited. His new store, Hank's Furniture Mart, was about to open. Hank had been in the furniture business for more than 10 years, first as a delivery and setup man and then as an in-store salesperson. This was his big chance to launch out on his own. Using some money that he inherited, various loans, and the investment of a silent partner, the mid-price range retail furniture store was ready for business.

Hank's Furniture Mart was located outside the city limits of a large metropolitan subdivision. Being outside the city limits meant customers would not have to pay city sales tax. The store was part of a large corner cluster. Hank's agreement with the other tenants was to stay out of the mattress and bedding business, because another retailer exclusively sold those items. He also agreed that he would not sell television sets or stereos, for the same reason. A "country-kitchen" chain restaurant was located across the parking lot from the retail stores. The entire shopping complex could easily be reached, because of its convenient location next to the interstate.

Hank knew any furniture store faced a variety of competitors. On the high end, stores such Ethan Allen attracted the affluent customers. On the lower end were large warehouse-style operations offering low prices and prompt delivery of lower-quality pieces. In the middle, several retail chains sold various furnishings. Specialty stores that focused solely on recliners were also close by.

Two advantages gave Hank hope that his store would be a grand success. The first was his extensive knowledge of the retail furniture business. He knew how various stores competed, whether it was through price, quality, offering "deals," or any other tactic. His knowledge extended to the various manufacturers. Hank knew which ones gave the best deals, which ones delivered merchandise on time (or late), and the quality levels of the pieces each sold.

The second advantage was Hank's extensive potential customer base. Hank had been working in the retail furniture marketplace for more than a decade. He believed he had a series of loyal buyers and that word-of-mouth would be a big help.

(continued)

At the same time, Hank knew he would have to advertise. He had set aside enough money to fund television spots, radio, newspaper, Internet, and specialty ads including direct mail. Hank had chosen a local agency to develop a consistent theme across all the store's ads. He suggested the tagline "Hank's Furniture Mart: Our prices are right and our deals are real."

1. What type of message strategy should Hank's Furniture Mart feature?

2. What type of executional framework should Hank's ads utilize? Which type of appeal will the framework feature?

3. Who should be the spokesperson for the store, Hank or a paid professional actor?

4. Design a print ad for Hank's Furniture Mart.

# ENDNOTES

1. Based on information found in Lisa Bertagnoli, "Duck Campaign Is Firm's Extra Insurance," *Marketing News* 35, no. 18 (August 27, 2001), pp. 5–6.

2. David Aaker and Donald Norris, "Characteristics of TV Commercials Perceived As Informative," *Journal of Advertising Research* 22, no. 2 (1982), pp. 61–70; Henry A. Laskey, Ellen Day, and Melvin R. Crask, "Typology of Main Message Strategies for Television Commercials," *Journal of Advertising* 18, no. 1 (1989), pp. 36–41.

3. Stephanie Thompson, "Mobile Meals Gaining," *Advertising Age* 74, no. 25 (June 23, 2003), p. 20.

4. Kenneth Hein, "Nintendo Takes Charge with DS," *Brandweek* 46, no. 6 (February 7, 2005), p. 15.

5. Bradley Johnson, "IBM Moves Back to Intel Co-op Deal," *Advertising Age* 68, no. 10 (March 10, 1997), p. 4.

6. Shailendra Pratap Jain and Steven S. Posavac, "Valenced Comparisons," *Journal of Marketing Research* 41, no. 1 (February 2004), pp. 46–56.

7. Dhruv Grewal and Sukumar Kavanoor, "Comparative Versus Noncomparative Advertising: A Meta-Analysis," *Journal of Marketing* 61, no. 4 (October 1997), pp. 1–15; Shailendra Pratap Jain and Steven S. Posavac, "Valenced Comparisons," *Journal of Marketing Research* 41, no. 1 (February 2004), pp. 46–56.

8. Naveen Donthu, "A Cross-Country Investigation of Recall of and Attitudes Toward Comparative Advertising," *Journal of Advertising* 27, no. 2 (Summer 1998), pp. 111–121.

9. Joseph R. Priester, John Godek, D. J. Nayakankuppum, and Kiwan Park, "Brand Congruity and Comparative Advertising: When and Why Comparative Advertisements Lead to Greater Elaboration," *Journal of Consumer Psychology* 14, no. 1/2 (2004), pp. 115–124; Grewal and Kavanoor, "Comparative Versus Noncomparative Advertising: A Meta-Analysis"; "Bring Back Brand X," *Advertising Age* 70, no. 46 (November 8, 1999), p. 60.

10. Joanne Lynch and Leslie de Chernatony, "The Power of Emotion: Brand Communication in Business-to-Business Markets," *Journal of Brand Management* 11, no. 5 (May 2004), pp. 403–420;

Karalynn Ott, "B-to-B Marketers Display Their Creative Side," *Advertising Age's Business Marketing* 84, no. 1 (January 1999), pp. 3–4.

11. Atifa Hargrave-Silk, "Microsoft Softening Up Hard-Edged Corporate Image," *Media Asia* (February 27, 2004), p. 8.

12. Tracy Krisanits, "GSK Rolls Out Corporate Ad Campaigns," *Medical Marketing & Media* 39, no. 4 (April 2004), p. 9.

13. Jim Hanas, "Rotscope Redux," *Creativity* 10, no. 1 (February 2002), pp. 40–41.

14. Karen Moltenbrey, "Horsing Around," *Computer Graphics World* 27, no. 3 (March 2004), pp. 28–29.

15. Michael L. Maynard, "Slice-of-Life: A Persuasive Mini Drama in Japanese Television Advertising," *Journal of Popular Culture* 31, no. 2 (Fall 1997), pp. 131–142.

16. Hillary Chura, "Maytag Airs Epic Drama for $35 Mil Range Intro," *Advertising Age* 70, no. 28 (July 5, 1999), p. 4.

17. Amilda Dymi, "Wachovia Claims First Place in Community Development," *Financial News* 28, no. 14 (December 29, 2003), p. 6.

18. J. Levine, "Fantasy, Not Flesh," *Forbes* 145, no. 2 (January 22, 1990), pp. 3–5.

19. Sam Bradley, "Marketers Are Always Looking for Good Pitchers," *Brandweek* 37, no. 9 (February 26, 1996), pp. 36–37.

20. Claire Murphy, "Stars Brought Down to Earth in TV Ads Research," *Marketing* (January 22, 1998), p. 1.

21. Roobina Ohanian, "Construction and Validation of a Scale to Measure Celebrity Endorsers' Perceived Expertise," *Journal of Advertising* 19, no. 3 (1990), pp. 39–52.

22. "Battle of the Net Worth Stars," *Brandweek* 45, no. 45 (December 13, 2004), p. 20–22.

23. Wayne Friedman, "Home Runs Kings Still, But Not with Ad Deals," *Advertising Age* 70, no. 28 (July 5, 1999), pp. 3–4.

24. Carolyn Tripp, Thomas D. Jensen, and Les Carlson, "The Effects of Multiple Product Endorsements by Celebrities on Consumers'

Attitudes and Intentions," *Journal of Consumer Research* 20 (March 1994), pp. 535–547.

25. David J. Moore and John C. Mowen, "Multiple Sources in Advertising Appeals: When Product Endorsers Are Paid by the Advertising Sponsor," *Journal of Academy of Marketing Science* 22, no. 3 (Summer 1994), pp. 234–243.

26. Raymond R. Burke and Thomas K. Srull, "Competitive Interference and Consumer Memory for Advertising," *Journal of Consumer Research* 15 (June 1988), pp. 55–68.

27. A. W. Melton, "The Situation with Respect to the Spacing of Repetitions and Memory," *Journal of Verbal Learning and Verbal Behavior* 9 (1970), pp. 596–606.

28. H. Rao Unnava and Deepak Sirdeshmukh, "Reducing Competitive Ad Interference," *Journal of Marketing Research* 31, no. 3 (August 1994), pp. 403–411.

29. Grewal and Kavanoor, "Comparative Versus Noncomparative Advertising: A Meta-Analysis."

# Advertising Media Selection

## Chapter Objectives

*Master* **the process of creating a media strategy.**

*Understand* **the roles media planners and media buyers play in an advertising program.**

*Utilize* **reach, frequency, continuity, impressions, and other objectives in the preparation of an advertising program.**

*Study* **and incorporate the advantages of various media in developing an ad program.**

*Recognize* **the value of an effective mix of media in an advertising campaign.**

## M&M'S: THE SWEET TASK OF MEDIA SELECTION

Can you remember the first time you ate M&M's? Most probably cannot, because it happened so early in life. The M&M's brand is one of the most famous and popular candies offered by Mars, Incorporated. Today, the brand enjoys an international presence that continues to grow.

M&M's began with a global flavor. According to legend, Forrest Mars Sr. was in Spain visiting soldiers fighting the Spanish Civil War. He noted that they were eating pieces of chocolate that were encased in a hard sugary coating. Using this as inspiration, Mars returned to the United States and refined the recipe for M&M's. The first packages were sold in 1941 in the United States. They were a favorite of many GIs serving in World War II. The original candies were sold in a cardboard tube. The famous brown and white label package didn't emerge until the late 1940s.

The legend of M&M's grew when colors were added to the original brown. In the 1960s, red, green, and yellow were created. Eventually, these and other colors developed into advertising spokescandies, including the egomaniac Red, the lovely female Green, the amazing Crispy Orange, Cool Blue, and, of course, nutty Yellow.

Red disappeared for a time from the M&M's mix after some research suggested concerns about red food dye, even though the problem was not associated with M&M's. In 1987, Red triumphantly returned, much to the joy of candy lovers around the world.

The advertising program for M&M's has been long-lasting, noteworthy, and award-winning. Practically any baby boomer remembers the original M&M's tagline: "Melts in your mouth, not in your hand." Television advertisements have long been the staple of M&M's. Using a natural tie-in with candy consumption at Christmas, an intense burst of M&M's advertising takes place each December. Most of these ads include a guest visit from Santa.

The effectiveness of the M&M's characters has allowed many additional forms of support advertising. Print ads featuring Red, Blue, Green, Yellow, and Orange are placed in magazines for both children and adults. The M&M's Web site celebrates the characters, even offering a bio for each individual color. The characters are featured in a "Virtual Hollywood" site that includes M&M's Studios. By 1996, the characters were more popular than Mickey Mouse and Bart Simpson. M&M's merchandise, such as stuffed "candy" pillows, are available online and in other retail locations.

Several exciting advertising and promotional programs have been used to advertise the M&M's brand. In 1998, M&M's became the "Official Spokescandies of the New Millennium," due, in part, to the good fortune of two "M"s (MM) being the equivalent of the Roman numeral for "2000." Also in 2000, the official candy name switched from M&M's *Plain* Chocolate Candies to M&M's *Milk* Chocolate Candies, a major victory for Red, who supported the more accurate brand name.

During the tragedy of September 11, 2001, M&M's were provided in a special package containing red, white, and blue colors only. The candies were distributed to rescue workers and others working near Ground Zero. Approximately $3 million of the proceeds from the sale of the limited edition were given to victims and survivors of the attacks.

At the close of 2004, all of the M&M's lost their color on Dick Clark's Rockin' New Year's Eve television show. The question was posed, "Will the colors come back?" Only black and white M&M's were on the market for about 2 months. Then, the colors returned with a grand celebration, noting, "Chocolate is better in color!"

Beyond advertising in print, electronic, and television media, M&M's are part of several charitable efforts. One is with the Special Olympics, in which a "Keep Wrappers to Keep Dreams Alive" promotion raised more than $1 million dollars for the charity. In 2003, M&M's "Groovy Summer" program was used to support the Susan G. Komen Breast Cancer foundation. Special pink and white candies were created as part of the effort.

The future of M&M's continues to be bright. Everything from a vote to choose a new color (purple won) to news that the candy flies on the Space Shuttle keeps M&M's a popular, memorable, fun brand in the eyes of candy lovers around the world.[1]

**overview**

If a tree falls in the forest, and no one is present, does it make a sound? This philosophical question has been asked for many years. In the world of advertising, one common problem is that too many "trees" fall as unheard and unseen advertisements. Successful marketing account executives help a firm identify target markets and then find media that reach the members of those markets, in both retail situations and business-to-business marketing efforts. Once they identify the right media, creatives design clever, memorable, exciting, and persuasive advertisements to help convince customers to purchase products.

This chapter explains the nature of advertising media selection. The topics include:

- The media strategy
- Media planning processes and the roles of the media planner and buyer
- Advertising objectives
- Media choices based on the advantages and disadvantages of each medium
- Media selection in business-to-business and international settings

Developing an advertising campaign within the framework of an integrated marketing communications program is a vital function that high-quality advertising agencies provide. Client companies depend on effective ads to attract customers and entice them into purchasing various goods and services. The goals are to build a firm's image and to create a larger consumer base. Advertising media selection is an important element in this process. A review of the elements of the selection process follows.

## MEDIA STRATEGY

One of the most important ingredients in matching an advertising campaign with the overall integrated marketing communications program is to prepare an effective media strategy. A **media strategy** is the process of analyzing and choosing media for an advertising and promotions campaign.

The average consumer reads or looks over only 9 of the more than 200 consumer magazines on the market. A radio listener usually tunes in to only 3 of the stations available in a given area. Television viewers watch fewer than 8 of the 30-plus stations available by cable or satellite, and average network prime-time ratings have declined by more than 30 percent throughout the last decade. Simply finding the right places to speak to potential customers is an increasingly challenging task (see the Communication Action box titled "Out with the Old: In with the New").

Also, to make the account executive and media buyer's jobs more difficult, prices for advertising time or space have not gone down and often have risen. Client budgets for advertising have not kept up with inflation, yet there are stronger demands for results and accountability. The marketing team faces many difficulties as they seek to provide the right media outlets for the company.

Once the media strategy is in place, other aspects of media selection can proceed. The first step is to prepare a thorough media planning program containing the firm's advertising objectives.

# COMMUNICATION ACTION

## Out with the Old: In with the New

To be successful in advertising in today's global market, many marketing teams must change their views of advertising. The old advertising model had three distinct concepts. The first was the idea that a "mass market" exists and can be reached through effective broadcast advertising. Second, the old model suggests that segmentation based on demographic factors such as age, income, gender, and education is sufficient to be able to create effective ads. Third, with enough repetition and reach to the mass markets, favorable impressions can be made. An analysis of the typical advertising budget using the old model shows the majority of advertising dollars spent on network television aimed at a mass audience with the goal of building brand equity, whereby consumers are led to believe that a given product or company has a distinct advantage in the marketplace. This perspective views brand awareness as the key, because it is the first step toward higher levels of brand equity. Therefore, advertisers felt regional and local advertising was not necessary. They were also not very interested in other media channels.

A revised view of advertising suggests a mass-appeal ad is not likely to be effective. Further, merely knowing a target market's demographic makeup is not sufficient, and using only network television does not automatically result in brand awareness, brand equity, and brand loyalty. The new method of advertising campaign development is based on the idea that it takes a more integrated approach based on an in-depth understanding of the target market. In addition to demographics, it is essential to know the lifestyles of the members of a target market, how these consumers think, what their opinions are, and to have a solid understanding of their media habits.

This new approach emerged when consumers became more sophisticated as they became exposed to a greater number of media outlets. Increased clutter created a highly refined ability to tune out ads and messages. To counter this tendency, the advertising agency chooses spots, magazine placements, newspaper sections, Internet links, and billboard locations based on the customer's strongest interests. In those situations, the individual is more likely to listen to, watch, or read an ad and actually process the information. The old method is simply "zapped" too easily, as consumers become increasingly better at ignoring mass-appeal approaches.

**Source:** Gary Blake, "Tune In to the New Face of Advertising," *Franchising World* 26, no. 5 (September–October 1994), pp. 8–10.

Developing a successful media strategy is the key to successful brands.
*Source:* Courtesy of Candie's, Inc.

# MEDIA PLANNING

Media planning begins with a careful analysis of the target market. While developing the media plan, it is important to:[2]

▸ Focus on consumer behavior

▸ Create plans that reflect the consumer's (or business's) purchasing process

▸ Influence consumers in the marketplace

- A favorite wake-up radio station or one listened to during the commute to work
- A favorite morning news show or newspaper
- Trade or business journals examined while at work
- A radio station played during office hours at work
- Favorite computer sites accessed during work
- Favorite magazines read during the evening hours
- Favorite television shows watched during the evening hours
- Internet sites accessed during leisure time
- Shopping, dining, and entertainment venues frequented

**FIGURE 8.1**
**Examples of Times Workers Are Exposed to Advertisements**

One method of addressing media planning is to study the media choices that members of a specific, defined target market might make during the course of a day. Some of the more common are listed in Figure 8.1.

Specific details of this type are extremely valuable when developing a media strategy. Simply knowing demographic information such as age, sex, income, and education is not enough to determine the media habits of a person in a target market. Information about the viewing patterns of customers helps the marketing team design messages that appeal to the right people. The message can also be made available at the best times and in the best places.

No two media plans are alike. Each plan should integrate the overall IMC strategy with specific marketing tactics. The typical components of a media plan include the following elements:

- A marketing analysis
- An advertising analysis
- A media strategy
- Media scheduling
- Justification and summary

A *marketing analysis* is a comprehensive review of the fundamental marketing program. It includes a statement of current sales, current market share, and prime prospects to be solicited (by demographics, lifestyle, geographic location, or product usage). These elements should reflect a compatible pricing strategy based on the product, its benefits and distinguishing characteristics, and an analysis of the competitive environment.

An *advertising analysis* states the fundamental advertising strategy and budget to be used in meeting advertising objectives. The *media strategy* spells out the media to be used and the creative considerations. The *media schedule* notes when ads will appear in individual vehicles. The *justification and summary* states the measures of goal achievement. It also states the rationale for each media choice. Each of the media plan's elements is described in greater detail in the upcoming sections.[3]

Several individuals are involved in media planning. In addition to account executives and creatives, most agencies utilize *media planners* and *media buyers*. In smaller agencies, the media planner and media buyer can be the same person. In larger companies, they usually are different individuals. A discussion of the main tasks performed in these positions follows.

## Media Planners

The **media planner** formulates a media program stating where and when to place advertisements. Media planners work closely with creatives, account executives, agencies, and media buyers. It is important for the creative to know which media will be used. The choices have a major impact on how advertisements are designed. Television ads are constructed in a different way from radio or newspaper ads.

Media planners provide extremely valuable functions and are in high demand. The issue of accountability for advertising results combined with need to create a "return on investment" of marketing dollars has led to a shift in more power now being held by the media buying side and less held by the creative side. Media planning drives much of the strategic planning process as advertising and marketing campaigns are developed. Marketing experts at companies such as Procter & Gamble and Unilever consider media planning to be the heart of a communications strategy. In the Unilever division of P&G, the first step is to set brand priorities and objectives. Next, a media channel communications plan is agreed upon before the actual communications plan and creative brief are prepared.[4] The challenge for media buyers in this environment, according to Carl Fremont of worldwide media services company Digitas, is "to integrate marketing messages across a range of media, and sometimes this involves working with several agencies to accomplish the client's goals."[5]

In most instances, the media planner conducts research to help match the product with the market and media. If a product's target market is 18- to 25-year-old males with college degrees who love the outdoors, then the media must have a high percentage of its audience in the 18- to 25-year-old, male, college-educated, outdoor category. It is no accident that a fishing magazine contains advertisements for a bass boat and fishing gear next to articles about the summer feeding habits of bass and other fish. A successful media planner identifies these ideal locations for the client's advertisements. The New Balance running shoe ad on this page was placed in *Runner's World* near an article about running. The media plan should be designed to find the best ways to reach the client's customers.

Part of the media planner's research is devoted to gathering facts about various media. This includes newspaper and magazine circulation rates and demographic groups other media reach. Besides demographic information, media planners want to know as much as they can about the lifestyles, opinions, and habits of each medium's audience. For instance, the audience for a television show may be quite different from those of a radio station or a magazine. Careful research improves the chances of selecting appropriate media for the campaign.[6]

Almost everyone has heard of S.O.S. soap pads. A few years ago, however, S.O.S. sales had begun to decline. The product was no longer the top-of-mind brand for many consumers. The task of rebuilding awareness for the S.O.S. soap pads in Canada was assigned to the Palmer Jarvis DDB agency. The agency's media planners began by examining the media habits of the primary target market for S.O.S. soap pads. The group consisted of women, ages 35 to 54, who work, have kids, and are in a busy, active household. Women in this target group are heavy magazine readers. They have interests in home décor, entertaining, gardening, and cooking. As a result, media buys were made in *Canadian Living, Cooking at Home, Canadian House & Home*, and *Homemaker's*. These magazines were the best match of product, market, and media habits of the main consumer group.[7]

An advertisement featuring New Balance shoes that was placed in *Runner's World* magazine.
**Source:** Courtesy of New Balance Athletic Shoes Inc. Photograph by Paul Wakefield.

"SUBURBAN DEW" (KM 55) :25/:05 - DEALER TAG
2005 STIHL Television

| VIDEO | SOUND |
| --- | --- |
| Early morning. Beautiful, picturesque house. | SFX: tension; foreboding music |
| Shots of dew on grass, dew on bushes, dew on tree leaves. | AVO: You think that's dew? |
| | AVO: Think again. |
| Energy picks up as tool fires up and begins trimming. | AVO: That's what's called a cold sweat... |
| Shots of different attachments being taken off, put on and used. | AVO: ...'cause our guy has the STIHL KombiSystem. |
| More shots of tool being used | AVO: One tool. Multiple attachments. AVO: Tremble with fear little yard. Tremble with fear. |
| Cut to beauty shot of tool and attachments hanging on pegboard. | AVO: The STIHL KombiSystem. |
| Are you ready for a Stihl? 1-800-GO-STIHL www.stihlusa.com | AVO: Are you ready for a STIHL? |

To order this TV spot, call Red Letter Communications @ 1-800-732-0054 and ask for Part # 0463-901-0319 for a 3/4" or Beta SP tape for broadcast use and Part # 0463-901-0320 for a VHS tape for viewing purposes.

The primary task of the media planner is to match the product's target market with the correct media and programs within the chosen media.
*Source:* Courtesy of STIHL Incorporated.

## Media Buyers

After the media are chosen, someone must buy the space and negotiate rates, times, and schedules for the ads. This is the work of the **media buyer**. Media buyers stay in constant contact with media sales representatives. They have a great deal of knowledge about rates and schedules. Media buyers also watch for special deals and tie-ins between different media outlets (e.g., radio with television, magazines with the same owner, etc.).

To ensure that promotional dollars are spent wisely, the media planner works with the media buyer, the creative, and the account executive in the design of an advertising campaign. Each plays a critical role in the development of an integrated marketing communications program. The challenge of coordinating the efforts of these individuals intensifies when they are from different companies.

The size of the advertising agency or media buying firm alone does not ensure effective media purchases. Although it would seem logical to assume that larger agencies have greater bargaining power with media outlets, it is not always true. There is little connection between the size of an advertising firm and the prices they can negotiate. In fact, in one study the differences in media costs were based on the time the actual purchase was made (closer to the day the ad was to run) rather than the size of the agency.[8] Other major factors in cost differences are knowledge of the marketplace and the ability to negotiate package deals. Spot television media plans vary by as much as 45 percent in the price of the spot. A **spot ad** is a one-time placement of an ad on a local television station. Rates are negotiated individually by the times ads appear with individual stations. For example, a media plan costing one firm $10 million can cost another firm $15.3 million. Radio time slots vary by as much as 42 percent and national print ads by as much as 24 percent.[9]

More importantly, differences in effectiveness of advertising are often related to:

▶ Quality media choices (the right ones) made by each agency
▶ Creativity
▶ Financial stewardship ("bang" for your advertising buck)
▶ Agency culture and track record
▶ Computer systems to analyze data
▶ Relationships between the agency and the medium's sales representative

The negotiated price is only one element in the success of an advertising program. Effectiveness in advertising is also determined by quality of the selections made by the marketing team and the content of the ad itself. Media should be selected and purchased with specific advertising objectives in mind. These goals assist marketing team members in choosing the right media and combining them effectively to achieve the desired results.

# ADVERTISING OBJECTIVES

In selecting media, it is important to review the communications objectives established during the development of the IMC program. These objectives guide media selection decisions as well as the message design (see Chapters 6 and 7). Several concepts or technical terms are used in media objectives, including:[10]

- Reach
- Frequency
- Opportunity to see (OTS)
- Gross rating points
- Cost per rating point
- Cost
- Continuity
- Impressions

These ingredients are the key features of an advertising program. **Reach** is the number of people, households, or businesses in a target audience exposed to a media vehicle or message schedule at least once during a given time period. A time period is normally 4 weeks. In other words, how many targeted buyers did the ad reach?

**Frequency** is the average number of times an individual, household, or business within a particular target market is exposed to a particular advertisement within a specified time period, again, usually for 4 weeks. Or, how many times did the person see the ad during the campaign? A regular viewer sees the same ad shown each day on *Hollywood Squares* more frequently than an ad shown once on *The Apprentice,* even though the program has a far greater reach. In media planning, instead of frequency, **opportunities to see (OTS)** is commonly used. Opportunities to see refer to the cumulative exposures achieved in a given time period. For example, if a company places two ads on a television show that is televised weekly, then during a 4-week period there are 8 OTS (4 shows x 2 ads per show).

**Gross rating points (GRP)** are a measure of the impact or intensity of a media plan. Gross rating points are calculated by multiplying a vehicle's rating by the OTS, or number of insertions of an advertisement. GRP gives the advertiser an idea about the odds of the target audience actually viewing the ad. By increasing the frequency, or OTS, of an advertisement, the chances of a magazine reader seeing the advertisement increase. It makes sense that an advertisement in each issue of *Time* during a 4-week period is more likely to be seen than an advertisement that appears only once in a monthly periodical.

*Cost* is a measure of overall expenditures associated with an advertising program or campaign. Another useful number that can be calculated to measure a program's costs is its **cost per thousand (CPM)**. CPM is the dollar cost of reaching 1,000 members of the media vehicle's audience. The cost per thousand is calculated by using the following formula:

$$CPM = (Cost\ of\ media\ buy/Total\ audience) \times 1,000$$

Table 8.1 shows some basic cost and readership information. The first three columns of the table provide the name of the magazine, the cost of a 4-color full-page advertisement, and the magazine's total readership. The fourth column contains a measure of the CPM of each magazine. The cost per thousand (CPM) for *National Geographic* is $16.44. This means that it takes $16.44 to reach 1,000 *National Geographic* readers. Notice the CPM for *Sports Illustrated* is $71.11 and for *Travel & Leisure,* $83.09. The readership of *Travel & Leisure* is the lowest, and yet its CPM is the highest of all eight magazines. In terms of cost per thousand readers, the best buy is *Southern Living,* at only $1.98 per thousand.

Another cost calculation can be made besides CPM. One critical concern is the cost of reaching a firm's target audience. Therefore, a measure called the **cost per rating**

| Magazine | Cost for 4-Color Full-Page Ad | Total Readership (000s) | CPM Total | Target Market (20M) | |
|---|---|---|---|---|---|
| | | | | Rating (Reach) | Cost per Rating Point (CPRP) |
| National Geographic | $ 346,080 | 21,051 | $16.44 | 16.1 | $21,496 |
| Newsweek | 780,180 | 15,594 | 50.03 | 12.2 | 63,949 |
| People | 605,880 | 21,824 | 27.76 | 9.4 | 64,455 |
| Southern Living | 11,370 | 5,733 | 1.98 | 2.4 | 4,738 |
| Sports Illustrated | 965,940 | 13,583 | 71.11 | 10.5 | 91,994 |
| Time | 1,324,282 | 21,468 | 61.69 | 15.9 | 83,288 |
| Travel & Leisure | 183,216 | 2,205 | 83.09 | 2.3 | 79,659 |
| U.S. News & World Report | 100,740 | 8,929 | 11.28 | 8.3 | 12,137 |

**TABLE 8.1**

Hypothetical Media Plan Information for Select Magazines

point **(CPRP)** was developed. The cost per rating point is a relative measure of the efficiency of a media vehicle relative to a firm's target market. **Ratings** measure the percentage of a firm's target market that is exposed to a show on television or an article in a print medium. To calculate the cost per rating point, the formula is

$$CPRP = Cost\ of\ media\ buy/Vehicle's\ rating$$

Table 8.1 ratings were generated for potential buyers of a 35 mm camera (see the case at the end of this chapter). The table shows the CPRP for *National Geographic* is $21,496. This is the average cost for each rating point or of each 1 percent of the firm's target audience (35 mm camera buyers). Not all readers of a magazine are part of the firm's target market. The CPRP more accurately measures an advertising campaign's efficiency than does CPM. Notice that the CPRP is the lowest for *National Geographic, Southern Living,* and *U.S. News & World Report.*

CPRP provides a relative measure of reach exposure in terms of cost. For example, it costs $21,496 to reach 1 percent, or 200,000, of the 20 million in this firm's target market using *National Geographic.* To reach 1 percent, or 200,000, using *Sports Illustrated* costs $91,994. To reach 1 percent, or 200,000, using *Southern Living* costs only $4,738. Because *Southern Living* is so efficient, why wouldn't a media planner just do all of the advertising in that magazine? The answer lies in the rating for *Southern Living.* Advertising in only that magazine reaches just 2.4 percent of the target audience, meaning 97.6 percent of the target market does not read *Southern Living.* Thus, another magazine or media outlet is necessary to reach them. This example explains why diversity in media is essential to reach a large portion of a firm's target market.

To further study whether or not an ad has reached the target market effectively, a **weighted (or demographic) CPM** figure may be calculated, as follows:

$$Weighted\ CPM = \frac{Advertisement\ cost \times 1,000}{Actual\ audience\ reached}$$

For example, if the cost of an advertisement in *Sports Illustrated* is $115,000, and the magazine reaches 4,200,000 readers, the standard CPM would be $27.38. If the ad targets parents of Little League baseball players, and research indicates that 600,000 of *Sports Illustrated's* readers are Little League parents, the result would be:

$$Weighted\ CPM = \frac{\$115,000 \times 1,000}{600,000} = \$191.66$$

This figure could be compared to figures for *Sporting News, ESPN Magazine,* and other sports magazines.

**Continuity** is the exposure pattern or schedule used in the ad campaign. The three types of patterns used are continuous, pulsating, and discontinuous. A **continuous campaign** uses media time in a steady stream. The Skechers ad shown on this page could be presented on a continuous schedule. To do so, the media buys would be for ad space in specific magazines for a period of 1 to 2 years. By using different ads and rotating them, readers will not get bored because they will see more than one ad for the same product. A **pulsating schedule** means there is a minimal level of advertising at all times but there are also increases in advertising at periodic intervals. A retailer such as JCPenney might advertise throughout the year but increase the number of advertisements in small, short bursts around holidays, including Christmas, Thanksgiving, Memorial Day, Labor Day, Mother's Day, Father's Day, and Easter. The goal of pulsating advertising is to reach consumers when they are most likely to make purchases or buy special merchandise, such as during the holiday shopping season. Thus, a Blockbuster advertisement just prior to Christmas can encourage consumers to purchase Blockbuster gift cards. A **flighting (or discontinuous) campaign schedule** places advertisements at special intervals with no advertising between. A ski resort is following a flighting advertising schedule when it runs several ads during the fall and winter seasons but none during the spring and summer.

A Christmas advertisement by Blockbuster promoting a gift card as the "perfect holiday gift."
***Source:*** Courtesy of Blockbuster Entertainment Group.

A Skechers advertisement promoting shoes.
***Source:*** Courtesy of Skechers USA Inc.

The final objective advertisers consider is the concept of *impressions*. The number of **gross impressions** is the total exposures of the audience to an advertisement. It does not take into consideration what percentage of the total audience may or may not see the advertisement. Table 8.1 indicates that the total readership of *National Geographic* is 21,051,000. If six insertions were placed in *National Geographic,* multiplying the insertions by the readership would yield a total of 126 million impressions.

## ACHIEVING ADVERTISING OBJECTIVES

One continuing issue facing advertisers is deciding how many times a person must be exposed to an ad before it has an impact. Most agree that a single exposure is not enough. Discovering the actual number has inspired a great deal of debate. Some argue it takes three exposures. Others say as many as 10. The basic rule, developed by Herbert Krugman, states that it takes a minimum of three exposures for an advertisement to be effective. This is the *three-exposure hypothesis*. Most media planners have assumed it for many years.[11]

Now, many advertisers think three exposures are not enough to create an impression in the consumer's mind, primarily because of the amount of clutter that exists. Clutter also affects the types of objectives firms try to accomplish. For instance, increasing brand awareness is usually easier than building brand image. Attention-getting is easier than holding someone's interest long enough to make a point about the firm's image. Also, a well-known brand that is the first choice of the majority of consumers can accomplish its objective with fewer ad exposures than a less well-known brand.

Seeking to discover the minimum number of exposures needed to be effective is based on two concepts: effective frequency and effective reach. **Effective frequency** refers to the *number of times* a target audience must be exposed to a message to achieve a particular objective. **Effective reach** is the *percentage of an audience* that must be exposed to a particular message to achieve a specific objective. The concept of effective reach implies that some minimum number of exposures exists.

Effective frequency and effective reach are crucial. Too few exposures means the advertiser will fail to attain its intended objectives. On the other hand, too many exposures wastes resources. The goal is to discover the optimal reach and frequency mix to accomplish the intended objectives without experiencing diminishing returns from extra ads. Remember that the optimal mix for an objective dealing with brand recognition is different than if the objective involved is brand recall.

When the objective is to increase brand recognition, the emphasis will be on the visual presentation of the product and/or logo. The goal is to create or strengthen a linkage in the person's knowledge structure between the brand and other nodes of knowledge that already exist. Rather than have the individual recall the brand name from memory, the advertiser wants the person to recognize the brand name and logo at the retail store or in an advertisement. In this situation, advertisers want to increase reach, exposing a maximum percentage of the target audience to the brand's name, logo, and selling point. Media that are good at maximizing reach include television, billboards, magazines, the Internet, and direct mail.[12]

When the objective is to increase brand recall so the brand name becomes a part of the person's evoked set, then frequency is more important than reach. Repetition is required to embed a brand name in the consumer's cognitive memory. Repetition increases the odds that a particular brand will come to mind when a person thinks about a product category. The more often a consumer hears the brand name, the greater the probability it will be remembered. When the name of a restaurant is mentioned seven times in a 30-second commercial, it is more likely the name will be remembered than if it is stated only once or twice. In terms of media selection, television, radio, newspapers, and the Internet offer the potential for high frequency.[13]

Other elements can also enhance effective frequency and effective reach. They include the size, placement, and the length of an ad. A small magazine advertisement does not create the same impact as a larger ad. In television advertising, a spot in the middle of an ad sequence usually has less of an impact than the ads shown at the beginning and end of the series. If a firm uses 15-second television ads, effective frequency may require six exposures. In comparison, a longer 45-second spot may only require only four exposures to be remembered.

Another important factor that affects these objectives is the number of different media used in an advertising campaign. In general, a campaign featuring ads in two types of media, such as television and magazines, has greater effective reach than a campaign in only one medium, such as magazines only. A recent survey of Australian automobile buyers indicated that for customers of a particular car manufacturer or dealership, newspaper advertising was the most popular method for receiving promotional information followed by direct mail. For noncustomers of a particular auto brand, however, television was rated as the most preferred source of promotional information, followed closely by newspapers and direct mail.[14] The media mix is described in greater detail later in this chapter.

In recent years, numerous media companies have designed computer models to optimize reach and frequency. One of the more popular is *Nielsen SAVE*. The program examines cable TV alternatives and calculates the value of each using criteria such as Nielsen TV audience data (ratings), product purchasing information, customer preference cluster data, and specific systems data. Another version, *ADPlus* software, combines reach and frequency information with media mix information, budgeting data, and customized information for the individual advertiser. *Adware* provides Arbitron and Nielsen rating information, calculates media costs, and is designed to project GRP.

These and other software programs help the marketing team evaluate effective reach and frequency. They are based on probability theory. The programs help the marketing team allocate advertising dollars and may also show where interaction effects are present. An interaction of an attention-getting television ad with a magazine ad with copy explaining a product's features may have a synergistic effect. This means the ads in two media work together and are more potent than the impact of either ad alone.

## Recency Theory

A new theory concerning reach and frequency challenges the traditional three-exposure hypothesis. The approach, called *recency theory*, suggests that a consumer's attention is selective and focused on his or her individual needs and wants.[15] The traditional three-exposure hypothesis is based on the *intrusion value* of advertisements and the idea that advertisements can make an impact on an audience regardless of individual needs or wants. **Intrusion value** is the ability of media or an advertisement to intrude upon a viewer without his or her voluntary attention.

Recency theory states that consumers have selective attention processes as they consider advertisements. They give the most attention to messages that might meet their needs or wants. The closer or more recent an ad is to a purchase, the more powerful the ad will be. Also, when a consumer contemplates a future purchase of the product being advertised, it becomes more likely that the consumer will pay attention to and react favorably toward the ad. This means that a member of a buying center from a business in the market for a new copier will more readily notice copier advertisements. An individual who is not in the market for a copier ignores the same ad. The same is true in consumer markets: An individual needing a new pair of jeans notices clothing ads, especially ones that feature jeans.

Recency theory suggests that it is a waste of money when ads reach either individuals or businesses that are not in the market for a particular product or have no interest in it. Advertisers should carefully target ads to individuals who want or need a firm's goods and services. In other words, advertising life insurance to teenagers wastes promotional

The size and placement of this Palm-Aire magazine advertisement will have an impact on its effective frequency and effective reach.
*Source:* Courtesy of Konica Minolta Business Solutions U.S.A., Inc.

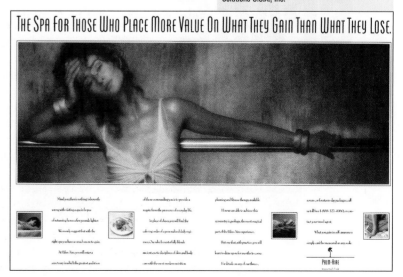

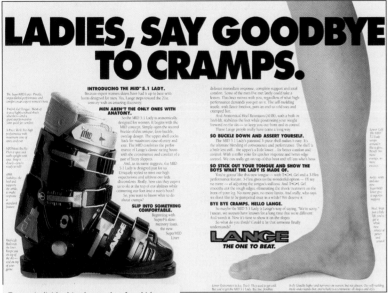

For an individual in the market for ski boots, one exposure to this advertisement may be enough to get her attention.

*Source:* Courtesy of Skis DYNASTAR, Inc.

A business advertisement for Polycom.

*Source:* Courtesy of Polycom Inc.

funds. At the same time, advertising supplemental health insurance to the elderly on social security is highly likely to be noticed and have a profound impact on that target market.

One primary difference in recency theory is the idea that one ad exposure is enough to affect an audience when that person or business needs the product being promoted. Additional exposures actually may not be necessary. The advertising strategy that matches recency theory spreads the message around using a variety of media, each one providing only one exposure per week or time period. In the case of selling supplemental health insurance to the elderly, magazines such as *Senior Living*, televisions spots on local news and weather programs, and newspaper ads close to the obituary section can quickly reach the target audience in a cost-effective manner. Such an approach, which maximizes reach, accomplishes more than increasing frequency.

In the business-to-business arena, applying recency theory means that ads should appear in a number of outlets rather than running a series of ads in one trade journal. Many times, a number of individuals are members of the buying center. Each has different interests and responsibilities. To make sure each one sees the ad, placing ads in all of the journals that might be read by a given buying center member is the secret to success. To facilitate the purchasing process for a company seeking to buy an audioconferencing system, the media buyer purchases space in trade journals, human resource journals, sales journals, and business journals. This increases the odds that the message will effectively reach various members of the buying center. Recency theory suggests that one exposure might be enough for each member, because the member is looking for information and is ready to make a purchase decision. To reach business personnel while traveling, Polycom recently placed an advertisement in the Delta Airline's *Sky* magazine, because of the higher odds that more than one buying center member might see the ad while flying with Delta.

Once the media buyer, media planner, account executive, and company leaders agree about basic objectives of the advertising campaign, they can select the actual media. Marketing experts consider each medium's distinct pros and cons as well as logical (and illogical) combinations of media. The next section examines media that an advertising program can use, leading to the final selection of media for the company's campaign.

## MEDIA SELECTION

There are many choices of advertising media. Effectively mixing these media is an important part of designing quality advertising. To do so, the advantages and disadvantages of each individual medium must be understood so that an advertising campaign features successful combinations.

| | |
|---|---|
| ▶ Word-of-mouth | 63% |
| ▶ Sampling | 45% |
| ▶ In-store | 32% |
| ▶ Mass media | 27% |
| —TV, radio, newspapers, magazines, outdoor | |
| ▶ Sponsorship | 23% |
| ▶ Alternative media—Viral, guerrilla | 18% |
| ▶ Public relations | 15% |
| ▶ Online | 10% |
| ▶ Direct mail | 7% |

**FIGURE 8.2**
**Percentage Indicating They Are "Very Attentive" to Brand Messages by Various Media**

*Source:* David Kaplan, "Study: Masses Still Tuned In to Mass Media," *Adweek* 44, no. 42 (October 27, 2003), p. 12.

It also helps to know how attentive consumers are to various media. The degree of attention varies considerably. Factors such as the target audience, product category, and media programming all affect how closely an ad is watched. A recent study conducted by MediaVest USA sheds some light on the how attentive consumers are to brand messages in different methods of communication. Word-of-mouth messages were at the top of the list. Of the survey sample, 63 percent said they pay more careful attention to brand messages conveyed by word-of-mouth. Second was sampling (45%), followed by in-store messages (32%), and mass media advertisements (27%). Mass media includes TV, radio, newspapers, magazines, and outdoor advertising.[16] The complete list is displayed in Figure 8.2.

## Television

For many years, television held the reputation of being the most glamorous advertising medium. A company featuring a television advertising campaign enjoyed a more prestigious reputation. To some, television advertising is still the best option. It is wise, however, to carefully consider whether or not a television advertisement is the optimal medium.

Table 8.2 lists the advantages and disadvantages of television advertising. As shown, television offers advertisers the most extensive coverage and highest reach of any of the media. A single ad can reach millions of viewers simultaneously. Even though total cost of running the ad is high, the cost per contact is relatively low. This low cost per contact justifies, for example, spending $2.5 million for a 30-second spot on the Super Bowl.

Further, television has the advantage of intrusion value, which is the ability of a medium or advertisement to intrude upon a viewer without his or her voluntary attention. Television ads with a catchy musical tune, sexy content, or humor can quickly grab a viewer's attention. Television provides many opportunities for creativity in advertising design. Visual images and sounds can be incorporated to capture the viewer's attention and present persuasive messages. Products and services

| Advantages | Disadvantages |
|---|---|
| 1. High reach | 1. Greater clutter |
| 2. High frequency potential | 2. Low recall due to clutter |
| 3. Low cost per contact | 3. Channel surfing during commercials |
| 4. High intrusion value (motion, sound) | 4. Short amount of copy |
| 5. Quality creative opportunities | 5. High cost per ad |
| 6. Segmentation possibilities through cable outlets | |

**TABLE 8.2**
**Television Advertising**

can be demonstrated on television in a manner not possible in print or using radio advertisements.

Clutter remains the primary problem with television advertising, especially on syndicated programs. The average for syndicated programs is 13 minutes and 56 seconds of commercials per hour. Among the broadcast networks, ABC runs the most nonprogramming materials. ABC shows 12 minutes and 29 seconds of nonprogramming materials per hour. CBS has the lowest rate at 11 minutes and 17 second per hour. On the cable side, Headline News shows more commercials than syndicated programs. The rate is 14 minutes and 51 seconds per hour. Other cable channels high on the list are E!, TBS, and MTV.[17] On average, a 30-minute television program is packed with between 12 and 15 commercials. Many viewers switch channels during these long commercial breaks. Thus, messages at the beginning or near the end of the break have the best recall. Those in the middle often have virtually no impact. Therefore, clutter makes it difficult for a single message to have much influence.[18]

Television commercials have short life spans. Sixty-nine percent of the national ads produced during the past year were 30-second ads. Occasionally an advertiser purchases a 15-, 45- or 60-second ad, but those are rare. Another disadvantage of television is the high cost per ad not only for the media time but also in terms of production costs. Outstanding commercials often are expensive to produce. The average cost to produce a 30-second national ad is $358,000. Production fees account for the largest portion of the cost, an average of $236,000. Other costs include director fees ($23,000), editing and finishing the ad ($45,000), and creative/labor fees and music ($34,000).[19]

Another disadvantage of television advertising is that the spots are shown so frequently that they can quickly lose the ability to attract the viewer's interest. Companies are forced to replace the ads with something new before consumers get tired of them and tune them out. At the same time, the marketing team wants to run an ad long enough to recover the production costs.

In recent years, choosing the best television advertising outlets for an ad has become more challenging. A variety of options exist. Advertisers try to select the programs and channels that are most likely to be viewed by members of the target market audience. It is advisable to match a firm's target audience with specific shows. Each television network and each television show tends to attract a specific type of audience. A cable television program can provide a well-defined audience consisting of a more narrowly defined target market.

To gain a quick sense of how well an advertisement fared in terms of reaching an audience, a given program's *rating* can be calculated. The typical ratings formula is:

$$\text{Rating} = \frac{\text{Number of households turned to a program}}{\text{Total number of households in a market}}$$

In the United States, the total number of households with television sets is approximately 109.7 million. To calculate the rating of an episode of *American Idol,* if the number of households tuned to the season finale was 17.8 million, then the rating would be:

$$\text{Rating} = \frac{17,800,000}{109,700,000} = 16.2$$

Next, if the advertiser were interested in the percentage of households that actually were watching television at that hour, the program's share could be calculated. If 71 million of the 109.7 million households had a television turned on during the hour in which *American Idol* aired, the share would be:

$$\text{Share} = \frac{\text{Number of households tuned to } American\ Idol}{\text{Number of households with a television turned on}} = \frac{17,800,000}{71,000,000} = 25$$

| TV Show | Cost (30-Second Ad) | Nielsen Rating |
|---|---|---|
| *American Idol* | $658,333 | 16.2 |
| *Survivor* | $412,833 | 10.8 |
| *CSI: Miami* | $374,231 | 10.0 |
| *Everybody Loves Raymond* | $315,850 | 9.8 |
| *Two and a Half Men* | $249,017 | 9.6 |
| *Law and Order* | $227,500 | 8.3 |

**FIGURE 8.3**
Cost of a 30-Second Ad
and Nielsen Rating

*Sources:* "Average Price of a 30-Second Ad for Fall 2004," *The Futon Critic* (www.thefutoncritic.com, March 29, 2005); "Nielsen Media Research Top 20," (http://tv.yahoo.com/nielsen, March 29, 2005).

A 16.2 rating would mean 16.2 percent of all televisions in the United States were tuned to *American Idol.* A 25 share means 25 percent of the households with a television actually turned on were watching the program.

Of course, there is no guarantee that the viewers saw the commercial. Ratings and share are only indicators of how well the program fared against the competition. They are used to establish rates for advertisements. The higher a show's rating over time, the more that is charged for an advertisement. For example, *American Idol* had a rating in March 2005 of 16.2, and a 30-second spot cost $658,333. *Survivor* had a rating of 10.8 with a 30-second ad costing $412,833. Figure 8.3 provides the cost and ratings of other TV shows.

The primary organization that calculates and reports rating and share is the ACNielsen. The company also provides local channel information regarding shares of stations in local markets known as *designated marketing areas* (DMAs). Data gathering techniques used by Nielsen include diaries written by viewers who report what they watched, audience meters that record what is being watched automatically, and people meters that allow the viewing habits of individual members of families to be tracked.

These numbers can be further refined to help advertisers understand whether an advertisement reached a target market. Within rating and share categories, the viewers can be subdivided by certain demographics, such as:

▶ Age

▶ Income

▶ Gender

▶ Educational level

▶ Race or ethnic heritage

Organizations that prepare this kind of information include Nielsen Media Research; Starch INRA; Hooper, Inc.; Mediamark Research, Inc.; Burke Marketing Research; and Simmons Market Research Bureau. An advertising team may find it extremely helpful to know that viewers of *The West Wing* tend to be college-educated, older than the age of 40, and have annual incomes of more than $50,000. If psychographic information can be added in (such as that the show is mostly watched by people who voted for Democrats in the previous election), then the advertiser has a good sense of whether this is the best audience for a given advertisement or campaign.

For local and regional advertisers, spot TV is the best option for television advertising. In many cases national brands supplement national commercials with spot TV purchases in select markets. Media planners do this primarily because of the high cost of national ad time and because 75 percent to 80 percent of prime-time slots are sold out during the spring, shortly after they go on the market. By selecting local early news, late news, and local prime access, a media planner can generate higher GRP at a lower cost than if only national ad time is purchased.

Two measures, called the *brand and category development indices* (*BDI* and *CDI*), can be used to help pick spot TV times. The *brand development index* is the market's percentage

This advertisement for *Men's Fitness* also prominently displays the magazine's Web site.

*Source:* Courtesy of *Men's Fitness*, American Media Inc.

exposed to an advertisement, the frequency of that exposure, and if the person has interacted with the ad in any way. Further, advertisers can actually determine how an individual interacted with an ad, which sections of the ad, and what they did. This type of feedback is not available with any other medium.[35]

Internet clutter is one disadvantage. The explosion of Internet advertising means many sites show numerous ads several layers deep. Web surfers quickly bypass these ads. In addition, a Web site filled with advertisements that delay its loading causes many surfers to become impatient and move on to other sites.

To counter the clutter, Audi of America designed a unique Web ad campaign for the A4 Sedan. Potential buyers were required to identify nine of the car's improvements via an online scavenger hunt. Every customer who found all nine improvements was entered into a contest. The prize was a 2-year lease of an Audi A4. The clues were clear and easy to find. The goal of the contest was to embed the Audi band name and features of the A4 sedan in the buyer's mind. The event was tied in with the NCAA men's basketball tournament and was aimed toward 28- to 35-year-old men with annual incomes of more than $75,000.[36]

Another problem is that Internet ads have short life spans. The wear-out time for Internet ads seems to be even shorter than that for other media.[37] This means advertisers must spend more time updating the advertisements if they hope to retain the audience's attention.

Unlike television, the Internet tends not to have intrusion value. Web surfers do not have to pause on an advertisement as one would have to do when looking at a magazine or newspaper. To get surfers to stop (i.e., to intrude upon individuals), ads featuring streaming videos and flashing displays have been developed and have proven to be less controversial than pop-up ads. Some advertisers have developed what is called *interstitial advertising*, which interrupts a person on the Internet without warning. These types of ads have to be clicked off to remove them from the screen, and they are extremely controversial. Although they have intrusion value, they also are annoying. Interstitial ads can come onto a person's computer even after logging off the Internet or come on the screen the next time the person logs on.[38] Although untested at this time, interstitial advertising could prove extremely valuable to business-to-business marketers. Targeted ads could be sent to members of the buying center even after they log off the computer. The chances of capturing some level of attention increase because these ads must be clicked off. Also, if the business buyer has been searching for information about a product and an advertisement for that product pops onto the screen, the individual will likely study the ad to see what is being offered.

The Internet is the fastest-growing medium in history. It took television 13 years to reach 50 million viewers. It took radio 38 years to reach 50 million. Experts estimate it took only 5 years for the Internet to reach 50 million users.

It is too early to know for sure the full impact of Internet advertising. If it is measured by the number of click-throughs, whereby the ad is quickly zapped, Internet advertising appears not to be as successful as advertisers first thought. Studies have shown that Web users tend to ignore banners, and most Internet users can't even remember the last banner

| Advantages | Disadvantages |
|---|---|
| 1. High market segmentation | 1. Declining readership (some magazines) |
| 2. Targeted audience interest by magazine | 2. High level of clutter |
| 3. Direct-response techniques (e.g., coupons, Web addresses, toll-free numbers) | 3. Long lead time |
| 4. High color quality | 4. Little flexibility |
| 5. Availability of special features (e.g., scratch and sniff) | 5. High cost |
| 6. Long life | |
| 7. Read during leisure time (longer attention to ad) | |

**TABLE 8.6**

**Magazine Advertising**

they clicked on. Some studies indicate that Internet advertising is ineffective. Other studies reveal the Internet is a successful method of advertising. A study by Millward Brown International concluded that brand awareness using Internet brand banners increased between 12 percent and 200 percent. Compared to brand awareness studies of television and radio ads, Internet banners generated greater ad awareness with a single exposure than did either television or radio.[39]

Internet advertising programs are certain to grow in the future. Chapter 13 is devoted to Internet marketing and e-commerce.

## Magazines

For many advertisers, magazines have always been a second choice. Recent research, however, indicates that in some cases magazines are actually a quality option. A study by the Magazine Publishers of America concluded that every dollar a company spends on magazine advertising yields an average of $8.23 in sales. The return on investment for all other media is $3.52 per dollar spent on advertising. The reason given for this huge difference is the magazine advertising's ability to target consumers more efficiently by demographics and lifestyles.[40] Naturally, the validity of these results has been staunchly debated by executives from other media. In any case, evidence exists that magazine advertising can be effective. Table 8.6 displays the pros and cons of magazine advertising.

One major advantage of magazines is the high level of market segmentation available. Magazines are highly segmented by topic area. Specialized magazines are much more common than general magazines with broad readerships. Even within certain market segments, such as automobiles, a number of magazines exist. Magazines are so highly differentiated that high audience interest becomes another advantage. An individual who subscribes to *Modern Bride* has some kind of strong attraction to weddings. People reading magazines also tend to view and pay attention to advertisements related to their needs and wants. Often, readers linger over an ad for a longer period of time because they read magazines in waiting situations (e.g., doctor's office) or during leisure time. This high level of interest, segmentation, and differentiation are ideal for products with precisely defined target markets.

Magazines allow a brand such as Tree Top to develop ads targeted to a highly segmented audience, such as this ad targeted to mothers of infants.
*Source:* Courtesy of Tree Top Apple Juice.

An advertisement encouraging people to purchase the spring issue of *Grace Magazine*.

*Source:* Used with permission of *The Joplin Globe*, Joplin, Missouri.

Trade and business journals are a major medium for business-to-business marketing. Businesses can target advertisements to buying center members. The ad copy can then provide a greater level of detail about products. Readers, if interested, take time to read the information in the ad. Ads can provide toll-free telephone numbers and Web addresses so that interested parties can obtain further information.

Magazines offer high-quality color and more sophisticated production processes, providing the creative with the opportunity to produce intriguing and enticing advertisements. Motion, color, and unusual images can be used to attract attention. Magazines such as *Glamour, Elle*, and *Cosmopolitan* use scratch-and-sniff ads to entice women to notice the fragrance of a perfume or cologne. Even car manufacturers have ventured into this type of advertising by producing the smell of leather in certain ads.

Magazines have a long advertising life that reaches, lasting beyond the immediate issue because subscribers read and reread them. This means the same advertisement is often seen by more than one person. It is not unusual for an avid magazine reader to examine a particular issue several times and spend a considerable amount of time with each issue. This appeal is attractive because advertisers know the reader will be exposed to the ad more than once and is more likely to pay attention. In addition, magazine ads last beyond the current issue. Weeks and even months later, other individuals may look at the magazine. In the business-to-business sector, trade journals are often passed around to several individuals or members of the buying center. As long as the magazine lasts, the advertisement is still there to be viewed.

One major disadvantage facing magazine advertisers is a decline in readers. The Leo Burnett Company's *Starcom Report* stated that magazines lost 61 million readers from the 18- to 49-year-old age bracket in just a year. Most moved to the Internet. Mediamark Research Inc. recently reported that magazine readerships declined by 5.9 percent for the same year. Of the 200 magazines examined, 56 gained readers while 144 lost readers.[41]

Although circulation continues to decline, ad revenue has rebounded in recent years and seen a steady increase; as a result, ad revenue is becoming a larger portion of a magazine's revenue. In 2004 advertising as a percentage of a magazine's total revenue was 53.7 percent; by 2008, it will rise to 59.5 percent. Part of this increase is due to the rising cost for a magazine ad. For national magazines, color ad rates now run approximately $10,000 per ad page for every 100,000 circulation. A magazine such as *Sports Illustrated*, therefore, charges $243,000 for a full-page color ad; *Parade* (newspaper supplement) charges $830,000. The full-page rate for *Better Homes and Gardens* is $339,000. *LIFE* magazine charges $310,000, and *ESPN, the Magazine* costs $148,000.[42]

Clutter is another big problem for magazine advertisers. A recent 318-page issue of *Glamour* contained 195 pages of advertising and only 123 pages of content. Ads can be easily lost in those situations. To be noticed, the advertisement must be unique or stand out in some way.

Long lead times are a major disadvantage of magazines, because advertisements must be submitted as much as 6 months in advance of the issue. Consequently, making changes in ads after submission is very difficult. Also, because of the long life of magazines, images or messages created through magazine advertising have long lives. This is good for stable goods or services, but not for volatile markets or highly competitive markets wherein the appeal, price, or some other aspect of the marketing mix changes more frequently.

Magazines continue to proliferate even with the problems of declining readership. The wide variety of special interests makes it possible to develop and sell them. Many advertisers still can target audiences and take advantage of various magazine features, such as direct-response Internet addresses and coupon offers. This is especially true in the business market. Although business-to-business marketers increasingly use other media, trade journals and business magazines remain an effective method of reaching their target markets. As a result, the nature of advertising in magazines may change, but individual companies still will find effective uses for the outlets.

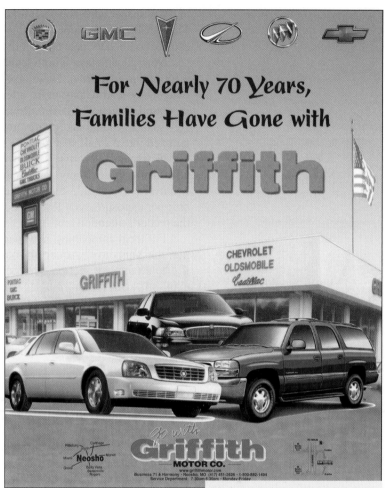

This award-winning advertisement was prepared by the staff of *The Joplin Globe*. *Source:* Used with permission of *The Joplin Globe*, Joplin, Missouri.

## Newspapers

When *USA Today* was launched, few believed a national daily newspaper could succeed. Obviously it has. The nature of news reporting has changed. Many small local papers no longer exist and conglomerates such as Gannett own most major city newspapers. Still, daily readership continues.

For many smaller local firms, newspaper ads, billboards, and local radio programs are the most viable advertising options, especially if television ads are too cost prohibitive. Newspapers can be distributed daily, weekly, or in partial form as the advertising supplements found in the front sections of many grocery stores and retail outlets. Table 8.7 displays the basic advantages and disadvantages of newspaper advertising.

Many retailers rely heavily on newspaper ads because they offer geographic selectivity (local market access). Promoting sales, retail hours, and store locations is easy to accomplish

| Advantages | Disadvantages |
|---|---|
| 1. Geographic selectivity | 1. Poor buying procedures |
| 2. High flexibility | 2. Short life span |
| 3. High credibility | 3. Major clutter (especially holidays) |
| 4. Strong audience interest | 4. Poor quality reproduction (especially color) |
| 5. Longer copy | 5. Internet competition with classified ads |
| 6. Cumulative volume discounts | |
| 7. Coupons and special-response features | |

**TABLE 8.7**

**Newspaper Advertising**

in a newspaper ad. Short lead time allows retailers to change ads and promotions quickly. This flexibility is a major advantage. It allows advertisers the ability to keep ads current. Ads can be modified to meet competitive offers or to focus on recent events.

Newspapers have a high level of credibility. Readers rely on newspapers for factual information in stories. Newspaper readers hold high interest levels in the articles they read. They tend to pay more attention to advertisements as well as news stories. This increased audience interest allows advertisers to provide more copy detail in their ads. Newspaper readers take more time to read copy, unless simply too much information is jammed into a small space.

Newspaper advertisers receive volume discounts for buying larger *column inches* of advertising space. Many newspapers grant these volume discounts, called *cumulative discounts*, for 1-month, 3-month, or even year-long time periods. This potentially makes the cost per exposure even lower, because larger and repeated ads are more likely to garner the reader's attention.

For local companies, newspapers offer an effective means of advertising. For example, the Vancouver Aquarium placed an ad featuring its spring break schedule in the life/entertainment section of a local newspaper. Parents flipping through the paper were exposed to a humorous message along with a list of events at the aquarium. A local newspaper ad for Healthy Inspirations Weight Loss & Lifestyle Centers generated 6 to 12 phone calls. The calls netted an average of 2.5 memberships per ad. The company calculated the acquisition cost for a new membership to be $92. After switching to freestanding insert in the paper, the number of phone calls rose to more than 30. This reduced the company's acquisition costs to $63 per new membership.[43]

There are limitations and disadvantages to newspaper advertising. First, newspapers cannot be targeted as easily to specific market segments (although sports pages carry sports ads, entertainment pages contain movie and restaurant ads, and so forth). Newspapers also have a short life. Once read, a newspaper normally is cast to the side, recycled, or destroyed. If a reader does not see an advertisement during the first pass through a newspaper, it probably will go unnoticed. Readers rarely pick up papers a second time. When they do, it is to continue reading, not to reread or rescan a section that has already been viewed.

Newspaper ads often have poor production quality. Many companies do not buy color ads because they are much more expensive. Photos and copy tend to be harder to read and see clearly compared to other print media, especially magazines. Newspaper ads tend not to be wild or highly creative. Newspaper editors normally avoid and turn down anything that may be controversial, such as Calvin Klein ads featuring more-or-less naked models. Newspapers are very careful about offending their readers.

Newspapers suffer poor national buying procedures. For a national advertiser, this means contacting numerous companies and using rate cards that vary by market. Also, newspapers tend to favor local companies instead of national firms. Local businesses generally receive better advertising rates than do national advertisers, because local companies advertise on a more regular basis and receive volume discounts. Also, newspapers want to have a strong local appeal. By favoring local companies in ad rates, they can meet this goal and seem more desirable to local patrons. To counter this difficulty, the Newspaper National Network (NNN) and Newspapers First have been formed to make national buys. NNN helps national advertisers reach virtually every daily U.S. newspaper with one buy and one bill. Another company, Newspapers First, is a cooperative that places ads in more than 40 large, daily newspapers.[44] As a result, national advertising, which makes up only 17 percent of all newspaper ad spending, is growing faster than any other category of newspaper advertising.[45]

Newspapers are used by many food manufacturers to promote their products. *Source:* Used with permission of *The Joplin Globe*, Joplin, Missouri.

## Direct Mail

Another major advertising medium is direct mail. Many companies send ads directly to target markets of customers through carefully constructed mailing lists. Other companies will blanket a region with direct mail information about more general products.

A few years ago, General Motors sent out 6 million direct-mail pieces as part of a 24-Hour Test Drive program. The mailing notified recipients that they could keep a vehicle overnight. GM also used the mailing to promote a $50 million giveaway. The idea was to generate traffic to GM showrooms and to build awareness of GM vehicles.

Frito-Lay relies on direct mail to increase awareness of new products. To introduce its new Naturals line of products, Frito-Lay mailed 500,000 coupons. To sell a new Sensible Snacks line, Frito-Lay mailed 400,000 coupons.

Direct mail is used by a variety of companies. According to Mark Siegel of AT&T Wireless, "There is an intimacy and personalization and therefore an impact with direct communication with a customer that you just don't get anywhere else." Average overall response to direct mail offers is 2.5 percent. Packaged-good manufacturers have the highest response rate (5.36%). Retailers have the second highest at 4.45 percent.[46]

The major advantage of direct mail is that it normally lands in the hands of the person who opens the mail, who usually makes a significant amount of family purchasing decisions. Many mail offers include direct-response programs, so results are quickly measured. Direct mail also can be targeted to geographic market segments.

The primary disadvantages of direct mail include costs, clutter, and the "nuisance" factor. To be noticed, direct-mail advertising usually requires a color brochure, making the mailings more expensive to produce. As postage rates continue to rise, so do the costs of direct mail. Mailings tend to clutter post office boxes and become more prevalent during key seasons, such as Christmas. Many people are genuinely annoyed by "junk mail" and actively seek to have their names taken off mailing lists, especially for catalog-type operations.

Direct mail suits well-known local or national firms seeking a more immediate response (e.g., coupon redemption) or when the company wants to reinforce ads presented in other media. Direct mail reaches some customers who do not buy newspapers. Record clubs, book clubs, and others have used direct mail effectively over the years. It is likely that many firms will continue to use direct mail in the future.

Direct mail remains a favorite marketing tool for business-to-business marketers. It provides a method of bypassing gatekeepers when the names of actual members of the buying center can be obtained. Direct mail can be one method of reaching businesses when they are in a straight rebuy situation with another vendor and not open to calls by salespeople. Even if the direct mail is ignored when it is received, many people often file it away for future use. Although the cost per contact is high for direct mail, so is the response rate as compared to other media. The key to success for businesses is to make sure that the direct-mail piece gets into the hands of the right person in the buying center and that it is attractive enough to grab attention.

## Alternative Media

Besides all of the "traditional" and new (Internet) media discussed, numerous alternative ways are available for companies sending out advertisements. The key, as always, is to make certain the ads reach the right target market with the proper message. Some examples of additional forms of advertising—some that are new and some that have existed for many years—include:

- Leaflets, brochures, and carry-home menus
- Ads on carry-home bags from stores (grocery stores and retail outlets)
- Ads on T-shirts and caps (promotional giveaways and products sold)
- Ads on movie trailers both in theaters and on home video rental products
- Small, freestanding mall signs

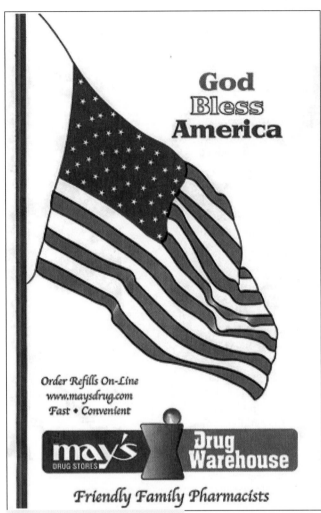

God
Bless
America

Order Refills On-Line
www.maysdrug.com
Fast • Convenient

may's
DRUG STORES

Drug
Warehouse

Friendly Family Pharmacists

May's Drug Stores placed this patriotic advertisement on all of the company's pharmacy bags to enhance the brand name.
*Source:* Courtesy of May's Drug Warehouse.

▶ Self-run ads in motel rooms on television, towels, ice chests, and other places

▶ Yellow pages and phone book advertisements

▶ Mall kiosk ads

▶ Ads sent by fax

▶ Ads shown on video replay scoreboards at major sports events

▶ In-house advertising magazines placed by airlines in seats

▶ Ads on the walls of airports, subway terminals, bus terminals, and inside cabs and buses or transit advertising

Each of these has additional benefits and problems. For example, yellow-page advertising has become more difficult as additional firms enter into the phone book preparation market. Mall kiosk ads are placed in high-traffic areas, but are easily defaced by vandals. Ads sent by fax are low cost and can be highly targeted (luncheon specials faxed to local companies just before noon). Still, many business owners become angry when their fax machines are tied up receiving ads. Ads on replay scoreboards have high intrusion values, yet can be ignored or even "booed" by those attending the game. Nonetheless, advertisers must consider all of the possibilities as they prepare advertising campaigns. The goals of reach, frequency, cost, and continuity must all be considered as individual media are selected and groups of media formulated into a campaign mix.

One of the more widely used alternative media programs is called **guerrilla marketing**, which is a focus on low-cost, creative strategies to reach the right people. Guerrilla marketing means the marketing team looks for ways to reach individuals and small groups in a unique way that will cause them to take notice. Creativity is the key to guerrilla marketing. For example, a booth at a golf tournament may be set up to allow customers to hit a tee shot and have a computer estimate the distance and accuracy of the drive. When the customer is handed a small piece of paper with the information, the paper contains not only the golf shot information, but also the advertiser's brand, tagline, and logo. This piece of paper will be kept and shown to others, thereby increasing awareness of the advertiser at a low cost, plus those shown the paper will be interested golfers, which is the target market.

Many national products are also displayed as part of a television program or movie. These are called *product placements*. Ford trucks appeared in the *Extreme Makeover* show hauling trailers and carting away refuse. A Ford Super Duty truck was also in the family's garage. Placements are relatively low-cost methods of achieving additional product exposures during a television program or film. Typical fees charged by film companies are $20,000 for showing the product, $40,000 for mentioning it, and $60,000 for the actor to actually use the product. Not all companies are willing to pay for a product placement. John Deere & Co. provides tractors and equipment for placement in movies and television shows, but does not pay to have them in the show. Company leaders also screen the show to make sure that it fits with the marketing image John Deere wishes to portray.[47]

Another form of placement is the purchase of advertising space in what will be key camera shots during sporting events. For instance, many Major League Baseball teams now allow ads to be displayed behind home plate, so that a center-field camera shot of the pitcher and the batter will also reveal the advertisement. Professional golfers, not to be outdone, are paid fees for wearing caps carrying the names of various companies. Tiger Woods wears a cap featuring the Nike swoosh, and Phil Mickelson wore one for KPMG Consulting for several years.

---

## ETHICAL ISSUES

### Media Selection for Adult Products

In 2002, NBC began accepting money to run advertisements for liquor products with alcohol contents that were stronger than beer or wine. Almost immediately, a host of critics argued that it would be unwise to subject minors to such ads. Eventually the network decided against running the ads. The debate once again raises questions about free speech and free enterprise and why the tobacco and alcohol industries are banned from advertising on specific media when other product categories do not face this media restriction.

After television tobacco advertising was banned by the government, marketers have created a series of tactics to make certain company products are mentioned on the air. Sponsorship of the Virginia Slims Tennis Tournament and Marlboro Cup Racing have come under congressional scrutiny, because sportscasters must state the names of the products while reporting scores and results. Is this ethical?

Many adult products require tasteful advertising and marketing programs, even when they are free to be shown through any medium. Feminine hygiene, condoms, and other personal adult products may be featured in practically any medium. It is the responsibility of the marketing professional to select media that are appropriate as well as create ads that will not be offensive.

In the international arena, this responsibility becomes even greater. In many Islamic countries, advertisements for personal hygiene or sexually related products would be highly offensive. It is important for company leaders to explore these cultural differences before undertaking any kind of marketing campaign.

---

One of the more creative approaches to establishing an alternate method of reaching customers involves using what is essentially "flip card" technology in subways. Instead of riders seeing barren walls, 20- to 30-second commercial messages appear through the windows. Target was among the first advertisers to utilize this unique new method for reaching customers.

The use of alternative media has risen dramatically in the past 20 years. Clutter and consumer disinterest in traditional advertising methods have driven marketing teams to look for new, distinctive ways to reach customers. They may be tied to traditional advertisements or stand-alone. They must, however, match the company's brand, image, and theme to be successful.

## MEDIA MIX

Selecting the proper blend of media outlets for advertisements is a crucial activity. As campaigns are prepared, decisions are made regarding the appropriate mix of media. Media planners and media buyers are both excellent sources of information about the most effective type of mix for a particular advertising campaign. It is the challenge of the creative to design ads for each medium that speak to the audience and that also tie in with the overall theme of the integrated marketing communications program.

Table 8.8 shows considerable differences in media mixes used by various industries. Notice that retailers spend more on newspaper advertising (41.3%) than they do on any other media. Apparel manufacturers spend 71.6 percent of budgets on magazines; restaurants spend 84.8 percent of advertising funds on television. Choosing the appropriate advertising channels and then effectively combining outlets requires the expertise of a media planner who can study each outlet and match it with the product and overall message.

Recent studies by Millward Brown and ACNielsen highlight the benefits of combining different media.[48] In a telephone survey, Millward Brown found that ad awareness was 65 percent when consumers viewed the ad both on television and in a magazine. It was 19 percent for those who saw only the magazine ad and 16 percent for those who saw only the television ad. The increased impact of using two or more media is called

**TABLE 8.8**

Advertising Expenditures
by Categories

|  | Magazines | Newspaper | Outdoor | Television | Radio | Internet |
|---|---|---|---|---|---|---|
| Retail | 8.4% | 41.3% | 1.8% | 37.0% | 4.6% | 6.9% |
| Automotive | 11.9% | 34.1% | 1.8% | 48.6% | 2.4% | 1.2% |
| Food and beverages | 24.2% | 0.6% | 0.8% | 70.6% | 2.7% | 1.0% |
| Airlines, hotels, car rental | 23.1% | 34.3% | 5.6% | 27.4% | 2.5% | 7.1% |
| Restaurants | 2.6% | 3.6% | 5.0% | 84.8% | 3.6% | 0.4% |
| Apparel | 71.6% | 1.1% | 0.9% | 22.9% | 0.7% | 2.8% |
| Total Domestic Ad Spending | 20.9% | 21.4% | 2.2% | 47.2% | 3.0% | 5.3% |

*Source:* "100 Leading National Advertisers," *Advertising Age* (June 29, 2004), pp. 1–5.

**TABLE 8.8**

Advertising Expenditures
by Categories

a **media multiplier effect**, which means the combined impact of using two or more media is stronger than using either medium alone. Business-to-business firms can apply this concept by buying ad space in places other than traditional trade journals. The key is finding effective combinations of media when designing a media mix.

Figure 8.5 shows possible linkages between various media. Consider the many possible options and combinations. Media experts work continually to decide which go together for individual target markets, goods and services, and advertising messages.

## MEDIA SELECTION IN BUSINESS-TO-BUSINESS MARKETS

Identifying differences between consumer ads and business-to-business ads is becoming more difficult, especially in television, outdoor, and Internet ads. In the past, it was easy to spot business-to-business ads. The content was clearly aimed toward another company, and television, outdoor, and the Internet were seldom used. Currently, about 56 percent of all business advertising dollars are spent in nonbusiness environments.[49]

Several items explain this shift to more nonbusiness media. First, business decision makers are also consumers of goods and services. The same psychological techniques used to influence and gain consumer attention can also be used for business decision makers.

Second, and probably the most important, business decision makers are very difficult to reach at work. Gatekeepers (secretaries, voice mail systems, etc.) often prevent information flow to users, influencers, and decision makers. This is especially true for straight rebuy situations whereby orders are given to the current vendor. If a company is not the chosen vendor, it is extremely difficult to get anyone's attention. To avoid various gatekeepers, business-to-business firms try to reach the members of the buying center at their homes, in their cars, or in some other nonbusiness venue.

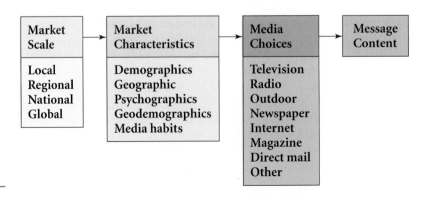

**FIGURE 8.5**
Developing Logical Combinations
of Media

A third reason for this shift to nonbusiness media is that the clutter among the traditional business media has made it more difficult to get a company noticed. Business advertisers recognize that a strong brand name is a major factor in making a sale. Taking lessons from brand giants such as Nike, Campbell's Soups, Wal-Mart, and Procter & Gamble, business marketers see the value of strong brand name, because the name helps a company gain the attention of members of the buying center.

Office Depot recently launched an advertising campaign directed toward their business customers, which make up approximately 80 percent of the company's customer base. The campaign, titled "Takin' Care of Business," highlighted the company's commitment to business customers. The ads ran as TV spots, along with radio, print, online, and search marketing ads. Office Depot also signed a sponsorship deal to be the official office products partner of NASCAR.[50]

In the past, business ads were fairly dull, but now they look much more like consumer ads. Creative appeals and the use of music, humor, sex, and fear, similar to consumer ads, are used. The boldest business ads sometimes include nudity or other more risqué material. In fact, many consumers cannot tell the difference.

B-to-B ads are now regular advertisers on the Super Bowl. At $2.5 million per 30-second ad, this is seen by many observers as a very risky venture. But considering that last year's Super Bowl audience totaled 86.1 million, others see it is a viable alternative to trade publications and an opportunity to reach business buyers. Evaluation evidence of the impact of the B-to-B ads would indicate they are a good buy. FedEx's 45-second spot in the 2005 Super Bowl featuring Burt Reynolds and a talented bear generated 186 broadcast mentions and publicity valued at $1.3 million. The three spots for Careerbuilder.com generated 250 broadcast mentions and generated $3.4 million worth of publicity.[51]

Figure 8.6 identifies how business-to-business advertising expenditures are divided among the various media. Figure 8.7 lists the top six business-to-business advertisers. As shown, trade journals remain the number-one media used in business settings. Approximately 43 percent of all B-to-B advertising dollars are spent here. Trade journals offer a highly targeted audience.

Trade journals provide an opportunity to reach members of the buying center whom salespeople cannot reach. Gatekeepers typically do not prevent trade journals from reaching different members of the buying center. Unfortunately, if the firm is in a straight rebuy situation, it is doubtful the ad will be noticed. If the firm is in a modified rebuy and the buying center is in the information search stage, then the ad has a better chance of success.

In addition to trade journals, business-to-business advertisers also use business magazines such as *BusinessWeek* and consumer magazines. A total of 53.9 percent of the advertising budget goes for magazines. When newspapers are added to this list,

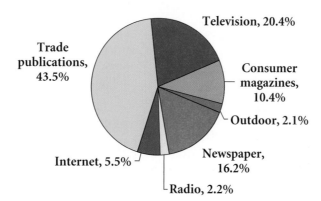

**FIGURE 8.6**
**Business-to-Business Advertising Expenditures**

*Source:* Reprinted with permission from *BtoB Magazine,* 2003. Copyright Crain Communications Inc.

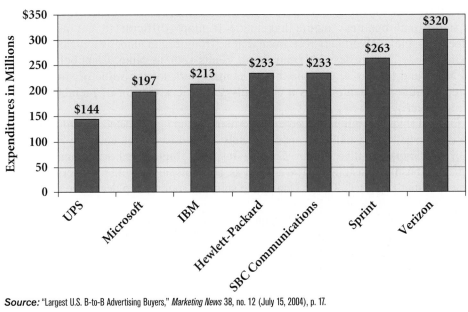

**FIGURE 8.7**
**Top Six Business-to-Business Advertisers**

*Source:* "Largest U.S. B-to-B Advertising Buyers," *Marketing News* 38, no. 12 (July 15, 2004), p. 17.

An advertisement for Internet banking.
*Source:* Courtesy of WingspanBank.com.

It works because
it was built from the Internet up.
Not from a bureaucracy down.

Checking
Credit Cards
Loans
CDs
Bill Pay
Mortgage Finder
Investing
Planning Tools

**WINGSPAN**
BANK.COM™

While traditional banks trundle online with the same old thinking, we're harnessing the power of the Internet to give you new financial power. Like loan answers in 51 seconds. Electronic bill pay. Even a credit card that saves 5% at leading web merchants. Someone has to lead banking in a new direction. Why not you?

www.WingspanBank.com ©1999. Bank products by FCC National Bank. Member FDIC. Investments through Wingspan Investment Services, Inc. Member NASD/SIPC.
INVESTMENTS NOT FDIC INSURED. MAY LOSE VALUE. NO BANK GUARANTEE.

print media accounts for 70.1 percent of all business-to-business dollars spent. The primary reasons for these high levels of expenditures in print media are because they have highly selective audiences and the ads have longer life spans in print. Business decision makers and members of the buying center spend more working time examining print media than any other medium. Business buying center members are more likely to notice the WingspanBank.com ad shown to the left when it is located in a trade journal than they would if the same ad ran in a more general-audience type magazine such as *Time*. A trade journal's readers are more likely to notice and read the advertisement because they are more likely to have been working with or thinking about banking or financial services within their companies.

Many goals in business-to-business advertisements are the same as those devoted to consumers. It remains important to identify key target markets, to select the proper media, and to prepare creative, enticing ads resulting in some kind of action, such as a change in attitude toward the company or movement toward a purchase decision. Many of the variables shown in Figure 8.5 apply equally well to business advertising.

## MEDIA SELECTION IN INTERNATIONAL MARKETS

Understanding media viewing habits in international markets is important for successful advertising programs. In Japan, television is a major advertising tool; in other countries, it is not as prevalent. In Europe, the best way to reach consumers is through newspapers. Magazines are also used more often in Europe; direct

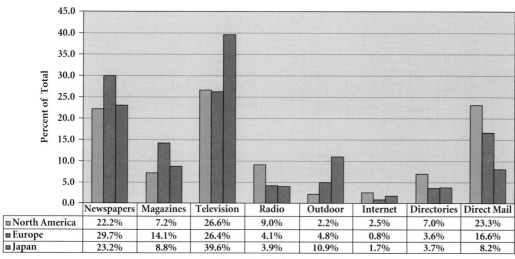

| | Newspapers | Magazines | Television | Radio | Outdoor | Internet | Directories | Direct Mail |
|---|---|---|---|---|---|---|---|---|
| North America | 22.2% | 7.2% | 26.6% | 9.0% | 2.2% | 2.5% | 7.0% | 23.3% |
| Europe | 29.7% | 14.1% | 26.4% | 4.1% | 4.8% | 0.8% | 3.6% | 16.6% |
| Japan | 23.2% | 8.8% | 39.6% | 3.9% | 10.9% | 1.7% | 3.7% | 8.2% |

*Source:* "Global Adspend Trends: Global TV Advertising," *International Journal of Advertising* 22, no. 4 (2003), pp. 567–568.

**FIGURE 8.8**
**Media Usage in North America, Europe, and Japan**

mail is used more often in North America. Figure 8.8 illustrates differences in media usage in North America, Europe, and Japan.

Just as media viewing differs, media buying in other countries often differs. For example, the trend in France is to farm media buying out to international media specialists. France's largest advertiser, PSA Peugeot Citroen, hired Euro RSCG's Mediapolis to do its media buying. Another advertising agency, the Danone Group, chose Carat Media Services France to handle its media buying. Several international companies operating in France follow this trend. Nestlé used to have its own internal company, Societe Publi Edition Distribution Courtage, to purchase media. Now it uses Optimedia, a media specialist firm.[52]

In other countries, the reverse may be true. Top advertising agency executives in Brazil fiercely oppose all independent media buying groups. They have even pushed for a change in the law that would prohibit the payment of agency commissions and discounts from media buying to any firm that is not a full-service advertising agency. In India, the Advertising Agencies Association passed a stern resolution requiring members to stop handling media-only accounts or risk expulsion from the association. The Advertising Agencies Association of India believes it is critical for the full-service agency to be involved in all aspects of a brand's advertising, including media buying. The resolution and opposition of the Advertising Agencies Association to media buying independents is aimed at Carat Media Services India—India's first independent media buying service. Carat successfully persuaded Charagh Dink, India's largest shirt maker, to move its entire media buying account to Carat while hiring a freelancer to do the creative work. Carat also captured business from BBC World, Cadbury India, and Virgin Music. To prevent expulsion from the Advertising Agencies Association of India, agencies such as Madison DMB&B, which handles media buying for firms such as Coca-Cola, have added small creative departments.[53]

In international settings, it is important to understand the media habits of consumers as well as their daily lifestyles. McCann-Erickson Worldwide launched a multinational media research effort named Media In Mind in Europe. The goals of this research were to: (1) improve media effectiveness by matching a firm's advertising to the time of day the audience will be most receptive and (2) select the correct medium. Such firms as Motorola, Johnson & Johnson, General Motors, Coca-Cola, and Boots Healthcare International use Media In Mind. They report increases in media effectiveness by as much as 20 percent more than those firms that do not use Media In Mind.

One aspect of Media In Mind's research in Europe has focused on consumer moods throughout the day. Boots Healthcare International used this research in the advertising of headache remedies. The research revealed that in Poland the people classified in the "headache" category were more likely to have a headache from the time they woke up until around noon. Thus, Boots Healthcare advertises on billboards that people see on their way to work or at lunch. The company also advertises on radio during the morning hours.[54]

In general, many tactics used to develop advertising campaigns in the United States apply to international advertising. What differs is the nature of the target markets, consumer media preferences, and the processes used to buy media. Also, companies must carefully attend to cultural mores to make sure the buying process does not offend the cultural and religious attitudes prevalent in any given region. It is important to carefully screen clothing, gestures, words, symbols, and other ingredients as a company purchases advertising time or space and prepares ads.

# SUMMARY

The traditional view of advertising has been to design a message that will accomplish the intended IMC objective and then find the best media channel. This view is slowly being replaced as the roles of media planners and media buyers grow in importance. According to Bob Brennan, chief operating officer of Chicago-based Leo Burnett Starcom USA, in the past, "Ninety-five percent of your success was great creative and 5 percent was great media. Now it's much closer to 50–50."[55]

This chapter reviews the media selection process. A media strategy is the process of analyzing and choosing media for an advertising and promotions campaign. Media planners and buyers complete much of this work. The media planner's primary job is to formulate a program stating where and when to place advertisements. Media planners work closely with creatives and account executives. Media buyers purchase the space, and they negotiate rates, times, and schedules for the ads.

The goals of reach, frequency, opportunity to see, gross rating points, effective rating points, cost, continuity, and impressions drive the media selection process. Reach is the number of people, households, or businesses in a target audience exposed to a media vehicle or message schedule at least once during a given time period. Frequency is the average number of times an individual, household, or business within a particular target market is exposed to a particular advertisement within a specified time period. Gross rating points (GRP) measure the impact or intensity of a media plan. Cost per thousand (CPM) is one method of finding the cost of the campaign by assessing the dollar cost of reaching 1,000 members of the media vehicle's audience. Cost per rating point (CPRP) is a second cost measure, which assesses the efficiency of a media vehicle relative to a firm's target market. Ratings measure the percentage of a firm's target market that is exposed to a show on television or an article in a print medium. Continuity is the schedule or pattern of advertisement placements within an advertising campaign period. Gross impressions are the number of total exposures of the audience to an advertisement.

In addition to these basic concepts, advertising experts often utilized the concepts of effective frequency and effective reach. Effective frequency is the number of times a target audience must be exposed to a message to achieve a particular objective. Effective reach is the percentage of an audience that must be exposed to a particular message to achieve a specific objective.

In seeking advertising goals, marketing experts, account executives, and others must assess the relative advantages and disadvantages of each individual advertising medium. Thus, television, radio, outdoor billboards, the Internet, magazines, newspapers, and direct mail should all be considered as potential ingredients in a campaign. Other new media can be used to complement and supplement the more traditional media outlets. Logical combinations of media must be chosen to make sure the intended audience is exposed to the message. The three-exposure hypothesis suggests that a consumer must be exposed to an ad at least three times before it has the desired impact; other experts believe even more exposures are necessary. In contrast, recency theory suggests that ads truly reach only those wanting or needing a product and, therefore, only one exposure is necessary when someone is "on the hot spot" and ready to buy.

In business-to-business settings, companies can combine consumer media outlets with trade journals and other business venues (trade shows, conventions, etc.) to attempt to reach members of the buying center. In many cases, enticing ads using consumer appeals such as sex, fear, and humor have replaced dry, dull, boring ads with an abundance of copy.

When designing business advertising, remember that advertising is just one component of the integrated marketing communications plan. It must be integrated with the sales force, sales promotions, trade promotions, and public relations. Business-to-business advertising using traditional consumer media cannot accomplish all of the communications objectives a business needs to accomplish. They help develop brand awareness and build brand equity, but are usually not the best for providing information the buying center needs.

International advertising media selection is different in some ways from that which takes place in the United States, because media buying processes differ as do media preferences of locals in various countries. At the same time, the process of media selection is quite similar: Marketing experts choose media they believe will reach the target audience in an effective manner.

Media selection takes place in conjunction with the message design and within the framework of the overall IMC approach. Effective media selection means the company spends enough money to find the target audience and does not waste funds by overwhelming them with the same message. Account executives, creatives, media planners, media buyers, and the company's representative must all work together to make certain the process moves as effectively and efficiently as possible.

## REVIEW QUESTIONS

1. What is a media strategy? How does it relate to the creative brief and the overall IMC program?

2. What does a media planner do?

3. Describe the role of media buyer in an advertising program.

4. What is reach? Give examples of reach in various advertising media.

5. What is frequency? How can an advertiser increase frequency in a campaign?

6. What are gross rating points? What do they measure?

7. What is the difference between CPM and CPRP? What costs do they measure?

8. What is continuity?

9. Describe the three-exposure hypothesis.

10. How is recency theory different from the three-exposure hypothesis?

11. What is effective frequency? Effective reach?

12. What are the major advantages and disadvantages of television advertising?

13. What are the major advantages and disadvantages of radio advertising?

14. What are the major advantages and disadvantages of Internet advertising?

15. What are the major advantages and disadvantages of magazine advertising?

16. What are the major advantages and disadvantages of newspaper advertising?

17. Is the strong intrusion value of television an advantage? Why or why not?

18. Name a product and three media that would mix well to advertise that product. Defend your media mix choices.

19. What special challenges does media selection present for businesses? What roles do gatekeepers play in creating those challenges?

20. What special challenges does media selection present for international advertising campaigns? What differences and similarities exist with U.S. media selection processes?

## KEY TERMS

**media strategy** The process of analyzing and choosing media for an advertising and promotions campaign.

**media planner** The individual who formulates the program stating where and when to place advertisements.

**media buyer** The person who buys the space and negotiates rates, times, and schedules for the ads.

**spot ad** A one-time ad placed on a local television station.

**reach** The number of people, households, or businesses in a target audience exposed to a media vehicle or message schedule at least once during a given time period.

**frequency** The average number of times an individual, household, or business within a particular target market is exposed to a particular advertisement within a specified time period.

**opportunities to see (OTS)** The cumulative exposures to an advertisement that are achieved in a given time period.

**gross rating points (GRP)** A measure of the impact or intensity of a media plan.

**cost per thousand (CPM)** The dollar cost of reaching 1,000 members of the media vehicle's audience.

**cost per rating point (CPRP)** A measure of the efficiency of a media vehicle relative to a firm's target market.

**ratings** A measure of the percentage of a firm's target market that is exposed to a show on television or an article in a print medium.

**weighted (or demographic) CPM** A measure used to calculate whether an advertisement reached the target market effectively.

**continuity** The schedule or pattern of advertisement placements within an advertising campaign period.

**continuous campaign** Media buys that result in a steady stream of advertisements during a particular time period.

**pulsating schedule** A minimal level of advertising punctuated by increases at periodic times.

**flighting (or discontinuous) campaign schedule** Placing ads at special intervals with no advertisements shown between those intervals.

**gross impressions**   The number of total exposures of the audience to an advertisement.

**effective frequency**   The number of times a target audience must be exposed to a message to achieve a particular objective.

**effective reach**   The percentage of an audience that must be exposed to a particular message to achieve a specific objective.

**intrusion value**   The ability of media or an advertisement to intrude upon a viewer without his or her voluntary attention.

**guerrilla marketing**   Focusing on low-cost, creative strategies to reach the right people in a market area.

**media multiplier effect**   The combined impact of using two or more media is stronger than using either medium alone.

## CRITICAL THINKING EXERCISES

### Discussion Questions

1. To be effective, multiple media should be chosen and integrated carefully. Individuals who are exposed to advertisements on combinations of media selected from television, radio, the Internet, and billboards are more inclined to process the information than when only a solitary medium is used. Fill in the following chart. Put your probability of being exposed to an advertisement from each medium into the appropriate column. The percentages across each row should add up to 100 percent.

| Product | Television | Radio | Newspaper | Magazine | Outdoor | Internet | Direct Mail |
|---|---|---|---|---|---|---|---|
| Movie | | | | | | | |
| Restaurant | | | | | | | |
| Clothing | | | | | | | |
| Jewelry | | | | | | | |
| Dry cleaner | | | | | | | |

2. Billboard advertising in Times Square is so popular that space has already been sold for 10 years. Coca-Cola, General Motors, Samsung, Prudential, NBC, Budweiser, and The New York Times are paying rates in excess of $100,000 per month to hold these spaces. Inter City is building a 50-story hotel at Broadway and 47th Street. The building will accommodate 75,000 square feet of advertising. Even before the completion of the hotel or tower, companies including FedEx, Apple Computers, AT&T, HBO, Levi Strauss, Morgan Stanley, and the U.S. Postal Service purchased space. Why would companies pay so much for outdoor advertising? What are the advantages and disadvantages of purchasing billboards at Times Square?

3. Repetition and a short, catchy name are the keys for an effective radio spot. Sports equipment retailer Fogdog.com has been very successful with its radio spots. The URL is easy to remember and is reinforced with the sound of a howling dog. People don't have to fumble with finding a pencil to write it down. After a few repetitions, they remember it.[56] Another Web company, Sandbox.com, which is a fantasy sports game site, is looking to develop a radio and billboard campaign. Prepare a radio and a billboard advertisement that will catch people's attention and that will be easy to remember. What are the advantages of combining a radio campaign with billboards?

4. Xerox offers a color printer that sells for $1,200. The goal is to market it to business buyers. What media mix would you suggest for a $20 million advertising campaign? Justify your answer.

## INTEGRATED LEARNING EXERCISES

1. From the following tables, choose either the cosmetics companies or the clothing companies. Access each firm's Web site. Indicate how many advertisements you have seen in each of the media listed within the last month. Then discuss each company's media plan. Does the company project an integrated message? What target market does the Web site attract? Does the Web site convey the same message broadcast in the other media?

### Cosmetics Companies

| Company (Web Address) | TV | Radio | Newspaper | Magazine | Outdoor | Internet |
|---|---|---|---|---|---|---|
| Estee Lauder (www.esteelauder.com) | | | | | | |
| Maybelline (www.maybelline.com) | | | | | | |
| Sephora (www.sephora.com) | | | | | | |
| Clinique (www.clinique.com) | | | | | | |
| Revlon (www.revlon.com) | | | | | | |

### Clothing Companies

| Company (Web Address) | TV | Radio | Newspaper | Magazine | Outdoor | Internet |
|---|---|---|---|---|---|---|
| Polo (www.polojeansco.com) | | | | | | |
| Pepe (www.pepejeans.com) | | | | | | |
| Squeeze (www.sqz.com) | | | | | | |
| Guess (www.guess.com) | | | | | | |
| Lee (www.leejeans.com) | | | | | | |
| Wrangler (www.wrangler.com) | | | | | | |

2. The following table provides the population of the top 10 demographic marketing areas (DMAs). The target market for a particular company is yuppie boomers, or those 35 to 54 years old who are professionals or managers. Based on the percentage of adults in each DMA that fits the target market profile, calculate the size of the target market in each DMA. Washington has been completed for you. If you had funds to advertise in only five of the 10 DMAs, which five would you choose? Why?

| DMA | Population | DMA Percent | Number in Target Market |
|---|---|---|---|
| Washington | 3,965,200 | 18.4% | 729,600 |
| San Francisco–Oakland | 4,824,600 | 14.2 | |
| Boston | 4,495,600 | 13.6 | |
| Dallas–Ft. Worth | 3,669,900 | 13.3 | |
| Houston | 3,251,100 | 13.1 | |
| New York | 14,432,500 | 12.0 | |
| Chicago | 6,483,800 | 11.7 | |
| Philadelphia | 5,655,800 | 11.6 | |
| Los Angeles | 11,391,200 | 11.3 | |
| Detroit | 3,549,600 | 11.1 | |

3. A major supplier of media research information is Nielsen Media Research. Access its Web site at www.nielsenmedia.com. Go to the "About Us" section and then access the information available. Read "What TV ratings really mean" and summarize what TV ratings mean. From "Ratings 101," determine how ratings are calculated. What other types of services does Nielsen Media offer?

4. In Canada, a valuable source of information is BBM (Bureau of Broadcast Measurement). Access this Web site at www.bbm.ca. What type of information is available on the site? How can it be used to develop a media plan for Canada?

5. Achieving advertising media objectives normally requires a blending of the various media within the advertising plan. Access Benchmark Communications at www.bmcommunications.com and examine the information that is provided in the site, especially about the traditional media of newspapers, radio, and television. What types of services does Benchmark Communications provide? How can Benchmark Communications assist in the development of a media plan?

6. Two Web sites that are important for radio advertising are the Radio Advertising Bureau at www.rab.com and the top 100 radio sites at www.100topradiosites.com. Access both sites. What information is available in each site? Discuss how the information can be used to develop an advertising plan using radio.

7. A major company for outdoor advertising is Lamar Advertising Company. Access its Web site at www.lamar. com. Access the outdoor component of the company and locate the rates for your area. What type of outdoor advertising is available? Access the transit component of the company. What services does Lamar offer? What other services does Lamar offer?

8. One of the best sources of information for business-to-business advertisers is *Advertising Age's* Net B2B Web site at www.netb2b.com. What type of information is available at this Web site? How can it be used? What benefits would a B-to-B advertiser derive from the Web site?

# STUDENT PROJECT

## IMC Plan Pro

Picking the right advertising media is a vital step in creating an effective advertising and promotions campaign. You can use the IMC Plan Pro disk and booklet available from Prentice Hall to assist in the task of choosing an effective mix of media. Remember, you will need to consider the more traditional advertising locations such a television, radio, and magazines along with the proper mix of new media, such as Internet programs and other alternative media.

## CASE 1

**CREATING A PHOTO OP**

Manuel Ortega was placed in charge of an advertising campaign for a new 35 mm camera. His company was going to compete directly with Nikon and Yashica. As the account manager, Manuel was given a $12 million budget for the first phase of the campaign, which was to run for 3 months.

The objective of the campaign is to explain the firm's version of disk technology. Images recorded on computer disks rather than film are sharper and easier to use. The complexity in conveying the details of the new technology and the benefits to consumers makes the campaign more difficult. Manuel consulted carefully with his media planner, media buyer, and creative after receiving the contract from the company. They agreed to use magazine ads to be followed up with television spots.

Part of their reasoning for choosing magazines was the profile of the target market for this particular type of camera. The company's research indicated that the target buyer is between 18 and 44 years of age, has completed at least 2 years of college, and has a family income in excess of $30,000. These individuals read magazines at home and subscribe to most of the magazines they read. Manuel knew that individuals who subscribe to a magazine pay more attention to advertisements than do those who purchase the same magazine from a store. The other major characteristic of this group is that they have purchased a 35 mm camera in the past. The company believed those who had not purchased a 35 mm camera in the past were unlikely to buy into this new technology.

The company believed that 20 million individuals in the United States fit the target market profile for the 35 mm camera, and 3.22 million of those individuals read *National Geographic*. Manuel explained to the company's leaders that by dividing the percentage of the total target market by those who read *National Geographic,* the yield is 16.1 percent. In other words, 16.1 percent of the target market for this camera reads *National Geographic* and would be exposed to an advertisement placed in the magazine. As shown in Table 8.9, the percent sign is dropped and the reach for *National Geographic* is listed simply as 16.1. In the advertising industry, this number is the rating for that particular vehicle and can be obtained from commercial sources.

Table 8.9 indicates that *National Geographic* and *Time* magazines have the largest ratings. *Travel & Leisure* and *Southern Living* have the smallest ratings. Two things explain the difference in ratings: (1) the size of the circulation of the various magazines and (2) the percentage of readers who fit the target audience. For example, the total circulation for *National Geographic* is

**TABLE 8.9**

Creating a Photo Op Case Study

| Magazine | Cost for 4-Color Full-Page Ad | Total Readership (000s) | CPM Total | Target Market (20 M) | |
|---|---|---|---|---|---|
| | | | | Rating (Reach) | Cost per Rating Point (CPRP) |
| *National Geographic* | $ 346,080 | 21,051 | $16.44 | 16.1 | $21,496 |
| *Newsweek* | 780,180 | 15,594 | 50.03 | 12.2 | 63,949 |
| *People* | 605,880 | 21,824 | 27.76 | 9.4 | 64,455 |
| *Southern Living* | 11,370 | 5,733 | 1.98 | 2.4 | 4,738 |
| *Sports Illustrated* | 965,940 | 13,583 | 71.11 | 10.5 | 91,994 |
| *Time* | 1,324,282 | 21,468 | 61.69 | 15.9 | 83,288 |
| *Travel & Leisure* | 183,216 | 2,205 | 83.09 | 2.3 | 79,659 |
| *U.S. News & World Report* | 100,740 | 8,929 | 11.28 | 8.3 | 12,137 |

(continued)

21,051,000 readers, compared to only 2,205,000 for *Travel & Leisure.* Not all readers of *National Geographic* fit the target profile for this 35 mm camera. In fact, only 15.3 percent of *National Geographic's* readers fit this profile compared to 20.8 percent of *Travel & Leisure's* readership. (Manuel calculated these percentages by multiplying the rating times 20, then dividing by the readership of the magazine in millions.)

The advertising team decided that two primary factors would determine the reach of the campaign. First was the number and diversity of media being used. A media plan using the eight magazines would have a greater reach than a media plan using only five magazines. Notice that the total reach for the eight magazines is 77.1. Thus, 77.1 percent of the target market for this 35 mm camera would be exposed at least once during the next 4-week time period to an advertisement. In addition to the quantity, the diversity of media will have an impact. Magazines that are different from each other tend to overlap less than magazines that are not different. Advertising only in sports magazines, for example, would overlap considerably because the same individuals probably read the various sports magazines. Reach measures the unduplicated percentage of a firm's target market exposed to an advertisement. Ads in media with nearly identical target markets do not reach as many people as advertising in vehicles with different target markets.

1. Use the information provided in the case and Table 8.9 to develop the magazine media selection plan for the print advertising campaign for Manuel Ortega. Each magazine must have at least one advertisement insertion but no more than eight insertions.

   Use Table 8.10 to calculate the gross rating points for the magazine campaign and the total cost. As noted in the case, Manuel has a $12 million budget to work with. To illustrate how to calculate the gross rating points and total cost, the first magazine, *National Geographic,* has already been completed. The goal is to maximize the gross rating points while staying within the constraints of the $12 million budget. (Those familiar with linear programming can solve this problem using a linear program to maximize the gross rating points. It also can be solved using a spreadsheet and what-if analysis.)

2. Justify the solution, especially in terms of frequencies chosen.

3. Is television a logical medium for the next phase of the campaign? Why or why not? If not television, which medium would be best?

**TABLE 8.10**

**Media Plan for Case Study Creating a Photo Op**

| Magazine | Cost for 4-Color Full-Page Ad | Rating | Number of Insertions | GRPs | Total Cost |
|---|---|---|---|---|---|
| *National Geographic* | $ 346,080 | 16.1 | 8 | 128.8 | $2,768,640 |
| *Newsweek* | 780,180 | 12.2 | | | |
| *People* | 605,880 | 9.4 | | | |
| *Southern Living* | 11,370 | 2.4 | | | |
| *Sports Illustrated* | 965,940 | 10.5 | | | |
| *Time* | 1,324,282 | 15.9 | | | |
| *Travel & Leisure* | 183,216 | 2.3 | | | |
| *U.S. News & World Report* | 100,740 | 8.3 | | | |
| | Total | | | | |

*Note:* The goal is to maximize the GRPs within the $12 million budget. There is a minimum of one insertion per magazine and a maximum of eight per magazine. Based on a linear programming solution, the optimal number of *National Geographic* insertions is eight. *National Geographic's* information has already been completed.

4. If the client wanted to have a fully integrated communications media package, what package of media would be most likely to succeed? Explain the choices.

5. For a long-term project, investigate similar costs for television and radio advertising in your local area. Construct a budget and develop a media buying plan for each medium.

# CASE 2

## OPRYLAND AMERICA

Mark Jones was about to begin an interesting aspect of his advertising career. His agency had been chosen to represent a new client—Opryland America. The country and western, gospel, and bluegrass music show was located near the Lake of the Ozarks, in central Missouri.

For many years, Opryland America was not only the best choice for live country and western music, but it was also the only choice. Visitors came from nearby towns such as Jefferson City and Columbia, Missouri, and from the Kansas City and St. Louis metropolitan areas. In the years between 1960 and 1980, Opryland thrived using a small television advertising program for the local markets and in the metropolitan areas. Word-of-mouth brought in a great deal of business. Campers and lake-lovers who visited the Lake of the Ozarks would drive by the music theater as they reached the Bagnell Dam area, creating another set of potential audience members.

The 1990s brought new challenges to the show. First, the Lake of the Ozarks area had evolved from a "family" area to a major hangout for college students (especially from the University of Missouri, which was about 60 miles away) and 20-somethings looking for a place to party on the weekends. The natural draw of families had declined.

The bigger problem was new, regional competitors. Among the most dangerous was the new music mecca called Branson. The Branson region featured several cleaner, less crowded lakes along with other family enti-cements, especially the Silver Dollar City theme park. Silver Dollar City's advertising stretched across the Midwest and attracted many visitors who would then attend one of the many music shows nearby. Market research indicated that people attend Branson music shows for three reasons: nostalgic fun, religion, and patriotism. Many political candidates (especially Republicans) scheduled campaign stops in Branson. For several years Branson had also been a satellite site for the Jerry Lewis Muscular Dystrophy Telethon during the Labor Day weekend.

Other competitors were also beginning to advertise on a wider scale, especially Pigeon Forge, Tennessee, which was close to the Dollywood theme park. Nashville also became more of a threat as roads to the city were widened. Access to quality country and western music had become much easier, for people in Missouri, Tennessee, Arkansas, and other nearby states.

Mark's challenge was to find a way to bring people back to Opryland. Essentially, he had a much smaller budget than the competition. He needed to find a way to attract local music lovers and reach the tourists who still came to the Lake of the Ozarks.

Opryland had two major advantages. First, those who had seen the show over the years were loyal fans. These people would bring their children and grandchildren to see the program. Second, Mark knew that the actual music and show were every bit as good as those offered by competitors, who charged higher prices. Tickets to prime shows with good seats in

(continued)

Branson, Pigeon Forge, and Nashville ran in excess of $40. Opryland still only charged $25 for the best seats in the house.

Against this backdrop, Mark began to think about his media choice options. He knew the future of Opryland America might very well depend on the quality of the advertising program he developed.

1. Which media should Mark use in advertising Opryland America? Defend your choices.

2. What should be the primary message sent out in Opryland's advertising?

3. Besides advertising, what else should Opryland do to bring back business and find new customers?

# ENDNOTES

1. Mars Incorporated, M&M's homepage (www.mms.com, accessed May 4, 2005).

2. Mark Dominiak, "Open Your Mind to Consumer's View," *Television Week* 23, no. 42 (October 18, 2004), p. 47.

3. Mickey Marks, "Millennial Satiation," *Advertising Age* 14 (February 2000), p. S16; J. Thomas Russell and W. Ronald Lane, *Kleppner's Advertising Procedure,* 15th ed. (Upper Saddle River, NJ: Prentice Hall), 2002, pp. 174–175.

4. Larry Percy, John R. Rossiter, and Richard Elliott, "Media Strategy," *Strategic Advertising Management* (2001), pp. 151–163.

5. Kate Maddox, "Media Planners in High Demand," *B to B* 89, no. 13 (November 8, 2004), p. 24.

6. Jack Neff, "Media Buying & Planning," *Advertising Age* 70, no. 32 (August 2, 1999), pp. 1–2.

7. Melanie Johnston, "That Little Blue Pad," *Marketing Magazine* 107, no. 4 (April 8, 2002), p. 10.

8. Arthur A. Andersen, "Clout Only a Part of Media Buyer's Value," *Advertising Age* 70, no. 15 (April 5, 1999), p. 26.

9. Ibid.

10. R. F. Dyer and E. H. Foreman, "Decision Support for Media Selection Using the Analytic Hierarchy Process," *Journal of Advertising* 21, no. 1 (March 1992), pp. 59–62.

11. Herbert E. Krugman, "Why Three Exposures May Be Enough," *Journal of Advertising Research* 12, no. 6 (1972), pp. 11–14.

12. Larry Percy, John R. Rossiter, and Richard Elliott, "Media Strategy," *Strategic Advertising Management* (2001), pp. 151–163.

13. Ibid.

14. Maria Nguyen, "Best Media for Car Marketers," *B&T Weekly* 54, no. 2493 (October 15, 2004), p. 21.

15. Betsy Tabor, "Is Your Advertising Strategy Obsolete?" *Mississippi Business Journal* 20, no. 34 (August 24, 1998), p. 28.

16. David Kaplan, "Study: Masses Still Tuned In to Mass Media," *Adweek* 44, no. 42 (October 27, 2003), p. 12.

17. Gene Accas, "Commercial Overload," *Broadcasting & Cable* 130, no. 2 (January 1, 2000), p. 34.

18. Chuck Ross, "Now, Many Words from Our Sponsors," *Advertising Age* 70, no. 40 (September 27, 1999), pp. 3–4.

19. "AAAA Survey Finds Eight Percent Hike in Cost to Produce 30-Second TV Commercials," *Film & Video Production & Postproduction Magazine (ICOM)* (www.icommag.com/november-2002/november-page-1b.html, accessed January 14, 2005).

20. Roger Baron, "Spot TV Strategy No Simple Matter," *Television Week* 23, no. 39 (September 27, 2004), p. 57.

21. Stephanie Thompson, "Food Marketers Stir Up the Media," *Advertising Age* 70, no. 42 (September 11, 1999), p. 18.

22. Kate Fitzgerald, "Beer, Auto, Retail Energizing Radio Airwaves," *Advertising Age* 76, no. 5 (January 31, 2005), p. S–6; Gary Fries, "Radio Is the Tool to Tune Into Ethnic Consumers," *DSN Retailing Today* 43, no. 22 (November 22, 2004), pp. 10–11.

23. Arlena Sawyers, "GM Certified Offers Dealer Ads," *Automotive News* 79, no. 6138 (March 14, 2005), p. 58.

24. Stephanie Thompson, "Arden Scores with Radio Promotions," *Advertising Age* 75, no. 47 (November 22, 2004), p. 8.

25. Camille Alarcon, "War of Words over Radio Ads," *B&T Weekly* 54, no. 2508 (February 25, 2005), p. 9.

26. Deborah L. Vence, "Outdoor Ads Leverage New Technology," *Marketing News* 38, no. 5 (September 15, 2004), pp. 11–13.

27. Dana Wood, "The Great Outdoors," *WWD: Women's Wear Daily* 188, no. 121 (December 10, 2004), p. 6.

28. Katy Bachman, "The Big Time," *Adweek Western Edition* 49, no. 38 (September 20, 1999), pp. 50–51.

29. "Starbucks Revs Up Advertising with Taxi Rooftop Campaign," *Marketing News* 38, no. 5 (September 15, 2004), pp. 7.

30. "Mobile Billboards Get Exposed in Traffic," *Marketing News* 38, no. 14 (September 1, 2004), p. 12.

31. Carol Krol, "Look Up! Seeing Is Believing," *Advertising Age* 70, no. 32 (August 2, 1999), p. 2.

32. "Why Internet Advertising?" *Adweek Eastern Edition* 38, no. 18 (May 5, 1997), pp. 8–12.

33. Diane Cassavoy and Edward N. Alero, "Ads Get Flashier, More Personal," *PC World* 2, no. 2 (February 2005), p. 22.

34. Brain Morrissey, "Marketers Find Search Ads Pay Off Beyond Online Sales," *Adweek* 46, no. 11 (March 14, 2005), p. 12.

35. Richard Karpinski, "Online Advertising: Key Metrics," *B to B* 89, no. 7 (June 8, 2004), p. 23.

36. Catherine P. Taylor, "Audi Sends Users on Scavenger Hunt," *Adweek* 46, no. 11 (March 14, 2005), p. 12.

37. Kathy Sharpe, "Web Punctures the Idea That Advertising Works," *Advertising Age* 70, no. 38 (September 13, 1999), p. 44; Shaffer, "Listen Up! Pay Attention! New Web Startups Want Ads That Grab You."

38. Ibid.

39. "Why Internet Advertising?"

40. Jamie LaReau, "Magazines Are Pricey—But a Bargain, Publishers Say," *Automotive News* 79, no. 6139 (March 21, 2005), p. 46.

41. Ann Marie Kerwin, "Magazines Blast Study Showing Reader Falloff," *Advertising Age* 70, no. 10 (March 8, 1999), pp. 3–4.

42. Lisa Granatstein, "Ups and Downs," *Brandweek* 45, no. 34 (September 27, 2004), p. SR11; Jamie LaReau, "Magazines Are Pricey—But a Bargain, Publishers Say," *Automotive News* 79, no. 6139 (March 21, 2005), p. 46.

43. Casey Conrad, "Back to Basics with Newspaper Options," *Club Industry* 19, no. 12 (December 2003), pp. 42–44; Sandy Stein, "The Intimate Medium," *Marketing Magazine* 108, no. 28 (August 11, 2003), p. 19.

44. Pete Wetmore, "National Ads Kick It Up a Notch," *Advertising Age* 75, no. 16 (April 19, 2004), p. N–4.

45. Todd Shields, "Slow Growing," *Brandweek* 45, no. 34 (September 27, 2004), p. SR–12.

46. Patricia Odell, "Mail Box Mania," *PROMO SourceBook 2005* 17 (2005), p. 16.

47. Sean Callahan, "Marketers Explore Product Placement," *B to B* 89, no. 13 (November 8, 2004), p. 13.

48. Lindsay Morris, "Studies Give 'Thumbs Up' to Mags for Ad Awareness," *Advertising Age* 70, no. 32 (August 2, 1999), pp. 16–17; Rachel X. Weissman, "Broadcasters Mine the Gold," *American Demographics* 21, no. 6 (June 1999), pp. 35–37.

49. "2002 B-to-B Ad Spending," *B to B* 88, no. 10 (September 15, 2003), p. 19.

50. Carol Krol, "Office Depot Puts Focus on 'Business' in New Year," *B to B* 90, no. 1 (January 17, 2005), p. 3.

51. Mary Ellen Podmolik, "B-to-B Super Bowl Ads Took Chances, Scored Big," *B to B* 90, no. 2 (February 14, 2005), p. 3.

52. Larry Speer, "Nestlé Joins Trend of Farming Out Media Buys in France," *Advertising Age International* (October 1999), p. 1.

53. Laurel Wentz and Mir Maqbool Alan Khan, "The Backlash Against Indies in Brazil," *Advertising Age International* (October 5, 1998), p. 14.

54. Suzanne Bidlake, "Consumers Under Microscope," *Advertising Age International* (February 8, 1999), p. 21.

55. Neff, "Media Buying & Planning."

56. Noah Liberman, "Web Marketers Use Radio to Net Audience Members," *Atlanta Business Chronicle* 22, no. 16 (September 24, 1999), p. 73A.

# 9 Trade Promotions

## Chapter Objectives

*Recognize* **the important relationship between trade promotions programs and the other parts of the promotions mix.**

*Understand* **the difference between trade promotions and consumer promotions.**

*Utilize* **trade promotions tools to build strong ties with members of the marketing channel.**

*Know* **when and how to use each trade promotions tool.**

*Overcome* **the barriers and obstacles to effective use of trade promotions.**

## SEALY: MADE FOR SLEEP

Mattress-shopping can be stressful. You might even lose some sleep over it. One company that works hard to make the mattress-buying process a little less daunting is Sealy. CEO David McIlquham notes that finding the right mattress can be confusing and difficult. The wide variety of mattress choices (regular, pillow top, standard, queen-size, king-size, air mattress, water beds, and adjustable frames) means there is a great deal to consider before even going to the store. Then, bedding materials are sold by numerous types of retailers, including furniture stores, mattress specialty shops, department stores, and mass merchandisers. Price, quality, delivery, and warranty comparisons can all drive the purchase decision, and the market is bombarded with messages sent out by more than 700 mattress manufacturers.

The approach taken by Sealy is to remain the largest bedding manufacturer in North America by building quality products with excellent warranties and marketing them by featuring a strong brand presence. In the United States, the three main product lines offered by the company are Sealy, Sealy Posturepedic, and Sealy Posturepedic Luxury Collection.

The Sealy name and the Posturepedic brand are among the most well-known in the domestic market. The name Posturepedic was first used in 1950, with the idea that a Sealy mattress offered the best possible back support while you sleep. This powerful image helps pull the line into numerous retail stores, where conventional bedding still represents 85 percent of all purchases made.

To maintain this strong presence in the bedding marketplace requires quality relationships with retailers. Sealy makes product information widely available to both consumers and those in the market channel. A great deal of advice and facts about mattresses can be found not only on the company's Web site but also in marketing materials used by retail outlets. Sealy also makes it easy for consumers to find the company's products. A prime feature of the Sealy Web site is a Store Locator page.

The Sealy company relies on a variety of advertising techniques. The firm builds on an innovative base, which includes running the first national prime-time television commercials in the 1960s. Cooperative advertising programs with retailers help Sealy maintain positive contacts with various types of stores. Many innovative programs revolve around Sealy's tagline: "It's Made for Sleep. It's a Sealy."

Two additional strong markets for Sealy products are the hospitality industry and institutional buyers. Sealy has strong marketing programs aimed at hotel and resort customers. The company also customizes products to be purchased by hospitals.

The new millennium has led to a great deal of change for Sealy. After being purchased in a leveraged buyout in 1989, the company operated as a privately held corporation for several years. More recently, the Kohlberg, Kravis Roberts Company acquired Sealy. All the while, the company continued to expand by creating manufacturing facilities and individual national brands in a variety of countries. Sealy's world brand names include Crown Jewel, Correct Comfort, BackSaver, Posture Premier, Stearns & Foster, Carrington-Chase, reflexion, BedTime, and Meyer. Manufacturing operations are carried out in the United States, Canada, Mexico, Puerto Rico, Brazil, Argentina, France, and Italy.

Sealy strengthens relationships with customers and members of the market channel by emphasizing four concepts: (1) first, (2) best, (3) most, and (4) improving. The company's vision statement states that Sealy should be first in product and quality service, best in meeting customer needs, most in every facet of business relationships, and driven to improve by continually examining the company's operations.

In the future, Sealy's plans are to continue to expand by looking at new international opportunities including greater use of licensing arrangements. At the same time, the company's roots remain. Most beds are purchased one-at-a-time by individual consumers in retail stores that have names other than "Sealy." Maintaining a strong brand presence is the key to Sealy's goal of providing the world with "a good night's sleep."[1]

arketing goods and services can, at times, seem fairly glamorous. Creating television commercials and radio spots, developing Web sites, and being involved in other advertising activities is an enticing prospect for someone interested in a highly visible marketing career. Remember, however, that effective integrated advertising and marketing communications programs include both highly visible and somewhat more subtle ingredients. Sometimes a subtle element of a marketing program can actually end up being the key factor in a purchase decision.

This section of the textbook explores the less visible elements of an IMC program. These critical components add significantly to the impact of any marketing effort, especially when they are executed correctly. As shown in Figure 9.1, a successful IMC program is built on the foundation that was described in Chapter 1 of this textbook. Consumer markets are defined, business-to-business customers are identified, and various buyer behaviors are studied. Next, advertising campaigns are formulated to reach all key customers. Then, trade promotions and the others parts of the promotions mix can be structured to support and enhance the IMC message. When the marketing team fails to incorporate the other parts of the promotions mix into the IMC plan, it is incomplete and the odds of success are diminished.

In this chapter, trade promotions are described. Other promotional programs, including consumer promotions, direct marketing programs, and Internet marketing are described in Chapters 10, 11, and 12. The goal is to create a truly integrated promotions mix. When this occurs, the company's internal and external publics all speak with the same voice. Employees know what the organization is trying to achieve with the marketing program. The advertising agency can design messages that portray the company speaking with one clear voice. As a result, both individual customers and business buyers are keenly aware of the company's goods and services. This, in turn, bodes well for the future of the firm.

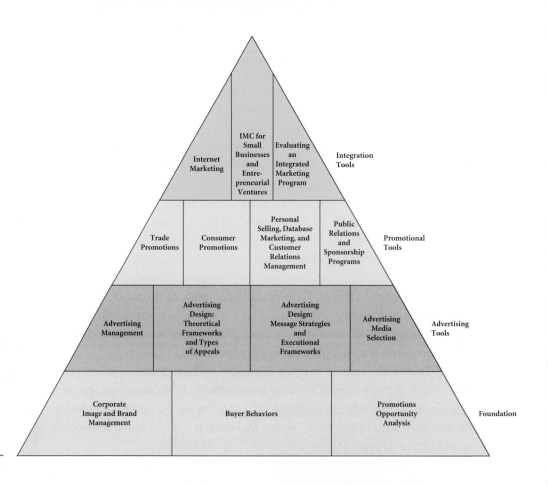

**FIGURE 9.1**
**An IMC Plan**

# THE NATURE OF TRADE PROMOTIONS

More than 80 percent of all marketing dollars are spent on marketing activities other than consumer advertising. As shown in Figure 9.2, only 18 percent of a typical promotions budget is spent on consumer advertising. Fifty-four percent is spent on trade promotions. **Trade promotions** are the expenditures or incentives used by manufacturers and other members of the marketing channel to help push products through to retailers.

The best way to understand trade promotions is to note that they are incentives members of the trade channel use to entice another member to *purchase goods for eventual resale.* In other words, trade promotions are aimed at retailers, distributors, wholesalers, brokers, or agents. A manufacturer can use trade promotions to convince another member of the trade channel to carry its goods. Wholesalers, distributors, brokers, and agents use trade promotions to entice retailers to purchase products for eventual resale.

The difference between trade promotions and consumer or sales promotions is that the latter involves a sale to an *end user or customer.* When a manufacturer sells products to another business for end use, the enticements involved are business or sales promotions tools. On the other hand, when a manufacturer sells to another business for the purpose of having the goods resold, then trade promotions tools are being used.

The primary role played by trade promotions is building stronger relations with members of the market channel. When a retailer stocks the merchandise a manufacturer promotes, consumers have the opportunity to buy the product. The same is true for distributors, wholesalers, brokers, or agents. When these members of the channel decide to carry a product, they help push it on to retailers.

Trade promotions incentives account for a significant percentage of a supplier's or retailer's gross revenues. In 2004, manufacturers gave nearly $16 billion in incentives aimed at moving items on to retailers.[2] The amount spent on trade promotions grew from 38 percent of total promotional expenditures in the 1980s to approximately 54 percent today.

Currently, many manufacturers devote more money to trade promotions than to any other promotional tool. Some company leaders would like to reduce these expenditures or cut them entirely. What they find, however, is that they can do neither. Resistance from retailers, directions from sales managers, and pressures from competitors that still offer trade promotions mean that any cutback in trade promotions is likely to have a negative impact on profits.

Consequently, trade promotions should be an integral part of an IMC program. Unfortunately, in some companies, the individual handling trade promotions is not involved in the IMC planning process. Leaders in these firms often view trade promotions as being merely a means for getting products onto retail shelves or satisfying some channel member's request. As a result, little consideration is given to the other components of the IMC program when trade promotions programs are developed.

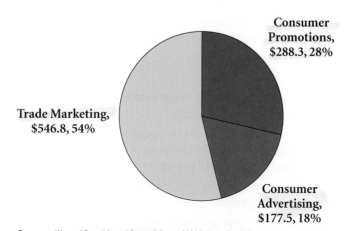

Consumer Promotions, $288.3, 28%

Trade Marketing, $546.8, 54%

Consumer Advertising, $177.5, 18%

**FIGURE 9.2**
**Breakdown of Marketing Expenditures (in Billions of Dollars)**

*Source:* "Upward Bound Annual Report," *Promo 2004 Industry Trends Report* (www.promomagazine.com, April 2004), pp. AR 3–5.

▶ **Trade allowances**
▶ **Trade contests**
▶ **Trade incentives**
▶ **Training programs**
▶ **Vendor support programs**
▶ **Trade shows**
▶ **Specialty advertising**
▶ **Point-of-purchase advertising**

**FIGURE 9.3**
**Trade Promotions Tools**

To solve this problem, the marketing executive must explain the benefits of a systematic approach to all parts of the marketing mix to company executives. Tie-ins between ad campaigns and trade promotions programs can help companies achieve more "bang" for their marketing bucks. The account executive also has a vested interest in bringing the trade promotions program in line with the other parts of the IMC plan, because the goal is to generate tangible sales and other measurable outcomes.

A variety of trade promotions tools exist. These items are used by manufacturers as well as other members of the trade channel. Figure 9.3 lists the most common trade promotions tools.

## TYPES OF TRADE PROMOTIONS

Individual companies select trade promotions techniques based on several factors. These factors include the nature of the business (manufacturer versus distributor), the type of customer to be influenced (e.g., selling to a retailer versus selling to a wholesaler), company preferences, and the objectives of the IMC plan. Each type of trade promotion offers various benefits. A review of the major categories follows.

### Trade Allowances

The first major type of trade promotion manufacturers and others use in the channel is a trade allowance. The purpose of **trade allowances** is to offer financial incentives to other channel members in order to motivate them to make purchases. Trade allowances can be packaged into a variety of forms, including the four described in Figure 9.4. Each one makes it possible for the channel member to offer discounts or other deals to customers.

**Off-invoice allowances** are financial discounts given for each item, case, or pallet ordered. They are designed to encourage channel members to place orders. Approximately 33 percent of all trade dollars are spent on off-invoice allowances. This makes them the largest single type of expenditure among trade promotions tools.[3]

Companies often use off-invoice allowances during holiday seasons. This encourages retailers to purchase large quantities of various items. Orders must be placed by a

▶ **Off-invoice allowance:**  A per-case rebate paid to retailers for an order
▶ **Drop-ship allowance:**  Money paid to retailers who bypass wholesalers or brokers for preplanned orders
▶ **Slotting fees:**  Money paid to retailers to stock a new product
▶ **Exit fees:**  Money paid to retailers to remove an item from their SKU inventory

**FIGURE 9.4**
**Trade Allowances**

specific date to receive a holiday off-invoice allowance. Manufacturers also can place a minimum order size as a further condition.

A second type of trade allowance is called a drop-ship allowance. A **drop-ship allowance** is money paid to a retailer who is willing to bypass wholesalers, brokers, agents, or distributors when making preplanned orders. Passing the middle members of the channel benefits both the manufacturer and retailer, because this can increase profit margins for both organizations. The retailer can pass along the savings to consumers by lowering prices instead of just keeping the discount.

Drop-ship allowances have several advantages. Shipping merchandise directly to the retailer can create a stronger relationship with the manufacturer. The manufacturer does not have to rely on an intermediary agency to handle a transaction. Remember that when wholesalers represent several manufacturers, they either push every manufacturer equally or, more likely, push the brand that makes them the most money. A drop-ship allowance means that the manufacturer is not forced to try to make sure the intermediary company will push its brand.

The primary disadvantage of bypassing a wholesaler or distributor is that a wholesaler who handles other products for the manufacturer may retaliate by either dropping the manufacturer or not emphasizing its other products. Manufacturers must seek to avoid damaging relationships with wholesalers when using drop-ship allowances.

The most controversial form of trade allowance is a slotting fee. **Slotting fees** are funds charged by retailers to stock new products. Eighty-two percent of retailers charge slotting fees. These companies justify charging the fees in several ways.[4] First, retailers spend money to add new products to inventories and to stock merchandise. A product that is not successful means the retailer's investment in inventory represents a loss, especially when the retailer has stocked the product in a large number of stores.

Second, adding a new product in the retail store means giving it shelf space. Most shelves are already filled with products. Adding a new product means either deleting a brand or product or reducing the amount of shelf space allocated to those products. In both cases the retailer spends both time and money on making space available for a new product.

Third, slotting fees make it easier for retailers to finalize decisions about new products. A typical supermarket carries 40,000 SKUs (stockkeeping units). The supermarket's managers must evaluate at least 10,000 new products per year. Seventy percent of new products fail. Consequently, retailers believe charging slotting fees force manufacturers to weed out poor product introductions. The average total cost in slotting fees for a nationally introduced product ranges from $1.5 million to $2 million.[5] Consequently, retailers contend that slotting fees force manufacturers to conduct careful test marketing on products before introducing them. Such testing reduces the number of new products offered each year. This, in turn, drastically reduces the number of new product failures.

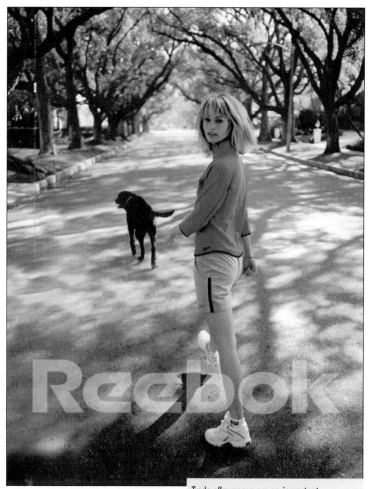

Trade allowances are an important component of Reebok's integrated marketing plan.
*Source:* Courtesy of Reebok.

New products, such as a new salad dressing (even from an existing line such as that offered by Ott's), are charged slotting fees.
*Source:* Used with permission of *The Joplin Globe*, Joplin, Missouri.

Get Carried Away... with Ott's

Fourth, and finally, slotting fees add to the bottom line. Many products have low margins or markups. Slotting fees provide additional monies to support retail operations. It has been estimated that between 14 and 27 percent of trade promotion monies given to retailers go directly to the retailer's bottom line.[6]

The other side of the argument comes from manufacturers, who claim slotting fees are practically a form of extortion. Many manufacturers believe slotting fees are too costly and are unfair in the first place. These fees compel manufacturers to pay millions of dollars to retailers that could be used for advertising, sales promotions, or other marketing efforts.

Slotting fees can prevent small manufacturers from getting products onto store shelves simply because they cannot afford them. Some large retail operations have small vendor policies; however, getting merchandise on the shelves is still extremely challenging. For example, one small manufacturer experienced a drop in sales from $500 per day to only $50 per day when its shelf space was reduced. A large national manufacturer paid the store a large slotting fee, which took space away from the smaller firm.[7]

In addition to keeping small manufacturers out of the market, slotting fees favor incumbent suppliers. New entrants into the market face tremendous investment of up-front money already, and then must add on slotting fees. Unless company leaders are absolutely certain the new brand can compete, the firm may not enter a market simply because of slotting fees.

A fourth approach to granting a trade allowance is called an exit fee. **Exit fees** are monies paid to remove an item from a retailer's inventory. This approach is often used when a manufacturer introduces a new size of a product or a new version, such as a 3-liter bottle of Pepsi or Pepsi Diet Vanilla. PepsiCo already has products on the retailer's shelves. Adding a new-sized container or new variety of the product involves lower risk and is not the same as adding a new product. Rather than charging an up-front fee such as a slotting allowance, retailers ask for exit fees if the new version of the product fails or if one of the current versions must be removed from the inventory. Only 4 percent of retailers use exit fees, compared to the 82 percent that use slotting fees.[8]

### Disadvantages of Trade Allowances

Although trade allowances are key incentives used to build relationships with retailers, there are some disadvantages. These include:

1. Failing to pass along allowances to retail customers
2. Forward buying
3. Diversion

First, in extending trade allowances to retailers, manufacturers assume that a portion of the price reduction will be passed on to consumers. This occurs only about 52 percent of the time. In 48 percent of the cases, retailers charge consumers the same price and pocket the allowance.[9] When a portion of the price allowance is passed on to consumers, retailers often schedule competing brands, so they can have at least one special offer going at all times. It is not an accident that one week Pepsi offers a reduced price and the next Coke offers a discount. The two products are rarely promoted **on-deal** (passing along trade allowance discounts) at the same time. By offering only one on-deal at a time, the retailer always has a reduced price competitor for the price-sensitive consumer. The retailer also can charge the brand-loyal consumer full price 50 percent of the time. While accomplishing these goals, the retailer receives special trade allowances from both Pepsi and Coke.

Another problem trade allowances create is the practice of forward buying. **Forward buying** occurs when a retailer purchases extra amounts of a product while it is on-deal. The retailer then sells the on-deal merchandise after the deal period ends, saving the cost of purchasing the product at the manufacturer's full price. Forward buying provides two options to the retailer. First the retailer can choose to extend price savings to customers by selling the product cheaper than its competitors. The second option is to charge full price for the product. This increases the retailer's margin of profit on the product, because the company purchased the merchandise at a reduced price.

POP displays are those integrated with other marketing messages. Logos and message themes used in advertisements should appear on the POP. The POP display should reflect any form of special sales promotion. Customers more quickly recognize tie-ins with current advertising and promotional themes as they view displays. Recent research indicates that POP displays increase sales when they have the following elements:

▶ Brand signs

▶ Base wrap under the display

▶ Standee (base of support)

▶ An inflatable component or mobile above the POP display

▶ A tie-in to a sport, movie, or charity shown on the display

Of these, a tie-in adds most significantly to sales.[28]

The POP display should make a clear, succinct offer that customers immediately understand. Many times the POP display only has three-tenths of a second to capture the customer's attention. If it fails, the customer simply moves on to other merchandise. Colors, designs, merchandise arrangements, and tie-ins with other marketing messages are critical elements of effective POP displays.[29] Figure 9.10 lists some additional pointers for point-of-purchase advertising. Three new trends are present in the use of POP displays:

1. Integration with Web site programs

2. Displays that routinely change messages

3. Better tracking of POP results

Each of these items represents key changes in POP programs. A review of these issues follows.

The first new trend is integrating POP displays with the Internet site and Web address of the company. For example, Tucker Federal Bank distributed POP materials to its 14 branch banks, encouraging people to sign up for a free checking service. The display encouraged people to go to the bank's Web site. The URL, **www.justrightbank.com**, was integrated with the advertising tagline, "Not too big. Not too small. Just right." Customers who visited the bank's Web site could complete and submit the application for free online checking. Effective integration of e-messages involves more than just printing a Web address on the POP display. The company should encourage customers to go there for a specific reason, such as was the case with Tucker Federal.[30]

The second trend in POP advertising is developing displays with the capability of changing the message. Messages are changed daily, weekly, or, in some extreme cases, several times per day. One method manufacturers use to accomplish these changes is by featuring LED electronic signs, which can be changed via computer. This allows the manufacturer or retailer to frequently present new messages to keep the POP fresh to consumers. To the retailer, the major advantage is that messages can be localized and designed to meet changing local needs. To the manufacturer, it offers an opportunity to partner with retailers looking for ways to maximize sales.

---

▶ Integrate the brand's image into the display

▶ Integrate the display with current advertising and promotions

▶ Make the display dramatic to get attention

▶ Keep the color of the display down so the product and signage stand out

▶ Make the display versatile so it can be easily adapted by retailers

▶ Make the display reusable and easy to assemble

▶ Make the display easy to stock

▶ Customize the display to fit the retailer's store

**FIGURE 9.10**
**Effective POP Displays**

The third issue is accountability. Both retailers and manufacturers look for methods to measure the effectiveness of POP displays. Retailers have limited space and can set up only a fraction of the displays sent to them. They want to use the most effective displays. Manufacturers invest money into building, shipping, and promoting POP displays. The manufacturer wants its display to be utilized and not set in a storeroom or simply thrown away. Thus, it is in the best interests of both parties to develop methods for measuring effectiveness.

One method to measure results is tying the POP display into a point-of-sale (POS) cash register. Items on the display are coded so that the POS system picks them up. Then individual stores measure sales before, during, and after a POP display program by using cash register data. The data also help the retailer decide that it is time to withdraw or change a POP display because sales have begun to decline. This technology allows retailers to identify the POP displays with the largest impact on sales. A retailer even could use this method to test-market different types of POP displays in various stores. The most effective displays can then be used nationally.

From the manufacturer's viewpoint, using POS data can help improve POP displays. The data can also be used to strengthen partnerships with retailers. These bonds help the manufacturer weather poor POP showings. Retailers are more willing to stay with a manufacturer that tries to develop displays that benefit both parties.

Internet trading may have reduced some retail store traffic. Still, many customers shop and window-shop frequently. A POP advertising program remains an important ingredient in selling to the end user and in strengthening bonds with retailers as part of a larger trade promotions effort.

## OBJECTIVES OF TRADE PROMOTIONS

The trade promotions manager should be included in the planning stages of the IMC program. This increases the chances that trade promotions and incentives will be effectively coordinated with the other components of the IMC process. Regrettably, the process is more difficult than it appears, because manufacturers and retailers have objectives that differ from each other and from those of distributors.

For manufacturing operations, the primary goal is to increase sales of company brands. Retailers, on the other hand, try to increase the market shares of individual stores. Retailers are not concerned with which brand sells the most. Instead, they promote the brand that has the highest sales or contributes the most to profits. Often retailers play one manufacturer against another to see which one will offer the best deal. The manufacturer's marketing team must decide which trade promotions to use and offer them to the right retailers. The decision becomes more complicated when a wholesaler or distributor is involved. These organizations also have goals that are different from those of both retailers and manufacturers.

Figure 9.11 lists the major objectives of trade promotions from the manufacturer's perspective. At times one takes precedence instead of another. Each one may be a key goal for a given trade promotions effort. These objectives are described next.

> ▶ Obtain initial distribution
> ▶ Obtain prime retail shelf space or location
> ▶ Support established brands
> ▶ Counter competitive actions
> ▶ Increase order size
> ▶ Build retail inventories
> ▶ Reduce excess manufacturer inventories
> ▶ Enhance channel relationships
> ▶ Enhance the IMC program

FIGURE 9.11
Objectives of Trade Promotions

## Obtaining Initial Distribution

When a firm begins operations, enters a new territory, or seeks to expand into global markets, one primary concern is finding retail outlets to carry the product. The company must be able to develop a distribution network through either a "pull" or a "push" strategy. *A pull strategy* occurs when advertising and publicity causes consumers to become aware of a product's availability. These individuals then ask retailers if they carry the product, which leads the retailer to become more interested in it. A *push strategy* is the result of aggressive marketing efforts by the manufacturer to entice retailers to consider placing the product on its shelves. One goal of a trade promotions effort is to assist in this form of push strategy. Trade shows, slotting fees, vendor support programs, specialty advertising, and point-of-purchase displays help a manufacturer gain a wider audience for a new product.

## Obtaining Prime Retail Shelf Space or Location

Retail shelf space is critical in selling merchandise. Simply stated, a manufacturer that cannot get its products onto retailer shelves will not sell merchandise. Quality spots of shelf space mean higher sales. A manufacturer who has 24 inches of prime shelf space is likely to do better than a company given only 10 inches of shelf space. To get quality space and more space means manufacturers normally must be willing to provide incentives to retailers in the form of trade promotions in addition to providing products with high consumer demand. Trade allowances, contests, training programs, and trade incentives can assist in capturing and maintaining quality shelf space.

## Supporting Established Brands

Trade promotions efforts often are used to increase shelf space for current, well-established products. Even in situations where the manufacturer merely tries to maintain current shelf space, trade promotions are needed to keep competitors from taking retail space. More often than not, the competition continually tries to find ways to offer retailers a better deal. This forces manufacturers to make sure they stay on top of what is happening in order to maintain quality shelf space and lead the retailer to support established brands. For instance, if a new competitor were to enter the potato chip market, that manufacturer would logically spend considerable funds seeking to push out more established brands, such as Lays and Frito-Lay. These chip suppliers would be interested in maintaining superior locations on grocery store and convenience store shelves. Every trade promotions tool can be used to support established brands.

## Countering Competitive Actions

Manufacturers often use trade promotions to counter an action taken by a competitor. A rival company may, for example, offer a trade promotion deal to retailers or a consumer promotion of some type that requires a response. Trade promotions can be used to lessen the impact of a competitor's aggressive advertising campaign. To ensure channel members do not emphasize the competition in selling products, a manufacturer's marketing team may offer a trade promotion to match the competition's effort or one that is more attractive to channel

Companies such as Keebler often use trade promotions in conjunction with consumer promotions such as coupons.
*Source:* Courtesy of Keebler Company.

members. Unfortunately, this can lead to a vicious spiral in which manufacturers pump more and more dollars into trade promotions just to keep up with each other.

On the other hand, failing to fend off competitive threats can have even greater consequences. There are other competitive responses beyond simply raising the funds spent on trade promotions. A firm helps its own cause by taking care of other parts of the business relationship. This includes meeting delivery deadlines, providing support services to retailers, accepting returns without problems in crediting retailer accounts, entering into cooperative advertising agreements, and finding other ways build stronger ties between the two organizations. Then, when the competition acts, the manufacturer can choose either to offer the same trade promotions tactic or take a different approach in order to counteract the competition's efforts.

## Increasing Order Sizes

Another goal of trade promotions programs is to push an individual brand through the channel of distribution in such a way that order sizes increase. Manufacturers primarily use trade allowances and sales contests to increase order sizes. The objective may be to increase the order size from either the retailer or the distributor. Occasionally, a POP will induce a larger order from the retailer, if the display features a major advertising campaign or is offered during a key season for the product, such as starter fluid for barbecue grills featured in the summer.

## Building Retail Inventories

Another marketing goal can be to build retail inventories, thus preempting the competition. A large retail inventory of a particular brand should result in the retailer pushing that particular brand instead of competing brands. Trade allowances that lead to forward buying or diversions may actually help reach the goal of larger retail inventories. Other parts of the IMC plan, such as advertising and consumer sales promotions, also drive the retailer to hold larger inventories in anticipation of increased retail sales.

## Reducing Excess Manufacturer Inventories

Trade promotions help manufacturers reduce inventory levels. This often occurs near the end of a fiscal year or near the end of an evaluation period when sales have not met forecasts. To ensure a quota is met, a manufacturer offers retailers an especially attractive trade promotions deal. This in turn helps reduce excess manufacturer inventories.

Trade promotions are important in developing international markets.
*Source:* Courtesy of Electrolux.

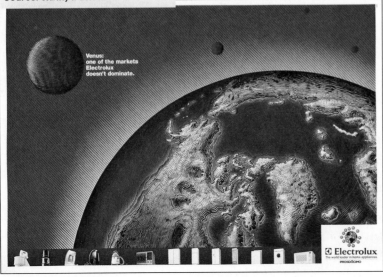

## Enhancing Channel Relationships

Manufacturers utilize trade promotions to enhance relationships with other channel members. Contests, allowances, incentives, giveaways, and training all make the relationship between the manufacturer's sales rep and the company's buyers more personal and intimate. Maintaining positive relationships is especially important if the competition also is heavily involved in granting trade promotions.

## Enhancing the IMC Program

Finally, trade promotions should be used to enhance other IMC efforts. If a manufacturer plans a massive consumer promotion campaign, it makes sense to support the consumer sales promotion effort with trade promotions. The same is true for a major advertising campaign. Manufacturers spending large amounts of money on advertising campaigns want to be sure products are available in stores. A manufacturer's marketing team should try to entice retailers to promote the product with desirable shelf space or an end-of-aisle display. Obtaining these more desirable locations normally requires a more concerted trade promotions effort. It is important to remember that the company's image and theme should be enhanced not only through clever advertisements but also through the other elements of the promotions mix, including trade promotions incentives.

## CONCERNS IN USING TRADE PROMOTIONS

Every member of the marketing channel should find ways to incorporate trade promotions into an overall IMC effort. This occurs only when top management buys into the integrated marketing communications concept and insists on including the trade promotions manager on the marketing team. The manager must also make sure all the team members work together with a common marketing agenda.

In most organizations, employee pay structures encourage the use of trade promotions irrespective of the IMC plan. Sales managers face quotas, and if sales fall behind, the easiest way to boost them is to offer retailers a trade deal. Further, companies often evaluate brand managers based on the sales growth of a brand. The easiest way to ensure continuing sales growth is to offer trade deals. The pattern of using trade deals to reach short-term quotas rather than long-term image and theme-building will not change until top management adopts a new approach. The IMC model only succeeds when a long-term horizon is considered and compensation structures change to accommodate this view of success.

To illustrate why a change in management philosophy is necessary, consider the following situation: A sales manager or brand manager has about a month left in the fiscal year and is 12 percent behind on a sales quota. To ensure the quota is reached, the sales manager requests a trade deal to encourage retailers to buy excess merchandise. In the short term, the goal has been achieved. In the long run, however, the brand's image may have eroded. It takes a long-term perspective for management to say that increasing trade promotions to meet the quota is not part of the IMC plan and should not be done. Eroding brand image to meet short-term goals is not in the company's best long-term interest. A strong brand image will cause retailers to stock the product even when fewer trade deals are offered. This is because a strong brand by itself can help pull customers into retail stores. For example, if a customer believes Sony is a strong brand name in the stereo marketplace, an electronics retailer stocking Sony has an advantage, even when no current trade promotions are on the table.

Meanwhile, as company leaders consider ways to include trade promotions into the IMC plan, they should be aware of other potential problems associated with trade promotions programs. These include costs, the potential impact on small manufacturers, and the tendency to rely too much on trade promotions to move merchandise

The first of these concerns is the cost of trade promotions. Manufacturers spend billions of dollars each year on trade promotions. These costs are often passed on to consumers in the form of higher prices. It is estimated that 11 cents out of every dollar spent for a consumer product goes directly for the cost of trade promotions.[31] The goal should be to keep trade promotions cost at a reasonable level. Money should be spent wisely, rather than simply getting into "bidding wars" with competitors. Trade promotions dollars are best used when they build relationships and help achieve other key IMC goals.

The second major concern with trade promotions is the potential impact on small manufacturers. When the cost to get a new item stocked in retail stores ranges from $1.5 million to $2 million, the large manufacturer has a major advantage. Larger companies can afford to invest more heavily in trade allowances. Only 8 of the top 15 retailers in the United States have programs that allow small vendors opportunities to stock merchandise. Figure 9.12 displays both types of retailers. Although these retailers have special programs for small manufacturers, there is no guarantee they will get shelf space when a large manufacturer such as General Mills offers millions of dollars in trade incentives

| Retailers with Small Vendor Programs | Retailers with No Small Vendor Programs |
|---|---|
| ▶ Wal-Mart | ▶ Circuit City |
| ▶ Sears | ▶ Consumer-Electronic |
| ▶ Sam's Warehouse | ▶ Office Depot |
| ▶ Price Costco | ▶ Service Merchandise |
| ▶ Target | ▶ Wal-Mart Supercenter |
| ▶ Home Depot | |
| ▶ Toys "R" Us | |

**FIGURE 9.12**
**Retailers and Small Vendor Programs**

such as slotting fees and cooperative advertising programs (including coupon redemption programs).[32] Small-scale manufacturers must discover creative ways to gain shelf space, both in major retail chains and through smaller vendors. It is clearly a challenging part of the process, but one that must be addressed in order to achieve long-term success.

The third major concern is that the use of trade promotions has led to a situation in which merchandise does not move until a trade promotions incentive is offered. In the grocery industry, an estimated 70 percent to 90 percent of all purchases made by retailers are on-deal with some type of trade incentive in place. The constant use of deals has trimmed manufacturer margins on products and created competitive pressures to conform. If a manufacturer tries to quit or cut back on trade promotions, retailers replace the manufacturer's products with other brands or trim shelf space to allow more room for manufacturers offering better deals. Recently, Procter & Gamble cut back on trade promotions in an effort to sell more products off-deal in order to boost profit margins. In a retaliatory action, Safeway cut some of the less popular P&G sizes and brands from its stores. Curbing trade promotional expenditures is extremely difficult because trade promotions are a critical part of moving goods from manufacturers to retailers.[33]

The best way to correct these problems is to spend more on advertising focused on building or rebuilding a brand's image. Also, it is important to be certain promotions fit the brand's image. "If it doesn't fit," writes Brian Sullivan in *Marketing News,* "don't use it."[34] Unfortunately, to spend more on advertising means cutting trade promotions incentives. The risk becomes that other competitors will move in by offering trade promotions to retailers, and shelf space will be lost as a result. Then, the vicious cycle begins again.

The management of trade promotions programs is a challenging part of the marketing planning process because such a large percentage of the marketing budget is spent on trade promotions. Effective IMC programs achieve a balance between all elements of the promotions mix and identify clear goals and targets for trade promotions programs. Only then is the company able to compete on all levels and not just through a cycle of trade promotions bidding wars.

## SUMMARY

The marketing mix consists of four basic components: (1) advertising, (2) trade promotions, (3) consumer promotions, and (4) personal selling. Trade promotions are the primary tools that members of the marketing channel use to push products onto retailer shelves. Any time a product is being promoted for resale, a trade promotions program is being utilized.

A wide variety of trade promotions programs exist, including trade allowances, trade contests, trade incentives, training programs, vendor support programs, trade shows, specialty advertising, and point-of-purchase displays. Several major factors affect the choice of promotional tool, most notably:

▶ Standard practice in the industry

▶ Competitive pressures

▶ Company preferences

▶ Marketing goals and objectives

Common objectives for trade promotions programs include obtaining distribution for new products, gaining prime retail space, supporting established brands, countering the competition, increasing order sizes, enlarging retailer inventories or reducing manufacturer inventories, enhancing channel relationships, and building on other parts of the IMC program. Various trade promotions tools match with these goals.

The major issue facing marketers who work with promotional programs is making sure the promotions match overall IMC goals. They should be coordinated with advertising expenditures and campaigns and balanced with other parts of the promotions mix. Trade promotions are costly and place enormous pressures on small manufacturers. Many wholesale and retail firms simply will not place orders for merchandise until a trade promotions incentive is offered. Company

leaders must work diligently to build and maintain brand image and not fall into the trap of simply engaging in competitive trade promotions bargaining to retain retail space. Instead, brand image and strong relationships with various vendors can counterbalance competitor attempts to steal space merely by offering a short-term price discount.

As with all of the other ingredients of an IMC plan, the primary task is to develop a coordinated and balanced plan of attack to reach the marketplace with one clear message. Trade promotions must be included in the process and not dominate marketing expenditures to the point that other aspects of the marketing mix are neglected. When this balance is achieved, the company can compete in the long term for better position with other members of the channel as well as retail customers. Maintaining the vision to seek long-range goals is one key element in managing trade promotions.

## REVIEW QUESTIONS

1. What is a trade promotions program? How is it related to other elements of the marketing mix?
2. What is the difference between trade promotions and consumer sales promotions?
3. Describe the four main types of trade allowances and the goals they are mostly likely to achieve. Which is the most controversial? Why?
4. What is forward buying? Why is it a problem for manufacturers?
5. What is a diversion tactic? Why are diversions used less frequently than forward buying?
6. What is spiff money?
7. Name and briefly describe the various forms of trade contests. Which is the least likely to be used?
8. Name and briefly describe the major forms of trade incentives. Which ones involve retailers paying some of the costs first, before receiving compensation?
9. Why are training programs considered to be a form of trade promotion? What objectives will a quality training program be most likely to achieve?
10. What is a billback program?
11. What advantages do cooperative advertising programs hold for manufacturers? For retailers?
12. Why have smaller specialty trade shows begun to replace larger, more general shows?
13. How are international attendees different from local attendees at a trade show? What should a manufacturer do to meet these differences?
14. What are the five top giveaways associated with specialty advertising? How are they related to the concept of reciprocation?
15. What are the characteristics of a high-quality, effective POP display?
16. What are the major objectives manufacturers try to achieve with trade promotions programs? Are these objectives different from those of wholesalers or distributors? Why or why not?
17. What problems are associated with trade promotions programs? How can manufacturers overcome these problems?
18. How should a retailer respond to trade promotions incentives? Should retailers try to get manufacturers involved in bidding wars? Why or why not?
19. What role should trade promotions play in the overall IMC plan?

## KEY TERMS

**trade promotions** The expenditures or incentives used by manufacturers and other members of the marketing channel to help push products through to retailers.

**trade allowances** Financial incentives offered to other channel member to motivate them to make purchases.

**off-invoice allowance** Financial discounts given for each item, case, or pallet ordered.

**drop-ship allowance** Money paid to a retailer that is willing to bypass wholesalers, brokers, agents, or distributors when making preplanned orders.

**slotting fees** Funds charged by retailers to stock new products.

**exit fees** Monies paid to remove an item from a retailer's inventory.

**on-deal** When a price allowance is being given as part of a trade promotions program.

**forward buying** When a retailer purchases excess inventory of a product while it is on-deal to sell later when it is off-deal.

**diversion** When a retailer purchases a product on-deal in one location and ships it to another location where it is off-deal.

**spiff money** Rewards given as contest prizes to brokers, retail salespeople, retail stores, wholesalers, or agents.

**trade incentives** Enticements given when the retailer performs a function in order to receive the discount or allowance.

**cooperative merchandising agreement (CMA)**   A formal agreement between the retailer and manufacturer to undertake a two-way marketing effort.

**calendar promotions**   Promotional campaigns the retailer plans for customers through manufacturer trade incentives.

**corporate sales program (CSP)**   A form of trade incentive offered by highly specialized manufacturers.

**producing plant allowance (PPA)**   A trade incentive in which the retailer purchases a full or half truckload of merchandise in order to receive a major discount.

**back haul allowance (BHA)**   A trade incentive in which the retailer pays the cost of shipping and furnishes the delivery truck for a truckload of discounted merchandise offered by a manufacturer.

**cross-dock or pedal run allowance**   Monies paid to retailers for placing a full truck order that is then divided among several stores within the same geographic region.

**premium or bonus pack**   Given by offering the retailer free merchandise rather than a discount on the price.

**billback**   The manufacturer pays the retailer for special product displays, advertisements, or price cuts.

**cooperative advertising program**   The manufacturer agrees to reimburse the retailer a certain percentage of the advertising costs associated with advertising the manufacturer's products in the retailer's ad.

**reciprocation**   A psychological concept that whenever someone receives a gift, the human desire is to return a gift or favor.

**point of purchase (POP)**   Any form of special display that advertises merchandise.

# CRITICAL THINKING EXERCISES

## Discussion Questions

1. One type of trade show that has received considerable publicity recently is a gun show. Although some gun trade shows are restricted to only retailers, others allow anyone to attend. What is your evaluation of gun shows? Should they all be restricted to only retailers?

2. Three common problems with trade allowances are that retailers fail to pass along allowances to retail customers, forward buying, and diversion. From the perspective of the retailer, defend these practices and explain why they are not unethical.

3. Debate has continued for many years about the use of slotting fees by retailers. Recently, the U.S. Congress examined the practice when it considered them to potentially restrict free trade. Using an academic search engine, locate recent articles about slotting fees. Should they be permitted, or should laws be passed restricting or even eliminating them?

4. Study a recent Sunday or Wednesday newspaper. How many cooperative advertisements are present? What brands does the

retailer's advertisement promote? Are these advertisements effective from the viewpoint of the manufacturer? How effective are they for the retailer?

5. Go to a nearby retail store. How many POP displays are present? Which ones are the most impressive? Why? Which ones did not succeed in gaining your interest? Why? Return to the same store a week later. How many new POP displays are there? Which ones are still up?

6. Interview a retail store manager about trade promotions used at his or her store. Especially discuss POP displays and trade allowances. Find out what percentage of the POP displays received are not used. Why are others not used? What criteria does the store manager use in deciding?

7. From the list of stores in Figure 9.12, pick one that is close by. Interview the manager about the store's small vendor program or lack of a small vendor program. Report the findings to your class.

# INTEGRATED LEARNING EXERCISES

1. AgrEvo Environmental Health held a trade contest to launch a new line of DeltaGard low-dose formulations. DeltaGard is an insecticide sold to pest control companies and retailers. To encourage pest control companies to purchase DeltaGard, AgrEvo teamed up with Harley-Davidson and developed the DeltaGard Win-a-Harley Sweepstakes. Entry forms were available only to licensed pest control companies and were featured at the annual National Pest Control Association trade show, at official AgrEvo DeltaGard distributors, on the AgrEvo Web site, and in a series of advertisements that ran during the trade contest. First place was a Harley-Davidson motorcycle valued at over $12,000. Second place was a Harley-Davidson leather jacket. Third place was a Harley-Davidson wristwatch.[35] Was

this trade contest a good idea? Would every pest control company be motivated by the prizes offered? Could this trade contest be improved to create greater participation?

2. The Trade Promotion Management Association (TPMA) is a national organization that focuses on the development and administration of program allowances provided by manufacturers and suppliers to retail and wholesale customers. Access the Web site at **www.tradepromo.org**. What type of services does TMPA offer? How can the association benefit manufacturers? Would the association be beneficial to retailers? Why or why not?

3. Point-of-purchase displays should be an important component of a firm's IMC program. Research indicates that effective

POP displays have a positive impact on sales. Access the following firms that produce POP displays. Which firm's site is the most attractive? Which firm would be the best from the standpoint of developing displays for a manufacturer? Why?

   **a.** Acrylic Designs, Inc. (www.acrylicdesigns.com)

   **b.** Vulcan Industries (www.vulcanind.com)

   **c.** Display Design & Sales (www.displays4pop.com)

4. Many firms turn to specialty agencies or full-service agencies to handle trade promotions programs. The same agency often handles the consumer promotion component as well in order to ensure the two mesh. Examine the following companies by accessing their Web sites. What appears to be the strengths of each agency? Which company would you feel the most comfortable with to handle trade promotions? Why?

   **a.** Little & King Co. LLC (www.littleandking.com)

   **b.** CCI (www.coopcom.com)

   **c.** TradeOne Marketing (www.tradeonemktg.com)

   **d.** Sable Advertising (www.sableadvertising.com)

5. Access the Trade Show News Network at www.tsnn.com. Pick one trade show from each of the following categories:

   **a.** Apparel

   **b.** Boating and yachting

   **c.** Gender specific

   **d.** Photography

   **e.** Physical fitness and health

Find out the following information about each trade show. Evaluate it as being potentially successful or a waste of time for the exhibitor and the attendee.

   **a.** Type of show

   **b.** Location of show

   **c.** Show date

   **d.** Number of exhibitors

   **e.** Number of attendees

   **f.** Names of exhibitors

   **g.** Names of the attendees

6. Access the Trade Show News Network at www.tsnn.com. Pick one category of trade shows from the list in Exercise 5. Assume you are a small manufacturer in that industry. Locate five trade shows that would be feasible to attend as an exhibitor. Evaluate each one. If you could afford to attend only one, which show would you choose? Why?

## STUDENT PROJECT

### IMC Plan Pro

Individual customers are only part of the target when an IMC campaign is being designed. Your IMC plan is not complete until a program for reaching members of the distribution channel is in place. The IMC Plan Pro disk and booklet available from Prentice Hall are designed to make sure you examine the ways to reach channel members that will push the company's products through to retailers and end users. An effective trade promotions program means being in the right places, such as trade shows, and offering the right enticements to other firms in the marketing channel.

# CASE 1

## HOT ROD MARKETING

Terry Walsh knew the time was right to move from being a small, "garage-based" company to a much larger enterprise. After spending years as a research chemist, Terry had launched out on his own. His goal was to develop a top-of-the-line fuel injector cleaner for both domestic and foreign automobiles. For 2 years, he worked with various formulas until the right one emerged. The product was named Hot Fire Fuel Injector Cleaner, and the company's name was Hot Fire. Terry was positive Hot Fire would perform well against any competitive product.

The market for fuel injector cleaners is diverse. Numerous backyard mechanics sell limited amounts of their concoctions to local merchants and over the Internet. Several formulas are even available on eBay. There is no guarantee of quality for these products, some of which may actually harm engine performance. At the other extreme, major companies such as STP, Gumout, and Dupont offer various grades of cleaners, from low-end products selling for around $3 per unit up to high-end versions priced as high as $30. The primary price determinant is the degree to which the product reduces congestion in a fuel injector. The higher priced entries are more powerful and remove more "gunk."

Terry's Hot Fire Fuel Injector Cleaner was at the high end. The price would be $17 wholesale, per can. He hoped that dealers would charge no more than $25 as a retail price. Hot Fire sold in single containers as well as in multipacks of 6 and 12 cans. Each can held two treatments or applications.

Several potential markets are available for fuel injector cleaners. The first is auto repair shops, including simple "lube and oil" change stores and more traditional repair shops. Many times the proprietors of these stores welcome the idea of a small display of an auto repair or maintenance product, as long as the owner believes the product actually works.

The second type of outlet consists of all of the retailers that sell replacement parts and auto supplies, such as Napa Auto Parts, Dallas Auto Parts, and O'Reilly Auto Parts. Most of these retailers only sell nationally-based products from major manufacturers. Getting them to stock Hot Fire would be a major victory.

A third potential customer base is convenience stores. Again, the primary challenge would be convincing a chain, such as 7-Eleven or Circle K, to carry Hot Fire along with other, cheaper products such as STP's and Gumout's low-end products.

Terry knew that buyers in all of these outlets are extremely price sensitive. At the same time, the buyers want to be sure the product works and will not harm other engine parts. Once these objectives have been reached, the goal is to convince them to order larger quantities and continually stock the product. To encourage sales, seasonal discounts, such as for the summer driving season, may move more product to the shelves.

Hot Fire currently employs 20 workers in the production department and has a sales force of 5 people to cover the entire country. The company's Web site is designed to attract people who are willing to buy auto products online and to provide information to business customers.

Terry had a large enough budget to do some advertising. He mostly bought ads in magazines that featured high-performance cars and trade journals for auto body shop managers. One major advantage that had emerged was that Hot Fire sold well locally and was emerging as a product known by local and regional race-car drivers. Hot Fire decals were placed on cars at races across the region.

With some additional funding, it was now time to try to move Hot Fire to national prominence. Winning over each type of retailer was the key to success.

1. What should be the main trade promotions objectives for Hot Fire Fuel Injector Cleaner? What challenges or obstacles might keep the company from reaching those objectives?

2. Design a trade promotions program for Hot Fire Fuel Injector Cleaner.

3. Create a magazine advertisement and tagline for Hot Fire that ties in with the trade promotions program.

# CASE 2

## THE CHRISTMAS RUSH

Musa Pinar, the promotions trade manager for Galactic Toys, knows his firm is in for a new experience. Galactic Toys is a highly successful company in its home country, Turkey. In that region, the toy business is not as strongly dictated by the successes and failures of films and is not quite as dominated by the Christmas season. In an effort to build sales and "test the waters," Musa has been asked to study the U.S. toy market to see if the firm's biggest-selling line, Galaxy Conquest toys, could compete effectively.

In the United States, each year more than half of all toy purchases are made at the retail level during November and December. The summer movie schedule provides some clues as to which "fad" toys are most likely to succeed. Any new *Star Wars* film boosts sales of its figures, and the same is true for *Shrek, Toy Story,* and many others. A second set of toys has a more annual and traditional base, including Barbie, GI Joe, and standard board games and more generic products such as Lincoln Logs and Legos. These products are updated to keep them more current and are staples for several manufacturers in the industry.

Seasonal toys are featured in major trade shows every summer. Major companies set up booths and hold extravagant release campaigns for new products and other innovations. The media are invited and a feature story can become the lifeblood of a new fad product. Cabbage Patch Dolls, Teenage Mutant Ninja Turtles, Tickle Me Elmo, and Furby toys have created near riotous conditions in various retail outlets following successful media campaigns in the pre-Christmas publicity season. Toys tied to movies enjoy the additional benefits of the Halloween costume season ahead of actual toy sales.

Toy buyers can be distributed roughly into four categories. First, those who buy for small children tend to rely on major name brands, such as Fisher-Price and Playskool. At a slightly older age, Tonka toys are big sellers. Second, grade-school-age children constitute the primary market for fad and trendy toys. Parents view many of these products as "status symbols" as much as they are playthings for kids. Thus, owning a Furby represents not only a fun toy, but a major one-upmanship factor for parents who want their kids to have everything, as well. The third set of buyers tends to purchase more staple toys. These shoppers are often lower-income families who cannot afford the more extravagant prices paid for the season's hottest item or parents who simply withdraw from the "keeping up with the Joneses" mentality associated with high-status toys. Fourth, junior-high-age kids now buy more sophisticated technology-based toys, especially Nintendo products.

Galactic Toys would normally be placed in the GI Joe–*Star Wars* section of toy store shelves. Individual products are high quality, but reasonably priced for more staple buyers who are less driven by trends and more

(continued)

inclined to seek out items that do not break easily. The problems Musa believes the company will experience are:

▶ Gaining attractive booths at major trade shows

▶ Breaking through the publicity campaigns of major fad toys to build interest by various stores

▶ Convincing retailers that Galactic Toys are more year-round, and less seasonal, products (e.g., toys for birthday gifts and other minor celebrations or occasions)

To succeed, Musa thinks he should start with the trade shows themselves. He attended a few shows and noticed glamorous women dressed in attractive fashions showing off dominos and checkerboards. He watched the video presentations, saw giveaways, and examined other attention-seeking devices. Next, Musa subscribed to all key trade journals and solicited information about prices, locations in magazines, and other information about ads. Third, Musa has been looking for tie-ins with other products, such as breakfast cereals, T-shirts, and others. Still, in his report to company leaders, Musa wrote that making headway in such a tough marketplace is going to be a challenge, even with the company's best efforts.

1. Assess Musa's report.

2. Design a trade promotions campaign and integrate it with a larger IMC program and theme for Galaxy products.

3. Besides trade shows, are there any other trade promotions tools Galactic Toys can use to increase sales?

4. Are there any other special challenges that a Turkish toy company will encounter when trying to compete in the United States? What are they?

## ENDNOTES

1. Sealy (www.sealy.com, accessed May 19, 2005).

2. Walter Heller, "Promotion Pullback," *Progressive Grocer* 81, no. 4 (March 1, 2002), p. 19; "Study: Trade Dollars Up," *Frozen Food Age* 50, no. 2 (September 2001), p. 14.

3. "Study: Trade Dollars Up," *Frozen Food Age* 50, no. 2 (September 2001), p. 14.

4. Leonard Kile, "Slotting Fees Vary Among Products," *Food Logistics*, no. 65 (January/February 2004), p. 6; Walter Heller, "Promotion Pullback," *Progressive Grocer* 81, no. 4 (March 1, 2002), p. 19.

5. Leonard Kile, "Slotting Fees Vary Among Products," *Food Logistics*, no. 65 (January/February 2004), p. 6.

6. "Study: Trade Dollars Up," *Frozen Food Age* 50, no. 2 (September 2001), p. 14.

7. Martin Hoover, "Supermarket 'Slotting' Leaves Small Firms Out," *Business Courier: Serving the Cincinnati–Northern Kentucky Region* 16, no. 25 (October 8, 1999), pp. 3–4.

8. Walter Heller, "Promotion Pullback," *Progressive Grocer* 81, no. 4 (March 1, 2002), p. 19.

9. "Study: Trade Dollars Up," *Frozen Food Age* 50, no. 2 (September 2001), p. 14.

10. "Cruise Selling Season Kicks Off with Agent Promotions and Optimism," *Travel Agent* 319 (January 3, 2005), p. 9.

11. Laurie Watanabe, "Duel at Dawn," *Dealernews* 33, no. 12 (November 1997), p. 59.

12. Michele Marchetti and Andy Cohen, "In Search of Microsoft's Softer Side," *Sales and Marketing Management* 151, no. 12 (December 1999), p. 20.

13. Roger A. Slavens, "Getting a Grip on Co-Op," *Modern Tire Dealer* 75, no. 3 (March 1994), pp. 34–37.

14. Shawn Clark, "Dual Destiny," *Adweek* 41, no. 21 (May 22, 2000), pp. 60–66.

15. Roger A. Slavens, "Getting a Grip on Co-Op," *Modern Tire Dealer* 75, no. 3 (March 1994), pp. 34–37.

16. Dana Blankenhorn, "Memphis Company Solves Co-Op Ad Accounting Problem Online," *Advertising Age's Business Marketing* 83, no. 12 (December 1998), pp. 3–4.

17. Julie Cantwell, "Mazda and Co-Op Gets Mixed Reviews," *Automotive News* 75, no. 5932 (May 28, 2001), p. 3.

18. Jim Martyka, "Sports Trade Shows Shrink, Specialize," *City Business: The Business Journal of the Twin Cities* 17, no. 13 (August 27, 1999), p. 10; Laurie Freeman, "B-to-B Marketing Communications Budgets Grow 14.5 Percent As Overall Spending Reaches $73 Billion," *Advertising Age's Business Marketing* 84, no. 5 (May 1999), pp. S3–S4.

19. Matthew Flamm, "Alien Influences," *Crain's New York Business* 15, no. 46 (November 15, 1999), pp. 35–36.

20. Ibid.

21. Jennifer Gilber, "The Show Must Go On," *Sales & Marketing Management* 155, no. 5 (May 2003), p. 14; Martyka, "Sports Trade Shows Shrink, Specialize."

22. Alastair Goldfisher, "Firms Give Away Everything to Capture Trade-Show Traffic," *Pacific Business News* 37, no. 3 (April 2, 1999), p. 21.

23. Bob Lamons, "Gimmes Provide a Distinct Advantage When Done Right," *Marketing News* 34, no. 22 (October 23, 2000), p. 14.

24. Hilary S. Miller, "P-O-P Has High Recall, Survey Shows," *Beverage Industry* 85, no. 12 (December 1994), pp. 15–16; Matthew Martinez and Mercedes M. Cardona, "Study Shows POP Gaining Ground As Medium," *Advertising Age* 68, no. 47 (November 24, 1997), p. 43.

25. Ibid.

26. "POP Sharpness in Focus," *Brandweek* 44, no. 24 (June 6, 2003), pp. 31–36; David Tossman, "The Final Push—POP Boom," *New Zealand Marketing Magazine* 18, no. 8 (September 1999), pp. 45–51.

27. Betsy Spethmann, "Retail Details," *PROMO SourceBook 2005* 17, (2005), pp. 27–28.

28. "Signposts: The Power of Point-of-Purchase," *Marketing News* 35, no. 1 (May 21, 2001), p. 3.

29. Alf Nucifora, "Point-of-Purchase Advertising Now a Marketing VIP," *Business Journal [Phoenix]* 19, no. 49 (September 17, 1999), p. 32.

30. Dana James, "Seeing Green," *Marketing News* 33, no. 24 (November 22, 1999), p. 19.

31. Walter Heller, "Promotion Pullback," *Progressive Grocer* 81, no. 4 (March 1, 2002), p. 19.

32. Susan Greco, "Selling the Superstores," *Inc.* 17, no. 10 (July 1995) pp. 55–61.

33. Jack K. Kasulis, "Managing Trade Promotions in the Context of Market Power," *Journal of the Academy of Marketing Science* 27, no. 3 (Summer 1999), pp. 320–332.

34. Brian Sullivan, "Make Sure Promotional Items Fit Brand Perfectly," *Marketing News* 35, no. 19 (September 10, 2001), p. 15.

35. "Harley Sweepstakes Kicks Off AgrEvo's DeltaGard Promotion," *Pest Control* 65, no. 9 (September 1997), pp. 28–29.

# Consumer Promotions

## Chapter Objectives

*Be* aware of the goals, advantages, and disadvantages for each consumer promotions program.

*Tie* consumer promotions with trade promotions and other elements of the promotions mix and then match them with the overall IMC program.

*Seek* out quality uses of consumer promotions for sales to business-to-business buyers.

*Understand* the limitations that are present when consumer promotions programs are developed for international customers.

## TIME-SHARE VACATION PROPERTIES

### Half-Product Half-Service Promotions

Leisure time activities and recreation generate major revenues for the economies of various regions, states, and even nations. Many types of companies attempt to lure tourists into various areas. Hotels, restaurants, theme parks, water sports, and other activities all improve the odds visitors will come. One of the most lucrative parts of tourism is that vacationers spend money in different ways while on trips. Items ordinarily considered too expensive or simply unnecessary are more readily purchased.

One type of company that has taken advantage of the desire for quality leisure time is found in the time-share industry. Basically, time-share property holders own blocks of time for condominiums, apartments, townhouses, or motel rooms in resort towns. Normally a block lasts for a week. Time-shares are "goods" in the sense that a person buys ownership of a real piece of property at a given location for the specified time period. A deed is prepared, and usually the ownership can be resold or passed along to heirs.

Time-shares also are services. The typical time-share agreement includes a clause stating that the owner will pay a "maintenance" fee each year. The fee covers housekeeping, lawn care, and other services the time-share company provides. More importantly, other aspects of time-shares make them truly unique. These time allocations can be traded across nationwide networks of time-share locations. A person can exchange a week in Santa Cruz, California, for a week in Branson, Missouri. The trade involves paying a fee for the swap. The fee is charged by the company running the trading network.

Various weeks of time have more or less "value" depending on the season. For instance, a time-share week in New England during the autumn, when the leaves are changing into spectacular colors, has more value than a week in the winter. A week in New Orleans during the Mardi Gras season has more value than a week in the middle of summer. Most firms

declare weeks of ownership to have one of three levels: (1) peak, (2) regular, or (3) off-season. Peak season weeks may be traded for all three types, and off-season can usually be exchanged only for off-season times.

Promotion of time-shares involves a variety of tactics. First, the firms advertise heavily in tourist magazines and magazines devoted exclusively to properties. Second, the typical time-share program includes granting a prospective buyer a small period of time (usually for a night up to a full weekend) to stay free at a time-share property. The prospect must agree to tour the facility and hear the sales pitch in order to receive the free night(s) of lodging. Often, small gifts are given. Meals, fruit baskets, bottles of wine, and other small tokens such as T-shirts and lawn chairs are part of the package.

The tour involves showing the client the property in detail, plus a presentation of all the additional benefits of time-sharing, including the exchange network. Then, at the close of the sale, the prospect is usually offered a one-time, must-buy-today discount to purchase a week of time.

To beef up prospect lists, members of the time-share community are given gifts for bringing in potential buyers. A member may receive extra days or weekends of time for finding prospects. Some are even given "upgrades" for their weeks (e.g., from off-season to regular) for identifying someone who might visit the area.

The exchange program also offers vacations to non–time-share areas, along with coupons and discounts for tours and other activities in tourist areas, such as coupons for meal discounts and reduced-price boat rides at lake resorts.

There is even an after market for time-shares. Many can be resold. Firms that resell time-shares can work either separately from or in conjunction with the time-share management team. These properties normally do not offer the free visits and gifts used to entice first-time buyers of the property.

Competition in the time-share market is intense. Many hotel chains, including Sheraton, Hilton, and Radisson have now entered into the time-share marketplace. As a result, some locations do not sell enough time slots for each room. These companies quickly encounter cash flow problems.

Some critics argue the free time-share visits are simply "bait and switch" techniques that cause people who cannot afford to make purchases to spread themselves too thin. Those who enjoy time-share privileges argue the programs are among the best investments in leisure time. As the baby boom generation continues to age and accumulate additional disposable income, the odds are high that time-share companies will continue to prosper. At some point, you may find yourself tempted by a free vacation, a few goodies, and a very polished sales rep seeking to lure you into the exciting world of vacation property ownership.

## o v e r v i e w

**C**onsumer **promotions** (sometimes called *sales promotions*) are incentives aimed at a firm's customers. These customers can be end users of the good or service, or they may be other businesses. As noted in Chapter 9, the difference between consumer promotions and trade promotions is that trade promotions are directed at firms that resell the manufacturer's or firm's products. Consumer promotions are directed toward individuals or firms that use the product and do not resell it to another business. Thus, consumer promotions can be used in both consumer markets and business-to-business markets.

One of the primary goals of a consumer promotion is to entice the customer to take the final step and make a purchase. Advertising creates the interest and excitement that brings the consumer into the store. Marketers then use other tactics in conjunction with advertising programs. In addition to leading to the final decision to by an item, consumer promotions programs can be highly effective in bringing traffic into a store and generating brand loyalty.

The two most general categories of promotions are: (1) *consumer franchise-building promotions* and (2) *consumer sales-building promotions.* Consumer franchise-building promotions are designed to increase awareness of and loyalty to a brand. The goal is to build a favorable image by pointing out unique features and selling points, with the goal being reduced reliance on discounts to entice sales. Sales-building promotions focus on immediate sales, rather than brand equity or loyalty, through discounts, prizes, or other enticements.

Marketers have traditionally believed that any type of sales promotion, whether consumer or trade, eroded brand equity and encouraged customers, businesses, and the distribution channel to focus on price. Recently, however, that view has changed. Many company leaders now recognize that a consumer promotion can be used to differentiate a brand from the competition. This increased differentiation builds brand awareness and can improve a brand's image. This is especially true for franchise-building promotions. Consumers who are exposed to franchise-building promotions tend to develop higher levels of brand awareness and stronger perceptions of brand equity. Although the sales-building promotions also increase awareness, the impact on brand equity is not as positive.[1]

A marketing manager must carefully design a consumer promotional program that will meet IMC goals and that support a brand's position in the marketplace. In the early stages of a product's life cycle, promotions should match advertising and other efforts designed to achieve brand awareness, create opportunities for trial purchases, and stimulate additional purchases. Later, the goal may shift to strengthening a brand, increasing consumption, fending off competition, or finding new markets. In terms of brand positioning, a company should use more franchise-building promotions that do not focus on price for high-image brands; for lower image brands, sales-building promotions are more applicable.

As with other parts of the promotions mix, consumer promotions should be tied into the integrated marketing communications plan. Many large advertising agencies seldom

> ▶ Coupons
> ▶ Premiums
> ▶ Contests and sweepstakes
> ▶ Refunds and rebates
> ▶ Sampling
> ▶ Bonus packs
> ▶ Price-offs

**FIGURE 10.1**
**Types of Consumer Promotions**

actually prepare consumer promotions within the agency. Some agencies have relationships with subsidiary consumer promotions agencies. For example, the New York–based advertising agency DDB Needham handles advertising for brands such as Budweiser, Volkswagen, American Airlines, and Sony. Louis London, a sales promotion subsidiary agency of DDB Needham, handles the sales promotion aspect of these accounts. Others agencies have a separate internal division to handle consumer promotions.

The recent push toward more fully integrated marketing communications programs has led some clients to seek out firms that can manage every aspect of the communications program, including consumer sales promotions. This has led some specialty consumer promotion firms to add services, much in the same way that large advertising agencies are branching out into consumer promotions.

Regardless of which type of agency is used, full-service or specialty, the trend for both is to expand offerings to allow for a greater degree of integration of the consumer promotion component with the other elements of the IMC plan. Figure 10.1 lists the most common consumer promotions. A review of each type follows.

## COUPONS

A coupon is a price reduction offer to a consumer. It may be a percentage off the retail price such as 25 percent or 40 percent, or an absolute amount (50 cents or $1). In the United States, 336 billion coupons were distributed and 3.7 billion redeemed within just a year. The 1.1 percent redemption rate represents approximately $3 billion in savings for consumers, or about 81 cents per coupon. Approximately 78 percent of all U.S. households use coupons, and 64 percent are willing to switch brands with coupons.[2] Figure 10.2 provides a more detailed breakdown of coupon usage.

Approximately 80 percent of all coupons are issued by manufacturers. Figure 10.3 lists the various forms of coupon distribution. Nearly 90 percent of all coupons are sent out through print media. Approximately 84 percent, or 251 billion, are distributed through **freestanding inserts (FSIs)**. FSIs are sheets of coupons distributed in newspapers, primarily on Sunday. An average U.S. citizen receives 850 freestanding inserts per year.

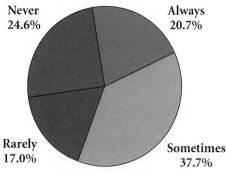

Never
24.6%

Always
20.7%

Rarely
17.0%

Sometimes
37.7%

**FIGURE 10.2**
**Percentage of Consumers
and Coupon Usage**

*Source:* Karen Holt, "Coupon Crimes," *PROMO* 17, no. 5 (April 2004), pp. 23–29.

▶ **Print media**

▶ **Direct mail**

▶ **On- or in-package**

▶ **In-store**

▶ **Sampling**

▶ **Scanner delivered**

▶ **Cross-ruffing**

▶ **Response offer**

▶ **Internet**

▶ **Fax**

▶ **Sales staff**

**FIGURE 10.3**
**Methods of Distributing Coupons**

Other methods of distribution include in-store, on-shelf, and electronically dispensed coupons, along with coupons attached to free samples of a product. The remaining coupons are distributed in or on product packages, by direct mail, and in magazines and newspapers.[3]

There are several reasons for using FSIs and print media to distribute coupons. First, a consumer must make a conscious effort to clip or save the coupon. Second, coupons create brand awareness. The consumer sees the brand name on the coupon even when the coupon is not redeemed. Third, FSIs encourage consumers to purchase brands on the next trip to the store. Consumers are more likely to purchase a couponed brand and remember the brand name when they redeem a coupon, which helps move the brand to a consumer's long-term memory. The consumer is more likely to recall the brand and buy it the next time the need arises, even without a coupon.

## Types of Coupons

Coupons are often distributed in retail stores and placed on or near packages. The consumer immediately can redeem the coupon while making the purchase. This type of coupon is called an **instant redemption coupon**. These coupons often lead to trial purchases and purchases of additional packages of a product. Many grocery stores allow a company to cook a new food product and offer free samples along with coupon giveaways. Coupons also are placed in dispensers near various products, which provide convenient access for customers. All of these are forms of instant redemption coupons, because customers can use them immediately.

Coupons also can be placed inside packages so that customers cannot redeem them quite as quickly. This approach encourages repeat purchases. These coupons are called **bounce-back coupons**.

Some companies issue coupons at the cash register. These are called **scanner-delivered coupons**, because they are triggered by an item being scanned. The coupon that is delivered is often for a competitor's product. This approach is designed to encourage brand switching the next time a consumer makes a purchase.

**Cross-ruffing** is the placement of a coupon for one product on another product. A coupon for a French onion dip placed on a package of potato chips is a cross-ruff coupon. Cross-ruff coupons should be on products that fit together logically and that are often purchased and consumed simultaneously. Occasionally, a manufacturer uses cross-ruffing to encourage consumers to purchase another one of its products. For example, the Kellogg company may place a coupon on a Rice Krispies box for another cereal, such as Frosted Flakes or an oatmeal product. This type of couponing tactic encourages consumers to purchase within the same brand or family of products.

**Response offer coupons** are issued following requests by consumers. Coupons then are mailed, faxed, or sent by Internet to the consumer. A fax is the most common method of response offer coupon in the business-to-business sector. Office supply companies and other vendors use them to entice business customers to make purchases or place orders. Some firms distribute coupons through sales representatives. This creates instant redemptions, because the salesperson also takes the order.

Another form of coupon is one that is *electronically delivered.* Nearly 50 percent of the electronically delivered coupons are requested via the Web. Twenty-eight percent were requested after a consumer viewed a television ad. Another 18 percent were requested after the consumer heard about the coupon from a friend. The redemption rate for e-coupons is considerably higher than for any other type of coupon. With rising Internet access, the use of e-coupons should also increase.[4]

## Coupon Responses

Coupon response rates are slightly more than 1 percent. Recently, coupon distribution has continued to increase, however, redemption rates have steadily declined.[5] Redemption rates for Internet-delivered coupons have fared the best, with an average more than 20 percent redeemed.

Research into coupon redemptions helps the marketing team understand consumer response patterns. Coupons are not used equally among various ethnic groups. African-Americans and Hispanics tend to redeem coupons less often than the population as a whole, because there is a lower distribution rate to many ethnic groups. Freestanding inserts in Sunday papers account for 80 percent of the distribution of coupons. Minority groups tend to read ethnically-oriented newspapers and magazines and are less inclined to subscribe to publications aimed at the general population. Consequently, FSIs do not reach them. Magazines and newspapers targeting individual ethnic groups contain fewer coupon offers than do more general-appeal print media. Lower redemption rates can make ethnic groups appear to be less attractive and, therefore, they receive fewer direct-mail coupons. To correct this cycle, manufacturers and other distributors can improve target marketing by sending out coupon offers through ethnic publications.[6]

## Problems with Coupons

There are drawbacks to the use of coupons as a promotional tactic. They include:

- Reduced revenues
- Mass-cutting
- Counterfeiting
- Misredemptions

Many current customers with a strong brand preference will redeem that brand's coupon with the next purchase. This reduces full-price revenues. Customers who already have a preference for a brand redeem approximately 80 percent of all coupons.[7] Some argue that offering a price discount to customers who are willing to pay full price does not make sense. Manufacturers, however, point out that these consumers may be willing to stock up on the item, which means they won't use the competition's coupons. Consequently, manufacturers recognize that these brand-preference customer redemptions are a "necessary evil" if mass distribution is used. Some firms use direct mail to distribute the coupon primarily to nonloyal customers. The goal is to target nonusers and the competitor's customers. The primary disadvantage of this method is the high cost of direct mail, especially in light of the low response rate associated with direct-mail coupons.

Of the $3.6 billion paid annually for coupon redemptions, $500 million is in the form of illegal reimbursements, according to Coupon Information Council estimates.[8] A common form of coupon fraud is *mass-cutting.* Coupons are "redeemed" through a fraudulent, nonexistent retail outlet, which is a mailbox set up by an illegal coupon-redemption ring. At \$.50 to \$3 per coupon, mass-cutting of coupons can be lucrative. Many times these rings take advantage of charitable organizations and religious groups that think they are helping a worthy cause by sending in coupons to the mailbox to receive a percentage of the proceeds. Instead, they actually are aiding an illegal activity.

*Counterfeiting* occurs when coupons are copied and then sent back to the manufacturer for reimbursement. The manufacturer pays for phony coupons. Newspaper-generated black-and-white coupons are the easiest to counterfeit. Color copiers, however, have made other forms of counterfeiting easier. The major source of counterfeiting is the Internet. Web and high-quality printer technology makes it possible for people to create bogus coupons and then sell or distribute them via the Internet. In most cases the counterfeit coupons are sold in bulk and often it is for inflated discounts or even free merchandise. Under pressure from the Grocery Manufacturers of America and the Food Marketing Institute, both Yahoo! and eBay banned coupon sales. This has not stopped mass distribution of counterfeit coupons. Still, some progress has been made.[9]

A number of retailers have refused to accept Internet coupons. Soon after, however, these companies bowed to pressure from customers who had legitimate coupons. After investigating the problem further, a number of retailers such as Publix Super Markets and Ukrops noticed the primary counterfeit problem was for free merchandise rather than a discount on a product. Therefore, the policy was modified to accept reasonable Internet coupons, but not coupons for free merchandise or for an unusually large percentage of the purchase price. Wal-Mart only accepts Internet coupons that include a valid expiration date, remit address, and bar code.[10]

Retailers usually are not involved in mass-cutting or counterfeiting of coupons. They can, however, engage in the *misredemption* of coupons. For instance, a coupon for soup often states the size of can for which the discount applies. If the discount is used for another size, such as a 12-ounce can instead of the 24-ounce can, then a misredemption occurs. This may be due to an error on the part of the clerk who did not check the coupon carefully. Or, the clerk might have known it was the wrong-size can but did not want to bother finding the correct size or risk making the customer mad by denying the coupon. Other times, clerks honor coupons for merchandise that was not purchased when they take the coupon and subtract it from the customer's total without matching it to any actual product.

Some misredemptions are performed by retail "clearinghouses" that collect money for coupons even when they were not actually redeemed by customers. Other retailers submit coupons for reimbursement rather than placing them on the shelf or some other location in the store. The typical supermarket redeems hundreds of coupons per day. As a result, there is ample opportunity for errors, mistakes, and fraud.

## Tactics to Improve Coupon Effectiveness

Three factors influence attractiveness of a coupon. The first is the face value of the coupon. A higher face value makes the coupon more attractive and more likely to be redeemed.

Second is the distribution method. Research indicates that FSIs are the most attractive to consumers because they can choose coupons in the privacy of their homes. In-store coupons are less attractive because consumers do not want to take time to process information while in the store.

Understanding that coupons sent to consumer homes are more effective, Valpak mails coupons in the company's customary blue envelope to high-income households consisting of educated adults and households with children. In an effort to boost sales, several heating, air-conditioning, and refrigeration companies now use coupons circulated by Valpak. One such company, Front Range Mechanical Services, generated considerable inquiries using a \$10 off coupon. Another company, Lancaster Plumbing & Heating, saw profits increase from \$1,420 to \$19,036 using coupons circulated by Valpak.[11]

The third attractiveness factor is whether the coupon is for a preferred brand or at least for a brand that is already in the consumer's evoked set (readily recalled brands). Coupons for the preferred brand or one from the evoked set tend to be more attractive than those for unknown or unrecognized brand names.

# PREMIUMS

A second form of consumer promotion is the offer of a premium. Premiums are prizes, gifts, or other special offers consumers receive when purchasing products. When a company offers a premium, the consumer pays full price for the good or service, in contrast to coupons, which grant price reductions. Some marketing experts believe the overuse of coupons damages a brand's image. Conversely, premiums can actually enhance a brand's image. The key is to pick the right type of premium. Premiums can be used in the attempt to boost sales; however, they usually are not as successful as coupon sales. Nevertheless, premiums remain a valuable consumer promotional tool. In the United States, over $4.5 billion is spent on premiums each year.[12] There are four major types of premiums:

1. Free-in-the-mail
2. In- or on-package
3. Store or manufacturer
4. Self-liquidating

**Free-in-the-mail premiums** are gifts individuals receive for purchasing products. To receive the gift, the customer must mail in a proof of purchase to the manufacturer, who then mails the gift back to the consumer. Sometimes more than one purchase is required to receive the gift. Notice the premiums being offered in the Fisher Boy advertisement shown on this page. Consumers collect points from the front of Fisher Boy packages to be redeemed for "cool" prizes. To further encourage sales, the advertisement has a coupon attached.

Credit card companies use premiums to entice individuals to sign up for credit cards. Instead of providing a proof of purchase, the consumer needs only to activate the card to receive the incentives, which can range from cash back on purchases to merchandise and frequent-flier miles.

**In- or on-package premiums** are usually small gifts, such as toys in cereal boxes. Often the gift is disguised or packaged so the consumer must buy the product to find out which premium it contains. The most famous of these may be Cracker Jack's prizes. At other times the gift is attached to the package, such as package of blades with the purchase of a razor.

**Store or manufacturer premiums** are gifts given by either the retail store or the manufacturer when the customer purchases a product. Fast-food restaurants offer children a toy with the purchase of a child's meal. To entice individuals to purchase high-end homes and real estate in Prime Nature Villa in Thailand, unique premiums were offered by contractors. The premium was a 525i BMW automobile offer to individuals who purchased land plots larger than 1,600 square meters in the company's luxury-home project area. Individuals who purchased smaller plots, between 800 and 1,600 square meters, received gift certificates for diamond jewelry.[13]

The fourth major type of premium is called the **self-liquidating premium**. These premiums require the consumer to pay an amount of money for a gift or item. For example, the premium may be offered for only $4.99 plus shipping and handling and two proofs of purchase from boxes of Cheerios. The premium is called *self-liquidating* because the $4.99 covers the cost of the premium. The

A free-in-the-mail premium offer for Fisher Boy seafood.
*Source:* Courtesy of Fisher Boy.

manufacturer also receives money for shipping and handling. This means that consumers are paying most or all of the actual cost of the item.

## Problems with Premiums

The two major problems associated with premium programs are: (1) the time factor and (2) the cost. Premiums tend to have short life spans. Many companies try to find items that are in vogue and adopt them. The problem is that by the time the marketing material is developed and the merchandise arrives, the item may no longer be popular. Many companies have warehouses full of premiums that turned out to be busts because either they waited too long to order the merchandise or the product they thought would be a great premium turned out to be no longer exciting for customers. A few years ago, KFC tried to take advantage of the popularity of Pokémon after seeing Burger King's success with the cartoon character. KFC offered Pokémon beanbags. The program turned out to be a disaster. Most KFC stores still had huge stocks of the beanbags 6 weeks after the end of the promotion.[14]

The second problem connected to premiums is the cost. A premium exclusively offered often increases the demand for the item. For example, numerous Disney tie-ins with fast-food restaurants are exclusive contracts. In these arrangements, Disney promises not to sell the premium to any other vendor or restaurant. Yet it may offer the merchandise to other types of businesses or to retail outlets. This type of deal normally raises the price of the item and cost to the firm. Consequently, a rising scale exists. Lower-cost premiums generate less interest and probably fewer sales. Higher-cost premiums create more sales, but cost more to provide.

## Building Successful Premium Programs

Figure 10.4 highlights the primary keys to building successful premium programs.[15] First, and most important, is to match the premium to the target market. For a target market such as older, high-income individuals, the premium may be china or fine crystal. If the market is children, a cartoon figure or a character from Disney or Sesame Street would be attractive. The premium should match the desires and interests of target market members.

Next, the best premiums are those that reinforce the firm's image in some way. They should not be low-cost trinkets. Offering cheap merchandise insults customers and can damage the image of a firm.

Premiums are more likely to succeed when they are tied in with the firm's products. These items can enhance the image of the product as well as the image of the firm. For instance, Sears offered a 20-piece Pfaltzgraff dinnerware set to every consumer who purchased a Kenmore microwave. Customers had a choice of four different patterns. In just 6 weeks, 4,000 premiums were redeemed. Offering the dinnerware dishes with the purchase of a microwave reinforced the idea that Sears' products are of high quality. The quality of the dishes reinforced Kenmore's brand image.[16]

Premiums should be integrated with the other components of the IMC program. Premiums are an excellent means of adding value to a product instead of slashing prices or using coupons. They can reinforce the brand's image. Premiums can serve as a "thank you" to current customers or to attract new customers. *Sports Illustrated* has a rich

FIGURE 10.4
Keys to Successful Premiums

▶ Match the premium to the target market

▶ Carefully select the premiums (avoid fads, try for exclusivity)

▶ Pick a premium that reinforces the firm's product and image

▶ Integrate the premium with other IMC tools (especially advertising and POP displays)

▶ Don't expect premiums to increase short-term profits

*Source:* Based on Don Jagoda, "The Seven Habits of Highly Successful Premiums," *Incentive* 173, no. 8 (August 1999), pp. 104–105.

history of premium programs, from videos to watches to phones, which are presented for either renewing a subscription to the magazine or ordering one for the first time.

There are three principles to remember when using premiums. First, premiums should build rational involvement in some way with the good or service. A moving company giving out tote bags that say, "No job too large or small" communicates the point that the mover can help any size household. Second, premiums should build emotional involvement, such as feeling more warm and secure or simply happy about the item given. Third, the premium must build involvement with the product, not just the premium.[17]

Although premiums are an excellent method of adding value or enhancing a brand, they are not as effective at increasing profits. Therefore, a clear relationship between the premium's intention and IMC goals should be established. Logically the goal should be more about image than profit.

## CONTESTS AND SWEEPSTAKES

Contests and sweepstakes are popular forms of consumer sales promotions. Approximately $2 billion are spent on various games, contests, and sweepstakes each year.[18] Both are used in consumer markets as well as business markets. A primary factor that determines the success rates of this type of appeal is the prize list. Members of the target market for the contest or sweepstakes must believe the prizes are desirable enough to entice them to participate. A prize that is perceived to be of low or no value does not work.

The words *contest* and *sweepstakes* tend to be used interchangeably, yet there are some differences, primarily legal. *Contests* normally require the participant to perform some type of activity. The winner is selected based on who performs best or provides the most correct answers. Often, contests require a participant to make a purchase to enter. In some states, however, it is illegal to force a consumer to make a purchase to enter a contest. It is important in developing contests to know the different state and federal laws that apply.

Contests range from the controversial bikini or suntan contests at local nightclubs to popular television shows such as *Jeopardy* or *Survivor* in which contestants must answer

---

### ETHICAL ISSUES

#### Consumer Promotion Activities

One of the fastest-growing problems in the United States is addiction to gambling by young people. Access to gaming facilities and gambling opportunities has never been greater, as individual states set up lotteries, dog tracks, casinos, and other operations. Many college students gamble regularly.

In this environment, does a marketing team worsen the problem by offering contests and sweepstakes? Currently, many consumers do not recognize that gambling can be a problem. Offering a contest may cause an individual to buy more products simply to obtain the chance to win a big prize. Is the marketing team comfortable with this possibility?

Another ethical concern in the area of promotions is coupon redemptions. Should stores honor coupons that have been created fraudulently, thereby risking alienating a store's customer base? Retailers also face the issue of honoring coupons for the wrong size of a product, such as one aimed at a 10-ounce size rather than a 15-ounce one. Again, the retail store's customer is happy, but the coupon provider loses money.

Manufacturers trust retail stores to accurately and honestly follow the rules of consumer promotions for contests, sweepstakes, premiums, coupons, or bonus packs. The difficulty is that manufacturers have no way of being certain that the rules have been followed. With so many retailers being involved, it is impossible for them to police all of the activity. In this type of environment, it becomes tempting for a retailer to violate rules if it will increase the retailer's profit or satisfaction levels of customers.

Looking for a leg up?

**Enter the Grace Fund Essay Contest...**

All women and women's organizations are eligible. Please forward an essay, 500 words or less, on what, when, where, and why you would like to be awarded one of four monetary awards ($500 minimum) from the Grace Fund. It may be to propel a dream or enhance an established venture.

Grace Magazine
P.O. Box 7 • Joplin, MO 64802
gracemagazine@joplinglobe.com
Entries must be submitted by March 15, 2004.
Recipients will appear in the April issue of Grace Magazine.

questions or win competitions to earn prizes. Although some contests are mostly chance (e.g., *Wheel of Fortune*), others require skill. For example, ACH Food Companies, Inc., sponsored a Karo Syrup Recipe Contest for students. To enter, students had to create original recipes using Karo syrup. In a similar type of contest sponsored by Florida's Tomato Association, participants created original recipes utilizing tomatoes. The grand prize winner for the latter contest was Steve Barnhart's "Fresh Florida Tomato Orange Soup."[19]

No purchase is required to enter a *sweepstakes*. Consumers can enter as many times as they wish, although it is permissible for firms to restrict customers to one entry per visit to the store or some other location. The chances of winning a sweepstakes are based on a probability factor. The probability of winning must clearly be stated on all point-of-purchase (POP) displays and advertising materials. In a sweepstakes, the probability of winning each prize must be published in advance. This means the firm must know how many winning tickets, as compared to total tickets, have been prepared.

People enter contests and sweepstakes that they perceive as being worth their time and attention. Consumers do not enter every contest or sweepstakes they encounter. Instead, they selectively choose. The decision is often based on the perceived value of the contest or sweepstakes prize combined with the odds of winning. The greater the perceived odds of winning, the more likely a person will play the contest or enter the sweepstakes.

The perceived value of a prize has two components: (1) extrinsic value and (2) intrinsic value. The extrinsic value is the actual attractiveness of the item (a car versus a free sandwich). The greater the perceived value, the more likely the person will participate. Intrinsic values are those associated with playing or participating. A contest requiring the use of a skill, such as the one with recipes or an essay contest, entices entry by individuals who enjoy demonstrating a skill. In that case, extrinsic rewards become secondary. Instead, participants enjoy competing and demonstrating their abilities, which in part explains the popularity of fantasy football and baseball leagues and "pick the winner" sports contests.

## Problems with Contests and Sweepstakes

Company leaders must seek to overcome three issues in order to create successful promotional programs. The problems associated with contests and sweepstakes are:

▶ Costs
▶ Consumer indifference
▶ Clutter

Contests and sweepstakes require companies to provide prizes, entry forms, legal statements, supportive advertising and other promotional activities, and often enticements to retailers to set up POP displays and other contest-related materials. Failure to support a contest fully means the odds of success diminish. Companies must be prepared to undertake all of the necessary expenditures associated with the program.

Consumers are increasingly indifferent to many contests and sweepstakes because of the rising availability of gambling opportunities. State lotteries, casinos, riverboat gambling, and Internet gambling make it possible to play games of chance and skill frequently. As a result, a contest offering a prize of a free dinner or $100 may not seem very exciting.

Clutter results from the number of firms promoting contests at any given time. With so many legal and illegal places to play games of chance, the idea of making a purchase or trip to the store to enter one more contest is less appealing.

## Creating Successful Contests and Sweepstakes

One factor in the success level of a contest is finding the right prize. Firms can be creative in trying to reach this goal. For example, in Ohio a sweepstake was created for a small, local company called Velvet Ice Cream Company. Ohio was a gateway to the West in the early 1800s. A number of inns were built along stagecoach routes traveling through the state. Many of these inns still exist. Six inns were solicited and agreed to participate in the sweepstakes. The inns provided prizes, which consisted of one free night stay for two, dinner, and a dessert containing Velvet Ice Cream product. Each winner also received a booklet with pictures of the inn, a brief history of the inn, and various recipes for Velvet Ice Cream products. The sweepstakes ran from Memorial Day to Labor Day and was considered a rousing success by Velvet, as well as the six inns that participated. Traffic and revenues for all participants increased during the sweepstakes.[20]

A second ingredient in a successful contest can occur when a company takes advantage of a special event, such as a sports contest or a celebration. Local companies sometimes create a contest in conjunction with a local celebration, such as a town's 100th birthday or at an annual event such as an ethnic festival.

A third method for creating a successful contest or sweepstakes is using the popularity of the Internet. The Internet can provide opportunities for individuals to play contests and sweepstakes for their intrinsic value. It also can be used to create interactive games that can challenge the contestant's ability. The Internet provides promoters with data-capturing capabilities. Internet contests are less costly to set up and run than other types of promotions.[21]

Yoyodyne Entertainment has designed more than 100 contests and games for companies such as H&R Block, MCI, American Express, Fox TV, and *Rolling Stone* magazine. H&R Block's contest was called "We'll Pay Your Taxes." The contest was designed to

## COMMUNICATION ACTION

### Mobile Phone Fun

Young people ages 18 to 24 are not watching much television nor are they reading newspapers. Teens and "tweens" are more likely to be instant messaging a friend than to be viewing any form of media. Wanting to reach members of these valuable target markets, companies looked to the mobile phone for creative ways to contact them. With the rise in popularity of instant messaging, a number of innovative marketing firms launched various marketing campaigns via cell phones. The most successful were those campaigns that incorporated some type of game, contest, or fun into the message.

Hip Cricket, a mobile marketing and event company based in Essex, Connecticut, developed the Mobile Emmy Trivia Challenge for the Television Academy. The challenge was a series of 2-part trivia quizzes that ran just prior to the Emmy Awards on ABC in September. To play, cell phone users sent a text message to the Emmys with the keyword "PLAY." It cost each player 50 cents to enter, per day, except for Sprint users, who did not have to pay the charges. The game was designed to draw 18- to 34-year-olds back into the Emmy audience. The winner won a trip to the following year's Emmy show in Los Angeles.

Hip Cricket prepared an even more intriguing sweepstake for Miller Brewing Company's Icehouse brand. The sweepstakes was the first to be conducted live, during a rock concert. Music fans, 21 years old or older, could enter the sweepstakes by text messaging the words "Pick Me" during the concert. At 10:00 P.M., one concertgoer, Melissa Hasty, received word via text message that she had won the grand prize, a 5-day, 4-night Caribbean cruise on the "Rock Boat." Other concert fans won secondary prizes throughout the night, again, receiving notification via their cell phone's instant messaging system. Winning is always fun. For Melissa and others at the concert, winning instantly was even more exciting.

**Source:** Kathleen Joyce, "Not Just a Novelty," *PROMO* 17, no. 12 (November 2004), pp. 52–56.

FEELING LUCKY?

www.luckysurf.com

**PLAY LUCKYSURF.COM**
The free game that's like playing the lottery every day. A daily $1 million jackpot. A no-hassle, no-cost way to turn a little luck into an obscene amount of money. Play today. So you can quit your job tomorrow. And be in Fiji by the weekend.

LuckySurf.com

A new media trend for contests and sweepstakes is offering them over the Internet.
*Source:* Courtesy of LuckySurf.com.

drive traffic to the H&R Block Web site. Through a series of weekly e-mail messages, players were directed to H&R Block's Web site for the answers. Each e-mail message contained brief product messages from H&R Block. The game ran just 2 months but averaged 46,000 hits per week, more than H&R Block had the entire previous year.[22]

To encourage consumers to continue playing a contest, the extrinsic values of prizes can be increased by allowing small, incremental rewards. A consumer who wins a soft drink or a sandwich in a sweepstakes at Subway is more likely to continue playing. Scratch-and-win cards tend to be effective because the reward is instant. The mobile phone promotions discussed in the Communication Action box in this section provided instant notification of winning via text messaging. As with coupons, instantly redeemed prizes are more popular with consumers than are delayed rewards. Using special Java technology, scratch-and-win cards can even be used on the Internet so that consumers can receive instant prizes.

To fully ensure the success of the contest or sweepstakes, it is important to coordinate the promotion with the advertising, POP displays, and other marketing tools. All of these elements must be directed toward the same target audience and convey a united message. These features add to the cost of the contest, however, such integration is a crucial ingredient in achieving the desired goals.

When the contest or sweepstakes program features a tie-in with another company, the two firms should carefully coordinate activities. It is a daunting task to include all creatives, trade promotions managers, consumer promotions managers, media buyers, and media planners, but it is also necessary in order to create a successful program.

The primary goals of contests and sweepstakes are to encourage customer traffic and boost sales. There is no doubt that a contest or sweepstakes increases customer traffic. The question is whether they actually boost sales. Some do, others do not. Marketers are beginning to realize that intrinsic rewards tend to draw consumers back. This means many Internet games are exciting prospects, because they can be structured to create intrinsic rewards.

Marketing research has demonstrated that brand awareness increases with multiple exposures to an advertisement or contest. Therefore, although contests and sweepstakes may not boost sales in the short run, they can be a driving force behind brand awareness and brand image development for longer periods of time, such as the McDonald's Monopoly game promotion that ran for several years. As a result, these games are often key weapons in the marketing arsenals of many organizations.

## REFUNDS AND REBATES

Refunds and rebates are cash returns offered to consumers or businesses following the purchase of a product. Consumers pay full price for the product but can mail in some type of proof of purchase. The manufacturer then refunds a portion of the purchase price. A *refund* is a cash return on what are called "soft goods," such as food or clothing. *Rebates* are cash returns on "hard goods," which are major ticket items such as automobiles and appliances. Normally refunds are smaller and rebates are larger. For example, the typical refund offered on a food item may be $1; the typical rebate on a car may be $500, $1,000, or more, depending on the price and size of the car.

Only about 30 percent of all rebates are ever claimed. For rebates valued at $50 or more, however, the percentage of claims rises to about 65 percent. The major reason for the low response rate is the inconvenience associated with getting the rebate. Too many steps or long waiting times because of "snail mail" are common complaints about rebates. It is not unusual for consumers to wait up to 6 months to receive a rebate check. Recently, the number of complaints to the Better Business Bureau concerning rebates rose by 21 percent in just a single year.[23]

Rebates are common in the computer and electronics industries. In fact, computer retailers have reduced expenditures on advertising of computers and relied more on rebates to drive sales. Rebates are now offered for approximately 66 percent of all desktop computers on the market. Rebates are also used in the business-to-business sector. Most electric utilities offer rebates to companies that design and build more energy-efficient buildings. The rebates also apply to retrofitting inefficient buildings with energy-efficient lighting systems, motors, air conditioners, heating systems, and insulation.[24]

## Problems with Refunds and Rebates

The problems associated with refunds and rebates include the costs, the paperwork involved, and diminished effectiveness. The retail outlet must carefully document manufacturer rebates so that the customer is reimbursed. To hold down the paperwork, many automobile manufacturers have the rebate assigned to the dealer and deduct the amount from the sales price. This often lessens the "impact" of the rebate, because no check is ever delivered to the customer.

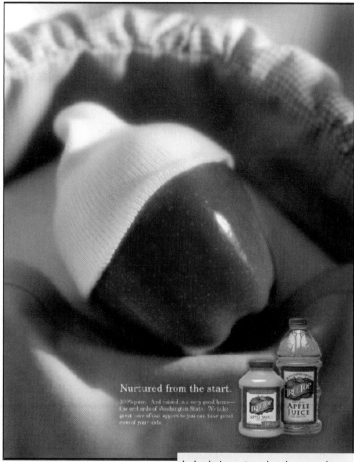

Nurtured from the start.

In developing a strong brand name such as Tree Top, it is important to choose the right consumer promotion.
*Source:* Courtesy of Tree Top Apple Juice.

The cost of a refund or rebate is the lost revenue from the sale price combined with the mailing and record-keeping costs involved. Further, a promotional or advertising campaign emphasizing the offer must be developed, or the program goes unnoticed. These extra promotional expenditures further add to the costs of the plan.

Many rebate programs suffer from diminished effectiveness, because consumers have come to expect them. For example, many car dealers find that customers won't buy until rebates are offered. As a result, there is no new purchase activity associated with the rebate, but rather a delay in the purchase process as consumers "wait out" auto manufacturers. According to J.D. Power and Associates, slightly more than 60 percent of all vehicle purchases in the United States involve some type of cash rebate.[25] Further, increasing the amount of a rebate no longer seems to spur additional sales activity, yet discontinuing or reducing rebate levels tends to have an immediate negative impact on sales.

## Creating Effective Refund–Rebate Programs

To generate an effective refund or rebate program, the offer must have:

▶ Visibility

▶ Perceived newness

▶ An impact

The refund should be visible. Customers must find out about the program before they can take advantage of it. Refunds and rebates achieve the greatest successes when they are perceived as being new or original. When they are an entrenched part of doing business, they have simply become an expected discount. Rebates and refunds must have the impact of changing the buyer's behavior, either by leading to more immediate purchases or by causing the customer to change brands.

Retailers tend to like refunds and rebates because the retailer maintains its margin or markup on the product, which means the item or service is sold at full price. Recently,

An advertisement by Nature's Plus offering consumers a free sample.

*Source:* Courtesy of Natural Organics, Inc.

Iomega offered a $50 rebate on its Zip drive that sold for $199. Retailers responded favorably to the Iomega rebate because it was easy for consumers to understand, the display materials were attractive, and implementing the rebate was easy for retailers. Also, the rebate was large enough to stimulate sales and encourage consumers to choose the Iomega brand.[26] Consequently, effective rebate programs are an option for various companies seeking to heighten the buying excitement levels associated with products.

## SAMPLING

One popular method that is used to encourage consumers to try a new product is sampling. Sampling is the actual delivery of a product to consumers for their use or consumption. Most samples are provided free of charge. A coupon or price-off incentive is often given with the sample to persuade the consumer to purchase a larger version of the product, such as a full-size package.

In business-to-business markets, samples of products are often given to potential clients. Sampling also can be used in the service sector. For example, a tanning salon may offer an initial visit free to encourage new customers to try its facilities. Dentists and lawyers use sampling when they offer an initial consultation free of charge.

Figure 10.5 lists various ways samples are distributed. The most common consumer method is *in-store distribution,* such as when food product companies have personnel cooking the food and passing it out to individuals in the store. *Direct sampling* is a program in which samples are mailed or delivered door to door to consumers.

Various demographic target markets can be identified for free samples. In the business-to-business sector, salespeople often deliver direct samples. *Response samples* are made available to individuals or businesses responding to a media offer on television, on the Internet, from a magazine, or by some other source. *Cross-ruff* sampling plans provide samples of one product on another. A laundry detergent with a free dryer sheet attached to the package is a cross-ruff sample. *Media sampling* means the sample is included in the media outlet. For example, a small sample of perfume can be included in a magazine advertisement or with a newspaper. *Professional samples* are delivered by professionals, such as when doctors provide patients with free drug samples. These are

- ▸ **In-store distribution**
- ▸ **Direct sampling**
- ▸ **Response sampling**
- ▸ **Cross-ruff sampling**
- ▸ **Media sampling**
- ▸ **Professional sampling**
- ▸ **Selective sampling**

**FIGURE 10.5**
**Types of Sampling**

given out, for example, by doctors who receive free samples from a drug company. *Selective samples* are distributed at a site such as a state fair, parade, hospital, restaurant, or sporting event. For instance, many times Power Bars are given to people attending football or basketball games. There is a tie-in between the product (nutrition) and the event (athletics).

The target audience determines the best method of sampling to use. Direct sampling is generally the ideal for business-to-business situations. Other methods tend to work better for consumers. Women tend to prefer mail samples they can examine at home. Men prefer samples given to them at a store or an event. The advantage of passing out samples at an event is that the person receiving the sample receives the personal touch.

Sampling is an effective method to entice consumers to try a product.

A smile, a greeting, and additional information can be conveyed along with the sample. Also, if the consumer liked the event, then he or she may transfer the good feelings toward the event to the sampled product.[27]

In recent years, marketers have increased usage of FSIs for the distribution of samples. A variety of products have been distributed in newspapers, such as breakfast bars, coffee, shampoo, snacks, tea, and automotive cleansers. Companies using newspapers like the FSI insert method because it breaks through the clutter and gets the attention of consumers. The newspaper is an "invited medium." Therefore, consumers are more receptive when samples distributed are with the paper.[28]

Internet-based response sampling programs have also become popular with both consumers and manufacturers. Bristol-Myers/Squibb was one of the first companies to utilize the Internet for product sampling. The company offered a free sample of Excedrin to individuals who requested the sample and were willing to provide their names, addresses and e-mail information. In addition to the 12-pack sample of Excedrin, consumers received coupons for additional Excedrin purchases along with the quarterly *Excedrin Headache Relief Update Newsletter.* The advantage of this form of response sampling is that only consumers who requested the product received it. Also, companies normally can gather additional information to be added to a database. Seventy percent of consumers who requested a sample online were willing to complete a survey to receive the sample.[29]

## Problems with Sampling

Product sampling is an effective way to introduce a new product and generate interest in that product. The primary disadvantage is the cost. Often a special sample-size package must be developed. The package must be very similar to the regular-size pack, so consumers will be able to identify the product after using the sample. Many times samples are mailed, adding to the expense of the program. A sample given out in a store requires an individual to distribute it and some kind of permission from the store.

To fully cover an area with samples requires careful planning of the distribution. Many times people simply discard the sample without even trying the product. Therefore, careful market research should be used before undertaking a sampling program.

## Effective Use of Samples

As with the other consumer promotions, sampling must be a central part of the IMC plan. The primary purpose of sampling is to encourage a trial use by a consumer or a business. Sampling is most effective when it introduces a new product or a new version of a product to a market. Samples also help promote a current product to a new target market or to new prospects.

**WAITING ISN'T WORKING.**

Videoconferencing never looked so good.

With today's reduced budgets and increased travel times, now more than ever Polycom's award-winning videoconferencing products are essential, must-have tools for getting business done. With the only end-to-end solutions that efficiently integrate video, voice, data and web collaboration, Polycom lets you be there without going there. As the industry leader, we can show you how our state-of-the-art video and audio quality redefines the concept of face-to-face meetings. And how our solutions can be tailored to fit any room and any budget. So isn't it time you got Polycom and stopped waiting in line?

**RISK-FREE TRIAL!**
TRY ANY POLYCOM VIDEOCONFERENCING SYSTEM FREE FOR 30 DAYS.*

Call today 1-877-POLYCOM
Go to www.polycom.com/see

* 100% financing available on all Polycom systems.

**POLYCOM**

Sampling is important in the business-to-business market to encourage trial usage of a product. Polycom offers companies a free 30-day, risk-free trial.
*Source:* Courtesy of Polycom.

The key to successful sampling is targeting the right audience. Mass sampling is not nearly as cost-effective as targeted sampling. Recently, Green & Black launched a sampling campaign for organic chocolates at 21 outdoor concerts in England. Each audience member was given a bar of Green & Black's organic chocolate at the entrance. More than 80 percent of the audience, a total of 105,000 people, received sample bars. A tasting marquee was also set up in the concert area so that concert attendees could try other flavors. The goal was to build a brand experience between concert attendees and the Green & Black brand name and to boost sales, which it did. Sales of the organic chocolate bar increased 79 percent in the months immediately following the concerts.[30]

## BONUS PACKS

When an additional or extra number of items are placed in a special product package, it is called a bonus pack. When a consumer buys four bars of soap for the price of three, it is a bonus pack promotion. Recently, Rayovac offered three free AA batteries in a bonus pack containing nine batteries. Typical bonuses range from 20 percent to 100 percent of the normal number of units in a package. A 30 percent bonus is the most common.

Figure 10.6 identifies the major objectives of bonus packs. Increasing the size or quantity of the package can lead to greater product use. For example, if a cereal box is increased in size by 25 percent, the consumer is likely to eat more cereal, because it is readily available. This is not true for products that have a constant rate of consumption. For instance, if Colgate increases the size of a toothpaste container by 25 percent, consumers will not use more toothpaste. In effect, what this does is delay the customer's next purchase. Still, manufacturers do offer these types of bonus packs, because they may help preempt the competition. A consumer with a large quantity of the merchandise on hand is less likely to switch to another brand, even when offered some type of deal, such as a coupon.

A firm's current customers often take advantage of a bonus pack offer. When customers stockpile a quantity of a particular brand, it discourages purchasing from a competitor. Bonus packs reward customer loyalty by offering, in effect, free merchandise.

Bonus packs rarely attract new customers because the consumer is less likely to have previously purchased the brand. Obtaining an extra quantity does not reduce the purchase risk. In fact, it adds to the risk, especially when the customer does not like to waste a product by throwing it away if he or she is dissatisfied with the product.

Bonus packs can lead to brand switching if the consumer has used the brand previously. Facing purchase decisions, consumers may opt for brands that offer a bonus pack at the regular price. These products have an advantage that competitive brands are not offering.

▶ Increase usage of the product
▶ Match or preempt competitive actions
▶ Stockpile the product
▶ Develop customer loyalty
▶ Attract new users
▶ Encourage brand switching

**FIGURE 10.6**
**Reasons for Using Bonus Packs**

## Problems with Bonus Packs

Some marketing research indicates that consumers are skeptical of bonus pack offers. When the bonus is small (20 percent to 40 percent), consumers often believe the price has not truly changed. Unfortunately, when the bonus is large, such as a two-for-the-price-of-one sale, consumers tend to believe that the price was first increased to compensate for the additional quantity. Even though increasing the size of a bonus, catches the consumer's attention, it may not convey the desired message.[31]

Bonus packs are costly because additional amounts of product sell for the same or a similar price. Also, they may incur new packaging and shipping costs. Cash flows may slow down, because customers buy larger quantities and therefore purchase the item less often.

## Using Bonus Packs Effectively

Bonus packs tend to be popular with manufacturers, retailers, and customers. A retailer can build a good relationship with a manufacturer that uses a bonus pack to increase brand switching and stockpiling. Retailers gain an advantage because the bonus pack is a "bargain" or "value" offered through the retail outlet. Customers like bonus packs because they get additional product at the same price. For ongoing products with high competition, the bonus pack approach is one way to maintain brand loyalty and reduce brand switching at a minimal cost.

A bonus pack offer for two packages of Lean Slices by Carl Buddig.
*Source:* Courtesy of Carl Buddig & Company.

## PRICE-OFFS

A price-off is a temporary reduction in the price of a product to the consumer. A price-off can be physically marked on the product, such as when a bottle of aspirin shows the regular retail price marked out and replaced by a special retail price (e.g., $4.99 marked out and replaced by $3.99). Producing a label with the price reduction premarked forces the retailer to sell the item at the reduced price. This ensures the price-off incentive will be passed on to the consumer. At other times, the price-off is not on the actual item, but on a POP display, sign, or shelf.

Price-offs are excellent at stimulating sales of an existing product. They can entice customers to try new products because the lower price reduces the financial risk of making the purchase. They can encourage customers to switch brands in brand parity situations or when no strong brand loyalty exists. In cases where consumers do have a brand preference, a price-off on a favorite brand encourages stockpiling of the product and possibly increased consumption of the item.[32] A consumer who purchases additional breakfast bars because of a price-off tends to consume more. Again, this will not be true for products such as deodorant or toothpaste. Stockpiling for those types of products just delays the next purchase. It does not increase consumption. Similar effects are seen in the business-to-business arena when price-offs are used.

The retailer can initiate a price-off promotion. Retailers usually offer price-off discounts to draw traffic into the store. The idea is for customers to purchase additional items other than those on sale. During the holidays and other times of the year, price-off sales are very common. Retailers advertise major price-off sales at Christmas, Thanksgiving, and Presidents' Day. Many use Presidents' Day sales to reduce inventories of winter clothes and unsold Christmas merchandise.

A special price-off offer by Papa John's.
**Source:** Courtesy of Papa John's International.

## Problems with Price-Off Promotions

Price-offs are easy to implement and can have a sudden impact on sales. They can also cause problems. Although a price-off offer may increase sales, it can have a negative impact on a company's profit margin. It normally takes at least a 20 percent increase in sales to offset each 5 percent price reduction.

Another danger is that price-off programs encourage consumers to become more price-sensitive. In the same way that customers respond to rebates, they can either wait for a price-off promotion or choose another brand that happens to be on sale. An estimated 25 percent of consumers base purchase decisions on price. Price-offs are often necessary because of competitive and trade pressures. Individual firms must be careful not to overrely on price-offs.[33] Remember, however, that too many price-off offers can also have a negative impact on a firm's image.

## Using Price-Off Offers Effectively

Price-off programs can be used to increase store traffic and generate sales. They work better with higher markup items and for goods or services that normally do not offer discounts. The goal should be to create new interest in the product to entice buyers to take a second look. Loyal customers may be attracted to a price-off discount and buy to stock up, but they should not be the primary targets for price-off programs. Instead, new users or customers who have drifted away to other products should be the target market.

Price-offs have proven to be successful consumer promotions for two reasons. First, the price-off has the appeal of a monetary savings to consumers. Second, the reward is immediate. Unlike rebates, refunds, contests, sweepstakes, and other promotional incentives, consumers do not have to wait for the reward. As always, price-off programs should be incorporated into the firm's overall IMC program.

## OTHER ISSUES IN PROMOTIONS PROGRAMS

The major forms of consumer sales promotions programs are coupons, premiums, contests, refunds, sampling, bonus packs, and price-off offers. Each has distinct advantages and problems. The marketing account executive's goal should be to help the company select a consumer sales promotion approach that matches its trade promotions efforts, advertisements, and personal selling tactics. The entire promotions mix can then be structured to mesh with a more integrated IMC plan.

At times companies combine two or more consumer promotions activities into a single campaign, called an *overlay*. For example, to attract Chinese consumers in Canada, Tropicana combined sampling with coupons. Free samples (50,000 cups of orange juice) were given out along with 30,000 coupons at a Chinese New Year's celebration in Vancouver. Asians who live in the United States and Canada are not typically large users of coupons; however, Tropicana Canada's research showed that the Chinese consider oranges to be harbingers of good luck. A few weeks after the promotion, 40 percent of the coupons were redeemed, and sales of Tropicana orange juice among the Chinese community in Canada increased considerably.[34]

Another common strategy is to develop a consumer promotion with another product or company such as in the ad featuring General Mills Betty Crocker brand and Tyson in this section. This is called a *tie-in. Intracompany tie-ins* are the promotion of two different products within one company using one consumer promotion. An alternative method is with another company, such as General Mills and Tyson, which is an intercompany tie-in. Fast-food restaurants often use tie-ins with movies and toys to creative attractive children's promotions. Whether a promotion is a stand-alone, overlay, or tie-in program, careful attention must be given to planning the event to maximize its effect.

## PLANNING FOR CONSUMER PROMOTIONS

In planning the consumer promotions component of the IMC, it is vital that the promotions support the brand image and the brand positioning strategy. To ensure this occurs, it is first necessary to bear in mind the target audience of the program. Then research must be conducted to identify the core values present in the target audience as well as opinions regarding the firm's products, especially as they relate to the competition. Once this information is gathered, the firm is ready to finalize the consumer promotions plan. In terms of promotions, consumers can be divided into three general categories:

▶ Promotion prone
▶ Brand-loyal
▶ Price-sensitive

**Promotion prone consumers** regularly respond to coupons, price-off plans, or premiums. They are not brand loyal and purchase items that are on-deal. A **brand-loyal consumer** purchases only one particular brand and does not substitute regardless of any deal being offered. Few consumers are completely promotion prone or brand loyal. Instead, buying is more like a continuum anchored at its ends by promotional proneness and brand loyalty. People tend toward one approach or the other, but sometimes lapse into the other approach. The tendency toward being promotion prone or brand loyal may depend on the product being purchased. A beer drinker may be extremely promotion prone; a wine drinker may be quite brand loyal. The same beer drinker may be extremely loyal to a pizza brand, and the same wine drinker may be quite promotion prone when it comes to buying potato chips.

For the **price-sensitive consumer**, price is the primary if not the only criterion used in making a purchase decision. Brand names are not important and these individuals will not pay more for a brand name. They take advantage of any type of promotion that reduces the price. It is important to identify the set of promotion prone or price-sensitive consumers who will be targeted by a consumer promotions program.

For brand-loyal consumers, sales promotions can be crafted to boost sales and reinforce the firm's image. For example, a small local restaurant has a monthly drawing for a free meal for two. To enter, patrons place a business card in a jar upon leaving. Each month the restaurant draws a name. The more often a person dines at the restaurant, the greater the chance of winning. A simple promotion such as this can boost sales for the restaurant by tying chances of winning with additional meals. The additional cost to the restaurant to run this promotion is minimal and can result in excellent goodwill from customers.

In planning promotions, it is important for manufacturers to understand retailers' incentives in using promotions. It does little

Southwest Airlines is promoting their swavacations.com Web site with tie-ins for hotels, car rentals, and other vacation activities.
*Source:* Courtesy of Southwest Airlines.

An intercompany tie-in by Betty Crocker with Tyson.
*Source:* Courtesy of Betty Crocker and Tyson.

She loves her home
(saved 20% on painting supplies)

fresh flowers
(saved $5 on a mixed bouquet)

family pictures
(saved 50% on enlargements)

and the blue envelope.

*There's something in it for you.*®

Discover great savings like these inside the envelope and online at www.valpak.com.
To advertise, call 800-355-9642, today.

A Valpak advertisement soliciting other businesses to offer consumer promotions within the Valpak mailer.
**Source:** Courtesy of Valpak.

good to create a promotion that is popular with consumers if retailers are not willing to work with the manufacturer to enhance the promotional offer. Retailers want promotions that will benefit them in some way. The primary reasons retailers give for supporting a manufacturer's consumer promotions program are to:[35]

▶ Increase store traffic

▶ Increase store sales

▶ Attract new customers

▶ Increase the basket size

In planning promotions programs, it is important to tie the promotions program with the theme of the IMC plan while keeping in mind the retailers where the promotions will be seen by the consumer. Specific goals associated with the product, the target market, and the retail outlets should be formulated. For instance, building brand image is more of a long-term goal; generating sales is more short range. Price-based offers normally are designed to: (1) attract new customers or (2) build sales. Other consumer promotions such as high-value premiums can be used to enhance a firm's image.

## BUSINESS-TO-BUSINESS PROGRAMS

Consumer promotions are also used in the business-to-business area. In fact, 18.7 percent of business-to-business marketing budgets are spent on promotions directed to business customers, who are not part of the distribution channel. Manufacturers are the most inclined to offer some type of promotion to business customers.[36]

Consumer promotions in the business-to-business arena are not monies or incentives offered to retailers, wholesalers, distributors, or agents who stock the manufacturer's products for resale. Those funds are trade promotions monies. Instead, manufacturers offering some type of special promotion to customers (other businesses) are involved in business-to-business promotions. For example, a manufacturer needing paper for copy machines may be enticed to buy from a paper company offering a promotional incentive. The paper itself is necessary for the company, but is not used in making products and is not resold.

*Coupons* often are used in the business-to-business sector. For example, an office supply company may fax or mail coupon offers to business customers. A pest control business may offer an introductory coupon to encourage businesses to sign up for its services. Microsoft offered a $99-off coupon on a 1-day training session about installing and supporting BackOffice SBS. The offer was designed for small- to medium-size businesses. The coupon was made available only to CPAs who were official members of the American Institute of Certified Public Accountants (AICPA).[37]

Though FSIs and print media work well for consumer promotions aimed at end users, direct mail, fax, or coupons distributed by sales staff work best for business markets. In business-to-business promotions, one key is to make sure the promotion reaches the right person. Few business buyers would see or use an FSI coupon. Instead, a coupon sent by mail or fax can be directed to the purchasing agent or someone with the authority to make the purchase decision.

*Premiums* also can be offered in business-to-business markets. They can be additional merchandise given to the firm for making a purchase. A company such as Quaker

State can offer a free case of motor oil for placing an order within a specified time period or for a specific size of order. John Deere used Christmas ornaments, toy tractors, and John Deere trading cards as premiums for business customers. These gifts should match the products being sold.

*Contests and sweepstakes* can be used to attract purchases in much the same way as they are used in consumer markets. Business buyers are just as interested in winning prizes as are retail customers. A central part of Office Depot's Small Business Month integrated marketing campaign was an Office Makeover Contest. The integrated campaign consisted of more than 350 weekly newspaper inserts, direct mailings, catalogs, newsletters, e-mails, radio promotions, television ads, and print ads. The goal of the campaign was to drive small-business owners and business technology buyers into Office Depot stores. To enter the Office Makeover Contest, someone from a small business with less than 20 employees had to send pictures into Office Depot along with an essay explaining why their business office was most in need of a makeover.[38]

*Sampling* is an excellent method to encourage a business to try a product. For example, an office supply store offers a company the use of a copier for a month in an effort to land a contract to supply all of the firm's copiers. A company can provide a process or raw material sample to a perspective business client. Such a sample has the advantage of giving the engineers an opportunity to analyze the materials to see if it meets company standards. The goal is to get the engineers to believe that the material is superior to the product the company currently uses. Sampling is an effective method of placing a company's products in the hands of the individuals who are the influencers in business purchase decisions.

*Bonus packs* also can be part of business-to-business marketing. Offering a prospective business a bonus pack may attract new users. The lure of additional merchandise at no extra cost appeals to cost-conscious business buyers.

Price is often a negotiated item in the business-to-business sector. Consequently, *price-off programs* are seldom used. Many business relationships are formalized by a contractual agreement, and the price is fixed by that contract. Price-off discounts can be offered by vendors seeking to obtain a new business contract by enticing the business customer to at least consider the firm making the offer. Also, a vendor can offer a price-off program to tempt customers to purchase additional merchandise. Price-offs can be used to preempt competitive deals. The latter situations occur when there is no formal contract between the firm and the vendor. Firms furnishing operating supplies normally operate without contracts and use price-offs as part of their marketing programs.

Business-to-business consumer promotions programs play vital roles in an IMC program. Marketing managers should integrate them with all other parts of the promotions mix, for both business buyers and other customers.

## INTERNATIONAL CONSUMER PROMOTIONS PROGRAMS

As was first discussed in Chapter 1, an international integrated marketing communications program requires an overall, global approach. At the same time, there must be flexibility to match the needs of each region or country, so that marketing activities, including consumer promotions, can be adapted to fit local conditions.

It is not possible to have a totally centralized, global consumer promotions program. Customs, laws, and views toward various types of consumer promotions differ throughout the world. Even in Europe, the laws governing consumer promotions are not consistent. In France and England, contests offering free prizes are legal; however, in Germany, The Netherlands, and Belgium, they are illegal. In Japan, the maximum value of a premium is either 10 percent of the selling price or 100 yen (80 cents). Thus, it would not make sense to use a premium in Japan. Although many marketers prefer to use the same sales promotional tactics around the world in order to gain economies of scale, it is not likely.[39]

Coupons are not as prevalent in the United Kingdom as they are in the United States. Culturally, coupon redemption is associated with being underprivileged in England. Some customers in the United Kingdom fear that using coupons will cause the cashier to

**TABLE 10.1**

Couponing in Selected Countries

| Media | Redemption Rate | | | | Distribution Method | | | |
|---|---|---|---|---|---|---|---|---|
| | England | Italy | Spain | United States | England | Italy | Spain | United States |
| Newspaper | 1.9% | – | 1.4% | 0.8% | 26% | – | 10.0% | 1.9% |
| Magazine | 2.8 | 1.4 | 1.4 | 0.3 | 13 | 5.7 | 14.7 | 4.2 |
| Door to door | 11.0 | 13.7 | 12.9 | – | 18 | 2.0 | 43.0 | – |
| In/on pack | 25.1 | 20.3 | 30.7 | 9.2 | 15 | 63.2 | 25.2 | 2.5 |
| In store | 27.7 | 32.3 | 28.2 | 6.8 | 19 | 22.1 | 5.5 | 1.9 |
| FSI | 12.0 | – | – | 1.4 | 1 | – | – | 85.4 |
| Mailing | – | 6.6 | – | 3.6 | – | 6.5 | – | 1.1 |
| Overall average | 6.8 | 14.3 | 16.0 | 2.0 | | | | |

**Sources:** "International Coupon Trends," *Direct Marketing* 56, no. 4 (August 1993), pp. 47–49; "FSI Coupon Redemption Rate for Frozen Foods," *Frozen Food Age* 47, no. 3 (October 1998), p. 70.

judge them to be poor and needy.[40] Still, coupon redemption rates are higher in Europe than they are in the United States. Table 10.1 compares redemption rates and distribution methods of the United States with three European countries: England, Italy, and Spain. As shown, the overall redemption rates are 14.3 percent in Italy and 16 percent in Spain as compared to only 2 percent in the United States. Coupons are legal in all European countries except Germany. At the same time, German laws allow on-pack price reductions and gifts inside of a package.[41]

In Japan, restrictions on print media carrying coupons were not lifted until 1990. Retailers and consumers are still reluctant to use coupons. In 1991, Japanese newspapers were allowed to carry freestanding inserts, but the average redemption rate still is only 1.2 percent. To encourage retailers to redeem coupons, Japanese supermarkets are offering checkout coupons. Checkout coupons issued for competing products have had some success.[42]

In order to manage the consumer promotions function within a global market successfully, a company should retain an experienced international sales promotion coordinator or manager. Some of the major responsibilities of this coordinator are:[43]

1. Promoting the transfer of successful consumer promotion ideas among the company's brands from one country to another
2. Proposing and soliciting ideas for consumer promotions within and across each region or country
3. Developing and presenting training on consumer promotions planning to each local region that is responsible for developing them
4. Gathering performance data on each sales promotion program and making the information available to each regional sales promotion manager
5. Developing methods for measuring the effectiveness and efficiency of the various consumer promotions
6. Coordinating relationships with all sales promotions agencies that are being used
7. Coordinating efforts among advertising agencies, media buying agencies, and any other agencies or firms that are working with sales promotions in a region or country
8. Making sure all consumer promotions fit into the firm's overall IMC program

Effective management of a global IMC program is one of the keys to long-term success. Using sales promotions tactics wisely is a key ingredient. A truly integrated marketing communications program pulls together all elements of the marketing mix so that the firm's voice is heard clearly in all areas in which it competes.

# SUMMARY

An IMC program highlights all four elements of the promotions mix. In the previous section of this textbook, advertising was carefully considered because it is often the main "voice" of the IMC message. At the same time, other parts of the mix including trade and consumer promotions play crucial roles in the success or failure of the overall marketing program.

This chapter reviews the techniques available to attract consumers to the company by using consumer sales promotions. These tactics include coupons, premiums, contests and sweepstakes, refunds, rebates, samples, bonus packs, and price-off deals. These items should be combined with specific promotional goals to have the right impact on customers.

Consumer promotions are often used to boost sales. They can be an excellent short-term method to increase sales or a firm's market share. They can also be an excellent means of introducing new products. Often a consumer promotion prompts consumers to at least try the product where selling it at the regular price will not. Coupons and contests have been successful tactics for attracting new customers. Consumer promotions can boost sales of a particular brand, and evidence suggests that they increase sales of the overall product category rather than just take sales away from competitors.

Sales promotions also can be used to increase the household inventory of the item being promoted. Consumers with more of a particular product in their house experience fewer home "stockouts" and often increase their usage of the product. In other words, having more potato chips on hand means people in the home might eat them at a faster rate.[44]

Unfortunately, many sales promotions still are not part of the integrated marketing communications plan. They start out being part of the IMC program and may be carefully designed to support the IMC plan and firm's desired brand image. As long as sales increase and the goals of the firm are being met, all is fine. If, however, sales slump and target goals are not met, marketers often turn to additional sales promotion tactics, seeking a quick remedy. Yet, as was discussed in Chapter 9, money spent on promotions and taken away from advertising often dilutes the brand's image. When the brand image is tarnished, consumers then base purchase decisions on criteria such as price or a promotional offer rather than brand name or perceived brand quality. Although increased use of sales promotions techniques often provides a short-term solution to slumping sales, their overuse can damage the brand's image in the long run.

The most crucial step in planning an integrated consumer promotions program is to match the firm's target market, specific marketing goals, and promotional tactics together. Goals range from quick boosts to sales, to increased brand awareness, to improved brand image, to establishing solid relationships between manufacturers and members of the marketing channel, specifically retailers. Consumer promotions programs also can expand the reach of the company into the business-to-business market. Again, carefully set goals combined with well-chosen tactics are the key.

Internationally, consumer promotions programs can be used when they are chosen based on the characteristics, attitudes, laws, regulations, and cultural nuances of a given geographic region. The primary objective of any promotions program must always be to enhance the message sent forth in other aspects of the IMC program in a manner that helps the company reach its long-term marketing objectives in a cost-effective and positive fashion.

# REVIEW QUESTIONS

1. What is a consumer sales promotion? How is it different from a trade promotion?

2. What is an FSI? What kind of sales promotion is distributed through FSIs?

3. Name and describe five types of coupons. Which is the most popular with manufacturers? Which has the highest redemption rate?

4. What are the various ways consumers request electronically delivered coupons?

5. What problems are associated with coupon programs?

6. How can companies most successfully utilize coupons?

7. What is a premium? What four types of premium programs can companies use?

8. What are the disadvantages of premium programs?

9. How can companies enhance the odds of success of a premium program?

10. What is the difference between a contest and a sweepstakes?

11. What problems are associated with contests and sweepstakes?

12. What tactics can be used to improve the success rates of contests and sweepstakes? What role might the Internet play in this process?

13. How is a refund different from a rebate?

14. What problems are associated with refunds and rebates?

15. What can be done to make rebate programs more successful?

16. Name and describe six types of sample programs that manufacturers can employ.

17. What disadvantages are there to sampling programs?

18. What can be done to enhance the odds of success of a sampling program?

19. What is a bonus pack? How is it different from samples?

20. What problems are associated with bonus pack programs?

21. What bonus pack plans are most effective?

22. What is a price-off sales promotion?

23. What are the disadvantages of price-off programs?

24. How can manufacturers most successfully employ price-off discounts? How can retailers most successfully use price-off discounts?

25. Describe sales promotion tactics in business-to-business settings.

26. What problems must be overcome when developing international sales promotions programs?

# KEY TERMS

**consumer promotions** (sometimes called *sales promotions*) Incentives designed for a firm's customers.

**freestanding inserts (FSIs)** Sheets of coupons distributed in newspapers, primarily on Sunday.

**instant redemption coupons** Coupons that customers can redeem immediately when making a purchase.

**bounce-back coupons** Coupons that customers cannot redeem instantly but instead must be used at a later purchase.

**scanner-delivered coupons** Coupons issued at the cash register, which are triggered by an item being scanned.

**Cross-ruffing coupons** The placement of a coupon for one product on another product.

**response offer coupons** Coupons are issued (or mailed) following requests by consumers.

**free-in-the-mail premiums** Gifts given to individuals for purchasing products; however, the customer must mail in a proof of purchase to the manufacturer to receive the gift.

**in- or on-package premiums** Small gifts, such as toys in cereal boxes, often disguised or packaged so the consumer must buy the product to find what the gift is.

**store or manufacturer premiums** Gifts given by either the retail store or the manufacturer when the customer purchases a product.

**self-liquidating premiums** Gifts that accompany purchases whereby consumers must pay an amount of money for them.

**promotion prone consumers** Individuals who are not brand loyal and regularly respond to promotions, such as coupons price-off plans, or premiums, only purchasing items that are on-deal.

**brand-loyal consumer** Someone who purchases only one particular brand and does not substitute regardless of any deal being offered.

**price-sensitive consumer** A consumer for whom price is the primary, if not the only, criterion used in making a purchase decision.

# CRITICAL THINKING EXERCISES

## Discussion Questions

1. According to Kim James, sales promotion manager for Eckerd Drug, "The teen and preteen segments are important because they (teens) are developing buying habits and loyalties during these ages and are our future loyal consumers." In addition to established brands such as Cover Girl and Maybelline, Eckerd Drug now stocks brands such as Bonne Bell, Jane, and Naturistics.[45] Which consumer promotions would be the best to attract teens and preteens to the cosmetics department of Eckerd Drug? What tie-ins or overlays would you recommend?

2. Many manufacturers believe the best method for differentiating company brands from competitors is advertising. It is true that consumer and trade promotions cannot replace advertising in brand development. At the same time, well-chosen promotional tactics can support brand differentiation. Discuss which consumer promotions a manufacturer should and should not use to develop a brand. Justify your answer.

3. Design a magazine advertisement with a detachable coupon or premium for one of the following products. Compare your offer with those of other students in your class. Discuss the differences between the offers.

   a. SunBright Tanning Salon

   b. Dixie Printing

   c. Hamburger Haven

   d. Blue Bell Ice Cream

4. The Rawlings Sports Equipment Company plans to increase sales of baseball gloves this season. The company intends to use a coupon program. Discuss the pros and cons of each method of distributing coupons for Rawlings listed in Figure 10.3. Which methods should be used? Why?

5. To maintain its strong brand image, Revlon's marketing team decides to use a premium for each of its lipstick products. What type of premium would you suggest for Revlon for each of the target markets listed here? Which premium would you use? Justify your answers.

   a. Caucasian females, ages 50+

   b. African-American females, ages 14 to 19

   c. Hispanic females, ages 25 to 40

   d. Professional females, ages 30 to 50

6. Meet in groups of four to six students. Ask each group member to identify the last contest and the last sweepstakes he or she entered. What was the enticement to enter? What was the extrinsic reward? What was the intrinsic reward?

7. Video games generate huge revenues for many companies. One manufacturer decided to use sampling as a method to reach the primary target market, males between ages 15 and 30. The sampling could have been distributed in one of two ways. First, the actual game could be loaded on a computer for targeted individuals. Second, potential customers could be sent an abbreviated version of the game. Which sampling method would be the best? Using Figure 10.5, discuss the pros and cons of each sampling method in terms of this new video game. Which type and method of sampling would you recommend? Why?

8. Consumers can be divided into three broad categories in terms of how they respond to consumer promotions: (1) promotion prone, (2) brand loyal, and (3) price sensitive. Identify two services or goods that would fit into each category for you personally. For example, you may be promotion prone when you buy soft drinks (your favorite brand is "What's on Sale") but be very brand loyal when you buy shoes (Nike, Reebok). Compare your completed list with those of other students. Discuss the differences you observe.

9. Interview three people who have lived in another country about the use of consumer promotions in those countries. Make a list of those promotions heavily used and those not used. Present your findings to the class.

10. As with the other consumer promotions, international expansion requires understanding the laws and customs of each country and culture. In Saudi Arabia and other Muslim countries, Clinique had to modify its sampling techniques. In the United States and Western cultures, Clinique provides cosmetics samples in retail outlets for customers to try. In the United States, females normally sell retail cosmetics; in Saudi Arabia, males do. At the same time, Muslim custom prohibits a male from touching a female. Female customers must either apply the cosmetics themselves or bring their husbands to the store with them.

Asking a female customer "What color are your eyes?" constitutes a grave offense in Saudi Arabia, because the eyes are believed to be the gateway to the soul. Asking her about skin tone does not make sense, because females keep their faces covered after they reach the age of 14. Sampling is very important for Clinique in Saudi Arabia.[46] How would you organize a sampling program in light of these cultural factors? What other consumer promotions could be used? If you have someone in your class from a Muslim country, ask your classmate to discuss the use of consumer promotions in his or her home country.

## INTEGRATED LEARNING EXERCISES

1. Coupons are one of the most popular forms of consumer promotions. Access three of the following Web sites. What are the advantages and disadvantages of each, to a consumer? How do the Web sites impact manufacturers? How do they impact retailers?

   a. Eversave (www.eversave.com)

   b. CoolSavings (www.coolsavings.com)

   c. SmartSource (www.smartsource.com)

   d. Valpak (www.valpak.com)

   e. Coupons (www.coupons.com)

   f. Coupon Country (www.couponcountry.com)

2. Sweepstakes and contests are excellent methods for building customer traffic to a retail outlet and for building interest in a brand. Certain firms can assist in the development of sweepstakes and contests. This is important due to a variety of legal restrictions imposed by different states. Access the following web sites. What types of services does each offer? How can the companies assist in developing a contest or sweepstakes? Which firm would you choose if you were responsible for developing a contest or a sweepstakes program?

   a. SweepstakesBuilder (www.sweepstakesbuilder.com)

   b. Promotions Activators Inc. (www.promotionactivators.com)

   c. Centra Marketing (www.centramarketing.com)

   d. Ventura Associates (www.sweepspros.com)

3. Many companies offer special consumer promotions on company Web sites. Examine the following company Web sites. What types of promotions are available? What are the objectives of the various consumer promotions? Do the promotions on the Web sites mesh with the company's advertising and consumer promotions at retail outlets?

   a. Taco Bell (www.tacobell.com)

   b. Hershey's (www.hersheys.com)

   c. Quaker Oats (www.quakeroats.com)

   d. Papa John's (www.papajohns.com)

4. One widely read journal featuring promotional marketing is called *PROMO*. Access the Web site at www.promomagazine.com. Examine the table of contents and access the various areas. After exploring the site, write a short report on what is available at the Web site and how it can be used to assist companies wanting to develop various promotions.

## STUDENT PROJECT

### IMC Plan Pro

Sometimes an ad will get customers to the Web site or retail store, but they still need a little push to help them make the actual purchase. Consumer promotions such as coupons, premiums, price deals, contests, and others are necessary to complement the total communications program. You can use the IMC Plan Pro disk and booklet available through Prentice Hall to help choose the best consumer promotions for your IMC campaign.

# CASE 1

## SUNNY SUCCESS

Jessica Corgiat faced a difficult challenge as she took control of the Sun Products, Inc., account. As a relatively new account executive, Jessica knew it was important to establish measurable results when conducting various marketing communication campaigns. Sun Products sells items primarily oriented toward beach-related activities, the most successful of which is the company's line of sunscreen products.

The tanning industry faces a unique set of challenges as a new generation of consumers emerges. First, more than ever consumers are aware of the dangerous long-term effects of tanning. These include more wrinkles along with vastly increased chances of developing skin cancer in later life. In Australia, where the ozone layer is the most depleted, exposure to the sun is even more hazardous. More importantly, however, is a potential shift in cultural values regarding appearance.

A few generations ago in Europe, completely white skin was a sign of affluence. Those who were forced to work outside developed tans. Those who lived as royalty or as the wealthy class could show their high social standing by simply keeping out of the sun.

As the new millennium commences, it is possible that a certain set of consumers will begin to believe that tanning is equal to foolishness—or, at least, that a suntan is no longer as "sexy" as it has been for many years. Beach bums and bunnies continue to run counter to this trend. The question remains, however, whether a national obsession with being browner continues in the general population.

One way to counter this problem is by developing new products designed to screen out the sun rather than enhance the sun's tanning properties. Lotions with higher SPF (sun protection factor) values generally sell at higher prices. Higher-quality sunscreens do not wash off in a pool or while swimming. Further, items containing herbal ingredients and new aromas are designed to entice new interest. Sun Products with aloe vera and vitamin E may help reduce the pain and heal a sunburn more quickly. Products that "tan" without exposure to the sun are being developed for those who want the beach look without doing time in the sand.

At the same time, to promote more "traditional" products to college students on spring break and others who still enjoy a deep, dark tan requires careful promotion. Advertisements often stress the "fun" aspects of being outdoors.

Hawaiian Tropics, one of the chief competitors in the tanning industry, has taken a unique approach to the promotion of its products. The company holds an annual contest in which the Tropics team of beach girls is chosen to represent the firm. Contestants are female, beautiful, and have good tans. Those who win the contest tour the country promoting Hawaiian Tropics products and appear on television programs.

At individual events held at beaches across the United States and in other locations, free samples of Hawaiian Tropics may be given out, along with coupons and other purchase incentives. Giveaways of beach towels and other beach equipment are used to heighten interest in the product at various stores.

Jessica is considering how to respond to this quickly changing marketplace. Besides product development, she needs to describe a "theme" the company can use, either oriented toward "safety" or "sexy" or "safety with sexy." She is considering the entire range of promotional possibilities, from coupons for new products, to premiums as giveaways for existing products, to contests, sampling, bonus packs (with various ranges of SPF values in the same pack), to refunds for higher-priced lotions. She knows the key is to maintain a message and theme for this company, which will help it stand out in the crowd of Coppertone, Bain de Soleil, and Hawaiian Tropics. She realizes that to succeed she needs Sun Products' POP displays placed prominently in as many places as possible, from drugstores to swimming specialty stores.

1. Which consumer sales promotions items will be least helpful to Jessica and Sun Products?

2. Which consumer sales promotions items will be most helpful to them?

3. Design an IMC program for Sun Products, Inc., focusing on advertising themes, trade promotions, and consumer sales promotions. Explain how it will differentiate the company from other suntan product companies.

## CASE 2

# BEN'S COMPLETE LAWN CARE SERVICE

Ben Folds had turned a part-time college job into a full-time business. As a student, he maintained a solid client list of people using his lawn-mowing service. Following graduation, he knew the type of business that best matched his skills and personality: a complete lawn care service.

Lawn care is typically divided into three main types of companies: (1) ones that mow lawns and provide trimming, (2) firms that provide fertilizers, insect control, and weed control, and (3) sod and seeding companies. Ben's idea was to provide every single aspect of lawn care, from the first spring feeding, to mowing, trimming, weeding, leaf removal, and even a winter fertilization program. He would also offer sod and seed services for lawns with bare spots or brand new lots.

Ben's vision was to service two main types of customers: (1) residential homeowners who didn't want to do lawn work, either because they didn't enjoy it or because they didn't have the time for it, and (2) businesses requiring lawn care, including any construction contractors and house builders who wanted to subcontract out the grass-growing part of finishing a home.

Companies that provide lawn-mowing services tend to compete with price and quality. Most offer free bids for a residential mowing job. The more successful firms were those who made a lawn look as good as possible, including trimming around hard-to-reach spots.

Fertilization, weed control, and insecticide providers normally offer a full price and then discount in a variety of ways. Prepayment discounts are given for those who pay in advance. Quantity discounts are given for customers who use the services more frequently, such as a price-per-treatment for eight summertime treatments that is substantially lower than the price-per-treatment for a customer who only schedules four. Referral discounts are given when a customer finds a new client for the company. Specials are run for extra services when needed. The major national companies will also offer larger price discounts to those customers who decide to terminate services. A follow-up call is made or a coupon is sent to the customer, proposing substantial price discounts to get the reluctant customer to reestablish a relationship with the company.

Sod and seeding companies charge what the market will bear. A customer with only a few options pays more for sod and seed than those where there are more competitors. Many sod companies primarily service wealthy homeowners and contractors.

Ben knew there were several challenges facing his company. First was brand-name awareness. He had to reach a wide audience of potential buyers. Second would be convincing homeowners to use his services rather than those of national chains. His biggest advantage was being a full-service lawn care facility offering more than just one or two types of services. Ben's

(continued)

Complete Lawn Care Service began operations in Minneapolis in the winter. The company had four employees. Ben knew that he had to build a strong client list quickly and keep those clients happy so that word-of-mouth referrals would help his firm grow in the future.

1. What kinds of promotions are used by Ben's competitors?

2. Design a consumer promotions campaign for Ben's Complete Lawn Care Service.

3. What types of advertisements should be used in conjunction with the company's consumer promotions campaign?

# ENDNOTES

1. Mariola Palazon-Vidal and Elena Delgado-Ballester, "Sales Promotions Effect on Consumer-Based Brand Equity," *International Journal of Market Research* 47, no. 2 (2005), pp. 179–205.

2. "Do Coupons Make Sense," *Incentive* 177, no. 5 (May 2003), p. 19; "DSN Charts: Coupons," *Discount Store News* 38, no. 9 (May 3, 1999), p. 4.

3. Noreen O'Leary, "Dealing with Coupons," *Adweek* 46, no. 8 (February 21, 2005), p. 29; Jack Neff and Joseph Gatti, "Coupon Distribution Up, But Web Dispersal Still Scanty," *Direct Marketing* (October 2003), p. 1.

4. "Coupons and Samples 'Key' to E-Marketing," *Marketing Week* 28, no. 4 (January 27, 2005), p. 17.

5. Noreen O'Leary, "Dealing with Coupons," *Adweek* 46, no. 8 (February 21, 2005), p. 29.

6. Corliss L. Green, "Media Exposure's Impact on Perceived Availability and Redemption of Coupons by Ethnic Consumers," *Journal of Advertising Research* 35, no. 2 (March–April 1995), pp. 56–64.

7. Elizabeth Gardener and Minakshi Trivedi, "A Communication Framework to Evaluate Sales Promotion Strategies," *Journal of Advertising Research* 38, no. 3 (May–June 1998), pp. 67–71.

8. Karen Holt, "Coupon Crimes," *PROMO* 17, no. 5 (April 2004), pp. 23–29.

9. Ibid.

10. Ibid.

11. John R. Hall, "Contractors Try Direct Mail Alternative," *Air Conditioning, Heating & Refrigeration News* 223, no. 16 (December 20, 2004), p. 12.

12. "Upward Bound," *PROMO* 17, no. 5 (April 2004), pp. AR3–5.

13. Srimalee Somluck, "Prime Nature Villa: Cars, Jewelry on Offer," *The Nation (Thailand)* (www.nationmultimedia.com, accessed September 29, 2004).

14. Theresa Howard and Terry Lefton, "KFC Units Buried in Beanbags," *Brandweek* 40, no. 4 (January 25, 1999), pp. 4–5.

15. Don Jagoda, "The Seven Habits of Highly Successful Promotions," *Incentive* 173, no. 8 (August 1999), pp. 104–105.

16. Kate Bertrand, "Premiums Prime the Market," *Advertising Age's Business Marketing* 83, no. 5 (May 1998), p. S6.

17. Alexander Haim, "Match Premiums to Marketing Strategies," *Marketing News* 34, no. 20 (October 25, 2000), p. 12.

18. Patricia Odell, "Flatlining," *PROMO* 17, no. 21 (2005), p. 21.

19. "Contest News," *Restaurant Hospitality* 89, no. 2 (February 2005), p. 110.

20. Lee Esposito, "Sweepstakes Can Run As Smoothly As Velvet," *Frozen Food Age* 53, no. 7 (February 2005), p. 46.

21. Patricia Odell, "Flatlining," *PROMO* 17, no. 21 (2005), p. 21.

22. Rodney J. Moore, "Games Without Frontiers," *Marketing Tools* (September 1997), pp. 38–42.

23. Sandra Block, "Rattled About Rebate Hassles? Regulators Starting to Step In," *USA Today* (March 22, 2005), p. 3b.

24. Doug Olenick, "Retailers Trust Rebates to Pull in PC Customers," *TWICE: This Week in Consumer Electronics* 17, no. 26 (November 11, 2002), p. 42; Jim Lucy, "Robust Rebates," *Electrical Wholesaling* 86, no. 3 (March 2005), p. 3.

25. Lindsay Chappell, "Rebates Eventually Become Ho-Hum, Researcher Says," *Automotive News* 79, no. 6133 (February 7, 2005), p. 36.

26. Aaron Ricadela, "Rebates Bundles Promote Margins," *Computer Retail Week* 167 (April 21, 1997), pp. 41–42.

27. Alison Wellner, "Try It—You'll Like It!" *American Demographics* 20, no. 8 (August 1998), pp. 42–43.

28. Pete Wetmore, "Inserts Branch Out Beyond Print Fliers," *Advertising Age* 75, no. 16 (April 19, 2004), p. N-6.

29. Betsy Spethman, "Introductory Offer," *PROMO* 16 (2004), p. 27; Jennifer Kulpa, "Bristol-Myers Squibb Breaks Ground with Direct Response Product Sampling Website," *Drug Store News* 19, no. 7 (April 7, 1997), p. 19.

30. Jennifer Hiscock, "The Two Faces of Sampling," *Event* (April 2004), pp. 25–26.

31. Beng Soo Ong and Foo Nin Ho, "Consumer Perceptions of Bonus Packs: An Exploratory Analysis," *Journal of Consumer Marketing* 14, no. 2–3 (1997), pp. 102–112.

32. David R. Bell, Ganesh Iyer, and V. Padmanaghan, "Price Competition Under Stockpiling and Flexible Consumption," *Journal of Marketing Research* 39, no. 3 (August 2002), pp. 292–304.

33. Mike Ogden, "Price-Based Promotions May Hurt Your Bottom Line," *Washington Business Journal* 18, no. 6 (June 18, 1999), p. 54.

34. Showwei Chu, "Welcome to Canada, Please Buy Something," *Canadian Business* 71, no. 9 (May 29, 1998), pp. 72–73.

35. Walter Heller, "Promotion Pullback," *Progressive Grocer* 81, no. 4 (March 1, 2002), p. 19.

36. Christine Bunish, "Expanded Use of Collateral Material, Catalogs Boost Sales Promotions," *Advertising Age's Business Marketing* 84, no. 5 (May 1999), p. S11.

37. "Microsoft, CPAs Unite on Market," *Computer Reseller News,* no. 766 (December 1, 1997), p. 66.

38. Beth Snyder Bulik, "Office Depot Targets Small-Business Sector," *B to B* 89, no. 12 (October 25, 2004).

39. Allyson L. Stewart-Allen, "Cross-Border Conflicts on European Sales Promotions." *Marketing News* 33, no. 9 (April 26, 1999), p. 10.

40. Allyson L. Stewart-Allen, "Below-the Line Promotions Are Below Expectations," *Marketing News* 29, no. 19 (September 11, 1995), p. 9.

41. "International Coupon Trends," *Direct Marketing* 56, no. 4 (August 1993), pp. 47–49.

42. "Targeting Supermarket Shoppers," *Target Marketing* 19, no. 10 (October 1996), p. 44; "International Coupon Trends."

43. Kamran Kashani and John A. Quelch, "Can Sales Promotion Go Global?" *Business Horizons* 33, no. 3 (May–June 1990), pp. 37–43.

44. Kusum L. Ailawadi and Scott A. Neslin, "The Effect of Promotion on Consumption: Buying More and Consuming It Faster," *Journal of Marketing Research* 35, no. 3 (August 1998), pp. 390–398.

45. Liz Parks, "Chains See Today's Wealthy Teens as Tomorrow's Loyal Customers," *Drug Store News* 21, no. 15 (September 27, 1999), p. 84.

46. Vanessa Friedman, "Planet Clinique," *Elle* 13, no. 9 (May 1998), pp. 218–219.

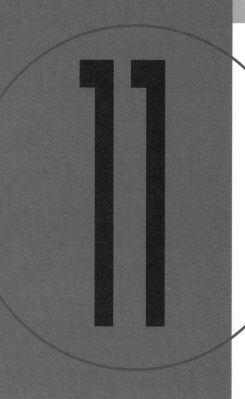

# Personal Selling, Database Marketing, and Customer Relationship Management

## Chapter Objectives

*Understand* the role personal selling plays in the success of both retail outlets and manufacturing operations.

*Examine* the role of personal selling in buying decision-making processes of retail customers, other businesses, and international customers.

*Learn* how to match a database program with an IMC program.

*Use* a database to improve direct marketing, permission marketing, and frequency programs.

*Apply* the database to customer relationship management (CRM).

## LEVI STRAUSS & CO.

### Using Quality Information to Build Relationships

Levi Strauss & Co. has been in business since 1853, when a Bavarian immigrant by the name of Levi Strauss opened his clothing operation. Since that time, the firm has continued to operate guided by four principles: empathy, originality, integrity, and courage. Of these, the goal of integrity has led to a strong emphasis on social responsibility. Empathy and originality fit with the design of innovative clothes and knowing customers. Courage is the desire to take bold steps that company leaders believe are right, such as the move toward providing health insurance to employees with same-sex domestic partners in a household.

The company's three primary brands are Levi's, Dockers, and Levi Strauss Signature. The Dockers brand is targeted at older customers. The brand helped maintain sales to consumers who need a little more room in a pair of pants. The Dockers line was created to build a bridge between jeans and a dress suit or dress slacks, featuring pants that could be worn to work. Dockers are sold at Sears, JCPenney, and slightly more upscale clothing stores that don't necessarily target just teenage buyers. The Levi Strauss Signature brand is emphasized in Europe and other foreign countries.

For many years, the original Levi brand was a dominant force in the U.S. teenage and young adult marketplace. In the past 2 decades, however, some brand erosion has taken place. Many younger buyers began to express the sentiment that Levi's were the jeans worn by their parents. Firms such as Old Navy, Calvin Klein, and other brands were gaining sales at Levi's expense, because Levi's were viewed by some as not being hip enough to suit the younger consumer.

The company was able to respond these challenges by developing a strong database marketing program. Levi's marketing team recognized that to be effective, a company's database must be much more than a collection of names and addresses. Levi's

reacted by emphasizing relationship marketing. This meant trying to understand what consumers want and then giving them a voice to be heard by company leaders. To meet these objectives, the firm identified five consumer groups for a pilot program by using a major survey.

Using the database that was already in place, the company's marketing team contacted various shoppers and enticed them to fill out questionnaires. In total, nearly 100,000 consumers completed questionnaires, which were distributed at stores, colleges, the Lilith Fair, and via customer service lines. Levi's carefully recorded the "doorway" each respondent used and tied it to other information, which eventually yielded the five major groups of shoppers. Each of the five groups expressed differing needs when it came to jeans.

Next, Levi's targeted the groups individually. Promotions were structured to match the nature of the customer profile that emerged. For example, one group, known as Valuable Shoppers, represented individuals who were willing to spend $60 or more on a pair of pants. These patrons were sent thank-you gifts following purchases of custom-fit jeans. The gift was a planter with flower bulbs and a card signed by the clerk who took the fitting. Responses from this group were impressive. A Valuable Shopper who received a gift purchased, on average, 2.3 more pairs of jeans within the next few weeks.

Online shoppers, who largely came from a group identified as Generation Y, or persons ages 15 to 25, were not sent this type of premium. Instead, this group was enticed with fashion messages. The goal was to match the promotional approach with the buyer group's characteristics.

By contacting consumers through questionnaires, gifts, promotions, and service lines, Levi's marketing team believed it was able to establish a more intimate form of communication with the company's clientele. This, in turn, helped the company combat declining interest in Levi's products.

Levi's success started with having a fairly well-established database to begin the program, enhancing the database, and listening to what consumers had to say. Any organization that is willing to utilize the talents and programs made available from an effective database management team may be in the position to reap similar rewards.[1]

**o v e r v i e w**

An integrated marketing communications program relies heavily on the employees who have the most interactions with customers. These individuals are the "face" of the company. Quality relationships between representatives of the company and buyers are crucial. Intimate, trusting, and friendly interactions create long-term bonds that help a firm build and maintain a strong market share. A positive purchasing experience often causes the buyer to provide word-of-mouth recommendations to as many as six other people, such as family members or friends. An unhappy customer is likely to tell as many as 11 other people about a bad experience.[2] This makes personal selling a key factor in the success or failure of a company's IMC program.

In this chapter, three closely related topics are studied. First, personal selling is described. Second, database marketing programs are examined. Third, customer relationship management (CRM) programs are explained. The goals of these activities are to make certain they match with other IMC efforts and to make sure they mix well with each other. When this occurs, the company's message reaches the customer through both personal (sales rep) and impersonal (media) channels.

## PERSONAL SELLING

Personal selling is sometimes called the "last 3 feet" of the marketing function, because 3 feet is the approximate distance between the salesperson and the customer on the retail sales floor as well as the distance across the desk from the sales rep to a prospective business customer. A bond or partnership between a sales representative and a client can be a valuable asset. Personal selling takes place in two major categories: (1) retail sales and (2) business-to-business selling.

## RETAIL SALES

Sales to consumers are facilitated by retail salespeople. Transactions occur on the sales floor, in checkout lines, on the telephone, and in other places. What ties these selling activities together is that the salesperson "is" the company as far as the customer is concerned. Retail selling and its connection to the overall IMC program are vitally important to marketing success. Retail selling occurs in three general categories:

1. Selling in retail outlets
2. Selling services
3. Telemarketing

### Selling in Retail Outlets

The most common form of retail selling is a **single transaction**. The salesperson assists the customer until the sale is finalized or the person decides to shop somewhere else. There is no relationship with the customer, other than the one purchase. Most retail stores feature single transaction sales, as do automobile dealerships and other bigger-ticket item stores.

A new type of retail selling that is rapidly replacing single transactions is the order-taker form. **Order-takers** are individuals who perform tasks as simple as filling an order at Burger King to more involved orders in hardware or lumber yards. Many retail order-takers also serve as the *cashier*. Large operations such as Lowe's, Target, and

Wal-Mart separate cashier work from order-taking; however, in a smaller setting such as a bookstore one person provides both functions.

## Selling Services

Selling of services can be divided into two categories. First, some services are sold by a sales representative, and that is the fundamental activity driving the relationship. Insurance sales are an example of this kind of selling. The insurance agent writes the contract. The insurance company is responsible for processing claims and most other aspects of the relationship with the customer. This type of selling is often a single transaction, but also can be a **repeat transaction** type of relationship, when customers routinely return to the same company and salesperson. Often this form of selling includes *problem solving* for customers making purchases.

The second type occurs when the person doing the selling also performs the service. Many individuals sell or perform services for retail customers. Lube and oil shops both sell oil and provide oil change services. Many people sell the services they render, including such personal services as hair care, massage therapy, and lawn mowing. These service providers require *repeat business* to succeed, making loyalty and trust crucial. These individuals must be skilled at providing the services and interact well with customers.

## Telemarketing

Another type of retail selling involves telemarketers. These employees use the telephone to make sales calls and presentations. **Inbound telemarketing** occurs when employees handle customer calls. They do not make initial contacts. These employees respond to telephone orders or inquiries and serve primarily as order-takers. Many toll-free numbers are designed to attract inbound calls.

**Outbound telemarketing** means sales representatives call prospective customers or clients. Typical consumer products sold in this manner include long-distance services, credit cards, service contracts for appliances previously purchased, and an endless variety of aluminum siding to college fund-raising campaigns. Many people consider such calls invasive and annoying

Many experts believed that telemarketing would die out after the National Do-Not-Call Registry was created. Instead, telemarketing continues. There has been some shift from outbound calling to inbound call center operations. Even after the Do-Not-Call legislation, however, telemarketing still sells more products than any other direct-response marketing method. In 2004, nearly 66 million consumers purchased at least one item through a telemarketer. Remember that the National Do-Not-Call Registry does not apply to current customers of a firm. Calls can still be made to ongoing customers or anyone who had a previous relationship with the company.[3]

Text messaging to cell phone users is the newest version of telemarketing. The advantage is the ability to reach on-the-go consumers anywhere, at least those who have given permission. Many companies using text messaging have experienced positive results. Snapple recently sent a text message to 18- to 24-year-old consumers alerting them to a contest in which numbers were placed on 225 million bottle caps of Snapple iced tea, pink lemonade, and other drinks. Winners received overseas trips and walk-on parts on TV shows. Some found the text message to be annoying; however, nearly one-third of the message's recipients soon purchased a Snapple drink. Twenty-four percent sent a message back requesting additional information. Fourteen percent forwarded the message to friends. Reebok, Time Warner in the United States, Coca-Cola, and British Airways in Europe, Asia, and the United Kingdom have used similar text messaging campaigns. Only 20 percent of the nation's 169 million cell phone users utilize text messaging. This means there is ample opportunity for growth.[4] Currently only those cell phone users who have given advertisers permission receive ad messages.

**FIGURE 11.1**
**Consumer Buying Process**

▶ Problem recognition
▶ Information search
▶ Evaluation of alternatives
▶ Purchase decision
▶ Postpurchase evaluation

## RETAIL SALES PRESENTATIONS

A retail sales presentation includes more than just closing a deal. Objectives include gathering information and developing future relationships. A well-managed IMC program stresses the importance of quality contacts between retail salespeople and customers. There are five steps in the consumer buying process, as shown in Figure 11.1.

From a *selling* perspective, the salesperson must effectively handle each stage. During problem recognition, the salesperson knows the customer is not completely aware of what he or she needs. In this stage the sales rep helps the customer clarify the need. A person buying a refrigerator considers the amount of freezer space, ice maker and cold water features, and colors before thinking about a brand.

The sales rep assists the information search by providing facts about models, designs, and options. This often occurs while favoring his or her company's brand. As the customer evaluates the alternatives, the salesperson may discuss the benefits of all brands and show how his or her company's option is superior. When the purchase decision is made, the rep stops selling the product and starts selling other related items, such as service contracts. It is important to make sure the customer believes the product was a great choice.

Unfortunately, many salespeople in single transaction settings use high-pressure tactics to make sales. They also fail to recognize the importance of the first three steps of the buying decision-making process. Doing so costs the company repeat business and causes shoppers to walk out before a purchase because they are confused and frustrated by not having sufficient information.

A retail sales presentation is primarily made to end users. Courtesy, attentiveness, and a pleasant demeanor are the main ingredients needed to become a successful retail salesperson. Marketing executives should emphasize that personal selling is a key element of an IMC approach. Salespeople execute the final phase of a successful IMC program—completing the transaction.

Understanding the consumer buying process is very important for sales staff at Green-Yates when selling large-ticket items such as refrigerators.

***Source:*** Used with permission of *The Joplin Globe,* Joplin, Missouri.

**GE PROFILE ARCTICA™**
**The Ultimate in Refrigeration**

• Express Chill™
  Chill Beverages in Minutes, Not Hours.
• Express Thaw™
  Defrost Food in Half the Time
• Quick Ice™
  Provides Ice Up to 40 Percent Faster Than Normal
  for Parties and Social Gatherings

All While Using Up To 40 Percent Less Energy!

FREE AREA DELIVERY!
FREE INSTALLATION!

**GREEN ⒼⒺ YATES**
35 YEARS OF SERVING THE JOPLIN AREA    1821 Main    623-5125    WE SERVICE WHAT WE SELL

### The Manufacturer's Dilemma in Retail Selling

From the manufacturer's perspective, one problem remains: More than half the time, a customer finalizes a purchase decision while *in the store.* The retail salesperson has a tremendous impact on that decision, yet the manufacturer has little or no influence over that retail employee. A retail salesperson who prefers Amana refrigerators steers customers toward those models, even when General Electric, Coldspot, and others are available.

To combat this problem, manufacturers rely on three strategies. First, the manufacturer can provide training to retail salespeople, emphasizing the manufacturer's products. Second, advertising may be used to gain the attention of both customers and retail salespeople. Third, contests and incentives may be used to emphasize the manufacturer's products. Many manufacturers also employ **missionary salespeople,** who seek to develop goodwill, stimulate demand, and provide training incentives to enhance the manufacturer in the retailer's mind. Missionary salespeople are also called *merchandisers* and *detailers.*

## Cross-Selling

**Cross-selling** involves the marketing of other items following the purchase of a good or service. Many banks also offer insurance, loans, and other financial services in addition to checking and savings accounts. Inbound telemarketing calls are a good time to cross-sell goods and services. Customers are not defensive because they have initiated the call. Resolving the problem or answering the question that prompted the call makes the customer feel better. The inbound telemarketer often has access to customer information as the call takes place.

Successful cross-selling involves collecting quality customer data, integrating information technology, utilizing specialized software and computerized decision models, hiring and training the right type of salespeople, and creating a selling culture within the company. Forum Credit Union in Indianapolis tripled company revenue in 4 years by using cross-selling techniques. The firm's success resulted from a 3-pronged approach that included:[5]

When consumers evaluate alternatives, salespeople have the opportunity to discuss the benefits of brands such as Keepsake.
*Source:* Courtesy of Keepsake.

- ⫸ An automated cross-selling software system
- ⫸ A customer relationship management program
- ⫸ A selling culture

A technology called *Total Account Processing System (TAPS)* provided employees of Forum Credit Union with information about a customer's creditworthiness and existing relationships with the credit union. The program was designed to suggest cross-selling programs for individual customers. The recommendations were immediate, and credit decisions were delivered within 60 seconds due to the quality of the TAPS software.

Forum Credit's management team also established a customer relationship management (CRM) program. CRM programs will be described in detail later in this chapter. The Forum Credit version helped salespeople make calls based on knowing when a customer has just finished paying off a loan.

The third component was creating a selling culture. Forum's Credit's management team made sure the company's employees understood that selling is just the beginning of a relationship with a customer. With the aid of technology, selling the various products offered by the Credit Union was easier because sales calls could be based on information about each individual customer's relationship with the credit union

## BUSINESS-TO-BUSINESS PERSONAL SELLING

Personal selling is the vital link between a vendor and a client. An effective presentation to a business customer builds sales and creates a positive long-term relationship with the vendor. The three primary forms of business-to-business selling are: (1) field sales, (2) in-house sales, and (3) technology-based programs.

**Field sales** occur when the salesperson visits the customer's place of business. Presentations are made to develop new customers or to encourage repeat business from ongoing customers. Field salespeople are classified as **order-getters** because they actively seek out new customers and sales.

The Good Housekeeping Seal takes the guesswork out of buying a faucet.

Every Peerless® kitchen and bath faucet comes with the Good Housekeeping Seal, and the Peerless pledge that the quality inside matches the quality outside. You have our word on it. And theirs.

**PEERLE∬**
The Do-It-For-Yourself Faucet.®

Good Housekeeping Promises

Although advertising can develop a strong brand name like Peerless, salespeople at a hardware store often influence which brands are finally purchased.
*Source:* Courtesy of Delta Faucet Company. Photograph by John Welzenbach.

*In-house sales* mean salespeople work from the company's office. They handle phone-in orders, faxes, and Internet accounts. Occasionally the rep makes the initial contact with the customer; however, normally these reps merely respond to or take orders from ongoing customers.

Technology-based programs include telemarketing and Internet sales. Telemarketing includes both inbound and outbound calls. Internet programs and Web sites help firms develop more sophisticated linkages with various customers.

## Buyer–Seller Relationships

Personal selling plays a major role in creating successful business-to-business marketing programs. Figure 11.2 displays various forms of buyer–seller relationships. The degree of interaction and length of the relationship vary dramatically depending on the form involved.

*Single transaction* sales are made in new-buy situations, where the buyer is making a purchase of an item for the first time. Depending on the complexity of the purchase, it may be one salesperson (such as a real estate agent helping a company buy or sell a building) or a team of marketing professionals. If the potential contract is long and involved, more individuals will be involved in the single transaction sale.

*Occasional transactions* are often modified rebuy situations in which a company has purchased the product before but is now considering both the old vendor and other competitors. Business buyers will consider new possibilities when technologies change or when product improvements are common. In those circumstances, the buyer examines several options before making a purchase.

*Repeat transactions* occur when buyers purchase on a regular basis. These types of purchases are often straight rebuys. Raw materials and component parts for machines are often repeat transactions in the business sector

*Contractual agreements* are used to guarantee that the price and delivery of the good or service will remain stable for the length of the contract. With a contractual relationship, the seller does not need to worry about competitors until the next contract period. It is important to create as much mutual trust as possible in these relationships.

*Trust relationships* move beyond contracts. The two parties have interacted and worked together so well that both parties believe they benefit from the relationship, and each party trusts the other.

An *electronic data interchange (EDI) relationship* expands the levels of trust to include the sharing of data. EDI relationships occur when one company provides full access to another in order to manage orders, purchases, shipping information,

Strategic Partnerships
EDI Relationships
Trust Relationships
Contractual Agreements
Repeat Transactions
Occasional Transactions
Single Transactions

**FIGURE 11.2**
**Types of Selling Relationships**

production data, and other relevant materials. EDI relationships are much more exclusive than other forms and have become common between various businesses and suppliers.

A *strategic partnership* is the most intimate buyer–seller relationship. The goal is to collaborate on plans to benefit both parties and their customers. The seller looks for ways to modify or engineer products to improve the other company's position in the marketplace.

Each of these forms represents a different selling perspective. The potential value of each customer is evaluated as the firm develops relationships. Those with low potential do not evolve into more trusting situations; those with the greatest potential evolve to the higher order relationships.

The movement from single transactions to the strategic partnership begins with the customer becoming aware of a vendor's capabilities. Initial trial purchases are made by the customer at the transaction level with no commitment from either party. If the experience is positive for both sides, then the relationship is expanded through growing commitments made by the parties. This may or may not involve an actual contract. Continued growth in the relationship moves it to a trust relationship, which may involve EDI interchanges between the two parties depending on the nature of the product being sold. Moving to the highest order of relationships occurs with the sharing of people, resources, data, and mission to accomplish a unified goal that benefits both parties.[6]

An advertisement by Ceco Building Systems encouraging business customers to contact them to discuss their needs.
*Source:* Courtesy of Robinson & Associates, Tupelo.

## MANAGING THE BUSINESS-TO-BUSINESS SELLING PROCESS

Chapter 3 described the steps involved in business buying behavior as well as the individuals involved (members of the buying center). Understanding the process and reaching these individuals is best managed through the personal selling process displayed in Figure 11.3. No matter which type of salesperson is involved (field sales, in-house, or telemarketing), the steps involved are quite similar.

### Identifying Prospects

Prospects are potential customers. The idea is to quickly narrow prospects down to the most viable candidates. First, however, the pool must be created. Figure 11.4 lists some of the most common places salespeople find prospects. Customer referrals are one of the best sources for leads, because the buyer already has some level of satisfaction with the seller. Databases, as described in the next section, help fine-tune lists of prospects for

▶ **Identifying prospects**
▶ **Qualifying prospects**
▶ **Knowledge acquisition**
▶ **Sales presentation**
▶ **Follow-up**

**FIGURE 11.3**
**Personal Selling Process**

"Northeast Louisiana's only health club exclusively for ages 5-17"

2718 N. 7th St.
West Monroe, LA 71291
388-1365 voice
????????? Fax

**Chris Thurmon**
**Certified Personal Fitness Instructor**

chris@juniorfitnessacademy.com

An important component of a sales presentation is an attractive business card.
*Source:* Courtesy of Sartor Associates, Inc.

In an effort to increase sales, American Express offers products such as Gift Cheques as incentives.
*Source:* Courtesy of American Express Incentive Services.

## Sales Presentations

There are four main types of sales presentations: (1) stimulus-response, (2) need-satisfaction, (3) problem-solution, and (4) mission-sharing. Each may be used effectively in the proper context.[11]

A **stimulus-response sales approach** uses specific statements (stimuli) to solicit specific responses from customers, similar to what is called a "canned" sales pitch. Often the salesperson memorizes the stimulus statement (the pitch). Telemarketers, retail salesclerks, and new field sales reps often use this method.

The goal of the **need-satisfaction sales approach** is to discover a customer's needs and then provide solutions that satisfy those needs. The salesperson must be skillful at asking the right questions. Quality relationships with customers make it easier to discover their needs.

The **problem-solution sales approach** requires employees of the selling organization to analyze the buyer's operations. A team including engineers, salespeople, and other experts is often utilized to investigate a potential customer's operations and its problems, and to offer feasible solutions. This approach matches well with complex new-buy situations.

In a **mission-sharing sales approach**, two organizations develop a common mission. They then share resources to accomplish that mission. This partnership resembles a joint venture as much as a selling relationship.

The primary determinant of the sales approach to be used is the form of buyer–seller relationship that is present. The stimulus-response approach is used in the lower order relationships, such as single and occasional transactions. The need-satisfaction approach matches mid-level relationships involving repeat transactions and contractual agreements. The problem-solution approach is useful for higher order relationships including repeat transactions, contractual agreements, trust relationships, and EDI relationships. The mission-sharing approach is typically found in strategic partnerships. It can also be used with EDI relationships and trust relationships on rare occasions.

Additional factors that have an impact on the selling approach to be used include the nature of the product being sold, the buyer's personality, and the buying situation. Smaller purchases may result in a stimulus-response or a need-satisfaction sales approach. Major purchases are more likely to require a higher order sales approach, such as the problem-solution approach.

In terms of the buyer's personality, a strategic value buyer responds best to the mission-sharing approach. An extrinsic buyer responds to either the needs-satisfaction or problem-solution sales approaches. For the intrinsic buyer, normally using the stimulus-response yields the best results.

The purchase situation is the final factor in the choice of a sales approach. In new-buy situations, the salesperson can improve the odds of making a sale by helping the customer establish product specifications. This allows the rep to display concern and expertise. It is also possible to structure specifications to promote the rep's company. To do this, a higher level sales approach, such as the problem-solution approach, would typically be used.

## Follow-Up

The follow-up is the final crucial element of a sales presentation. Keeping a customer happy after the purchase will result in repeat business and brand loyalty. It is much more cost-effective to retain customers than to continually find new ones. Unfortunately, following-up is often neglected by the sales staff. The salesperson does not want to spend time on the activity, because commissions come from new sales, not following up on old ones.

The best method to create a favorable environment so that follow-up calls are made by the sales force is proper education. Salespeople should be taught that brand loyalty is the quickest path to repeat sales. Next, salespeople must be motivated. Retaining part of a commission until a follow-up call has been made is one approach. It is also possible to simply pay for or grant other credits for follow-up calls. Some companies are able to have experienced reps show new employees the value of follow-up calls, both because they lead to monetary rewards in terms of commissions and because they reduce the stress of continually trying to find new customers.

Managing the business-to-business selling process is a crucial part of an IMC program. The sales manager and key sales reps should be included in the IMC planning process. The inputs and advice provided by these individuals are valuable assets in the overall marketing program.

## NEW TRENDS IN BUSINESS-TO-BUSINESS PERSONAL SELLING

Several new marketing trends affect personal selling. Product parity has become more common. When consumers see fewer distinguishable differences between brands, it is important to understand how to create a strong brand and brand loyalty. Other new selling trends are summarized in Figure 11.7.

In addition to a sales call, potential customers of Polycom's Videoconferencing System can contact Polycom through the Internet or by calling 1-877-POLYCOM.
*Source:* Courtesy of Polycom.

## Decline in the Number of Salespeople

Some sources estimate that the number of sales positions present in the United States will decline by as much as 50 percent in the next decade.[12] Technology makes it possible to employ fewer salespeople. As a result, sales managers must adapt by making sure the reps that remain have both the technical and selling skills necessary to meet consumer needs.

## Expansion of Sales Channels

Many buyers now purchase products or make orders without ever contacting a salesperson. The Internet and EDI technology make it possible to place orders electronically. Special selling enticements are delivered in new ways, such as through faxes and e-mails. Customers contact companies by phone, in person, and through e-mail. People at these contact points should stress the firm's IMC message and theme. It is also important to track customer contacts to make sure customer needs are being met. Accounts should be regularly reviewed to make sure no client is left without service and follow-up attention.[13]

> ▸ Decline in the number of salespeople
> ▸ Expansion of selling channels
> ▸ Long-term relationships and strategic partnerships
> ▸ Team selling

**FIGURE 11.7**
**Trends in Personal Selling**

## Long-Term Relationships and Strategic Partnerships

Buyers in many companies are trying to reduce the number of vendors they deal with, and they seek stronger relationships with those who remain. Fewer vendors means larger order sizes with greater quantity discounts, and the potential exists to establish a better flow of materials from the seller to the buyer. When a company deals with a single vendor, the vendor must make certain the buyer receives all purchases in a timely fashion. A manufacturer missing one component part due to a late delivery must stop production. Therefore, logistics management becomes a crucial element of a strategic partnership or any other long-term, more exclusive relationship.[14]

## Team Selling

The movement toward using fewer vendors and stronger commitments to those vendors has led to more team-based rather than individual selling. These teams include engineers as well as salespeople in order to provide better service to the buyer. Salespeople and engineers are trained to work together to become better problem-solvers and consultants.

Some teams are not made up of different types of individuals. HomeBanc is a mortgage lender that developed a team-based selling approach consisting of groups of two to five salespeople. Commissions were paid to team members based on experience and on each member's contribution to the team. In the new system one salesperson who had generated $40 million in sales the previous year sold $103 million as part of a team. Customer satisfaction also rose, leading to many word-of-mouth endorsements. HomeBanc paid 15 to 25 percent more in commissions after the switch to a team approach.[15]

### ETHICAL ISSUES

## Deceptive Sales Practices

For many consumers, the statement "salespeople cannot be trusted" applies to more than just car salespeople. From a business-to-business perspective, many buyers believe that salespeople will say or promise anything and everything to close a deal. Often this creates an adversarial situation where cooperation should exist. There are good reasons to avoid deceptive practices, such as:

1. Repeat business is important to the salesperson and the company.
2. Word-of-mouth is a key part of creating new clients and customers.
3. Complaints may be filed with the Better Business Bureau.

Unfortunately, there are also times when a salesperson is less concerned about being deceptive. These include:

1. The selling situation is a one-time sale.
2. The salesperson and/or company believe there is an unending supply of new customers available.
3. The salesperson is about to leave the job or company.

Many laws have been enacted because of these concerns. In real estate transactions, new "disclosure" forms must be completed indicating that the seller is willing to reveal known problems associated with a house or property before making the sale. The seller is financially responsible when known defects are not disclosed. Consider other industries and sales situations. Are "disclosures" possible in places other than housing sales? Which ones?

# PERSONAL SELLING IN INTERNATIONAL MARKETS

Personal selling in international markets is challenging. A series of problems must be overcome in order to succeed. These include language problems as well as regional differences in cultures, customs, and mores. Often suspicion, doubt, and mistrust are present. It takes time to build long-term, trusting relationships in many international settings.

There is always a choice to be made when setting up an international personal selling system. The firm can hire and manage local members of the community to make sales calls, or company leaders can elect to send their own sales force overseas. The salesperson must understand the vendor company while at the same time taking advantage of any expertise in working with the local culture.

International competition has forced many companies to examine selling functions closely. Cold calls are difficult to justify because of the high cost. Marketing teams are willing to spend more time and money qualifying prospects in order to increase success rates of the sales force. Freelancers, specialists, and other firms are available to provide assistance to companies seeking prospects in new regions.

The secret to managing personal selling in international settings is to carefully plan out the approach, account for the culture, and follow up when difficulties arise. As the world becomes smaller, more and more experts are available to help deal with the various nuances present in individual countries.[16]

# DATABASE MARKETING

Database development and database marketing programs are often used to supplement personal selling activities. Developing an IMC database is not the same thing as database marketing. **Database development** is creating a database to support the overall company, IMC program, and total marketing effort. The steps involved in developing a database are described in Figure 11.8.

## Determining Objectives

The objectives and role of the database in the marketing and communication programs determine much of what will take place as the data are generated. The typical questions posed concerning data collection include:

- What kinds of data are currently available?
- When (or how often) will information be collected?
- What additional data are needed?
- Where will the data be located or stored?
- Why do we need certain data and not other types?
- How will the data be used and who will use it?

Answers to these questions allow the marketing and information systems departments to design the database. It is important to make sure the information helps the

- Determine objectives.
- Collect data.
- Build the data warehouse.
- Mine data for information.
- Develop marketing programs.
- Evaluate marketing programs and data warehouses.

**FIGURE 11.8**
Steps in Developing a Database

company maintain a successful IMC program. Typical objectives for an IMC database include:

▶ Provide useful information about a firm's customers.

▶ Create information about why customers purchase the products they do.

▶ Share information about customers with creatives as they prepare advertisements and promotional materials.

▶ Reveal contact points to be used in direct-marketing programs.

▶ Yield information about members of various buying centers in business-to-business operations.

▶ Track changes in purchasing behaviors and purchasing criteria used by customers.

These objectives may change or be modified as time passes. The essential information, however, remains relatively consistent.

## Collecting Data

After the objectives of the IMC database have been determined, the firm is ready to seek out potential sources of data. Most firms use both internal and external sources. Customers are an internal source, as well as is survey data collected from customers. External sources include commercial database services, channel members, and governmental data sources.

*Internal customer data* can be a rich source of information. Modern information technology makes it possible to collect more than just names and addresses. Through scanning technology, the purchasing behaviors of buyers can be examined. This information helps the marketing team identify and profile the company's best customers, cross-sell goods and services to key customers, and create profiles of consumers who might be enticed to become new company customers. Internal customer data should answer the questions posed in Figure 11.9. If they do not, the firm's marketing team should look for ways to expand the database and data collection techniques.

Internal customer data may not be sufficient to meet all the needs of an IMC program. *External data* are also required. Psychographic, lifestyle, and attitudinal information can be valuable external data that are used to supplement what was collected from regular customers. The sources of secondary data include *commercial database services.* These services offer demographic information, such as data regarding income, age, race, marital status, and household type for various groups. Profiles such as *neighborhood lifestyle clusters* are offered by commercial database services.

Commercial databases are also available in the business-to-business sector. Chain Store Guide of Tampa, Florida, recently introduced a new state-of-the-art online searchable database for the retail and food service industries. Manufacturers, retailers,

---

▶ Where are the customers located?

▶ What have they purchased?

▶ How often have they purchased?

▶ How did they initially make contact?

▶ How do they order or purchase (in person, Web, mail, phone, etc.)?

▶ What is known about their families, occupations, payment histories, interests, attitudes, and so forth?

▶ In business-to-business situations, who are the influencers, users, deciders, and purchasers?

▶ In business-to-business, is it a corporate office or a branch office?

**FIGURE 11.9**
**Internal Data Information**

distributors, and service providers can utilize the database to generate prospect lists. The information in the database is updated weekly. It now contains information about 200,000 retailers, food service operators, distributors, and wholesalers in the United States and Canada.[17]

Another source is *survey data* collected from customers. To prevent bias in the surveys, it is often helpful to hire an external marketing research firm to conduct the interviews. A major advantage to hiring an external firm is that the company can supplement current customer data with non-customer data. Then, the two groups can be compared.

Information obtained from *channel members* is helpful because channel members are often customers. Wholesalers and retailers are the manufacturer's primary customers and should be able to provide useful information about end users.

Finally, there are times in which the organization can collect information from *governmental data sources.* The government makes economic information available. Also, the Bureau of Vital Statistics and the Census Bureau offer information about various individuals.

Simply collecting data does not place them into useful form. The next step is to construct a system that makes the information helpful to the marketing team and others involved in the company's operations.

Dialog is an online database service that can be used by companies in the development of a database.
*Source:* Courtesy of Dialog.

## Building a Data Warehouse

Constructing a useful data warehouse requires an understanding of all the various ways members of the organization might use data. Some of the more common uses are:

▶ Targeting customers for a direct-marketing program

▶ Developing a system so that field salespeople have access to important customer information while making sales calls

▶ Making it possible for internal salespeople to be able to access the database when a customer calls to place an order

▶ Giving the service department and customer relations department access to customer data as they deal with inquiries and complaints

In building a data warehouse, internal information is often combined with external data. One common method of enhancing internal information is through **geocoding,** which is the process of adding geographic codes to each customer record so the addresses of customers can be plotted on a map. Geocoding is especially helpful when decisions are made about placements of retail outlets or when direct marketing to a specific geographic area. It is also useful when combining demographic information with lifestyle data. This helps the marketing team select media where ads will be most likely noticed (e.g., newspapers, radio stations, television programs).

One version of geocoding software is named *CACI Coder/Plus.* The software identifies a cluster in which an address belongs. A group such as Enterprising Young Singles in the CACI system would contain certain characteristics, such as enjoying dining, spending money on videos and personal computers, and reading certain magazines. A retailer could then target this group with mailings and special offers.[18]

A data warehouses can provide company leaders with mountains of information that can be used for a variety of purposes. Data that are properly organized and easily accessible makes it possible to conduct quality data mining programs.

## Data Mining

**Data mining** normally involves one of two approaches: (1) building profiles of customer groups, or (2) preparing models that predict future purchase behaviors based on past purchases. Data mining can be used to develop a profile of the company's best customers. The profile, in turn, helps identify prospective new customers. The profile can be used to examine "good" customers to see if they are candidates for sales calls that would move them from "good" to a higher value. Companies offering different types of goods and services will develop multiple profiles. These profiles are used to target sales calls and to look for situations in which cross-selling is possible.

The marketing team at First Horizon National used data mining to expand the company's wealth management business by studying consumer groups. Data about existing customers from the mortgage side of the firm's business made it possible to locate the best prospects for the firm's investment services. The data mining program combined with cross-selling resulted in an increase in company revenues from $26.3 million to $33.8 million in 1 year.[19]

American Eagle used data mining to study how consumers responded to price markdowns. The information helped the marketing team determine when to cut prices and by how much in order to optimize sales. Markdown programs were geared to individual stores, because consumers responded differently in each outlet.

Goody's data mining program analyzed baskets of merchandise purchased by individual shoppers. The goal was to determine the types of items customers purchase together.[20] The information helped the marketing team develop advertising and consumer promotions programs, point-of-purchase displays, and store layouts.

The second approach to data mining is to develop models that predict future sales based on past purchasing activities. Staples, Inc., used a modeling program to examine the buying habits of the company's catalog customers. The program identified the names of frequent buyers. Customized mailings were sent to those customers.

The method used to mine data is determined by specific informational needs. A direct-mail program to current customers is different from one designed to attract new customers. Profiles and models assist in designing the database best suited for each purpose or program.

## Developing Marketing Programs

Once the data have been mined for information, individual marketing programs can be designed. The data provide clues about the best approach for each customer group. A quality database helps the marketing team decide on types of sales promotions to be used, advertising media to be selected, and the type of information that will spark the interest of a particular group of customers.

Marketing programs may also enhance customer loyalty. For example, if a hotel's check-in person knows in advance that a business traveler prefers a nonsmoking room, a queen-size bed, and reads *USA Today,* these items could be ready when the person arrives. Training hotel clerks and other employees to use the database helps them to provide better service, thereby building loyalty from regular customers.

In the modern marketplace, account executives are increasingly interested in making sure someone from the client's database department is part of any project team. By supplying creatives

This advertisement for men's clothes was placed in several women's magazines after analysis of the data indicated that many women are the ones who are actually choosing or purchasing the men's clothes.
*Source:* Courtesy of Haggar.

with information such as psychographics, attitudes, purchase behaviors, lifestyles, and trends, the advertising agency is able to prepare messages with the best appeal to the most valuable customers.

Other marketing programs can result from database analysis. Internet programs, trade promotions, consumer promotions, and other marketing tactics can be facilitated by carefully using the database.

## Evaluating Marketing Programs and the Data Warehouse

A high-quality data warehouse contains information about as many customers as possible. Each transaction is recorded. This allows for the analysis of various purchasing trends among customer groups and even of individual customers. Continually collecting information makes it possible to evaluate the overall IMC program. Questions to be answered can be as general or as specific as the ones that follow.

▶ Do our customers know our overall theme and image?

▶ Have we moved toward greater brand equity in the past year?

▶ Which items are our customers most inclined to buy? Which are not selling well? Do we know why?

▶ Is our customer base changing? Is this because we have changed, or is it because a new group is better suited to our products?

▶ What should be done to improve our position?

This evaluation is necessary to determine which programs work and which do not. Then, the marketing program can be modified to better meet customer needs. One application of this database is to market directly to consumers or businesses that purchase the product.

## DIRECT MARKETING

One program that is closely tied to database marketing is direct marketing. **Direct marketing** is vending products to customers without the use of other channel members. According to the Direct Marketing Association, about 60 percent of a typical direct-marketing

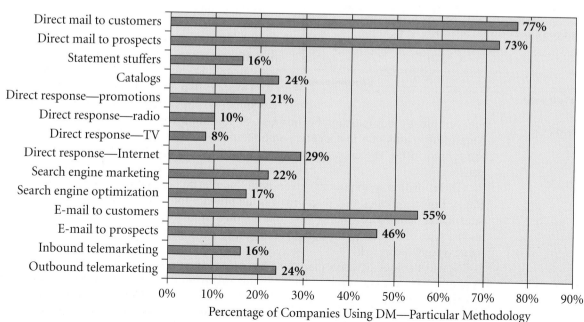

**FIGURE 11.10**
**Methods of Direct Marketing**

Percentage of Companies Using DM—Particular Methodology

*Source:* Richard H. Levey, "Prospects Look Good," *Direct* 16 (December 1, 2004), pp. 1–5.

Congratulations! You've been chosen as one of a few select homeowners to receive **this special coupon valued at $250!** As you've heard on television, radio, and in the newspaper, Diamond Security and Communications, northeast Louisiana's fastest growing security company, is offering their most popular home security system for **only $99.95 installed!** Well, if you act now, not only will you get this incredible home security system by First Alert for an amazing price, you'll also get **two 3-button remote controls absolutely free!**

That's right! **Free!** But you must act now. This offer by Diamond Security and Communications is available only to homeowners and business owners who agree to a 48 month monitoring contract with Diamond (only $29.95/month) before January 15, 2004! That's less than a month away, so call now! And don't forget to present the coupon below for **two 3-button remotes**, absolutely **FREE!**

By the way, if you already have a security system, **you can still save with a Diamond Security monitoring contract.** Switch to Diamond before January 15, 2004, and we'll give you the **first three months FREE** with a 24 month contract (at only $18/month). Use that money to pay off Christmas or other recurring bills!

Don't let this valuable offer get away! Call us at 322-0880, or 1-866-790-0880 and SAVE! We're looking forward to meeting you and helping make your home even more valuable and secure.

Sincerely,

Paul Fontenot          Thomas Eddleman

**P.S.**
**Don't miss this chance to increase the value of your home, while bringing you and your loved ones peace of mind! This offer expires January 15, 2004! Call now 322-0880, or 1-866-790-0880!**

A direct-mail piece sent out by Diamond Security Communications.
*Source:* Courtesy of Sartor Associates, Inc.

budget is used for prospecting for new customers; the other 40 percent is used to retain current customers.[21]

Figure 11.10 identifies the most typical forms of direct marketing and percentages of companies using them. Many companies use multiple forms of direct marketing to increase response rates and sales. In every type of program, a toll-free number and the company's Web site address are frequently displayed so that consumers know how to contact the company for additional information and also to place orders.[22]

Dell Computers has built a strong brand name and reputation through direct marketing. Dell's primary direct-marketing tool is its catalog. Several versions of the catalog are mailed each month to current customers and small and medium-size businesses. The catalog program is supplemented by television advertising focused either on the Dell brand or on direct-response offers. Dell's marketing team recently discovered that the company's television spots had a much greater impact on sales than was anticipated. Television generated the largest number of responses, as measured by inbound calls and hits on the company's Web site after seeing an advertisement. Dell also places ads in freestanding inserts (FSIs) in newspapers and on the radio. Both have also proven to be more successful than anticipated in driving traffic to Dell's Web site.[23]

## Mail

The most common form of direct marketing is still through the mail. Direct mail is sent to both consumers and business-to-business customers. A company's database can help limit the total number of pieces sent out by identifying the best possible prospects, thereby reducing the costs of mass mailings.

Direct mail can be easily targeted to various consumer groups. Also, the impact is easily measurable by comparing the number of mailings to the number of responses. Marketing teams can test every component of a direct-mail campaign, including the type of offer, the copy in the ad, graphics used, color, and the size of the mail packet.

Direct mail is an important driver of the Internet and online sales. A recent study by Pitney Bowes revealed that direct mail is the primary tool for promoting company Web sites. Direct mail was used to advertise a firm's Web site by 70 percent of firms with annual sales of at least $1 million. In addition, 43 percent of Internet sales were driven by some type of direct mail.[24]

The technology of direct marketing has greatly improved. It is now possible to create mailings that are customized to the individual recipient through **digital direct-to-press**, which is a software program that instructs the computer to send a tailor-made message. Digital direct-to-press is popular in the business-to-business sector because the pitch can

# COMMUNICATION ACTION

## Cysive Nails Down New Accounts

Cysive is a company that develops e-business systems. Cysive's e-systems are designed by engineers with inputs from the company's clients. A few years ago, the company's leaders created an innovative and highly successful direct-mail marketing program.

While looking for a way to market Cysive, John Saaty, the company's vice president of marketing, compared creating an e-system to constructing a building. A firm needing a state-of-the-art facility would hire a professional contractor to do the work. The same should be true for building an e-system. It should be constructed by expert engineers. According to Saaty, "Seventy percent of all e-commerce projects fail because of lack of expertise of those constructing the Web site."

Using the construction analogy, advertisements for Cysive featured a hammer hitting an *e-nail,* which was a message in the shape of a nail. The slogan "E-business systems built like nobody's e-business" was supported by ad copy highlighting how the system would be built by senior engineers and would be scalable, expandable, and secure. The advertisements ran in *The Wall Street Journal, BusinessWeek,* and *Fortune.* The two main objectives of the campaign were to develop brand awareness and produce leads.

The second part of the campaign was a direct mailing. According to Saaty, "The first step is to understand your target market, and you must have a specific target market in mind when developing a direct-mailer." The Cysive direct mailing was sent to CEOs of large firms, especially those in the *Fortune* 500. CEOs were targeted for two reasons. First, the type of system that Cysive builds costs millions of dollars. Therefore, it is likely that the CEO would be involved in the decision-making process and in negotiations. Second, if the CEO's attention could be captured, even if he or she is not involved in the decision process, the CEO may be willing to ask someone in the office to contact Cysive for further information.

Typical direct-mail pieces would not work, because CEOs of *Fortune* 500 companies would simply ignore them. The mailing had to include something special. Cysive's direct-mailer was a box containing a real hammer. The Cysive logo was placed on the hammer. On the outside of the box were the words "Some e-business systems are held together with bubblegum and spit." Inside was the hammer with the phrase "We take a different approach." Approximately 500 hammers were mailed to CEOs.

"We needed something different, something symbolic of building an e-business system. We also wanted something the CEO would not throw away but would be useful. While mailing the actual hammer was 10 times more expensive than the traditional approach, it got the CEO's attention," Satty noted.

The results were impressive. A follow-up survey of the CEOs contacted indicated the hammer was well received. Cysive was contacted by 10 to 15 companies—a 2 to 3 percent response rate. Salespeople followed up every lead generated by the direct mailing. One of those firms eventually signed a multimillion-dollar contract with Cysive. According to Saaty, "Just that one contract covered the cost of the direct-mail program."

Finally, salespeople contacted the CEOs and companies that did not respond. In almost all cases, the hammer opened the door to talk to the CEO or some other high-ranking official.[25]

be designed and customized for each customer. The program is expensive, which limits the number of companies that can afford it.[26]

The primary disadvantage of direct mail is clutter. Most consumers are bombarded with direct-mail ads on a daily basis. Therefore, one key aspect of direct marketing is to make certain only viable prospects receive mailings.

## Catalogs

Many consumers enjoy catalogs, because they view them at their leisure. Catalogs have a longer-term impact because they are kept and shared. Catalogs are a low-pressure direct-marketing tactic that allows consumers time to consider goods and prices. Many marketers believe that online shopping has replaced catalog mail-order shopping; however, research by the U.S. Postal Service reveals that although the number of consumers purchasing online has increased, consumers continue to prefer having catalogs mailed to them. In many cases, receiving a catalog is the first step in the buying cycle.[27]

Successful cataloging requires an enhanced database. Many catalog companies such as L.L.Bean, Spiegel, and JCPenney create specialty catalogs geared to specific market segments. The items have a lower cost and a higher yield, because they target individual market segments.

Catalogs are essential selling tools for many business-to-business marketing programs. They provide more complete information to members of the buying center as well as prices for the purchasing agent. When combined with the Internet, a catalog program can provide a strong connection with individual customers.

## Mass Media

The most common forms of mass media used in direct marketing are television, radio, magazines, and newspapers. Television ads can be targeted to various programs or cable channels. Infomercials may also be designed to entice an immediate "call now" response. Radio does not have the reach of television, but can be targeted by the type of station format. Radio ads must repeat the response number frequently so consumers can make contact. Print media can be sent to various market segments with quick-response messages regarding Web site information and toll-free numbers.[28]

Valpak offers businesses a unique way to reach consumers, who are, in turn, more likely to make purchases.
*Source:* Courtesy of Valpak.

## Alternative Media

Direct-marketing programs using alternative media represent new ways to reach consumers. **Package insert programs (PIPs)** are materials placed in order fulfillment packages, such as when a record club includes direct-response order forms for jewelry, customized checks, or CD players in a package of CDs or tapes. **Ride alongs** are materials that are placed with another company's catalog or direct-mail piece, such as the additional marketing materials packaged with a record club's catalog. A **card pack** is a deck of 20 to 50 business reply cards, normal 3 1/2" x 5", placed in a plastic pack. These can be sent to consumers or as part of a business-to-business program.[29] Another successful alternative media program is offered by Valpak, which creates what are called "cooperative direct mail" products. Advertisers place ads into a 9 3/4" x 4 1/2" envelope, called "The Blue Envelope of Savings." Postage is shared among the advertisers. Consumer responses have been favorable and strong.

## The Internet

The Internet provides another channel for direct marketing. With growing consumer confidence about security, many individuals and businesses are willing to make purchases online. Internet direct-marketing programs are fast, and the goods and services can be suggested to consumers based on past purchasing or click-stream behaviors.

### E-Mail

In addition to Web sites, many companies are developing e-mail direct-marketing campaigns. One recent success story was generated by Williams-Sonoma, Inc., a retailer of cookware and household goods. E-mail was used to promote an online bridal registry. Approximately 5 percent of the customers contacted by e-mail visited the store. This total was considerably higher than any previously used direct-mail campaign.[30]

## PERMISSION MARKETING

A relatively new form of direct marketing is **permission marketing**, which is promotional information that is sent only to consumers who give the company permission to do so. Permission marketing programs can be offered on the Internet, by telephone, or through direct mail. Response rates are often higher in permissions programs, because consumers are receiving only marketing materials they have asked for. The steps of a successful permission marketing program are:

1. Obtain permission from the customer.
2. Offer the consumer an ongoing curriculum that is meaningful.
3. Reinforce the incentive to continue the relationship.
4. Increase the level of permission.
5. Leverage the permission to benefit both parties.

Permission is normally obtained by providing an incentive for volunteering. Information, entertainment, a gift, cash, or entries in a sweepstakes are common incentives. The curriculum of information is primarily educational and is focused on the company's product or service features. Reinforcing the incentive involves an additional new incentive beyond the original gift. Permission levels are increased by obtaining more in-depth information about a consumer, such as hobbies, interests, attitudes, and opinions. Information is leveraged into additional purchases in which the participant gets a special deal, which creates a win–win situation for both parties.

Quris, Inc., of Denver, Colorado, solicited travelers and frequent fliers for an e-mail permissions marketing program. The permission marketing e-mails were opened and read regularly by 54 percent of the enrollees into the program. In one year, 64 percent made an online purchase that was directly the result of the e-mail permission marketing program. Frequent fliers who participated in the online e-mail permission program spent an average of $1,210 per year online, beyond air travel purchases.[31]

An important key to success in a permission marketing program is to make sure the recipients have agreed to participate. Unfortunately, some consumers have been tricked into joining permission marketing programs without realizing it. This often occurs as a customer completes an online survey or makes an online purchase. To opt out of the permission marketing part of the program, the person must uncheck a box on the site. These techniques are likely to create negative feelings toward the company.

It is also important to make sure the e-mail marketing piece is relevant to the consumer receiving it. Too many people have joined a permission marketing program that turned into a situation where the consumer has no input and is bombarded with extraneous marketing messages. A recent survey revealed that 80 percent of consumers stopped reading permission e-mails from some companies because they were shoddy or irrelevant. Another 68 percent said the e-mails came too frequently and

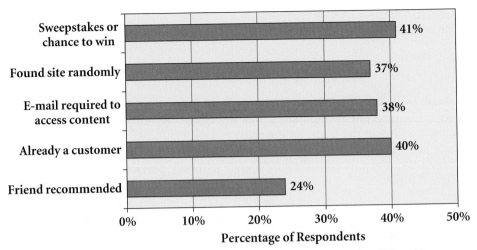

**FIGURE 11.11**

**Reasons Consumers Opt Into an E-Mail Frequency Program**

*Percentage of Respondents*

*Source:* Joseph Gatti, "Most Consumers Have Reached Permission E-Mail Threshold," *Direct Marketing* (December 2003), pp. 1–2.

51 percent said they lost interest in the goods, services, or topics of the e-mails. On the whole, consumers delete an average of 43 percent of permission e-mails without ever reading them.[32]

What attracts consumers to an e-mail permission marketing program? Figure 11.11 lists the top reasons for opting into e-mail programs. At the top of the list is a chance to win something in a sweepstakes. Also when the individual is already a customer of the company, the person feels favorably predisposed to the company's products.[33]

When asked what motivates them to remain loyal to a permission marketing relationship, consumers shift their answers. The most frequent reason is the content of the e-mail is particularly interesting, followed by account status updates. Contests and sweepstakes remain an important factor at 34 percent. Figure 11.12 provides the complete list.[34]

Permission marketing programs have the potential to build strong, ongoing relationships with customers when the program offers something of value to the customer. To optimize permission marketing, firms must feature empowerment and reciprocity.[35] Empowerment means consumers believe they have power throughout the relationship and not just at the beginning when they agreed to join the program. They can make decisions and have choices about what is received. To maintain positive attitudes, consumers should be given instant rewards along the way, not just at the beginning. This creates feelings of reciprocity. One mistake that is often made is rewarding

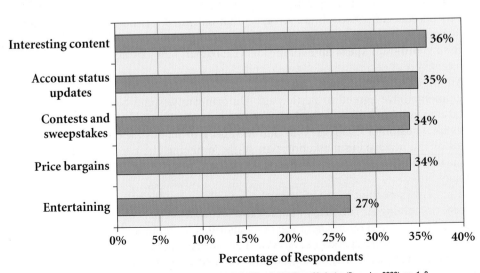

**FIGURE 11.12**

**Reasons Consumers Remain Loyal to a Permission Relationship**

*Percentage of Respondents*

*Source:* Joseph Gatti, "Most Consumers Have Reached Permission E-Mail Threshold," *Direct Marketing* (December 2003), pp. 1–2.

▶ **Maintain sales, margins, or profits.**

▶ **Increase loyalty of existing customers.**

▶ **Preempt or match a competitor's frequency program.**

▶ **Induce cross-selling to existing customers.**

▶ **Differentiate a parity brand.**

▶ **Preempt the entry of a new brand.**

**FIGURE 11.13**
**Frequency Program Objectives**

*Source:* Grahame R. Dowling and Mark Uncles, "Do Customer Loyalty Programs Really
Work?" *Sloan Management Review* 38, no. 4 (Summer 1997), pp. 71–82.

consumers only for joining a permission marketing program. Empowerment and reciprocity lead the customer to believe the company values the relationship. This enhances the quality of the program and increases the chances that the consumer will remain an active participant in the program.

## FREQUENCY PROGRAMS

A **frequency program** is an incentive plan designed to encourage customers to make repeat purchases. When brand parity exists, such as in the airline industry, a frequent flyer program is one method to encourage repeat business. Figure 11.13 lists various reasons for developing frequency programs. Frequency programs were first developed to differentiate one brand from its competition; however, now they tend to be common across all competitors in an industry (airline, hotel, etc.).

Company leaders develop frequency programs for two reasons. The first is to develop loyalty from customers. The second is to match or preempt the competition. Keeping customers creates repeat purchases and makes it possible to cross-sell other goods and services.

Three principles are used in building a loyalty program. The first is to *design the program to enhance the value of the product.* It should add value to what the product offers or provide a unique new feature. When frequent flyer miles are given for using a credit card, the feature is unique, just as the cash-back feature is for the Discover card.

The more effort a customer must expend to participate in a frequency program, the greater the value of the reward should be. Many consumers are willing to put forth greater effort to obtain luxury rewards as opposed to necessity rewards. Shoppers at a grocery store are more likely to be willing to give a higher level of effort in order to receive a free overnight stay at nearby local resort than they would for a $50 gift certificate for food.[36]

The second principle in building a loyalty program is to *calculate the full cost of the program.* Make sure all record keeping is considered as part of the cost. Many times the cost of maintaining a frequency account is greater than the profits earned.

The third principle is to *design a program that maximizes the customer's motivation to make the next purchase.* Moderate users of a product are most likely to be enticed by a frequency program. The added incentive encourages loyalty to a particular company or brand.

An advertisement for the Southwest Airlines
Rapid Rewards frequent flier program.
*Source:* Courtesy of Southwest Airlines.

When You Use Your Free Ticket To Fly To Any One Of Our Great Destinations, You'll Have Plenty Of Money For Other Things.

With Southwest Airlines' Rapid Rewards, it only takes eight roundtrips within 12 consecutive months to earn a free ticket. That means there's no counting miles or waiting forever to get your free trip. And with 52 cities to choose from, including some of the most popular vacation spots you want to visit, it also means your souvenir collection should grow pretty fast.

**SOUTHWEST AIRLINES RAPID**REWARDS**
A SYMBOL OF FREEDOM™

An advertisement by Southwest Airlines highlighting the benefit of being a member of their Rapid Rewards program.
*Source:* Courtesy of Southwest Airlines.

Harrah's Entertainment is one of the world's largest casino operators. The company generates $4 billion annually through 45,000 slot machines in 28 different casinos.[37] Seventy-five percent of Harrah's 250,000 daily customers are members of the company's rewards program and use what is called a "loyalty card." With every push of a button and every swipe of the loyalty card, data are sent to Harrah's computing center. Over 100 million pieces of data are collected daily. A Harrah's loyalty card can be used track the machines or games a customer plays, how much that customer spends, how long the person stays at a particular machine, and how often the customer goes to a Harrah's casino. The marketing team can track the gambling behaviors of 30 million people. This information is combined with slot records to determine which games are the most popular with various groups, such as men, women, tourists, and locals. In addition, Harrah's staff knows which slot machines are hot and which are not. The information is used to place slot machines in the best locations at each casino. Other data help determine which types of machines should be purchased and which machines should be phased out. Finally, the information is also used to determine which customers should receive frequency rewards such as room upgrades, show tickets, or free dinner vouchers.[38]

Frequency programs are also used in the business-to-business sector. Bell Atlantic has developed a frequency program for corporate customers called "Business Link." Members save approximately 15 percent on direct-dial calls when their monthly usage exceeds a minimum amount. Business customers also earn points that can be redeemed for various items such as gift certificates to restaurants and tickets to shows. The information collected from the rewards program helps Bell Atlantic's marketing team identify buying center members in various companies.[39]

## CUSTOMER RELATIONSHIP MANAGEMENT

One of the newest trends in the application of data to the selling process is called **customer relationship management (CRM)**. These programs are designed to build long-term loyalty and bonds with customers through the use of a personal touch facilitated by technology. CRM programs go beyond the development of a database and traditional selling tactics. They include product modifications to meet the needs of individual customers.

CRM works best when customers have highly differentiated needs, highly differentiated valuations, or both. CRM has three technological underpinnings:

1. Database technology, including the ability to analyze and map data
2. Interactivity through Web sites, call centers, and other means of contacting customers
3. Mass customization technology, or the ability to customize a good or service to better meet a customer's needs[40]

Typically, creating a CRM program requires four steps.[41]

The first step of CRM is to *identify the firm's customers.* This may be accomplished by using standard data collection techniques and the firm's database.

Second, *differentiate customers in terms of their needs and their value to the selling company.* There are two CRM metrics involved: (1) the lifetime value of the customer and (2) share of customer. The **lifetime value** is based on the idea that customers who generate revenues throughout their lifetimes are more valuable than those who only make one transaction. To calculate a customer's lifetime value, the average number of visits per year is multiplied by the average amount of money spent per visit multiplied by the average life span of a customer. From this total, deduct the costs of acquiring and servicing the customer and add in the value of people this customer refers to the company. The final figure is the lifetime value of the customer.

The second underlying principle of CRM is that some customers are more valuable to the firm than others and that over time the amount of money a customer spends with a firm can increase. **Share of customer** means the potential value that could be added to a given customer's lifetime value. In other words, if more is invested in developing this relationship, what will the yield be over time? When a customer makes only 25 percent of her purchases of a particular product with a specific vendor, increasing the share of the customer would mean increasing that percentage from 25 percent to a higher level, thus generating additional sales revenues. The ultimate goal would be leading the customer to make 100 percent of her purchases with one vendor. A CRM program involves understanding what various kinds of customers contribute to profits over time.[42]

Third, *interact with customers in ways that improve the cost efficiency and the effectiveness of these contacts.* A company must provide what the customer wants in a timely fashion so that neither the company nor the customer wastes time. One company that has reached this goal is JBoss, an open-source software developer. JBoss sends out 20 e-mail campaigns a month highlighting the company's goods and services. The e-mails generate an average of 10,000 leads per month. Prior to installing a CRM program, these 10,000 leads were handled manually, by only 25 salespeople. Many leads were never followed up and considerable business was lost. Now JBoss's CRM program software sorts the leads based on e-mail and Internet opens and click-through rates. Using predetermined metrics, the most qualified leads are sent automatically to the sales staff for follow-up. E-mails and correspondence sent to these prime leads automatically become a part of the CRM database. The CRM software also records the products a customer examines and any materials that the customer downloads. This information is extremely valuable when the salesperson makes contact with the customer. JBoss now follows up on all 10,000 leads per month and provides a higher level of service to each individual customer.[43]

As part of its CRM program, Glaxo has pharmaceutical professionals available to provide information about company products.

*Source:* Courtesy of West & Vaughan, Inc.

Fourth, *customize some aspect of the goods or services being offered to the customer.* These products should better meet the needs of the customer, who in turn rewards the company with long-term loyalty. For example, Barnes & Noble has a database program in which book buyers' long-term purchasing habits are recorded. The sales force receives a prompt when, for example, a customer has purchased all books written by one author except for one title. In that case, the customer is contacted and offered the outstanding book at a discounted price. In the future, the customer is contacted when the author publishes any new title.

Seth Godin, author of *Permission Marketing,* writes, "Instead of trying to find new customers for the products you've got, you find new products for the customers you've already got."[44] American Airlines' customization technology is used in the firm's AAdvantage program. Frequent flyers are able to create personalized travel profiles and customized travel packages based on those profiles. This leads to more sales to the same customers.[45]

CRM programs do not always succeed. The Gartner Group, a research and advisory firm, notes that 55 percent of all CRM projects do not produce results. Failures are normally attributed to four factors. First, the program is often implemented before creating a solid customer strategy. Market segments must be identified so that customization programs can proceed. Failing to understand market segments creates a "ready, fire, aim"—type approach.[46]

Second, rolling out a CRM program before changing the organization to match it will create problems. A CRM program affects views of how to treat customers as well as how to deliver goods and services to them. This means a new management philosophy is essential. Failing to educate the entire staff about this new perspective and approach quickly leads to problems.

Third, becoming technology-driven rather than customer-driven causes the failure of some CRM programs. Technology can only assist in record keeping and some aspects of order fulfillment. The rest is the responsibility of the employees, who must understand the customer and develop customized approaches.

Fourth, CRM programs fail when customers feel like they are being "stalked" rather than "wooed." Trying to build a relationship with a disinterested customer will be more annoying than helpful. For example, the *Dallas Morning News* discovered that its telemarketing program to gain subscribers was annoying people rather than winning them over. Moving to direct mail was costly, but yielded better results. The marketing team must identify those customers who wish to become partners and then reach them in ways that add value.

Mitchell's of Westport is a high-end clothing store that has made effective use of a CRM program. The company has data available to the sales staff regarding customer preferences, sizes, previous purchases, and other data. Purchases are followed up with thank-you notes, and customers are notified of sales and given invitations to special events when specific products are available. Loyalty to the store is very high. Even customers who have moved to new cities return to the store to buy clothing.[47]

CRM programs must be customized to fit each company's needs. When the possibility of building relationships is low and there is little difference in valuations of customers, the program is less likely to succeed. Each marketing team should assess the company's profile before investing in a CRM plan.

# SUMMARY

Personal selling takes place in several major and important ways. First, manufacturers as well as small companies put products into the hands of end users and customers. Second, many relationships exist between salespeople and clients in other businesses.

Retail clerks interact directly with customers. These relationships ordinarily take place on a transactional level; however, effective store employees can influence customer attitudes toward the retail outlet. Competent, friendly, and helpful store clerks encourage customers to return in the future.

In business settings, it is important to identify key needs and then to sell products that fulfill those needs. Relationships that are strengthened over time move from single or occasional transactions toward more strategic alliances with business customers. A sales force must adjust to international settings by understanding the natures of international customers and by working within the norms, customs, and laws of a foreign country.

Personal selling is enhanced by the effective use of the company's database. Managing a database begins with establishing clear goals for the program. Data sources, both internal and external, must be evaluated so that those offering the most vital information are used. Then a data warehouse can be built, and data mining can begin.

One of the most important applications of a database program is direct marketing. These efforts may be made by mail, catalog, phone, fax, mass media, the Internet, or e-mail. Geocoding identifies individuals with similar attributes by zip code. Others are identified when they contact the firm by telephone or through the company's Web site.

Permission marketing is a selling approach in which the customer agrees to receive promotional materials in exchange for various incentives. Frequency programs are incentives customers receive for repeat business. Both are designed to create customer loyalty over time.

Customer relationship management is a program designed to build long-term loyalty and bonds with customers through the use of a personal touch facilitated by technology. CRM programs go beyond the development of a database and traditional selling tactics. They include product modification to meet the needs of individual customers.

As the role of personal selling evolves, the use of technology to facilitate marketing efforts is likely to rise. An effective IMC program incorporates people skills, understanding of customer needs and wants, and technology into a seamless program designed to differentiate the company and build customer loyalty.

# REVIEW QUESTIONS

1. What is a single transaction sale? What mistakes do sales reps make when finalizing this type of sale?

2. Describe the personal selling aspect of marketing services.

3. How is a retail sales presentation related to the steps of the consumer buying decision-making process? What is the manufacturer's dilemma in this process? How can a missionary salesperson help?

4. What is cross-selling? How is it related to inbound telemarketing calls?

5. What are the three basic forms of business-to-business personal selling? How do they relate to the various types of buyer–seller relationships?

6. What are the steps involved in managing the business-to-business selling process? How do intrinsic value buyers differ from extrinsic value buyers and strategic value buyers when going through these steps?

7. Name and briefly describe the four selling approaches. Which is the most intense and interpersonal? Why?

8. What trends are present in personal selling? How should marketing managers respond to those trends?

9. What issues, problems, and opportunities exist in international selling?

10. Describe database development and its relationship to an IMC program.

11. What is the primary source of internal database information? How can this data be collected?

12. What is geocoding? What role does it play in database programs?

13. Describe the various methods that can be used to facilitate direct-marketing programs.

14. Describe a permission marketing program. What are the key benefits of this approach?

15. What are the steps involved in an effective permission marketing program?

16. Describe a frequency program. Which type of user pays off the best in a frequency program—light, medium, or heavy users?

17. What is customer relationship management? What are the four steps involved?

18. What is the lifetime value of a customer? Why is the concept crucial to a CRM program?

19. When is a CRM program most likely to be effective? What problems can cause the program to fail?

# KEY TERMS

**single transaction**   Occurs when the buyer and seller interact for the purpose of a solitary purchase.

**order-takers**   Salespersons whose primary tasks are to take orders.

**repeat transactions**   Sales that occur when buyers purchase on a regular basis.

**inbound telemarketing**   Selling in response to inbound telephone calls.

**outbound telemarketing**   Selling by making outbound calls to consumers or businesses.

**missionary salespeople**   Members of the sales force who try to develop goodwill, stimulate demand, and provide the training and incentives needed to enhance the manufacturer in the retailer's mind.

**cross-selling**   The marketing of another item following the purchase of a good or service.

**field sales**   A form of marketing in which the salesperson travels to the customer's place of business or home.

**order-getters**   Salespeople who go out and solicit orders.

**intrinsic value buyers**   Customers who understand the product, know how to use it, and view the product as a commodity-type item.

**extrinsic value buyers**   Customers who focus more on product attributes and the solution a particular product can provide.

**strategic value buyers**   Customers who seek out partnerships with suppliers.

**stimulus-response sales approach**   Using specific statements (stimuli) to solicit specific responses from customers (sometimes called a "canned" sales pitch).

**need-satisfaction sales approach**   Discovering a customer's needs and then providing solutions that satisfy those needs.

**problem-solution sales approach**   Analyzing a buyer's operation and offering solutions through various goods and services.

**mission-sharing sales approach**   A relationship in which two organizations develop a common mission and then share resources to accomplish that mission.

**database development**   The creation of a database to support the overall company, IMC program, and total marketing effort.

**geocoding**   Adding geographic codes to customer records to make it possible to plot the addresses of customers on a map.

**data mining**   An analytical process to sift through information to help the firm better understand customers.

**direct marketing**   Vending products to customers without the use of other channel members.

**digital direct-to-press**   Software that instructs the computer to create a tailor-made direct mail messages to a customer.

**package insert programs (PIPs)** Marketing materials placed in order fulfillment packages.

**ride alongs** Marketing materials that are placed with another company's catalog or direct-mail piece.

**card pack** A deck of 20 to 50 business reply cards, normally 31/2 by 5 inches, placed in a plastic mail pack.

**permission marketing** A form of database marketing in which the company sends promotional materials to customers who give the company permission to do so.

**frequency program** A marketing plan designed to cause customers to make repeat purchases by offering them incentives.

**customer relationship management (CRM)** Programs designed to build long-term loyalty and bonds with customers through the use of a personal touch facilitated by technology.

**lifetime value** The sales revenue of a customer throughout the lifetime of a relationship.

**share of customer** The percentage of purchases of a product that a customer makes with a particular firm.

# CRITICAL THINKING EXERCISES

## Discussion Questions

1. Personal selling in retail stores varies greatly depending on the type of outlet. Discuss the differences in selling approaches between a retail salesperson in a discount store (Wal-Mart) versus a retail salesperson at a high-end department store (Macy's or Saks Fifth Avenue).

2. Visit a nearby local retail store. Ask the manager to describe the tactics that manufacturers use to encourage retail store salespeople and clerks to push a specific manufacturer's brand. Ask individual salespeople to specify the brands they encourage customers to purchase. Based on your conversations, discuss the challenges manufacturers have in encouraging sales in the retail store.

3. For classes that have international students, ask these individuals to discuss retailing in their home countries. Do store clerks sell in the same way as in the United States? Discuss mores or cultural traditions in each country, and try to explain how they would affect personal selling. If any students have experience as a field salesperson or know of someone in their home country who is a field salesperson, ask them to discuss how it is different from field selling in the United States.

4. Assume you are the account executive at a database marketing agency. A music retailer has asked you to develop a database for the company. How would you go about building a data warehouse? What type of data mining would you do for the music retailer?

5. Form a group of four to five classmates. Ask each person in the group to list the catalogs that came into his or her home during the past 2 weeks. Have each person discuss why he or she receives certain catalogs. Next, discuss how often each of you order something out of a catalog and how the order was placed. Is anyone in the group accessing the Internet for information given in a catalog or ordering from a catalog after accessing a Web site? Discuss how important the catalog market is to you and what you see as the future of catalog marketing.

# INTEGRATED LEARNING EXERCISES

1. A variety of companies are available that claim to help retail salespeople do a better job. Go to the following Web sites to observe what each of these companies offers:

   **a.** Business Training Media.com Inc. (www.business-marketing.com)

   **b.** Robertson Training Group (www.robertsontraining group.com)

   **c.** Sales Keys (www.saleskeys.com)

2. Almost all hotels have some type of frequency or loyalty program. Examine the loyalty programs of the following hotels. Critique each one. Which ones are best? Why?

   **a.** Best Western (www.bestwestern.com)

   **b.** Days Inn (www.daysinn.com)

   **c.** Doubletree Inn (doubletree.hilton.com)

   **d.** Holiday Inn (www.basshotels.com/holiday-inn)

   **e.** Marriott (www.marriott.com)

   **f.** Radisson (www.radisson.com)

   **g.** Wyndham Hotels & Resorts (www.wyndham.com)

3. Examine the methods of direct marketing highlighted in Figure 11.10. Evaluate each method for the following types of businesses. Which ones would be the best? Which ones would not work as well? Justify your answers.

   **a.** Shoe store

   **b.** Printing service

   **c.** Internet hosiery retailer (sells only by the Internet)

   **d.** Manufacturer of tin cans for food processing companies

   **e.** Tractor parts dealer

4. Discuss how a customer relationship management (CRM) program could be developed for a local retail clothing store. How would a CRM program be developed for a national retail clothing store? What are the similarities and differences? What about manufacturers such as Guess who sell to clothing stores? How would they develop a CRM program? Go to www.guess.com. How does the site address customers?

merchandise or bidding on goods. Instead, eBay message boards were filled with statements of grief.

Responding quickly, the eBay executive team decided to turn part of the site into the world's biggest fund-raising effort on behalf of the victims of the attacks. The program, called "Auction for America," was designed to raise $100 million in 100 days. Customers were invited to sell off anything possible, with proceeds donated to the fund. eBay waived all fees, as did VISA, an active partner of the company.

The Auction for America program was launched on September 17, just 6 days after the attacks. CEO Meg Whitman stood with New York Mayor Rudolph Giuliani and Governor George Pataki to announce the drive. The NFL offered to sell football memorabilia and Jay Leno volunteered to sell one of his Harley-Davidson motorcycles, covered with autographs of numerous celebrities. Everything from Vietnam War medals to dinosaur teeth became part of the program. The success of the Auction for America program helped restore confidence in the rest of eBay's operations. The company continued expansion plans into new markets, meeting with great success.

The new global atmosphere has caused some change. The company has taken gun listings off the board, as well as firecrackers, police badges, and tobacco products. Anything that might be considered "hate commerce" is also off-limits.

The continuing success of eBay must be attributed, in part, to the kindhearted nature of the company and the family-like atmosphere of its clients. Although the World Trade Center is gone, Meg Whitman and many others believe that eBay has become the virtual World Trade Center that represents all of the positive ingredients of a "global economic democracy."[1]

The traditional marketing mix consists of advertising, sales promotions, personal selling, and public relations efforts. At this point in the textbook, the first three elements in the mix have been presented. This chapter is devoted to the fourth element, public relations. Closely related to public relations issues are sponsorship programs and obeying marketing regulations.

Public relations efforts, sponsorship programs, and legal concerns are all part of the overall integrated marketing communications approach. The same unified message appears in every marketing endeavor, from the appearance of the company's letterhead and stationery, to advertisements, promotional items, information in press releases, and in any sponsorship program. The goal of an IMC plan is to make sure that each component of a firm's communication plan speaks with one voice. Extending this goal to public relations, sponsorships, and legal concerns can be difficult, but is an important task for the marketing team.

This chapter begins with a discussion of the nature of a public relations function within an integrated marketing plan. Second, sponsorship programs and event marketing tactics are outlined to show how the company can make quality contacts with existing customers, new prospects, vendors, and others. The goal of these activities is to reach the general public with the same clear voice that has been developed in other marketing activities. Third, government and industry regulations are discussed. The challenge is to build an ethical and legal foundation for the company. Among the benefits of this type of attitude is that the company is much more likely to be able to avoid lawsuits as well as any other accusation about illegal activities. When the company succeeds at building positive public relations and sponsorship programs and acts in an ethical and legal manner, the firm's image is enhanced and its brands are better known and perceived more favorably in the marketplace.

## PUBLIC RELATIONS

In Hollywood, one well-worn phrase is "There's no such thing as bad publicity." This may be true for a bad-boy actor trying to get his name out to the public, however, in the world of marketing and communications, bad publicity is *worse* than no publicity. Many business organizations spend countless hours fending off negative news while trying to develop positive and noticeable messages and themes.

The **public relations (PR) department** is a unit in the firm that manages publicity and other communications with every group that is in contact with the company. Some of the functions performed by the public relations department are similar to those provided by the marketing department. Others are quite different. Often the public relations department is separate from the marketing department. The two may cooperate with and consult each other, yet each has a separate role to perform.

Some marketing experts argue that public relations should be part of the marketing department, just as advertising, trade promotions, and sales promotions are under the jurisdiction of the marketing manager. Others suggest that public relations activities are different and cannot operate effectively within a marketing department. Instead, a member of the public relations department should serve as a consultant to the marketing department. Still others contend that a new division, called the "department of communications," should be created to oversee both marketing and public relations activities.

In any case, the first major decision company leaders must make concerning public relations is who will handle the various activities involved. They can be managed by an internal public relations officer or department. Other companies hire public relations firms to handle either special projects or all of the public relations functions. When a public relations agency is retained, normally someone is placed in charge of internal public relations, because most public relations firms deal only with external publics.

The decision criteria used in selecting advertising agencies can be applied to selecting a public relations firm. It is important to develop a trusting relationship with the public relations agency and to carefully spell out what the firm expects from the agency.

One common goal of a public relations firm is to get hits. A **hit** is the mention of a company's name in a news story. Hits can be positive, negative, or even neutral in terms of their impact on a firm. The concept behind getting hits in the news is that the more a consumer sees the name of a company in a news-related context, the higher the brand or company awareness will become. This may be true, but it is important to consider the type of image that is being developed. It may be a wiser strategy to seek fewer hits and to make sure that those hits project the company in a positive light that also reinforces the firm's IMC theme.

Consequently, when a public relations firm is used, the agency's personnel must be familiar with the client's IMC plan. Then, members of the public relations firm are able to work on ideas that reinforce the plan. Special events, activities, and news releases can be developed to strengthen the "one voice" concept needed to build a successful IMC program. The following sections describe public relations functions that must be performed, including reaching all of the targets of various company communications.

## PUBLIC RELATIONS FUNCTIONS

Many public relations activities are not considered typical marketing functions. This is because the marketing department concentrates on customers and the channel members en route to those customers, such as wholesalers and retail outlets. In contrast, the public relations department focuses on a variety of internal and external stakeholders including employees, stockholders, public interest groups, the government, and society as a whole.

Five key public relations functions are displayed in Figure 12.1. Each represents the tasks given to public relations personnel, whether they are internal employees or members of a public relations company hired to perform those functions.

## IDENTIFYING STAKEHOLDERS

All the recipients of company communications are important. Any constituent who makes contact with a company should receive a clear, unified message. In this section, the stakeholders who are targets of public relations efforts are described. A **stakeholder** is a person or group that has a vested interest in the organization's well-being. A vested interest can be a variety of items, including:

- Profits paid as common stock dividends
- Loan repayments that a lending institution seeks to receive
- Sales to the company or purchases made from the company
- Wages paid to employees
- Community well-being
- A special-interest topic

In other words, any number of things can give a person or another company a stake in the firm's well-being.

To understand the nature of public relations programs, it is helpful to begin by identifying the publics that make contact with various companies. Figure 12.2 identifies the primary internal and external stakeholders that the public relations department should monitor.

We are a company of Americans.

32,000 men and women who grieve with our nation.

32,000 men and women who are proud of our country and our company.

32,000 men and women with a mission: to keep America flying.

Nothing can keep our country or Southwest Airlines from moving ahead.

**SOUTHWEST AIRLINES**

The Public Relations Department placed this advertisement in *USA Today* immediately after the terrorist attacks of September 11, 2001.
*Source:* Courtesy of Southwest Airlines.

---

- ▌ Identify internal and external stakeholders
- ▌ Assess the corporate reputation
- ▌ Audit corporate social responsibility
- ▌ Create positive image-building activities
- ▌ Prevent or reduce image damage

**FIGURE 12.1**
**Public Relations Functions**

| | |
|---|---|
| ▶ Employees | ▶ Media |
| ▶ Unions | ▶ Local community |
| ▶ Shareholders | ▶ Financial community |
| ▶ Channel members | ▶ Government |
| ▶ Customers | ▶ Special-interest groups |

**FIGURE 12.2**
**Stakeholders**

Communications to each of these stakeholder groups is important. To ensure consistency, the company should develop a clear communication strategy that fits well with the firm's IMC plan and corporate image that is to be conveyed. The overall message to each stakeholder should be same. Still, each message has to be tailored to meet the different expectations of the various audiences. By tailoring the content, style, and channel of communication, each stakeholder group receives a message that best resonates with them, yet is consistent with other messages that are delivered and with the image of the company.

In addition to sending communications to each of the stakeholders, the public relations department must closely monitor the actions and opinions of each group. When changes in attitudes, new views, or serious concerns develop, the public relations department should be ready to address the problem. Most importantly, it is the responsibility of the public relations department to be certain that all forms of communications to each of these publics remain consistent with the firm's IMC plan and the image the firm seeks to project.

Motorola's theme is that the company's "Wireless Communication Centers help you stay connected." The theme should be used by employees in all communications.
*Source:* Courtesy of Motorola, Inc./Personal Communications Sector. © 1999.

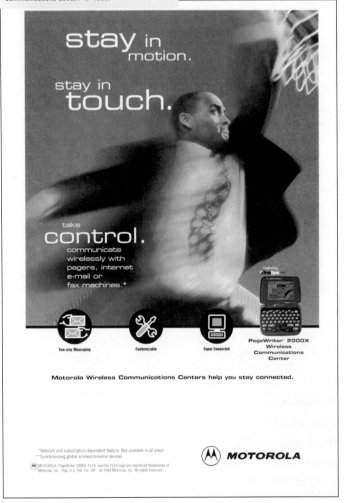

## Internal Stakeholders

Company leaders should not underestimate the importance of internal communications. Employees are a potentially powerful channel of communication to people outside of the organization and can either enhance the firm's reputation or damage it. What employees say to those around them has a much higher level of credibility than what a company says about itself. Word-of-mouth communications, even informal ones through employees, impact decisions about purchasing and investing.[2]

Employees should receive a constant stream of information from the company. The same is true for other internal stakeholders, such corporate shareholders and any labor unions. Many of these individuals are quite distant from the marketing and public relations departments. They should be made aware of what the company is trying to achieve with its IMC program, even if this means only basic knowledge. Those closest to the marketing department, such as employees serving customers, are going to be more acutely aware of the nature of the IMC plan, including how the company's message theme is being sent to all other constituents.

The Motorola advertisement shown on this page states that the company's "Wireless Communications Centers help you stay connected." Employees who are aware of Motorola's theme can communicate the same message when dealing with customers, vendors, and other publics.

To work effectively in communicating with employees, the public relations department must work closely with the human resource (HR) department. Publications and communications aimed at employees must be consistent with the image and message that the firm is espousing to customers and other groups. For example, any firm that uses advertising to suggest that employees are always ready to assist customers should make sure those employees are aware of the message. Employee behaviors should then be consistent with the advertising theme that is being conveyed to customers. The HR department should hire the kind of worker who is attracted to such an approach and structure performance appraisals and rewards to favor those who "buy into" the company's overall IMC approach. The emphasis on providing information about company activities must logically extend to every public relations event and sponsorship program.

## External Stakeholders

Overseeing external communications is a daunting task, because the company has little or no influence on how these publics perceive organizational activities. External stakeholders include groups such as the media, local community, financial community, government, and special-interest groups. The company usually has little power over what these groups say or how they interpret information about the company. It is important, therefore, for the company to disseminate positive information and quickly react to any negative publicity or views that are expressed.

In general, a totally integrated communications program accounts for all types of messages that an organization delivers to both internal and external stakeholders. Every contact point provides the opportunity for a message to be sent. The marketing department tends to create contact points with customers and potential customers. To complement this effort, the public relations department deals with the myriad of contact points that are not created or planned, yet are just as critical as those that are planned. An unplanned contact point such as a news story or an individual talking to an employee of the firm at a social gathering allows the firm to build a positive image or reduce any negative messages that are being passed along. Naturally, it is more difficult to deal with unplanned contact points, because they cannot always be anticipated. The key is to monitor constantly what is going on around the firm in order to keep constituents as happy and satisfied as possible.

An advertisement by Wal-Mart directed to its employees, local communities, and other stakeholders.
*Source:* Courtesy of Wal-Mart.

## ASSESSING CORPORATE REPUTATION

A corporation's reputation is extremely vulnerable. It also is extremely valuable. Well-received corporate and brand names can enhance businesses during the good times and protect them when a crisis or problem occurs. Consumer preferences about which brands to purchase are influenced by a company's reputation. People make decisions about where to invest based on corporate reputations. Potential employees decide where to apply and where to work based company reputations.

In one recent survey, 66 percent of those who responded believed that most businesses would take advantage of consumers if they thought they wouldn't get caught.[3] Corporate scandals, accounting fraud, and CEO greed have damaged more than just the few companies involved. People are leery of big business, suspicious of business motives, and unsure if any company can be trusted. Perceptions of corporate reputations by external publics are at an all-time low. As one homemaker stated, "I'm very

*Thank You*
To Our
Consumers
& Team
Members
For
Having Us
At
Your Table!

*Championship brands
trusted around the world.* . . . . . . . . . .

TEAM JOPLIN

**GENERAL MILLS**
BAKERIES & FOODSERVICE

An advertisement placed in *The Joplin Globe*
by General Mills, thanking customers and
employees.
*Source:* Courtesy of General Mills, Inc.

disappointed in how money can rob the goodness in people." She went on to state that putting money under her mattress would be a safer place than investing in today's corporations.[4]

Assessing and managing a company's reputation is as important as promoting its products. Yet, with all that is at stake, less than half of the companies in the United States have someone assigned to monitor corporate reputation. This means company leaders have little idea what consumers, investors, employees, and the public think about the firm. A public relations program is impossible to pursue effectively if company leaders do not know what other people think about the organization.

Assessment begins when company leaders take the time to conduct surveys and interviews to find out what people think of the organization. These efforts can be completed internally or be performed by an outside company, such as a public relations firm. The process of assessment should include internal views of the corporation's reputation as well as opinions held by those outside the company.

## AUDITING CORPORATE SOCIAL RESPONSIBILITY

**Social responsibility** is the obligation an organization has to be ethical, accountable, and reactive to the needs of society. Figure 12.3 outlines some of the general areas in which firms can become more ethical and reactive to society's needs.

In general, business experts agree that socially responsible firms are more likely to thrive and survive in the long term. Companies engaged in positive activities generate quality publicity and customer loyalty that result in a positive image of the firm. Firms that work strongly toward reductions in unfair practices, pollution, harassment, and other negative activities are more likely to stay out of court, and the company will suffer fewer negative word-of-mouth comments by unhappy consumers. By managing these activities properly, a firm can reduce damage to its public image and increase positive public perceptions of the organization.

A corporate social responsibility audit is usually undertaken by the organization's management team in conjunction with department managers. Often, external agencies provide

**FIGURE 12.3**
**Examples of Activities that
Affect a Company's Image**

| Image-Destroying Activities | Image-Building Activities |
|---|---|
| ▶ Discrimination | ▶ Empowerment of employees |
| ▶ Harassment | ▶ Charitable contributions |
| ▶ Pollution | ▶ Sponsoring local events |
| ▶ Misleading communications | ▶ Selling environmentally safe products |
| ▶ Deceptive communications | |
| ▶ Offensive communications | ▶ Outplacement programs |
| | ▶ Supporting community events |

guidelines. The purpose of a social responsibility audit is to make sure the organization has clear-cut ethical guidelines for employees to follow and that the company acts to serve the interests of all publics. Guidelines include use of a corporate or professional code of ethics, specifying activities that would be construed as being unethical, and statements about the positive activities a company will pursue. Many firms also have access to "ethical hotlines," where employees can call or write e-mails to discuss specific ethical dilemmas.

If a firm is found to be deficient during a social responsibility audit, clear steps should be outlined to show how the issues will be resolved. Firms without codes of ethics should start by setting up committees or groups to develop them. Companies without other ethical guidelines should move quickly to establish them.

It is the task of the public relations department to make sure internal publics are aware of a corporation's social responsibility efforts. The department can then inform the general public about these activities to help enhance the firm's image.

## CREATING POSITIVE IMAGE-BUILDING ACTIVITIES

In an effort to positively influence the views that consumers and other stakeholders have about a company, many firms have turned to cause-related marketing and green marketing. These *planned events* are designed to draw positive attention to the organization as a solid corporate citizen, one committed to social responsibility. The public relations department can then send out messages in the form of press releases and hold press conferences to highlight these positive, image-building activities.

An advertisement promoting a local social cause, sponsored by Howard Publishing Co.
*Source:* Courtesy of Sartor Associates, Inc.

## Cause-Related Marketing

**Cause-related marketing** is a program in which a firm ties a marketing program in with some type of charity in order to generate goodwill. American businesses pay over $600 million each year for the right to use a not-for-profit organization's name or logo in company advertising and marketing programs. This type of partnership agreement between a not-for-profit cause and a for-profit business is based on the idea that consumers are more likely to purchase from companies that are willing to help a good cause.

As noted previously, brand parity is the norm for many goods and services. Customers perceive that there are few notable differences between products and the companies that sell them. Many marketers use cause-related marketing to help develop stronger brand ties and to move consumers as well as businesses toward brand loyalty. A recent survey revealed that nearly half of all of consumers have switched brands, increased their usage, or tried or inquired about new products that were connected to companies supporting specific causes. In the same survey, 46 percent said they felt better about using the product, service, or company that supported a particular cause.[5]

One difficulty businesses can encounter is that what is a "good" cause to one customer may be disliked by another. Dayton Hudson found a large number of picketers outside company stores objecting to contributions the company made to Planned Parenthood, even as others praised Dayton Hudson's involvement.[6]

Would you stop to give someone directions?
If you were walking that way,
would you guide them?
What if it was out of your way?
One mile.
Two miles.

Two thousand miles,
directly inland from the Skeleton Coast,
to a one-room schoolhouse in the foothills of Namibia.
What if you were the teacher in that schoolhouse?
Would you travel that far to teach someone?
To learn something yourself?

Peace Corps.
Life is calling. How far will you go?

Call 800.424.8580 | Visit peacecorps.gov

The Peace Corps is a social cause supported by a number of companies.
*Source:* Courtesy of Peace Corps. Scott Lowden, photographer, Magnum Photos.

In the past, a number companies donated to causes with little thought to the impact or benefit of such gifts. These philanthropic efforts were expected of big business. Currently, most companies want to know what the benefit will be. Although company leaders believe a charity is worthwhile, supporting that charity must, in some way, result in a tangible benefit. Otherwise the company should not give support. Possible benefits include:

▶ Additional customers
▶ Increased profits
▶ Consumer goodwill for the future
▶ Better relations with governmental agencies
▶ Reduced negative public opinion

These benefits lead companies to get involved. Relationships that do not yield positive benefits to the business sponsor do not last long. Figure 12.4 highlights the top five areas consumers want businesses to consider as they seek causes to support.

In choosing a cause, the marketing team focuses on issues that relate to the company's business. Supporting these efforts is more credible to consumers. When the company supports an unrelated cause, consumers may feel that the business simply is trying to benefit from the not-for-profit's reputation. This may lead some consumers to stop buying the company's products or to believe the company is trying to cover up unethical behavior. Consumers are becoming very skeptical about the motives behind the increased emphasis given to various charities. Even though most people understand that a business must benefit from the relationship, they still tend to develop negative views when they believe that the business is exploiting a relationship with a not-for-profit.

When a good fit exists, positive reactions emerge. For example, a cosmetic dentist established partnerships with a homeless shelter for battered women and a residential education center for former substance abusers and ex-convicts. The dentist offered free services to these centers. Before each event, he contacted the local media. Several TV and newspaper reporters showed up to observe him treating patients. Individuals who had been in pain for months were interviewed. When they stated that cosmetic dental work gave them relief, positive feelings in the community were the result. The publicity was

| | |
|---|---|
| ▶ **Improve public schools** | **52%** |
| ▶ **Dropout prevention** | **34%** |
| ▶ **Scholarships** | **28%** |
| ▶ **Cleanup of environment** | **27%** |
| ▶ **Community health education** | **25%** |

**FIGURE 12.4**
**Causes Consumers Prefer**

*Source:* Bevolyn Williams-Harold and Eric L. Smith. "Spending with Heart," *Black Enterprise* 28, no. 12, (July 1998), p. 26.

extremely valuable. The dental services were something neither the centers nor individuals who were living in the centers could afford.[7]

Cause-related marketing is also important for not-for-profit organizations. Competition has increased in both the business world and the not-for-profit world. An increasing number of not-for-profit organizations currently compete for contributions and gifts. Stra-tegic relationships with businesses can boost contributions for a not-for-profit organization considerably. For example, the American Cancer Society sold its logo to the Florida Department of Citrus for $1 million per year. The American Cancer Society also endorses the Nicoderm nicotine patch produced by SmithKline Beecham for $1 million per year. The American Lung Association received $1.25 million per year in a deal with Nicotrol, a patch produced by McNeil Consumer Products that competes with Nicoderm. The American Heart Association receives $2,500 per product the organization certifies as healthy. Each year the association receives $650 for recertification of the product.[8] These relationships with businesses result not only in direct increases in revenues but also in greater publicity for the not-for-profit organization.

The public relations aspect of cause-related marketing is tricky. To benefit from cause-related marketing, companies need publicity about what is being done. Yet, if the company publicizes too much, people will think the cause is simply being used for commercial gain. In a survey of British consumers, 86 percent said a company should spend funds on communications about their cause-related efforts. The same survey indicated that 69 percent said the amount that should be spent should not be significant. At the same time, the majority of those surveyed said their purchase decisions are influenced by the causes a company supports. This makes informing people about what a company is doing important; however, doing so involves walking a thin line between publicizing and what might be perceived as self-aggrandizement.[9]

A Wal-Mart advertisement highlighting a social cause.
*Source:* Courtesy of Wal-Mart.

## Green Marketing and Pro-Environmental Activities

**Green marketing** is the development and promotion of products that are environmentally safe. When asked, most consumers strongly favor the concept of green marketing. One recent survey indicated that 58 percent of Americans try to save electricity, 46 percent recycle newspapers, 45 percent return bottles or cans, and 23 percent buy products made from, or packaged in, recycled materials.[10]

Although consumers favor green marketing and environmentally safe products, actual purchases of such products only occur when all things are considered equal. Most consumers are not willing to sacrifice price, quality, convenience, availability, or performance for the sake of the environment. In fact, according to a recent study, about 40 percent of consumers say they do not purchase green products because they believe the products are inferior to regular goods.[11]

To benefit from green marketing, the company should identify market segments that are most attracted to environmentally-friendly products. Figure 12.5 divides Americans consumer into five segments based on the propensity to use green products and attitudes about environmental issues. Notice that only 9 percent of American consumers are classified as "True Blue Greens" and another 6 percent are classified as "Greenback Greens."

**COMMUNICATION ACTION**

## Building Positive Publicity Can Be a Tough Sell

Philip Morris began as a tobacco company. Many of its products remain in that industry. In addition, the company has acquired the Miller Brewing Company and 7-Up. One continuing concern is that many of Philip Morris's products are considered "vices." Consequently, the company has a strong vested interest in creating as many positive contact points as possible.

One program devised to generate goodwill is the "We Card" campaign. In conjunction with the Coalition for Responsible Tobacco Retailing, Philip Morris sends out placards to retailers suggesting that they ID any customer who looks to be 27 years old or younger. All 50 states have a minimum purchase age of 18, except Alabama, Alaska, and Utah, which require customers to be 19 years old. Philip Morris has heavily advertised its involvement with the We Card effort. This may be, in part, due to complaints that the tobacco industry targets young people to attract new business.

The We Card program also allows Philip Morris to build more positive ties with retail outlets along with local police officers. Combating underage purchases is easier with the We Card kits. In addition, the company provides training to retailers regarding crime prevention.

Another major thrust developed by the public relations team is the food program for the elderly. This venture combines Philip Morris with the National Meals on Wheels Foundation. Again, substantial positive publicity results from this type of effort.

In the area of disaster relief, Philip Morris employees volunteered their time on several occasions to help provide food and water to those who had been flooded or struck by hurricanes or ice storms. Miller Brewing used its facilities to provide fresh water to those whose systems had been contaminated during storms. Advertisements showing Miller beer trucks rushing to deliver fresh water emphasized the company's involvement in helping people during times of personal crisis.

Beyond these efforts, the Marlboro team is linked with programs to reduce domestic violence, as well as disaster relief, hunger, and youth access to tobacco. These may seem like conflicting messages, yet the company may be able to convince consumers that the company is not out just to push products on unsuspecting members of the public. Doing so may be one of the keys to success in the future, as tobacco suit settlement agreements drive up cigarette prices and continuous negative press bombards the organization.

**Sources:** "Philip Morris to Provide More Than 1 Million Meals to the Elderly in All 50 States," *Fund Raising Management* 30, no. 6 (August 1999), p. 1; Philip Morris press releases (December 19, 1995; March 23, 2000); Philip Morris Web site; and Lori Dorfman, "Polishing Its Image or Preventing Domestic Violence—What's Philip Morris Really Doing?" *Off Our Backs* 31, no. 10 (November 2001), pp. 28–29.

**FIGURE 12.5**
**U.S. Consumers Segmented on Their Attitudes Toward and Support of Green Marketing**

- **True Blue Green (9%)**—Have strong environmental values and are politically active in environmental issues; heavy users of green products
- **Greenback Greens (6%)**—Have strong environmental values, but are not politically active; heavy users of green products
- **Sprouts (31%)**—Believe in green products in theory, but not in practice; will buy green products, but only if equal to or superior to nongreen products
- **Grousers (19%)**—Are uneducated about environmental issues and cynical about their ability to effect change; believe green products are too expensive and inferior
- **Basic Browns (33%)**—Do not care about environmental issues or social issues

*Source:* Jill Meredith Ginsberg and Paul N. Bloom, "Choosing the Right Green Marketing Strategy," *MIT Sloan Management Review* 46, no.1 (Fall 2004), pp. 79–84.

The True Blue Greens are active environmentalists who support environmentally safe products and shop for brands that utilize green marketing. The Greenback Greens purchase environmentally safe products, but are not politically active.

Company leaders must carefully choose a green marketing strategy that matches the target audience. In making the decision on how much emphasis to put on green marketing, managers should ask three questions. First, what percentage of the company's customer base fits into the green marketing segments? Second, can the brand or company be differentiated from the competition along green lines in such a way that it can become a competitive advantage? Third, will the company's current target audience be alienated by adopting a green marketing approach?

Almost all firms say they are pro-environment and provide information on company Web sites about environmental activities. The amount of effort given to publicize these activities varies widely.[12] For example, Coca-Cola tries to protect the environment, but most people are unaware of the company's efforts. Coca-Cola has invested heavily in various recycling programs and recyclable package designs. The activities are not publicized because there is some fear that it would reduce the product's appeal to some of the company's audience. Overemphasizing the green aspects of Coca-Cola's operation may actually hurt sales.

An alternative approach to being pro-environment is to promote the direct, tangible benefits of a product first. The environmental benefits are only presented as a secondary factor. Recently, the Toyota Prius was launched and the emphasis was on fuel efficiency. Consumers were told they would spend less on gas. The fact that the Prius was an environmentally advanced, fuel-efficient hybrid vehicle was mentioned, but not stressed. The idea was that strong environmentalists would believe a hybrid car is important. For those who were not strong environmentalists, it did not matter because the car delivered fuel efficiency.

For a few companies, environmental activities are fully integrated into the business' design and marketing approach because the primary customer base is True Blue Greens and the Greenback Greens. Examples of these types of companies include The Body Shop, Patagonia, and Honest Tea of Bethesda, Maryland. For Honest Tea, social responsibility is embedded in every company activity, from the manufacturing process to the marketing of products. Honest Tea uses biodegradable tea bags, organic ingredients, and community partnerships. The focus of Honest Tea's marketing program is the company's concern for and support of both environmental and social issues.

Every company should be involved in protecting the environment and creating green products, however the marketing emphasis each one gives will vary. If company leaders believe new customers will be gained or product sales will rise, the company will be more likely to aggressively promote its environmental stance. Other companies, such as Coca-Cola, may be less willing to make such bold statements. Each company's marketing team will decide whether or not green marketing should be a central part of the IMC message and how to position itself in terms of the environment.

## PREVENTING OR REDUCING IMAGE DAMAGE

One of the most important public relations functions is damage control. **Damage control** is reacting to negative events caused by a company error, consumer grievances, or when unjustified or exaggerated negative press appears. Corporate and brand images are quickly damaged by negative publicity and events. A strong company image, which took years to build, may be destroyed in just a few weeks or months. ExxonMobil still suffers from an event that occurred nearly 20 years ago. The 1989 *Exxon Valdez* accident, in which 11 million gallons of crude oil were spilled into the bay at Prince William Sound, Alaska, has resulted in a great deal of animosity toward the company. There are still consumers who will not buy Exxon gas. Many do not believe any messages from ExxonMobil about what the company is doing for the environment. ExxonMobil may not recover until a new generation of drivers grows up.

In 2005, Wendy's sales dropped dramatically for several months when a customer claimed to find a detached finger in a bowl of chili, even though the incident turned out to be a fraud. Bad news travels quickly and hits hard.

**FIGURE 12.6**
**Damage-Control Strategies**

Not all negative publicity is generated by the media. Sometimes negative publicity comes from word-of-mouth communication from customers, employees, or other individuals connected with the company. With the Internet, bad experiences and negative talk can be posted and spread to thousands, even millions, within a very short time.

Damage control is used in two situations. The first occurs when the firm has made an error or caused legitimate consumer grievances. The second takes place when unjustified or exaggerated negative press appears. Defending an organization's image and handling damage control take two forms: (1) proactive prevention strategies and (2) reactive damage-control strategies (see Figure 12.6).

## Proactive Prevention Strategies

Proactive prevention means that rather than waiting for harmful publicity to appear and then reacting, many firms work hard to minimize the effects of any bad press. These approaches may prevent negative publicity from starting in the first place. Two proactive prevention techniques are entitlings and enhancements.[13] **Entitlings** are attempts to claim responsibility for positive outcomes of events. **Enhancements** are attempts to increase the desirable outcome of an event in the eyes of the public.

Entitling occurs when a firm associates its name with a positive event. For example, being the official sponsor of a U.S. Olympic team that wins a gold medal attaches the company's name to the athletic achievements of people who don't work for the firm, yet the firm can claim responsibility for some aspect of their successes.

Enhancements occur when a bigger deal is made out of something that is relatively small. For instance, many products now claim to be *fat free,* which makes it sound like they are diet foods. In fact, many fat-free products have just as many calories as do products that contain fat. At the same time, the fat-free label helps convince customers that the company tries to help with eating healthy food, and watching their weight at the same time.

## Reactive Damage-Control Strategies

Company leaders often must react to unforeseen events, because they cannot anticipate every possible contingency. In these instances, managers must work diligently to blunt the effects of unwanted bad publicity by every means possible. Crisis management and other techniques should be designed to help the firm cope with circumstances that threaten its image. Reactive damage-control strategies include Internet interventions, crisis management programs, and impression management techniques.

**Internet interventions** are designed to combat negative word of mouth. With the rise of the popularity of the Internet, new forums for sharing negative word of mouth and spreading bad experiences have arisen, including e-mail, chat rooms, rogue Web sites, and Internet blogs. All provide an environment in which consumers from every part of the world can share horror stories. Individuals can put any information they desire on the Internet, even when it unfairly portrays certain industries, companies, or brands.

The Internet has opened an entirely new venue for people to vent emotions, which can be devastating to a company's reputation. Unfortunately, few companies monitor these communications and even fewer do anything about them. A survey by Hill & Knowlton, a public relations firm, revealed that only 16 percent of firms closely monitor the Internet, 30 percent check it periodically, and 43 percent do not watch the Web at all.[14]

Vigilant company leaders realize the power of the Internet and what it can do to an organization's reputation. These leaders make sure someone monitors what is being said. When they see messages criticizing a company unjustly or proclaiming untruths, company representatives take action. Some log into a chat room and immediately identify themselves as company representatives. They then attempt to explain the company's point of view and try to correct misconceptions. In other situations, the company's public relations department prepares public statements and press releases. Not every activity warrants formal reaction. Still, monitoring the Internet keeps the company's leadership informed about what people are saying and what they are thinking.

**Crisis management** involves either accepting the blame for an event and offering an apology or refuting those making the charges in a forceful manner. A crisis may be viewed as either a problem or an opportunity. Many times a crisis contains the potential to improve the firm's position and image. For example, when PepsiCo encountered claims that hypodermic needles were being found in its products, the management team quickly responded with photographs and video demonstrating that such an occurrence was impossible because the bottles and cans turn upside down before being filled with any soft drink. Next, footage of a con artist slipping a

Demonstrating to the public how Pepsi cans and bottles are filled was important in dealing with the crisis.
*Source:* Courtesy of Pepsi.

needle into a can was shown. This fast and powerful answer eliminated the negative publicity, and Pepsi was able, at the same time, to make a strong statement about the safety of its products. Pepsi's reaction was quite effective in dealing with this particular crisis.

Unfortunately, some company leaders manage only to make matters worse, as was the reaction of Ford and Bridgestone to the faulty tires on the new Ford Explorers. Instead of immediately seeking to correct the problem, both denied a problem existed and tried to put the blame on others. Ford CEO Jacques Nasser blamed Bridgestone/Firestone, Inc., for the tire separation problems. Bridgestone blamed consumers, saying they did not inflate the tires to the correct pressure. This finger-pointing ended Ford's 100-year relationship with Firestone. Bitter words were exchanged and the public did not buy either excuse. The outcry was so strong that both companies lost sales, suffered image damage, and eventually Nasser lost his job at Ford.[15]

An **apology strategy** is another reactive form of crisis management and damage control. If the end result of the investigation is the revelation that the firm is at fault, an apology should be offered quickly. A full apology contains five elements, as shown in Figure 12.7.[16]

Apologies are most often used either in situations in which the violation is minor or ones in which the firm or person cannot escape being found guilty. It is also a good strategy for creating a strong emotional bond with the public. It is more difficult to be angry with a company that admits a mistake was made. If people feel the apology is sincere and

| |
|---|
| 1. An expression of guilt, embarrassment, or regret |
| 2. A statement recognizing the inappropriate behavior and acceptance of sanctions for wrong behavior |
| 3. A rejection of the inappropriate behavior |
| 4. Approval of the appropriate behavior and a promise not to engage in inappropriate behavior |
| 5. An offer of compensation or penance to correct the wrong |

**FIGURE 12.7**
**Elements of an Apology Strategy**

heartfelt, they not only will forgive the company, but they may also feel more positive about the company afterwards.

The tendency to protect one's self-image is called **impression management** or "the conscious or unconscious attempt to control images that are projected in real or imagined social interactions."[17] In order to maintain or enhance self-image, individuals and corporations attempt to influence the identities they display to others. The goal is to project themselves in such a manner as to maximize access to and the visibility of positive characteristics while minimizing any negative elements.

Any event that threatens a person's self-image or desired identity is viewed as a predicament. When faced with such predicaments, individuals make concerted efforts to reduce or minimize the negative consequences. If the predicament cannot be avoided or concealed, then an individual engages in any type of remedial activity that reduces the potentially harmful consequences. Remedial tactics include expressions of innocence, excuses, justifications, and other explanations.[18]

An *expression of innocence* approach means company leaders provide information designed to convince others (clients, the media, and the government) that they were not associated with the event that caused the predicament. In other words, they say, "We didn't cause this to happen. Someone (or something) else did."

*Excuses* are explanations designed to convince the public that the firm and its leaders are not responsible for the predicament or that it could not have been foreseen. Thus, they should not be held accountable for the event that created the predicament, e.g., "It was an act of God. It was totally unavoidable."

*Justifications* involve using logic designed to reduce the degree of negativity associated with the predicament. Making the event seem minor or trivial is one method. Making the argument that the firm had to proceed in the way it did ("We pollute because if we don't we'll be out of business, and our employees will lose their jobs") is another form of justification.

*Other explanations* may be created to persuade individuals that the cause of the predicament is not a fair representation of what the firm or individual is really like. In other words, the case was the exception rather than the rule, and customers should not judge the firm too harshly as a result. You will hear comments such as "This was a singular incident, and not indicative of the way we do business."

Each company's management team, marketing department, and public relations specialist should be acutely aware of how quickly events can cause great damage to a firm's image. Both proactive and reactive measures should be used to make sure the firm survives negative publicity without major damage.

## SPONSORSHIPS AND EVENT MARKETING

To build brand loyalty and other positive feelings toward a company, many marketing leaders rely on sponsorships and event marketing. These programs make it possible to meet with prospects, customers, vendors, and others in unique situations. People who attend sponsored activities or special events already have favorable feelings about the activity taking place. These positive attitudes are easily transferred to a company that has provided funding. In this section, sponsorship programs and event marketing are described in greater detail.

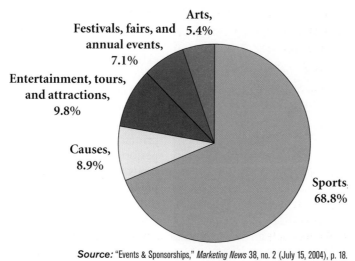

*Source:* "Events & Sponsorships," *Marketing News* 38, no. 2 (July 15, 2004), p. 18.

**FIGURE 12.8**
**Breakdown of Marketing Expenditures on Sponsorships and Events**

**Sponsorship marketing** means that the company pays money to sponsor someone, some group, or something that is part of an activity. A firm can sponsor a practically unending list of groups, individuals, activities, and events. For years, firms sponsored everything from local little league baseball and soccer teams to national musical tours, NASCAR drivers, and placing names on sports stadiums.

Approximately $9 billion a year is spent on sponsorships and events. Figure 12.8 provides a breakdown of how the money is spent. Sports represent nearly 70 percent of all sponsorships. Sporting events are highly popular and often attract large crowds. In addition to the audience attending the game or competition, many more watch on television. Popular athletes can be effective spokespersons for various products. If possible, the firm should be the exclusive sponsor of the person or team. It is much easier to be remembered if the firm is the only sponsor rather than one of multiple sponsors.

Gillette's sponsorships are a major component of the company's marketing program. Gillette spends millions of dollars each year on various sponsorships, many of which are sports-related. The company has an employee whose job description is to manage sponsorship activities. A recent Gillette sponsorship was the 2004 FIFA World Cup, combined with a $50 million global promotion featuring soccer star David Beckham. In 2003, an integrated marketing campaign featured a $20 million Gillette Young Guns Campaign musical concert tour tied with six NASCAR drivers and a sampling and couponing program at the concerts. In 2001, Gillette acquired the naming rights for the New England Patriots football stadium (Gillette Stadium) in Foxboro, Massachusetts. The team's two Super Bowl victories in 3 years added to Gillette's national following.[19]

FedEx uses sponsorships to build customer loyalty. The company sponsors many sporting events and makes sure key customers not only get to attend them but also are allowed to go into places they could not get into on their own. This includes NFL locker rooms, trackside passes at the Daytona 500, and access to famous golf courses such as Pebble Beach. These unique experiences create strong bonds with FedEx.[20] In addition, the marketing department tracks revenues from these customers before and after each event. Company figures indicate these activities generate positive revenues along with customer loyalty.

FedEx sponsors a college football bowl game (FedEx Orange Bowl), sports teams, sporting events, and sports stadiums. The company has relationships with the NFL, NBA, NASCAR, the PGA Tour, horse racing, and the NCAA. These programs create a great deal of company exposure. The FedEx Orange Bowl generates $32 million worth of TV exposure. The NASCAR sponsorship costs $16 million but generates nearly $50 million in TV exposure. More recently, FedEx became the transportation carrier for many of the company's sponsored events. FedEx ships equipment for the halftime shows for the Super Bowl and Pro Bowl. The company also ships game films to every professional football team on a weekly basis.

At 24, I became the second youngest champion in NASCAR history. Here's another little-known fact. Of the 42 drivers who chase me at more than 200 mph, most don't get enough calcium. My advice? Drink three glasses of milk a day. Preferably while standing still.

**MILK**

Where's your mustache?"

In addition to milk, notice all of the corporate sponsors listed on Jeff Gordon's uniform.
*Source:* Courtesy of Bozell Worldwide, Inc.

Some organizations have moved away from sports sponsorships toward more cultural events, such as classical music groups and jazz bands, visual art exhibits by noted painters, dance troupes, and actors for various theater performances. Cultural sponsorships are not the best match for every firm. They are most effective for products sold to affluent members of society. Consequently, financial institutions are the primary sponsors of these types of performers and performances. In the past, many institutions provided funds without receiving much recognition. Now these philanthropic efforts are being leveraged by having the name of the company strongly associated with the cultural activity. This includes printing the name of the firm on programs and regularly mentioning the brand or corporate name as being responsible for arranging for the artist to be present at the cultural event. Also, sponsors usually receive choice seats at performances that can be given to key clients.

In choosing a sponsorship, it is important to match the audience profile with the company's target market. A firm sponsoring a participant at an event attended mainly by females is best when the company's primary customers are female. Marketing executives also consider the image of the individual participant or group and how it relates to the firm's image. For instance, a contestant in an "upscale" competition, such as a beauty contest, should be sponsored by a tuxedo or formal gown company.

To maximize the benefits of a sponsorship effort, it is important to define the primary goals of the program. As with the other marketing tools, the goals of the sponsorships should be integrated with the firm's overall IMC theme. The public should easily recognize the link between the person or group being sponsored, the activity, and the company involved. To achieve the maximum impact for the sponsorship, the message should be combined with other advertising and promotional efforts, such as a sampling program or a giveaway (T-shirts, caps, etc.). Sampling is an effective method for encouraging people to try a product. Unless a sponsorship is surrounded by supporting marketing efforts, the money invested may not accomplish as much.

It may be hard to measure the impact of a sponsorship program directly. Sponsorships are designed to accomplish many different objectives for organizations. Sponsorships can be used to:

▶ Enhance a company's image.

▶ Increase a firm's visibility.

▶ Differentiate a company from its competitors.

▶ Showcase specific goods and services.

▶ Help a firm develop closer relationships with current and prospective customers.

▶ Sell excess inventory.

One company that attempted to build visibility and image through the use of a sponsorship was the Great Florida Bank of Miami. After being open for just 11 months, Great Florida signed on as a sponsor of the NBA's Miami Heat for the 2005 playoffs. Great Florida marketed itself as the "Official playoff bank of the Heat." The bank's name appeared on the team's official "Red Zone" playoff logo, on billboards, game programs, print ads, and signs inside the American Airlines Arena, where the Heat play home games. The sponsorship program may have seemed like a dangerous approach because it came with a hefty price tag. The marketing team at Great Florida Bank felt it was worth the money to gain such huge exposure in a short time period. When the team almost made the NBA finals, Great Florida Bank had received wide exposure for nearly a month, because the Heat played in numerous home playoff games.[21] Time will tell how well the sponsorship succeeded.

The best sponsorship programs include a method of assessment. The idea is to follow up to see if the goals that were set have been reached. In the case of Great Florida Bank, for example, market research could be undertaken to see how much brand awareness increased following the playoffs. In each sponsorship program, there should be an attempt to gather tangible evidence that the sponsorship is worthwhile.

## Event Marketing

Sponsoring the right event can provide a company with brand-name recognition and help develop closer ties with vendors and customers. Events can also help boost morale for the employees who participate in or attend them. Sponsoring local events such as the Special Olympics provides a company with the potential to generate free publicity. These events may also be used to enhance the company's image in the local community.

## COMMUNICATION ACTION

### Beach Volleyball's Rise

In the 1990s, professional beach volleyball became practically a sponsor's dream. What better venue than sponsoring buff, nearly naked athletes on sunny beaches competing against each other? As the decade progressed, however, the athlete-run Association of Volleyball Professionals (AVP) drifted toward bankruptcy. The association alienated athletes, television broadcast partners, and the most critical financial element, the sponsors. In stepped Leonard Amato. He purchased the AVP and immediately set out to right the ship. Under his leadership, the AVP brought back the athletes, the broadcast companies, and the sponsors.

In 2004, the Swatch women's tour totaled $2.47 million in prizes to competitors and the men's tour totaled $2.83 million in prizes. Over the years, Amato brought new sponsors on board. The new list included Nissan, Wilson, Bud Light, Paul Mitchell, McDonald's, Aquafina, Nautica, Nature Valley, Xbox, and Swatch. Other companies, such as Speedo, signed sponsorships with individual players, such as Kerri Walsh, to wear its swimwear while playing in tournaments. In addition to paying Walsh a sponsorship fee, Speedo also contributes annually to the Kerri Walsh foundation, a nonprofit organization.

To entice sponsors, the AVP offers several event sponsorship package opportunities. At the official level, the sponsor provides use of AVP marks and logos, sand-level center-court signage, extensive outer-court signage, a tent interactive display, public address announcements, on-court promotions, AVP Web site presences, and VIP hospitality passes. The lowest level of sponsorship, called the "exhibitor level," provides only a tent interactive display, public address announcements, and VIP hospitality passes.

According to AVP, beach volleyball now has 20.3 million fans, of which 51 percent became interested in the sport within the last 2 years. More than 800,000 fans attended various AVP events in 2004, an increase of 43 percent over 2003 attendance. The fan base is a highly desirable, lucrative target market for the sponsor companies. In terms of demographics, 71 percent of AVP fans are 18 to 34 years old, 51 percent are male (49% female), 84 percent attended or are currently attending college, and 70 percent have incomes greater than $50,000 a year.

**Source:** Deborah L. Vence, "Serves Them Right," *Marketing News* 39, no. 2 (February 1, 2005), pp. 13, 16; AVP (www.avp.com, May 26, 2005); "In Brief," *WWD: Women's Wear Daily* 188, no. 119 (December 8, 2004), p. 2.

The Peach Fest, held in Ruston, Louisiana, is an example of an event that can be sponsored by local companies.
*Source:* Courtesy of Sartor Associates, Inc.

Event marketing is similar to sponsorship marketing. The major difference is that sponsorship marketing involves a person, group, or team. **Event marketing** occurs when the company supports a specific event. Event marketing is closely related to *lifestyle marketing,* which is more fully described in Chapter 14. Both often include setting up a booth or display and having some type of physical presence at an event.

As is the case with sponsorships, many event marketing programs feature sports. Other events are more related to lifestyles. A rodeo sponsored by Lee Jeans or a music concert put on by a radio station are marketing events. More segmented events can also be held. A Hispanic food festival funded by a food company is event marketing, as is a health fair conducted by a local hospital (e.g., "An Affair of the Heart" wellness program sponsored by Freeman Medical Hospital).

There are several key steps to take when preparing an event. Therefore, to ensure the maximum benefit from event sponsorships, companies should:[22]

1. Determine the objective(s) of sponsoring events.
2. Match each event with customers, vendors, or employees.
3. Cross-promote the event.
4. Make sure the company is included in all event advertising and brochures.
5. Track results.
6. Evaluate the investment following the event.

The first step is to determine the *marketing objectives* to be accomplished before becoming involved in a particular event. When the objective is to reward customers, it is crucial to find an event major customers would be interested in attending. Objectives that are more internally oriented, especially those designed to get employees involved and boost morale, should be met by finding events internal members will enjoy. Many times, the goals of sponsoring an event are to: (1) help the firm maintain its market share, (2) build a stronger brand presence in the marketplace, or (3) enhance the product or firm's image.

To meet these goals means carefully selecting an event to sponsor that matches the firm's *customers, vendors,* or *employees.* Different companies will have customers who are more likely to attend certain events. Vendors and employees may also favor different events.

**Cross-promotions** are often used to boost the impact of an event marketing program. Recently, eBay partnered with Sony and Baskin-Robbins to create a unique event called "Camp eBay." During the summer months consumers are typically outdoors enjoying the warm weather and not logged onto the Internet, so eBay decided to go to consumers. Camp eBay was eBay's first attempt at event marketing. The aim was to create awareness in and to educate people who do not use eBay. The program was also designed to encourage existing buyers and sellers to be more active in the summertime.

The Camp e-Bay program began with the purchase of a refurbished school bus that was sent out on a mobile marketing tour to six high-traffic areas: the Indy 500, Country Music Fanfest, eBay Live, Taste of Chicago, the Ohio State Fair, and the Minnesota State Fair. The school bus classroom drew 52,000 people who attended 30-minute sessions on how to use eBay. Participants earned badges redeemable for prizes that were furnished by Sony and Baskin-Robbins. The prizes were worth a total of $85,000. In addition, eBay pitched tents at 20 Clear Channel Entertainment venues that hosted nearly 400 concerts. The impact of the event marketing program was that 45 percent of existing users increased their purchases leading to an overall increase in sales of 2 percent during the promotion and 9 percent after the event.[23]

Sponsoring participants in an event should insist on *placement of the company name,* logo, and other product information in every advertisement and brochure for the event. Many attendees of special events keep the program as a souvenir or as something to show others. Placing the sponsor's name and message on the program generates an ad with a long life span. The sponsoring business must work to maximize brand-name exposure by connecting the firm's name with the event's marketing program. Working closely with the event management team is vital to seeing that the sponsor's name receives prominent attention in all materials associated with the event.

Some events turn out better than others for the sponsor. To determine the best events, the marketing team should *track results.* In addition to sales, employees can monitor how many pieces of literature were given to attendees, the number of samples distributed, and the number of visitors to the sponsor's display booth. Further, marketing research can be conducted to measure brand awareness before and after the event to discover if any new brand recall or brand awareness developed.

Results and marketing information allow the business to *evaluate the investment* in the event. Company leaders and marketing managers then can decide if sponsoring a particular event was beneficial and whether to sponsor the event in coming years or similar events in the future. When Victoria's Secret launched a new brand, called "Pink," it was coupled with a unique event marketing promotion during spring break. The goal was to reach 18- to 24-year-old females. The event began when a 3-story pink box was set up on a Miami beach. Advertisements, postings, street teams of employees giving out fliers, aerial signs, signs in nearby hotels, and public relations press releases built excitement during the 5-day countdown. On March 17, 2005, 5,000 spring breakers showed up at the pink box. They were treated to a fashion show and a live concert by No Mercy. After the concert, Victoria's Secret Pink gift cards were passed out and the company hosted nightclub parties. The unique marketing event spurred sales of both the new Pink brand and other Victoria's Secret brands. The Victoria's Secret marketing team completed the evaluation stage and discovered that the Pink brand sales increase in the Miami area was huge and the other Victoria's Secret brand sales also rose dramatically.[24] As a result, the evaluation suggested the event was a major success.

Sponsorship programs are connected to a wide variety of events.

Sponsorship programs and event marketing have increased in popularity during the past decade due to their potential to reach consumers on a one-to-one basis. In the future, sponsorships and event marketing tie-ins with other media, especially the Internet, will rise. Rock concerts, boat shows, music fairs, and a wide variety of other, more specialized programs are likely to be featured by various companies. Many marketing experts believe that making contact with customers in personalized ways that do not directly involve a sales call are valuable activities. Event marketing and sponsorship programs make these contacts much easier to create.

## MARKETING COMMUNICATIONS REGULATIONS

The U.S. federal government has passed a great deal of legislation designed to keep companies from taking advantage of consumers. Various states also regulate for-profit companies and other organizations. Many of these federal and state laws are enforced by regulatory agencies. In this section, governmental actions are reviewed in the areas of legislation and regulation of company marketing practices.

### Unfair and Deceptive Marketing Practices

One of the major areas that the government regulates is unfair or deceptive marketing practices. Consumers may be misled by advertisements, mailings, corporate literature, labels, packaging, Internet Web site materials, and by oral and written statements made by salespeople. Numerous ordinances have been enacted to defend consumers from these wrongful practices. Other laws have established regulatory agencies for enforcement.

At the federal level, the *Wheeler-Lea Amendment* (1938) to Section 5 of the Federal Trade Commission Act prohibits false and misleading advertising. A firm can violate the act even when the company did not expressly intend to deceive. An advertisement or communication is deemed to be deceptive or misleading when:

---

### ETHICAL ISSUES

## Alcohol and Minors: Ethics, IMC, and the Brewing Industry

By the age of 18, the average American teen has viewed more than 100,000 beer commercials. Critics of the brewing industry and marketing agree: Many beer commercials are designed to encourage underage drinking and build brand loyalty or brand switching in a population that is not even supposed to use the product. This can lead to an addiction in a few months, because underage drinkers are less developed mentally, physically, and emotionally.

Young males are often the targets of ads prepared for baseball, football, basketball, and auto racing telecasts. Use of sexuality and social acceptance are common themes, along with humor. Recent testimony in Congress suggests the brewing industry is walking a fine line.

The questions becomes: Do a few public relations ads, such as the "Know When to Say When" campaign authorized by Budweiser and the "21 Means 21" advertisement sponsored by Coors, represent a real attempt to reduce underage drinking, or are they designed to placate the government and critics?

Drunken driving, diminished performance in school, health problems, and even death by binge drinking are all part of the problem. In the alcohol industry, as in many other circumstances, the role of public relations should be real and genuine, not just designed to keep the government away. Marketing professionals will continue to confront this issue in the coming years.

1. A substantial number of people or the "typical person" is left with a false impression or misrepresentation that relates to the product.

2. The misrepresentation induces people or the "typical person" to make a purchase.

These conditions lead to the conclusion that a violation has occurred. Both individuals and businesses can sue. In the case of a business-versus-business lawsuit, the competing firm must show either infringement of a trademark or false advertising.

## Claims Versus Puffery

Before going any further into a discussion about misleading advertising, it is important to point out that firms can use what is called puffery in advertisements and messages. **Puffery** exists when a firm makes an exaggerated statement about its goods or services. The key difference, in terms of the Federal Trade Commission (FTC) and the courts, between puffery and a *claim* is that puffery is not considered to be a *factual statement*. On the other hand, a claim is considered to be a factual statement that can be proven true or false. Firms are entitled to make puffery statements without proving them; claims must be substantiated or proven in some manner.

Terms normally associated with puffery include words such as *best, greatest,* and *finest.* Therefore, it is acceptable to state "our brand is the best" or "our signature dishes use only the finest ingredients." Courts and the regulatory agencies view these statements as puffery and believe that consumers expect firms to use them routinely in their advertisements. The Tree Top advertisement shown on the next page states that Tree Top apple juice is "twice as good." The statement is puffery and is acceptable because "twice as good" is not a factual statement that can be proven true or false. The subheadline states, "Tree Top puts 2 apples in every glass. And nothing else." This part of the ad is a claim that could be tested.

The words *best* and *better* are more vague and have recently been tested through the FTC, the National Advertising Division of the Better Business Bureau, and the courts. Papa John's use of the phrase "Better Ingredients, Better Pizza" was found to be puffery, as was the phrase "Only the best tomatoes grow up to be Hunt's."

A few years ago, Progresso used the phrase "Discover the Better Taste of Progresso" in company advertisements. The statement was challenged by Campbell's Soup Company, which argued that Progresso's "better taste" phrase was not puffery. Campbell's representatives argued that it is possible to determine if one food does taste better than other brands through the use of taste tests. The courts agreed and forced Progresso to either modify the phrase or prove that Progresso soups do taste better.[25]

Obviously quite a bit of gray area exists between puffery and a claim that must be substantiated. Consequently, lawsuits are filed and governmental agencies are forced to address complaints and suspected violations of the law. These agencies and their rulings strongly affect individual marketing practices as well as company actions.

An advertisement for Cruex using puffery.
*Source:* Courtesy of Novartus Consumer Health Inc.

# Twice as Good

*Tree Top puts 2 apples in every glass. And nothing else.*

Every delicious glass of Tree Top apple juice is made from the juice of two fresh,
Washington state apples. Nothing added (not a single granule of sugar). And nothing taken
away. It's simply pure apple juice. Pasteurized. And naturally sweetened by the sun.

An advertisement for Tree Top apple juice
with the claim that it is "Twice as Good."
**Source:** Courtesy of Tree Top Inc.

## Governmental Regulatory Agencies

Numerous governmental agencies serve as watchdogs to monitor for potential violations of the law, some of which are only partially related to marketing. For example, the Food and Drug Administration (FDA) regulates and oversees the packaging and labeling of products. The FDA also monitors advertising on food packages and advertisements for drugs, yet its primary responsibilities are ensuring food quality and drug safety.

The Federal Communications Commission (FCC) regulates television, radio, and the telephone industry. The primary responsibility of the FCC is to grant (and revoke) operating licenses for radio and television stations. The FCC also has jurisdiction over telephone companies. The FCC does not have jurisdiction over the content of advertisements transmitted by mass media. Further, the FCC does not control which products may be advertised. The organization is, however, responsible for monitoring advertising directed toward children. Under FCC rules, TV stations are limited to 12 minutes per hour of children's advertisements during weekdays and 10 minutes per hour on weekends. Recently, Viacom agreed to pay $1 million for programming on Nickelodeon that violated the time limitation 600 times in the span of 1 year. Under the same FCC investigation, Walt Disney Company agreed to pay $500,000 for children's commercials that aired beyond the time limit on its ABC Family Channel.[26]

The U.S. Postal Service (USPS) has jurisdiction over all mailed marketing materials. The USPS also investigates mail fraud schemes and other fraudulent marketing practices. The Bureau of Alcohol, Tobacco and Firearms (ATF) rules when the sale, distribution, and advertising of alcohol and tobacco are at issue. Ordinarily, the governmental agency that examines incidents involving deceptive or misleading marketing tactics is the Federal Trade Commission (FTC). These agencies are listed in Figure 12.9. The next section examines the FTC in greater detail.

## THE FEDERAL TRADE COMMISSION

The federal agency that presides over marketing communications is the **Federal Trade Commission**, or FTC, which was created in 1914 by the passage of the Federal Trade Commission Act. The act's original intent was to create an agency to enforce antitrust laws and protect businesses from one another. It had little authority over advertising and marketing communications except when an advertisement would be considered unfair to the competition and therefore restrict free trade.

In 1938, Congress passed the Wheeler-Lea Amendment to increase and expand the authority of the FTC. The agency then had the ability to stop unfair or deceptive advertising

---

▶ **Food and Drug Administration (FDA)**

▶ **Federal Communications Commission (FCC)**

▶ **U.S. Postal Service (USPS)**

▶ **Bureau of Alcohol, Tobacco and Firearms (ATF)**

▶ **Federal Trade Commission (FTC)**

**FIGURE 12.9**
**Government Regulatory Agencies**

practices and to levy fines when necessary. The law also granted the FTC access to the courts to enforce the law and ensure that violators abide by FTC rulings.

## How Investigations Begin

Various types of complaints can trigger an FTC investigation. These include problems noticed by:

▶ Consumers

▶ Businesses

▶ Congress

▶ The media

Each can raise questions about what appears to be an unfair or deceptive practice. Most investigations by the FTC are confidential at first, which protects the agency and the company being investigated. When members of the FTC believe a law has been violated, a **consent order** is issued. If company leaders sign the consent order, they agree to stop the disputed practice without admitting guilt. Most FTC investigations end with the signing of a consent order.

An example of this process involves the "Ab Force" belt produced by TELEBrands Corporation. The Ab Force is an electronic belt that was advertised to stimulate the abdominal muscles and provide a full workout, with no exercise required. The ad further promised weight and fat loss as well as firm and sculpted muscles simply by wearing the belt and doing no other exercises or diet modifications. The FTC found these claims false and misleading, and in a consent agreement TELEBrands agreed to stop making such false advertising claims about the Ab Force belt.[27]

If a consent agreement cannot be reached, the FTC issues an **administrative complaint**. At that point a formal proceeding similar to a court trial is held before an administrative law judge. Both sides submit evidence and render testimony. At the end of the administrative hearing, the judge makes a ruling. If the judge feels a violation of the law has occurred, a *cease and desist order* is prepared. The order requires the company to stop the disputed practice immediately and refrain from similar practices in the future. If the company is not satisfied with the initial decision of the administrative law judge, the case can be appealed to the full FTC commission.

The *full commission* holds hearings similar to those before administrative law judges. Rulings are made after hearing evidence and testimony. Companies not satisfied with the ruling of the full FTC commission can appeal the case to the U.S. Court of Appeals and further to the highest level, the U.S. Supreme Court. The danger for companies that appeal cases is that consumer redress can be sought at that point. This means companies found guilty of violating laws can be ordered to pay civil penalties.

## Courts and Legal Channels

Occasionally, the FTC uses the court system to stop unfair and deceptive advertising and communications practices. This occurs when a company violates previous FTC cease and desist orders or when the actions of a company are so severe that immediate action is needed. The latter situation was the case involving the National Consumer Council (NCC), a debt reduction and negotiation firm based in Santa Ann, California. The FTC investigation found that the National Consumer Council encouraged consumers to stop paying their debts once they signed up with NCC for debt reduction. At the same time, NCC did not normally start negotiation with debtors for 6 months. By then, the customer's debtors were irate and not willing to negotiate. In the meantime, the NCC customer had been making payments into a fund at NCC. Charges and monthly fees were being withdrawn for payment to NCC. Many customers did not know NCC was making the charges. Eventually, the customers discovered that not only did NCC ruin their credit ratings, but they were also deeper in debt than when they signed on. Almost all of them were forced to declare bankruptcy. Due to the severity of

NCC's activities, the FTC obtained a restraining order from a federal court to immediately close NCC's operation. The FTC also obtained a restraining order against the London Financial Group, which provided telemarketing, accounting, and management services to NCC.[28]

The FTC also works with other legal entities, such as state and federal attorneys general. The FTC, Orange County (CA) district attorney, and the California State Attorney investigated Body Wise International, Inc., for false and deceptive advertising and for violating a consent agreement between Body Wise International and the FTC that was made in 1995. The complaint against Body Wise involved the alleged medical benefits of a product called "AI/E-10." Body Wise International advertised that AI/E-10 could prevent, treat, and cure diseases such as cancer, HIV/AIDS, and asthma. Body Wise supported these claims through the expert testimony of a physician, Dr. Stoff. The FTC investigation revealed that Stoff was receiving royalties from every bottle that was sold and that he did not have sound, medical substantiation for any of the claims being made. The FTC order not only banned Body Wise International from making such claims, but it also prohibited Stoff from misrepresenting the existence of tests and studies concerning AI/E-10. In the final settlement, Body Wise International agreed to pay $2 million to the FTC in civil penalties and $1.5 million in civil penalties to the State of California. Further, the final agreement contained a $358,000 monetary judgment against Dr. Stoff.[29]

## Corrective Advertising

In more severe instances of deceptive or misleading advertising, the FTC can order a firm to prepare **corrective advertisements**. These rare situations occur only when the members of the FTC believe that discontinuing a false advertisement is not a sufficient remedy. When the FTC concludes that consumers believed the false advertisement, it can require the firm to produce corrective ads to bring consumers back to a neutral state. The goal is for consumers to once again hold beliefs they had prior to the false or misleading advertisement.

A few years ago, the FTC ordered corrective advertising in a judgment against Novartis Corporation. The judgment was based on false and deceptive advertisements of a product called Doan's analgesic. During the investigation, members of the FTC concluded that Doan's claim of greater efficiency than competing products was not properly substantiated. The FTC ordered Novartis to immediately cease comparative advertising and to make the following statement in corrective ads: "Although Doan's is an effective pain reliever, there is no evidence that Doan's is more effective than other pain relievers for back pain." Novartis was ordered to spend $8 million advertising the statement and include it for 1 year in all advertisements, except for 15-second broadcast ads. Unhappy with the order, leaders at Novartis filed a lawsuit in federal court against the FTC, but the federal court upheld the FTC order.[30]

## Trade Regulation Rulings

The final type of action the FTC takes is called a **trade regulation ruling**, which applies to an entire industry in a case of unfair or deceptive practices. Normally the commission holds a public hearing and accepts both oral and written arguments. The commission then makes a ruling that applies to every firm within an industry. As with other FTC rulings, decisions can be challenged in the U.S. Court of Appeals.

In 1984 and again in 1994, the FTC investigated pricing practices within the funeral home industry and subsequently issued a trade regulation ruling. The ruling requires funeral homes to provide an itemized list of funeral goods and services that state both the price and a detailed description of the good or service. As part of the itemization, the ruling requires all funeral homes to disclose the following four statements to consumers: (1) Consumers have the right to select only the goods and services they desire. (2) Embalming is not always required by law. (3) Individuals desiring cremation of a loved one can use alternative containers for the remains. (4) The only fee a consumer can be required to pay is the nondeclinable basic service fee. A trade regulation ruling is designed to keep firms in industries from conspiring or colluding to become involved in the kinds of misleading or deceptive practices that also occur in individual companies.

## Substantiation of Marketing Claims

FTC rules cover every aspect of marketing communications. Regardless of the type of communication, the FTC prohibits unfair or deceptive marketing communications. Marketers must be able to substantiate claims through competent and reliable evidence. If companies use endorsers, these statements must be truthful and represent their experiences or opinions. If they use expert endorsements, these statements must be based on legitimate tests performed by experts in the field. All claims must reflect the typical experience that a customer would expect to encounter from the use of a good or service, unless the advertisement clearly and prominently states otherwise. Kleenex used actual touch tests by consumers as evidence that its brand was softer. The company then used engineering or lab tests to show that Kleenex tissue is made with 24 percent more cottony, soft fiber.

One of the keys to FTC evaluations of advertisements and marketing communications is the idea of **substantiation**. Firms such as Kleenex must be able to substantiate (i.e., prove or "back up") any claims made. Failure to do so can result in some form of FTC action. Substantiation is not always easy. To increase the probability the substantiation will be accepted by the FTC and courts, company leaders can use the following principles.[31]

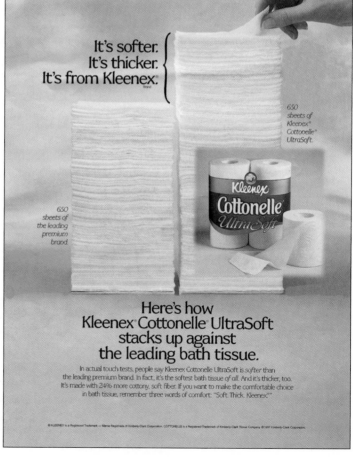

An advertisement by Kleenex Cottonelle using a substantiated claim.
*Source:* Courtesy of Kimberly-Clark Corporation. The illustrated advertisement, all copyrights thereto and rights to the trademarks appearing therein are the property of Kimberly-Clark Corporation and used with its permission.

1. The federal government assumes consumers read ads broadly and don't pay much attention to fine print and qualifying language. Thus, hiding a qualifier at the bottom of the ad or using words such as *usually, normally,* or *under typical situations* somewhere in the ad is not normally accepted as substantiation.

2. The evidence has to be for the exact product being tested, not for a similar product, regardless of the similarity.

3. Evidence should come from or be accepted by experts in the relevant area of the product, and would be considered valid and reliable by the experts. Studies conducted by the company or something found on the Internet is not acceptable.

4. The FTC and courts will consider the totality of the evidence. If the company has one study that supports the claim but there are four studies by other independent organizations that indicate something different, then the evidence will not be accepted as valid substantiation.

Kentucky Fried Chicken (KFC) signed a consent agreement with the FTC concerning two ads the FTC investigated and believed were not adequately substantiated. In the first, the FTC held that KFC made false claims in an advertisement that stated eating two Original Recipe fried chicken breasts had less fat than the Burger King Whopper. It was true that the chicken did have slightly less total fat and saturated fat than the BK Whopper; however, the chicken had more than three times the trans fat and cholesterol, more than twice the sodium, and had more calories. Thus, to the FTC the claim was inadequately substantiated. In the second ad, Kentucky Fried Chicken claimed that one

FIGURE 12.10
Industry Regulation

> ▶ **Better Business Bureau**
> ▶ **National Advertising Division (NAD)**
> ▶ **National Advertising Review Board (NARB)**

Original Recipe chicken breast had only 11 grams of carbohydrates and 40 grams of protein, compatible with a "low carbohydrate" weight-loss program. The FTC found the ad misleading because the "low carbohydrate" weight-loss programs such as the Atkins Diet and the South Beach Diet specifically recommend against eating breaded, fried foods.[32]

## INDUSTRY REGULATION OF NEGATIVE MARKETING PRACTICES

It is clear that federal regulatory agencies cannot oversee all industry activities. Although various industry regulatory agencies have no legal power, they can reduce the load on the FTC and the legal system. Many allegations or complaints about unfair and deceptive advertising and marketing communication are handled and settled within the industry system. Although each industry has its own system of regulating marketing communications, the three most common are: (1) the Better Business Bureau, (2) the National Advertising Division, and (3) the National Advertising Review Board (Figure 12.10).

The Better Business Bureau is a resource available to both consumers and businesses. Consumers and firms can file complaints with the bureau about unethical business practices or unfair treatment. The bureau compiles a summary of all charges leveled against individual firms. Customers seeking information about the legitimacy of a company or its operations can contact the bureau. The bureau gives them a carefully worded report that will raise cautionary flags when a firm has received a great number of complaints and reveals the general nature of customer concerns. The Better Business Bureau is helpful to individuals and businesses that want to make sure they are dealing with a firm that has a low record of problems.

Complaints about advertising or some aspect of marketing communications are referred to the National Advertising Division (NAD) of the Better Business Bureau for review. The role of the NAD is to discover the real issue. The NAD collects information and evaluates data concerning the complaint to determine whether the advertiser's claim is substantiated. If it is not, the NAD negotiates with the business to modify or discontinue the advertisement. If the firm's marketing claim is substantiated, then the complaint is dismissed.

Individuals and companies both can file complaints about unfair ads. Sometimes,

The NAD would expect statements such as "half the carbs of Bud Light" to be supported by data.
*Source:* Courtesy Miller Brewing Company.

however, they do not receive the ruling they are seeking. For example, Verizon Wireless filed a complaint with the NAD concerning an advertisement by Nextel Communications, Inc., that promoted a $50 Direct Connect "Free Incoming" plan that included "Unlimited Push to Talk Walkie-Talkie" calls "Across Jersey and Across the Country." The NAD's role in such a case is to investigate the marketing claim for substantiation. In the view of the NAD, Nextel was able to support the marketing claims made in the Direct Connect advertisement. The NAD did recommend, however, that Nextel modify its pricing information to "more accurately explain the services that are included in the monthly fees in a clear and conspicuous manner."[33]

The Nextel decision was a somewhat atypical NAD recommendation. In the majority of cases, the NAD concludes that the advertisement being investigated is false or misleading and that it should either be modified or halted. Of the 118 cases heard in 2004, the NAD ruled that cases were not properly substantiated in 65 cases. Only in six of the cases did the NAD rule the ad was fully substantiated.[34]

When a complaint is not resolved by the NAD or the advertiser appeals the NAD's decision, it goes to the National Advertising Review Board (NARB). The NARB is composed of advertising professionals and prominent civic individuals. If the NARB rules that the firm's advertisements are not substantiated, it then orders the firm to discontinue the advertisements. This is very similar to the consent order by the FTC, but is issued by this private advertising board. If the business firm being accused refuses to accept the NARB ruling, then the matter is turned over to the FTC or an appropriate federal regulatory agency.

The NARB has been involved in numerous business-versus-business disputes. For instance, Minute Maid orange juice was ordered to modify its ads because the ad copy claimed that consumers preferred Minute Maid to Tropicana by a 2:1 margin. Tropicana originally lodged the complaint about the ad and won when it was heard by the NAD. Minute Maid disagreed with the NAD ruling and appealed to the NARB. Minute Maid complained that the decision by the NAD placed an unnecessary and unfair burden on comparative advertising because all claims relative to a competitor must be substantiated. The NARB supported the NAD decision and forced Minute Maid to comply with the ruling.[35]

The NARB seldom refers a case to the Federal Trade Commission. In fact, such an action has been taken only four times in the last 25 years. The last was a case dealing with Winn-Dixie, which made direct price comparisons with competitors. The NARB found that Winn-Dixie was using prices that were sometimes up to 90 days old. The NARB ruled that any price comparisons made in an advertisement by Winn-Dixie must use prices that are no more than 7 days old. The decision to forward the case to the FTC was made when Winn-Dixie refused to modify its ads and accept the NARB ruling.[36]

These industry-based actions are designed to control the marketing communications environment and prevent legal actions by either the courts or a regulatory agency. Effective management, however, should become proactive rather than reactive. Company leaders should work to create an image of a socially responsible firm rather than a firm that must constantly be watched by consumers and regulatory agencies.

An advertisement for Progresso Soups.
*Source:* Courtesy of General Mills, Inc.

THIS SOUP'S GOT FEWER NET CARBS THAN THE CRACKERS FLOATING ON TOP.

INTRODUCING PROGRESSO CARB MONITOR™ SOUPS, WITH 6-7g NET CARBS* PER SERVING.
Discover Progresso's Carb Monitor™ soups: Chicken Vegetable, Beef Vegetable, Chicken Cheese Enchilada Style, and Tuscan-Style Meatball. They're a great way to cut the carbs without cutting the taste.

# SUMMARY

The public relations department plays a major role in an integrated marketing communications program, whether the department is separate from marketing or combined as part of a communications division. Public relations efforts are primarily oriented to making sure that every possible contact point delivers a positive and unified message on behalf of the company. This includes assessing a corporation's reputation and involvement in socially responsible activities.

There are many stakeholders inside and surrounding a company. Any person or group that has a vested interest in the organization's activities is a stakeholder. Internal stakeholders include employees, unions, and stockholders. External publics include members of the marketing channel, customers, the media, the local community, financial institutions, the government, and special-interest groups.

To reach all intended audiences, the public relations department has a series of tools available. These include company newsletters, internal messages, public relations releases, correspondence with stockholders, annual reports, and various special events. Even the bulletin board in the company's break room can be used to convey messages to internal stakeholders.

In the attempt to build a favorable image of the company, the public relations department develops special events such as altruistic activities and cause-related marketing programs. Due care must be given to making certain that these acts are not perceived with cynicism and skepticism. This means being certain that any good deed matches with company products and other marketing efforts. A natural fit between an altruistic event and the company's brand is more readily accepted by various members of the public.

Sponsorship programs enhance and build the company's image and brand loyalty. A sponsorship of an individual or group involved in some kind of activity—whether it is a sporting event, a contest, or a performance by an artistic group—can be used to link the company's name with the popularity of the player involved. Sponsorships should match with the firm's products and brands.

Event marketing occurs when a firm sponsors an entire event. A strong physical presence at the event is one of the keys to successfully linking an organization's name with a program. To do so, the firm must determine the major objective of the event sponsorship, match it with company customers and publics, and make sure the firm's name is prominently displayed on the literature accompanying the event.

Managing public relations, sponsorships, and event marketing programs requires company leaders to carefully assess both the goals and the outcomes of individual activities. A cost–benefit approach may not always be feasible, but the marketing team should be able to track some form of change, whether it is increased inquiries, the number of samples passed out at an event, or a shift in the tenor of news articles about the organization. The primary task of public relations is to be the organization's "watchdog," making sure those who come in contact with the company believe the firm is working to do things right and to do the right things.

The public relations team is also responsible for damage control when negative publicity arises. Both proactive and reactive tactics are available to maintain a positive image for the company. Damage control tactics include Internet interventions, crisis management programs, and impression management techniques.

To enforce fair standards in the areas of advertising and marketing communications, a number of governmental agencies are ready to take action when needed. These include the Federal Trade Commission, Food and Drug Administration, Federal Communications Commission, and others. Each tries to keep unfair marketing activities from taking place. The FTC is the primary agency assigned marketing communications and gives special effort to stopping instances of unfair or deceptive practices. In conjunction with the courts, the FTC and other governmental agencies regulate the majority of companies and industries in the United States. The FTC regulates cases of fraudulent practices targeted at individual consumers as well as conflicts between businesses. Through the use of consent orders, administrative complaints, cease and desist orders, and full commission hearings, the FTC is able to make its findings and rulings known to the parties concerned. Court actions and corrective advertising programs are utilized in more severe cases. Trade regulation rulings apply when an entire industry is guilty of an infraction.

The public relations department deals with the negative impression created by bad press. It therefore makes sense to avoid FTC investigations and to quickly make any changes demanded by the FTC rather than drag things out and create long-term damage to a firm's image and reputation.

# REVIEW QUESTIONS

1. Describe the role of the public relations department. How is it related to the marketing department? Should both departments be called the "department of communications"? Why or why not?

2. What is a stakeholder?

3. Name the major internal stakeholders in organizations. Describe their interests in the company.

4. Name the major external stakeholders in organizations. Describe the major interest in the company of each one.

5. What is social responsibility? How is it related to public relations activities?

6. What is cause-related marketing? How can company leaders create effective cause-related marketing programs?

7. What is green marketing? How do different companies promote environmentally friendly activities?

8. Name and briefly describe two proactive prevention strategies companies can use to create a positive image.

9. What reactive damage-control techniques are available to the public relations team?

10. What four forms of impression management are used to combat negative events?

**11.** What is sponsorship marketing? Name a pro athlete, musician or musical group, and performer of some other type who has been featured in a sponsorship program. Was the program effective or ineffective? Why?

**12.** Describe an event marketing program. What must accompany the event in order to make it a success?

**13.** What are cross-promotions? How are they related to event marketing programs?

**14.** When does an ad or message become false or misleading?

**15.** What is puffery? Should a company use a great deal of puffery in its ads? Why or why not?

**16.** What roles does the FCC play in marketing communication?

**17.** What role does the U.S. Postal Service play in marketing communication?

**18.** What are the steps of the process when the Federal Trade Commission investigates a claim of false or misleading advertising?

**19.** What is a consent agreement?

**20.** What is a trade regulation ruling? How is it different from other FTC rulings?

**21.** What does the term *substantiation* mean? How does a company know it has met the substantiation test in an advertisement?

## KEY TERMS

**public relations (PR) department** A unit in the firm that manages items such as publicity and other communications with all of the groups that make contact with the company.

**hit** The mention of a company's name in a news story.

**stakeholder** A person or group that has a vested interest in a firm's activities and well-being.

**social responsibility** The obligation an organization has to be ethical, accountable, and reactive to the needs of society.

**cause-related marketing** Matching marketing efforts with some type of charity work or program.

**green marketing** The development and promotion of products that are environmentally safe.

**damage control** Reacting to negative events caused by a company error, consumer grievances, or unjustified or exaggerated negative press.

**entitlings** Attempts to claim responsibility for positive outcomes of events.

**enhancements** Attempts to increase the desirable outcome of an event in the eyes of the public.

**Internet interventions** Confronting negative publicity on the Internet, either in Web site news releases or by entering chat rooms.

**crisis management** Either accepting the blame for an event and offering an apology or refuting those making the charges in a forceful manner.

**apology strategy** Presenting a full apology when the firm has made an error.

**impression management** The conscious or unconscious attempt to control images that are projected in real or imagined social situations.

**sponsorship marketing** When the company pays money to sponsor someone or some group that is participating in an activity.

**event marketing** When a company pays money to sponsor an event or program.

**cross-promotion** A tie-in between a company's product and an event.

**puffery** When a firm makes an exaggerated claim about its products or services without making an overt attempt to deceive or mislead.

**Federal Trade Commission** A federal agency that regulates marketing communications.

**consent order** A directive that is issued when the FTC believes a violation has occurred.

**administrative complaint** A formal proceeding similar to a court trial held before an administrative law judge regarding a charge filed by the FTC.

**corrective advertisements** Ads that bring consumers back to a neutral state, so consumers once again hold beliefs they had prior to being exposed to a false or misleading advertisement.

**trade regulation ruling** Findings that implicate an entire industry in a case of unfair or deceptive practices.

**substantiation** Firms must be able to prove or back up any claims made in their marketing communications.

## CRITICAL THINKING EXERCISES

### Discussion Questions

**1.** Watch the news on television or read your local paper for news about a local or national business. Was the report positive or negative toward the firm? Did the news report affect your attitude toward the company? Watch one of the many special investigative shows, such as *60 Minutes*. What companies did it investigate? If you were the firm being featured, what would you do to counteract the bad press?

**2.** The public relations officer for a small but highly respected bank in a local community was charged with sexual harassment by a female employee. What type of communications should be prepared for each of the constituencies listed in Figure 12.2? Which of the constituencies would be the most important to contact?

3. How important is the local community for a manufacturing firm that sells 99 percent of its products outside the area? Does it really matter what the local people say or believe about the manufacturer as long as the firm's customers are happy?

4. What causes do you support or are special to you? Do you know which corporations sponsor or support the causes? If not, see if you can find literature or Web sites that contain that information. Why do you think the corporations choose a particular cause to support? What benefits do corporations receive from sponsorships?

5. When Starbucks opened its first coffee shop inside a public library, 10 percent of all proceeds from coffee sold there went to support the operation of the library. Do you think a public library should allow a for-profit organization such as Starbucks to sell products inside the building? Is this a conflict of interest for governmentally sponsored organizations such as libraries? What if the local doughnut shop wanted to sell doughnuts at the library? Should it be allowed to do so? How does a library manager decide?

6. Managers often are the most difficult group for the public relations department to reach. To entice employees to reach departmental goals, managers often communicate using memos or verbal messages. These messages may conflict with the IMC theme. For example, in an effort to trim costs, a manager may send a memo to all employees telling them to use only standard production procedures. Through verbal communications, employees learn that anyone caught violating or even bending the policy to satisfy a customer will be immediately reprimanded. The manager's action suggests that even though he wants employees to provide customer service, in actuality, they had better not do anything that is not authorized. Employees soon get the message that management cares only about costs, not the customer. Employees will perceive any advertising message about customer service as a big joke. Write a memo to employees that supports the IMC goal of high customer service, yet alerts them to the need to follow standard operating procedures. Is there anything else you would do to ensure that this is not a conflicting message being sent to employees?

7. Baskin-Robbins recently utilized public relations efforts to reach potential new franchise operators. In each market targeted for expansion, Baskin-Robbins prepared news releases announcing plans to open a specified number of stores. These news articles normally appeared in the business section of the local newspapers, often on the front page. The news articles contained more details than the classified ads that Baskin-Robbins used to attract franchise operators.[37] What advantage does Baskin-Robbins gain by combining the articles with the ads? Why would newspapers print an article about Baskin-Robbins wanting to open franchises? Is this really newsworthy information?

# INTEGRATED LEARNING EXERCISES

1. Although some firms handle public relations activities internally, many firms retain public relations firms to work on special projects and to handle unique situations. The Public Relations Society of America (PRSA) is one of the major associations for PR individuals. In Canada, the primary association is the Canadian Public Relations Society. Access the Web sites of these two organizations at www.prsa.org and www.cprs.ca. What type of information is available? What types of services are offered? How would these organizations be beneficial to various companies?

2. *PRWeek* magazine is an excellent publication. Access the online version at www.prweek.net. What type of information is available? How would this site be valuable to a PR individual? How could it be used by a firm seeking a public relations agency?

3. Cause-related marketing is an important component of IMC programs. Access the Cause Related Marketing (CRM) Web site for the United Kingdom at www.crm.org.uk. Access the various components of the Web site to learn what is available. What type of information is provided? How can this site be used? By whom?

4. For a different perspective on cause-related marketing, access the National Charities Information Bureau (NCIB) at www.give.org. The mission of this Web site is to inspire responsible, informed giving by corporations to charities. What type of information is available and who would use it?

5. Event marketing is used by many organizations to accomplish various objectives. Access the following companies that assist firms with event marketing. What type of services does each offer? What is your evaluation of each of the companies?
   a. Advantage International, LLC (www.advantage-intl.com)
   b. Pierce Promotions and Event Management, Inc. (www.ppem.com)
   c. RPMC Event and Promotion Agency (www.rpmc.com)

6. Corporate sponsorships are very important to not-for-profit organizations. Without their financial assistance, many causes would not exist. Look up two organizations from the following list of not-for-profit organizations. Who are their corporate sponsors? What benefits do the profit-seeking companies receive from these sponsorships?
   a. American Cancer Society (www.cancer.org)
   b. Arthritis Foundation (www.arthritis.org)
   c. Multiple Sclerosis Society (www.mssociety.org.uk)
   d. United Cerebral Palsy (www.ucp.org)
   e. Alliance for the Wild Rockies (www.wildrockies alliance.org)
   f. National Wildlife Federation (www.nwf.org)
   g. Trout Unlimited (www.tu.org)

7. The Federal Trade Commission is the primary federal agency that oversees advertising and other marketing-related communications. Access the Web site at www.ftc.gov. What type of information is available at the Web site for consumers? For businesses? Access the "Formal Actions" portion of the Web site and locate a recent case you find interesting. What was investigated and what was the final decision of the FTC?

# STUDENT PROJECT

## IMC Plan Pro

A successful IMC program includes making sure that every aspect of the firm's reputation is considered. Public relations programs should assist the marketing team in creating and sending a consistent message about the company's products and its good intentions. Using the IMC Plan Pro disk and booklet available from Prentice Hall will help you establish positive media relations and create targeted sponsorships and events that reach the right people with the right message.

# CASE 1

## CAN THIS RESTAURANT BE SAVED?

If there is any one industry in which word-of-mouth can do great damage in a hurry, that industry would be food service, especially restaurants. A single round of food poisoning can drive away customers for months. Any tale of contamination or unsanitary conditions that circulates in a local community creates a major crisis for a restaurant owner.

Juan and Bonita Gonzales knew the risks when they opened their new restaurant, The Mexican Villa, in a small shopping center in North Canton, Ohio. With the recent wave of Mexican immigrants to the area, two other successful Mexican restaurants had opened across town. The couple believed that if they provided high-quality food in a pleasant atmosphere, their restaurant could succeed.

The business opened in the fall of 2003. First-year sales were better than expected. A mixture of Hispanic and Caucasian customers regularly dined at The Mexican Villa. The restaurant had two distinct serving areas: the dining room and the cantina. In the dining room, authentic Mexican music played softly in the background. There was plenty of room between tables. The floors were carpeted and clean. Servers were dressed in bright colored clothing and were carefully trained to be pleasant, efficient, and helpful. In the cantina the music was louder. The floors were tile. Smoking was permitted in a bar-type atmosphere. Television sets were tuned to sports programs. In both areas, customers were quickly greeted and served salsa and chips at no charge. The menu was the same for both areas.

Both the cantina and the dining room had regular customers who ate at the Villa as often as once a week. The Villa also had a strong luncheon business, where a lighter menu with lower prices was featured. The restaurant was near a business district and shopping center, which provided access to many potential lunch guests.

The crisis occurred after The Mexican Villa had been open for 15 months. In the spring of 2005, one of the Villa food preparers contracted an infectious case of hepatitis. Hepatitis is highly contagious and dangerous. The local health authorities discovered the problem and forced the Villa to close for 7 days. Word was sent out in the newspaper, on the radio, and on the local television news that anyone who had eaten at the Villa in the past 2 weeks should contact the governmental health authorities to be tested. Word spread quickly through North Canton about the episode both in the Spanish-speaking community and to other groups.

Fortunately, no one was infected. The employee had worn protective gloves while preparing food. The safety precautions used at the restaurant had kept the disease from spreading to others.

Juan and Bonita had a limited budget for advertising. Once the news stories had run, the media quickly lost interest. It was impossible for the couple to capture the same audience to tell people that the health crisis had passed. The number of customers who returned after the week long closure dropped dramatically. Sales had been down for more than a month. The couple began to wonder if people would ever come back.

1. What kinds of public relations tactics should be used to help The Mexican Villa?

2. Is there any kind of cause-related or event marketing program that might bring people back to the restaurant?

3. Do you believe The Mexican Villa can be saved, or is it a lost cause? Why?

# CASE 2

## FOURTH OF JULY MARKETING: MORE FIREWORKS THAN THEY NEEDED

Station manager Jim Jefferson decided it was time to pull the plug. For the past 12 years, his television station (KSNN) had proudly sponsored the local annual Fourth of July Festival. Until recently, the event had been a solid promotional marketing tool that generated sales and goodwill for a variety of vendors. Now, however, Jim believed the hassles had begun to outweigh the benefits.

The first KSNN Fourth of July Festival was a modest affair. One sponsor, a dynamite factory located in the community, chipped in money for a small fireworks display, and the local college allowed the event to be held in an open area of the campus. As time passed, the scale and scope had grown into the single largest attraction in the area each year.

First, corporate sponsors were added. Each provided funding for various aspects of the program. Some paid for the actual fireworks and were rewarded with the company's logo lit up in a display to start each year's show. Other sponsors kicked in money so that relatively famous entertainers could be brought in. Local vendors paid money to sell food and drinks during the course of the event.

When the event initially began, the festivities started at about 7:00 P.M. with only a fireworks display. As the show evolved, the gates were opened at 2:00 P.M., and programs started around 4:00 P.M., led by a welcoming proclamation from the mayor. Bands played, local choirs sang patriotic songs, parachute jumpers swooped into the arena. The local college opened its football stadium to accommodate parking, seating, restroom facilities, and other amenities.

KSNN developed a tie-in with an area radio station. Beginning in the sixth year of the event, the fireworks were set up in time with music piped through stadium speakers with a simulcast on the radio. KSNN even broke into network programming to provide pictures of the fireworks show for the city.

The event generated a considerable amount of money for KSNN. Sponsors were required to buy ads promoting the event for 2 weeks prior to the Fourth of July weekend. The college was given free advertising time throughout the year in exchange for opening its facilities. By the 10th year, nearly 40,000 people were at or near the school, seeing the ads and visiting the booths and displays set up by the various sponsors.

KSNN also benefited from the football stadium setup. Key sponsors and their guests were given seats inside the air-conditioned press box during the day. KSNN served food and drinks to these individuals as part of their pampered exposure to the show. The guests could then move to the roof of the press box when the actual fireworks display took place. The school's president was thrilled to be able to schmooze with major corporations in the area each year and in fact had generated donations to the college based on these relationships.

Unfortunately, in the 11th year, vandalism associated with the event reached an all-time high. The school's football field, which was made of AstroTurf, was badly damaged by hoodlums who infested the event. Traffic jams caused so many problems that the local police department began asking to be reimbursed for all the overtime it was forced to pay to keep officers on duty to direct traffic and solve other problems.

Also, some of the sponsors began to object to the rising fees they were being charged to be associated with the event. KSNN's revenues had risen, but the station was also paying higher expenses each year.

The tide turned when the college rejected KSNN's bid to return for a 13th show. The president reported that replacing the football field surface made it too cost prohibitive for the college to be involved. KSNN was forced to move the event to a local city golf course, over the objections of golfers and

(continued)

several members of the city council, who feared destruction of the greens, fairways, and tee-boxes would be a major expense.

In the same year, two sponsors dropped out, citing costs as their key concerns. Food and drink vendors expressed frustrations that they would not have good places to set up to sell products, and the remaining sponsors balked at bad locations for their booths. Many attendees had to ride shuttle buses to get close enough to see the show, and they completely bypassed the booths on the ride.

The growing number of headaches with the city, sponsors, and others caused the local newspaper to write articles about problems the show created. Jim decided the negative publicity was not what his station needed.

Following intense negotiations, KSNN withdrew after the show. Another local television station took over sponsorship of the event, but pared it down to a simple fireworks display at a local auto racetrack, to be held in conjunction with a day of racing.

1. Did KSNN wait too long before pulling out? Should the company's leaders have tried to solve the problems on their own, rather than just giving up?

2. What benefits accrued to KSNN, the sponsors, and the college when the show was going well?

3. Do you think the college was wise to withdraw from the show? Why or why not?

# ENDNOTES

1. George Anders, "eBay Learns to Trust Again," *Fast Company*, no. 53 (December 2001), pp. 102–107; Steve Smith, "eBay's Whitman Shares Opinions on Web at Annual CEA Dinner," *This Week in Consumer Electronics* 17, no. 3 (January 28, 2002), pp. 1–2; "Meg Whitman," *BusinessWeek*, no. 3631 (May 31, 1999), p. 134.

2. Jenny Dawkins, "Corporate Responsibility: The Communication Challenge," *Journal of Communication Management* 9, no. 2 (November 2004), pp. 106–117.

3. "Random Sample," *Marketing News* 38 (August 15, 2004), p. 3.

4. Ronald J. Alsop, "Corporate Reputation: Anything But Superficial—The Deep But Fragile Nature of Corporate Reputation," *Journal of Business Strategy* 25, no. 6 (2004), pp. 21–30.

5. "Consumers Back Companies on CSR," *Business & the Environment with ISO 14000 Updates* 16, no. 4 (April 2005), pp. 9–10.

6. Brad Edmondson, "New Keys to Customer Loyalty," *American Demographics* 16, no. 1 (January 1994), p. 2.

7. Steven Van Yoder, "Make It Mean Something," *Successful Meeting* 53, No. 2 (February 2004), pp. 27–29.

8. Brian K. Miller, "Many Companies Give Generously, But with a Catch," *Business Journal Serving Greater Portland* 14, no. 43 (December 19, 1997), pp. 28–29.

9. Jenny Dawkins, "Corporate Responsibility: The Communication Challenge," *Journal of Communication Management* 9, no. 2 (November 2004), pp. 106–117.

10. Jill Meredith Ginsberg and Paul N. Bloom, "Choosing the Right Green Marketing Strategy," *MIT Sloan Management Review* 46, no. 1 (Fall 2004), pp. 79–84.

11. Ibid.

12. Examples based on Jill Meredith Ginsberg and Paul N. Bloom, "Choosing the Right Green Marketing Strategy," *MIT Sloan Management Review* 46, no. 1 (Fall 2004), pp. 79–84.

13. Marvin E. Shaw and Philip R. Costanzo, Theories of Social Psychology, 2nd ed. (New York: McGraw-Hill, 1982), p. 334.

14. Ronald J. Alsop, "Corporate Reputation: Anything But Superficial—The Deep But Fragile Nature of Corporate Reputation," *Journal of Business Strategy* 25, no. 6 (2004), pp. 21–30.

15. "Jac Nasser Out As Ford's CEO," *Tire Business* 19, no. 16 (November 15, 2001), p. 1.

16. Marvin E. Shaw and Philip R. Costanzo, *Theories of Social Psychology,* 2d ed. (New York: McGraw-Hill, 1982), p. 334.

17. Ibid, p. 329.

18. Ibid, p. 333.

19. Jack Neff, "Gillette Amps Up Sponsorships," *Advertising Age* 75, no. 36 (September 6, 2004), pp. 4–5.

20. Tom Weir, "When You Absolutely, Positively Need $$$$$," *USA Today* (December 29, 2004), p. 03C.

21. Laura Thompson Osuri, "Little Bank, Very Big Guys," *American Banker* 170, no. 91 (May 12, 2005), p. 8.

22. Kim Pryor, "Events As Incentives," *Incentive* 173, no. 8 (August 1999), pp. 102–103.

23. Diane Anderson, "eBay's Campy Road Tour: One on One, No Mosquitoes," *Brandweek* 46, no. 10 (March 7, 2005), p. R6.

24. Betsy Spethmann, "A Winning Season," *PROMO* 18, no. 1 (December 2004), pp. 32–41.

25. Bart Lazar, "This Column Is the Best One You'll Ever Read," *Marketing News* 38, no. 13 (August 15, 2004), p. 8.

26. "Broadcasters Breach Kids Rules," *Marketing Magazine* 109, no. 35 (November 1, 2004), p. 4.

27. "FTC Buckles Down on 'Ab Force' Belt," *Response* 13, no. 2 (November 2004), p. 10.

28. "FTC Takes Aim at Another Credit Counseling Firm," *Mortgage Servicing News* 8, no. 7 (August 2004), p. 21.

29. "Body Wise International to Pay $3.5 Million to Settle Federal and State Deceptive Advertising Charges," *Federal Trade Commission* (www.ftc.gov, accessed September 20, 2005).

30. Debbi Mack, "FTC Use of Corrective Advertising Upheld," *Corporate Legal Times* 10, no. 108 (November 2000), p. 80.

31. Gary D. Hailey and Jeffrey D. Knowles, "Claiming Sufficient Substantiation Is No Easy Task," *Response* 13, no. 4 (January 2005), p. 50.

32. "KFC's Claims That Fried Chicken Is a Way to 'Eat Better' Don't Fly," *Federal Trade Commission* (www.ftc.gov/opa/2004/06/kfccorp.htm, accessed June 30, 2002).

33. Dan Meyer, "Nextel Adjusts Only Pricing Claims in Ads Following Ad Review," *RCR Wireless News* 23, no. 49 (December 6, 2004), p. 17.

34. Jim Edwards, "NAD a Not-So Challenging Forum for Ad Challengers," *Brandweek* 45, no. 45 (December 13, 2004), p. 5.

35. "Minute Maid Complains, But NARB Forces Change," *Advertising Age* 68, no. 15 (April 14, 1997), p. 51.

36. "NARB Sends Winn-Dixie Complaint to FTC," *Advertising Age* 67, no. 52 (December 23, 1996) p. 2.

37. Betsy Nichol, "Integrated Marketing: The Cluster-Buster," *Franchising World* 26, no. 5 (September–October 1994), pp. 15–17.

# 13 Internet Marketing

## Chapter Objectives

*Understand* **who uses the Internet and how it is used.**

*Adapt* **every marketing communications function to Internet programs.**

*Develop* **a strong e-commerce program to complement and supplement other selling and promotional activities.**

*Make* **sure every component of an e-commerce approach is carefully integrated and designed to attract customers to a Web site and to eventually make purchases.**

*Be* **aware of the ramifications of Internet programs for business-to-business customers and for international marketing efforts.**

## GOOGLE: A NEW WORLD ORDER?

Every once in awhile, a product or a company's name becomes so famous it gets added to our vocabulary. A generation ago, people started making "xerox" copies. Before that, people started taking "aspirins" instead of "pain medicine" and covering wounds with "band aids" rather than "adhesive strips."

Today, it is common to hear someone say they "googled" something. The name "Google" was taken from the word *googol*. A googol is a 1 followed by 100 zeros. The company's primary edge is its ability to organize a vast amount of information into a system that can be easily accessed using the Web.

Google has achieved success in a world that was first filled with failures—Internet companies (dot-coms). Google works because it uses a different business model. Google provides information for free. The company sells advertising that is linked to the free information. The search engine provides access to a vast variety of Web sites that help connect customers with information about products, ideas, social trends, and an endless variety of additional services. Need something translated from Russian to English? Go to Google, and numerous free translation services are quickly at your disposal. Of course, those translation services are more than willing to sell you courses to help you learn various foreign languages at the same time.

A "search" according to Steve Cohen, a VP in charge of products at Basis Technology, "is made up of two stages: indexing and retrieval." One primary advantage held by Google is that the company has been able to expand indexing and retrieval searches into nearly 100 languages. It was not an easy task. For example, many Asian languages, in their print forms, do not have spaces between words. This created a major challenge for word box search engines. Using basis technology programming, Google is able to offer searches in Asian and other challenging languages. The net result is a global company with a worldwide reach.

The year 2004 was especially significant at Google. The company sold stock for the first time, raising $1.67 billion in capital. The stock price then soared. Annual revenues exceeded $5 billion dollars on a global scale, and 2005 opened as strongly as 2004 closed. Many major firms have learned that advertising on a search engine like Google provides a targeted audience with profitable results. Naturally, advertising dollars are quick to follow, and in this case they moved to Google, the market leader in search engine use. One industry leader commented that Google has created almost a "new world order" in advertising.

To maintain its strong pattern of growth, executives at Google have expanded into new territories. First, the firm began advertising to build brand strength. Previously Google relied solely on word-of-mouth. Now the company advertises using radio and print in numerous markets. Next, Google is entering the "local search market." Local classified advertising is a major source of revenue for many companies. Google's technology makes it possible to see all of the dry cleaners in just one city. The primary challenge in this expansion effort has been brand awareness. Google's marketing team has moved to solve the problem by using local advertising. A final launch in 2005 was in the area of business computing.

Google's management team is acutely aware of competitors. Microsoft and Yahoo! are two main search engine providers that could affect Google's share. New competitors emerge every day. Firefox, Opera, and Apple's Safari are some of the latest entrants. Still, given Google's power in the marketplace makes company leaders believe the future remains exciting. In the new world Internet businesses (they don't like to be called "dot-coms" anymore), Google is an excellent example of how to succeed using creativity, energy, and an effective marketing program.[1]

The final section of this book is called "IMC Integration Tools." These tools are found at the top level of the IMC pyramid (Figure 13.1). There are three elements of integration described in this section. First, the roles of the Internet and e-commerce are described. Next, a chapter is devoted to the special issues and IMC concerns present in entrepreneurial and small-business ventures. Finally, methods to evaluate IMC programs are examined. The goal is to provide a complete picture of the final ingredients in an IMC program. When these fundamentals are successfully applied, the company, whether small or large, is in the best position to know and understand customers and to meet their needs efficiently and effectively.

This chapter explores the Internet and e-commerce in greater detail. It is clear that two inventions had a profound impact on business in the latter half of the twentieth century: (1) the computer and (2) the Internet. Using a computer to access the Internet, a business in practically any location can compete in the global marketplace. The size of an organization's operation makes little difference, because the Internet is an open environment. Similar companies compete against one another while being only a mouse-click away. A buyer can locate numerous sellers offering similar merchandise, similar prices, and similar offers in a very short time period. As more people and businesses become comfortable with the Internet, the marketing landscape will continue to evolve. The presence of the Internet and e-commerce is so dramatic that the various applications of Web technology are now essential elements in any fully integrated marketing communications program.

The first part of this chapter examines the nature of Internet users as well as marketing functions on the Internet. Next, a description of e-commerce and the elements necessary to build a successful e-business, including the types of incentives required to build a base of customers, is provided. Then, various IMC topics, such as brand development, brand loyalty, sales support, service efforts, and promotional programs using the Internet, are presented. In each of these areas, implications for business-to-business marketing programs as well as international concerns are suggested.

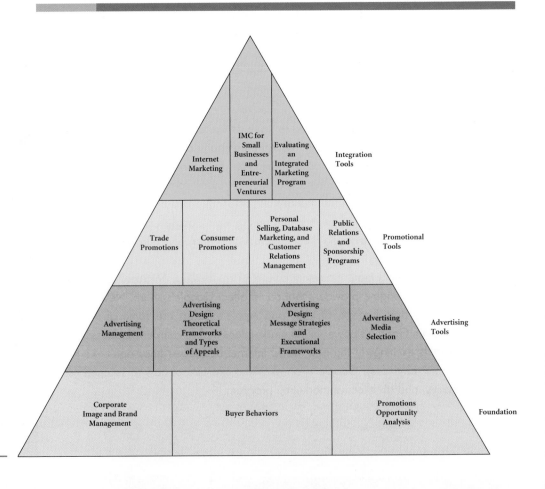

**FIGURE 13.1**
**An IMC Plan**

# WHO USES THE INTERNET?

Use of the Internet to reach consumer and business-to-business markets has exploded during the past decade. Although experts still debate the ultimate future of the Internet, no one doubts its impact on the current marketing environment. Here are some facts about the Internet that highlight its tremendous growth and presence in society:

▶ Approximately 48 percent of Americans, 47 percent of Canadians, and 36 percent of Britons access the Internet daily.

▶ Communication via e-mail, online chat, or instant messaging is the most common use of the Internet.

▶ Voice over Internet Protocol (VoIP) is used by 1 million individuals and is anticipated to grow rapidly.

▶ A large number of people communicate over Web blogs through the 2 million active blogs.

▶ Global Internet retail sales total over $144 billion annually, which is nearly 7 percent of all retail sales.[2]

The first companies to make profits using the Internet were primarily business-to-business marketers. Today, the Web has become the communication tool of choice for many business-to-business companies. The Internet provides opportunities for communication, customer service, sales support, collaboration, and e-commerce. Some companies employ the Internet in every aspect of the business including taking orders, inventory control, production scheduling, communications plans, sales programs, service departments, and support programs. The change from traditional communication channels such as salespeople, telephone, and "snail mail" to the Internet and e-mail happened quickly in some companies and more slowly in others. Most top managers are well aware of the potential of Internet marketing. At the same time, there is a still a lack of Internet expertise in parts of the business community. As a result, many companies are turning to marketing agencies for guidance. Figure 13.2 identifies some of the Internet services marketing agencies now provide.

# MARKETING FUNCTIONS ON THE INTERNET

The Internet has a major impact on sales, marketing, and distribution systems. These three activities typically account for 20 percent to 30 percent of the final cost of a good or service. What makes the potential of the Internet enticing is that companies can save 10 percent to 20 percent of these costs by using the Web instead of traditional marketing channel activities. This means that rather than paying for packing, shipping, and transporting products to a retail site, the products can be sent directly to customers. The producer can pocket the markup the retailer would ordinarily receive. Alternatively, the producer can mark down the price of an item, saving customers money and generating more purchases. Shipping costs may be charged to customers for e-commerce purchases. As a result, the manufacturer does not need to absorb these costs, which are normally part of the price charged to retailers.[3]

A variety of marketing activities can be provided by the Internet. Figure 13.3 identifies the primary functions a business Web site can provide. The marketing team should carefully consider each of these components when designing and managing an Internet program.

▶ **Building databases for e-mail campaigns**
▶ **Designing e-mail campaigns linking customers to Web site information**
▶ **Creating fun and innovative games to attract and keep customers coming back to the Web site**
▶ **Creating incentive programs**
▶ **Translating printed documents, catalogs, brochures, and newsletters for the Internet**
▶ **Adding graphics to the Web site**

**FIGURE 13.2**
Internet Services Offered by Marketing Agencies

*Source:* Ellisor, "Business-to-Business Offers WWW Opportunities," *Houston Business Journal* 30, no. 7 (September 17, 1999), p. 18B.

**FIGURE 13.3**
**Functions of the Internet**

▶ Advertising
▶ Sales support
▶ Customer service
▶ Public relations
▶ E-commerce

The design of a Web site should be guided by the IMC plan and the specific objectives the site seeks to accomplish. A flashy Web site designed to attract attention is created when the goal is *advertising*. Many firms use Web sites to promote individual products as well as the overall company. Most movies now are advertised through traditional media (television, magazines) but also have Web sites for e-moviegoers to view.

Advertising is usually incorporated with other marketing functions. Some Web sites offer *sales support*. In those instances, information about products is made accessible through a link to another page on the Web site or by using a message system that connects the buyer with a salesperson. These types of Web sites are used more routinely by business-to-business customers rather than retail consumers. Effective sales support sites must be useful for engineers and other members of the buying center who require additional product information. The actual sale is normally made via a salesperson. The final price and other terms can be negotiated separately.

A *customer service* Internet site provides a different function. The goal of a customer service Web site is to support the customer after the sale. In this instance, documentation and operating information are provided. Customers who have questions can use the e-mail function to obtain information or scroll through the **FAQs (frequently asked questions)** people have about various items or services. Portions of these sites may be password protected in order to ensure that only customers who have purchased products can access certain information.

Another purpose for a Web site is to create a positive *public relations* image. Information about not-for-profit and philanthropic causes that a company supports can be placed on the firm's Web site. Individuals then see not only what the company is doing but also may be able to volunteer for or donate money to a cause, such as when the contributions were made to support the tsunami victims in 2005. At times these sites are separate from the company's primary site. In others, a hyperlink within the site is developed. A public relations message may be prepared to react to bad publicity. This gives the firm the opportunity to refute a charge or to explain the company's side of the story.

These marketing functions clearly indicate the potential of the Internet to be a valuable component of the company's IMC program. The next section provides a more complete description of the final item in Figure 13.3, e-commerce.

## E-COMMERCE

**E-commerce** is selling goods and services on the Internet. E-commerce can take on many different forms. A retail store can vend items to consumers through the Internet when there is no handy outlet nearby or simply as a convenience for some shoppers. E-commerce also can be a retail operation that sells entirely on the Internet

A Travelocity ad encouraging consumers to make travel arrangements using the Internet.
***Source:*** Courtesy of Visa USA, Inc.

BOOK A TRIP

Travelocity.com
Powered by SABRE

WITHOUT
MAKING ONE

Too busy to book your hotel room, air travel, car rental?
Book your next trip on-line with Visa.
It's fast. It's safe. It's a four-star destination for travelers.

**VISA**

Worldwide. Webwide. Visa® It's everywhere you want to be®

© 1999 Visa U.S.A. Inc.                                           www.visa.com

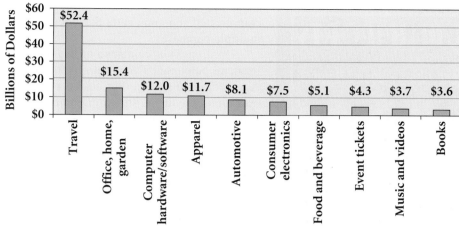

*Source:* Adapted from "Cyber Shopping," *License* 7, no. 10 (November 2004), p. 12.

**FIGURE 13.4**
**Top 10 Cyber Shopping Categories**

without any physical store or even inventory. Services are offered, deals are mediated, and products are shipped through this range of e-commerce operations. Instead of investigating all of the various forms of e-commerce, the purpose of the section is to provide a short synopsis of why and how setting up an e-commerce site benefits an organization. Figure 13.4 identifies the top 10 cyber shopping categories.

In the past, individual businesses approached e-commerce in various ways. At one extreme was the business that jumped into e-commerce immediately, because the organization's leaders decided it was the trend of the future. These individuals concluded that the day would come when there would be no retail stores, and everything would be purchased over the Internet or through an interactive television setup. The other extreme included those who thought that e-commerce was a fad that would soon pass away. These business leaders believed that consumers prefer dealing with people and therefore would always go to retail stores to make purchases. In reality, neither extreme was the case.

To the established retail operation, e-commerce offers customers an alternative mode for making purchases. Not every customer uses the Internet, but many do. As time has passed, more people have become comfortable with online shopping. Without an e-commerce site, these customers are lost to retail operations with established online retail sites.

Quite often, consumers make purchases at retail stores after first using the Internet to gather information. For example, a shopper may research stereos on the Internet and then go to the store with a list of "finalists." Another person may get on the Internet and find a fishing rod with a special set of features. Using the Internet store locator, the individual identifies the closest store offering the product to make the actual purchase. In that case, even though the customer did not make the purchase via e-commerce, he or she has used the Internet as part of the buying decision-making process. Consequently, the leaders of most established businesses know they must develop high-quality e-commerce sites in order to remain competitive.

## E-Commerce Components

E-commerce programs have three components. The first is a *catalog.* The catalog may contain a few items or be a complex presentation of thousands of products. The nature of the firm's operation determines the type of catalog required. In every case, customers should be able to easily locate products of interest. Photos, streaming videos, and product information are important in creating appealing online catalogs. If the company has a printed catalog, it is important to tie the printed catalog with the Web catalog. Victoria's Secret has a "catalog quick order" system that allows customers to enter the product number from the print catalog and then go straight to checkout. The shopping program saves considerable time in trying to find and buy a product on the Web.[4]

Second, each site contains a **shopping cart** to assist consumers as they select products. Again, the shopping cart can range from just checking a circle for an item

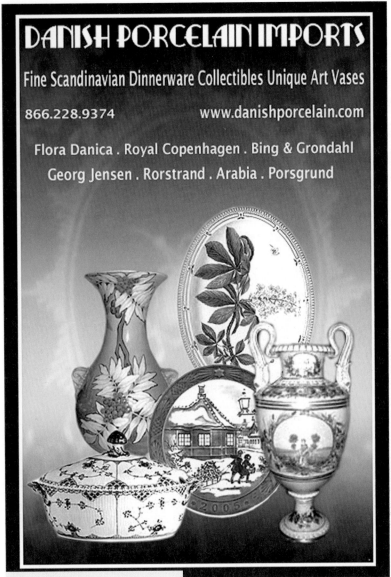

Consumers may access information on a Web site, but go to an actual retail store to make the purchase.
*Source:* Courtesy of Danish Porcelain Imports.

when only a few products are offered to more complicated shopping carts that keep records of multiple purchases.

Third, each site contains a method of *payment* for items purchased. For consumers, this normally is a credit card system. For business-to-business operations, payments are normally made using a voucher system. In other situations, a bill is generated or a computerized billing system is used so that the invoice goes directly to the buyer. In more trusting relationships, the invoice is added to the customer's records without a physical bill ever being mailed.

Many consumers are still wary of purchasing products via the Internet. There are two reasons for this reluctance: (1) security issues and (2) purchasing habits.

## Security Issues

Consumer fears about security are based on worries about a credit card number being stolen as well as identity theft. Others are concerned about fraud, where a retailer takes the money but does not ship the merchandise. Both can cause people to resist making Internet purchases.

To resolve these problems, a review of the past may be helpful. When telephone orders were first encouraged by mail-order firms, people were hesitant because of fears about giving out a phone or credit card number to a stranger they couldn't see. Now, nearly everyone is willing to provide the information while placing orders on the phone. Also, it wasn't that many years ago when credit cardholders expressed anxiety about various store employees stealing those numbers. Originally, customers were instructed to "take the carbon" from a credit card purchase to make sure it was torn into shreds in order to prevent an employee from using the credit card number later.

The same pattern is likely to follow with Internet shopping. As more consumers become accustomed to using the Web, fears about giving out credit card information will be no greater than they are for telephone orders or credit card sales. Credit card companies have created a series of independent television commercials designed to calm and reassure people about the quality of their Internet security programs; however, these efforts are set back each time a major virus is released.

## Purchasing Habits

The second issue has strong ramifications for the ultimate success of e-commerce. Currently, many consumers are most comfortable when they buy merchandise at retail stores. Some are also comfortable buying through catalogs. It will take time to change these habits, especially the preference for retail shopping.

At the retail store, consumers can view and touch the merchandise. They can inspect it for defects and compare brands. Clothes can be tried on to make sure they fit. In addition, the customer can see how the clothing item looks while being worn. Changing these habits requires the right kinds of incentives. Consumers and businesses must have valid reasons for switching to making purchase through the Internet instead of through traditional methods (at the retail store or following a call from a salesperson). To overcome this obstacle, many e-commerce firms have developed incentives to attract customers to make purchases in this new format.

# E-COMMERCE INCENTIVES

Three incentives can be used to encourage consumers to make online purchases. They are the same incentives that lead people to use ATMs and to phone in mail-order purchases. The three types are: (1) financially-based, (2) convenience-based, and (3) value-based incentives.

## Financial Incentives

Persuading an individual or business to buy via e-commerce often requires a financial incentive. A first-time purchaser may be attracted to a monetary incentive, which can take the form of a reduced price, an introductory price, or an e-coupon. Financial incentives are profitable for most firms because of the reduced costs of doing business online. Once the individual or company makes the switch, continuing the financial incentive may not be necessary because the conveniences and added-value features of an e-commerce program will help keep that customer.

When consumers or businesses buy over the Internet, the company often saves time and money. The firm is then able to pass along savings. A firm that fills orders via the Internet saves in several ways, including:

▶ Lower long-distance telephone bills

▶ Reduced shipping costs, because the costs are passed along to the buyer

▶ Decreased labor costs associated with stocking shelves

▶ Lower personnel costs (sales force) paid for waiting on in-store customers or field salespeople calling on retailers and other channel members

In business-to-business settings, purchases via e-commerce also make it possible to offer financial incentives. The company may be saving the cost of a field sales call, which is often more than $300 per call. Passing these savings on to customers can be a very effective means of encouraging customers to switch from their current mode of purchasing to e-commerce.

One special type of financial incentive is known as cyberbait. **Cyberbait** is some type of lure or attraction that brings people to a Web site. The bait may be a special offer such as a pair of jeans sold as a loss leader. It may be a game that consumers can play, or it can be a weekly or daily tip on some topic. For example, for a business-to-business health insurance site, a weekly tip on how to reduce health risks and job-related injuries may be cyberbait that attracts prospects to the site. To entice consumers and businesses to return to the site on a regular basis, additional cyberbait is needed. E-shoppers find it easy to surf the Internet and search competing sites. Therefore, these individuals need some reason to return on a regular basis.

The Bluefly.com ad on this page states that the company is "the outlet store in your home." Bluefly.com is a successful New York–based upscale apparel and home

E-commerce retailers like Bluefly.com provide the opportunity for consumers to shop in the convenience of their homes, at any hour of the day or night.
*Source:* Courtesy of Bluefly.com.

furnishings discounter. The company's philosophy, according to Ken Seiff, CEO, is that "more site traffic equals more business." To build a client list, Bluefly.com made several cyberbait offers. One was a weekly contest with smaller prizes such as a $1,000 Bluefly shopping spree and high-end prizes including the highly demanded Hermes Birkin bag, which was valued at $20,000. Web surfers were allowed to enter the sweepstakes every day to increase the odds of winning, but to be eligible to win the visitors had to supply e-mail addresses. This information was used to send weekly e-mails highlighting specials and exclusive deals to those who had registered. A second form of cyberbait was price-based. Discounts as great as 60 percent on brand-name merchandise such as Gucci, Donna Karan, Prada, and Polo were offered to first-time buyers. The cyberbait programs were quite successful. The company currently carries over 1 million names in its database. More importantly, the average cost of acquiring these new customers was only $23.07 per person, compared to the average order of $154 made by each new buyer.[5]

Typically, the most effective financial incentives are free shipping with orders, free freight, and dollar discounts, such as $5 or $10 off. Some retailers have also had success offering free gifts with orders over a minimum amount. Sport Supply Group offers the members of its loyalty program double frequent-buyer points if they purchase online rather than through the catalog. Babystyle not only offered free shipping, but also a $10 price-off on orders of $50 or more.[6] Whatever financial incentive is used, two things should be kept in mind. First, the incentive must be meaningful to individuals visiting the site. Second, the incentive should be changed periodically to encourage new visitors to buy and to encourage repeat purchases by current visitors.

## Convenience Incentives

Convenience is a second incentive that encourages customers to switch to e-commerce. Instead of making a trip to a retail store, a consumer can place the order in the office or at home. More importantly, the order can be placed at any time; 24-hour availability is also a major reason why ATMs are popular. Convenience is also an issue when the consumer looks for information about a product. The Internet can be quicker and easier than using *Consumer Reports* or talking to salespeople.

For businesses, ordering merchandise, supplies, and materials via the Internet can save purchasing agents considerable time. In addition to ordering, businesses can check on the status of an order, shipment information, and even billing data. In most cases, doing so online is considerably quicker than making a telephone call. In the fast-paced world of business, convenience is a highly attractive incentive for many companies.

To get consumers to return, a Web site must be updated and changed regularly. It is important to keep the site current. Prices and product information must always be up-to-date. In addition, the appearance of the site should be routinely changed so consumers will return to see what is new. The front page of a Web site should be revised just as a display at a retail store is regularly altered. The difference, however, is that in changing the Web site, the marketing team must be careful not to change links or location of merchandise. Consumers become accustomed to finding things on the site. It is best not to make it hard for them to locate familiar items. Just as a grocery store seldom moves merchandise around just to create a different look, designers also must be aware that shoppers will become annoyed if they can't find their favorite products. Consequently, convenience remains an important feature as a Web site is being redesigned. The Web site should also consistently emphasize the IMC theme and the company's image.

By providing an interactive Web site, Preference Video Introductions makes it convenient for consumers to gather information about the company before deciding to use it to meet someone.

*Source:* Used with permission of *The Joplin Globe,* Joplin, Missouri.

As company leaders become more Internet-savvy, new types of e-commerce programs have emerged. For example, many retail stores now offer Web access for couples who are about to marry so that wedding gifts can be examined, purchased, and registered online. This feature helps make sure the couple will receive gifts without duplicates. Out-of-town friends can conveniently choose, wrap, and ship presents to the couple. Victoria's Secret has a gift guide that lists various items either by price or popularity. Apparel cataloger J. Crew has easy-to-use "how to measure" charts to assure consumers that what they are buying will fit.[7] All of these types of conveniences stimulate sales and encourage visitors to return to the company's Web site.

## Value-Added Incentives

Value-added incentives are used to cause consumers to change purchasing habits over the long term. The added value may be personalized shopping, whereby the software system recognizes patterns in customers' purchasing behaviors. The same specialized software informs customers about special deals. These offers are matched to past purchasing behaviors or a customer's search patterns. For example, a consumer going through the mystery section of an online bookstore may see a banner pop up advertising a special deal on a new mystery novel. In addition to instant banners, consumers and businesses also may receive e-mails offering new information and other special deals that are available.

One common value-added approach many e-retailers offer is merchandise on the Web site that is not available in a print catalog. Design Within Reach, a modern furniture retailer, advertises "our Web site offers numerous products not always included in the catalog, as well as weekly features of new items." An antique hardware retailer places sales items and new products on the Web site before including them in the print catalog.[8]

Barnes & Nobles, Charles Schwab, and others have launched a value-added service that is proving to be extremely popular—free education. Barnes & Noble offers free online courses on subjects such as guitar playing and Shakespeare through Barnes & Noble University. More than 50 courses per year are offered, each tied to a book in its

## COMMUNICATION ACTION

### Getting Involved with Soap and Sauce

Most people see a logical connection between the Internet and companies that can sell products directly to consumers. Products such as music CDs, books, and airline tickets sell well over the Internet. But what about low-involvement products such as Tide or Ragu spaghetti sauce? These products would not be purchased via the Internet because it is not financially feasible for the consumer or the company to offer them. No one particularly needs a box of detergent shipped in by FedEx or UPS. Still, the Internet can be a valuable tool for both products in terms of brand development.

Tide has sites at www.clothesline.com and www.tide.com. Instead of offering information about Tide and using the Internet site as an advertisement for Tide, Procter & Gamble uses the Tide Web site to assist consumers. The Web site provides helpful hints on removing stains from garments as well as other laundry tips. Consumers can ask the "Stain Detective" for help on specific stains by providing information about the type of fabric, color, and other information.

Ragu spaghetti sauce, on the other hand, has a highly entertaining site where a made-up personality known as "Mama" nags you about eating right. Browsers have the option of giving their e-mail address so they can receive coupons, updates on the site, and information about new products that are introduced.

The key, in both cases, is creativity. Firms that can discover ways to augment communication programs with quality Web sites gain a major advantage in the marketplace. Thus, even soap and sauce are quality candidates for an Internet presence.

inventory, which must be purchased by students. Classes are often taught by the authors and consist of assigned reading materials, communication with classmates, and quizzes. Since June 2000, over 500,000 students have taken classes, with the average student enrolling in two classes. Charles Schwab has more than 50 online courses through its Charles Schwab Learning Center. Some courses are self-paced online courses; others are live, virtual classrooms that use conferencing software such as WebEx Communications. Since December 1999, more than 200,000 people have enrolled, with recent enrollments averaging 1,000 per week.[9] These types of value-added incentives encourage repeat visitors who are more likely to make purchases and become regular customers.

# BUSINESS-TO-BUSINESS E-COMMERCE

Business-to-business e-commerce spending totaled $767 billion in 2004, up from $40 billion in 1998.[10] Figure 13.5 shows business-to-business e-commerce spending since 1998. Although spending in the B-to-B area has not grown as fast as some experts thought it would, it still is a large component of Internet marketing. Steady growth in B-to-B e-commerce is expected for many years to come.

For business-to-business organizations, e-commerce may be as critical as it is in consumer markets. In many buying situations, purchasing agents can go to the Internet and compare prices and product information. Once a business account is established, a business customer finds it very easy to place orders. This approach works well for products such as office supplies, maintenance supplies, and for repair and operation products. The orders are simple because the product does not have to be modified for the buyer. Also the dollar cost-per-item is relatively low. A seller with strong brand name has an advantage when all other factors are equal. Buyers are willing to purchase from companies that they know provide superior service, on-time delivery, and other attributes. As a result, to compete in e-commerce, a business-to-business firm must have: (1) an effective e-commerce site, and (2) work to establish a strong brand name that stands out.[11]

Financial, convenience, and value-added incentives that are similar to consumer incentives are offered to business buyers. In the iGo.com Internet advertisement shown on the next page, a 10 percent discount is offered for orders placed via the Internet at www.igo.com or by telephone. The same 10 percent discount applies to any product or service provided at www.employeesavings.com.

A growing form of e-commerce in the business-to-business sector is online exchanges and auctions. These exchanges allow business buyers to purchase a variety of commodities and goods at bargain prices. The Internet enables vendors to speed up time to the market, to sell directly to other businesses, and to cut transaction and inventory costs. Buyers can find both nonproduction goods such as office supplies as well as production-related supplies, raw materials, and equipment. There are also sites where oil, natural gas, electricity, coal, chemicals, steel, and other raw materials are made available.

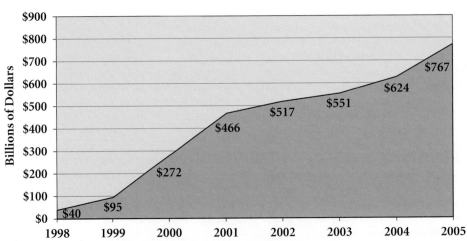

**FIGURE 13.5**
**E-Commerce Spending in the Business-to-Business Sector**

*Source:* Reprinted from *BtoB Magazine*, copyright © 2005 Crain Communications Inc.

Many online markets are run by intermediary companies that simply match buyers and sellers. EqualFooting.com is a privately held company whose purpose is to give small manufacturers and construction businesses an equal footing with large companies in terms of purchasing, financing, and shipping. Members of EqualFooting.com can purchase industrial and office supplies, obtain loans, sign leases, and schedule freight delivery through vendors listed with EqualFooting.com. The company offers distributors, lenders, and shippers access to its small manufacturing and construction database. The service is free to buyers, but sellers pay EqualFooting.com a small commission on all sales. EqualFooting.com now has a relationship with 2,500 distributors and approximately 35,000 buyers.[12] Without the Internet, providing these types of services would be virtually impossible.

Selling commodity-type products on the Internet has become especially popular. The average business-to-business sale made by a salesperson starts with $300 per-sales-call costs. In the process of wining and dining that client, a company can spend several thousand dollars to get the sale and then additional money is paid in the form of commissions. These costs can be greatly reduced using the Internet. Still, it is important to maintain sales support staff for Internet programs. In-house salespeople are often needed to handle online negotiations.[13]

E-commerce operations have other uses. A Web site should provide store location information to buyers, because consumers may want to make purchases in a physical store. A similar process takes place in the business-to-business marketplace. Vicinity Corporation's SiteMaker and Business Finder software display the location of the closest outlet for these businesses, complete with a map and directions showing how to get to there. A business needing specialized parts, supplies, or maintenance equipment immediately is able to find the nearest location where the merchandise is sold.[14]

An Internet advertisement for iGo.com featuring a financial incentive to encourage business or consumer purchases.
*Source:* Courtesy of iGo.com.

Cross-selling additional goods and services is a tactic used by many business-to-business firms. As more transactions were being made over the Internet, it seemed possible that cross-selling was doomed. The marketing team at Wells Fargo discovered a creative way to cross-sell on the Internet when the company launched its Commercial Electronic Office (CEO) feature. CEO is a one-stop shop for corporate accounts with revenues of $10 million or more. CEO makes a large range of services available to these accounts through the Web site. Services including foreign exchange, loan servicing, and quarter-million-dollar wire transfers are available. The CEO technology exposes these high dollar accounts to all of Wells Fargo's banking products each time a customer logs in. Bank personnel also remind these high-end clients of the services that are available online. Clients gradually added more banking products. Now each high-end customer that uses Wells Fargo as its primary bank uses an average of five Wells Fargo products. The success of CEO is based on its convenience, instantaneous account information, and, most importantly, the software's powerful security and access controls.[15]

Many business-to-business companies are expanding into international operations. Minolta recently added multilingual options for distributors and retailers to its B-to-B Web site. The site guides Minolta's thousands of resellers and its 50 distributors through the sales process. Resellers are able to order directly from the Web site. In addition, Minolta is able to access to the reseller's Web site to cross-sell products. For instance, an individual who buys a printer from the reseller would be offered ink cartridges. The multilingual site started with European operations and has now expanded to Asia.[16]

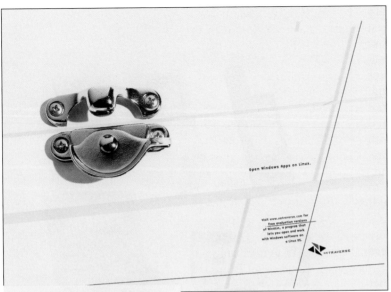

Open Windows Apps on Linux.

Visit www.netraverse.com for
free evaluation versions
of WinaLin, a program that
lets you open and work
with Windows software on
a Linux OS.

NETRAVERSE

To encourage businesses to use its software, Netraverse allows a company to access a demonstration version on the firm's Web site.
*Source:* Courtesy of West & Vaughan.

In all of these applications, it has become clear that e-commerce is a major force in business-to-business marketing programs. It seems highly likely that there will be continual growth in the uses of the Internet in business-to-business transactions, especially as businesses expand internationally.

## INTERNATIONAL E-COMMERCE

One of the major advantages e-commerce has when compared to bricks-and-mortar retail stores is the ability to reach consumers everywhere, even in other countries. Unfortunately, in 2004 almost 46 percent of the existing Internet companies turned away international orders because they did not have processes in place to fill the orders. Therefore, although the Internet makes it possible for a company to sell items in an international marketplace, many companies are not prepared to go global. Many obstacles to selling across national boundaries exist. They include communications barriers, cultural differences, global shipping problems due to a lack of sufficient infrastructure, and varying degrees of Internet capabilities in other countries.[17]

One key to an effective launch of a global e-commerce site is preparing methods to make international shipments. Air transport is affordable for smaller products. DHL Worldwide Express, FedEx, and UPS offer excellent shipping options. Larger merchandise normally is shipped by some type of freight forwarder, who finds the best mode of delivery, from ships to trucks or by rail. Both air transport companies and freight forwarders offer specialized logistics software and provide the proper documentation and forms to meet the importing and exporting regulations in every country they serve. Internet companies must follow local export and import laws.

Shipping arrangements are not the only concern. Payment mechanisms must also be installed. Each country has a different currency and methods of payment also vary. For example, in Europe, debit cards are preferred to credit cards. Europe also has a high rate of credit card theft, which increases the risks associated with accepting them.

Another task in the international arena is developing a Web site that appeals to the audience in each country. This includes adding information that someone in another country would need, such as the country code for telephone numbers. It also requires removing or changing any colors, words, or images that might be offensive to a particular group of people in another country. Figure 13.6 identifies some cultural misunderstandings that have occurred in the past.

New globalization software has been developed for companies expanding into other countries. One software package translates an English Web site into a large number of foreign languages. Another valuable feature that the software offers is called "cultural

**FIGURE 13.6**
**Cultural Disasters to Avoid in International Internet Marketing**

▶ Using black in backgrounds and graphics has sinister connotations in Asia, Europe, and Latin America.

▶ The thumbs-up sign and the waving hand are rude gestures in Latin America and the Middle East, respectively.

▶ Showing a woman with exposed arms or legs is offensive in the Middle East.

▶ Using a dog as a company logo is not successful in Korea because dogs are used for food.

*Source:* Lynda Radosevich, "Going Global Overnight," *InfoWorld* 21, no. 16 (April 19, 1999), pp. 1–3.

adaptation," which adjusts a Web site's terminology, look, and feel to suit local norms. The software also has a feature in which the content that is developed in one location can easily be deployed to all sites around the world. This provides a more consistent look to the Web sites, so that someone does not have to spend time modifying every foreign Web site. A Web site prepared in the proper native language that also conforms to local customs is much easier to create because of this new globalization software.[18]

The technical side of international e-commerce remains a difficult challenge. Software compatibility is an unresolved technical issue. Eventually, the hope is that these various technologies will be merged into one system. Currently, the bandwidth for handling Internet traffic varies considerably. Information technology (IT) people must be involved in every step of an internationalization process in order to overcome all of the potential technical glitches.

Another major key to successful global e-commerce is a coherent IMC strategy utilizing local input from the various countries involved. The brand on an Internet site must be consistent from one country to the next. Each site should also consistently present the company's primary marketing message. For IBM, this meant using local companies in each country to design the Web site and provide the information used on the site. To ensure consistency, IBM designs the main marketing messages at its central office, but then local companies translate the messages and add reseller contact and pricing information.

A unique aspect of e-commerce is that small companies can compete as effectively as large companies. Trebnick Systems and Greyden Press are excellent examples. Trebnick Systems is a printing business located near Dayton, Ohio. The company employs 10 people, yet its Web site has attracted customers from Japan, Germany, Spain, and Ireland. Greyden Press employs only 25 people but uses the Internet as its primary marketing tool. Customers can request quotes and submit jobs online. The majority of customers Greyden serves are not located in Columbus, Ohio, where the organization's facility is physically located. In both cases, e-commerce helped a small company expand its customer base beyond a local area.[19]

In the future, the growth of international e-commerce is likely to be explosive. Firms that "get in on the ground floor" are likely to have a major marketing advantage.

## IMC AND THE INTERNET

The Internet is an important component of a quality integrated marketing communications plan. The most critical decision facing businesses is choosing the functions the Web site should serve. It is extremely difficult to design a Web site that provides every function mentioned in Figure 13.3. If multiple functions are to be served, it may become necessary to create separate Web sites for some of them. These different sites can be connected by links. Still, the marketing team should resist the temptation to create a Web site that attempts to be everything to everyone.

The Internet is a critical component of BMW Motorcycles' IMC plan.
*Source:* Courtesy of BMW Motorcycles.

In addition to incorporating the Internet into the IMC plan, it is vital for the information technology (IT), human resource, production, and shipping departments to be included as the marketing team develops the program. If they are not, disasters can happen. For example, marketers at a major consumer goods company launched a highly successful Web site that created 3,000 customer queries a day. The problem was that no one had been hired by HR to handle the queries. Several years ago, Victoria's Secret announced its Internet fashion show during the Super Bowl. The site drew more than 1 million hits. Unfortunately, no one told the IT department that the commercial was going to air. In fact, members of the IT department found out about the Internet fashion show when they saw the Super Bowl ad. The result was that

**START LOOKING FORWARD TO RUSH HOUR**

Introducing the F 650 CS. Just try not to snicker at those guys in sports cars hitting a top speed of 5 mph as you whip by. And if that doesn't turn heads, there are a few other things about this bike that will. Like an optional audio system with waterproof loudspeakers. Or if you prefer, use the built-in storage bay to hold an overnight bag trust us, you'll be spending a lot less time at home. Put it this way: for you, getting around town is about to be the best part of city living.

To find out when and where you can get ahold of the new F 650 CS just call 1-800-345-4BMW, or visit bmwmotorcycles.com.

| | |
|---|---|
| ▶ Internet content search | 38% |
| ▶ Word-of-mouth | 30% |
| ▶ Internet banner | 20% |
| ▶ Television ad | 7% |
| ▶ Print ad | 5% |

**FIGURE 13.7**
**What Drives People to a New Site?**

*Source:* Don Jeffrey, "Survey Details Consumer Shopping Trends on the Net," *Billboard* 111, no. 22 (May 29, 1999), p. 47.

the Victoria's Secret system crashed. To avoid this type of problem, it is essential to communicate with other departments when formulating an Internet strategy.[20]

Coordination between the IT department and other areas involves a variety of activities. Changes can be made quickly on individual Web sites, and marketers must think about how each change can impact other activities in the company. The marketing department should coordinate each advertising campaign with the IT department so that software capabilities are addressed to ensure smooth operations. The company must work hard to avoid glitches that affect operations. Also, members of the call center need to know when additional telephone calls and e-mail inquiries may result from a special Internet offer. It takes time and effort to coordinate marketing changes with IT and other departments, but any delay in implementation will be offset by a smoother, more efficient operation.

A recent poll, called the "World Wide Internet Opinion Survey," examined the factors that drove people to Internet Web sites for the first time. These results are highlighted in Figure 13.7. As shown, a search engine is the primary method consumers use to discover new Web sites. As a result, it is important for companies to make sure they are listed under as many search engines as possible and also to use the right keywords. Notice that television and print ads are the least successful in driving someone to an Internet site for the first time, finishing far behind word-of-mouth.

Travel Alberta used search engines and some advanced Internet technology to boost visitors to the organization's Web site and to Alberta, Canada. The marketing team purchased 600 keyword searches on AOL and Google. Software called "WebTrends" was used to record the effectiveness of each search word. The search words that did not attract visitors to the site were dropped and other words were chosen to replace them. The WebTrend software helped the marketing team at Travel Alberta to tailor its approach to the interests and location of the visitor. The approach was successful. Alberta had more than 1.5 million annual visitors from both the United States and Canada, one-third of them as a result of the e-marketing program.[21]

Many experts believe the traditional banner ad has little influence on people. Not surprisingly, Web designers are trying to attract attention through fancier banners. Graphics, flashing images, and streaming videos are used to garner attention. Interstitial or pop-up ads were created, which forced Web browsers to react. Unfortunately, these types of ads have become highly controversial and many view them as offensive. The truth is, however, that pop-up ads work significantly better at attracting buyers than do traditional banner ads. This success has led many Internet companies to develop superstitials that work after a person leaves a Web site or even shuts off the computer. The ad appears the next time the person logs onto the Internet. E-mail advertisements also are being created with full graphics and videos that are sent overnight to customers who were on a particular Web site. Although the ethical implications of such advertising tactics are being debated, the fact is that they work. Consequently, their use will continue to increase.

E-mail advertisements have begun to lose their luster. Part of the reason is the huge number of junk e-mails everyone receives, both consumers and businesses. Since the CAN-SPAM Act went into effect in January 2004, unsolicited e-mails have increased to 80 percent or more of all e-mail sent.[22] Instead of stopping e-mails, the law simply made it legal to spam, as long as you meet the guidelines, which are relatively easy for many companies to do. Also, catching and prosecuting spammers is extremely difficult and costly.

A recent survey indicated that the 70 percent of the people interviewed complained that they receive too many e-mails. The number of respondents who reported they delete the ads without even looking at them rose from 31 percent to 55 percent during a 2-year time period. The percentage of respondents who agreed that e-mail offers were "a great way to find out about new products and promotions" declined from 48 percent to 25 percent during that time. Therefore, marketing managers must be wary of these feelings about e-mail advertisements. As an alternative, businesses have shifted to B-to-B newsletters, which have enjoyed some success. These newsletters, which are sent monthly, have the benefit of being filled with more information and are perceived as better than both banner ads and e-mail.[23]

A relatively new method of promoting Web sites, brands, and products is the blog. A blog provides a venue for companies to promote products in a nonadvertising, word-of-mouth, off-beat way. Blogging can be used to give the company or product a "personality." Dr. Pepper/Seven Up, Inc., used a 4-month blogging campaign to introduce the company's new flavored milk products. The target of the blog was 18- to 24-year-old consumers. The blog featured a cow that was tired of white milk. The cow broke out of its barn and was raging across the country, encouraging young adults to break out of their white-milk mode and try flavored milk, such as Berry Mixed Up, Pina Colada Chaos, Chocolate Caramel Craze, and Jamocha Frenzy Flavors. The blog was written in the voice of Generation Y, using such phrases as "Ho hee, we did it! Fate was on our side that night—the moon was in its final quarter." The blog was so popular with Generation Y consumers that in just a single day, 20,800 people logged on.[24] Although blogs are not for every consumer or for every product, they are a new, unique way for companies to reach consumers outside of the traditional channels.

In business-to-business markets, the number of hits at a B-to-B Web site is directly related to the amount spent on advertising and sales promotions. A large business-to-business company went from 20,000 visits per month to 80,000 visits per month during a 6-month period by doubling the company's annual advertising budget for print, direct mail, and trade shows. A small company went from 2,000 to 6,000 hits per month by increasing the company's budget for print ads from $25,000 to $65,000 per year. Dynamic Web, a high-tech Web company, saw company Web site traffic increase 250 to 300 hits per week immediately following participation in a trade show featuring the company's Web site.[25]

The Internet affects a firm's IMC program in numerous ways. This section presents the Internet's impact on several activities. Each is part of the total IMC program. The areas to include in an Internet program include:

- Branding
- Brand loyalty
- Sales support
- Customer service

The goal is to bring the firm's Internet programs into line with the rest of its marketing communications efforts. A review of these IMC topics follows.

## Branding

Brand image is a major factor in the success of a company. Powerful brands are also vital to Internet success. In one survey, 82 percent of the respondents said that a brand name has an impact in their online purchases.[26] The design of a Web site and the information it provides are key variables that affect perceptions of the brand. An IMC plan that emphasizes that the brand is a product with high quality should maintain the same theme on the Web site. Also, a Web site should reinforce the integrated communications theme that is presented in other media. When this is accomplished, the Internet becomes a valuable tool in the development of the brand.

Creating an effective brand presence online requires more than a Web site with an e-commerce capability. Cyberbranding involves integrating online and off-line branding

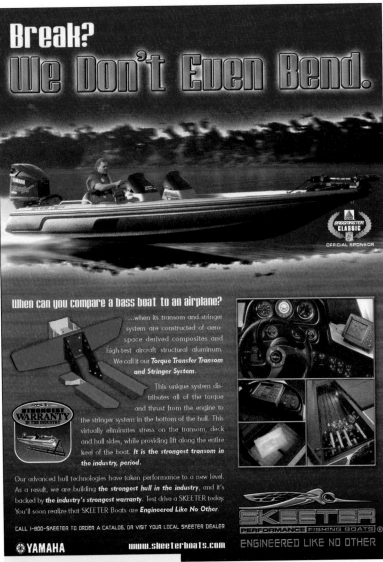

**Break?**
**We Don't Even Bend.**

When can you compare a bass boat to an airplane?

...when its transom and stringer system are constructed of aerospace derived composites and high-test aircraft structural aluminum. We call it our *Torque Transfer Transom and Stringer System*.

This unique system distributes all of the torque and thrust from the engine to the stringer system in the bottom of the hull. This virtually eliminates stress on the transom, deck and hull sides, while providing lift along the entire keel of the boat. *It is the strongest transom in the industry, period.*

Our advanced hull technologies have taken performance to a new level. As a result, we are building *the strongest hull in the industry*, and it's backed by *the industry's strongest warranty*. Test drive a SKEETER today. You'll soon realize that SKEETER Boats are *Engineered Like No Other*.

CALL 1-800-SKEETER TO ORDER A CATALOG, OR VISIT YOUR LOCAL SKEETER DEALER

**YAMAHA**          www.skeeterboats.com

SKEETER PERFORMANCE FISHING BOATS ®
ENGINEERED LIKE NO OTHER

The brand name is important to consumers in making purchases as well as providing access to additional information on the Web. *Source:* Courtesy of Newcomer, Morris & Young, Inc.

tactics that reinforce each other to speak with one voice.[27] The most common method of building an online brand presence is through an off-line technique called brand spiraling. **Brand spiraling** is the practice of using traditional media to promote and attract consumers to an online Web site. From television, radio, newspapers, magazines, and billboards to simple shopping bags, consumers are encouraged to visit the firm's Web site. One goal of each advertising campaign should be to encourage traffic to the site and enhance brand recognition. The interactive nature of the Internet makes it possible for a firm to learn more about each customer. This information can then be used to target more specific messages. The magazine advertisement on the next page for WeddingChannel.com is designed to encourage traffic to the Web site. Once there, WeddingChannel.com requests information from viewers in an effort to learn more about them and their particular needs.

Figure 13.8 identifies some of the techniques used to advertise business-to-business Web sites. As shown, the most common method is displaying the Web address on all printed and promotional material. Next is placing ads promoting the Web address in various trade publications. More than 70 percent of the companies register keywords with search engines, because business buyers often look for a specific product. The odds of making a sale increase substantially when a firm's Web site is cited after a keyword is typed into the search engine. The least used method is placing banners on other sites. Seldom do business customers go to a site when they are at another site. The primary effect of placing banners on other sites is to develop brand awareness and brand knowledge rather than to attract customers.

Companies with strong off-line brands benefit from what is called a **halo effect**. A well-received brand leads more customers to try new goods and services that are being offered by the company on the Internet. These same customers are also more willing to provide information that can be used for greater personalization of messages. This halo effect results from the credibility of the firm's brand being transferred to an individual's evaluation of the Web site. Barnes & Noble and Toys "R" Us were late entrants into e-commerce. Still, both companies built successful Internet businesses because of strong brand names.

A company such as Amazon.com, which was an Internet start-up, is likely to use traditional advertising media to help develop a brand name. Brand-name power cannot be created solely through advertising on the Internet. To achieve a strong brand name, Amazon.com invested a half-billion dollars in traditional media. In each case, a strong brand name is simply a "must" in a marketing and IMC program.

## Brand Loyalty and IMC Internet Programs

An effective Internet program creates several benefits. For one, the Internet makes it easier to communicate with loyal consumers. This makes it possible to strengthen relationships with them. To take advantage of the Internet, begin by identifying heavy users. Remember that being a heavy user does not always mean the buyer feels strong brand loyalty. Some individuals or companies are heavy users because of price or convenience or for some other reason. When another firm emerges offering a better price or an improved delivery schedule, these heavy users will switch while a brand-loyal consumer will not.

Brand-loyal consumers make purchases for reasons beyond the price, the convenience, or the product itself. Often they experience a type of "psychic" or positive affective feeling toward the brand or company. Also, in nearly every instance of brand loyalty, consumers believe the brand is superior in quality. Inferior items are not likely to create brand loyalty. Lower quality products are more likely to generate repeat purchase behaviors rather than loyalty.

The experience or feelings a consumer develops toward a brand are often the result of marketing communications between the firm and the consumer. Although advertising is a major component or communication channel used to develop brand loyalty, the Internet is becoming increasingly valuable.

A magazine advertisement for WeddingChannel.com designed to encourage visits to its Web site.
*Source:* Courtesy of Della.com.

| | |
|---|---|
| ▶ Putting the Web address on printed materials and promotional items | 91% |
| ▶ Advertising in trade journals | 74% |
| ▶ Registering the Web site with search engines for keywords | 72% |
| ▶ Buying banners on other sites | 25% |

**FIGURE 13.8**
**B-to-B Techniques to Boost Web Site Awareness**

*Source:* Robert Harvin, "In Internet Branding, the Off-Lines Have It," *Brandweek* 41, no. 4 (January 24, 2000), pp. 30–31.

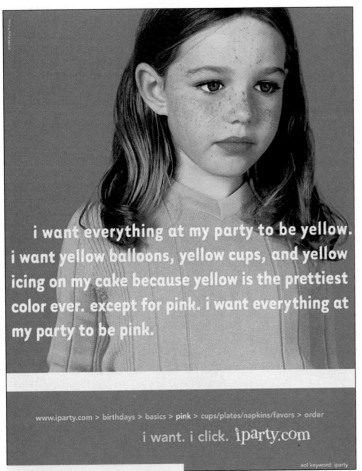

i want everything at my party to be yellow. i want yellow balloons, yellow cups, and yellow icing on my cake because yellow is the prettiest color ever. except for pink. i want everything at my party to be pink.

www.iparty.com > birthdays > basics > **pink** > cups/plates/napkins/favors > order

i want. i click. iparty.com

aol keyword: iparty

This advertisement by iparty.com highlights the convenience of finding all of the party needs a consumer would need to have that special event.
*Source:* Courtesy of iparty.com/Kirsenbaum Bond & Partners.

The Inglenook ad prominently displays the Web address.
*Source:* Courtesy of Sartor Associates, Inc.

Free* Mats and Glass
ON ALL CUSTOM FRAMING

The Inglenook
A CUSTOM FRAME GALLERY
200 Hudson Lane, Suite 2
Monroe, LA 71201
nglenook@bellsouth.net

*Regular single mat and glass only

The Internet provides three opportunities that are not possible with advertising. First, the Internet can be designed to make shopping and other contacts more pleasurable experiences. Buyers return to the Web sites because they enjoyed the experience previously. These feelings may be similar to what a customer encounters at Starbucks. Consumers are loyal to Starbucks because of the total experience and atmosphere of the establishment. Not only is the coffee good, but much more is also involved in the feelings of loyalty toward the company.

The second opportunity the Internet provides is the ability to establish one-to-one communication between the consumer and the firm. This communication can take on two forms: e-mail and personalization of shopping. Speed is extremely important in converting a visitor to a Web site to a buyer. E-mails should be sent immediately, welcoming visitors to the site and thanking them if they registered with the company while at the site. TravelSmith, a California-based cataloger of luggage and travel wear, conducted a test to determine if e-mails had an impact. Individuals who received e-mail follow-ups after registering with a sight generated an average of 15 percent more profit than individuals who did not receive e-mails.[28]

Remember that database technology can be used to assist the marketing team in developing a detailed history of groups of consumers as well as information about individual shoppers. Using these data, it is possible to develop a one-on-one connection between the consumer and the firm. These communications (special offers, customized ads, etc.) often move users toward brand loyalty. HPShopping.com used this approach through specialized software that was installed. The software automatically called up the visitor's previously browsed product rather than the company's homepage. This reminded the visitor why he or she had visited the sight. The company had 19 times as many orders from these visitors than from individuals who were sent to the homepage each time they logged on.[29]

Third, the Internet offers the potential to contact niche customers. Computer Economics research analyst Adam Harris notes that, "The Internet . . . offers a unique opportunity for companies to target specific markets." Potential niches include African-Americans, gays, women, Latinos, persons of Asian descent, and Christian or other religious Web surfers.[30]

In communicating with consumers, it is important to provide rewards for loyalty. These rewards are not promotions, but actual rewards. The gift or offer may be the same as for a promotion, but the dialogue with the consumer is different. For loyal consumers, these rewards are mentioned as a way to say "thank you" for that loyalty. On the other hand, consumer promotions are merely used to entice the price-sensitive consumer or the promotion-prone user to make a purchase. A reward helps the firm say that the person or business is important, and the psychological impact of this type of message can be powerful.

# Sales Support on the Internet

One key feature of any IMC program is sales support. The Internet can be used in various ways to help. Manufacturers that sell products through retailers and wholesalers must be careful to avoid having a Web site that is viewed as a threat. Many retailers and wholesalers are wary of manufacturing Web sites where customers can place orders. To prevent damaging relationships with retailers, manufacturers can offer product information, but actual orders for merchandise can go through the retailer or wholesale vendor.

The strategy of using a Web site for information only rather than for direct sales is found more frequently in the business-to-business sector. In that arena, each manufacturer has fewer customers. Therefore, it is critical for a manufacturer to maintain positive relationships with its retail or wholesale vendors. When a manufacturer sells through multiple vendors, it may be wise to offer a locator on the manufacturer's Web site that shows customers the nearest vendor. For example, a manufacturer of a depth finder for fishing boats could list the retail stores where that particular brand can be purchased. Through locator software, customers can find the closest retail store.

Often, the most important use of the Internet in the area of sales support is providing information about clients and products to the sales staff. The salesperson should be able to access all of the information the company has in its database about any given customer. In addition, data can be collected regarding which products are being examined by individual customers on a Web site. This gives the salesperson insight regarding what product to pitch and how to make the sales approach. The information also helps the company when a number of customers are accessing details about specific products. The **Web master**, or the person who manages a firm's Web site, can then add materials regarding that product in order to increase the odds of making a sale.

Further, the sales staff can utilize the Internet as a valuable resource tool in another way. Although experienced salespeople may have complete knowledge of all of the products sold, new salespeople may not. The salesperson can use the Internet to provide the information a client requests. Often this can be done in the client's office or within a short period of time while on the phone. The Internet also can be used when a customer is ready to place an order. The order can be sent immediately, and the salesperson with access to the firm's database can inform the customer of the shipping date. If the item is out of stock, the salesperson informs the customer that the item must be back ordered. Receiving this information at the time the order is placed is much better than getting a phone call or note later.

Customers can go online and also receive sales support. The Internet has the advantage of being available 24 hours a day, 7 days a week. Customers can access a Web site to obtain product information at the time that best suits them. A Web site can provide extensive sales support that can be transmitted to customers and prospects even when the salesperson is not available.

In the business-to-business market, both prospecting for and qualifying prospects can be facilitated through use of the Internet. A salesperson can locate companies that may be interested in a certain product. For example, Trebnick Systems, the printing service mentioned earlier in this chapter, discovered customers in Japan, Germany, Spain, and Ireland by examining 160 Web sites. Trebnick made contact and obtained orders. Once prospects have been located, whether through the Internet or through traditional channels, the Internet can help qualify prospects to see if they are good candidates for sales calls. If they are not, the salesperson may want to try an e-mail contact or turn the lead over to telemarketers to explore.[31]

The Internet provides valuable information for preparing a sales call. By examining a prospect's Web site first, the salesperson can discover information about the company, its products, and the personnel at the firm. Also, the sales rep can use a search engine to locate articles and press releases about a prospect company. Financial information is available for publicly held corporations. All of this information can be useful in the preparation of a sales call, and the sales rep is able to individualize and personalize a presentation.

## Customer Service and the Internet

The Internet offers a cost-effective method for companies to provide customer service. FedEx, the U.S. Postal Service (USPS), and VISA are companies that have made effective use of the Internet for customer service. FedEx and USPS customers can track packages through the Internet. It is more efficient to use the Internet to find a package. For the companies, the costs of telephone calls are reduced, because fewer human operators are needed when customers go to the Web first. VISA provides an ATM finder program for its consumers, which gives directions to the closest ATM when one is needed.

A recent survey indicates that the *response time,* or the time from when the customer e-mails a company for information or with a complaint to when he or she receives an answer, is a significant factor that will affect future purchase decisions.[32] Unfortunately, quick responses are not always the case. In one survey, only 37 percent of the respondents stated that they were generally satisfied with the online customer service, compared to 85 percent for traditional retailers. Older consumers were less satisfied with online retailers than the younger people. Only 26 percent of individuals age 45 or older said they were satisfied with online service support.[33] Clearly this is an area many companies must improve.

Communicating effectively is an important ingredient in quality customer service, regardless of the type of online business. In all, 92 percent of online businesses offer an e-mail channel for customers. Sadly, only 34 percent acknowledge receipt of a customer's e-mail, and one-third take 3 days or more to respond. About half of these companies answer a customer's e-mail query within 24 hours, and about one-third answer within 6 hours. An amazing 24 percent of e-mail questions or requests go unanswered.[34] With statistics like this, it is no wonder customers tend to be dissatisfied with online customer service and, as a result, prefer to use the telephone to make contact with an online business.

The Institute of Management and Administration (IOMA) offers six steps to improve an organization's customer service.[35] First, service representatives need to be knowledgeable. Second, it is important to confirm the customer's order or inquiry. Let them know the e-mail was received and, if possible, a time frame for a reply. Third, add a personal touch. In the reply e-mail, the service rep should address the person by name, tell the person that his or her business is important to the company, and then address the specific order, question, or concern that was the subject of the e-mail. Fourth, offer customers the opportunity to talk to you in person, if they so desire. Fifth, use good communication skills. Sixth, be aware of the work habits of customers. For instance, a customer in the Middle East was upset because he did not receive a reply within 24 hours. The problem was that Saturday and Sunday are not workdays in the United States and in many countries of the world; Thursday afternoons and Friday are often not workdays in the Middle East. By knowing that the customer was from the Middle East, the acknowledgment e-mail could have informed him that a reply would not arrive until the following Monday.

In addition to providing e-mail communication, it is important to provide an efficient Web site that is easy for customers to use. If company leaders want to encourage customers to use the Internet for information and transactions rather than the telephone or in person, then the Web site should be easy to navigate and information should be easy to access. When problems occur, customer service should be available. Wells Fargo recently introduced a new online customer service system that allows commercial customers to troubleshoot the problem with service representatives while online. The new customer service software allows both the customer and the Wells Fargo rep to see the screen that the customer is viewing. The co-browsing capability also allows either party to move to another screen or change entries. This capability allows the Wells Fargo employee to see what the customer is trying to do and provides direct assistance. Most problems are resolved within minutes and the customer does not have to try to explain by phone what he or she is doing and what is happening. The service is free with the Wells Fargo Commercial Electronic Office (CEO), described earlier in the chapter.[36]

Another approach some companies use to enhance customer service on the Internet is to put together discussion groups, chat rooms, or blogs. Many public relations people dislike chat rooms and blogs, even though they provide the opportunity for customers to interact with each other and with the firm in a somewhat controlled environment. One of the best ways for a firm to react to negative comments by consumers is to directly reply to complaints. Everyone reading the chat conversation sees the response. Discussion groups and blogs also allow consumers to interact with each other and may provide solutions to problems that the company had not considered. This type of situation can occur with computer software and highly technical products. Such open communication with customers tends to build a stronger bond between customers and the firm.

For business-to-business marketing, granting access to information within the seller's database can be especially beneficial. Each company with access has a password to gain entry. Providing information in this manner can save everyone considerable time, especially when there is a strong bond between the two companies. For example, a shipping company may allow its customers access to all of its database information concerning location of shipments and availability of trucks, trains, and ocean vessels. In scheduling shipments, this information is helpful to the logistics coordinator responsible for planning and coordinating movement of goods from the manufacturer to the retailer or wholesaler. Thus, by knowing that an ocean vessel currently has capacity for a 25-ton shipment, a logistics manager can reserve the space to ensure that a large shipment of merchandise arrives on time. Without the Internet, the logistics manager must make a series of telephone calls to obtain the information.

Many retailers now offer manufacturers access to databases via the Internet. The manufacturer's marketing team can study what products are selling. They also can see which colors, sizes, and styles are the most popular. They even can find out which stores have the highest levels of sales. Then the manufacturer can modify or set production schedules in order to make sure retailers have a steady supply of the right sizes, colors, and styles.

In general, the marketing team cannot underestimate the importance of customer service to an IMC program. Quality service conveys the idea to the customer that the company cares. Service programs also help every member of the marketing channel build strong bonds with its constituents.

## DIRECT MARKETING ON THE INTERNET

In Chapter 11, the Internet was noted an ideal medium for direct marketing because consumers and businesses can order directly from the company. Loyal Internet patrons can also be sent e-mails promoting specific products or discounts and other price incentives. Many Internet direct-marketing programs are tied in with other media.

Currently, direct mail is the most effective tool for getting customers to investigate a Web site and place an Internet order.[37] A print catalog that is mailed to a target audience of consumers and businesses can be highly effective. These customers will often exam the catalog during leisure time or while making a purchase decision at work. The order is placed using the Internet.

The iGo.com direct-mail piece shown on the right includes catalog, telephone, and Internet features. The mailing has a box the customer can check in order to receive a free iGo e-newsletter along with a response card used to request the iGo catalog. The mailing is designed to obtain names for a database. These names and addresses can then be used in future direct-mail and e-mail marketing programs. The mailing piece also encourages recipients to visit the iGo.com Web site to learn more about the company's Pocket mail service. Individuals making purchases receive 2 months of free e-mail service.

A direct-mail piece encouraging consumers to visit the iGo.com Web site and to receive the iGo e-newsletter.
*Source:* Courtesy of iGo.com.

The most recent trend in direct marketing via the Internet is **interactive marketing**. Interactive marketing is individualizing and personalizing everything from the Internet Web content to the products being promoted on e-mail messages. NCR produces software called "Relationship Optimizer and Prime Response" that uses powerful data analysis techniques to personalize direct offers. The NCR software analyzes customer interactions such as click-stream data traffic—any type of customer interaction with the firm—and combines it with demographic information from external or internal direct-marketing databases. As the data are being processed, the software can launch complex interactive and personalized Web and e-mail campaigns.

Levi Strauss uses similar software, called "Blue Martini E-Merchandising," to customize both the Levis.com and the Dockers.com Web sites. The Home Shopping Network uses Edify's Smart Options software to track user preferences and suggest products based on the customer's past activities and current purchases. These technologies blur the line between selling and marketing because the messages and products a customer sees are based on past purchasing and browsing activities. These programs are designed to increase the odds that the customer will see something he or she wants rather than being forced to wade through scores of products he or she has no interest in purchasing at a more standardized Web site.[38]

As new technologies emerge, other forms of direct-marketing programs will become possible. Also, as more people access the Web while on the move (through pagers and other carry-around devices), Web marketers undoubtedly will develop methods to reach customers with on-demand goods and services. It is likely that direct marketing has only scratched the surface of the potential the Internet offers.

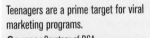

Teenagers are a prime target for viral marketing programs.
*Source:* Courtesy of RCA.

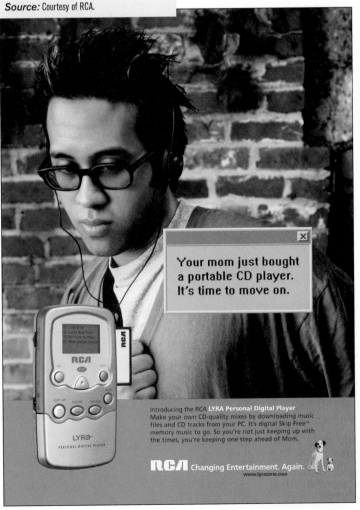

Your mom just bought a portable CD player. It's time to move on.

Introducing the RCA **LYRA Personal Digital Player**
Make your own CD-quality mixes by downloading music files and CD tracks from your PC. It's digital Skip Free™ memory music to go. So you're not just keeping up with the times, you're keeping one step ahead of Mom.

**RCA** Changing Entertainment. Again.
www.lyrazone.com

Remember, however, that sending unsolicited e-mails can alienate customers, who are already frustrated with the amount of spam they receive. Internet spam is the equivalent of junk mail sent to a general audience. An Internet e-mail direct-marketing program should be targeted at individuals who are most likely to be interested in a company and its products. For many Internet direct-marketing programs, the best idea is to first get the customer's permission. Obtaining this permission is easier when some type of reward or incentive is offered.

## VIRAL MARKETING ON THE INTERNET

Today's technology has created a new form of marketing. **Viral marketing** is preparing an advertisement that is tied to an e-mail. It is also a form of advocacy or word-of-mouth endorsement marketing. In other words, viral marketing takes place as one customer passes along a message to other potential buyers. The name *viral* is derived from the image of a person being infected with the marketing message, then spreading it to friends like a virus. The major difference, however, is that the customer voluntarily sends the message to others.

Viral marketing messages include ads for goods and services, hyperlinked promotions that take someone immediately to a Web site, online newsletters, streaming videos, and various games. Statistics indicate that about 80 percent of recipients who receive viral marketing messages pass them along to others. Almost 50 percent pass messages along to two or more people. Viral messages can be sent directly to friends and family using an e-mail forward. They can also be transmitted passively, when the message is simply attached to an e-mail. Viral marketing allows a firm to gain rapid product awareness at a low cost.[39]

Blue Marble, a viral marketing company, created a program for Scope mouthwash. Consumers were able to send a customized, animated e-mail "kiss" to their friends. The attached marketing message reinforced the brand message that Scope brings people "kissably close." People who received the e-mail kiss could then forward the message to someone else. Scope's tracking technology indicated most did forward the message.

Mazda also recently created a viral marketing campaign. The attachment was a video clip about parking cars, a Mazda, of course, and the differences between males and females. The clip and link were passed on to thousands and sparked an international debate on blogs and in other forums about male and female parking capabilities. Globally, the viral marketing campaign generated over a million views in less than a month. The video clip was located at **www.mazda.com**. As with other viral marketing campaigns, this one provided a high level of brand exposure at a very low cost to Mazda.[40]

An advertisement by *The Joplin Globe* offering local businesses Web site development services.
*Source:* Used with permission of *The Joplin Globe*, Joplin, Missouri.

## INTERNET DESIGN ISSUES

The primary issue in the design of a Web site is to make sure it functions properly. E-commerce companies spend an average of $100 to acquire each new customer, and some companies spend up to $500.[41] It may appear that developing an effective Web site is cheap. In reality it is not. As a result, it is essential that the firm specify the key function to be served by the Web site before it is created. In addition, the site should then be designed to effectively support the function that is to be provided. If the function is to *support e-commerce,* then the site should be easy for customers to navigate. Selecting products and making orders must also be simple. If the key function is to *support selling,* then the person designing the Web site should first talk with salespeople and determine their concerns.

Companies spend almost $20 billion per year on Internet advertising of Web sites. Just as with the other components of advertising, careful consideration should be given to where the advertisements will be placed. One approach is to focus on targeted Web sites with similar customer profiles. For example, a Web site for John Deere farm tractors and implements may also advertise on other agriculture-related Web sites. Another approach is to advertise on a broader array of sites to develop brand awareness. A company can advertise on a variety of Web sites in order to encourage different people to visit its Web site. Even if a person does not go to the site, the ad enhances brand awareness.[42]

A Web site should match the constituency it serves. Too often, a site is designed by a computer whiz who likes fancy graphics and images, but the users of the site hate it because they cannot find what they are looking for or the pages take too long to load. Figure 13.9 provides common Web site design problems.

The proliferation of e-commerce Web sites is challenging. The marketing team should avoid as many pitfalls as possible to achieve the goal of building a stronger company through Internet activities. In contrast to the don'ts listed in Figure 13.9, Figure 13.10 highlights some tips for creating winning Web sites.

FIGURE 13.9
Clues to Poor Design

▶ Clueless banners
▶ Slow loading front pages
▶ Forcing people to go through numerous screens
▶ Too much verbal information
▶ Too many technical terms
▶ Sites that are hard to navigate

FIGURE 13.10
Tips to Creating Winning Web Sites

▶ The Web site should follow a strategic purpose such as to acquire new customers, serve existing customers, or to cross-sell goods and services.
▶ Make the Web site easy to access and quick to load.
▶ Written content should be precise with short words, short sentences, and short paragraphs.
▶ Remember that content is the key to success, not fancy graphics and design.
▶ Be certain graphics support content, and do not detract from it.
▶ Make some type of marketing offer to encourage a response.
▶ Ask for site evaluation.
▶ Provide easy-to-use navigation links on every page.
▶ Use gimmicks such as moving icons or flashing banners to gain attention at the beginning but do not use them deeper in the Web site.
▶ Change the Web site on a regular basis to keep individuals coming back.
▶ Measure results continually, especially designs and offers.

*Source:* Based on Ray Jutkins, "13 Ideas That Could Lead to Successful Web Marketing," *Advertising Age's Business Marketing* 84, no. 6 (June 1999), p. 27.

# SUMMARY

Increased usage of the Internet by both consumers and businesses has led most marketing teams to develop some type of Internet site. Sometimes Web designers are being asked to design a Web page because it's the "thing to do," and little or no thought is given to the functions the Web site should perform. This chapter is designed to explain how an Internet Web site can be integrated into the overall integrated marketing communications plan and why it should.

The primary goals of various Web sites are for advertising, sales support, customer service, public relations, and e-commerce. An e-commerce Web site will include a catalog, a shopping cart, and a method to collect payments. In e-commerce and other Internet ventures, customers must feel the process is secure and be enticed to change their buying habits. Three incentives that help people alter buying patterns are financial incentives, greater convenience, and added value.

The Internet changes the traditional ways that buyers and sellers deal with each other. In business-to-business markets, field salespeople have traditionally called on customers and prospects. Information is shared, prices are negotiated, and orders are taken. On the Internet, buyers can purchase directly from suppliers. Middlemen can be eliminated. Buyers can obtain quotes from a number of vendors and obtain product information from each, all on the Internet. Although it saves the selling company money in

terms of sales calls, it also risks losing customers. Loyalty and strong relationships are endangered as buyers search the Web to meet their corporations' needs.

International markets may also be served by e-commerce enterprises, especially when cultural differences, shipping problems, and Internet capability problems can be solved. Information technology departments will play a key role in solving the Internet problems. Shipping issues and language differences also require attention in this lucrative and growing marketplace.

The Internet blurs many internal functional boundaries. An effective Internet Web site can advertise, send sales messages, provide public relations announcements, offer press releases to the media, talk about the company, provide answers to frequently asked questions, provide information to investors, dispense product catalogs complete with product descriptions and prices, take orders from customers, process payments, receive e-mail messages, handle customer service queries, and entertain Web viewers.

As always, the primary goal of an Internet program is to expand and enhance the message portrayed by the company's IMC plan. Careful attention must be paid to issues of brand image and loyalty. Web sites must be designed to support selling efforts and customer service programs, and deliver consumer promotions of value to potential buyers. Brand spiraling may be used to combine the Internet program with advertising in traditional media. The quality of a Web site is a primary factor in the success of the entire Internet program. Many company leaders are beginning to grasp the potential of these marketing efforts, as interest and activity on the Web continue to grow. In the end, the potential of the Internet may be limited only by what the company decides to do.

## REVIEW QUESTIONS

1. What percentage of U.S. citizens uses the Internet? What about Canadians? Does this have implications for IMC programs?

2. What marketing functions can be provided on the Internet?

3. Define *e-commerce*. What are the three common components of e-commerce programs?

4. What two issues must e-commerce providers overcome in order to build successful businesses?

5. Name and describe the three main incentives used to attract shoppers to e-commerce Web sites.

6. What is cyberbait? How must it be used to maintain it as an effective marketing tactic?

7. In business-to-business e-commerce operations, what obstacles occur? How can they be overcome?

8. What problems exist for international e-commerce operations? What can companies do to resolve them?

9. How can the Internet affect a brand? Brand loyalty?

10. What is brand spiraling? What is the primary goal of brand spiraling programs?

11. How can the Internet be used to provide sales support?

12. How can the Internet be used to provide customer service?

13. How can direct marketing be used most effectively to reach customers?

14. What is interactive marketing?

15. What is viral marketing? What is the goal of a viral marketing program?

16. What tactics should companies avoid in designing Web sites? What should they do to make effective Web pages?

## KEY TERMS

**FAQs (frequently asked questions)**   Questions people have about various items or services.

**e-commerce**   Selling goods and services on the Internet.

**shopping cart**   A component of e-commerce operations that allows the individual to mark items to purchase later as part of a complete order.

**cyberbait**   Some type of lure or attraction that brings people to a Web site.

**brand spiraling**   The practice of using traditional media to promote and attract consumers to an online Web site.

**halo effect**   A situation in which a well-received brand leads customers to try new company products and services that are being offered via the Internet.

**Web master**   The person who manages a firm's Web site.

**interactive marketing**   Individualizing and personalizing Web content and e-mail messages for various consumers.

**viral marketing**   Preparing an advertisement that is tied to an e-mail in which one person passes on the advertisement or e-mail to other consumers.

## CRITICAL THINKING EXERCISES

### Discussion Questions

1. What types of goods or services have you purchased over the Internet during the last year? Have your parents purchased anything using the Internet? If so, compare your purchases and attitudes toward buying via the Internet to theirs. If neither you nor your parents have used the Internet to make purchases, why not?

2. Access four different Web sites for one of the following products. Locate the FAQ section. Was the FAQ section difficult to find? How is the FAQ section organized? Does it provide effective answers for questions? Do the four sites have similar questions listed?

   a. Antivirus software

   b. Cosmetic surgery

   c. Automobile parts

   d. Cameras

   e. Financial services

3. First Energy Corporation, the nation's twelfth largest utility, purchases about 30 percent of its coal via the Internet. The purchasing process that normally took 60 days to complete has been compressed to just 2 weeks. Bidding takes place on a single day, and suppliers know within 2 to 3 days whether they have won the order.[43] What risks does First Energy take in purchasing coal over the Internet? How can those risks be minimized? Why would a supplier want to sell coal over the Internet instead of developing a strong personal relationship with First Energy Corporation?

4. Credit card security is an issue with many people. Interview five people of various ages and genders. Does age or gender make any difference in the person's feelings, especially about the fear of using a credit card to make purchases over the Internet? Are there specific products or Web sites that people do not trust? More importantly, how do you judge whether a Web site provides the necessary credit security?

5. Pick one of the following product categories. What types of financial incentives are offered on the company's Web site to encourage you to purchase? What about the other two types of incentives, greater convenience and added value? What evidence do you see for them?

   a. Contacts or eyeglasses

   b. Water skis

   c. Jeans

   d. Computers

   e. Camping supplies

# INTEGRATED LEARNING EXERCISES

1. To better understand who is using the Internet, access the CyberAtlas Web site at **www.cyberatlas.com**. What information is available under the "Stats Toolbox"? What other information is on the Web site? What type of articles does the Web site have? How can it be used by someone involved in e-commerce or other types of Internet marketing?

2. Best Buy Company was a late e-commerce entrant, but it has developed a strong e-commerce component. The key to Best Buy's success, according to Barry Judge, vice president of marketing, is, "We do a lot of one-to-one marketing. We're not overly focused on where the consumers buy." The Web site carries every product that Best Buy stocks. It uses personalized services, along with convenient pickup and fair return policies to entice consumers to shop. The consumer can purchase items on the Internet and either have them shipped directly to them or pick them up at the closest store. Shoppers can use the Internet to see if Best Buy stocks a particular item, what the item costs, and to gather product information.[44] What is the advantage to this philosophy? Access the Web site at **www.bestbuy.com**. Evaluate it in terms of ease of use and product information, and then locate the Best Buy closest to you. Next, access Circuit City's Web site at **www.circuitcity.com**. Compare it to Best Buy's site. Select one product such as a camcorder to compare the two Web sites.

3. Examine the advertisements in this chapter by iGo.com and then access the company's Web site at **www.igo.com**. Do the advertisements match the information on the Web site? How are they integrated? What parts are not well integrated?

4. Part of iGo's business is a workforce management service operation. Access the Web site at **www.employeesavings.com**. What services are offered? How would you promote this site through off-line advertising? What other venues or methods would you recommend for marketing this particular site?

5. The primary companies businesses use to ship small packages either overnight or 2-day delivery are FedEx, UPS, and the U.S. Postal Service. Access each of these Web sites (FedEx at **www.fedex.com**; UPS at **www.ups.com**; U.S. Postal Service at **www.usps.gov**). What guarantees do they make about delivery? Which site is the most user-friendly? Which site appears to offer the best customer service? In looking at the different functions of a Web site discussed in this chapter, indicate the function for which each Web site was designed.

6. Web sites serve a number of different functions. Access the following Web sites. What is the primary function of each? For each site, list other functions it offers.

   a. MVP.com (**www.mvp.com**)

   b. Travelocity (**www.travelocity.com**)

   c. Trebnick Systems (**www.trebnick.com**)

   d. Wells Fargo Bank (**www.wellsfargo.com**)

   e. Victoria's Secret (**www.victoriassecret.com**)

   f. WeddingChannel.com (**www.weddingchannel.com**)

   g. Saturn (**www.saturn.com**)

   h. Harley-Davidson (**www.harley-davidson.com**)

7. Customer interactive software is an important part of many Web sites. Access the following two companies that sell interactive software. What capabilities does each software package offer? What other services are available?

   a. Blue Martini Software (**www.bluemartini.com**)

   b. Edify (**www.edify.com**)

# STUDENT PROJECT

### IMC Plan Pro

If you want to keep up with the rapidly changing world of marketing, it will be important to incorporate a quality Internet program with the other elements of an IMC program. The IMC Plan Pro disk and booklet from Prentice Hall provides examples of companies that are using Internet marketing as part of the overall integrated communications effort.

# CASE 1

## THE CIRCULATION GAME

William Johnson was about to embark on a major new phase of his publishing career. He had begun as a writer for a small newspaper in New York; the newspaper had been oriented toward an African-American readership. From there, William had become an editor and eventually a publisher of a chain of small-town newspapers in Georgia. The cities the chain served also were predominantly African-American. Now, however, William's company had just made a successful bid to acquire newspapers in six cities in the upper Midwest. Suddenly William was about to become one of the largest minority newspaper owners in the United States.

The newspaper business has changed dramatically in the past half century. From a time when papers were the primary source of news for most Americans until the new millennium, where citizens are bombarded with news formats of all types, a major shakeout of news chains had occurred. Smaller local papers were forced to compete with national offerings, such as *USA Today* and *The Wall Street Journal.* Readership changed as well. In the latter half of the twentieth century, editors knew their readers were largely 18 years of age or older and reasonably well educated.

Currently, newspapers appear in several formats: tabloids, traditional papers, weekly magazines, and Internet news. They compete with radio news stations, network news, and cable news stations such as CNN, ESPN, and other more specific program formats. African-Americans can also tune in to one cable channel devoted more exclusively to them: the BET (Black Entertainment Channel), which offers some news programming. Satellites allow breaking news stories to appear instantly around the world, and people can access news via the Internet when a television is not nearby.

William's company, like most other paper chains, derives income from several sources. First, the "old-fashioned" subscriber forms the basis of the company's circulation numbers. Businesses buy advertising space, and many individuals and companies run classified ads. Weekly newspapers sell additional advertising space in these magazine-type papers. The newest source of revenue is advertising on Internet editions of the paper.

The biggest change in the newspaper business is the partnerships involved. Most papers are owned by media giants that also own radio and television stations. There is a cross-mix of reporting, polling, and other activities. In addition, most newspapers, even in small towns, find they must advertise the product in other markets. Thus, newspapers buy ads on television and on the radio to promote readership. The circulation department conducts telephone sales campaigns designed to entice people to buy home delivery. Others are distributed in vending machines and in newsstands throughout each city.

In this complex marketplace, William looks for ways to expand the reach of the paper and to compete with other media. He knows the future will witness increasing use of the Internet by most households, but there will continue to be a strong base of readers who want to wake up in the morning, go out to the front yard, pick up a paper, and read it over coffee or breakfast.

1. How can William's company cater to various minorities in its Internet division of the newspaper? Or should he avoid this type of tactic?

2. What special marketing and IMC challenges affect newspapers in both circulation (retail) and business-to-business (advertising) areas?

3. Find your local city's newspaper on the Internet. How is it different from a traditional "paper" newspaper? How is it similar?

4. Design an advertising program for William Johnson's local newspaper's Internet edition.

# CASE 2

## SHELLY'S CONNECTION

K. Michele Kacmar (who goes by Shelly) loved love. She enjoyed introducing people to see if any kind of spark would fire. She had "set up" several friends who wound up dating and even marrying each other. Shelly's other major talent was Web design. These two skills led Shelly to believe her calling was to set up an Internet dating service. She created one for the Los Angeles area, where she lived, called "Shelly's Connection."

Shelly's Connection had two twists. First, the site was designed only for local people, in Los Angeles and the surrounding counties. She was not trying to set up a national service. Second, besides simply making high-tech introductions, Shelly's Connection offered social events. These included evening "meet ups," where people sipping coffee or soft drinks circulated through the room and visited with 5 to 10 potential dating partners in a 90-minute time span. Also, Shelly's Connection had singles parties and mixers where people who had expressed interest in three or four potential dating partners could pay a cover charge and then attend the event; light snacks were served, dance music was played at a volume low enough for people to talk, and a cash bar was available. Shelly's marketing idea was to create a "fully integrated" dating program.

Internet dating services are not new. They are plagued by several problems. First, unless properly screened, married people sign up to start dating "on the side." Second, some people confuse dating services with online escort services and prostitution rings. Third, most dating services offer nationwide prospects rather than just local arrangements. Sifting through all of the clients to find one close to home can be a problem. Fourth, some people shy away from the services because they feel like joining makes them seem "desperate."

To combat these problems, Shelly believed a high-quality advertising campaign would be needed. The ad should clearly spell out what type of service she offered, warn away married people, and emphasize that dating and meeting people are time-consuming. Shelly's Connection was set up to offer convenience, help people who want to use their spare time wisely, and have fun. Armed with some venture capital from local investors, Shelly's Connection began operations. Time would tell if love would bloom and Shelly would enjoy a successful Internet business operation.

1. Are there any other potential problems that Shelly has not considered in creating her company?
2. Which media should Shelly use to promote her Web site?
3. Create the ad copy Shelly's Connection should use in its advertisements. Also, write an effective tagline for the ads.

# ENDNOTES

1. Heidi Gautschi, "Search in Any Language," *EContent* 28, no. 5 (May 2005), p. 29; "Google Is Standing on the Brink of Global Dominance," *Marketing Week* (April 28, 2005), p. 31; Thomas Claburn and Tony Kontzer, "Google Wants a Piece of the Business Market," *InformationWeek*, no. 1040 (May 23, 2005), p. 29; Mathew Creamer and Kris Oser, "Google Breaks Down and Decides to Advertise," *Advertising Age* 76, no. 18 (May 2, 2005), p. 3.

2. Linda Lyons, "Britons, Canadians Logging More Time Online," *Gallup Poll Tuesday Briefing* (February 15, 2005), pp. 1–3; "Online Activities," *World Almanac & Book of Facts* (2005), pp. 391–392.

3. Alan Mitchell, "Marketers Must Grasp the Net or Face Oblivion," *Marketing Week* 22, no. 3 (February 18, 1999), pp. 30–31.

4. David Sparrow, "Get 'em to Bite," *Catalog Age* 20, no. 4 (April 2003), pp. 35–36.

5. Ibid.

6. Mark Del Franco, "Mailers Say, Webward Ho!" *Catalog Age* 19, no. 4 (March 15, 2002), pp. 1–3.

7. David Sparrow, "Get 'em to Bite," *Catalog Age* 20, no. 4 (April 2003), pp. 35–36.

8. Mark Del Franco, "Mailers Say, Webward Ho!" *Catalog Age* 19, no. 4 (March 15, 2002), pp. 1–3.

9. Elisabeth Goodridge, "E-Businesses Hope to Learn That Edu-Commerce Pays," *InformationWeek,* no. 877 (February 25, 2002), pp. 76–77.

10. "Data," *B to B* 90, no. 5 (April 11, 2005), p. 5.

11. Bob Donath, "Web Could Boost Branding in B-to-B Marketing," *Marketing News* 32, no. 10 (May 11, 1998), p. 6.

12. Doug Harper, "Net Gains, Net Pains," *Industrial Distribution* 89, no. 9 (September 2000), pp. E4–6.

13. John Evan Frook, "Trading Hubs Drive Changes," *B to B* 85, no. 4 (April 24, 2000), p. 33.

14. Karen E. Hussel, "New Service Helps Brand Clicks with Bricks," *Advertising Age's Business Marketing* 84, no. 11 (November 1999), pp. 40–41.

15. "The Cross-Selling Machine," *Business 2.0* 4, no. 4 (May 2003), pp. 84–85.

16. Theo Mullen, "Minolta to Go Global with B2B Site," *InternetWeek,* no. 842 (December 18, 2000), p. 13.

17. Lynda Radosevich, "Going Global Overnight," *InfoWorld* 21, no. 16 (April 19, 1999), pp. 1–3.

18. "The Worldly Web," *CFO* 19, no. 7 (June 2003), p. 30.

19. Todd McCollough, "Online Services Make Ordering, Billing, Printing a Snap," *Business First* 15, no. 24 (February 5, 1999), pp. 19–20.

20. Julia King, "Online Marketing Tools Can Cause IT Disasters," *Computerworld* 33, no. 46 (November 15, 1999), p. 49.

21. Norma Ramage, "Searching for Visitors," *Marketing Magazine* 109, no. 33 (October 18, 2004), p. 8.

22. Tom Zeller, Jr., "Law Barring Junk E-Mail Allows a Flood Instead," *The New York Times* (February 1, 2005).

23. "A Little Restraint, Please," *Marketing News* 36, no. 11 (May 21, 2002), p. 4; "E-Mail Newsletters Click Better with Customers," *Marketing News* 35, no, 6 (March 12, 2001), p. 3.

24. Catherine Arnold, "Vox Venditori," *Marketing News* 38, no. 5 (March 15, 2004), pp. 1, 11–12.

25. Carol Patton, "Marketers Promote Online Traffic Through Traditional Media," *Advertising Age's Business Marketing* 84, no. 8 (August 1999), p. 40.

26. Alan Bergstrom, "Cyberbranding: Leveraging Your Brand on the Internet," *Strategy & Leadership* 28, no. 4 (2000), pp. 10–15.

27. Based on Robert Harvin, "In Internet Branding, the Off-Lines Have It," *Brandweek* 41, no. 4 (January 24, 2000), pp. 30–31.

28. David Sparrow, "Get 'em to Bite," *Catalog Age* 20, no. 4 (April 2003), pp. 35–36.

29. Ibid.

30. "Not Scratching the Niche," *Marketing News* 34, no. 14 (June 19, 2000), p. 3.

31. Todd McCollough, "Online Services Make Ordering, Billing, Printing a Snap," *Business First* 15, no. 24 (February 5, 1999), pp. 19–20.

32. "Yes, I Would Like Some Help, Thank You," *Marketing News* 26, no. 4 (February 18, 2002), p. 3.

33. "E-Tailers Offer Poor Customer Service," *New Media Age* (September 2, 2004), p. 10.

34. "Six Steps to Improve Your Organization's E-Service," *Report on Customer Relationship Management* 2002, no. 11 (November 2002), pp. 1–4.

35. Ibid.

36. Priya Malhotra, "Wells Offers Web Hand-Holding," *American Banker* 167, no. 189 (October 2, 2002), p. 20.

37. "Direct Mail Drives Internet Economy," *Graphic Arts Monthly* 72, no. 2 (February 2000), p. 94.

38. Jeff Sweat and Rick Whiting, "Instant Marketing," *InformationWeek* no. 746 (August 2, 1999), pp. 18–20.

39. Alf Nucifora, "Viral Marketing Spreads by 'Word of Net,'" *Business Journal* 14, no. 18 (May 5, 2000), pp. 25–26.

40. Justin Kirty, "Getting the Bug," *Brand Strategy,* no. 184 (July/August 2004), p. 33.

41. Donna L. Hoffman and Thomas P. Novak, "How to Acquire Customers on the Web," *Harvard Business Review* 78, no. 3 (May–June 2000), pp. 179–85.

42. Mie-Yun Lee, "Goal-Based Strategy Can Make Banner Ads Click," *Puget Sound Business Journal* 30, no. 21 (October 1, 1999), p. 18.

43. Hussel, "New Service Helps Brand Clicks with Bricks."

44. Tobi Elkin, "Best Buy Takes Cue from Retail Shops," *Advertising Age* 71, no. 10 (March 6, 2000), p. 8.

# IMC for Small Businesses and Entrepreneurial Ventures

## Chapter Objectives

*Develop* an understanding of the challenges facing entrepreneurs and small-business owners, especially in the area of marketing communications.

*Explain* the tactics used to reach small-business customers effectively.

*Utilize* programs, such as guerilla marketing, to manage costs while designing an effective message.

*Take* advantage of alternative media, lifestyle marketing, and other advertising programs to reach a small-business target market.

## THE PASTA HOUSE CO.

### Neighborhood Marketing Builds Big Profits

"The Hill" in St. Louis, Missouri, is nationally known for fine Italian dining. In the neighborhood where baseball legends Yogi Berra and Joe Gargiola grew up, numerous low-cost/high-quality restaurants are sprinkled among the houses and small businesses. In the middle of this competition, The Pasta House Co. has grown from a single unit in 1974 to more than 20 locations in St. Louis alone, along with franchises throughout the United States and internationally.

J. Kim Tucci, Joseph Fresta (shown in the photo, respectively) and their deceased partner John Ferrara, all sons of Italian immigrants, founded The Pasta House Co. The original decor featured Italian pop culture in a setting of an imaginary pasta factory. Nearly 30 pasta dishes, 10 entrees, and all-you-can eat salad are on the menu. Company profits grew, in part, due to a suggestive selling program in which add-ons such as appetizers, wines, specialty drinks, specialty breads, and desserts created larger ticket totals per customer. The Pasta House Co.'s cheese garlic bread is a popular favorite among regulars.

When it became apparent that demand was great enough to expand, a site selection group helped pick the next six locations. To make sure that each unit was successful, owners of The Pasta House Co. began a neighborhood marketing program. "It's a family-oriented business, and basically we do things for families," says J. Kim Tucci about the operations.

To build loyalty to individual stores, a frequent diner program was instituted in which a person who buys $250 worth of food is given a $25 gift certificate. The certificate can only be redeemed at the location where the person is a frequent diner member, to encourage neighborhood loyalty. Members of the club also get free

spaghetti and a dessert on their birthdays and a candlelight dinner for two on their anniversaries.

The Pasta House Co.'s outreach program has been another major source of brand recognition and customer loyalty. One plan, called the "Reading, Writing, and Ravioli" program, is targeted toward elementary students. A child reads a book, writes a book report, and receives a free dish of spaghetti or ravioli with a salad and Coca-Cola as a prize. Coca-Cola is a co-sponsor of the program. More than 400 schools and 4,000 teachers participate in the program. Since it began, over 6 million book reports have been turned in. Participating teachers receive a 50 percent discount coupon each month. "Inside every classroom is our logo and Coca-Cola's logo, a list of students, and how many books they've read," Tucci reports. He believes students are more loyal to The Pasta House Co. than to McDonald's as a result.

At the high school level, The Pasta House Co. sponsors a student art contest. To enter, students must recreate a great work of art with one addition—a plate of pasta. Winners and their schools receive prizes up to $1,000.

The Pasta House Co. also participates each year in the Jerry Lewis Muscular Dystrophy program, giving 30 cents for each order of toasted ravioli to "Jerry's Kids." Every 5 years, The Pasta House Co. sets up a "RavoMeter" thermometer to show how much money has been raised. The company also maintains its own not-for-profit organization, The Caring and Sharing program. The organization raises money and canned goods to distribute to locals during the Christmas season. Individual employees have a payroll plan in which money is given to St. Jude's Hospital in Memphis, Tennessee.

Further expansion now comes from franchising. There are 29 additional units beyond St. Louis. The first foreign franchise was established in the Dominican Republic. "The taste for Italian food is as universal as hamburgers and pizza, no question about it," Tucci says. Franchising agreements combined with local sales generated more than $55 million. Licensee training takes place in St. Louis.

In the future, The Pasta House Co. will expand into both domestic and foreign locations. From humble beginnings, many success stories similar to The Pasta House Co.

have emerged. Each one contains common elements of quality, reputation, specialization in one unique competitive advantage area, community outreach, an energetic and visionary ownership group, and a strong message theme that reaches the target market effectively.[1]

**overview**

Is owning your own business still the "Great American Dream"? The answer may depend on whom you ask. Projections are that new business ventures will create a substantial number of new millionaires in the next 2 decades. On the other hand, starting, owning, and maintaining a small business is still a high-risk venture, although it remains an attractive option for many individuals.

One of the keys to success in creating a new business is to stand out in the marketplace. Doing so means careful planning and disciplined implementation. A well-thought-out IMC program is an essential tool in the pursuit of success.

The purposes of this chapter are to: (1) describe the challenges associated with running a small business or entrepreneurial venture, (2) spell out how to create an IMC plan for this unique situation, one that is especially oriented to finding and attracting customers, and (3) present methods for creating and keeping loyal customers. As is the case in any size organization, it is vital for the operation to speak with one clear and distinct voice to cut through the clutter of the marketplace. For a new start-up business, this is even more critical.

The interior of a Pasta House Co. facility.

## TYPES OF VENTURES

All small businesses and new ventures are not the same; the range is quite large. Here are a few common types:

▶ A small family-owned business, such as a dry cleaner, a restaurant, a specialty shop (e.g., photo studio), or a one-stop convenience store, designed to provide the family with income

▶ A business start-up with growth in mind, either through increased product sales, multiple locations, or franchise agreements

▶ Corporate start-ups of entrepreneurial ventures, such wireless phone and Internet access services offered by long-distance companies

▶ Groups of physicians, dentists, or other professionals who go into practice together

Typically, **entrepreneurship** means a company is being formed with the express goal of becoming larger through an aggressive growth agenda. **Intrepreneurship** is a corporate spin-off or start-up. A **small business** is a family-owned company or consortium of professionals that is formed with specific objectives in mind. In most cases, aggressive growth is not as important as providing adequate income for the owners of a small business.

## MAJOR CHALLENGES

A new business faces many challenges. The common denominator is that the company is unknown in the marketplace. Some of the issues new ventures experience include:

▶ Consumers are not aware of the business.

▶ Consumers are cautious or wary of trying a new good, service, or company.

▶ Advertising and promotional clutter make it difficult to be recognized.

▶ Small budgets for marketing, advertising, and promotional activities make it difficult to compete.

▶ New businesses are especially vulnerable to negative word-of-mouth communications.

Many consumers are cautious about trying new goods, services, or companies. Purchases are often based on known brand names and familiar purchasing patterns. It is much easier for customers to purchase the same brand they have always purchased or another brand name they recognize or have used. To be considered, a new business name or brand must be recalled, and the memory must be positive enough to entice the person to try the product or company.

A major obstacle to overcome is the massive amount of marketing clutter that all companies face. Overcoming clutter is especially difficult for new firms with limited budgets for marketing and promotion. Traditional methods of advertising and consumer promotions may not be enough to get recognized.

Company leaders must be sure to deliver on promises and provide a high-quality experience, especially on the customer's first purchase. One bad encounter will often lead to negative word-of-mouth. A new business will probably not get a second chance if the customer has a bad experience.

To overcome these problems, a new company must develop a unique selling point and find a way to inform consumers about that advantage.[2] Everything from the brand name to the logo to company advertisements must capture the interest and attention of the consumer. It is important to remember that customers are interested in *benefits* as opposed to product or service *features,* or as one writer put it, "What's in it for me?" The new company must be able to clearly answer this question in order to survive and grow.[3]

## STARTING A COMPANY: THE MARKET ANALYSIS

A business may be started for many reasons, including one as simple as turning a hobby into something more profitable. Someone who loves computers may decide to open a computer retail store or computer repair service. The new entrepreneur can go it alone, form a partnership with someone who has the same interest, or start up a franchise operation such as Geeks On Call. By purchasing a franchise from Geeks On Call, an individual gains access to marketing materials, a business plan, and an established customer base.[4] In any case, no matter how the business begins, a careful market analysis is in order. This includes three steps (see Figure 14.1):

1. Understand and define consumer needs.
2. Establish a clearly defined product.
3. Develop a unique market niche.

Small businesses, such as Joplin Pool and Spa, are an important component of each community's local economy.

*Source:* Used with permission of *The Joplin Globe,* Joplin, Missouri.

In this advertisement, Merry Maids offers house-cleaning services to consumers.

*Source:* Courtesy of Merry Maids L.P.

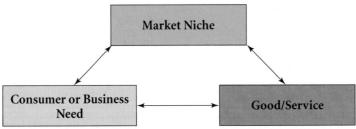

## FIGURE 14.1
### The Market Analysis

**Finding a target market means matching the needs of consumers or businesses with a good or service in a unique way.**

These three tasks proceed together as the creation of a business moves forward. Although the market analysis steps are combined in the actual practice, each is presented here separately.

## Understanding and Defining Consumer Needs

Understanding and defining needs means knowing more than just names, demographic characteristics, or psychological tendencies of target market segments. It means understanding what a particular group desires from a good or service that is not currently available. An ongoing and successful dot-com business is an Internet-based concierge service called VIPdesk. The company was created to serve an unmet need: Some people believe they can make better use of their time when certain tasks are "farmed out." VIPdesk buys theater tickets, sends flowers, and provides numerous "gofer" chores for customers of corporate clients such as MasterCard International and Citibank.[5] At the time the company was founded, the service was one that had never before been offered via the Internet. The market niche is corporate customers and individuals with greater levels of disposable income.

Chris Otto identified another unmet need when she created a mobile dog-grooming business and named it "Your Fairy Dogmother." First, Otto recognized that people did not like to transport a dirty dog to a grooming shop, leave it all day in a cage, and then have to rush back after work to pick the dog up and take it home. Your Fairy Dogmother goes to the customer's residence in a brightly painted van with the company's name boldly featured and grooms the dog. Otto says, her customers, " . . . love the service. They love the fact that the dog doesn't have to leave the house." In this case, the major factor in the decision to purchase the service is convenience, which made it easy to give the company a try. Also, the company's name suggests that the family pet is treated with extra special care. By understanding and then defining the needs of her customers, Otto has been able to develop a successful small business.[6]

Through careful research, the entrepreneurs who started Geeks On Call, VIPdesk, and Your Fairy Dogmother were able to identify a target market. Although the demographic characteristics of customers are helpful, a new start-up must go beyond demographics to include psychographic and purchasing behavior information. Understanding the needs, attitudes, interests, and opinions of individuals in the target market is important in developing a good or service. It is also important in preparing an IMC plan that will reach those consumers.

## Creating a Clearly Defined Product

A clearly defined product is one in which everyone knows exactly what the company intends to deliver. As Leslie Godwin, a career and life-transition counselor pointed out, it is just as important to say what your company *won't* do as what it will do.[7] She noted that a psychotherapist with a business card that says "Specializes in treating children, adults, adolescents, groups, and individuals" is overstating the professional's talents. Compared to an ob/gyn who claims she specializes in "women struggling with menopause," the differences are obvious.

A Cut-N-Heaven understands the needs of their customers.

*Source:* Used with permission of *The Joplin Globe*, Joplin, Missouri.

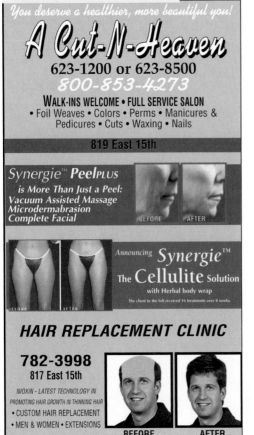

One doctor is trying to be all things to all people. The other has more logically spelled out a form of expertise that would be attractive to a specific set of people.

An entrepreneur must avoid falling into the trap of trying to please everyone. Doing so means there is no clear sense of identity for employees, customers, and company leaders. Instead, a simple question should be asked, "What do we do well?" The goal is to feature that good, service, or skill.

Once the product is clearly defined, it is important to carefully create a brand name, logo, and other word-based marketing elements such as the company's slogan and advertising tagline. These items must communicate the nature of the clearly defined good or service, or other efforts will not be as likely to succeed. Brand names such as The Pasta House Co. or Champion Dry Cleaners clearly spell out to customers what the business is all about. Although VIPdesk and Geeks On Call are easy to remember, it is less clear to consumers exactly what type of service is being provided. These companies had to expend greater effort in defining the business so that customers could see the advantage in giving the firm a try.

An advertisement by Chic Shaque defining the types of products that are sold.
*Source:* Used with permission of *The Joplin Globe*, Joplin, Missouri.

## Developing a Unique Market Niche

This process is also known as having a **unique selling position (USP)**. A USP is a feature that allows the newly formed company to stand alone and be distinct from all other competitors. The USP may be based on price, the offer of a service not previously available, or some other feature that is not easily duplicated. VIPdesk, which is used by 10.5 million people, offers services via the Internet, phone, or through a wireless device. No other concierge service is set up that way. Remember, a USP difference must be important enough for the customer to "sit up and take notice."

Simply competing by offering a minor price difference will not be enough. It must be a major difference. The success of the Midwestern chain Eureka Pizza was, in part, based on the "buy one—get two free" price advantage. This unique selling position was enough to get the company noticed in the strongly competitive pizza delivery market.

When the market analysis process is complete, other aspects of the IMC plan more readily fall into place. Finding a voice for a small business starts with defining the actual business and its market. Notice the relationship between these activities and the IMC foundation (see Figure 14.2). From there, other elements of the marketing plan can be delivered more effectively.

Butcher's Block offers the goods and services that meet the needs of target markets, both consumers and businesses.
*Source:* Used with permission of *The Joplin Globe*, Joplin, Missouri.

## FINDING CUSTOMERS: A CRUCIAL ELEMENT OF THE IMC PLAN

A new company's IMC plan must be created while bearing in mind the challenges present to entrepreneurial ventures. The person in charge of marketing, whether it is the new business owner or some other member of the company, often operates with

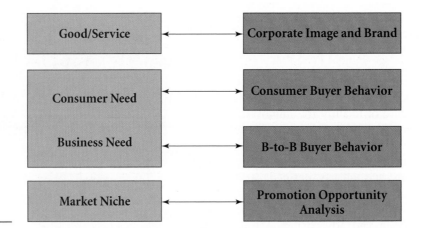

limited resources while trying to reach a cautious and skeptical public. Beyond the tasks completed in forming the company (need, niche, and good or service), the most crucial activities involved in creating an IMC plan for a small business or entrepreneurial venture include:

▶ Locating customers

▶ Making it easy for customers to reach the new company

▶ Reducing purchase risk for customers

Remember that all of the IMC activities must be performed. In the case of a new company, however, it is sometimes difficult to carry them out in traditional ways. A small business or start-up venture will not have a $10 million budget for marketing. There may only be $1,000 to $5,000 for very small firms or possibly $75,000 for a larger start-up. It is essential that a small business allocate sufficient resources to ensure success. A minimum of 3 percent to 5 percent of the firm's revenues should be devoted to marketing. Failing to provide sufficient funding for marketing creates a major disadvantage for the new firm.

Marketing funds are spent differently for small firms as opposed to multinational firms such as Procter & Gamble. The number of potential customers is often lower and more concentrated in a particular geographic area. Therefore, those responsible for marketing must be creative and careful in using resources.

## ETHICAL ISSUES

### Building an Ethical Reputation in a Small Business

Word-of-mouth is a key ingredient that often determines the success or failure of a new business. It works in both directions. Negative word-of-mouth can quickly ruin the reputation of a company and make survival difficult, if not impossible. Positive word-of-mouth can build a customer base and help establish the entrepreneur in the community so that other strong relationships can be created, including those with suppliers, employment agencies, and the local government.

Two ethical issues emerge as a firm begins to grow. One is the use of reciprocal relationships. Is it ethical to set up a series of "I'll buy from you if you buy from me" connections with other companies? It is legal, but it may build the perception that a firm doesn't mind competing in an unfair manner.

The other issue is hiring away employees. Many times entrepreneurs became disenchanted with their company. The individual goes into the exact same business that he or she left. When this happens, there is a strong temptation to drag along customers and former employees. Is it ethical to do so? Will it hurt the reputation of the new firm?

These and other tricky issues, such as not fully reporting income, surround the new business operator. This person often has a lifetime of savings invested. Remaining ethical is important, both for personal well-being and the long-term standing of the new operation.

## Locating Customers

The ideal situation for an entrepreneur starting a business is to hire a market research firm to assist in locating customers. Although some small businesses and start-ups may be able to afford this service, it can be expensive. A well-developed market research effort is likely to cost between $25,000 and $500,000. Consequently, alternative methods may have to be used for locating customers and determining the level of demand.

One good way to start is by assessing the various types of marketing activities in terms of their ability to generate leads and then the probability of the leads turning into sales. If possible, it is often helpful to examine the market for comparable goods or services to gather an approximate estimate of the market size. For example, to compete in the dine-in restaurant market, an entrepreneur could study sales of comparable companies, such as TGIFriday's, Applebee's, or Outback Steakhouse. The Pasta House Co. can estimate the market for its restaurant in a new city by looking at sales of other chain Italian restaurants, such as Olive Garden. The primary objective is to be certain the market is large enough and viable enough to sustain operations over time.[8]

Locating customers involves finding a road map to them that is cost-effective. Doing so with limited resources is challenging, but it is possible. One approach, known as **guerrilla marketing**, focuses efforts on low-cost, creative strategies to reach the right people. The approach was first described by Jay Conrad Levinson following his success in changing the

This advertisement for Mix 95.1 highlights the market niche served by the station.
*Source:* Used with permission of *The Joplin Globe*, Joplin, Missouri.

## COMMUNICATION ACTION

### Ethnic Targets

Many small-business owners have discovered that ethnic populations represent a rich new source of customers. In the next 20 years, the number of African-Americans in the United States is expected to increase by 25 percent, while the Asian-American population will grow by 68 percent, and the number of Hispanic Americans will increase by 64 percent. In the past, marketing to ethnic groups was largely the domain of major companies; however, this is beginning to change.

To effectively reach an ethnic target market, Ken Greenberg of AC Nielsen Homescan recommends several key practices. First, create or participate in special events that reflect an ethnic heritage. Sponsorships are one angle, but creativity should be used. For instance, DaimlerChrysler offers a "ride and drive" program that provides vehicles to those who attend the National Association of Black Journalists convention each year. The vehicles make it possible for attendees to see local attractions in the convention city. Free samples and demonstrations of products at ethnic fairs provide firsthand contacts with potential new customers.

Second, personalize products and services by incorporating language (such as Spanish) and endorsements from local community leaders. Also, it is crucial to employ individuals from various ethnic backgrounds within the company.

Third, target the media that will reach ethnic communities in a given location. In San Diego, a firm seeking to reach Hispanics and Latinos should be targeted to radio, newspaper, and other media that are geared to Spanish-speaking people from the area.

Fourth, and most importantly, carefully review all messages so they do not offend or alienate the target market. Patronizing language is just as bad as culturally insensitive messages. Be certain the intended message is the one that is likely to be received.

**Source:** Chuck Paustian, "Anybody Can Do It," *Marketing News* 35, no. 7 (March 26, 2001), p. 23.

EVERYBODY LOVES...

*The Pasta House Co.*

**EVERY SUNDAY**
*Kids Eat Free!*

**EVERY MONDAY**
*All-You-Can-Eat
Pasta & Salad!*

* For a limited time. Two children (12 years and under)
per paying adult. Not valid with any other offer.

- More than 20 Different Pastas
- Chicken & Seafood Entrees
- Choice USDA Steaks
- Children's Menu
- Open Everyday for Lunch,
  Dinner and Cocktails

| FREE PASTA COUPON | FREE PASTA COUPON |
|---|---|
| Purchase Any Large Order Of Pasta And Receive Any Order Of Pasta Of Equal Or Lesser Value, FREE. | Purchase Any Large Order Of Pasta And Receive Any Order Of Pasta Of Equal Or Lesser Value, FREE. |
| Cool Springs GALLERIA (615) 778-9440    1800 Galleria Blvd. Between Dillard's and Sears, next to "Hobby Instant Shoe Repair" Franklin, TN 37067 | Cool Springs GALLERIA (615) 778-9440    1800 Galleria Blvd. Between Dillard's and Sears, next to "Hobby Instant Shoe Repair" Franklin, TN 37067 |
| ITALIAN RESTAURANT | ITALIAN RESTAURANT |
| This offer good at The Pasta House Co. Restaurant in Tennessee and is not valid with any other offer. One coupon per item per customer. Gratuity and sales tax not included. Regular menu only. | This offer good at The Pasta House Co. Restaurant in Tennessee and is not valid with any other offer. One coupon per item per customer. Gratuity and sales tax not included. Regular menu only. |
| | Offer Expires: 10/14/01 |

The Pasta House Co. has successfully reached its local customers with both food products and quality services.
*Source:* Courtesy of The Pasta House Co.

image of Marlboro cigarettes from a woman's product into the now famous "Marlboro Man" approach. Levison argues that guerrilla marketing is designed to obtain instant results with limited resources using tactics that rely on creativity, good relationships, and the willingness to try unusual approaches.

One recent notable example of guerrilla tactics involved Van's Harley-Davidson franchise in Gloversville, New York. The company advertised a "cat shoot," to be held at the store. Local police, the Humane Society, the mayor, and the Society for the Prevention of Cruelty to Animals all inquired, and the event generated front-page stories for 3 straight days in local papers. The event was actually a 3-for-a-dollar paintball shoot at a 6-foot-tall cartoon cat, with proceeds benefiting the local Humane Society. It was tremendously successful in helping customers find their way to the store. Although bizarre, the approach used by Van's Harley-Davidson illustrates the concept of guerrilla marketing. The contrast between guerrilla marketing and traditional marketing are summarized in Figure 14.3.[9]

Guerrilla marketing is not so much a method of marketing as a different mentality. The goal is to find ways to reach individuals and small groups with a unique message that will cause them to take notice. Most small businesses do not have the money to send a marketing message to thousands of potential customers. Consequently, the owner must look for ways to make an impression. Every dollar that is spent on marketing should have a strong potential for locating potential customers. Techniques that can be successful include:

▶ Participation in trade shows
▶ Involvement in sponsorships
▶ Participation in public relations programs
▶ Use of alternative media
▶ Lifestyle marketing

Depending on the type of business, *trade shows* can be a major source of locating customers. The key, according to Doug Ducate, president of the Center for Exhibition Industry Research, is to follow up on sales leads created at the show. For example, an

| Traditional Marketing | Guerilla Marketing |
|---|---|
| ▶ Requires money | ▶ Requires energy and imagination |
| ▶ Geared to large businesses with big budgets | ▶ Geared to small businesses and big dreams |
| ▶ Results measured by sales | ▶ Results measured by profits |
| ▶ Based on experience and guesswork | ▶ Based on psychology and human behavior |
| ▶ Increases production and diversity | ▶ Grows through existing customers and referrals |
| ▶ Grows by adding customers | ▶ Cooperates with other businesses |
| ▶ Obliterates the competition | ▶ Aims messages at individuals and small groups |
| ▶ Aims messages at large groups | ▶ Uses marketing to gain customer consent |
| ▶ Uses marketing to generate sales | ▶ "You Marketing" that looks at how can we help "You" |
| ▶ "Me Marketing" that looks at "My" company | |

**FIGURE 14.3**
**Traditional vs. Guerilla Marketing**

exhibitor may offer "show prices," or discounts that are given to trade show participants that make purchases within 30 days of the exhibit. Also, many exhibitors offer some type of contest or drawing. The goal is to generate names of prospective customers in addition to generating interest in the business and the company's products. Leads obtained at a trade show make an excellent start for a database and may also lead to some purchases.[10]

Before participating in a trade show, it is important to define the primary objective. The goals can include generating leads, introducing a new good or service, finalizing deals with prospective customers who will be attending, or generating awareness of the company. The objective defines how the trade show booth will be constructed and manned. For example, if the goal is to generate awareness, then the exhibit should include an attention-getting feature. Bright lights, characters in colorful costumes, and music are ways to attract attention. If instead the goal is to generate customer interest in company products, then the products should be displayed in a manner that makes it easy for prospective customers to examine them. Also, the booth should be staffed by personnel with expertise and product knowledge.

*Sponsorships* can be another creative way to locate customers and place the name of the company in the consumer's mind. For a small business, a sponsorship program should be a local event or organization. It is important to make sure the image is consistent with the IMC theme of the sponsoring company. When established carefully, various goals may be reached, such as winning new customers or creating a positive image to attract new employees.[11]

Cost is a concern with sponsorships, however, there are many options. A restaurant or dairy store can sponsor a little league baseball or soccer team at a low cost. A furniture store may develop a relationship with an art gallery without spending significant funds. The primary objective in a sponsorship is to make certain the right people are exposed to the company. The right people are potential customers. It does not make sense to sponsor an event that does not match the firm's target customers. For example, sponsoring an infant beauty contest is not a logical fit for a music store aimed at teenagers.

*Public relations* programs are often closely tied to sponsorships. For example, a company that offers an in-house cancer screening for employees may wish to notify the local paper and count on word-of-mouth to send the signal that the firm cares about its workers. Public relations can also be separate events such as when the business owner or manager agrees to speak at a public event or writes an article for the local newspaper. An article about a new or trendy event in a particular industry and how it affects consumers can be an effective means of getting some free news coverage. For instance, a construction company owner may offer some tips about roof safety just before a forecasted major snowstorm. A clothing retailer may offer information about new

Little league baseball is an excellent sponsorship opportunity for local businesses.

Local companies such as Massey Music can increase exposure by offering free guitar or other types of music lessons.
***Source:*** Used with permission of *The Joplin Globe*, Joplin, Missouri.

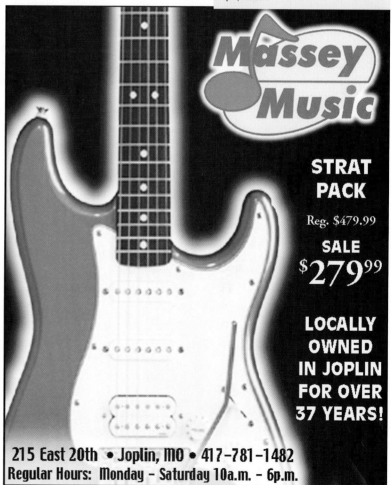

Farmers markets can be used as lifestyle marketing venues.

fashions and how fashion shows in New York and Paris translate into fashions seen on the street in a local community.[12]

A firm must look creatively for ways to become visible. Offering promotions for Valentine's Day, Mother's Day, July Fourth, Halloween, and Christmas are not likely to make a new business stand out. Compared to what a bigger business can offer, a small business will probably not be noticed, and the money spent on promotions is virtually wasted. Instead, the manager should look for unique opportunities for promotions. For example, Geeks On Call could offer a special promotion during October, which is Computer Learning Month. The company could offer free seminars to senior citizen groups or at a local elementary school. This would not only generate goodwill in the community but should also provide some free publicity for the firm.[13]

*Alternative media* are an excellent resource for small businesses. These include company logos on vehicles, ads on mall kiosks, billboards on little league baseball parks and soccer fields, T-shirt or baseball cap giveaways, and any other low cost and unique method of reaching potential customers. Many local firms fax coupons or special deals to targeted customers. Restaurants use faxes to offer lunchtime specials to employees of various nearby businesses.

One program that has captured the attention of many small-business owners is called **lifestyle marketing**. Rather than standing on a street corner giving out flyers or placing them on cars in a parking lot, lifestyle marketing means finding grassroots contact points for potential customers. For example, Flip Records in Los Angeles gives free samples of new music to specialty stores, tattoo shops, and at rock concerts in order to reach young people, who are the most likely to make purchases.[14]

Lifestyles marketing includes contacting consumers who attend farmers markets, bluegrass festivals, large citywide garage sales, flea markets, craft shows, and stock car races, and other distinct groups that are limited in size but contain large concentrations of potential customers. A fuel additive that makes cars run more smoothly may be marketed at a drag race or a stock car oval with good results. A new fertilizer may capture interest at a farmers market. The key is to match the product to the distinct group.

Locating customers must include both traditional and nontraditional elements. The marketing team cannot simply pursue standard methods, such as advertising, because of clutter and cost problems. Creativity and energy are tremendous assets in the introduction of a new good, service, or company to a local community.

## Helping Customers Reach the Company

There are additional communications channels and venues that make it possible for consumers to contact the new business. These include:

▶ Traditional methods
▶ Web sites
▶ Networking
▶ Lifestyle marketing

*Traditional methods* of helping customers reach the company include the firm's telephone service, mail, and in-store visits. Having a phone number that spells a word, such as 231-AUTO or 555-SHOP, will help the customer remember the number. Some firms ask for sequences of numbers, such as 885-1234 to assist in recall. Phone numbers, Internet addresses, and mail addresses should be prominently featured in all marketing communications when a new business opens. Customers must know how to reach and find the company in order to make purchases. Any mail and e-mail that is sent to the business should be opened and answered quickly, in order to maintain the perception of service quality.[15] Also, when a customer visits a retail store, it is vitally important to give prompt, courteous, and sincere service.

Businesses that use the Internet or are involved in e-commerce should select a *Web site* address that is easy to remember and related to the business. For instance, The Pasta House Co. has the Web site address **www.pastahouse.com**. The goal is to make it easy for customers to find and communicate with the company. A quality Web site is easy to navigate and provides pertinent information. It should offer an uncomplicated method for making purchases and provide a way for customers to contact the company with other concerns.

*Networking* begins with something as simple as attending a Chamber of Commerce, Lions Club, or other local civic group meeting with a handful of business cards. It is important to develop contacts and relationships with other local businesspeople, city officials, and other key citizens in the community. One method of strengthening these bonds is to become involved in committees and projects.

Networking provides the opportunity to meet other businesspeople, create leads, and personally promote a new company. Networking also offers an avenue for feedback from customers as well as other businesspeople. Relationships can be formed in many ways. A business owner's doctor, lawyer, butcher, dry cleaner, family, and friends should all be made aware of the new operation. They can pass along referrals and positive word-of-mouth.[16] When making new contacts, the business owner should exhibit tact and diplomacy. Seeming pushy is a negative in these kinds of relationships.[17]

Quality networks offer the possibilities of word-of-mouth endorsements and referrals. They can lead to not only more customers but also quality employees. Business-to-business sales of anything from flowers, to food, to computer repair and consulting services can greatly increase company revenues.

*Lifestyle marketing,* the guerilla marketing technique mentioned earlier in this chapter, is an excellent method of reaching customers. It also represents a major opportunity to receive feedback from those customers. A booth at a special event such as local street fair offers the chance to visit firsthand with potential customers along with those who have done business with the company. Some customers may even suggest product modifications or better methods to reach potential customers.

## Reducing Purchase Risk

Even after a potential customer has become aware of the company, the challenge of moving that person to buying remains. Purchasing from someone new normally creates a higher level of perceived risk. In some cases, such as a new restaurant, the risk is relatively low. One bad meal is pretty easily dismissed. At times, however, utilizing a new vendor is a major investment of time, energy, and money. The marketing plan must be adjusted to the degree of perceived risk. Typical enticements designed to attract the first purchase include:

▶ Samples

▶ Coupons

▶ Price discounts

▶ Referral discounts (for gaining a new customer)

▶ Free first consultation visits

▶ Money-back guarantees

Each must be structured to fit the price/quality relationship. Thus, an attorney opening a practice would not use coupons. Money-back guarantees work well with new services, such as hair care. The goal is to reduce the worry that a purchase is somehow a gamble.

The "Buy One Pair and Get Two Pair Free" promotion is an excellent method of reducing purchase risk for new customers.
*Source:* Used with permission of *The Joplin Globe*, Joplin, Missouri.

Once the initial purchase has been made, the focus shifts to repeat or return business. Small-business owners and especially new businesses spend considerable time, money, and effort in attracting and finding customers. To hold down future costs, the goal must be to keep those who have visited the location. Repeat business is vital to the long-term well-being of almost all small businesses.

## ADVERTISING SMALL BUSINESSES

Limited funds and lack of clout in the media marketplace make advertising a major challenge for a small-business owner. The tasks of advertising management, ad design, and media selection are often complicated because the company may not be able to afford an advertising agency. Even those with budgets large enough to afford an agency may not have as much money as the business would wish to spend on advertising. At the same time, advertising should not be abandoned. Careful and selective use of advertising funding is an important issue.

Ad design is critical to getting noticed among national ads that are created with large budgets. Although a national advertiser can spend a million dollars creating a 30-second spot, a local advertiser may be able to spend only $500. The challenge is to design an ad that speaks clearly and effectively. Under these circumstances, many small-business owners are tempted to put too much into the ad, trying to present all of the reasons consumers should purchase from them. This type of ad is too cluttered and overwhelms the viewer.

A small-business manager should develop a creative brief to aid in the development of company advertisements. When a business is new, the objective of advertising should be to create awareness. Creating persuasive or reminder ads should wait until there is a higher level of brand or company awareness.

Realizing that his company's brand name was mostly unknown, the owner of Southland Cleaning Services of Springdale, Arkansas, decided to tie the name to other, better-known companies in the area. At a cost of only $400, a 45-second ad was created featuring four local businesses that were Southland's clients. Two included short testimonials from clients; the other two featured Southland workers cleaning the facility. The ads ran on local television on a rotating schedule. Soon, Southland was getting phone calls from businesses, asking, "Are you the company that cleans Sears?" They were, because the ad featured Sears in the opening spot. Although businesses could not always remember the Southland brand name, they did tie it to Sears. What made the ad work was that the message clearly came across to the right people, who concluded, "If this company can keep Sears clean, they can keep my business clean."[18]

Once the ad message is defined, various media can be selected. A brief review of advertising media selection follows.

*Television* ad time is expensive, especially national and prime-time slots. Many small businesses are shut out unless they can utilize the forms designed for them. These include cooperative ads, where more than one company is featured in the same spot, as well as rotation buys from cable providers. When a company buys a set of rotating spots on cable, they are shown at all hours and on a variety of programs. Therefore, it is not possible to target the ad to a specific viewer audience. It may be run on shows that do not reach the target market or at times when members of the target market are not watching television. Under these circumstances, some of the advertising money is wasted, but this loss is offset by the

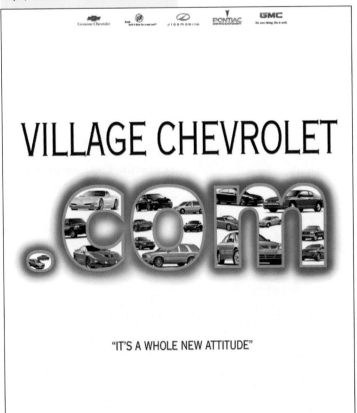

This award-winning ad ("Best Use of 4-color" and "Best of Show," Missouri Press Association Award Ceremony) is an excellent example of creating brand awareness for an automobile dealer's Web site.

*Source:* Used with permission of *The Joplin Globe,* Joplin, Missouri.

low cost. For example, an ad on a national television show such as *CSI* will cost as much as $450,000 for 30 seconds. A rotated cable spot may cost as little as $10 through a long-term contractual agreement in which the advertiser agrees to purchase a certain number of spots over a period of time, such as 12 months.

Retailers should explore cooperative advertising opportunities with manufacturers. Many manufacturers have co-op advertising programs that pay a portion of the cost of a local ad if the manufacturer's brand is prominently displayed. This can help the small business in managing the cost of advertising. Also, cooperative advertising with a national brand makes the small retailer more credible to the public.

*Radio* spots can be prepared at a relatively low cost, especially when a local DJ reads the copy. Listeners tend to have an affinity with radio personalities. This can create credibility when a DJ endorses a local company or brand. For local companies, radio is an excellent advertising medium because most radio stations have a limited broadcast area and tend to provide local coverage. For small businesses serving other businesses, radio can provide an opportunity to reach business buyers or other members of the buying center while at work or traveling in their vehicles.

A radio station's advertising personnel should have a solid knowledge of the station's listening audience. A local business owner can determine which station offers the best match. The costs of radio spots are higher during prime drive time in the morning and afternoon. For smaller national start-up companies, purchasing national radio advertising time is virtually impossible because there are limited national radio networks.

Most *newspaper* advertising is more expensive than local cable television and radio. Although there are discounts for buying more space, the cost of a half-page or full-page ad is often prohibitive compared to local cable TV or radio ads. For retail businesses, however, newspapers are an important advertising medium. This is especially true if a firm's target market consists of baby boomers or older Americans who are the primary readers of newspapers. It is also the best medium for reaching a local geographic area around a retail store.

Newspapers can be used to build brand awareness and to generate store traffic. Offering coupons and specials in newspaper ads can bring customers into a store. Newspaper advertising is more likely to be effective when it is tied to a consumer promotion and the ad encourages action.

*Magazines* have limited uses for local business advertising. Magazine ads are expensive and the magazine is likely to be aimed at a national, rather than local, audience. Magazine ads can be used by national start-up or entrepreneurial ventures. Some magazines offer regional editions that allow a business to advertise in a particular area. Also, if a business sells products via the Internet, magazine advertising can be used if the magazine readership matches the target market of the business and, more importantly, if the target market is willing to purchase the product via the Internet. In that situation the company must select highly targeted specialty magazines.

*Billboard* advertising features low CPM with long-term exposure. For local businesses, billboards are an excellent method of building brand awareness of the firm as well as informing local consumers where the business is located. Billboard space should be purchased along routes where potential customers live, work, and commute. Ads on vehicles such as buses, cabs, or in subways can reach many potential patrons. Many small businesses are able to make package buys on billboards

The newspaper is an ideal medium for both local consumer and business markets.
*Source:* Used with permission of *The Joplin Globe*, Joplin, Missouri.

A billboard advertisement promoting Valley Harley-Davidson as a place for sales, service, and fashions.
*Source:* Courtesy of DJ Media.

that are rotated throughout a city. Advertisements placed on the store itself may be effective if the business is located on a major road.

For some small and start-up businesses, *Internet* ads may be effective. A local company can often purchase ads on the community's Chamber of Commerce site or city's Web site. If ads cannot be purchased, having the firm's name on the site or linked to the site is important. For example, a new restaurant should make sure it is mentioned by the local visitor's bureau and Chamber of Commerce materials. Providing a link to the restaurant's Web site is even better because it allows locals as well as visitors or tourists to access the company directly. Another option is a reciprocal arrangement with another business. For example, a local pet store may offer to list local veterinarians on its Web site in exchange for the veterinarians listing the pet store on their Web sites.

The Internet can be a very powerful tool to provide information for prospective customers that cannot be placed in an advertisement. On the Web site, a firm can place information about the business, its goods and services, guarantees, current customers or clients, and special offers as well as prices. Television, radio, newspaper, magazine, and billboard ads all can identify the firm's Web site and encourage consumers and businesses to access it. When used properly, the Internet can be a beneficial form of advertising once consumers have been directed to it by some other form of advertising.

The company leader considering local advertising should use a "bang for the buck" criterion. Dollars must be spent judiciously. Also, low-quality ads may injure the reputation of the company. It is better to spend more money on developing a quality ad and less on the media reach of the ad than to create a poor advertisement that is the brunt of local jokes. Small and start-up companies must advertise, even though it is often a major challenge for the entrepreneur or business owner.

# MAKING CUSTOMERS ADVOCATES

A solid customer base is the difference between success and failure of a new business. It simply costs too much money and takes too much time to keep enticing new customers as old ones fall away. Once a customer base has been established, the goal is then to turn them into advocates for the business. An **advocate** is a customer who is loyal to the business and draws others through positive communications. Several methods can be used to keep customers and turn them into advocates. A discussion of these techniques follows.

## Database Management

A crucial feature of a new or small business is the development and maintenance of a database. Unfortunately, many small businesses and start-up ventures neglect this important component of an IMC plan. Creating a database is the most cost-effective method of keeping track of customers.

Developing a database does not have to be difficult, nor does it require a high level of expertise. An owner/operator of a small retail outlet will soon discover that there are idle hours while the store is open. Employees can use this time to help create a database. This can be accomplished by collecting business cards for drawings, pulling names and addresses from the tops of personal checks written for purchases, and soliciting information at the time of a purchase. The goal should be to try to enter every person who makes a purchase into the database. Once the customer is in the database, every purchase that the person makes should be recorded. Developing a history for each customer is a valuable asset in personalizing a marketing approach. This approach is cheaper than buying lists from credit card companies or other sources.

An old rule of thumb in business is that 80 percent of the business comes from 20 percent of the company's customers. Employees need to know who those 20 percent are, by name. These individuals should be notified of special discounts and sales, the arrival of new merchandise, or a new service that is being offered. For example, a hair salon may run a discount on perms. Long-standing customers should know about the special through some type of personal contact so they can take advantage of it. The small-business database is a key resource for keeping tabs on customers, monitoring purchasing patterns, and making contacts.

## Direct Marketing

One of the major benefits of a database is the ability to use direct marketing, which can be in the form of mail, e-mail, telephone, or personal contacts. Most small businesses think of only direct mail, but the customer base should be examined carefully. A telephone call, a fax, or an e-mail may be a more effective way of contacting customers.

According to the Direct Marketing Association, the average dollar spent on direct mail brought in $10 in sales.[19] When carried out correctly, direct mail is an effective method to increase revenues and build relationships with customers. Patrick Dineen suggests the following steps when creating a direct-marketing program:

1. Define the goals of the program and make sure those goals are more than simply generating sales.
2. Define the audience. A solid database helps this process.
3. Target the prospective customers to be contacted. Once again, a database is crucial to providing relevant information about customer characteristics.
4. Produce the art and copy. Make it simple, direct, and professional.
5. Print and mail the package.
6. Track responses for the future.

There is some debate as to whether a follow-up phone call is advisable. Dineen says it will generate additional sales. Others disagree, believing calls about mailings are viewed as a nuisance.[20] Keep in mind that although these suggestions were made for direct-mail campaigns, the same principles would apply to e-mail, telephone, or fax campaigns.

## Personal Selling

The "personal touch" remains an integral part of keeping customers, regardless of the size of the company. In the case of a small business, it is absolutely vital. Knowing the names of customers, their preferences, and other key information makes a sales call or visit to a retail operation a much more positive experience.

Employees who are trained to recall names and go the extra mile in delivering service, and who exhibit positive manners on the phone as well as in person are a major asset to a small business. Uncaring and unprepared salespeople and service personnel may cost the company business it simply cannot afford to lose.

## Trade and Consumer Promotions

Customers of small businesses need to know they are appreciated. To strengthen relationships with customers, company marketing leaders must be creative in the use of consumer and trade promotions, because marketing dollars are so limited. Specialty advertising is often helpful in trade promotions. Calendars, pens, cups, and other items help remind the customer of the small business. As the company grows, it will logically expand into other types of trade promotions such as discounts.

Personal selling is extremely important to local businesses, such as jewelry stores.
*Source:* Courtesy of Newcomer, Morris & Young, Inc.

Romantic Delights offers a "free gift" with a purchase as a means of generating store traffic.

**Source:** Used with permission of *The Joplin Globe,* Joplin, Missouri.

Consumer promotions should go beyond coupons. Creative use of premiums, contests or sweepstakes, samples, refunds, and rebates should be developed whenever possible. When created effectively, contests and sweepstakes can help the company build a database. Contestants should be asked to provide names and addresses in order to enter. A store owner may find it extremely helpful to deliver samples beyond the store. For instance, a small-town chocolate company that provides samples to other businesses and residences may expect increased traffic in return.

There are several things to remember when developing trade and consumer promotions. First, they should be cost-effective. Second, goals should be stated for the program (awareness, image, sales, etc.). Third, these promotions should reflect the position, image, and theme of the company.

## SUMMARY

Entrepreneurship means a company is being formed with the express goal of becoming larger through an aggressive growth agenda. Intrepreneurship is a corporate spin-off or start-up. A small business is a family-owned company or consortium of professionals formed with specific objectives in mind. In most cases, aggressive growth is not as important as providing adequate income for the owners.

Typical challenges to new businesses include the problem that consumers are not aware of the business. They are often cautious or wary of trying a new good, service, or company. Also, advertising and promotional clutter make it difficult to be recognized, and small budgets for marketing, advertising, and promotional activities make it difficult to compete. New businesses are especially vulnerable to negative word-of-mouth communications.

Starting a company consists of three intertwined activities: (1) understanding and defining consumer needs, (2) establishing a clearly defined product or service, and (3) developing a unique market niche. When finding customers, it is crucial to employ methods of research to locate interested clients, make it easy for consumers to reach the company, and reduce purchasing risk to whatever degree is possible.

Guerrilla marketing is a focus on low-cost, creative marketing methods to reach the right people. Other ways to reach potential customers include trade show participation, involvement in sponsorships, participation in public relations programs, and the use of alternative media. Lifestyle marketing is an alternative program designed to find grassroots contact points for potential customers.

Purchase risk can be reduced by using samples, coupons, price discounts, referral discounts, free first consultation visits, money-back guarantees, and other methods. The goal is to turn customers into advocates who are loyal to the business and draw others through positive comments.

Advertising a small or start-up business includes all standard media; however, limited budgets mean the dollars must be spent carefully. When attempting to reach customers, traditional methods of phone, mail, and in-store visits must be accompanied by networking, lifestyle marketing, and use of a Web site and e-mail.

Turning customers into advocates includes use of database management programs, direct-marketing tactics, quality personal selling, and effective trade and consumer promotions. All of the elements of an IMC program should be used in a small business setting; only the emphasis changes. Creativity, energy, quality, reputation, specialization, community outreach, and a visionary owner are the major assets in creating a successful new business operation.

## REVIEW QUESTIONS

1. Describe the differences between entrepreneurship, intrepreneurship, and a small business.

2. What are the major challenges to new businesses? What is the difference between a product benefit and a product feature?

3. What are the three components of a market analysis?

4. When defining a product, why is it important to say what a company won't do as much as what it will?

5. What is a unique selling position? Why is a USP so crucial to a new business?

6. What is guerrilla marketing? How is it different from traditional marketing?

7. Discuss the role trade shows, sponsorships, public relations programs, and alternative media play in locating customers.

8. What is lifestyle marketing? Name some local events or activities that could be used in lifestyle marketing programs.

9. How can a small-business owner maintain two-way communication with customers?

10. Describe the tactics small businesses can use to reduce purchasing risk.

11. Describe the use of television in advertising a small business.

12. How can radio be used effectively in advertising a small business?

13. What types of customers are best targeted with newspaper advertising in a small-business setting? What do newspapers offer that other media cannot?

14. Describe the limitations and uses of magazine advertising for small businesses.

15. What are the advantages of billboard advertising for small businesses?

16. How can Internet advertising enhance a small-business IMC program?

17. What is an advocate? How can small businesses turn customers into advocates?

## KEY TERMS

**entrepreneurship** The organization and operation of a business venture.

**intrepreneurship** A corporate spin-off or start-up company.

**small business** A family-owned company or consortium of professionals that is formed with the primary objective of providing adequate income for the owners.

**unique selling position (USP)** A feature that allows a newly-formed company to stand alone and be distinct from all other competitors.

**guerrilla marketing** A focus on low-cost, creative marketing strategies to reach a firm's target market.

**lifestyle marketing** Finding grassroots contact points for potential customers.

**advocate** A customer who is loyal to the business and draws others through positive communications.

## CRITICAL THINKING EXERCISES

### Discussion Questions

1. Identify a small business in your area. Talk to the owner of the business about how he or she markets the business. Compare your findings with those of your classmates. Are there any underlying themes?

2. Look at five advertisements in your local newspaper for small, local businesses. What consumer or business need are they attempting to meet? Does the advertisement do a good job of presenting the company's expertise?

3. In groups of three to five students, discuss needs or wants you have that are not being met adequately by a local business. Choose one need that stands out among you. Describe the unique market niche that a start-up business could develop to meet that need. Is the market large enough to support a business? How could other consumers with the same need be reached?

4. Pick one of the following types of businesses. Conduct an informal market analysis to determine if there is a sufficient

market for a new business. Who would be the firm's primary competitors? What unique selling proposition could they use to differentiate themselves from the competitor?

   a. Dry cleaner
   b. Tanning salon
   c. Laundromat
   d. Car wash
   e. Lawn service

5. Pick one of the services listed in Exercise 4. Discuss guerilla marketing techniques that a start-up business could use to locate customers.

6. Pick one of the services listed in Exercise 4. Discuss an advertising approach that would allow the small business to get the most "bang for its buck."

7. Pick one of the services listed in Exercise 4. Discuss ways the small business could turn customers into advocates for the firm.

## INTEGRATED LEARNING EXERCISES

1. Several Web sites, consulting firms, and organizations offer information, ideas, and support for entrepreneurs. Access the Entrepreneurship Centre at www.entrepreneurship.com. What type of information is available? What type of assistance does the Centre provide? Examine one of the successful companies listed and write a short report.

2. Access one of the following Web sites. Discuss what types of information are available and how a new business could use the Web site.

   a. Yahoo! Small Business (smallbusiness.yahoo.com)
   b. BusinessWeek Online (small business) (www.businessweek.com/smallbiz)
   c. Small and Home-Based Business Links (www.bizoffice.com)

3. Many entrepreneurs will go into business by purchasing a franchise operation. Examine the following Web sites for information about franchise opportunities. Pick a franchise

that appeals to you and look it up on all four Web sites. What did you learn? How did the Web sites differ in terms of information provided?

**a.** Franchise Solutions (www.franchisesolutions.com)

**b.** Own Your Own Franchise (www.ownyourownfranchise. com)

**c.** Franchise.com (www.franchise.com)

**d.** Franchises 4U (www.franchises-4u.com)

**4.** Understanding your customers' needs, finding the right market niche, and clearly defining your good or service are the basics of establishing a new business. Examine the Web sites of Geeks On Call (www.geeksoncall.com) and VIPdesk (www.vipdesk.com). In your opinion, why are these two businesses successful?

**5.** Guerrilla Marketing International has a resource for online marketing using the concepts of guerrilla marketing. Access the Web site at www.gmarketing.com. Examine the resources available. What is your evaluation of this Web site in terms of helping small business owners?

**6.** Access the Internet and locate the Web sites of two local businesses in your community. Evaluate their Web sites. What is good about the sites? What needs improvement?

## STUDENT PROJECT

### IMC Plan Pro

A small-business owner needs IMC every bit as much as big business. You can use the IMC Plan Pro booklet and disk available through Prentice Hall for any size organization. If the company is smaller, it may be helpful to think outside the box to find clever ways to reach customers at a low cost, but yet with a powerful and consistent marketing message.

# CASE 1

## MASON SURGICAL MASKS

Neil and Peggy Drees were beginning what they called "Our adventure of a lifetime." Neil had been a chemist in the fabric industry; Peggy had been a registered nurse for the past decade. They had just joined their talents to develop a "state-of-the-art, better than all the rest, surgical mask." The secret was in Neil's adaptation of microfiber technology. The mask he had developed would be superior at stopping both particulate and gaseous hazardous materials. Neil was well on his way to receiving patent protection. The couple purchased a "spec" industrial building from the local government in Edina, Minnesota, at a low price. The plant would also have some tax advantages granted by both the city government and the state of Minnesota.

Believing that their management and operational plan was solid, it was time to think about marketing. Neil and Peggy visited several local marketing professors, three successful local entrepreneurs, and two advertising agencies. With a limited budget for marketing programs, they needed to do as much as possible by themselves.

The first issue, in their minds, was to identify target markets. The couple decided there were three main groups. The primary group was medical supply services. It was clear that the masks could not be sold directly to hospitals and doctor's offices. Instead, linen services and other companies that sold either medical supplies (needles, thermometers, etc.) or nonmedical supplies (tissues, paper towels, sheets, pillow cases) to these organizations and individual physicians were the targets. A sale to one supplier would reach numerous physicians, hospitals, and clinics.

The second target market was any company that worked with hazardous items. These groups are served by a different type of supplier. Many construction workers are around hazardous materials, including concrete dust, solvents and cleaners, and other noxious fumes that required masks for protection. A second group consists of companies that are in the "cleaning" industries. Many of their employees also wear surgical masks. A third group within this cluster is any company that has employees wearing masks to protect the product from the employee, such as food preparation, medicines, and other companies where contamination is a concern.

The final target was retail stores that sell surgical masks to individual customers who want protection. This was the fastest growing market. An increasing number of people have begun wearing masks while gardening or mowing the lawn, or for protection on high smog days in larger cities.

The common denominator among the three groups was a need: Each wants the best possible protection from the elements at a reasonable price. Masks are disposable. Many times they are thrown away after only one use.

Peggy suggested the company and product brand name, Mason Surgical Masks, for two reasons. First, a mason is a bricklayer. She believed the image of something strong and impermeable was a good idea. Second, another popular product is a mason jar, which is well known for quality.

After gaining access to some venture capital to support the company and its marketing program, they were ready. The adventure was about to begin.

1. What is the unique selling proposition of Mason Surgical Masks?

2. Is the brand name Mason Surgical Masks a good one? Why or why not?

3. Would a company such as this be able to succeed in today's marketplace? Why or why not?

# CASE 2

The grocery store business is rapid-moving and risky. Customer preferences can evolve slowly or develop quickly. Hot new items can capture the fancy of some customers while others remain staunchly devoted to old "standbys." The entry of Wal-Mart into the grocery business has also changed the dynamics of the industry. Smaller stores find they must create and dominate a niche if they want to remain in business.

In each major city, one or more grocery chains continually battle to retain a base group of loyal customers while enticing others to at least occasionally visit the store. Heavy promotion of loss-leader pricing has been the standard in the industry for many years. At the same time, various chains and local stores have tried other gimmicks to keep and build a share of the market.

Bobby's Market was associated with an independent grocer chain. Bobby Mulvaney inherited the store from his father, Bobby Senior, 20 years ago. Bobby had watched as stores opened and closed, and fretted as Wal-Mart's Supercenter, located on the edge of town, began taking away business from his store and others in the area.

The grocer chain associated with Bobby's Market was wary of magnet-card, VIP programs that several groups had tried. These programs, which provided a great deal of data about individual customers and their purchases, seemed to create a kind of "backlash" effect. Those who didn't have the cards wondered why they couldn't receive the more favorable discounts given to VIP cardholders, and those holding the cards soon were bombarded with extra promotions besides the regular weekly ads placed in the newspaper and on television. Consequently, this chain decided not to become involved in any kind of VIP card promotion.

Instead, Bobby was sent a series of materials for a "Bonus Buy" club promotion. Each customer was given a punch card that contained a series of dollar amounts. As the individual bought items from the store, the value of the total purchase was hand-punched into the card. A fully punched card was an entry into a contest, where the prizes ranged from $1 to a $1,000 grand prize, given out each week. To make the process more enticing, various items throughout the store were marked as "Bonus Buy" items, and dollar values on the punch card were increased by $1, $5, or $10, depending on the item. Thus, a package of T-bone steaks was marked with a $10 bonus punch, so the customer received the value of the total purchase plus $10 for that trip to the store, meaning the person was going to gain more entries into the contest for frequently shopping at Bobby's Market. The person gained an even greater advantage if he or she was willing to buy larger numbers of bonus buy items.

One main feature of the contest was that cashiers would give punch cards to every shopper, unless the individual said that he or she did not want one. A person who forgot his or her card was allowed to "combine" punches from a series of cards to gain an entry in the sweepstakes. Therefore, even absent-minded customers could still win.

Two negatives were associated with this program. First, the company could not collect any data from those who did not participate. The punch cards did not require the customer to disclose anything until an entry was redeemed. Then, the individual was asked to add his or her address and phone number to the punch card. Still, this meant many people did not provide information, and their actual purchases could not be tracked. Only increases in sales of Bonus Buy items could be studied.

Second, punching each individual card dramatically slowed the check-out times for all shoppers. Those who didn't want to enter the contest became increasingly annoyed as cards were being punched and cash prizes were given by cashiers, who weren't ringing up items or sacking groceries while they took care of contest details. Even contest participants shopping at peak hours noticed the lines were longer and checkout times were rising.

As the contest wound down, Bobby wondered if it had been a good idea. He tried to figure out ways to discover if he should try the Bonus Buy plan again in 6 months. The grocery chain liked the program, because the marketing team could offer Bonus Buy points for overstocked items. Yet Bobby needed to know how all of his customers were reacting.

1. From a small-business perspective, which is more important, knowing more about customers or making some of those customers unhappy?

2. Are there any guerrilla marketing tactics Bobby could use to build the business?

3. What are the goals associated with the Bonus Buy promotion? Are these goals compatible with those of a small independent grocer trying to compete with Wal-Mart and other larger chains?

4. What type of message theme would work best for Bobby's Market? How can he get that message out to the right people?

## ENDNOTES

1. Carolyn Walkup, "Pasta House Co. Signs Licensees to First Foreign-Expansion Pacts," *Nation's Restaurant News* 34, no. 20 (May 15, 2000), p. 8; Bret Thorn, "The Pasta House," *Nation's Restaurant News* 36, no. 4 (January 28, 2002), pp. 152–54.

2. Arthur A. Thompson, Jr., and A. J. Strickland III, *Strategic Management: Concepts and Cases*, 12th ed. (New York: McGraw-Hill/Irwin, 2002).

3. Meir Liraz, "Ten Marketing Mistakes Small Businesses Make," *Air Conditioning, Heating, & Refrigeration News* 214, no. 9 (October 29, 2001), p. 24.

4. Debra Williams, "How to Turn Your Hobby into a Business," *Air Force Times* 62, no. 42 (May 13, 2002), pp. 2–3.

5. Toddi Gutner, "A Dot-Com's Survival Story," *BusinessWeek*, no. 3782 (May 13, 2002), p. 122.

6. Lee Zion, "Fairy Dogmother Service Carries on a Favorite Tradition," *San Diego Business Journal* 22, no. 2 (January 8, 2001), p. 32.

7. Karen E. Klein, "Find Your Niche—and Stick with It," *BusinessWeek Online* (March 22, 2002), www.businessweek.com, accessed September 25, 2005.

8. Bo Burlingham, "Where Are the Customers?" *Inc.* 24, no. 5 (May 2002), p. 110.

9. Shari Caudron, "Guerilla Tactics," *IndustryWeek* 250, no. 10 (July 16, 2001), p. 52.

10. Bob Lamons, "Trade Shows Still a Good Bet for Small Firms," *Marketing News* 36, no. 7 (April 1, 2002), p. 10.

11. Jenny Hirschkorn and Richard Cree, "The Perfect Match," *Director* 55, no. 8 (March 2002), p. 19.

12. Lisa Schalon, "Marketing Programs That Make Every Dollar Count," *San Diego Business Journal* 22, no. 18 (April 30, 2001), p. 19.

13. Risa B. Hoag, "Tips to Increase Visibility for Any Size Business," *Westchester County Business Journal* 36, no. 39 (September 29, 1997), pp. 15–16.

14. Jane Applegate, "Succeeding in Small Business," *Enterprise: Salt Lake City* 30, no. 5 (August 7, 2000), p. 11.

15. Kenneth E. Clow, Donald Baack, and Jerry D. Rogers, "The Impact of Effective Service Recovery Procedures on Satisfaction with City Services and Citizen Complaints About City Services," *Proceedings* (Washington, DC: American Marketing Association Summer Educator's Conference, 2001), p. 54.

16. Karen E. Klein, "Want New Customers? Go Guerrilla," *BusinessWeek Online* (April 29, 2002), www.businessweek.com, accessed September 25, 2005.

17. Alf Nucifora, "Networking Groups Still Best Source of Leads," *Fort Worth Business Press* 13, no. 37 (January 5, 2001), p. 7.

18. Interview with Kenneth E. Clow, president of Southland Cleaning Services (June 8, 2002).

19. Patrick Dineen, "Improving Direct Mail Prospecting," *Franchising World* 33, no. 7, (October 2001), p. 42.

20. John R. Graham, "Marketing and Sales Strategy: Ten Ways to Push Your Company Forward—By Doing It Backwards," *American Salesman* 46, no. 11 (November 2001), p. 6.

# Evaluating an Integrated Marketing Program

## Chapter Objectives

*Assess* **every level of IMC programs, from individual ads and coupon campaigns to the company's long-term growth and survival.**

*Develop* **both evaluations of messages and measures of behavioral responses when marketing tools are used.**

*Examine* **the quality of public relations efforts in conjunction with studies of other marketing programs.**

*Prepare* **a series of short- and long-term goals that are linked to the company's voice and theme.**

## PRETESTING FOR EFFECTIVENESS
### The New High-Tech World of Advertising Design

For many years, management and marketing specialists have known that the easiest way to fix many problems is to prevent them from occurring in the first place. The "rocket" analogy is the reasoning that is used. If a rocket is off course in the first few minutes after the launch, it will drift much farther off course as the trip proceeds. A correction early in the flight puts the rocket back on track and the ride goes much more smoothly.

The same is true in advertising design. If the ad is off course at the beginning, the company spends additional funding to develop a campaign that is doomed from the start. One new approach to making ads more effective is to send them through a series of pretests before the actual campaign begins. A company known as Decision Analyst is one of the leading international marketing firms in the world of advertising testing.

One program the company uses is based on Internet research. It is called CopyScreen™. To test an ad, a sample is drawn using 200 to 300 target audience consumers who are identified over the Internet. The subjects are shown preliminary versions of print ads and asked for opinions in four areas: (1) attention value, (2) Internet value, (3) purchase propensity, and (4) brand recognition. The responses are given mathematical scores, and a total is generated for the test ad. Those who go beyond a threshold score are deemed worthy of further development.

The ads moving on to the next stage may be tested through a program called CopyCheck®. This program provides more specific feedback concerning the ad's probable effectiveness. Questions CopyCheck attempts to answer include:

1. Will the ad capture the viewer's attention?
2. Will the brand name be noticed and remembered?

3. Does the ad increase the consumer's interest in buying the brand?

4. Does the ad trigger the intent to purchase?

5. How memorable is the brand name?

6. What are the key ideas in the ad?

7. What is missing from the ad (things viewers would like to know)?

8. What did viewers like about the commercial?

9. What did viewers not like about the commercial?

10. How could the commercial be improved?

Decision Analyst provides ad feedback about a week after an advertiser purchases the CopyCheck program. This type of program gives the company preparing the ad two major advantages. First, money is not wasted on ineffective ads. Second, the final ads have a much greater chance of stimulating the desired response.

The same company provides feedback regarding the potential for effectiveness of a completed ad as well as tests of recall for ads that have run. Even a rocket that is "in orbit" occasionally needs to have its course adjusted.

The use of computers, the Internet, and more sophisticated research techniques have made it possible for many companies to spend advertising dollars more wisely. In a world where marketing departments and advertising account managers are being asked to produce tangible results, the use of these types of programs is likely to continue to rise.[1]

John Wanamaker, a well-known nineteenth-century department store owner, was one of the first to use advertising to attract customers to his store. He once remarked, "I know half the money I spend on advertising is wasted, but I can never find out which half." It is difficult to evaluate advertising effectiveness.

Millions of dollars are spent each year on marketing communications programs. Consequently, it is very important for each company to attempt to evaluate these efforts. To spend a major amount on a marketing campaign without trying to find out if it had positive impact does not make sense. The problem, however, is finding the best ways evaluate the effectiveness of a marketing communications plan.

This final chapter is devoted to the various methods available for evaluating components of an IMC program. At the most general level, two broad categories of evaluation tools can be used to evaluate IMC systems: message evaluations and respondent behavior evaluations.

**Message evaluation techniques** are used to examine the message and the physical design of the advertisement, coupon, or direct-marketing piece. Message evaluation procedures include the study of actors in advertisements as well as the individuals who speak in radio ads. A message evaluation program is designed to consider both the cognitive components associated with an ad such as recall and recognition as well as emotional and attitudinal responses.

**Respondent behavior evaluations** address visible customer actions including making store visits, inquiries, or actual purchases. This category contains evaluation techniques that are measured using numbers, such as the number of coupons that are redeemed, the number of calls to an inbound telemarketing program, and changes in sales.

In today's IMC marketplace, many advertising companies are being asked to deliver compelling proof that the ads being designed actually work. Respondent behaviors provide such evidence. Higher sales, increases in store traffic, a greater number of daily Internet hits on a Web site, and other numbers-based outcomes appeal to many managers. Consequently, both forms of evaluation help the marketing manager build short-term results and long-range success.

## MATCHING METHODS WITH IMC OBJECTIVES

Methods of evaluation should be chosen because they match the objectives being measured.[2] When the objective of an advertising campaign is to increase customer interest in and recall of a brand, then the level of customer awareness should be measured. Normally this means the marketing team measures awareness before and after the ads are run. This procedure is commonly known as *pretest* and *posttest* analysis. At other times objectives vary. For instance, redemption rates measure the success of a campaign featuring coupons, so the behavior (purchasing) rather than the cognitive process (recall) is being tested. Redemption rates can be studied to discover how many items were purchased both with and without coupons.

Several levels of analysis are possible when evaluating an advertising or IMC program. They include the following factors:

▶ Short-term outcomes (sales, redemption rates)

▶ Long-term results (brand awareness, brand loyalty or equity)

▶ Product-specific awareness

▶ Awareness of the overall company

▶ Affective responses (liking the company and a positive brand image)

Keep in mind that many marketers overemphasize the first factor, short-term outcomes, without considering the long-term impact of a campaign or marketing program. The company must maintain a voice that carries across campaigns over time. For example, consider the "I love you, man" Budweiser ads of the late 1990s. The short-term success was indeed attractive because so many people thought the ads were funny. For many years, Anheuser-Busch has maintained a strong and consistent voice by using humor to promote products, from the Budweiser frogs and lizards to the "Whazzup" team and the subsequent "True" campaign.

In light of the overall marketing and advertising goals, then, the marketing manager can consider the various options for evaluating the advertising program. Often it is necessary to think about the evaluation procedure prior to launching a particular campaign. An ad placed in a trade journal may contain a code number, a special telephone number, or a special Internet site that can be used to track responses to a particular campaign. For coupons, premiums, and other sales promotions, code numbers are printed on each item to identify where it came from.

When assessing the effectiveness of an ad, even something as simple as the date or time the advertisement appeared is important. For example, an Internet banner ad campaign should be reviewed by keeping a record of inquiries or hits associated with the banner. In the same way, the date a magazine reaches the newsstands and when subscribers receive copies are important items used in evaluating magazine ads.

In general, careful planning prior to initiating an IMC program makes evaluation of the campaign easier and more accurate. At the same time, the evaluation of a specific advertisement or marketing piece is difficult, because many factors affect the outcome being measured. For instance, a retailer may run a series of newspaper and radio ads to boost store traffic. In order to measure the impact of the ads, the retailer keeps records of store traffic before, during, and after the ad campaign. Unfortunately, the traffic count may be affected by other factors, even something as simple as the weather. If it rains for 2 days, the traffic count will probably be lower. Further, the store's chief competitor may be running a special sale during the same time period. This would also affect

It is important to match the evaluation method with the objective of the ad.
*Source:* Courtesy of Newcomer, Morris & Young, Inc.

traffic. A TV program, such as the season finale of a major series, or even a special program at the local high school (commencement, school play), could have an impact. In other words, many extraneous factors can affect results. When reviewing an advertising program, it is important to consider these external factors.

More importantly, perhaps, is that one specific analysis does not assess the influence the ad may have had on the larger company image. For example, even though store traffic was low, the ad may have been stored in the buyer's long-term memory. At some future point, this may make a difference. Conversely, the same ad may have been awkward or in some way offensive, and the store owner may believe the weather affected the outcome instead of a poor advertising design. Consequently, company leaders must be reminded to consider both short-term consequences and long-term implications when they assess overall IMC programs.

One measure of effectiveness of this advertisement is the increase in the number of phone calls to schedule a Cool Touch consultation.

*Source:* Used with permission of *The Joplin Globe,* Joplin, Missouri.

# MESSAGE EVALUATIONS

Evaluation or testing of advertising communications can occur at any stage of the development process. They can be analyzed at the concept stage before an ad is ever produced. This testing normally involves soliciting the opinions of either a series of experts or from "regular" people. The ad can be tested after the design stage has been completed but prior to development. For example, a television ad may be produced using a storyboard. A **storyboard** is a series of still photographs or sketches that outline the structure of a television ad. After the television commercial is produced, then experimental tests can be used to evaluate the ad. At that point, a group of consumers can be invited to watch the ad in a theater-type setting. When this is done, the test ad is placed in a group of ads to disguise it. Viewers are then asked to evaluate all of the ads (including the test ad) to see if the test ad had the desired effect.

Before launching the campaign, the agency may show the ad in a *test market* area. Several tools can then be used to measure the quality and impact of the ad. These instruments will be presented in detail later in this chapter. The final stage of evaluation takes place after the marketing communication has been used. Information collected at this time helps the company's leaders and the advertising agency to assess what worked and what did not. These findings are then used in the development of future marketing campaigns.

Companies have several methods to investigate the message content of an advertisement or marketing communication piece. These methods are listed in Figure 15.1, along with when the technique tends to be used. Although most of the methods deal with the verbal or written components of the communication piece, peripheral cues are also important and should be part of the message evaluation.

The best method to use in a message evaluation scheme depends on the objective of the communication plan. Most market researchers employ more than one method to try to make sure the findings are as accurate as possible. Each evaluation tool is discussed separately in this section; however, in most instances more than one measure is used. Also, as mentioned earlier, pretests and posttests normally are used for the purposes of making comparisons before and after a series of ads has run.

## Concept Testing

**Concept testing** examines the proposed content of an advertisement and the impact that content may have on potential customers. Many advertising agencies conduct concept tests before spending money to develop an advertisement or promotional piece.

**FIGURE 15.1**
**Message Evaluation Techniques and When to Use Them**

| Message Evaluation Method | When the Test Is Normally Used |
|---|---|
| ❯ Concept testing | Prior to ad development |
| ❯ Copytesting | Final stages of development or finished ad |
| ❯ Recall tests | Primarily after ad has been launched |
| ❯ Recognition tests | After ad has been launched |
| ❯ Attitude and opinion tests | Anytime during or after ad development |
| ❯ Emotional reaction tests | Anytime during or after ad development |
| ❯ Physiological tests | Anytime during or after ad development |
| ❯ Persuasion analysis | Primarily after ad has been launched |

The average cost of producing a national 30-second television ad is $358,000.[3] Consequently, it is more cost-effective to test a concept at the early stages of an ad's development rather than after taping the commercial. Also, if changes must be made, it is less costly to complete them during the planning stage rather than after the marketing piece has been completed. Once the marketing communication item is finished, creatives and others who worked on the piece tend to feel a sense of ownership and become more resistant to making changes.

The most common procedure used for concept testing is a focus group. *Focus groups* normally consist of 8 to 10 people who are representative of the target market. These individuals are paid money or are given financial incentives such as gift certificates to entice them to participate. In most cases, it is wise to use independent marketing research firms to conduct focus groups. The goal is to prevent biased results. An independent company is more likely to report that a certain advertising approach did not work than is someone who developed the approach and has a vested interest in it.

The number of focus groups used to study an issue varies greatly. It can be as many as 50 or as few as one. Focus group reactions can be quite different. Results are affected by the makeup of the group and the way the session is conducted. As a result, it is risky to base a decision on just one focus group's final opinion. For example, a humorous ad may have a great deal of appeal to one group, yet another might not think the ad is funny or may even find it offensive. Therefore, it is a good idea to study the responses of several groups to see the impact of the humor on a series of individuals. Even trained focus group leaders experience varying results due to the composition of the group, the questions the group is asked to answer, and the degree of formality used in conducting a session. Also, one person's opinions may strongly influence the rest of the group. Therefore, most agencies use more than one group in order to ensure more reliable results. When several different focus groups arrive at the same conclusion, the finding is more reliable.

Several components of a marketing communications plan can be evaluated with concept tests. They include the:

- Copy or verbal component of an advertisement
- Message and its meaning
- Translation of copy in an international ad
- Effectiveness of peripheral cues, such as product placement in the ad and props used
- Value associated with an offer or prize in a contest

Two common testing instruments are called comprehension and reaction tests. *Comprehension tests* are used when participants in a study are asked the meaning of a marketing communication piece. The idea is to make sure viewers comprehend the message as intended. The moderator can then explore the reasons why the intended message was comprehended correctly or why it was not.

*Reaction tests* are used to determine overall feelings about a marketing piece, most notably whether the response is negative or positive. If the focus group reacts negatively to an ad or particular copy in an ad, the agency can make the changes before it is too late. It is possible for an advertisement to be correctly comprehended but elicit negative emotions. Therefore, exploring any negative feelings provides creatives with input to modify the marketing piece.

## Copytesting

A second form of message evaluation is copytesting. **Copytests** are used when the marketing piece is finished or in its final stages of development prior to production. They are designed to solicit

As a result of concept tests, Newcomer, Morris & Young Agency was able to create this advertisement.
*Source:* Courtesy of Newcomer, Morris & Young, Inc.

responses to the main message of the ad as well as the format in which that message will be presented. For a television ad, a copytest could be conducted using a storyboard format or a version that is filmed by agency members rather than professional actors.

The two most common copytesting techniques are portfolio and theater tests. Both tests place the marketing piece in with others. A **portfolio test** is a display of a set of print ads, one of which is the ad being evaluated. A **theater test** is a display of a set of television ads, including the one being evaluated. The individuals who participate in these studies do not know which piece is under scrutiny. Both techniques mimic reality in the sense that consumers normally are exposed to multiple messages, such as when a radio or television station plays a series of commercials in a row or when a set of newspaper ads appears on a single page. The tests also allow researchers the opportunity to compare the target piece with other marketing messages. For these approaches to yield the optimal findings, it is essential that all of the marketing pieces shown be in the same stage of development (e.g., a set of storyboards or a series of nearly completed coupon offers).

Copytesting can utilize focus groups as well as other measurement devices. An ad or coupon that is in the final stage of design can be tested with a **mall intercept technique**. The approach involves stopping people who are shopping in a mall. They are then asked to evaluate the item. The mall intercept technique can incorporate a portfolio approach. To do so, subjects are asked to examine the marketing piece, which is mixed in with others, normally 6 to 10 ads, coupons, or other marketing communications tools. This may be a better approach than showing an item by itself. The disadvantage of displaying only one item is that people tend to give it a more positive evaluation than if it is mixed in with others. Comprehension and reaction tests are commonly utilized in a mall intercept setting.

For television commercials, theater tests are often used. The test ad is placed among other ads within a television documentary or a new show, such as a pilot episode of a new comedy or drama. The advantage of using a new show is that it is better able to hold the subject's interest. At the end of the program, the individuals participating in the study are asked for their reactions to the ads that were shown. For more valid results, those participating in the study should not know which ad is being tested.

There is some controversy concerning copytesting. A number of advertisers and marketers feel strongly that copytesting only favors rational approaches to advertising messages. Recently, creatives working for brands such as Nike, Volkswagen, Budweiser, and Target have been allowed to skip the copytesting phase of advertising design and move straight into production. The idea was that copytests stifle the creativity that is needed to produce ads that will stand out in the clutter. Further, these agency leaders believe that copytests are likely to lead to ad messages about product benefits that are believable and understandable to members of a focus group. Most consumers know little, if anything, about how to create an effective ad. It may not make sense to have them serving as final judges of an ad's quality.

A mall intercept technique is often used for copytesting of advertisements and other communication pieces.

Although, marketing professionals do not favor using copytests, the majority think they are necessary, primarily due to accountability issues. When it is time to make a decision to go forward on a high-dollar campaign, advertising agency and company executives want evidence that supports the decision. A creative's "gut feeling" is difficult to justify in a corporate boardroom. The members of an advertising agency may feel an ad is good and that copytesting wastes time and money, but they still recognize that company clients seeking top management approval of an ad campaign need evidence the ad will succeed. As a result, the client will want the ads tested. The copytesting techniques that are currently available may not be perfect, but it seems likely they will continue to be used.[4]

> ▶ **Product name or brand**
> ▶ **Firm name**
> ▶ **Company location**
> ▶ **Theme music**
> ▶ **Spokesperson**
> ▶ **Tagline**
> ▶ **Incentive being offered**
> ▶ **Product attributes**
> ▶ **Primary selling point of communication piece**

**FIGURE 15.2**
**Items Tested for Recall**

## Recall Tests

Another popular method used to evaluate advertising is called a **recall test**. This approach involves asking an individual to recall what ads he or she viewed in a given setting or time period. Then, in progressive steps, the subject is asked to identify information about the ad. Figure 15.2 lists some of the parts of an advertisement that can be tested for recall.

The most common form of recall test is the **day-after recall (DAR)** test. The DAR method is often used to evaluate TV advertisements. Individuals who participate in the study are called by phone the day after the advertisement first appears. Normally, they are tested using an approach called **unaided recall**. In other words, the subjects are asked to name, or recall, the ads they saw or heard the previous evening, without being given any prompts or memory jogs. For magazines and newspaper ads, there are two approaches. In the first, consumers are contacted the day after the ad appeared. The individuals name the ads they recall and then are asked a serious of questions to discover the features of the advertisements they remember. In the second, an individual is given a magazine for a certain period of time (normally 1 week) and instructed to read it as he or she normally would during leisure time. Then, the researcher returns and asks a series of questions about which ads became memorable and what features the individual could remember. In the business-to-business sector, the second method is a popular way to test ads for trade journals.

The day-after recall method works best when the objective is to measure the extent to which consumers have learned or remembered the content of an ad. DAR is a valuable test because advertisers know that increased recall enhances the probability that the brand is becoming a part of the consumer's evoked set, or the primary choices that are remembered when purchase alternatives are being considered. A brand that is part of the evoked set is much more likely to be chosen when the purchase is made.[5]

The second type of recall test is the **aided recall** method. Aided recall means that consumers are prompted by being told the product category and, if necessary, names of specific brands in that category. The respondent still does not know which brand or ad is being tested. When the consumer states that he or she does recall seeing a specific brand being advertised, the person then is asked to provide as many details as possible about the ad. At that point, no further clues are given regarding the ad content.

Most researchers believe the unaided recall approach is superior to other evaluative tests because it identifies the times that an advertisement has become lodged in the person's memory. Unaided recall is also better than aided recall because some people may respond to a prompt by saying they do indeed remember an ad, even when they are uncertain. Recall scores are almost always higher when the aided recall method is used. Some ad agencies use both methods. First, they use unaided recall to gather basic information. Then, the researcher follows up with prompts to delve deeper into the memories that are present, even if it takes a little help to dig them out.

In both aided and unaided recall tests, if incorrect information is provided, the researcher continues the questioning. Individuals are never told they have given inaccurate answers. Incorrect responses are important data to record, however. Memory is not always accurate in both aided and unaided recall situations. Consequently, people give incorrect answers. In other words, they may mention commercials that did not actually appear during the test period, but rather were viewed at some other time. Although this may seem strange, bear in mind that the average person sees between 50 and 100 ads on a typical night of television viewing. It is easy to become confused.

An incorrect response is often triggered by exposure to a similar ad. For example, a person may remember seeing a commercial for Firestone tires when it was actually presented by Uniroyal. Seeing the Firestone ad triggered the recall of the Uniroyal brand because the individual is more familiar with Uniroyal or holds the brand in higher esteem. This type of error is more common in aided recall tests. In that situation, the individual is being provided with clues from a particular product category, which increases the odds of remembering the wrong brand.

Recall tests are used primarily after ads and marketing materials have already been launched to the public. At the same time, however, they can be used in the early stages of communication development. In these instances, participants in the study are recruited, and the test is more of the standard experimental design variety. For example, an agency that has created a new business-to-business ad may wonder if the ad would work when aired with consumer ads. Using a theater lab setting, the new ad can be placed in a documentary with other ads. At the end, either the aided or unaided recall method can be used to measure ad and brand awareness.

It is important to consider three factors when evaluating recall tests. The first is a person's general attitude toward advertising. Individuals who regularly watch ads, believe advertising helps them stay informed, and have positive attitudes toward advertising will have higher recall scores. It is important, therefore, to measure a person's general attitude toward advertising in evaluating recall scores.[6]

A second factor that impacts recall scores is the prominence of the brand name in the ad. Recall scores are highly sensitive to the presence of a brand name and its visibility or prominence in the ad. Television ad copy that mentions the brand name 7 times during the 30 seconds is likely to receive higher recall scores than an ad that states the brand name only once. In addition, an individual is more likely to remember a brand name that he or she uses regularly, especially if it is prominent in the ad. Also, an institutional ad normally receives a lower recall score because of the difficulty in remembering the company's name.[7]

The third factor is the age of the respondent used in the recall tests. Recall scores tend to decline with age. Older people do not remember things as well as those who are younger. Table 15.1 displays average recall scores for different age segments using both DAR and brand recall instruments.[8] There are several explanations for lower recall scores in older people:

▸ They have reduced short-term recall capacity.

▸ Older persons are more fixed in terms of brand choices, making them less easily influenced by advertisements.

▸ The TV ads used to develop Table 15.1 may have been targeted more toward youth.

For whatever reason, it appears that age does affect recall scores. Still, recall tests are valuable instruments used in testing to see if the ad has the potential to move into a person's long-term memory and affect future purchase decisions.

**TABLE 15.1**

**Impact of Age on DAR and Brand Recall**

| Day-After Recall | | Brand Recall | |
|---|---|---|---|
| Age Segment | Average Recall | Age Segment | Average Recall |
| 12–17 | 34% | 13–17 | 70% |
| 18–34 | 29% | 18–34 | 53% |
| 35–49 | 24% | 35+ | 36% |
| 50–65 | 22% | | |

*Source:* Based on Joel S. Debow, "Advertising Recognition and Recall by Age–Including Teens," *Journal of Advertising Research* 35, no. 5 (September–October 1995), pp. 55–60.

## Evaluation Programs

Advertising agencies and companies often hire research firms to evaluate the effectiveness of IMC campaigns as well as components of the IMC plan such as advertising, sponsorships, and consumer and trade promotions. Techniques such as recall tests, recognition tests, and attitude measures are used with a representative sample. Conducting these tests is costly, and the future of an IMC or advertising campaign may be dependent upon the result.

Many opportunities for unethical behavior are possible, ranging from selecting the sample to interpreting the results. If a client wants the results to come out a certain way, it is tempting for a research firm to manipulate the data until the desired outcome is obtained. Rather than spend money on selecting a random, representative sample, a firm may use a judgment or convenience sample even though it may not be truly representative. These concerns are heightened when the advertising agency that designed the ads is evaluating its own work.

When evaluating an IMC campaign or individual parts of an IMC plan, those doing the research must act in a responsible and ethical manner. Results should be reported accurately even if they do not reflect what management or the client wants.

## Recognition Tests

A **recognition test** is a format in which individuals are given copies of an ad and asked if they recognize it or have seen it before. Those who say they have seen the ad are asked to provide additional details about when and where the ad was encountered (e.g., specific television program, the name of the magazine, the location of the billboard, etc.). This information is collected to validate that it was indeed seen. Next the individual is asked a series of questions about the ad itself. This helps the researcher gather information and insights into consumer attitudes and reactions to the ad. Recognition tests are best suited to testing for comprehension of and reactions to ads. In contrast, recall tests tend to work well when testing brand and ad awareness. Recognition tests help when the advertiser is more concerned about how the ad is received and what information is being comprehended. This is especially important for ads using a cognitive message strategy, in which some type of reasoning process is invoked in persuading the consumer about the value of a product.

Unlike a recall test, a recognition tests is not a memory test. Recognition tests are an expression of a person's interest in a particular advertisement.[9] Ads that are of no interest do not register with the person and are not remembered. In a recognition test, it is as if the respondent is saying, "Yes, advertisements of that kind usually attract my attention, so I did pause and look at it when I went through the magazine." An ad that a person likes is about 75 percent more likely to be recognized than an ad the individual did not like. This is one reason celebrities are selected for ads, such as the milk ad featuring Spike Lee on the right. If an individual likes the celebrity in the advertisement, then he or she will be more likely to recognize the ad. For ads the respondent thought were interesting, the odds of recognition were about 50 percent higher than for ads that were not deemed interesting.[10]

Using celebrities such as Spike Lee increases recall and recognition through greater interest in and liking of the ad.
*Source:* Courtesy of Bozell Worldwide, Inc.

Further, when the consumer uses the brand being displayed in the ad, the likelihood of recognizing the ad rises. A person who uses a brand is about 50 percent more likely to recognize the ad than an individual who does not use the brand. This means researchers must look beyond the number of respondents who recognize a particular ad. Questions should be asked about the brands subjects normally buy in the product category, if they liked the ad, and if they found the ad to be interesting.

A recognition score is also affected by factors such as the color and size of the ad. Larger ads are more easily noticed, as are color ads (as compared to black and white).[11] As a result, the research team should also account for the size of the print ad, whether or not the ad is in color, and the length of the broadcast ad when studying ad recognition.

One difference between recognition scores and recall scores is that recognition scores do not decline over time, primarily because consumer interests remain relatively stable. If a person liked the milk ad with Spike Lee when he or she first viewed the ad, it is likely he or she will like the ad and recognize it in the future, even months after it first appeared.

Recognition and recall tests measure different things. Consequently, many research teams perform both tests on the same subjects. First, recall measures are used to start the interview, and then recognition tests are given at the end of the session. For instance, a subject may have viewed an ad during a particular TV show but does not mention the ad when undergoing a recall test. In this situation the respondent can then be given a recognition test to see if he or she remembers seeing the ad.

Recall and recognition do have things in common. For one, both help to establish the brand in the consumer's mind.[12] Loyalty and brand equity are more likely to result. Therefore, even though recall and recognition are more oriented toward the short-term impact of a given ad or campaign, the long-term consequences of a series of successful and memorable ads should be considered.

## Attitude and Opinion Tests

Many of the tests used to study advertisements and other marketing pieces are designed to examine attitudinal components. These types of instruments may be used in conjunction with recall or recognition tests. Attitude tests deal with both the cognitive and affective reactions to an ad. They are also used to solicit consumer opinions. Opinions are gathered from surveys or focus groups. They can be obtained as part of a mall intercept plan or even in laboratory settings. They can be used anytime during the ad development process or after the ad has been launched.

The content and format of attitude tests vary widely. Sometimes specific responses are requested in what are called **closed-end questionnaire** formats. Scales such as *1 = highly unfavorable* to *7 = highly favorable* are often prepared for respondents to answer. In other tests, the individual is allowed to discuss whatever comes to mind regarding some aspect of a product or its advertisements. These are called **open-ended questions**.

Roper Starch Worldwide developed a testing system called "ADD+IMPACT." It was created to study consumer reactions to advertisements before they are launched. As part of the testing process, Roper conducts one-on-one interviews with 60 or more consumers. Each participant responds to open-ended questions as well as more standardized closed-ended attitudinal questions. The results of the test, transcripts, and a quantitative analysis of the numbers-based responses are provided to clients within 2 weeks of the test. By testing the ad prior to a launch, advertisers are more likely to know what people think about the ad and what type of reaction to expect. Changing an ad at this point is much less costly than after a campaign has been launched.[13]

Conducting attitude tests would be important for *Family Circle* to ensure this advertisement will accomplish its stated objective.
*Source:* Used with permission of Gruner & Jahr USA Publishing (G&J).

There are many aspects to the buying decision-making process. Attitudes and opinions are connected to short-term behaviors and longer-term assessments of a company and its products. Therefore, in addition to simply remembering that a firm exists, advertisers and IMC planners should try to understand how people feel about the company in the context of larger, more general feelings.

## Emotional Reaction Tests

Many ads are designed to elicit emotional responses from consumers. Emotional ads are based on the idea that ads that elicit positive feelings are more likely to be remembered. Also, consumers who have positive attitudes toward ads would logically develop more positive attitudes toward the product. This in turn should result in increased purchases.[14]

It is difficult to measure the emotional impact of an advertisement. The simplest method is to ask questions about an individual's feelings and emotions after viewing a marketing communication piece. This can be performed in a laboratory setting or as a theater test. Also, the ad can be shown to focus groups. In all of these circumstances the test ad should be placed with other ads rather than by itself.

A **warmth monitor** is an alternative method developed to measure emotions. The concept behind the warmth monitor is that feelings of warmth are positive when they are directed toward an ad or a product. To measure warmth, subjects are asked to manipulate a joystick while watching a commercial. The movements track reactions to a commercial by making marks on a sheet of paper containing four lines. The four lines are labeled:

1. Absence of warmth
2. Neutral
3. Warmhearted or tender
4. Emotional

The warmth meter was developed to evaluate TV ads. It can be adapted to radio ads.[15]

A more sophisticated warmth meter was developed at the University of Hawaii. Individuals view advertisements in a theater-type lab featuring big-screen television. Those who feel negatively about what they are watching pull a joystick downward. Those who feel more positively push the joystick in the opposite direction. Thus, as they are watching the commercial, the subjects constantly move the joystick, thereby conveying their feelings during every moment of the ad. The results of the 20 participants are tallied into one graph and then placed over the commercial. This technology allows an advertiser to see which parts of the ad elicit positive emotions and which parts elicit negative emotions. After graphing the test results, the group can then be used as a focus group to discuss the ad and why group members felt the way they did at various moments of the ad.[16]

A similar technology has been developed by DiscoverWhy. The major difference is that DiscoverWhy provides the service on the Internet. DiscoverWhy can poll 1,000 or more people who look at an advertisement as it is shown on the Internet. As they watch the ad on streaming video, participants use a mouse to move a tab on a sliding scale from 1 to 10. If they like what they see, they slide the scale toward the 10. Those who don't like what they see, slide the scale toward the 1. After the data have been collected, a graph can be superimposed over the advertisement. This shows the advertiser the likable and non-likable parts of the commercial. A major advantage of using the Internet is that subjects selected for the study can provide their ratings at any time that is convenient. If the agency needs a focus group to discuss the ad, subjects can be selected from the participants. The focus group session can even be held online.[17]

Most of the time, emotions are associated with shorter-term events, such as the reaction toward a given advertisement. At the same time, emotions are strongly held in the memory banks of most consumers. Therefore, an ad that made a viewer angry may be retrieved, and the anger recreated, every time the individual remembers either the ad or the company. As a result, it is wise to attempt to discover emotional responses to various ads before they are released to be shown to the general public.

Emotional advertising based on a substantial amount of pretesting led to a highly successful antismoking campaign in Minnesota. Based on focus group information, ads were structured to show the devastating effects of smoking (lost vocal chords) and of secondhand smoke on children. The ads were shown to groups of smokers and nonsmokers before being released because they were so dramatic and graphic. The net result was much stronger attitudes favoring smoke-free environments and additional calls to the state's quit-smoking hotline.[18]

## Physiological Arousal Tests

Emotional reaction tests are *self-report* instruments. In other words, individuals report their feelings as they see fit. Although this may or may not be a flawed instrument, many marketing researchers are interested in finding ways to measure emotions and feelings without relying on people to self-report how they feel.

Physiological arousal tests measure fluctuations in a person's body functions that are associated with changing emotions. The primary physiological arousal tests are:

1. The psychogalvanometer
2. A pupillometric test
3. Psychophysiology

A **psychogalvanometer** measures a person's perspiration levels. As an individual reacts emotionally to a situation (in this case, an advertisement), the amount of perspiration he or she generates changes. Perhaps you have noticed that you sweat quite a bit more when watching an exciting movie or sports event. This arousal indicates you are interested and involved emotionally. An ad producing these effects may be more memorable and powerful than one that is boring or receives no emotional response.

The psychogalvanometer works by evaluating the amount of perspiration located in the palm and fingers. A very fine electric current is sent through one finger and returns to the galvanometer through another finger. Remember, a reaction can be negative or positive. The galvanometer simply measures the individual's physiological reaction. One benefit of the psychogalvanometer is that it can be used to assess emotional reactions to many different types of marketing communication pieces including television commercials, consumer promotions, and trade promotions.

A **pupillometric meter** measures the dilation of a person's pupil. Dilation levels also change with emotional arousal. A person who is frightened has wider pupils, as does someone who is excited. Pupil dilation can be studied as the subject views a television or print advertisement. Pupils dilate more when the person reacts positively to the ad or marketing communication. Pupils become smaller when the subject reacts negatively.

When conducting a test, the subject's head can be set in a fixed position. The dilation of the pupil can then be measured while viewing the ad. In this way, each aspect of the message can be evaluated for positive or negative responses. A graph can be superimposed on the commercial to show evaluators how each person responded to the advertisement.

In recent years, there have been significant advances in **psychophysiology**, which is a brain-image

Physiological tests can be used to test ads such as this one by Weight Watchers.
*Source:* Courtesy of Weight Watchers International, Inc.

measurement process. It tracks the flow and movement of electrical currents in the brain. One recent study demonstrated that the currents in a subject's brain indicate a preference for Coke or Pepsi that is the same as the product the person chooses in a blind taste test. According to neuroscientist Justin Meaux, "Preference has measurable correlates in the brain; you can see it." Richard Siberstein, an Australian neuroscientist, used physiological measurements of the brain to show that successful ads tend to generate higher levels of emotional engagement and long-term memory coding.[19]

To demonstrate how physiological tests work, consider an advertisement with a sexually attractive male or female. In a focus group, respondents may enjoy the ad but cover up these feelings, stating the ad is sexist and inappropriate. These reactions may be due to social pressure; they may also occur because the subjects want to be accepted by those around them. The same individual may not move the joystick to report his or her true feelings when participating in a study using the warmth monitor. The stigma attached to sex in advertising often affects self-reported reactions. Thus, a physiological arousal test may be a better indicator of a person's true feelings.

All three of these tests are based on the idea that emotions affect people physiologically and that these physical responses can be measured. Some researchers believe physiological arousal tests are more accurate than emotional reaction tests, because physiological arousal cannot easily be faked. As scientists gain a better understanding of physiological responses, the brain, and the electrical currents that move through the brain, use of these methods of evaluating ads and marketing pieces is likely to increase.[20]

Physiological arousal tests could be used to test the impact of this advertisement for Maidenform.
*Source:* By permission of Maidenform, Inc.

## Persuasion Analysis

The final type of message evaluation tool is designed to appraise the persuasiveness of a marketing communication item. There are other measures of awareness, emotions, liking, and physical reactions, however these do not measure the ability of the marketing piece to persuade the consumer. Persuasion techniques require pretest and posttest assessments.

A researcher analyzing the persuasiveness of a television ad would start by gathering a group of consumers in a theater. Measures of brand attitudes and purchase intentions are then gathered for the test brand and other brands put in the study. A series of commercials is shown as part of a program. Next, measures are taken to see if any changes in attitude or purchase intentions resulted from exposure to the ads. The amount of change indicates how well the persuasion in the advertisement worked.

One company that conducts persuasion analysis programs is ASI Market Research. A sample of 250 consumers is recruited to attend a new television program. Once they are in the ASI theater, the consumers are informed that prizes will be given away through a drawing. These individuals are asked to identify the specific brand they prefer in each product category. The subjects are then shown two new TV programs complete with commercials. At the end, the subjects are told that a product was inadvertently left off the initial survey, and they are asked to fill the form out again in order to enter the drawing. ASI compares before and after responses to the same questions in order to see if there were any changes in attitudes; the subjects are not aware of the intention of the study.[21]

Knowing the ad actually has persuasive power is a major advantage for the advertiser. Attempts to assess the impact of such ads before they are released to a wider audience are solid investments of marketing dollars.

## EVALUATION CRITERIA

For all of the programs mentioned thus far, it is important to establish quality evaluation criteria. One program helpful in doing so is **positioning advertising copytesting (PACT)**. PACT was created to evaluate television ads. It was formulated by 21 leading

# COMMUNICATION ACTION

## A Quick Quiz

Knowing what works and what doesn't is the key to assessing any IMC promotional piece effectively. A magazine titled *Tested Copy* appeared on a monthly basis for several years. It was oriented toward discovering the best methods for reaching customers. In one issue, the following quiz appeared. See if you can select the correct answers, which appear at the bottom of the page

*Question 1:* Which of the following does *Tested Copy* most consistently find as a failure in print advertising? The failure to:

    a. Animate the product and bring it to life

    b. Thoroughly describe the characteristics of the product

    c. Tell the readers what the product will do for them

    d. Give the readers sufficient information about the advertisers

*Question 2:* Which type of advertising is the most believable?

    a. Ads that feature real people who have used the product

    b. Ads that cite the results of user surveys

    c. Ads with a money-back guarantee

    d. Ads that name the competition and make comparisons

*Question 3:* What proportion of readers of women's magazines agrees with this statement: *I like the way scented ads make magazines smell?*

    a. 29%

    b. 44%

    c. 68%

    d. 80%

*Question 4:* On average, an ad with sans-serif type is more likely to earn higher readership scores than an ad with serif type.

    a. True

    b. False

To learn more about this type of marketing information, go to the Web site of Roper Starch Worldwide. Information about *Tested Copy* is also available online.

*Answers:*
1. c
2. c
3. d
4. a

**Source:** Alan Rosenspan, "Roper Starch Worldwide, Inc.," *Direct Marketing* 61, no. 4 (August 1998), p. 4.

U.S. advertising agencies.[22] Even though PACT was designed to examine the issues involved in copytesting television ads, the principles can be used for any type of message evaluation system and all types of media. Figure 15.3 lists the nine principles that were developed. These should be followed when a written or verbal marketing communication piece is being tested. A discussion of these principles follows.

First, no matter which procedure is used, it should be *relevant to the advertising objective being tested.* If the objective of a coupon promotion is to stimulate trial purchases, then the test should evaluate the coupon's copy in order to determine its ability to stimulate trial purchases. On the other hand, an evaluation of attitudes toward a brand would require a different instrument.

*Researchers should agree on how the results are going to be used* when selecting test instruments. They should also agree on the design of the test in order to obtain the desired results. This is especially true for the preparation stage in an advertisement's

▶ **Testing procedure should be relevant to the advertising objectives.**

▶ **In advance of each test, researchers should agree on how the results will be used.**

▶ **Multiple measures should be used.**

▶ **The test should be based on some theory or model of human response to communication.**

▶ **The testing procedure should allow for more than one exposure to the advertisement, if necessary.**

▶ **In selecting alternate advertisements to include in the test, each should be at the same stage in the process as the test ad.**

▶ **The test should provide controls to avoid biases.**

▶ **The sample used for the test should be representative of the target sample.**

▶ **The testing procedure should demonstrate reliability and validity.**

**FIGURE 15.3**
**Copytesting Principles of PACT**

*Source:* Based on PACT document published in the *Journal of Marketing* 11, no. 4 (1982), pp. 4–29.

development, because many tests are used to determine whether the advertisement eventually will be created.

The research team should also decide on a cutoff score to be used following the test. This will prevent biases from entering into the findings about the ad's potential effectiveness. Many ad agencies use test markets for new advertisements before they are launched in a larger area. A recall method used to determine if people in the target market remember seeing the ad should have a prearranged cutoff score. In other words, the acceptable percentage may be established so that 25 percent of the sample should remember the ad in order to move forward with the campaign. If the percentage is not reached, the ad has failed the test.

*Using multiple measures* allows for more precise evaluations of ads and campaigns. It is possible for a well-designed ad to fail one particular testing procedure yet score higher on others. Consumers and business buyers who are the targets of marketing communications are complex human beings. Various people may perceive individual ads differently. As a result, advertisers usually try to develop more than one measure so that there is greater agreement on whether the ad or campaign will succeed and reach its desired goals.

The test to be used should be *based on some theory or model of human response to communication.* This makes it more likely that the test will be a predictive tool of human behavior. The objective is to enhance the odds that the communication will actually produce the desired results (going to the Web site, visiting the store, or making a purchase.) when the ad is launched.

Many testing procedures are based on a single exposure. Although in many cases this is sufficient for research purposes, there are times that *multiple exposures* are necessary to obtain reliable test results. For complex ads, more than one exposure may be needed. The human mind can comprehend only so much information in one viewing. It is vital to make sure the person can and does comprehend the ad in order to determine whether the ad can achieve its desired effects.

Often ads are tested in combination with other ads to disguise the one being examined. Placing the test marketing piece in with others means the test subjects do not know which ad is being evaluated. This prevents personal biases from affecting judgments. To ensure valid results, *the alternative ads should be in the same stage of process development.* Thus, if ad copy is being tested prior to ad development, then the alternative ads should also be in the ad copy development stage rather than established ads.

Next, adequate controls must be in place to *prevent biases and external factors from affecting results.* To help control external factors, experimental designs are often used. When conducting experiments, researchers try to keep as many things as constant as possible and manipulate only one variable at a time. For instance, in a theater test, the temperature, time of day, room lighting, television program, and ads shown can all be the

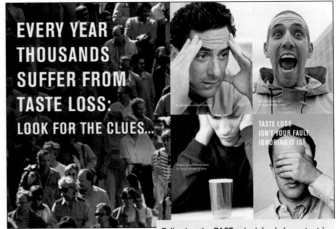

Following the PACT principles is important in evaluating ads such as these for Miller Lite beer.
*Source:* Courtesy of Miller Brewing Co.

same. Then, the researcher may display the program and ads to an all-male audience followed by an all-female audience. Changing only one variable (gender) makes it possible to see if the ad, in a very controlled environment, is perceived differently by men as opposed to women.

This does not mean field tests are ineffective. Testing marketing communications in real-world situations is extremely valuable because they approximate reality. Still, when conducting field tests, such as mall intercepts, those performing the testing must try to control as many variables as possible. Thus, the same mall, same questions, and same ads are shown. Then, age, gender, or other variables can be manipulated.

As with any research procedure, sampling procedures are important. It is crucial for the *sample being used to be representative of the target population.* For example, if a print ad designed for Spanish-speaking Hispanic Americans is to be tested, the sample used in the test normally will be in Spanish.

Finally, researchers must continually try to make tests *reliable and valid.* Reliable means "repeatable." In other words, if the same test is given five times to the same person, the individual should respond in the same way each time. If a respondent is "emotional" on one iteration of a warmth test and "neutral" when the ad is shown a second time, the research team will wonder if the test is reliable.

Valid means "generalizable." Valid research findings can be generalized to other groups. For instance, when a focus group of women finds an ad to be funny, and then a group of men reacts in the same way, the finding that the humor is effective is more valid. This would be an increasingly valuable outcome if the results were generalizable to people of various ages and races. Many times an ad may be reliable, or repeatable in the same group, but not valid or generalizable to other groups of consumers or business buyers.

The PACT principles are helpful when designing tests of short-term advertising effectiveness. They are also helpful when seeking to understand larger and more long-term issues such as brand loyalty and identification with the company. The goal is to generate data that document what a company is doing works. When this occurs, the company and its advertising team have access to invaluable information.

# BEHAVIORAL EVALUATIONS

The first part of this chapter has been devoted to message evaluations. These techniques provide valuable insights into what people think and feel. Still, some marketers contend that the only valid evaluation criterion should be *actual sales.* To these critics it is less important for an ad to be well liked. An ad that does not increase sales is ineffective. The same type of argument is often presented regarding the other marketing communication tools such as sales promotions, trade promotions, personal selling, and direct marketing.

There is some validity to the idea that tangible results should be the bottom line to any marketing program; however, not all communication objectives can be measured using sales figures.[23] Leaders of companies with low brand awareness may be most interested in the visibility and memorability aspects of a communication plan, even though a marketing program designed to boost brand awareness may not result in immediate sales.

Measuring the results of a sales promotion campaign featuring coupons using sales figures is easier to do than measuring the results of an advertising campaign on television. Consequently, effective promotions evaluations should involve the study of both message and behavioral elements. In this section, various behavioral measures are discussed. Figure 15.4 lists these techniques.

In evaluating this television advertisement for Maidenform, it is important that the sample used in the evaluation represent the target market of Maidenform.
*Source:* Courtesy of Maidenform.

## Sales and Response Rates

Measuring changes in sales following a marketing campaign is easier now than it was in the past. Universal product codes and scanner data are available from many retail outlets. These data are available on a weekly and, in some situations, daily basis. Many retail outlets even have access to sales information on a real-time basis, and the information can be accessed at any point during the day.

Scanner data make it possible for companies to monitor sales and help both the retailer and the manufacturer discover the impact of a particular marketing program. Bear in mind, however, that extraneous factors can affect sales. For instance, in a multimedia advertising program, it would be difficult to know which ad moved the customer to action. Further, a company may be featuring its fall line of jackets, and a cold snap may affect the region. If so, what caused the customer to buy—the ad or the weather? Firms utilizing trade and consumer promotion programs must account for the impact of both the promotion and the advertising when studying sales figures. Sales are one indicator of

> ❱ **Sales**
> ❱ **Response rates**
> ❱ **Redemption rates**
> ❱ **Test markets**
> ❱ **Purchase simulation tests**

**FIGURE 15.4**
**Behavioral Measures**

1960.

1968.

1975.

1980.

1986.

1990.

You always come back to the basics.

Scanner data could be used as one measure of the effectiveness of this Jim Beam advertisement.
*Source:* Courtesy of Jim Beam Brands Worldwide, Inc.

effectiveness; however, they may be influenced by any number of intervening factors.

Advertisements are probably the most difficult component of the IMC program to evaluate, for several reasons. These include:

1. The influence of other factors
2. A delayed impact of the ad
3. Consumers changing their minds while in the store
4. Whether the brand is in the consumer's evoked set
5. Brand equity considerations

First, as just discussed, it is difficult to distinguish *the effects of advertising from other factors.* This is because ads have short- and long-term effects, and consumers and businesses see ads in so many different contexts. Thus, the direct impact of one ad or one campaign on sales is difficult to decipher.

Second, *advertising often has a delayed impact.* Many times consumers encounter ads and are persuaded to purchase the product, but will not actually make the buy until a later time, when they need the item. Thus, a woman may be convinced that she wants to buy a new pair of jeans in response to a sexy and effective advertisement by Calvin Klein. Still, rather than buying them herself, she leaves several well-placed hints for her husband before her next birthday, which could be several months later. The problem is that her husband may have purchased another brand or a different gift. So, then she must wait until Christmas or Valentine's Day, but still the ad worked and led to a purchase. Measuring the impact of an ad in that setting is almost impossible.

Third, many times consumers may decide to make purchases based on an advertisement but *change their minds when they arrive at the retail store.* A competing brand may be on sale, the store could be out of the desired brand, or the salesperson could persuade the customer that another brand is better. In each case, the ad was successful on one level but another factor intervened as the purchase was made.

Fourth, *the brand being advertised may not be part of the consumer's evoked set.* Upon hearing or seeing the ad, however, the brand is moved into the evoked set. Thus, even when the brand is not considered at first, it will be in the future when the need arises or when the consumer becomes dissatisfied with a current brand.

Fifth, advertising is an essential component of building brand awareness and brand equity. Although sales may not be the result immediately, *the ad may build brand equity,* which in turn will influence future purchases.

It is easier to measure the effects of trade and consumer promotions, direct-marketing programs, and personal selling on actual sales. Manufacturers can study the impact of trade promotions by observing changes in sales to the retailers at the time the promotions are being offered. The same is true for consumer promotions such as coupons, contests, and point-of-purchase displays. Many manufacturers' reps push hard to get retailers to use the company's POP displays. At the same time, the retailer is more interested in the effects of the display on sales. Using scanner data, both the retailer and the manufacturer can measure the impact of a POP display. Retailers normally use POPs that have demonstrated the ability to boost sales.

To track the impact of POP displays, Anheuser-Busch, Frito-Lay, Procter & Gamble, and Warner-Lambert joined together as initial sponsors of a program developed by *Point-of-Purchase Advertising International (POPAI).* In the initial study, POPAI tracked 25 different product categories in 250 supermarkets nationwide. Sponsors paid between $50,000 and $75,000 to receive customized data about the POP displays featuring particular brands. One advantage of using POPAI data is that each firm not only can see the impact of the POP for its brand but also receive comparative data showing how well the display fared against other displays. The major advantage of the POPAI program is its

▶ **Changes in sales**

▶ **Telephone inquiries**

▶ **Response cards**

▶ **Internet responses**

▶ **Direct-marketing responses**

▶ **Redemption rate of sales promotion offers—**
**Coupons, premiums, contests, sweepstakes**

**FIGURE 15.5**
**Responses to Marketing**
**Messages That Can Be Tracked**

low cost. Sponsors of the POPAI program attained valuable data at a much lower cost than if they had sought the information on their own.[24]

There are a wide variety of responses to marketing communications programs besides sales. Figure 15.5 lists some of the responses that can be tracked. These items are described in the remainder of this section.

One method of measuring the impact of an advertisement—direct mailing, TV direct offers, or price-off discounts to a business customer—is to assign a *toll-free number* to each marketing piece. A great deal of information can be collected during an inbound call. Sales data can be recorded and demographic information gathered. Psychographic information then can be added by contacting various commercial services.

In business-to-business situations, a toll-free number provides contact names to help the vendor discover who is performing the various functions in the buying center. As a result, a toll-free number provides sales data to determine which marketing program is the best and also can be used to generate valuable customer information that can be tied to the sales data. Knowing who is responding to each offer helps a firm better understand its customers and the approach that should be used for each target group.

Another method for measuring behaviors comes from *response cards*. These customer information forms are filled out at the time of a inquiry. The primary disadvantage of response cards is that less data are obtained. Consequently, commercial sources will be needed to obtain additional demographic and psychographic information. This is because response cards solicited from current customers contain information the firm is already likely to have in its database.

*Internet responses* are excellent behavioral measures. By using "cookies," a firm can obtain considerable information about the person or business making the inquiry. In addition, many times the person or business responding is willing to provide a great deal of helpful information voluntarily. It is also possible to track responses to direct advertising through Internet views. For instance, the Canadian Tourism Commission tested direct-response ads that were placed on television, radio, direct mail, and online. Each ad used a different URL for viewers to access for additional information. To the tourist, there was no perceivable difference because each URL took the person to the designated Canadian Tourism site. The Tourism Commission could track easily which ad the person viewed and which URL the person used. This made it possible to count the number of visitors from each of the direct-response advertisements.[25]

To evaluate Internet advertising campaigns, AdKnowledge introduced an online management tool called "MarketMatch Planner." MarketMatch Planner software includes two components: (1) Campaign Manager and (2) Administrator. Campaign Manager records traffic to a site as well as performing postbuy analysis. Administrator integrates Web ad-buy data and performance analysis with the firm's accounting and billing systems. In addition, MarketMatch Planner has the capability of integrating third-party data including audience demographics from the following sources:

▶ MediaMetrix for basic demographics

▶ NetRatings for GRP and other ratings instruments

Counting the number of telephone inquiries or Web site visits following an advertising campaign such as this one for AG Edwards could be used as a measure of effectiveness.
*Source:* Courtesy of A.G. Edwards.

YOU CAN'T RIDE OFF INTO THE SUNSET IF YOUR NEST EGG WON'T CARRY YOU. We're big believers in a long-term retirement plan based on objective financial advice. And in having a financial consultant who can help you every step of the way. To see whether your nest egg could benefit from such Midwestern horse sense, visit agedwards.com or call 866-379-4243.

A.G. EDWARDS.
FULLY INVESTED IN OUR CLIENTS.

YOUR CLIENT CUT YOUR DEADLINE.
AT LEAST DINNER CAN GO ON AS PLANNED.

CHICKEN DIJON

Delicious Dijon sauce. Savory chicken breasts. All the makings of a mouth-watering meal, in just 25 minutes. So no matter what they do at work, it won't hurt your dinner plans. Look for it in our color-coded Meal Idea Center. For more chicken ideas, look for the yellow packages or click to www.mccormick.com.

**McCormick**
*The taste you trust™*

By using technology such as MarketMatch Planner, a company such as McCormick can track who goes to its Web site for recipes.
*Source:* Courtesy of McCormick & Co., Inc.

- Psychographic data from SRI Consulting
- Web site ratings and descriptions from NetGuide
- Web traffic audit data from BPA Interactive

New technologies have made it possible to quantitatively analyze Internet advertising. An e-company can see exactly how many hits an ad brings to a site. The company also can identify how many sales result and how much is spent per sale. Individual e-businesses can also identify demographic and psychographic information about customers. Internet advertising is much easier to evaluate quantitatively than any other advertising medium.

Internet data should be evaluated carefully. Results should be viewed in light of the IMC objectives that were set. An IMC objective of building brand awareness requires something other than Internet sales data to be assessed. An Internet ad can bring awareness to a brand but not lead to an online purchase. This might occur, for example, when a consumer or business uses the Internet to gather information but then makes the actual purchase at a retail store, by telephone, or by fax. When that happens, the impact of an Internet advertising campaign may not be able to reflect all of the brand awareness or sales that the campaign generated.

Various kinds of redemption rates can be used as behavioral effectiveness measures. *Coupons, premiums, contests, sweepstakes,* and *direct-mail pieces* are marketing communications devices that can be coded to record redemption rates. Comparing a current campaign with previous campaigns makes it possible for a firm to examine changes made in the design or execution of an ad. The results are reviewed in light of positive or negative changes in redemption rates.

Immediate changes in sales and redemptions are one form of behavioral evaluation. It is tempting for the advertiser and company to use them and fail to see "the forest for the trees." One campaign, advertisement, or promotions program should be viewed in the context of all other marketing efforts. Behavioral measures are best when the team sees them as part of the "big picture."

## Test Markets

A second form of behavioral response is a test market. Test markets are used when company leaders examine the effects of a marketing effort on a small scale before launching a national or international campaign. The primary advantage of test markets is that an organization can examine several elements of a marketing communication program. If the test market is successful, then it is likely that the national campaign also will be effective. It is also an excellent method of testing a campaign in a new country before launching a full-scale international campaign. Test market programs are used to assess:

1. Advertisements
2. Promotions and premiums
3. Pricing tactics
4. New products

Test markets are cost-effective methods to analyze and make changes in marketing efforts before millions of dollars are spent on something that will not accomplish the intended objectives. Ads can be modified, premiums revised, and pricing policies revisited before a more widespread program is under-taken. For example, McDonald's recently tested new ads that touted cleaner restaurants and friend-lier service. The goal of the ads was to test a cam-paign emphasizing McDonald's effort to improve in-store and drive-through service. Two television spots and one radio spot were produced and aired in Tampa and Seattle. Reactions from the test markets provided McDonald's marketing team and the advertising agency information about the impact of ad campaign, the parts of the ad that should be modified, and whether the campaign should be launched nationally.[26]

One major advantage of a test market is that it resembles an actual situation more than any of the other tests discussed thus far. The key is to make sure that the site selected for the test market strongly resembles the target population. A product targeted toward senior citizens should be studied in an area with a high concentration of senior citizens.

The Botany Shop could use Joplin as a test market by promoting a price-off sale.
*Source:* Used with permission of *The Joplin Globe*, Joplin, Missouri.

It is also important to design the test marketing campaign as close to the national or full marketing plan as possible. A lengthy time lapse may cause a company to experience differing results. The goal is to make sure the test market is a mirror image of the actual marketing program.

A test market can be as short as a few days or as long as 2 to 3 years. The longer the test market program runs, the more accurate the results. A test that is too short may yield less reliable results. On the other hand, if the test market is too long, the national market situation may change and the test market may no longer be a representative sample. The greatest fear, however, is that the competition is able to study what is going on. This gives competitors time to react to the proposed marketing campaign.

Competing companies can respond to a test market program in one of two ways. First, some firms may introduce a special promotion in the test market area in order to confound the results. This may reduce the sales for the product or campaign, making it appear less attractive. The second approach is not to intervene in the test market, but to use the time to prepare a countermarketing campaign. Firms that use this tactic are ready when the national launch occurs, and the impact may be that the test market results are not as predictive of what will happen.

Scanner data make it possible for results from test market campaigns to be quickly available. The figures can be studied to determine if test market results are acceptable. A firm also can design several versions of a marketing campaign in different test markets. Through scanner data, the firm can compare the sales from each test market to determine which version is the best. For example, in test market one, the firm may present an adver-tising campaign only. In test market two, the firm may add coupons to the ad program. In test market three, a premium and advertising can be used. Examining the results from each market helps the firm grasp which type of marketing campaign to use. Other test markets can be used with different prices in different regions to determine the price to charge and the elasticity associated with that price. It is also possible to vary the size of the coupon or premium to discover the impact. Rather than making a change at the national level, company leaders can modify the consumer promotion in selected markets to see what happens.

Through test marketing, firms have the opportunity to test communication ideas in more true-to-life settings. Test markets work best for trade and consumer promotions, direct marketing, and other marketing communication tools. They are not quite as accurate when assessing advertising because changes in sales take longer, and the test market program may not be long enough to measure the full impact. In any case, test markets are valuable instruments to use when examining specific marketing features and more general communications campaigns.

## Purchase Simulation Tests

A third behavioral approach available is purchase simulation tests. Consumers can be asked in several ways if they would be willing to buy products. For instance, they could be asked about purchase intentions at the end of a laboratory experiment. In this situation, however, intentions are self-reported and tend not to be an accurate predictor of future purchase behaviors. Test markets examine actual purchases, but are more costly because the marketing piece must be completed first. TV commercials cost a great deal to prepare. Even then, the impact of purchasing intentions and behaviors is hard to measure.

A useful and cost-effective approach to examine purchase behaviors is called a *simulated purchase test.* Research Systems Corporation (RSC) is a leading marketing research firm that specializes in purchase simulation studies. RSC tests the impact of commercials by studying consumer behaviors in a controlled laboratory environment.

RSC does not ask consumers to render opinions, describe their attitudes, or even ask if they plan to purchase the product. Instead, RSC creates a simulated shopping experience. Subjects are able to choose from a variety of products they would see on a normal store shelf. After completing a simulated shopping exercise, the subjects are seated and watch a television preview containing various commercials. The participants are asked to watch the TV preview as they would watch any TV show at home. The test ad is placed in with other ads, and the subjects do not know which ad is being tested.

When the preview is completed, the subjects are asked to participate in a second shopping exercise. Researchers then compare the products chosen in the first shopping trip to those selected in the second. Shifts in brand choices are at least partly due to the effectiveness of the advertisement, because it is the only variable that has changed.

A major advantage of this methodology is that the test procedures do not rely on opinions and attitudes. Among other things, this means that RSC's procedure can be used in international markets as well as domestic markets.[27] In some cultures, subjects tend to seek to please the interviewer who asks questions about opinions and attitudes. As a result, the answers are polite and socially acceptable. The same subjects may also seek to provide answers they think the interviewer wants to hear. By studying purchases instead of soliciting opinions, subjects are free to respond in a more accurate fashion.

Any methodology designed to tap into behaviors rather than emotions and feelings has a built-in advantage. Opinions and attitudes change and can be quickly affected by other variables in a situation. Observing behaviors and changes in behaviors gets more quickly to the point of the experiment, which is, can the buyer be influenced in a tangible way by a marketing communications tool?

In summary, the three systems designed to examine respondent behaviors are response rates, test markets, and purchase simulation tests. Many of these programs are used in conjunction with one another and also with the message evaluation techniques described earlier. None of these approaches is used in a vacuum. Instead, the data generated and findings revealed are tested across several instruments and with numerous groups of subjects. In that manner, the marketing department manager and the advertising agency can try to heighten the odds that both short- and long-term goals can be reached through the ads, premiums, coupons, and other marketing communications devices used. Even then, the job of evaluation is not complete.

## EVALUATING PUBLIC RELATIONS ACTIVITIES

Most public relations can be studied using one or more of the evaluation techniques that have already been described. Many times, however, company leaders use four additional methods. These evaluation techniques are:

1. Number of clippings
2. Number of impressions
3. Advertising equivalence technique
4. Comparison to PR objectives

The number of clippings occurs when a company subscribes to what is called a *clipping service.* The service scours magazines, journals, and newspapers looking for a client company's name. The number of clippings found is then compared to the number of news releases that were sent out. A firm that sends out 400 news releases and is told there are 84 clippings would conclude that the *percent return* is 21 percent.

The second approach, which became popular in the 1990s, is to calculate impressions. *Impressions* are counted as the total number of subscribers and purchasers of a print medium or the number of viewers of a broadcast medium in which the client company's name has been mentioned. For example, when a company's name is mentioned in a newspaper article with a circulation of 800,000 and newsstand sales of 150,000, then the total number of impressions is 950,000.

Although clippings tend to be the most frequently used measure of PR success, clippings, as well as number of impressions, ignore whether the article spoke positively or negatively about the company. Any clipping is counted when the company's name is mentioned, no matter the context. Unfortunately, this means an article criticizing the company counts as much as one praising the company. With impression counts, everyone who subscribes to or buys a magazine or newspaper is part of the total. No effort is made to see what percentage of those who bought the paper or magazine actually saw the company name or read the article.[28]

Firms that continue to use clippings and impressions should modify these techniques when possible. Clippings should be sorted into piles of positive and negative articles in order to see which occurs more frequently. Also, evaluators should summarize what was said in the article rather than simply noting that the company's name was mentioned. It is also wise to note if the article, whether negative or positive, appeared in a setting that would reach the company's customers or if it is "buried" somewhere with less importance.

For impressions, surveys should be conducted to indicate the percentage of the total audience that saw or heard the company's name. This can be accomplished by using recall or recognition tests, or both. In addition, attitude questions can be posed to see how people reacted to what was in the story. Again, merely counting impressions does not provide adequate feedback about a PR campaign.

The problems associated with clippings and impressions have led to a third method used to measure public relations effectiveness. The approach, called *advertising equivalence,* involves finding every place the company name was mentioned in print and broadcast media. Then, the market researcher calculates the cost of the time or space as if it was a paid advertisement. For example, if the company is discussed in an article that occupies one-half page of a magazine, the firm finds out the cost of a half-page ad. A similar approach is used for TV publicity. The cost of an ad running for the amount of time the company was discussed on the air is calculated. Again, this method makes the most sense only if positive publicity stories are counted.

The least used but best method involves examining the public relations piece in comparison to the company's PR objectives. Many times, the objective of a particular PR campaign is to increase awareness of the firm or product's name. Evaluation includes developing an index of awareness before a PR campaign begins. Then, after the PR event, awareness is measured a second time to see if it actually increased. This kind of information is valuable in the motion picture industry. When celebrities make personal appearances and visits to talk shows in the effort to generate publicity, awareness should increase.

In other situations, the goal of a PR campaign is to build a positive image for the company because of bad publicity or some other negative event. Again, the image should be measured before and after the PR campaign. The goal is to see if the image changed and, if so, to what degree. This approach is time-consuming and difficult. It may take time for a PR campaign to have a full impact. Still, many public relations teams are interested in knowing whether their efforts are working.

Each of these methods is based on the goal of discovering the impact of the PR program. When combined with assessments of the effectiveness of advertisements and behavioral responses, the company has a fairly solid grasp regarding what is going on in the current marketplace. Completion of a full IMC evaluation involves one more crucial process.

# EVALUATING THE OVERALL IMC PROGRAM

As has been noted throughout this textbook, the huge expenditures companies make on marketing communications has led CEOs and other executives to continue to push for greater accountability. These individuals, as well as stockholders and boards of directors, want to know what type of return results when a firm spends a large sum of money on an advertising campaign or other marketing activity. The idea is to try to discover the *return on investment (ROI)* of an advertising and promotions program.

The problem is that there is no agreement about what the ROI means when it is applied to a marketing program. There is also no consensus on how to measure marketing ROI. In one recent study, more than 70 percent of marketers said it would be difficult to measure the impact of advertising and marketing on sales. The same number predicted that it would be extremely difficult for the marketing industry to reach any agreement on what constitutes ROI for marketing. Table 15.2 lists some of the potential definitions of marketing ROI. The most commonly used descriptions of ROI are behavioral responses, such as incremental sales, total sales, and market share. Notice that the measures used to set prices for advertising time and space, such as gross rating points delivered and reach/frequency achieved, are not often considered the best definition of ROI.[29]

This confusion is likely to continue, even as company executives try to justify advertising and marketing expenditures. This means those in the marketing profession should keep trying to identify some way to measure the impact of marketing communications, ultimately in dollars and cents.

Many years ago, Peter Drucker outlined a series of goal areas that are indicative of organizational health. These goals match very well with the objectives of an IMC program and are listed in Figure 15.6.[30] As marketers struggle to find a way to measure ROI of marketing communication expenditures, understanding the various measures of overall health of an organization can provide valuable insight on how marketing communications contributes.

*Market share* has long been linked to profitability. It demonstrates consumer acceptance, brand loyalty, and a strong competitive position. A promotions opportunity analysis, as described in Chapter 4, should help the marketing team understand both its market share and the relative strengths and weaknesses of the competition. IMC programs are designed to hold and build market share.

*Innovation* is finding new and different ways to achieve objectives. This applies to many marketing activities, including new and unusual trade promotions devices (Chapter 9), consumer promotions (Chapter 10), public relations events and sponsorships (Chapter 12), Internet and e-commerce programs (Chapter 13), and, of course, the firm's advertising efforts.

*Productivity* is reflective of the industry's increasing emphasis on results. IMC experts are being asked to demonstrate tangible results from IMC campaigns. Both short- and long-term measures of the effects of advertisements and promotions demonstrate the

| Definition of ROI | Percent Using |
|---|---|
| Incremental sales from marketing | 66% |
| Changes in brand awareness | 57% |
| Total sales revenue from marketing | 55% |
| Changes in purchase intentions | 55% |
| Changes in market share | 49% |
| Ratio of advertising costs to sales | 34% |
| Reach/frequency achieved | 30% |
| Gross rating points delivered | 25% |
| Post-buy analysis comparing the media plan to its delivery | 21% |

**TABLE 15.2**

**Definitions of ROI for Marketing**

*Source:* Paul J. Cough, "Study: Marketers Struggle to Measure Effectiveness," *Shoot* 45, no. 29 (August 20, 2004), pp. 7–8.

▶ Market share

▶ Level of innovation

▶ Productivity

▶ Physical and financial resources

▶ Profitability

▶ Manager performance and development

▶ Employee performance and attitudes

▶ Social responsibility

**FIGURE 15.6**
**Measures of Overall Health**
**of a Company**

*Source:* Peter Drucker, *Management: Tasks, Responsibilities, Pratices* (New York: Harper and Row, 1974).

"productivity" of the organization, in terms of gaining new customers, building recognition in the marketplace, determining sales per customer, and through other measures.

*Physical and financial resources* are also important to an IMC program. Physical resources include the most up-to-date computer and Internet capabilities. The firm must provide sufficient financial resources to reach this goal. Scanner technologies and other devices that keep the firm in contact with consumers are vital elements in the long-term success of an IMC plan.

*Profitability* is vital for the marketing department and the overall organization. Many IMC managers know that more than sales are at issue when assessing success. Sales must generate profits in order for the company to survive and thrive.

*Manager performance and development* is possibly an overlooked part of an IMC program. Effective marketing departments and advertising agencies must develop pipelines of new, talented creatives, media buyers, promotions managers, database Web masters, and others in order to succeed in the long term. Also, new people must be trained and prepared for promotion for more important roles.

*Employee performance and attitudes* reflect not only morale within the marketing department but also relations with other departments and groups. As noted in Chapter 1, an effective IMC plan consists of building bridges with other internal departments so that everyone is aware of the thrust and theme of the program. Satisfied and positive employees are more likely to help the firm promote its IMC image.

*Social responsibility* was described in Chapter 12. It is clear that the long-term well-being of an organization rests, in part, in its ability to eliminate negative activities and expand its positive programs. Brand equity and loyalty are hurt when the firm is known for illegal or unethical actions. Therefore, marketing leaders should encourage all of the members of an organization to act in ethical and socially responsible ways.

When these goals are being reached, it is likely that the firm's IMC program is working well. Beyond these targets, IMC plans continually should emphasize the evolving nature of relationships with customers. Retail consumers and business-to-business buyers should be constantly contacted to find out how the company can best serve their needs.

Simply stated, every chapter in this book implies a series of key performance targets for IMC programs that should guide the actions of the marketing department and the advertising agency both in the short term and for the long haul. Firms that are able to maintain one clear voice in a cluttered marketplace stand the best chance of gaining customer interest and attention as well as developing long-term bonds with all key publics and stakeholders. An effective IMC program helps set the standards and measure performance and, in the end, becomes the model for marketing success for the entire organization.

Companies such as Koestler must use various methods to evaluate overall IMC programs.
*Source:* Courtesy of Sartor Associates, Inc.

**KOESTLER**
SINCE 1924
GRANITE & MARBLE

**2021 University Ave., Oxford, MS**

## SUMMARY

Assessing an IMC program often involves examining the effects of individual advertisements. These efforts are conducted in two major ways: (1) message evaluations and (2) evaluating respondent behaviors. A wide variety of techniques can be used. Most of the time, marketing managers and advertisement agencies use several different methods in order to get the best picture of an ad's potential for success. Advertisements are studied before they are developed, while they are being developed, and after they have been released or launched.

The guiding principles for any marketing tool include agreement on how test results will be used, pre-establishing a cutoff score for a test's results, using multiple measures, basing studies on models of human behaviors, using multiple exposures, testing marketing instruments that are in the same stage of development, and preventing as many biases as possible while conducting the test. Many times it is difficult for certain members of the marketing team to be objective, especially when they had the idea for the ad or campaign. In these instances, it is better to retain an outside research agency to study the project.

Public relations programs should be assessed in light of not only how many times a company is mentioned in the media but also what various ads and stories said about the company. Also, public relations efforts should be compared with the goals for the department in order to see if the company is achieving the desired effects with its publicity releases and sponsorship efforts.

IMC plans are general, overall plans for the entire company. Therefore, more general and long-term criteria should be included in any evaluation of an IMC program. When the IMC theme and voice are clear, the company is achieving its long-range objectives, the principles stated in this book are being applied efficiently and effectively, and the company is in the best position to succeed at all levels.

## REVIEW QUESTIONS

1. What is the difference between a message evaluation and respondent behaviors when assessing the effectiveness of an advertisement?

2. What does a concept test evaluate? How are storyboards and focus groups used in concept tests?

3. Describe the use of portfolio tests and theater tests in copytesting programs.

4. What is DAR? How are aided and unaided recall tests used in conjunction with DAR evaluations? What problems are associated with both types of tests?

5. What is a recognition test? How is it different from a recall test?

6. How are closed-ended questions and open-ended questions used in attitude and opinion tests?

7. What is a warmth monitor? What does it measure?

8. Describe how psychogalvanometers, pupillometric meters, and psychophysiology analysis techniques are used in evaluating advertisements.

9. How do the positioning advertising copytesting principles help advertisers prepare quality ads and campaigns?

10. What are the three forms of behavioral evaluations that can be used to test advertisements and other marketing pieces?

11. Name the measures of behavioral responses described in this chapter.

12. What items can be evaluated using test markets?

13. Describe a purchase simulation test.

14. Describe counting clippings and calculating the number of impressions as methods for assessing public relations effectiveness. What problems are associated with these two techniques?

15. Describe the advertising equivalence approach to assessing public relations programs.

16. Name and describe the criteria that can be used to assess the impact of the overall IMC program, as noted in this chapter.

## KEY TERMS

**message evaluation techniques**   Methods used to examine the creative message and the physical design of an advertisement, coupon, or direct-marketing piece.

**respondent behaviors techniques**   Methods used to examine visible customer actions including making store visits, inquiries, or actual purchases.

**storyboard**   A series of still photographs or sketches that outlines the structure of a television ad.

**concept testing**   An evaluation of the content or concept of the ad and the impact that concept will have on potential customers.

**copytests**   Tests that are used to evaluate a marketing piece that is finished or is in its final stages prior to production.

**portfolio test**   A test of an advertisement using a set of print ads, one of which is the ad being evaluated.

**theater test**   A test of an advertisement using a set of television ads, including the one being evaluated.

**mall intercept technique**   A test where people are stopped in a shopping mall and asked to evaluate a marketing item.

**recall tests**   An approach in which an individual is asked to recall ads he or she has viewed in a given time period or setting.

**day-after recall (DAR)**   Individuals participating in a study are contacted the day after an advertisement appears to see if they remember encountering the ad.

**unaided recall**   A test in which subjects are asked to name, or recall, the ads without any prompts or memory jogs.

**aided recall**   A test in which consumers are prompted by being told such information as the product category and if necessary names of specific brands to see if they recall an ad.

**recognition tests**   A test format in which individuals are given copies of an ad and asked if they recognize it.

**closed-end questionnaire**   A test in which subjects are asked to give specific responses to questions, and the answers are usually rated using some type of scale.

**open-ended questions**   A test in which subjects are allowed to discuss whatever comes to mind in response to a question.

**warmth monitor**   A method to measure emotional responses to advertisements.

**psychogalvanometer**   A device that measures perspiration levels.

**pupillometric meter**   A device that measures the dilation of a person's pupil.

**psychophysiology**   A brain image measurement process.

**positioning advertising copytesting (PACT)**   Principles to use when assessing the effectiveness of various messages.

# CRITICAL THINKING EXERCISES

## Discussion Questions

1. Create an idea for advertising one of the following products. Put that idea down in three or four sentences. Organize a small focus group of four other students in your class. Ask them to evaluate your advertising concept. What did you learn from the exercise?

   a. Retail pet store
   b. Baseball caps
   c. Computers
   d. Sweaters
   e. Watches

2. A very popular form of recall testing is day-after recall (DAR). Write down five advertisements you remember seeing yesterday. In addition to writing down the product and brand, note whatever else you can remember. Form into groups of four students. Compare your lists. How many commercials were recalled? How much could each of you remember about the commercial?

3. Pick out five advertisements you like. Conduct an aided recall test of these five ads. Ask 5 individuals, independently, if they saw the commercial. Mention only the brand name. If so, ask them to recall, in an unaided fashion, as much about the ad as they can. If they do not remember the ad immediately, give them cues. Be sure to record how much each person remembers unaided and how much each person remembers with aided information. Report your results to the class.

4. Form into a group of five students. Ask students to write down two advertisements they really like and their reasons. Ask students to write down two advertisements they dislike and their reasons. Finally, ask students to write down an advertisement they believe is offensive and their reasons. Ask each student to read his or her list comparing ads that were liked, disliked, and

offensive. What common elements did you find in each category? What were the differences?

5. How important are sales figures in the evaluation of integrated marketing communications? How should hard data such as redemption rates and store traffic be used in the evaluation of marketing communications? In terms of accountability, how important are behavioral measures of IMC effectiveness?

6. In some Asian countries it is improper to talk about oneself. Therefore, questions about feelings and emotions would be too embarrassing for citizens to answer. Those who answer the questions tend to provide superficial answers. Explain the advantages of a simulated purchasing test methodology in this situation. What other methods of evaluating feelings and emotions could an agency use in Asian countries?

7. From the viewpoint of a marketing manager of a large sporting goods manufacturer, what types of measures of effectiveness would you want from the $500,000 you pay to an advertising agency to develop an advertising campaign? Knowing that evaluation costs money, how much of the $500,000 would you be willing to spend to measure effectiveness? What type of report would you prepare for your boss?

8. A clothing manufacturer spends $600,000 on trade promotions and $300,000 on sales promotions. How would you measure the impact of these expenditures? If an agency was hired to manage these expenditures, what type of measures would you insist the company utilize?

9. Look through a magazine. Record how many advertisements have a method for measuring responses. How many list a code number, a toll-free number, or a Web site? Just listing a toll-free number or a Web site does not ensure the agency or firm will know where the customer obtained that information. How can the ad agency or firm track the responses from a specific advertisement in the magazine you examined?

# INTEGRATED LEARNING EXERCISES

1. Pick five print or television advertisements that provide Web sites. Go to each site. Was the Web site a natural extension of the advertisement? What connection or similarities did you see between the Web site and the advertisement? Do you think your response was tracked? How can you tell?

2. Decision Analysts, Inc., is a leading provider of advertising and marketing research; their Web site is www.decision-analyst.com. Access the Web site and investigate the various services the company offers. Examine the advertising research services that are available. Write a short report

about how advertising research services provided by Decision Analysts could be used.

3. DiscoverWhy offers ad testing through the warmth meter technology discussed in this chapter. Access the Web site at www.discoverwhy.com. Review how the company conducts advertising research. Write a report on when and how DiscoverWhy could be utilized for advertising research. What are the advantages and disadvantages of each research methodology?

4. Ipsos-ASI at www.ipsos-asi.com is an advertising research firm that has developed a high level of expertise in ad testing and measurements. Access the company's products and services. What services are offered? When would the various services be used? How would each be used?

5. AdKnowledge and comScore Networks are two firms that are excellent at measuring Internet traffic and Internet advertising. Access these Web sites at www.adknowledge.com and www.comscore.com. What services are offered by each company? Which company do you like the best? Why? Describe a research project that you feel each company could do successfully to assist in advertising or Internet research.

## STUDENT PROJECT

### IMC Plan Pro

Did you do a good job? An IMC program and campaign should be assessed during development as well as after launch. The IMC Plan Pro booklet and disk available through Prentice Hall will help you choose the best methods of evaluation for your company, the integrated marketing campaign you created, and its products.

# CASE 1

## CRUISING FOR INCREASED PROFITS

Adventure Cruises owns a fleet of ships that tour the Caribbean and the Bahamas and make trips to Hawaii. The company has been in operation for more than 20 years. Recently, there has been a drop in passengers on each voyage. Adventure's leadership believes increasing competition in the cruise ship industry combined with additional new leisure-time activities have led to the decline. Some worry that cruise ship tours are viewed as something "old people" do and that Disney has taken away the family cruise business.

To combat these problems, Adventure Cruises has decided on two tactics. First, the marketing department will present a new ad campaign highlighting the advantages the company has compared to other lines. Second, a new type of passenger will be recruited, a "working business vacationer."

Adventure rebuilt the staterooms on 10 of its ships to accommodate business travelers. These individuals can be members of a company or guests of the company. The idea is to get the customer alone on a ship to conduct business for a series of days, all the while being able to enjoy the many features of cruise travel, including fine dining, gambling, shows, and stops at various ports. The advantage to the company is that it has essentially a "captive audience" when a customer is given a free cruise in exchange for doing business with the company footing the bill. Adventure intends to take out ads in business magazines and journals, selling these new packages to various business buyers. Adventure president Henry Crouch points out, "Lots of companies pay really big bucks to rent luxury boxes in football stadiums. They get the customer for what, 4 or 5 hours? We can offer them a chance to keep a customer for 4 or 5 *days*."

Henry hired a large international advertising agency to prepare ads for both regular passengers and the new business-to-business market. Lauren Patterson was the account executive who signed the deal, by emphasizing that she would follow the Roper Starch copytesting principles. For cruise ship passengers, the ads would pass muster only if they met the following criteria:

1. *The eyes have it.* The ads must be clear and easy to follow.
2. *Never place copy above an illustration.* People see the picture first, so if the copy is higher, it's ignored.
3. *Great visuals work.* The idea is to capture attention and interest.
4. *Make sure the headlines and visuals blend with the copy.* Don't confuse the reader.
5. *Don't use confusing visuals.*
6. *Don't use confusing headlines.*
7. *Testimonials increase believability and readership.*
8. *Size matters.* The ad must be big.
9. *Keep it simple.* Readers are not as interested in the product as you are, so make the ad easy to follow.
10. *Break the rules.* Be creative.

In the business-to-business marketplace, three problems routinely occur. Lauren is going to insist that the ads avoid these problems. She calls them the ABC sins in business-to-business marketing. The problems are:

a. Ads that are not visually appealing
b. Ads that are abstract rather than designed with a human appeal
c. Ads that fail to emphasize the benefit to the business buyer

Henry realizes that these two markets (regular passengers and business customers) are somewhat distinct. Still he believes Adventure Cruises

(continued)

should speak with one voice. He believes his company has three major advantages: better food, unusual entertainment, and excellent service. He wants to be sure that Lauren incorporates those three elements into the ads that appear on television and in the trade journals that they select.

1. Design a print ad for Adventure Cruises' regular passengers.
2. Design a print ad for Adventure Cruises' business customers.
3. What type of testing should be done during the design phase of the advertisement?
4. What type of testing should be done after the ad is designed but prior to placing it in a magazine or other print media?
5. What type of testing should be done after the advertisement is launched? How can the effectiveness of the advertisement be measured?

# CASE 2

## WICKS AND MORE

Creating a strong brand name and presence in the specialty shop market is challenging. A single store located in a large mall has one advantage—regular traffic that passes by. At the same time, it takes just a little more encouragement to get customers to make a special trip just to shop for one item in a large mall.

Wicks and More is a candle shop. The store features a wide variety of candles, from simple scented candles to highly ornate candles that are used for decorations. Wicks and More also features candleholders, incense, and candlelighters of all kinds.

There are four major uses for candles. The first is to serve a functional purpose, providing light when the electricity goes out. Many people keep stocks of candles on hand just for those times. Second, candles are used for decorations. Third, candles can be burned to provide a romantic environment. Scented candles add to the experience of the warm glow of a candlelit bedroom. Other candles provide the perfect light for a romantic dinner. Fourth, candles are used as part of religious ceremonies.

The owners of Wicks and More have just contacted an advertising agency. They want to know if there is a way to make store advertising more effective. They typically run ads in the newspaper and occasional spots on local radio. Most of the store's radio advertising has been during the Christmas holiday season. Newspaper ads run all year.

The advertising agency was presented with four questions by Wicks and More's owners:

1. Is there a way to find out if our ads bring people into the store?
2. Which type of candle buyer is most likely to shop at Wicks and More?
3. Is it financially wise to advertise the special holiday candles that are part of various seasons? Wicks and More not only sells Christmas decoration candles, but it also sells candles for Easter, Saint Patrick's Day, Independence Day, and Thanksgiving.
4. What should be our primary message? How can we get everyone in town to think of Wicks and More when they want to buy candles?

The demographics for Wicks and More are fairly straightforward. Far more women buy candles than men. A typical customer is at least 20 years old. In terms of psychological characteristics, candle buyers tend to have a strong sense of fashion and decor. Many enjoy home decorating. Wicks and More's customers have enough disposable income to shop for nicer home decorations. Many are affluent, though it is not unusual for a middle class income shopper to stop into the store. People with lower incomes who want candles for power outages tend to buy them at Wal-Mart or a discount store.

Wicks and More has been in business for 3 years. The company has been profitable enough to keep going, but the owners believe an effective advertising program might help them build the business.

**1.** Design an advertising program for Wicks and More.

**2.** Which media should Wicks and More feature?

**3.** What types of evaluation should be used in the design and creation of advertisements for Wicks and More?

## ENDNOTES

1. Decision Analyst (www.decisionanalyst.com, accessed September 25, 2005); Patricia Riedman, "DiscoverWhy Tests TV Commercials Online," *Advertising Age* 71, no. 13 (March 27, 2000), pp. 46–47.

2. Gordon A. Wyner, "Narrowing the Gap," *Marketing Research* 16, no. 1 (Spring 2004), pp. 6–7.

3. "AAAA Survey Finds 8 Percent Hike in Cost to Produce 30-Second TV Commercials," *Film & Video Production & Postproduction Magazine (ICOM)* (www.icommag.com/november-2002/november-page-1b.html, accessed January 14, 2005).

4. Stefano Hatfield, "Testing on Trial," *Creativity* 11, no. 9 (October 2003), pp. 18–21.

5. David W. Stewart, "Measures, Methods, and Models in Advertising Research," *Journal of Advertising* 29, no. 3 (1989), pp. 54–60.

6. Abhilasha Mehta, "Advertising Attitudes and Advertising Effectiveness," *Journal of Advertising Research* 40, no. 3 (May–June 2000), pp. 67–72.

7. William D. Wells, "Recognition, Recall, and Rating Scales," *Journal of Advertising Research* 40, no. 6 (November–December 2000), pp. 14–20.

8. Joel S. Debow, "Advertising Recognition and Recall by Age—Including Teens," *Journal of Advertising Research* 35, no. 5 (September–October 1995), pp. 55–60.

9. William D. Wells, "Recognition, Recall, and Rating Scales," *Journal of Advertising Research* 40, no. 6 (November–December 2000), pp. 14–20.

10. Jan Stapel, "Recall and Recognition: A Very Close Relationship," *Journal of Advertising Research* 38, no. 4 (July–August 1998), pp. 41–45.

11. William D. Wells, "Recognition, Recall, and Rating Scales," *Journal of Advertising Research* 40, no. 6 (November–December 2000), pp. 14–20.

12. Jan Stapel, "Recall and Recognition: A Very Close Relationship," *Journal of Advertising Research* 38, no. 4 (July–August 1998), pp. 41–45.

13. Christina Merrill, "Roper Expands Testing," *Adweek Eastern Edition* 37, no. 45 (November 4, 1996), p. 6.

14. Steven P. Brown and Douglas M. Stayman, "Antecedents and Consequences of Attitude Toward the Ad: A Meta-Analysis," *Journal of Consumer Research* 19 (June 1992), pp. 34–51.

15. Douglas M. Stayman and David A. Aaker, "Continuous Measurement of Self-Report or Emotional Response," *Psychology and Marketing* 10 (May–June 1993), pp. 199–214.

16. Freddie Campos, "UH Facility Test Ads for $500," *Pacific Business News* 35, no. 23 (August 18, 1997), pp. A1–A2.

17. Patricia Riedman, "DiscoverWhy Tests TV Commercials Online," *Advertising Age* 71, no. 13 (March 27, 2000), pp. 46–47.

18. Steve Jarvis, "Minnesota Campaign Grabs Smokers by Throat," *Marketing News* 36, no. 8 (April 15, 2002), pp. 5–6.

19. Bruce F. Hall, "On Measuring the Power of Communications," *Journal of Advertising Research* 44, no. 2 (June 2004), pp. 181–188.

20. Bruce F. Hall, "On Measuring the Power of Communications," *Journal of Advertising Research* 44, no. 2 (June 2004), pp. 181–188.

21. David W. Stewart, David H. Furse, and Randall P. Kozak, "A Guide to Commercial Copytesting Services," *Current Issues and Research in Advertising,* James Leigh and Claude Martin, Jr., eds. (Ann Arbor: Division of Research, Graduate School of Business, University of Michigan, 1983), pp. 1–44.

22. Based on PACT document published in *Journal of Marketing* 11, no. 4 (1982), pp. 4–29.

23. "Aiming for an Accurate ROI," *Marketing News* 35, no. 15 (July 16, 2001), p. 11.

24. Amanda Beeler, "POPAI Initiates Study Tracking Effectiveness of Displays," *Advertising Age* 71, no. 15 (April 10, 2000), p. 54.

25. Chris Dillabough, "Web Lets Canadian Tourism Test Media Effectiveness," *New Media Age* (October 31, 2002), p. 12.

26. Kate MacArthur, "McDonald's Tests Ads That Focus on Service," *Advertising Age* 74, no. 1 (January 6, 2003), p. 3.

27. Tim Triplett, "Researchers Probe Ad Effectiveness Globally," *Marketing News* 28, no. 18 (August 29, 1994), pp. 6–7.

28. Kay Bransford, "Just Measure," *Communication World* 22, no. 1 (January 1, 2005), pp. 16–20.

29. Paul J. Cough, "Study: Marketers Struggle to Measure Effectiveness," *Shoot* 45, no. 29 (August 20, 2004), pp. 7–8.

30. Peter Drucker, *Management: Tasks, Responsibilities, Practices* (New York: Harper & Row, 1974).

# Photo Credits

# Name/Organization Index

# Subject Index

Unfair marketing practices, 390–391
Unique market niche, 200, 441
Unique selling position (USP), 441, 452
Unique selling proposition, 200, 223
Unpaid spokespersons, 213
Usage segmentation, 52
Use or application (positioning), 52
Users, 76

## V

Validity, 474
Value-added incentives (e-commerce), 415
Values, 67–68, 87
Values and lifestyle model (VALS), 113, 143, 156
Variability theory, 221, 223
Vendor audit, 81–82
Vendor selection, 82
Vendor support programs, 285
Verbal and visual images, 169, 170
Verbally biased ad, 170
Viral marketing, 428–429, 431
Visibility (refund-rebate program), 319
Visual consistency, 219, 223
Visual esperanto, 170, 190

Visual imagery, 170
Voice-overs, 213
Vulnerability (fear appeal), 171, 190

## W

Warmth monitor, 469, 485
Warranties, 154
Wear out effects, 102–103, 122
Web master, 425, 531
Web site creation, 429–430
Web sites, 447
Web site ratings, 478
Web traffic audit data, 478
Weighted CPM, 283, 265
What we can afford method (budgeting), 105, 122
Wheeler-Lea Amendments, 392–393
White space, 162, 190
Whole egg theory, 137
Word-of-mouth, 382

## Y

Yellow page advertising, 258
Younger boomers, 115–116